Changing Families

RELATIONSHIPS IN CONTEXT

Third Canadian Edition

Anne-Marie Ambert
York University

Toronto

Editor-in-Chief: Michelle Sartor
Acquisitions Editor: Matthew Christian
Sponsoring Editor: Joel Gladstone
Marketing Manager: Lisa Gillis
Program Manager: Madhu Ranadive
Developmental Editor: Charlotte Morrison-Reed
Lead Project Manager: Susan M. Johnson
Project Manager: Sarah Gallagher
Media Editor: Marisa D'Andrea
Media Producer: Bogdan Kosenko
Production Services: Rashmi Tickyani, Aptara®, Inc.
Compositor: Aptara®, Inc.
Permissions Project Manager: Daniela Glass
Photo Permissions Researcher: Krystyna Sperka Borgen, PreMediaGlobal
Text Permissions Researcher: Sam Bingenheimer, Electronic Publishing Services Inc.
Interior Designer: Aptara®, Inc.
Cover Designer: Suzanne Behnke
Cover Image: justaa/Shutterstock.com

Credits and acknowledgments for material borrowed from other sources and reproduced, with permission, in this textbook appear on the appropriate page within the text.

Original edition published by Allyn & Bacon, Inc., a division of Pearson Education, Inc., 160 Gould Street, Needham Heights, MA 20494. Copyright © 2001 by Allyn & Bacon, Inc.

If you purchased this book outside the United States or Canada, you should be aware that it has been imported without the approval of the publisher or the author.

Library and Archives Canada Cataloguing in Publication
Ambert, Anne-Marie, author
   Changing families: relationships in context/Anne-Marie Ambert,
York University.—Third Canadian edition.
   Includes bibliographical references and index.
   ISBN 978-0-321-90163-7 (pbk.)
   1. Families—Textbooks.   I. Title.
   HQ560.A34 2014   306.85   C2013-906010-3

9 17

ISBN 978-0-32-190163-7

Brief Contents

Preface   xii

PART 1 FOUNDATIONS OF FAMILY STUDIES

1   Introduction to Family Studies   1
2   History and Cultural Diversity of Canadian Families   34
3   Contemporary Changes in Family Life   67

PART 2 SOCIAL AND CULTURAL FAMILY CONTEXTS

4   Effects of Economic Changes and Inequalities on Families   93
5   Impacts of Neighbourhoods and Housing Conditions on Family Life: Contexts of Social Inequalities   121
6   Roles of Educational Institutions and Religious Participation in Family Life   148

PART 3 PATTERNS OF PARTNERING AND FAMILY FORMATION

7   Couple Formation and Sexual Relations   181
8   Patterns of Family Formation and Planning   217

PART 4 COUPLE AND FAMILY RELATIONSHIPS

9   Spousal Relationships   254
10   The Parent-Child Relationship and Child Socialization   284
11   Siblings: Relationships, Nature and Nurture   315

PART 5 FAMILY CHALLENGES AND SOLUTIONS

12   Divorce, Widowhood, and Remarriage   341
13   Family Violence, Abuse, and Neglect   374
14   Family Futures and Social Policies   407

Glossary   434
Bibliography and Author Index   438
Subject Index   497

Contents

Preface   xii

PART 1   FOUNDATIONS OF FAMILY STUDIES

1   Introduction to Family Studies   1

HOW CAN FAMILIES BE DEFINED?   3

Nuclear Families   6

Extended Families   6

Types of Union and Marriage   7

Polygamy as a Conjugal and Family Type   7

WHAT THEORETICAL PERSPECTIVES INFORM FAMILY STUDIES?   10

Structural Functionalism   10

Political Economy Theories   11

Social Exchange and Rational Theories   13

Social Constructionism   16

Feminist Theories   20

Developmental (Life Course) Perspectives   22

Symbolic Interactionism   25

Interactional-Transactional Perspectives   26

Behaviour Genetics   26

WHAT ARE THE MAIN THEMES IN THE TEXT?   28

WHAT METHODS ARE USED IN FAMILY RESEARCH?   29

An Example of Qualitative Methods: Students' Autobiographies   32

CONCLUSIONS: UNITY IN DIVERSITY   32

Summary   33

Analytical Questions   33

2   History and Cultural Diversity of Canadian Families   34

CANADIAN FAMILIES OF THE PAST   36

Early First Nations Families   36

Families of New France   38

Families during British Colonial Rule   41

First Nations Families under French and British Rule   43

Early Black-Canadian Families   44

Families during Industrialization and the Settling of the West   46

CURRENT DIVERSITY OF CANADIAN FAMILIES   50

Aboriginal Families   50

Québécois Families   54

Black-Canadian Families   56

Chinese-Canadian Families   58

Indo-Canadian Families   61

CONCLUSIONS: EVOLVING CANADIAN FAMILIES IN DIVERSITY   64

Summary   65

Analytical Questions   66

3 Contemporary Changes in Family Life   67

HAS THE FAMILY LOST
ITS RELEVANCE?   69

Functions That Have Remained with
the Family   70

New Responsibilities Imposed upon
Families   71

Additional Responsibilities Taken on
by Some Families   73

An Overabundance of Family
Responsibilities   73

FAMILIES AND COUPLES
LIVING APART   75

Transnational Families   75

Military Families   76

Couples Living Apart (LAT)   79

THE AUDIOVISUAL/SOCIAL MEDIA
AND FAMILY LIFE   79

Television: A Historical Overview   80

The Continued Effects of the Audiovisual
Media: The Internet and Cellular
Phone   82

CONCLUSIONS: THE FAMILY AS A
"PRIVATE" INSTITUTION SUBSIDIZES
THE ECONOMY   91

Summary   92

Analytical Questions   92

**PART 2 SOCIAL AND
CULTURAL FAMILY
CONTEXTS**

**4 Effects of Economic Changes
and Inequalities on Families   93**

OVERVIEW OF ECONOMIC
CHANGES   95

EFFECTS OF ECONOMIC CHANGES
ON FAMILIES   97

The Rise of Feminine Employment and the
Dual-Income Family   98

Domestic Division of Labour along Gender
Lines   100

Economic Realities and Changing Family
Time   102

The Rise of Consumerism in Family
Life   104

FAMILY POVERTY   105

SOURCES OF FAMILY POVERTY   106

Current Structural Sources of
Poverty   108

Sociohistorical Sources of Poverty   110

Sociopersonal Sources of Poverty   110

CONSEQUENCES OF FAMILY
POVERTY   113

For Mothers   114

For Fathers   115

For Children   116

CONCLUSIONS: THE COSTS OF
FAMILY POVERTY   119

Summary   120

Analytical Questions   120

**5 Impacts of Neighbourhoods and
Housing Conditions on Family
Life: Contexts of Social
Inequalities   121**

AFFLUENT NEIGHBOURHOODS   124

LOW-INCOME
NEIGHBOURHOODS   125

When Social Problems Are Added   126

Risk Factors for Children in Low-Income
Areas   128

ETHNICITY AND RACE IN
NEIGHBOURHOODS 131

HOMELESS FAMILIES 132

The Sources of Homelessness 133

The Effects of Homelessness on Mothers
    and Children 134

RURAL AREAS AND FAMILY LIFE 135

Farm Families 136

Vacation Areas 139

FAMILIES' HOUSING CONDITIONS
AND VARIETY 140

Condos: The New Trend 141

Mobile Homes 142

Family Privacy and Overcrowding 143

RESIDENTIAL MOBILITY 144

CONCLUSIONS: NEIGHBOURHOODS
AND HOUSING AS CONTEXTS 146

Summary 146

Analytical Questions 147

6 Roles of Educational Institutions
and Religious Participation in
Family Life 148

THE EDUCATIONAL SYSTEM:
AN OVERVIEW 150

CHILD CARE: QUALITY AND
OUTCOMES 151

The Effects of Child Care on
    Children 153

Early Childhood Education for Children in
    Low-Income Families 154

The Effects of Child Care on Parents 156

SCHOOLS AND FAMILIES 157

Parental Involvement 158

Family-School Compatibility 163

Schools and Antisocial Behaviour 164

Minority-Group, Immigrant, and
    Aboriginal Children 165

PRIVATE EDUCATION 167

Private Schools 167

Home Schooling 168

RELIGIOUS PARTICIPATION AND
FAMILY LIFE 170

THE ROLE PLAYED BY RELIGIOSITY
IN FAMILY LIFE 174

Religiosity Correlates with
    Well-Being 174

Religiosity Scaffolds the Parental
    Role 175

Religiosity Relates to Marital Quality and
    Stability 177

Limitations of Religion for Nonconventional
    Families 178

CONCLUSIONS: THE BALANCING ACT
OF FAMILY RESPONSIBILITIES 179

Summary 179

Analytical Questions 180

PART 3 PATTERNS OF
PARTNERING AND
FAMILY FORMATION

7 Couple Formation and Sexual
Relations 181

DATING AND SEXUAL
RELATIONSHIPS 183

Heterosexual and Same-Sex
    Dating 184

Interracial Couple Formation 185

Internet Dating 187

DATE AND PARTNER SELECTION 188

Elements in Partner Selection 188

COHABITATION 190

Relationship Stability and Reasons for
Entering into Cohabitation 193

Relationship Aspects 194

For Older Adults 196

HETEROSEXUAL MARRIAGE 197

SAME-SEX MARRIAGE 200

SINGLEHOOD 201

SEXUAL RELATIONS 203

Adolescent Sexuality 204

SEXUAL IDENTITIES AND
SEXUALITIES 210

Marital and Cohabitational Sexual
Relations 211

Extracouple Sexual Relations 213

Media Portrayals of Infidelity and
Pornography 214

CONCLUSIONS: THE CHANGING
PROFILE OF COUPLES AND
SEXUALITY 215

Summary 216

Analytical Questions 216

8 Patterns of Family Formation
and Planning 217

OVERVIEW OF FAMILY
STRUCTURE 218

FAMILY FORMATION VIA
MARRIAGE 220

FAMILY FORMATION VIA
COHABITATION 221

SAME-SEX-PARENT FAMILY
FORMATION 222

FAMILY FORMATION BY SINGLE
PARENTS 225

Family Formation by Adolescent Mothers 226

Multi-Partnered Fertility and Responsible
Parenthood 229

Children Born to Single Mothers 229

DELAYED PARENTHOOD 231

FAMILY PLANNING, BIRTHS,
AND FERTILITY 233

Births and Fertility 233

Infertility and Childlessness by Choice 235

Abortion 236

REPRODUCTIVE ALTERNATIVES 238

Donor Insemination 239

In Vitro Fertilization and
Transplantation 239

Surrogate Mothers 241

FAMILY FORMATION VIA
ADOPTION 242

The Social Construction of
Adoption 242

Adopted Children's Development 243

The Diversity of Adoption 246

FOSTER FAMILIES: FAMILY
RESTRUCTURING 249

CONCLUSIONS: FAMILY FORMATION
ALTERNATIVES IN CONTEXT 251

Summary 252

Analytical Questions 253

PART 4 COUPLE AND FAMILY
RELATIONSHIPS

9 Spousal Relationships 254

TYPES OF MARRIAGE AND
HOW THEY CHANGE 256

The Vital and Total Relationships 257

The Devitalized Relationship 258

The Congenial Relationship 258

The Conflict-Habituated Relationship 259

The Congenial Reproductive-Familial
   Relationship 259

The Cultural Reproductive-Familial
   Relationship 260

Marriages Evolve over Time 260

**ASPECTS OF SPOUSAL
RELATIONSHIPS 261**

Marital Happiness, Satisfaction, and
   Success 261

Communication Issues 263

Partner Conflict and Problems 264

Marital Quality through the Decades 266

The Next Time Around: Remarriage 266

The Conjugal Relationship in Later
   Life 267

**DIVISION OF LABOUR AND
INEQUALITY 269**

A Classification of the Domestic Division
   of Labour 269

The Effect on Marital Quality: Overview
   of Recent Changes 272

Division of Labour in Remarriages
   with Stepchildren 273

**THE SILENT DIVISION OF LABOUR:
EMOTIONAL WORK 274**

**SAME-SEX-COUPLE
RELATIONSHIPS 275**

**THE EFFECT OF CHILDREN ON THE
COUPLE RELATIONSHIP 276**

**THE EFFECT OF THE PARENTAL
RELATIONSHIP ON CHILDREN 277**

Conjugal Quality Fosters Supportive
   Parenting 279

The Role of Learning and Personality 280

Genes and Within-Family
   Environment 280

The Larger Environment Affects Marriage
   and Childrearing 281

**CONCLUSIONS: DEFINITIONS OF
RELATIONSHIP QUALITY ARE
CULTURE SPECIFIC 281**

Summary 282

Analytical Questions 283

**10 The Parent-Child Relationship
and Child Socialization 284**

**PARENTS' SOCIALIZATION PRACTICES:
REFLECTIONS OF THE ECONOMIC
ENVIRONMENT 287**

Authoritative and Authoritarian
   Parenting 288

"No-Nonsense" Parenting 289

Permissive and Uninvolved Parenting 290

Wavering-Negotiating Parenting 291

The Question of What Constitutes
   "Proper" Parenting 292

Determinants of Parents' Socialization
   Practices 294

**THE PARENT-ADOLESCENT
RELATIONSHIP 296**

The Social Construction of
   Adolescence 296

How Do Parents and Adolescents
   Get Along? 297

Cultural Determinants of Parental
   Influence 300

The Role of Peers in the Parent-Adolescent
   Relationship 301

**THE RELATIONSHIP BETWEEN
PARENTS AND ADULT CHILDREN 303**

When the Child Is a Young Adult 303

When the Child Is a Mature Adult 305

**AN EXTENSION OF PARENTING:
GRANDPARENTS 309**

Grandparents Who Raise
   Grandchildren 311

THE DEATH OF ADULTS' PARENTS 312

CONCLUSIONS: LIFE COURSE,
ECONOMY, AND PERSONALITY
IN THE PARENT-CHILD
RELATIONSHIP 313

Summary 313

Analytical Questions 314

11

Siblings: Relationships, Nature and Nurture 315

THE SIBLING RELATIONSHIP
BEGINS 317

Consequences of Family Size 319

CHILD AND ADOLESCENT SIBLING
RELATIONSHIPS 321

Sibling Influence 322

Supportive Sibling Relationships 324

DIFFERENTIAL PARENTAL
TREATMENT 325

Birth Order and Developmental Stage as
Factors 326

Gender as a Factor 327

Developmental Impact of Differential
Treatment 328

ADULT AND STEPSIBLING
RELATIONSHIPS 329

NATURE AND NURTURE 332

How Can Siblings Be
So Different? 332

Twins as Natural Experiments 333

THE CONTEXTS OF PARENTAL
INFLUENCE 336

CONCLUSIONS: NATURE AND
NURTURE 339

Summary 339

Analytical Questions 340

PART 5 FAMILY CHALLENGES
AND SOLUTIONS

12

Divorce, Widowhood, and Remarriage 341

DIVORCE RATES AND TRENDS 343

Age at Divorce and Duration of Dissolved
Marriages 346

Multiple (Serial) Divorces 346

Number of Children Involved 347

FACTORS CONTRIBUTING
TO DIVORCE 350

Sociocultural Factors 350

Demographic Factors 351

Reasons People Give for
Divorcing 353

ADULTS' LIFE AFTER DIVORCE 355

Changes in Ex-Spouses' Social
Networks 356

WHAT ARE THE EFFECTS OF DIVORCE
ON CHILDREN? 357

THEORIES EXPLAINING HOW DIVORCE
AFFECTS CHILDREN 360

Economic Explanation 360

Disruption of Parenting 360

The Role of Parental Conflict 361

Preexisting Child Conditions 362

Genetic Influence 363

WIDOWHOOD AND
BEREAVEMENT 363

Consequences of a Parent's Death
for Children 364

REMARRIAGE AND
REPARTNERING 365

Life after Remarriage and
Repartnering 365

What Are the Effects of Parental Remarriage
on Children? 368

GRANDPARENTING AFTER DIVORCE
AND STEP-GRANDPARENTING 370

CONCLUSIONS: THE FAMILIAL AND
SOCIAL IMPLICATIONS OF
DIVORCE 372

Summary 372

Analytical Questions 373

13 Family Violence, Abuse, and Neglect 374

DATING AND COURTSHIP
VIOLENCE 376

VERBAL AND PSYCHOLOGICAL ABUSE
OF PARTNERS 378

SPOUSAL AND PARTNER PHYSICAL
ABUSE 379

Factors Facilitating Spousal Abuse 381

The Effect of Spousal Violence on
Children 383

CHILD ABUSE AND NEGLECT BY
PARENTS 386

Child Abuse by Parents 387

Child Neglect by Parents 391

CHILD SEXUAL ABUSE BY
ADULTS 392

Who and Where Are the Sexual
Abusers? 393

Consequences of Sexual Abuse for the
Child: The Life Course Perspective 394

SIBLING VIOLENCE 396

Sibling Physical Violence 396

Sibling Sexual Abuse 398

PEER ABUSE 399

Peer Sexual Harassment and Abuse 400

ABUSE OF PARENTS BY
CHILDREN 401

Physical Abuse of Parents by Young
Children and Adolescents 401

Abuse of Elderly Parents by Adult
Children 402

CONCLUSIONS: THE LARGER CONTEXT
OF FAMILY VIOLENCE 404

Summary 405

Analytical Questions 406

14 Family Futures and Social Policies 407

SALIENT THEMES REVISITED 409

Social Inequalities and Gender
Stratification 409

Diversity of Families 409

A Surfeit of Family
Responsibilities 410

The Effective Community 411

The Cultural Context 411

WHAT DOES THE FUTURE
HOLD? 412

Fertility, Sex Ratio Imbalance, and
Age Distribution 412

A Crisis in Caring 413

Cohabitation, Marriage, and
Divorce 414

Singlehood and Family Formation
by Singles 415

Immigration and Transnational
Families 415

Families' Natural Environment 416

The Longer Time Frame 417

SOCIAL POLICIES PERTAINING
TO FAMILIES 417

Focus of "Family Policies" 418

REDUCING POVERTY AND ECONOMIC INEQUALITY 420

A Critique of Current Policies 420

Creating Green Jobs 422

Facilitating Adequate Housing 423

Expansion of Child Care Programs 424

After-School Care and Improved Schooling 425

Consequences and Limitations of Programs 426

SUPPORTING THE PARENTAL ROLE 427

FACILITATING THE CARE OF ELDERS 429

CONCLUSIONS: THE FAMILY IN CONTEXTS 431

Inertia of Political Systems 431

Family Responsibilities and Their Contexts 432

Summary 433

Analytical Questions 433

Glossary 434
Bibliography and Author Index 438
Subject Index 497

Preface

The field of family studies has recently benefited from an injection of innovative research from other areas of sociology as well as from other disciplines, particularly demography and psychology. *Changing Families: Relationships in Context* is the first family textbook, whether Canadian or American, to integrate this new body of knowledge—which also includes additional theoretical perspectives—in such a comprehensive manner. It follows that this book is different from others in terms of some of its contents. As well, some aspects of its format and organization are distinct. Further, this third edition includes *many new sections*.

NEW DIRECTIONS OF THE CONTENTS

In this third edition, the additions I have made reflect several of the more recent changes in family life and contexts for which more research has appeared in the past few years. These new trends have and will have a profound impact both on the present and especially the future of families, children, the elderly, and societies. The first and most obvious change is that western economies, including our own, have become much less secure, particularly in terms of earning a living and young people securing a foothold in our economy. In addition, economic power has become more concentrated in the hands of a relatively small number of families. While this has happened, living in Canada has become more expensive, particularly in terms of housing costs, so that a higher proportion of Canadians' income goes into mortgages and rents, leaving less for other expenditures and retirement. As well, technological developments have foisted upon us new "needs," such as smartphones, so that young people are less able to accumulate assets as their parents did. Rather, they accumulate debt. These changes have also led me to a return to **political economy theories**. The theoretical perspectives introduced in Chapter 1 have been linked to one another in a more holistic way throughout the chapters, in order to illustrate how family phenomena in contexts require multiple theories for their explanation—a reality that is generally not presented in texts favouring one theory.

The second development has been ongoing for well over a decade but has solidified recently in view of its long-term consequences: **low fertility** across the world, except for sub-Saharan Africa. Canadians, as well as Europeans, Chinese, South Koreans, Japanese, and many other nations, produce too few children to replenish their population with new generations of young people. Low fertility not only changes the current profile of families but it leads to the third development that is emphasized in this edition, the **aging of our population**. In other words, we are blessed with a longer lifespan but, at the same time, fewer young people are available to replace the retirees in the work force. Thus, we may experience a shortage of workers as well as a **crisis of caring**—not enough young people to provide for the caring of children, of the frail elderly, of the sick and disabled of all ages.

The fourth development is also related to this issue of fertility: It resides in the fact that some countries, particularly China and India, have a huge **sex ratio imbalance**. Many more boys than girls are born and survive. Girls are selected out—generally by abortion following gender screening via ultrasound technology—what Indian demographers refer to as **female feticide**. Of the many implications of this situation is that, in the affected countries, numerous males will never marry. Related to this type of systemic feminine discrimination is rape as an instrument of war.

The fifth development, which is specific to western countries, including Canada, has been ongoing for a few decades but has recently accelerated in terms of meaning: More young people are waiting longer before entering into a **first union**. Thus, entry into a committed union is delayed; more young adults are either living alone or remaining at home with their parents longer than in the past. More persons are remaining single, even in Asia and the Middle East. Of course, this development is also causally related to low fertility rates: Indeed, a later age at union formation, especially marriage, delays childbearing and thus reduces the number of children a woman or couple has. The sixth and related development is that, when couples are formed in the western world, it is more likely to be via **cohabitation** *first*. Furthermore, as cohabitations have become more institutionalized, they are becoming less of a risk factor for divorce when cohabitants marry each other.

The seventh development resides not only in the presence of more **immigrant families** in Canada (and in other countries as well), but in the fact that many of these families are **transnational** in the sense that the parents may live separately—one parent lives in Canada with the children or, yet, one parent arrives here first and the rest of the family follows later. What is new about this situation is that these families generally now stay in close and constant contact with the members who remain in the country of origin, such as grandparents, via the new technologies of communication and more affordable and reliable means of traveling.

Therefore, this third edition of *Changing Families: Relationships in Context* contains several chapters and many new sections that are entirely innovative and are not generally found in other family textbooks. In addition, I continue to include, particularly in Part 2, those topics that rarely appear in textbooks and that have been in the previous editions: The effects of the changing economy, neighbourhoods, and educational institutions on families and human development within these families. This is probably the only family sociology textbook on the market that focuses on these areas *combined*, including the role that religiosity plays in marriage and child socialization. As well, the media as a sociocultural context for family life is discussed more extensively than is done elsewhere and contains new material on video games and cell phones, for instance (in Chapter 3). I have, with each edition, tried to broaden the geographical scope to offer material on all the provinces and territories of Canada and other countries as well.

I have continued providing an entire chapter on siblings: their relationship, how they grow up to be different, and how they relate to their parents, with a special focus on genetics and environment or nature and nature. This third edition also expands on previously new sections on polygamy, online dating and infidelities, adolescent sexuality, casual sex, condo living, military families, and antisocial behaviours in and around schools, among others. It has also retained its substantial sections on adoption, foster families, reproductive technologies, the impact of children's peers on the family, same-sex-parent families, and ex-spouses' relationships after divorce. It includes new perspectives on cohabitation as well as more content on families' elders. Thus, this text contains a more complete overview of families and a greater diversity of domains relevant to family dynamics.

In the same vein, I have continued to introduce *a wide range* of theoretical frameworks. In addition to the better-known theories, such as structural functionalism and symbolic interactionism, others, including social constructionism, are much in evidence. For instance, interactional-transactional theories are used in the chapters on the parent-child relationship. Not only do we look at the socialization of children by parents but we also examine how children affect their parents' ability to raise them within specific environments—in other words, how parents, children, and their environment interact. Furthermore, I have borrowed from the field of behaviour genetics in order to acquaint students with new concepts, ideas, and explanations that are now regularly encountered in the area of family research and even in the popular media: the interaction between nature and nurture or genes and environment. Students can examine behaviour genetics within a critical sociological framework alongside other theories. Finally, I have added much material on more global perspectives, informed by political economy theories.

ORGANIZATION OF THE TEXT

The text of this book includes a great deal of qualitative sociology in the form of quotes, case studies, and summaries from my fieldwork. This material is an integral part of the contents. Moreover, I present a great deal of information, both quantitative and qualitative. How this information is obtained and research is carried out are important issues to me as an instructor. As a result, I have included at least one Family Research insert in most chapters: These Family Research features explain, "Here is how various researchers do it, and how they get their information on family life." In other words, these inserts illustrate various research methods that will allow students to get a better idea of the range of methods that are used in family studies, both qualitative and quantitative.

This third edition of *Changing Families: Relationships in Context* remains divided into five parts. Part 1, Foundations of Family Studies, introduces definitions, perspectives, and issues pertaining to families. This includes theoretical perspectives; a historical and cross-cultural overview; a discussion of current concerns about family functions; and contemporary developments, especially pertaining to the audiovisual media. Part 2, Social and Cultural Family Contexts, focuses on the macrosociological settings and conditions that affect family life and structure. These include the changing dynamics of the global and technological market economy, neighbourhoods and housing conditions, schools, and religious participation. The contents of Part 3 reflect its title, Patterns of Partnering and Family Formation, but also focus on sexual relations.

Part 4, entitled Couple and Family Relationships, introduces successive chapters on the spousal, parent-child, and sibling relationships. Part 5, Family Challenges and Solutions, begins with a chapter on divorce, widowhood, and repartnering, particularly remarriage. The next chapter examines violence, abuse, and neglect within the family. The last chapter re-examines the themes that have linked the contents and then focuses on future family trends. It then addresses social policies and suggestions designed to prevent or ameliorate problems faced by families. A special emphasis is placed on policies that could alleviate family poverty, improve child care, support conjugal units and the parental role, as well as provide a better environment for families' care of their elders.

PEDAGOGY

Each chapter begins with a detailed outline. Throughout the text, many concepts and themes are bolded or italicized in order to help students memorize key concepts and ideas and to note emphases. Concepts that might need additional explanation are further defined in the Glossary at the end of the book. This Glossary contains fewer but lengthier definitions to serve as a reference for students who have never taken a sociology course before. Each chapter has a clearly identified but brief conclusion that serves an integrative function. As is the convention, chapters end with a Summary and Analytical Questions. The online Student's Study Guide, available through MySearchLab, contains other useful material, such as Suggested Readings and Suggested Weblinks.

SUPPLEMENTS

The three supplements are an *Instructor's Manual*, a *Test Item File*, and a MySearchLab with *Student's Study Guide*. The instructor supplements are available for downloading from a password-protected section of Pearson Canada's online catalogue (**vig.pearsoned.ca**). Navigate to your text's catalogue page to view a list of available supplements.

Instructor's Manual: This manual contains a variety of additional instructor resources, including:

- **Additional Class Material** expands upon topics introduced in the text or adds new topics relevant to a chapter.
- **Chapter Linkages and Modules** help point out to students how various sections and themes in one chapter relate to their counterparts in other chapters.
- **Help with Analytical Questions** offers suggestions for those questions placed at the end of each chapter.
- **Suggestions for Discussion, Projects, Papers.**
- **Short Essay Questions.**
- **Suggested Media Options** are occasionally found.

Test Item File: Available in Microsoft Word/Adobe Acrobat format, this test bank includes almost 1,000 multiple-choice, true/false, and essay questions.

MySearchLab® (www.mysearchlab.com): A passcode-protected website that provides engaging experiences that personalize learning, MySearchLab contains an eText that is just like the printed text. Students can highlight and add notes to the eText online or download it to an iPad or Android tablet. MySearchLab also offers discipline-specific media and readings, access to a variety of academic journals, and Associated Press news feeds, along with a wide range of writing, grammar, and research tools to help hone writing and research skills.

The Student's Study Guide linked from the eText in MySearchLab contains the following *for each chapter*:

- **Learning Objectives** that help students focus on the main educational goals of each chapter. By the same token, these objectives will allow students to evaluate how successful they have been in terms of having acquired the knowledge and critical thinking required by each chapter. These objectives are useful both to orient students before they begin a chapter and as a self-evaluation of their own learning process after the chapter is concluded.
- **Questions Students Ask.** Often, students see certain results and statistics that may appear to be negative and want to know how these might apply to them, why they are not following the "averages," or they want to know why they have or have not been affected by given situations. A few of these questions are answered in this feature.
- **Relevance to Students' Lives.** This feature complements the section on Questions Students Ask. Students wishing to utilize this section will be encouraged to ask themselves how some of the contents of each chapter are applicable to their own lives and how they can situate themselves within the contexts presented by each chapter. This section may help students analyze their own family and partner situations or goals, and discover other alternatives, where relevant.
- **Work-Related Relevance.** This section will help students see where some of the contents of each chapter can be utilized in various types of work, such as clinical work with families and children, social work, teaching, health-related work, as well as research work.
- **Suggested Readings.**
- **Suggested Weblinks.**
- **Key Concepts and Themes.**

COURSESMART FOR INSTRUCTORS

CourseSmart goes beyond traditional expectations—providing instant online access to the textbooks and course materials you need at a lower cost for students. And even as students save money, you can save time and hassle with a digital eTextbook that allows you to search for the most relevant content at the very moment you need it. Whether it's evaluating textbooks or creating lecture notes to help students with difficult concepts, CourseSmart can make life a little easier. See how when you visit **www.coursesmart.com/instructors**.

COURSESMART FOR STUDENTS

CourseSmart goes beyond traditional expectations—providing instant online access to the textbooks and course materials you need at an average savings of 50%. With instant access from any computer and the ability to search your text, you'll find the content you need quickly, no matter where you are. And with online tools like highlighting and note-taking, you can save time and study efficiently. See all the benefits at www.coursesmart.com/students.

ACKNOWLEDGEMENTS

The following reviewers have provided extensive comments and suggestions that were greatly useful in guiding the structural and substantive improvements brought to the third edition: Andrew Buntin, George Brown College; Wei-Wei Da, Brescia University College; Elizabeth Dennis, University of the Fraser Valley; Denis Wall, Brock University. I still benefited from the suggestions of the reviewers for the second edition: Terry Murphy, College of the North Atlantic; Penny Poole, Fanshawe College; Denis Wall, University of Toronto; Adenike Yesufu, Grant MacEwan University. Their very detailed suggestions resulted in the elimination of two chapters and the addition of several sections as well as an improvement in the Supplements for both instructors and students. In addition, the following reviewers are acknowledged for their help and suggestions regarding the first edition: Paula Chegwidden, Acadia University; Debra M. Clarke, Trent University; Patience Elabor-Idemudia, University of Saskatchewan; Scott Kline, St. Jerome's University, University of Waterloo; Stephen Riggins, Memorial University; Noreen Stuckless, York University; Franc Sturino, York University; Alison M. Thomas, University of Victoria; Vappu Tyyskä, Ryerson University; and Mike Wahn, University of Winnipeg. These reviewers together have made me rethink and rework many sections and I am most grateful to them. I hope that I have done justice to their thoughtful input.

I also acknowledge the advice and help provided by Joel Gladstone and Matthew Christian, Acquisitions Editor at Pearson Canada, Stephen Kass, Editorial Assistant, Charlotte Morrison-Reed, who was my Developmental Editor, and that of Sarah Gallagher, who was the Project Manager. It was a pleasure working with each of them. Lila Campbell spent countless hours with the copy editing and had a sharp eye for my French way of turning English sentences . . . This also includes Susan Bindernagel who proofread the pages.

I am especially indebted to the hundreds of couples, ex-couples, as well as parents and children who have given so generously of their time and their hospitality for my various research projects over the past decades. Quotes and case studies from these families have greatly enriched this text, as has the material gathered from the over 1,500 students who wrote semi-structured autobiographies in my classes for more than 30 years. I am also indebted to the 232 adoptees, adoptive parents, and birth parents who, more recently, sent me unsolicited email information on their personal history and experience following an article I had published on a related website. As acknowledged at the beginning of Chapter 1, most of my research ideas and theoretical revisions throughout my career have been influenced by this spousal, parental, child, and student contribution to my knowledge of real life as lived by others in their diverse family situations.

Anne-Marie Ambert,
December 2013

Introduction to Family Studies

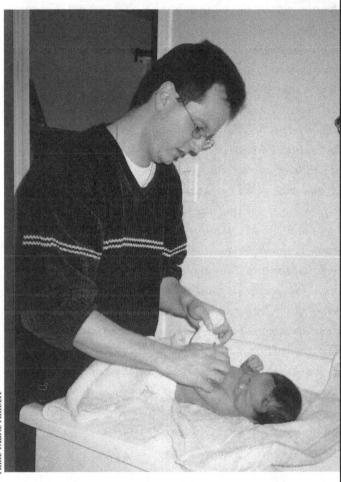

Anne-Marie Ambert

OUTLINE

How Can Families Be Defined?
Nuclear Families
Extended Families
Types of Union and Marriage
Polygamy as a Conjugal and Family Type

What Theoretical Perspectives Inform Family Studies?
Structural Functionalism
Political Economy Theories
Social Exchange and Rational Theories
Social Exchange Theory
Rational Theory
Social Constructionism
The Gendered Social Construction of Parenthood
Feminist Theories
Feminist Analyses of the Family
The Analysis of Gender Stratification and Gender Roles
Developmental (Life Course) Perspectives
Symbolic Interactionism
Interactional-Transactional Perspectives
Behaviour Genetics

What Are the Main Themes in the Text?

What Methods Are Used in Family Research?
An Example of Qualitative Methods: Students' Autobiographies

Conclusions: Unity in Diversity

Summary
Analytical Questions

My publisher suggested that I begin this chapter by answering a personal question: What in my own family life has led to my becoming interested in family studies? Simply put: I do not think that my early family life had much to do with this interest, although it certainly influenced my personal choices and values later on. Rather—and this may at first appear to be a strange answer coming from a sociologist—I am convinced that my interest largely stems from my genes, because I clearly recall being fascinated by family matters as young as age six. Yet, when I was small, there was no environmental reason for this interest because my family life was then uneventful for me. As well, the sociocultural climate of the time and place in which I lived was certainly not conducive to fostering the intellectual curiosity I was developing—at any rate, girls were not supposed to be "intellectual"!

Overall, what has most influenced my scholarly perspectives on family life, apart from readings, has been the fieldwork I have done for my research: learning about the lives of the hundreds of children, adolescents, parents, couples, and ex-couples I have interviewed, observed, and exchanged emails with. Further, as the reader will see at the end of this chapter, many of my students have written about their families in autobiographies and a large number of persons involved in adoptions provided me with a rich gamut of unsolicited (online) but welcome perspectives. These lives, put together, have shown me that the questions asked in family research, especially about the parent-child relationship, were often not the right ones. The theories were too limited and did not always fit the facts I was discovering. This led me early on to search for and consider a wider range of theoretical perspectives, including feminist theories in the late 1960s, interactional approaches in the 1970s and 1980s, as well as social constructionism and behaviour genetics in the 1990s and 2000s. The currently evolving economic situation led me to a return to political economy theories, already a focus of my undergraduate studies at the Université de Montréal, to complete the theoretical orientation to families within their contexts.

Notice that the title of this book contains the word *families* rather than *the family*; indeed, several types of families exist under one rubric. Despite this diversity, families can be analyzed as an **institution***N. In fact, families are the most basic institution of any society: It is within their folds that citizens are born, sheltered, and begin their

NOTE: Words are bolded to accentuate key concepts and themes or to serve as additional subtitles within a section: These words do *not* necessarily appear in the Glossary. Words appearing in the Glossary have an asterisk sign (*) next to them.

socialization. **Socialization*** is the process whereby children learn how to think and behave according to the ways of the society and the group in which they are born and raised. Children are not, however, passive recipients in this process: They respond according to their personalities, needs, and accumulated experiences. They accept, reject, or transform the cultural messages that they receive from parents and others. It is thus through this process that a society transmits its culture, with some or many modifications, to the next generation. *It is also through socialization that a society perpetuates and reconstructs its gender, racial, and economic structure as well as the roles that flow from it.*

Why are families called an institution (Durkheim, 1895)? An *institution* is a recognized area of social life that is organized along a system of widely accepted norms that have developed over time to regulate behaviours. The elements of organization and norms contribute to the predictability of life: People know what to expect—it is a shared culture. Over time, each society evolves a set of norms or rules that guides the behaviours of family members toward one another and toward other institutions. Other key institutions in a society may be the economic, legal, religious, educational, as well as the political, the military, or even the police. We will study some of these institutions as they intersect with families in subsequent chapters, particularly in Part 2 and in the last chapter. These institutions are not equally important throughout the world's societies. In some countries, educational institutions are quasi absent or are reserved mainly for males, as in Afghanistan, or reserved for the more affluent classes. Social institutions are at various stages in different countries: In some, the political institutions are new and just developing; in others, the military and police play a fundamental role. Thus, families are not affected in a similar way across the world by other major institutions.

In nearly all large societies of the world, change has become part of the institution of the family. This situation leaves many people uncomfortable about the future of the family and raises concerns in their minds about its fragility. But, as we will see in Chapter 2, although family forms may change, *the institution itself remains* while its responsibilities evolve and even multiply.

HOW CAN FAMILIES BE DEFINED?

The task of defining what families are is a difficult one these days. Experts do not all agree in this respect. Some want to eliminate the institutional aspect from the definition and replace it with a focus on close and sexually intimate relationships, however temporary. Others include networks of friends as a kind of family. For them, the emphasis is on the voluntariness ("chosen") and the relational aspects of the relationships. For the purpose of the census, Statistics Canada broadened its definition in 2002 in order to reflect some of the current processes. For instance, its definition (Statistics Canada, 2002a) includes a couple, of any sexual combination, with or without children, married or cohabiting, as well as "a lone parent of any marital status, with at least one child living in the same dwelling," or a grandparent raising a grandchild.

In this book, the definition adopted reflects current changes but also retains the institutional aspect and focuses on the **intergenerational** dimension of families: A family is a social group, an institution, and an intergenerational group of individuals related to one another by blood, adoption, or marriage/cohabitation. *It is a group that endures over several generations* (White and Klein, 2002). The minimum requirement to meet this definition at the nuclear level (see Table 1.1) is the combination of two generations in one household, or the nuclear family. Or it can refer to persons living together who are related to one another through another generation, such as siblings or cousins. Finally, it should be added that families existed among pre-humans and still exist among primates and other animals. It is an evolutionary and necessary system for the care of the young and helpless, and for the survival of the species (Sprey, 2009). In this respect, families should not be equated with marriage, which is a late cultural invention in the history of humanity—even though many animal species are monogamous for life (Durkheim, 1895).

Therefore, the typology of families presented here does *not* include unrelated single people living together, even though they constitute a **household** unit or share an address. Such persons are members of their families of origin or of procreation but do not themselves constitute a family. Although this definition is restrictive in terms of what constitutes a family (not a couple, not roommates sharing a house, not friends), it is quite inclusive as to the number and sex of parents present and takes recent social changes into consideration. In contrast, past definitions of the nuclear family did not include unmarried mothers or same-sex-parent families, for instance. This definitional distinction is important, not only in terms of accuracy but also because it carries family policy implications.

As mentioned, some critics opt for a much broader definition of the family. This definition includes any person one wishes to recognize as such or feels close to or shares a household with. Thus, best friends can become a family, and so can neighbours who help each other a great deal, as well as former partners, ex-spouses, and friends' relatives. The emphasis is on "intimate relations," which, it is argued, are more egalitarian and inclusive than families. This broad inclusiveness as to what constitutes a family, while positive at the emotional and social levels, is quite problematic for analytical and social policy purposes.

To begin with, such an inclusive family group overlaps with the concepts of **social networks** and support networks. Second, social policies designed to facilitate family life do need a modicum of definitional precision. Third, if we so broaden the definition of the family, it runs the risk of becoming useless. Basically, if we choose to include anyone we are close to at the moment, the concept of family will become so elastic that it will be meaningless and will have no continuity over time. As O'Brien and Goldberg (2000) put it, membership in a family is an **ascribed status*** while friendship networks are acquired: "Status ascription is one of the reasons that family relations tend to be enduring, whereas friendships change over time, especially when significant changes take place in a person's life" (p. 136). As well, a *family is enduring* (Stott, 2006). For instance, when a couple has children and separates, each ex-spouse remains part of their children's families as parents. The children then have a binuclear family and remain in both nuclear family groups. By using an intergenerational perspective, this text repositions procreation, adoption, and related linkages as central to the definition of families—no matter the gender or number of parents.

TABLE 1.1	**Typology of Families and Unions**

Type	Description
Families	
Nuclear family	*At least* one parent and one child living together
Conjugal	Husband, wife, and child(ren)
	Cohabitants with child
	Same-sex parents with child
Single parent	One parent and his or her child living together
Grandparent/grandchild	One grandparent or two grandparents and grandchild living together
Reconstituted	Remarried spouses or cohabiting spouses when at least one had a child from a former union
Horizontal	Sisters or brothers or cousins living together without the parent generation
Extended family	All the members of a family, including child, parents, grandparents, and other ascendants, plus uncles, aunts, and cousins (by blood, adoption, or marriage)
In one household	Generally involves three generations: at least one parent and his or her child living with another relative, usually the child's grandparent or aunt or uncle
In multiple households	Members of a family, including child, parents, grandparents, and other ascendants, plus uncles, aunts, and cousins (by blood, marriage, or adoption) living in separate dwellings and interacting on a regular basis
Unions	
Legal marriage	Socially/legally/religiously sanctioned union, which is generally heterosexual but could also be of same-sex partners, depending on the jurisdiction involved
Cohabitation	Consensual union that is not legally (common-law) sanctioned but is legally protected in Canada: It can involve same-sex or opposite-sex partners
Living apart together (LAT)	Union in which the two partners maintain separate residences
Monogamy	A legal marriage or cohabitation involving only two partners
Serial monogamy (serial polygamy)	Sequence of spouses or partners over time as in the sequence of marriage, divorce, and remarriage; spouses or cohabitants succeed each other
Polygamy	Multiple partners or spouses at the same time
Polygyny	One man married to more than one woman at the same time
Polyandry	One woman married to more than one man at the same time

Nuclear Families

A parent and his or her children as well as two parents with their children form the most elementary type of family—referred to as the nuclear family. When a person or a couple has a child, whether by birth, adoption, or surrogacy, a nuclear family of **procreation** is formed. What is important is that *a new generation is added*. Under this definition, a grandmother who raises her granddaughter, a single man who adopts a son, a lesbian couple who share children with a gay man, and a polygamous man with his wives and their children each also constitute a nuclear family. However, a husband and wife, a cohabiting couple, and a same-sex couple fall under the category of **couples** (see the lower panel of Table 1.1). They constitute a nuclear family only upon the arrival of their first child. These couples are, however, members of their own families of **origin** or **orientation**. That is, they "belong to" or originate from their parents and their parents' families.

This said, who constitutes a nuclear family and under what circumstances calls for some flexibility. For instance, when young adults move out of their parents' house and set up a new household, are they still part of the parents' nuclear family or do the parents become their extended family? One has to consider the fact that parents and their adult children who live separately may still consider themselves a nuclear family. Similarly, in a situation of divorce, children may experience what is termed a **binuclear** family; that is, half of their nuclear family is constituted by themselves and their mother and the other half by themselves and their father. When brothers and sisters share a household together without their parents, this is often referred to as a **horizontal** nuclear family because there is only one generation involved—but this generation originates from that of the parents.

Extended Families

Other relatives constitute the *extended* family or *kinship* group: grandparents, aunts, uncles, cousins, and in-laws (Milardo, 2009). There is fluidity between nuclear and extended families. It is not an either-or category (see upper part of Table 1.1). Most people belong to an extended family as well as to a nuclear family. Contrary to what is often believed, extended families living together under one roof (**multi-generational households**) have never been the norm in Canada, except among certain Aboriginal groups. English and French people arrived here with a tradition of "nuclearity" (Thornton, 2005). Even rural Quebec was an exception rather than a rule when, in the 19th and early 20th centuries, most elderly parents lived with *one* of their many children when widowed or ill.

Three-generational households have increased in Canada in the past two decades, largely as a consequence of the return home of adult children with their own children and immigration from Asia. The majority of these extended families live in cities, and in 48 percent of the cases such families contain one or two grandparents with a single parent and his or her children. Yet, despite this increase, in 2011, only 4.8 percent of Canadians lived in multi-generational households (Statistics Canada, 2012b). It is estimated that only about 7 to 10 percent of adult children in Canada live with an *elderly* parent (Mitchell, 2003).

The level of exchange taking place between the nuclear family and the extended family varies by coresidence, proximity of neighbourhood, and even for emotional and cultural reasons. In North America, most relationships between members of an extended kin system are optional—perhaps with the exception of communities in Newfoundland and Labrador because of the historical isolation of these fishing communities, the harsh environment, and dangerous subsistence activities. All these led to a greater reliance on kin and near kin. But, overall, in North America, for example, if two brothers and their wives or children do not get along, they are not forced to see each other, particularly if they live at a distance. In contrast, the kinship group is still a key organizational unit in many African and Asian societies today. For instance, in many cultures of Africa, children are still fostered to kin for their socialization (Twum-Danso Imoh, 2012). As we see in Chapter 2, most newly arrived families are more kinship oriented than are average Canadian-born families. Among the former, the extended family is more institutionalized: They often entertain higher values of reciprocity and have more exact rules of behaviour concerning their extended kin (Barrow, 1996; Yax-Fraser, 2011).

In some ethnic groups—of Latin American descent, for instance—friends may be assimilated into the family as they become godparents to children. In the Mexican vernacular, this is the system of *compradrazgo*. When a father's friend is a frequent visitor to the house, he may be called an uncle (*tio*) and a mother's friend becomes an aunt (*tia*), thus creating what some researchers call **fictive kinship** bonds, which were very important for the well-being of Chinese male immigrants to Canada in the mid to late 1800s (Marshall, 2011). Many Inuit groups similarly extend their kin system to the kin of kin (Miller, 2005:177).

Types of Union and Marriage

As indicated in Table 1.1, there are several types of union and marriage in the world. In Canada, the only two types of marriage and common-law union that are legally accepted are between *one* man and *one* woman or between *two* persons of the same sex. Polygamy in the form of *polygyny* (a man married to two or more women) became illegal in 1878 both in Canada and the U.S. *Polyandry* (a woman married to two or more men) is less frequently encountered across the world and tends to be localized in smaller societies.

Polygamy as a Conjugal and Family Type

Polygamy, in the form of a man married to two or more wives (polygyny), has resurfaced as an issue both in Canada and the U.S. in the past few years. It received wide media attention between 2008 and 2011, particularly with respect to Bountiful, British Columbia, and even Toronto (Javed, 2008). Indeed, an unknown number of polygamous Mormon families still exist in the U.S. and Canada, although they are not recognized by the mainstream Utah-based Church of Jesus Christ of Latter Day Saints. In 2009, 81 percent of Canadian adults disapproved of polygamy: 90 percent of women and 70 percent of men (MacQueen, 2009).

Polygyny was far more widespread throughout the world in the past and is mentioned in the Old Testament. It could be found in Asia, Europe, in non-Muslim parts of Africa, and some of the First Nations of the Americas. It is recognized in the Qur'an and accepted as a practice but *not* as a requirement (Ward, 2010). Today, polygamy is a minority phenomenon, even in countries that recognize it legally, such as South Africa (Stacey, 2011). It is said to be practised mainly by well-to-do men. The Qur'an specifies that a husband has to have the means to support all his wives. But some men in poverty resort to it. Generally women are more likely to enter a polygamous marriage when they are rural, have little education, and come from a disadvantaged family (Al-Krenawi et al., 2006). Historically, polygamy was rooted in agrarian societies where men who owned a great deal of land, for instance, benefited from the help of several wives and an extensive progeny. Wives and children were signs of wealth and producers of wealth. Plural marriages were also useful for the purpose of integrating widows and their children into another household in countries where women had no independent standing.

Today still, polygamy tends to be practised more in rural areas where agricultural activities can benefit from the birth of many sons and where co-wives have more space in which to establish quasi-separate residences with their children within the patrilocal compound (Stacey, 2011). It is not coincidental that, both in Canada and the U.S., polygamy exists mainly in rural enclaves isolated from mainstream culture. One can, therefore, ask how polygamy fits in societies that are highly urbanized and technological; need an educated workforce, including women's labour outside the home; and have a high population density. Within this analysis, polygamy can be seen as an outdated institution that no longer provides any economic benefit. In fact, more and more Asian and African societies are limiting its scope; some are introducing a gradual reduction in the number of wives permitted, while others are outlawing it outright (Coontz, 2006).

At the demographic level, and disregarding the issue of equity, there is a question of **sex ratio*** **imbalance** that arises where polygamy is practised by a segment of the population, even if it is a minority one. That is, as a proportion of men acquire more than one wife, there are not enough potential wives left. As a result, other men, generally the less fortunate ones, cannot marry, or have to wait until they are much older to do so. Or, yet, they may have to take a very young bride, or one who would not otherwise be "marriageable." Consequently, female age at marriage is generally low, often as low as the 9- to 14-year range, as occurs in Afghanistan and Yemen, for instance. As a result of this scarcity of women, parents may focus on the girls' role in the marriage market to the detriment of their education. In offshoot Mormon communities in the west of Canada and the U.S., many teenage boys have been expulsed from their familial enclaves and rejected from their group so that they would not compete for wives with the more senior males. This demographic situation is similar to what happens in countries such as China and parts of India where **female feticide*** (abortion of female fetuses) is practised: The male-to-female ratio increases, leaving many men unmarried and childless (Attané, 2006; Das Gupta et al., 2009; Guilmoto, 2009).

At the interpersonal level, the results of polygamy differ and may be more positive for men than women (Tsai and Dzorgbo, 2012). There may be competition between co-wives for a husband's attention and, especially, for material necessities. Which of their children the husband will favour is also a great and divisive concern (Ward, 2010). Indeed, the mother of a favourite son can expect a more comfortable old age. In some African societies, the fosterage of children to a wife's kin is often seen as a protection against co-wives' maltreatment (Twum-Danso Imoh, 2012). Yes, many co-wives learn to enjoy the benefits that additional hands bring to household labour, child care, chores related to small-business ownership, and help in horticultural activities. They may together obtain concessions from their shared husband and exercise a certain degree of power in the household and status in the community. In some countries, the senior wife, especially when she has had sons, benefits from having a co-wife: This raises her status and she may even help her husband in selecting subsequent wives. When co-wives are sisters or kin, their relatedness may help them adapt to each other and offers a certain level of protection (Yanca and Low, 2003). Even in American polygamous communities, many women report benefiting from the help and companionship they provide to one another (Forbes, 2003).

What about the children? It is very difficult to assess the research literature in this respect because the effects of polygamy on children certainly depend on the cultural and socio-economic context in which it is embedded. Therefore, the studies that exist in Africa and Asia cannot be applied to the cases found in Canada, the U.S., or Great Britain, where polygamy is not institutionally supported (Campbell, 2005). For instance, a focus group study of polygamous families in Jordan found that mothers, fathers, and children felt that children were normally treated (Khasawneh and Hijazi, 2011).

When polygamous families immigrate to western cities, as has been the case for a long period in France, they cannot afford a separate residence for each wife and her children. As a result, family members live in crowded conditions fostering stress and conflict between co-wives and their children. "There have been reports of women treated in Paris hospitals for physical injuries resulting from confrontations among family members, often co-wives" (Campbell, 2005:2). It is impossible to estimate how many polygamous families are in Canada as a result of recent immigration from African and Asian countries. Two women students mentioned it in their autobiographies in 2005; in one case, one of the two wives had arrived here as the "sister" of her husband in order to be accepted by Canadian Immigration. In the other case, the older wife, who was the student's mother, had been left behind ten years earlier with few resources.

> *"I am working very hard to get a good job to sponsor my mother* [who was only 38 years old] *and we will live together . . . I'll find a job for her, not too hard because she always slaved for my father and his side of the family and I want her to have some happiness. I won't tell my father because he might claim her to use her. . . . When I get married I'll take her with me because she couldn't survive alone, she's too inexperienced with life . . . I'll have to be very careful because my father may want to marry me off as soon as I graduate here and I should count myself lucky that this hasn't already happened but I don't think that he'll ship me off back home for this but just in case, I've made contacts with a group of women and I'm planning on moving to* [deleted] *as soon as I save money but the other problem will be to hide my pay check from my father. . . ."*

When the law of a society such as Canada does not allow for multiple wives, one of the wives who is not the "legal" one may be unprotected—even though some provincial laws, such as the *Ontario Family Law Act*, provide spousal support and welfare benefits. But these women may not be aware of these benefits and it is more than likely that their husband would not want them to know. This is one of the key questions that some Canadian legal experts are debating (Bala et al., 2005): Such wives may have no recourse in terms of support for themselves and their children after a religious divorce; they may even lose their children, especially when they are left behind in the home country. Hence, polygamous immigrant families face multiple challenges: Not only do they have to adapt to a new country but they also have to adapt to a different legal family situation and the criminalization of wife abuse.

Basically, throughout the world, the success of polygamy in terms of individualism (that is, how happy and well functioning the spouses and their children are) depends on the sociocultural context within which a polygamous family lives, including the fair treatment received by women within this type of family—a difficult balance to achieve (Hassouneh-Phillips, 2001; Madhavan, 2002). Al-Krenawi et al. (2006) concludes that "problematic family functioning is more characteristic of polygynous families than monogamous families" (p. 184)—perhaps a result of the greater complexity of this type of family structure (Al-Krenawi et al., 2002). A sophisticated analysis of the evolution of social inequalities shows that polygamy is a key indicator* of inequality in societies throughout the world (Nielsen, 2004).

WHAT THEORETICAL PERSPECTIVES INFORM FAMILY STUDIES?

The study of families requires a *multidisciplinary* approach, from demography and economics to psychology and social work. In the same vein, several theoretical perspectives are necessary to guide and explain family research (White, 2005). A **theory*** is a set of interrelated propositions that explains a particular phenomenon and guides research. In this section, some of the main theoretical perspectives that are encountered in the sociological study of families in western countries are examined. Two others are added that, although psychological in origin, are sociologically oriented and inform several discussions in this text. *Each theory that follows explains certain aspects of family life, but no theory alone explains it in its entirety and all its contexts.* Often, two or three theories combined provide a more thorough explanation of reality. However, all the extant theories were developed in the context of individualistic and capitalist societies in the western world. As such, they are imbued with the values of this economic system (Bahr and Bahr, 2001). As well, how these theories apply to non-western countries, especially less developed rural ones, remains to be tested (Arnett, 2008).

Structural Functionalism

Structural functionalism analyzes a society's organization, its structure, and the linkages between its various systems (Merton, 1968). Its protagonists were initially influenced by Durkheim (1893, 1897). Within this model, the family is an important unit that fulfills key **functions*** for society, such as child socialization. In turn, a society's social structure provides the overall cultural and organizational contexts that influence family life. The analogy is organic: An organism (the society) is a system with many subsystems that collaborate or function together to optimize its success. The various systems fulfill functions or do things for one another.

The sociologist responsible for the propagation of structural functionalism was Talcott Parsons (1951). Structural functionalism was, to some extent, a theory with *assumptions of consensus or equilibrium*. It left little room to address and redress inequalities in the social structure, because these inequalities were perceived to be fulfilling necessary functions for the entire society. Thus, this framework was not sufficiently flexible to analyze family developments. The changing role of women, for instance, could not be adequately examined because, under this perspective, even maternal employment threatened families' equilibrium.

As well, the differentiation along gender lines between the **instrumental role** (father as the breadwinner responsible for linking the family to the society at large) and the **expressive role** (mother who cares for children, maintains relationships, and does the housework) was not sustainable with the return to paid employment of a majority of women, the changes in gender ideologies, and the increasingly expressive role of fathers (Luxton, 2009). It is interesting that, in this respect, Cristi (2012) has argued that Durkheim did not consider the female aspect of the social order. Nevertheless, if one rereads Parsons and Bales's *Family, Socialization and Interaction Process* (1955), their analysis of the family is still relevant in some respects. Particularly important is the view that, as agents of socialization, parents must "interpenetrate" other systems in order to be successful in their role (p. 35), a perspective that is linked to the discussion of family responsibilities in Chapter 3.

Political Economy Theories

Overall, political economy perspectives analyze social inequalities within the context of the historical development of the economy, particularly the capitalist market economy. They explain how families, roles, group world views and values differ according to the situation that each family and group occupies in the economic stratification* system. These perspectives are paramount in this text where inequalities between families are discussed, particularly in Parts 2 and 5: Families' living conditions, especially poverty, are analyzed through the political and economic arrangements of society (Coburn, 2010). Unlike functionalism, this interpretation does not defend the *status quo;* rather, it suggests the necessity for change at the global level.

Conflict theories (not to be confused with inter-personal conflict) have several roots, particularly Marxist theory; they include the political economy approaches. In a nutshell, these theories explain that conflict largely arises when there is an unequal distribution of scarce resources and power, whether between societies, men and women, the rich and the poor, as well as majority and minority* groups, particularly racialized groups (Galabuzi, 2006). Last century, Ralph Dahrendorf (1959) was the main sociologist to propose that theory should include both conflict theory and consensus theory. As well, in terms of feminist analyses, the perspectives presented by Frederich Engels' (1884) *Origins of the family, private property and the state* have been especially relevant along with Marx's best known work, *Capital* (1867). Engels' work was written within its 19th century context of a newly industrialized Europe, particularly England, and he was heavily influenced by Henry Morgan's *Ancient Society* (1877). As a result, Engels' *Origins* is at times incorrect in its details but, as Eleanor Leacock points out in her introduction, his key points that matrilineality preceded patrilineality and that "the position of women relative to men deteriorated with the advent of class society" are supported by evidence. But Engels' analysis failed at some basic level: He equated production with the male sphere and human reproduction and related activities with the female sphere (Luxton, 2006a:25).

What is particularly important for us to retain is the fact that Marx and Engels and those they have inspired, particularly feminist political theorists, argue that how the economy is organized throughout the centuries brings different types of human relations, gender roles*, and familial structures (Luxton, 2006a). These are often embedded in economic exploitation of labour, from slavery, to serfdom, to sweatshops and low-paid work, and are contextualized within racist and sexist contexts (Arat-Koç, 2011; Galabuzi, 2006). The development of agriculture thousands of years ago (however basic it was at the outset) brought surpluses, private property, control by the ruling class over the means of production and access to labour—all of which, in turn, created unequal roles between men and women as well as class divisions between families and groups.

As we see throughout this text, in the past few years, especially since the severe depression of 2008, many analysts of the international economic situation have used analytical frameworks that have been inspired by Marxism—which is particularly relevant to us because of the increasing gap between rich and poor families, the dismantling of the middle class, and the control over the economy by the "one percent," as seen in Chapter 4. This further inequality has even spread, in the form of state capitalism, to countries such as Russia and China that are labeled communist and are theoretically classless. Currently, the groups (classes) that own and control the means of production are IT companies, car and clothing manufacturers, agribusiness, "big" oil and gas, banks and financial institutions on Bay Street and Wall Street, as well as the professions that support them legally (Livesey, 2012). Further, it has been decades since the economy has been as insecure as it now is (Bartels, 2008; Rifkin, 2011) and as concentrated in terms of control in the hands of a few, even at the international level (Brenna, 2012; Mackenzie, 2012a; Yalnizyan, 2010). Large multinational corporations, always eager to maximize their profits, pit the labour forces of the western economies against those of lower-wage countries, such as China, India, Vietnam, and the Philippines. As wages rise in these regions (such as is the case for China currently), companies find other countries that have yet to be industrialized on a large scale. This shifting (or offshoring) of jobs to other countries creates unemployment in western countries. While resulting in higher employment and higher wages in countries such as China and India, and lifting millions out of poverty, this situation also perversely increases social inequalities in these same societies where the state and a very few families control access to and remuneration for all these new jobs (Acemoglu and Robinson, 2012).

Social inequalities are increasingly threatening our future (Stiglitz, 2012). Thus, the economic situation of families throughout the world is affected and, as we see in Parts 1, 2 and 5, so are gender roles, opportunities for health care, the education of children, the contents of this education, family time and resources, as well as housing and transnational families. There is, consequently, a close link between these theories and feminist perspectives, an amalgamation of which is constituted within the feminist political theory approach which, for instance, currently adds depth to the analysis of transnational families (e.g., Arat-Koç, 2011; de Wolff, 2006) with a particular focus on **social reproduction*** (Luxton, 2006a). At the personal level, we have become dependent on the market economy which destroys regulations (Kern, 2010), invents services and related language—what Arlie Hochschild (2012) calls the commodification of intimate and community life: "While market forces have eroded stability and fostered anxiety at work and at home, it is, ironically, mainly the market that provides support and relief" (p. 1). The market economy is colonizing our thought system and **commodifying*** care, whether child care or elder care (Macdonald, 2010).

As well, the dominant class or classes are able to control part of the political process (Bartels, 2008; Langille, 2009). The dominant class also controls the ideologies or ideas that guide the relationships of production; the "needs" of consumers; parts of the media contents, especially via advertising; and even the school system and educational contents, as we see in several chapters. Thus, political economy theories are very helpful in explaining, at least in part, the situation of families currently and in the past.

Social Exchange and Rational Theories

Both social exchange and rational theories are the products of the sociocultural environment of the 20th century and their development was influenced by the discipline of economics. For its part, exchange theory owes a great deal to the influence of the philosophical perspective of utilitarianism, which is based on the assumption of individual self-interests (White and Klein, 2002:33). Resources occupy a key role in both these frameworks.

Social Exchange Theory

The early proponents of exchange theory were psychologists John Thibaut and Harold Kelly (1959) along with sociologists George Homans (1961) and Peter Blau (1964). Homans and Blau agreed that all the parties involved in an exchange should receive something that they perceive to be equivalent; otherwise imbalance will occur: One person will have power in the relationship while the other will be at a disadvantage. In this context, Homans used the term "distributive justice" while Blau referred to "fair exchange." However, Blau saw exchange as a more subjective and interpretive phenomenon than did Homans.

The basic assumption behind social exchange theory is that people interact and make choices so as to *maximize* their own *benefits* or rewards and to *minimize* their *costs*. In the market metaphor of exchange theory, **resources** and **power** occupy a central position—a perspective anticipated in Blood and Wolfe's (1960) research design in the mid-1950s. As explained by Sabatelli and Shehan (1993), "Each spouse's resources and each spouse's dependence on the relationship must be taken into account, for example, when attempting to study marital power" (p. 386). The spouse who has alternatives outside a marriage weighs the advantages of these alternatives against those secured in the current marriage. This theory has also given rise to the equity model or the perception of equity (see Sprechner, 2001). Thus, social exchange theory focuses on rational choices. Its emphasis on resources, which is called capital in rational theory below, brings an element of commonality between the two theories.

Exchange theory has been particularly useful in explaining gender relations, the household division of labour, and why people enter into, remain in, or leave relationships (Sassler, 2010). See Chapters 7 and 9, for instance. As well, decisions concerning separation or divorce are affected by the relative resources of the spouses and the perceived alternatives. The spouse with the most alternatives may be the least committed (Blau, 1964). However, one can argue that this principle does not always apply in the decision to divorce because more women than men now decide to divorce despite the fact that they have fewer alternatives after. Yet, if women make this step, it is often because of a perceived inequity within their marriage.

This market or economic orientation to human relations presents some difficulties for researchers who may want to use theories focusing on altruism, collectivism, and reciprocity (Bahr and Bahr, 2001; Hansen, 2005; Nelson, 2005). It is difficult, for instance, to believe that western parents make so many sacrifices for their children on the basis of the expectation of rewards. In fact, there is often an imbalance of power in favour of children when parents raise adolescents who are particularly difficult (Ambert, 2007). This, in itself, flies in the face of another tenet of exchange theory: that social groups such as the family exist and endure because they allow individuals to maximize their rewards. In contrast, Becker's (1974) concept of altruistic motives was tied to a sense of duty or moral obligation (Rajulton and Ravanera, 2006b). As Carroll et al. (2005) point out, morality and altruism are key motivators, especially in family life: Social exchange cannot account for these. In fact, in some areas, particularly isolated coastal communities in Newfoundland and Labrador and among the Inuit, survival depended, and still does to some extent, on others' help and altruistic exchanges. Another critique of this orientation resides in the fact that people's choices are not always made purposively or objectively (Parsons, 2005:14).

Rational Theory

Resources are also a key element of rational theory, which is currently used in the study of certain domains of family life. James Coleman (1990a) has been at the origin of this theoretical interest in family research in North America, albeit preceded by the French sociologists Durkheim (1897) and Bourdieu (1977). What I have excised from this theory for the purpose of this book is the concept of capital—social, human, and cultural (Coleman, 1988, 1990b). These concepts, particularly evident in Chapter 6, are used extensively to explain the socialization outcomes of children of various social classes, for instance (Bourdieu, 1977). In this sense, rational theory is more one of capital and community than one of choice by individuals, as is the case for exchange theory.

Human capital* refers to abilities, skills, education, and positive human characteristics inherited or acquired by a person. This concept is of paramount importance

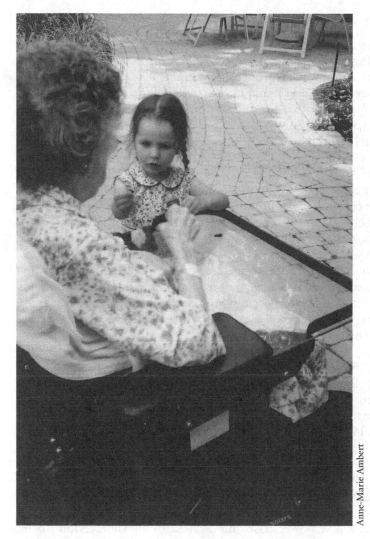

Anne-Marie Ambert

This three-year-old girl has five grandmothers: a grandmother and a great-grandmother on her father's side; a grandmother, great-grandmother, and great-great-grandmother on her mother's side. She knows each by name, "Gran Jeanne," "Gran Maria," and so on, and is well aware of their individual characteristics. She benefits from a rich web of intergenerational social capital.

in knowledge-based economies that require skills largely shaped by early childhood education (Bogenschneider and Corbett, 2010). **Cultural capital** (adapted from Bourdieu, 1977, 1984) refers to parents' general knowledge and aspects of their lifestyle that can promote their children's achievement. **Social capital***, a concept largely ignored by Bourdieu (Erickson, 1996), refers to resources that individual families are able to secure on the basis of membership in social networks (Portes, 1998; Statistics Canada, 2004l). In this text, social resources enhance families' sense of belonging, child socialization, and the acquisition of human and cultural capital. One type of social capital is evident when parents cooperate, agree, and share authority, which allows their children to learn norms more effectively. The same result occurs when the parental role is supported by a community. In both cases, **social closure** exists (White, 2005:71); that is, social networks are closed so that children are less subjected to conflicting norms. Another type of social capital refers to friendships, contacts with neighbours, and participation in volunteer work within communities, a key to well-being among older Canadians (Theurer and Wister, 2010).

Further, Coleman and Hoffer (1987) have been the proponents of the **effective community***, which I have adopted as one of the themes of this book. An effective community exists when neighbours are willing to take responsibility for all the children in their community (Sampson et al., 1999). This situation, whereby groups of parents share a particular prosocial set of values, enhances individual parents' social capital and contributes to the monitoring of all children (Aird, 2001). It allows for social closure and constitutes an element of *collective socialization*. In simple terms, parents are not alone and this refers us to the often-heard catch phrase that "it takes a village to raise a child."

Social Constructionism

There is diversity within constructionist positions (Crotty, 1998; Potter, 1996), and some are more psychological than sociological. Social constructionism has its roots in the classical sociology of knowledge, from Karl Mannheim's *Ideology and Utopia* (1936) through the better known Berger and Luckmann's *The Social Construction of Reality* (1966). The theory argues that various phenomena that are taken for granted and seem natural are actually culturally defined or socially constructed: A **social construct***** is a social and cultural creation or interpretation. A case in point is childhood, which has been redefined throughout the centuries according to prevailing *socioeconomic* changes (Ariès, 1962; Parr, 2003). William Kessen explained in 1979 how children are socially constructed by psychologists. He described the American child and psychology as two cultural "inventions," or social constructs. Badinter (2010) and Druckerman (2012) similarly describe how the French child is socially constructed with different socialization practices and impact on mothers than is the case in North America. As well, childhood is lived very differently in smaller, less stratified societies (Hewlett and Lamb, 2005). Gergen et al. (1996) also analyzed the discipline of psychology as a western product. Another example resides in the concepts of old age as well as elder abuse and neglect, as seen in Chapter 13 (Harbison et al., 2012). While social age rests on a biological reality, it nevertheless differs cross-culturally (Hareven, 2000:221).

Family life is socially redefined according to the socioeconomic needs of a society at any point in time (Ferree et al., 1999)—and it is currently being recast within a global market economy framework (Hochschild, 2012). This social construction of family life generally comes from those who are in **power** as well as from **experts** who produce the knowledge that is valued by a society at a particular time in its history (Dej, 2011; McCarthy, 1996). Such valued knowledge can be religious, medical, psychological, economic, or even legal expertise—all of which have evolved from a masculine power base. It is not surprising, then, that social constructionism is related to feminism (D. E. Smith, 1993). Both emphasize culture as an explanation for the definition of gender roles as well as masculinity and femininity. Both approaches present a critique of certain aspects of society (Calixte et al., 2010). Furthermore, this critique can in turn create a new power base and be used to alleviate certain social conditions created by the constructs, whether it be motherhood, fatherhood, adoption, adolescence, or the viability of same-sex-parent families, as examples.

The Gendered Social Construction of Parenthood

One of the most important influences on individuals' lives arises from the gendered social construction of parenthood. The overall social stratification by gender dictates that women and men fulfill different functions in their respective parenting roles. The consequent household division of labour is largely unequal and gives far more flexibility to males, who can choose the activities they engage in at home (Fox, 2001). However, as we see in Chapter 4, changes in the economy and at the cultural level are altering the framework within which fathers and mothers interpret their roles. As well, more fathers are sharing equally in parenting while others are their children's only visible parents (Doucet, 2006).

Motherhood

Probably the most salient metamorphosis that occurs in the formation of a new nuclear family is the transformation of a girl or a woman into a mother. Motherhood is, above all, a social and cultural phenomenon (Arendell, 2000): *It is socially constructed to serve the culture of the time and the economic system of a society—* and this returns us to political economy theories. It is also defined according to the prevailing definition of childhood and of children's needs and roles within that particular economic system (Wall, 2004). The "nature" of childhood is socially constructed and thus differs from culture to culture and from century to century. Thus, mothering is defined along with the nature of childhood, as the "needs" of children differ culturally (Ambert, 1994b; Badinter, 2010; Druckerman, 2012). For instance, in North America, it is believed that small children need to be talked to, given affection, allowed some autonomy, and prepared for school. As well, their self-esteem has to be nurtured, despite the fact that an overly high self-esteem may be detrimental (Menon et al., 2007) and can lead to narcissism (Twenge and Campbell, 2010). More and more, the emphasis is placed on the development of intellectual abilities and achievement from a young age, particularly among middle-class parents (Lareau, 2011). Such beliefs about children's needs place specific demands on how women mother (Hays, 1996). In other societies, such as the Efe and Bofi foragers and the Lese and Bofi farmers of Central Africa, small children are defined as needing assistance from older children, having to learn how to help in and around the house and how to get along with others (Fouts et al., 2005; Hewlett and Lamb, 2005). Such needs place fewer demands on mothers and bring vastly different socialization practices (Bornstein and Putnick, 2012).

Once there is agreement in a society or in a social class on what is "in the best interest of the child," that is, within a particular economy, what mothers should do and should be is implicitly and explicitly constructed (Miller, 2005). For instance, the Gusii in East Africa, an agrarian people, focus on the health and survival of their infants because of high mortality. The role of caregivers is accordingly scripted around child safety and feeding. Notions pertaining to the development of self-esteem, attachment, and intellectual abilities simply do not exist (in Hewlett and Lamb, 2005). Thus, the role description of Efe, Lese, and Gusii mothers does not include activities and concerns about these aspects of development. Whiting and Edwards (1988:94) have found that, in some societies, mothers initiate very few nurturing acts, such as cuddling; they leave these aspects of child care to older children. This observation led Whiting and Edwards to suggest that current stereotypes regarding the nature of the maternal role should be revised.

Further, in many western societies, it is believed that mothers are absolutely essential to children's well-being, and that women have a natural or "instinctual," rather than learned, aptitude for mothering (Eyer, 1992). Although it may be that mothers are indeed the most important persons and parents in a majority of children's lives in modern societies, this should not be taken to mean that *one* mother is a necessity of human nature. Indeed, the western focus on individual mothers at the core of children's development is not universal. Many anthropologists question it as an *ethnocentric* phenomenon* (LeVine, 1990). That is, motherhood is defined according to western criteria.

The reality is that multiple mothering and even **multiple parenting** are in the majority in many agrarian and gathering societies where several women in a community share in the care and supervision of children, particularly in Africa (Scarr, 1998; Twum-Danso Imoh, 2012). Members of the village are responsible for all children; older siblings or other youngsters are often small children's caregivers as well as their main source of psychological comfort and discomfort (Fouts et al., 2005). To some extent, one encounters multiple parenting among North American blacks and even more so in some Caribbean as well as in some Aboriginal communities (Barrow, 1996; Collins, 1992). The care of small children by older ones was widely practised in black families during slavery (Illick, 2002).

In contrast, many western societies, particularly the U.S. and Canada, require **intensive mothering**—mothering that is expert-guided, is labour intensive at the middle-class level, and emphasizes the child's psychological development, particularly the promotion of self-esteem and individualism (Harkness and Super, 2002; Lareau, 2011). The child is seen as a project that has to be perfected (Wall, 2001): The child becomes a product and motherhood (and soon fatherhood) becomes a performance to be evaluated and rated—yet again, a market economy vocabulary (Macdonald, 2010). Hays (1996) discusses the cultural contradictions of what is involved in this type of motherhood. She points out that this social construct requires mothers to expend a tremendous amount of time, energy, and money in raising their children. Yet, in consumerist western economies, two salaries are often necessary, so neither parent can afford to stay home and care for their children 24 hours a day. Thus, at the same time that the ever-demanding economy propels men and women into the workplace, it also requires of these parents that children be raised intensively. The end result is that the requirements of the current social constructions of motherhood and childhood compete (Hays, 1998). This may be reflected in the fact that, in a Canadian longitudinal* survey, having children at home was related to elevated risk of distress among women but a substantially reduced risk of such among men (Orpana et al., 2009). In many societies, women's main identity once they have a child is as a mother. In other societies, such as France, the woman comes before the mother—and this has been so for several centuries (Badinter, 2010).

Another example of the social construction of motherhood rests on the changes that have taken place regarding what is the **"proper" feeding of infants**. Before the 1970s, to breast-feed or bottle-feed was a choice on the part of mothers (Badinter, 2010). Since then, various "moral entrepreneurs" have transformed this choice into a directive highlighting the superiority, even the necessity, of breast-feeding—both for mothers and infants (Knaak, 2005). As a result, mothers who do not breast-feed are often led to feel guilty and inadequate, even "bad" mothers. Maternal needs are no longer considered and neither are cultural or economic barriers (Wolf, 2010). As Knaak (2005:23) puts it: "It is an ideological blanket . . . that undermines mothers' abilities to feel confident about" their decision and themselves.

Another anomaly inherent to the social construction of intensive motherhood in a society where women are employed resides in the division of labour between fathers and mothers (Luxton and Corman, 2001). As we see in Chapter 4, even a mother who has a career as demanding as that of her husband still spends more time in child care and housework than he does. This division of labour includes 24-hour-a-day maternal availability if the child is ill or needs special attention. Even the task of hiring nannies or locating daycare facilities is usually a woman's responsibility. Mothers also worry more about their children (Hays, 1996:104) and are blamed when a child "goes wrong" or develops problems (Ambert, 2001).

Mother blaming is an old phenomenon. It is also a very useful political tool to use when social policies and safety nets fail individual families (Robson, 2005). Mothers often become children's only safety net (Gazso, 2012). For instance, children with disabilities are more likely to live with a lone mother (Cohen and Petrescu-Prahova, 2006). Children themselves internalize the cultural definition of motherhood and behave accordingly: They demand more of their mothers than of anyone else in society, including their fathers (Dreby, 2010). Therefore, the transition to parenthood affects a **woman's role** in terms of daily activities and preoccupations far more than a man's role. A new father retains his primary identity as a worker, whereas a new mother acquires another identity that may supersede identities that she has devoted years to acquire by going to professional school, for instance. This is particularly evident among immigrant women who raise children in Canada and often become "invisible" as mothers and contributors to the new society (Yax-Fraser, 2011).

Fatherhood

The social construction of fatherhood has evolved substantially, particularly in the way researchers view it, and is affected by the ethnic and educational status of families (Coley, 2001). Although fathers are still defined as the chief breadwinners in two-parent families, the reality that mothers contribute heavily to the family's economy contradicts this social construction and brings considerable unease to a segment of men (Gazso, 2010). Thus, there has been a shift in the social construction of fatherhood, in great part as a result of women's increased participation in the labour force. The ideal father is now often described as the one who is involved with his children and shares household responsibilities with the mother (Doucet, 2006; Dubeau, 2002). Although many more fathers than before eventually take on child care and household responsibilities and become stay-at-home dads, generally reality clashes with this cultural shift, as paternal involvement in children's daily lives still remains comparatively low. This occurs in part because of the continuing persistence, particularly among employers, of the predominance of the provider role in the definition of fathers and the constraints this places on egalitarian parenting (Miller, 2011).

Further, a **dual practice of fatherhood** exists: one for intact families and one for what are called absent fathers (Eggebeen and Knoester, 2001). The more remote the *legal* paternity linkage to mothers, the less involved fathers are. Most are less involved after divorce, even though they may share legal custody, and are even less involved when the custody is not shared (Seltzer, 1998). When fathers remarry and have other biological children, they are much less likely to continue sharing the parenting of their first set of children (McGene and King, 2012). After separation, common-law fathers are far less likely to support their children than are divorced fathers. Finally, men who father children nonmaritally, especially when they have not lived with the mother, are the least involved of all parents. This particularly applies to fathers who have had children from several women (Bronte-Tinkew et al., 2009), as seen in Chapter 8.

In contrast, mothers generally maintain a high level of emotional investment with children, even during marital conflict and divorce. The role of fathers is less "scripted" and is consequently more influenced by situational variables (Doherty et al., 2000): Fathering is "a more contextually sensitive process than mothering" (Doherty et al., 1998). Thus, fathers' investment in children decreases as fathers' relations with mothers deteriorate (Taylor et al., 2012). Mothers constitute a key context for fathering (Doucet, 2006; Madden-Derdich and Leonard, 2000; Pasley et al., 2002): A husband who perceives that his wife has confidence in his parenting ability is far more involved in the care of their children. In contrast, motherhood exists on its own: A good relationship with the father helps, but does not determine the presence or absence of mothering. Fathering is also too closely related to the provider role, so that disadvantaged men, particularly black, are then unable to fulfill other aspects of fathering, such as nurturance and guidance (Anderson, 2008). We have to reconstruct fatherhood to find a way to legally and normatively de-couple the provider role from that of psychological and social involvement (Marsiglio and Roy, 2012).

Feminist Theories

The linkages between social constructionism and feminist theories as well as between political economy theories and feminism will become evident. There is a great deal of philosophical diversity within feminism ranging from liberalism to radicalism (Calixte et al., 2010; Hamilton, 2005). Feminist scholars, therefore, vary in the extent to which they emphasize certain elements over others (Luxton, 2009): Socialist feminists are more likely to seek to redress inequities in gender and class through changes in the state and in its policies and, as such, are linked to political economy theories. For these theorists, social reproduction is a key analytical concept linking productivity on the labour market and at home (e.g., Bezanson and Luxton, 2006; Luxton, 2006a). Liberal feminists seek equality of opportunity for women in "all areas of social, economic, legal, and political life" (Calixte et al., 2010:3). Radical feminists, for their part, focus on patriarchy and how women's daily lives are affected, whether through violence or pornography, as basic examples. This said, these theoretical distinctions are more ideal than real: Very few feminist scholars do not utilize more than one of these orientations, or, yet, have not emphasized one of these at some point in their lives while drifting into another later.

In summary, feminism is an interdisciplinary set of perspectives and theories united by a common analysis of the patriarchal organization of society. This social structure, initially created by a surplus and later continued via the market economy (Engels, 1884), privileges male attributes and male morality and leads to unequal gender roles in all social settings, beginning with the family (Thorne, 1992). These trends combined have provided most of the critique that has served as a basis for a reformulation of research on family life. Yet, it is still the case that only a minority of research on families utilizes feminist perspectives, even broadly defined (Wills and Risman, 2006).

There have been several waves of feminism in North America since the 19th century (Chunn, 2000), but ultimately feminist theories are woman-centred and aim at documenting and explaining the feminine experience (D. Smith, 1999). Feminist scholars have highlighted the fact that women's and men's experiences of life are largely different and unequal. This theme has a multitude of ramifications for family life even if feminists by and large, as Hilda Nelson (1997:3) points out, have neglected family issues other than the division of labour. Canadian theorists are, however, notable exceptions in this respect (see Krull and Sempruch, 2011; Little, 2011).

Feminist Analyses of the Family

Families cannot be understood outside of the forces in society that are dominated— at the political and economic levels—by a gendered as well as a racial structure (Ferree, 2010). The resulting division of labour by gender, both within society at large and within households, is a fundamental focus of feminist analyses (Bradbury, 1996). Thus, feminism emphasizes the fallacy of the family as an entirely private world that is untouched by society's inequities—as suggested by political economy theories. Feminists see the division of individuals' lives between the **public** and the **private spheres** as analytically flawed (MacKinnon, 2005). Not only is the private domain affected by the public (culture, economy, polity), but the private becomes a political issue. For instance, the notion that family relations, including wife battery, are purely a personal matter has been challenged by feminists and successfully placed on the social policy and legislative agendas. As well, private decisions—such as a woman's choice to have fewer children as a personal adaptation to having the major responsibility for those children—carry important social consequences (Kotkin, 2012).

Feminism also analyzes motherhood as a social construct rather than as a purely natural product. Thus, many aspects of feminist theories are related to social constructionism and have informed as well as expanded this perspective. Marriage is seen as an institution that generally contributes to feminine inequality and perpetuates it in private life. The gendered nature of marriage is particularly evident in the division of labour concerning household work and child care, one of the topics in Chapters 4 and 10. Other analyses examine the gap in parenting, what Jensen (1995) has called the "feminization of childhood," which links to the following discussion of how, in our type of society, the interests of women and children may be at odds (Presser, 1995).

However, feminist theories have been underutilized when studying older persons and their families (Chappell and Penning, 2001) and, especially, caretaking (Keating et al., 2003; McDaniel, 2009; Martin-Matthews, 2007). Further, feminist analyses have not sufficiently included women (and men) who might choose to be full-time parents to the exclusion of paid employment or those who have too little education to be competitive on the labour market and instead remain as homemakers (Evans, 1996; Marks, 2004). In a sense, feminist analyses have been developed by career-oriented women within an economic system of paid employment controlled by men and within a technology designed by men to serve the capitalist economy. These existential conditions have affected theory and research and may have unwittingly devalued "feminine" qualities and overvalued "masculine" ones as well as the male structure of work.

The Analysis of Gender Stratification and Gender Roles

Gender roles return us to social constructionism: They represent the social definition of what, in a society, is constructed as appropriately masculine or feminine in terms of behaviour. **Gender roles** are norms or rules that define how males and females should think and behave. They have the result of making men and women accept their proper place in society according to the dictates of the overarching structural arrangement by gender. The transmission of gender roles occurs at the interface of macrosociological* and microsociological* levels.

At the macro level, gender roles are supported by the masculine organization or *stratification* system of the society, which provides more resources, authority, and opportunities to men than to women (Ferree, 2010). In other words, men in general have more *power* and, at the micro level, this affects the way they think and behave—differentiated gender scripts and roles. Girls and boys are then socialized to occupy different roles in society, to think and feel differently, beginning with a preference for separate toys and activities. This process of socialization is so subtle that it is taken for granted as normal or as a result of nature, thus unavoidable. Consequently, on average, boys and girls grow up along divergent developmental paths and experience relationships as well as family life differently, even as adults. This fact is particularly relevant in the study of families. Feminist theories have influenced researchers who study men as well as the development of boys (Messner, 1997). For instance, there is a great deal of concern over the problems created and encountered by boys as a result of their masculine socialization emphasizing toughness, emotional distance, and even bravado (Garbarino, 1999).

Political economy feminist theories also contribute to the examination of social inequalities and diversities in general as well as in societies that have been subjected to colonization (e.g., Mohammed, 2002). As such, they are useful in the domains of state and social policies (Eichler, 1997; Luxton, 1997), particularly with regard to racism (Baca Zinn, 2007; Dua, 1999; Rezai-Rashti, 2004) and, more recently, gender and sexual differences (Baber, 2010) as well as transnational motherhood (Arat-Koç, 2011). Feminist theories have made it possible to examine the patriarchal structure of society from the perspective of anti-racism so as to study the impact of this double stratification on the lives of non-white women and on their families (Das Gupta, 2000), including from the perspective of Muslim women (Daneshpour, 2013; Mahmood, 2005; Zine, 2008:Chapter 6). This analysis has been extended to wars (masculine) and violence against women in zones of conflict (Giles and Hyndman, 2004; MacKinnon, 2006)—see Chapter 13. The phenomenon of immigration has been examined, including that of foreign domestic workers in Canada as well as the role played by gender and religion in the cultural adaptation of immigrant families (Bakan and Stasiulis, 1997; Dion and Dion, 2001; Zine, 2008)—see Chapters 3, 5, and 14.

Developmental (Life Course) Perspectives

As White and Klein (2002) point out, family development theory is the only sociological theory created specifically for the study of families. Paul Glick (1947) and Evelyn Duvall (1957) were the first to propose a sequencing to family life. Indeed, family **life stages** help structure Chapters 10 and 11 on the parent-child and sibling relationships. In this text, we see that families have a *life course* or trajectory that is now more fluid than it was in the past and not all families follow the same sequencing of events (Laszloffy, 2002). Developmental theories are both micro- and macro-sociological. At a more micro level, families are viewed as long-lived groups with a history of internal interactions as well as transactions with the rest of society. This theory has been particularly useful in the study of intergenerational phenomena and relations in the context of different historical periods. Indeed, at the macro level of analysis, families are considered within the **historical context** of their society (Hareven, 2000). Not only do families change and adapt, but they do so under the influence of more global social developments (McDaniel, 2002). The effect of technology on family life is a case in point (Chapters 3 and 8) as are the economy in general (Chapter 4) and a person's socioeconomic status (SES)* throughout the life course (Seabrook and Avison, 2012). It is at this juncture that the developmental perspective links with political economy theories. In turn, families and their members develop strategies throughout their life course to maximize their control over the historical changes of the decades they live in. As Hareven (2000) points out, "The life-course paradigm is developmental and historical by its own very nature. Its essence is the synchronization of 'individual time,' 'family time,' and 'historical time'" (p. 128–9).

One key contribution of the developmental perspective has been to present a more **longitudinal** or long-term framework for research on families at the methodological level (Aldous, 1996). Longitudinal studies follow individuals or families over time as opposed to interviewing them just once. Furthermore, the developmental perspective examines the careers of families within their particular socioeconomic context, and takes into consideration the dynamics between the various trajectories and life stages of its members (Elder, 1998). The concept of role recurs in this perspective as each individual's role evolves when additional members arrive, as children age and enter the economic system or depart, and as grandchildren are born.

Dynamic concepts include transition or passage from one stage to the next as well as individual transitions within a particular family stage, such as when an older child moves out while the other child remains at home (Macmillan and Copher, 2005). **Timing** is a key concept (Ravanera et al., 2004). For instance, today, normative timing includes a 25-year-old woman who marries and has her first child two years later. Less normative is the 17-year-old who has a baby. The first woman is "on time," whereas the second is "off time" (that is, too young according to the norms of society). Similarly, a 45-year-old woman who gives birth to her first child is considered to be off time, although such delayed transitions are becoming more common. Transitions may also include changes in family structure, such as the occurrence of divorce, with the recognition that parents' timing may not always mesh with the stage of life in which their children are (Chapter 12).

Developmental perspectives allow us to see how family stages relate to parents' own life course (Hareven, 2000). For instance, a couple who has their first child at age 28 compared to another one who is 40 to 50 when this event occurs are at the same stage in terms of **family development** but belong to two stages in terms of **individual development**. This difference has consequences on how they live this experience, on

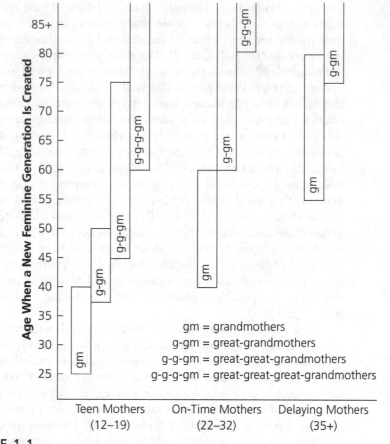

FIGURE 1.1

Generation Successions: How a Woman Creates Generations Depending on Her Age at the Birth of Her First Child

family dynamics, and even child development. It also means that the life course of the older couple's family may be less complex and contain fewer generations, as seen in Figure 1.1. Thus, mid-life is a particularly diverse life stage in individual development because it cuts across several different family life cycles (McDaniel, 2003).

Whether one looks at delayed or youthful generation creation, the life course perspective shows the extent to which the "circumstances experienced by one member of the family impact on the lives of other family members and create change for them" (Martin-Matthews, 2000:335). When a 16-year-old has a baby, she initiates a generational chain of events in her family. If she is her mother's first child to have a baby, she creates a young grandmother, as described in Figure 1.1, and may be creating a young great-grandmother and so on up the generational line. This family is **"age condensed"**: It has multiple generations closely succeeding each other. In the case of an on-time or yet older mother, the opposite occurs and the family has an **"age gap"** as the generations are less close in age (Milan and Hamm, 2003).

Early births accelerate family stages and stack up several generations of *young* people within a same family—young people who have had little time to devote to their own developmental tasks before creating another generation. In terms of rational theory, they have had little time to accumulate social and material resources or capital that could benefit both the youngest and the oldest generations (see East and Jacobson, 2000). With a young mother, the generational gap between mother and child is blurred: As the child ages, the young mother may act more like a peer or a sibling. Unless another adult takes over, this child can lack the benefit of having a parent who assumes moral authority and who can serve as a guide (Chapter 8). **Early fertility** that is repeated across generations contributes to an increase in social inequalities between families (Beaujot, 2004). The opposite is more likely to occur when adults become grandparents at an older age. The two older generations have had more time for education and asset accumulation, all of which can benefit the young and the frail elderly.

Symbolic Interactionism

Symbolic interactionism is favoured by qualitative family researchers and, as such, constitutes both a theoretical perspective and a methodological orientation. It is a sociopsychological theory in which the **self**, social self, and **role** occupy a singular position, as do societal contexts whose meanings and structures are perceived by individuals while interacting with one another. People develop their self-concepts and the definition of the roles they occupy through other people's views of them. The concepts of "reflected appraisals" and the "looking glass self" were originally used by Cooley in 1902 and Mead in 1934. Basically, individuals acquire their self-definition through interaction with **significant others**—that is, people who play an important role in that individual's life, such as parents. Parents, teachers, peers, and even sports figures, singers, and movie stars may become **reference groups*** for children. This means that children look up to these individuals and groups and use them as role models or as points of reference to guide their own behaviours, develop their sense of self, and interpret social contexts.

Symbolic interactionism is most suitable for the study of personal and familial phenomena that have not been sufficiently researched, such as love, jealousy, anger, disappointment, hurt, tolerance, and care (Daly, 2003). Families construct an environment based on the reflections of self and on the perceptions of significant others, all key themes of this theory. Families constitute their own symbolic world through myth and rituals (Gillis, 1996).

The best-known symbolic interactionists are George Herbert Mead (1934), Herbert Blumer (1969), and Erving Goffman (1959). Symbolic interactionism encompasses two orientations (White and Klein, 2002). The first focuses more on family processes. The second focuses more on roles, is more structural, and has been heavily influenced by Goffman. He became the most popular symbolic interactionist upon the publication of his *The Presentation of Self in Everyday Life* (1959), perhaps in great part because he focused on dramaturgy (using theatre or drama terms such as *roles, actors, frontstage,* and *setting*). This orientation indicates that role strain is reduced when individuals perceive greater consensus in the expectations surrounding their role. One can think of the role of parents here. If parents perceive that their role is well defined, they are less likely to feel insecure about it and role strain will be reduced. This will become important in Chapter 10 on the parent-child relationship.

Interactional-Transactional Perspectives

The interactional-transactional framework goes beyond symbolic interactionism: It posits that an individual creates his or her own environment, at the interpersonal level, at the same time that he or she is being shaped by this environment (Maccoby and Jacklin, 1983). It views socialization as a process whereby children participate in the formation of their identities. The perspective on the **child as a social actor** belongs to this theoretical perspective (Corsaro, 1997). This theory is particularly useful in the study of the parent-child relationship: It corrects the biases or flaws inherent to the earlier socialization and child development framework whereby children were seen as the passive recipients of their parents' actions. Instead, the child is studied as an active social actor with individual characteristics, as are parents (Ambert, 2001). *Interactions* between parents and children *feed back* on each other. Similarly, the socialization process involves the interaction between children's personalities and parental teachings. The child actively participates in the socialization process, albeit often unconsciously so. The child becomes **coproducer** of his or her own development.

The interactional causality model is multidimensional and **bidirectional**. It flows *both* from parents and children interacting with and reacting to each other and responding to the environment that affects them. Thus, the interactional perspective is also *transactional* in the sense that it involves a multiplicity of causality; in other words, it involves transactions between a child, his or her parent, and their environment within a **feedback model**. Interactional-transactional perspectives are very sensitive to the diversity of a family's environment, including culture and ethnicity (Sameroff, 2010). This theory applies equally well to other interactions within the family, such as between spouses or between siblings. Several chapters are informed by the interactional-transactional perspective, particularly Chapters 9 through 13.

Interactional theories are often developed within a larger framework whereby the various levels of a child's or a family's environment influence development and interactions (Sameroff, 2010). In other words, whereas children are coproducers in their development, both parents' and children's actions are enhanced, limited, and constrained by the larger **environment** in which they are situated (Bronfenbrenner, 1989), which is a tenet of transactional theories and is a guiding principle in this textbook. When the term "interactionist perspective" is used, it refers to the interaction between several variables whereas contributions from a social variable, such as poverty, to negative child outcomes is then combined with other parental or child variables to create further negative (or positive) child outcomes (Conger et al., 2010).

Behaviour Genetics

The framework of behaviour genetics, which was casually introduced in my autobiographical opener, is not well known to sociologists. It should not be confused with sociobiology, which explains human behaviours and social institutions on the basis

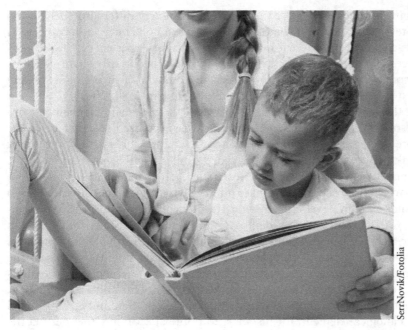

Both symbolic interactionist and interactional perspectives view the child as a social actor who coproduces his or her development. A mother can teach her child to read, for instance, only with the child's cooperation and active participation. In turn, the child's inherited abilities also enter in the equation and set limits or enhance the learning process.

SerrNovik/Fotolia

of evolution. Nor should it be equated with approaches that foster the notion of inequalities based on presumed genetic inferiority versus superiority between racial groups, for instance. Rather, the field of behaviour genetics studies *within*-family phenomena to explain how **nature and nurture** (or genetics and environment) *combine* and *interact* to produce personalities, parent-child interactions, the home environment, how parents raise their children, and why children grow up to be who they become (Barnes and Beaver, 2012; Beaver et al., 2009; Plomin et al., 2008).

Parents influence their children, both through their behaviours and attitudes, and also the genes they transmit to them and the indirect effect of their own genes on the family environment (Schnittker, 2008). Parents' genes are expressed through their personalities, their socialization practices, and the lifestyle choices they make for their families, all of which are even more influenced by their environment (Rutter, 2002). A parent's environment includes his or her economic and cultural situation and relationship with the other parent; it also includes his or her children, their personalities, and their behaviours, which in turn affect the parent and his or her socialization practices. In other words, in a family, *each person is part of the other's environment*. Behaviour genetics, then, is closely related to the multicausality model of interactional and transactional theories and can be embedded in life course perspectives (Seabrook and Avison, 2012; Wickrama and O'Neal, 2013).

Because of their different personalities, siblings in a family do not experience their **shared environment*** in exactly the same way (see Chapter 11). The shared environment consists of family events and circumstances in which everyone partakes, such as family outings, meals together, parental teachings, and even divorce (Booth et al., 2000). Therefore, depending on their own genetic predispositions, temperament, birth order, and spacing, siblings experience the shared environment differently (Belsky and Pluess, 2009; Steven et al., 2012). (There is a link with symbolic interactionism here in terms of the development of different meanings attached to experiences.) If one adds other experiences that children in the same family do not necessarily share—such as illnesses, classrooms, and peers (the **nonshared environment***)—it is not surprising that siblings grow up to be different to some extent (Lemelin et al., 2007).

The closer the genetic link between two persons, the more similar their personalities and personality-driven behaviours. Identical twins raised together resemble each other more than fraternal twins, as detailed in Chapter 11. Further, the closer the cultural link between two persons, the more similar their behaviours become. Therefore, identical twins raised together resemble each other behaviourally more than identical twins raised separately. Genes and the environment constitute the two engines that guide human development—*not* the environment alone and *not* genes alone (Meaney, 2010). For instance, high parental involvement (environment) can compensate for a child's genetic liabilities (Shanahan et al., 2008). Thus, behaviour genetics represents an important perspective for sociologists because nearly all the research on families has ignored the fact that human beings are biochemical entities that affect and are affected by their environment (D'Onofrio and Lahey, 2010). Behaviour genetics *complements* sociological perspectives (Sercombe, 2009) and adds a microsociological element, for instance, to political economy theories via the social and racial inequalities in which biological systems are embedded and affected (Wickrama and O'Neal, 2013).

WHAT ARE THE MAIN THEMES IN THE TEXT?

Within the theoretical perspectives just described, this book emphasizes several themes that provide the distinct conceptual framework and flavour or "voice" of this text. Social class or socioeconomic status (SES), gender, and race or ethnicity, which are key demographic variables as well as sources of inequalities, are woven into this multiple thematic framework.

The first theme of **structural social inequalities** is the dominant perspective of Part 2 and other chapters. This theme is informed by political economy theories and feminist theories as well as by social capital or rational theory. Based on their economic situation and their ethnicity, families have unequal access to the key resources of their society. Feminist analyses as well as social constructionism inform us that **gendered inequalities** and consequent **gender roles** cut across economic and ethnic stratification: Men and women have a differential access to societal resources and opportunities. Gender roles form the cornerstone of several specific discussions throughout the text, particularly the domestic division of labour, relationship maintenance, and kin keeping.

A second theme is related but not limited to the first one: **family diversity**—that is, diversity in structure, culture, and inequalities. Therefore, inequalities and diversity are the two overarching themes guiding Parts 1 and 2. Diversity also includes class, ethnicity, and religion as well as ideologies leading to distinct lifestyles (Biles and Ibrahim, 2005).

The third theme, which will be initially examined in Chapter 3, focuses on **family responsibilities**. The text will document that, not only has the family not lost its role, as is commonly believed, but it has actually acquired new responsibilities. Above all, the book will document how individual families are too often ill-equipped to fulfill their functions, in part because of a lack of social investment in families—an important social policy critique that recurs and is expanded upon in the final chapter.

A fourth theme running through the text is that of the **effective community***, particularly the role it plays or can play in child socialization and the successful integration of families in society. This theme, which is inspired by rational theories, emphasizes how effective communities constitute social capital that supports families. In turn, this social capital allows children to develop their own human capital: positive qualities, socially acceptable behaviour, and school completion and achievement, among others. An effective social community should also help in the care of frail elderly family members and of those with special challenges and disabilities so that women are not unavoidably the chief occupiers of this role—particularly women who are already caring for their nuclear family (Beaujot, 2000).

A fifth theme revolves around the **cultural context** and includes a recourse to *social constructionism*. An example is the social construction of adoption and how it can affect children's development (Chapter 8). Another example involves adolescence and the salience of age-segregated peer groups—all western phenomena that are not universal (Kağitçibasi, 2007; Kitayama and Cohen, 2007; see Chapter 10). The cultural context also involves the audiovisual media and its impact on family interaction and child socialization, a topic which first appears in Chapter 3. The cultural context joins the theme of diversity inasmuch as families belong to a wide range of religious, ethnic, and ideological spectra.

The sixth theme in this book is especially important for Parts 4 and 5 and has a double theoretical focus. First, it emphasizes the **interactional** aspect of family relations. This theme implicates feedback between environment, parents' characteristics and behaviours, and children's characteristics and behaviours. Second, this theme points to the complementary importance of paying attention to family members' embodiment and **genetic inheritance** as well as the interaction of genetic inheritance with the environment in creating personalities, meanings, and family relationships.

WHAT METHODS ARE USED IN FAMILY RESEARCH?

Let's briefly return to the matter of **theory**. As defined earlier, a theory is a set of interrelated propositions that explains a particular phenomenon and guides research. A good theory can be tested against facts with a set of hypotheses. A **hypothesis*** is a testable proposition or sentence. For instance, social exchange theory can give rise to the following hypothesis: Employed wives are less happy with their marriage when they perceive inequity in the household division of labour (Lavee and Katz, 2002). In methodological language, marital happiness is the *dependent variable*—it depends on the wives' perceptions of inequity. Inequity then becomes the independent variable, the one that will make marital happiness change. The independent variable (perceived inequity) is one of the presumed sources of the dependent variable (marital happiness).

TABLE 1.2	**Methods in Family Research**	
Surveys	Questionnaires given in groups (such as a classroom)	
	Questionnaires distributed to homes (includes Canadian census) and via the Internet	
	Face-to-face interviews in homes or elsewhere	
	Phone interviews	
Observations	Observation in natural settings (at homes, public places, village centres, streets)	
	Participant observation where the researcher plays a role in the life of the respondents	
	Laboratory observations (particularly of parent/child interactions) and one-way mirror; events are recorded as they occur	
Experiments	"Natural" experiments: the study of families before and after a social event or a natural phenomenon occurs (for instance, introduction of the Internet in the home; earthquakes)	
	Laboratory experiments (observations, questionnaires, interviews) before and after a variable is introduced or while the dynamics of an interaction are ongoing	
Evaluative research	May involve any of the above methods in order to study the impact of social policy initiatives and clinical interventions	
Content and secondary analyses	Content analysis of public documents, media programs, newspapers, books, songs, videos, video games, Facebook, Twitter, etc.	
	Content analysis of archives and personal documents such as diaries for historical research	
	Content analysis of diaries and autobiographies	
	Secondary analyses of surveys, the census, and other statistical sources (*secondary* refers to the fact that the researchers who do the analyses were not the ones who had designed the original study or data gathering)	

Theories inform the questions that researchers ask about families and provide explanatory models. **Methods** are the means or tools utilized to answer researchers' questions or obtain information. The methods utilized in family research are those of sociology, psychology, and demography in general. They are summarized in five categories in Table 1.2. This table will be useful throughout the following chapters where these methods are mentioned or are described in conjunction with various results found by researchers on a wide variety of topics in the special Family Research boxes appearing in most subsequent chapters.

The matter of methods is a serious one with great consequences: The utilization of inappropriate methods simply creates useless and even misleading or false results. As well, it is very important that social policies, including those that affect families, be evidence based. Many relevant surveys are used in this textbook, including the *National Population Health Survey* and the *National Longitudinal Survey of*

Children and Youth, both initiated in the 1990s. Thus, one can deplore the fact that the current government has stopped many excellent surveys carried out by Statistics Canada in order to save money (Bednar and Stabile, 2012).

Methods are generally separated into two large categories: quantitative and qualitative. *Quantitative methods* are based on numbers, percentages, and averages; they are shown in tables and charts and are expressed in statistical tests of significance such as time-series analyses or, at a more basic level, **correlations***. In contrast, *qualitative research* reports what family members say, write, and do in the form of extracts, quotes, case studies, and summaries, in order to describe and explain various family phenomena in depth and to arrive at conclusions. The reader will find many examples of such reports throughout the text, particularly in quotes from students' autobiographies, excerpts from conversations with parents during interviews, unsolicited email responses regarding adoption, and various case studies from my fieldwork. Above all, the methodological basis of qualitative methods focuses on a more holistic perspective, on letting respondents express their realities, and on informing theory. Many qualitative researchers use **grounded theory** (Corbin and Strauss, 2008). This is a *methodological* approach guiding the study of the family via qualitative methods (LaRossa, 2005). Grounded theory emphasizes individual experience from which to build research results and even theory (Gilgun, 2013). Qualitative methods are the preferred choice of researchers favouring symbolic interactionism as well as feminism.

Statistical designs generally begin with a set of hypotheses and usually consist of multiple-choice or "close-ended" questions. Qualitative researchers may also use the information they have gathered and summarize it numerically. For instance, they may present averages and percentages to provide an overall view of the themes and situations that have emerged in their narrative material. This is particularly useful when large samples are involved. Qualitatively-gathered material can lead to more sophisticated statistical analyses. Therefore, *the two methods do not need to be so entirely separate*. Qualitative and quantitative research methods are *equally scientific* and complement each other (Ambert et al., 1995); they are found within all five categories summarized in Table 1.2. In other words, both sets of methods can be used in surveys, observations, experiments, evaluative research, and content analysis (Gilgun, 2013). The latter includes historical documents. Both groups of methods can also be utilized to test hypotheses based on most theories described earlier.

Family sociologists should be concerned with choosing a research approach that can best describe the human reality they wish to study *within its social context*, whether it is a qualitative or quantitative approach or a combination of both. Methods should be selected depending on what is being investigated and on their ability to minimize the influence of social desirability (Whisman and Snyder, 2007). For instance, sensitive issues lend themselves well to audio-computer assisted self-interviews (Nooner et al., 2010). As well, if one wants to study the well-being of children in a country, then clearly a large sample is required and statistical analysis is needed. The Canadian **National Longitudinal Survey of Children and Youth** is a good example (Willms, 2002a,b). Statistics Canada's various **General Social Surveys** (GSS) are another. One salient problem in much of the research is that only one family member, or one parent, or one spouse, or one child, is generally interviewed.

An Example of Qualitative Methods: Students' Autobiographies

As pointed out in the Preface, one key source of qualitative material for this text is the research I have done from my students' autobiographies. This type of research falls under the rubrics of surveys and content analysis in Table 1.2. Throughout the years, students in some of my classes have written autobiographies that were semi-structured (i.e., in response to a set of **open-ended questions**). Such questions allow respondents to say anything they want. This project was first initiated when a format was tested on several hundred students. Two years later, students' responses had confirmed that the questionnaire was nonsuggestive, easily understood, and yielded answers that could be analyzed into themes. Questions have been added and some deleted throughout the years. More than 1,500 autobiographies have been collected.

The core of the autobiographies resides in the following questions: "When you look back on your early childhood (0–5 years), what is it that you like best to remember about it? (What made you the most happy?)" and "What is it that you remember being most painful to you? (What above all else made you unhappy?)" These two questions are repeated for the 6–10, 11–14, 15–18, and current age brackets. A great proportion of the autobiographical pages are devoted to these core questions as students utilize them to narrate the main themes of the story of their lives. There are other questions whose answers are used in this textbook. These result in descriptions of students' neighbourhoods and their relationships with parents, siblings, and peers within each age bracket. No question was asked about age, race, ethnicity, religion, or marital status, as these could help identify individual students. Nevertheless, most students provided this information somewhere in their narratives.

The autobiographies (as well as all other papers and tests) were submitted *anonymously,* via university identification number on the cover page only. After the autobiographies were read, the cover sheets were torn off, brought to class where the grades were entered on the class list in front of students. The autobiographies were an *option*; however, each year, only one or two students chose to do a conventional research paper instead. A formal evaluation of this assignment indicated that students not only trusted the anonymity of the procedure but also felt that they generally had benefited from the experience (see also Dorais, 2002:179). Students' answers indicated that they had tried very hard to project themselves back into the particular age brackets: "Of course, when I think about this now, I laugh, but it was really a terrible problem for me at that age." Other analyses I performed showed the trustworthiness (validity) of their efforts.

CONCLUSIONS: UNITY IN DIVERSITY

Families are tremendously diverse but they are united under the rubric of the family as an *intergenerational institution*. The theories used to study and explain the family are numerous but they form a totality that allows one to see the family in its entirety— to study families in the plural and yet to find important similarities among them. Furthermore, the various theories discussed in this chapter illustrate the fact that the family is an ideal phenomenon for a linkage between the macro and micro levels of sociological analysis. That is, some of the chapters that follow are placed within a societal framework (macro level), specifically Chapters 2 through 6 on ethnicity, the economy, neighbourhoods, and educational institutions, as well as religion.

On the other side of the coin, some chapters have a microsociological framework. Cases in point are the "relationship" chapters in Part 4 and much of the two "challenges" chapters in Part 5. Yet, these relationships and challenges are situated within and are explained by their larger contexts. Similarly, the themes that form the basis of this text, although diverse, are unified because, when placed together, they present a holistic view on family life. This view can then be translated into social policies pertaining to supporting the family as an institution and consequently supporting individual families, however diverse they are in terms of structure, social class, and culture.

Summary

1. The family is defined as an institution and an intergenerational group of individuals related by blood or adoption. The nuclear family is generally enclosed in an extended network of kinship. Polygamy is examined as a conjugal and family type in its social contexts.

2. The main theoretical perspectives informing family research are as follows: structural functionalism, political economy theories, social exchange and rational theories, social constructionism, feminist theories, developmental or life course perspective, symbolic interactionism, interactional-transactional perspectives, and behaviour genetics.

3. This text emphasizes six themes that recur throughout the chapters: social inequalities, including gender inequalities and roles; family diversity; family responsibilities; the effective community; the cultural context and social constructionism; interactional and behaviour genetics perspectives.

4. Qualitative and quantitative research methods in family research are equally scientific and complement each other. The description of students' autobiographies used in this text is presented as an example of a qualitative study.

5. The chapter concludes by emphasizing the unity in the family as an institution that exists amidst the diversity of levels of analysis and theoretical as well as thematic approaches to the study of the family.

Analytical Questions

1. Some instructors prefer to teach "Intimate Relations" rather than Families classes; some say that teaching about "families" is obsolete. How can you respond to this position?

2. Which of the theories described in this chapter interests you the most? Be prepared to make a reasoned case for your response.

3. Choose two theoretical perspectives and explain how they relate to or complement each other.

4. Link each of the main themes of this book to a theoretical perspective and analyze how these themes unite some of the theories herein presented.

5. How do qualitative and quantitative methods differ and complement each other? What are their respective limitations for the study of families?

CHAPTER 2

History and Cultural Diversity of Canadian Families

Anne-Marie Ambert

OUTLINE

Canadian Families of the Past
Early First Nations Families
Plains Cree and Nadouek Families
Families of New France
European and Native Precursors
Settlement and Colonial Families
Families during British Colonial Rule
*Families in Upper Canada and the
Maritimes*
Quebec Families under British Rule
First Nations Families under French and
British Rule
Early Black-Canadian Families
Families during Industrialization and the
Settling of the West
*Childhood: A New Social Construct
in Context*
*The Beginning of Family Ethnic and
Religious Diversity*

Current Diversity of Canadian Families
Aboriginal Families
Québécois Families
Black-Canadian Families
Chinese-Canadian Families
Marriage and Fertility in China
Chinese Families in Canada
Indo-Canadian Families

**Conclusions: Evolving Canadian Families
in Diversity**

Summary
Analytical Questions

"I find it difficult here at the university because there are not many Native persons like me and I don't even look like the stereotypical Native that people have in mind because my mother is part Native and my father's family was from Scotland and no one in my family looks alike but we speak English different, sort of slow and quiet and we live at the edge of town many of us together but we travel back and forth to visit our relatives north of here. . . . I am the first person in my family to go to university and my mother is very proud of this but at the same time this makes me different than my people . . . and I know for a fact that many Natives that got an education in the past have assimilated themselves into the rest of Canadians, so it's all very difficult to fit in anywhere completely." [A female Aboriginal student, one of only three who were ever enrolled in my classes while teaching at York University for more than 30 years; see also Mayer, 2008.]

"At that age [10–14] it was total rebellion at home: My parents were first-generation immigrants but I was born here and I wanted nothing to do with being different, poor, them having an accent, not being allowed out at night with the others. . . . Now looking back I realize that it must have been a horrible time for my parents: They only wanted the best for me."

"I am very happy to be in Canada because the country where I come from does not value girls. In Canada I can be anything I want. I just have to study hard. Even my father respects his daughters now."

"Things are different for my younger brother and sister than for me because they mix much more than I do with kids from backgrounds other than Chinese whereas in my time we had to work harder and we lived in Chinatown so it was difficult to meet other children and it's still difficult for me now. But I can see how different things have become in just 10 years even in my own family, especially now that we have moved out and up."

These students' comments exemplify the number of ways in which ethnic, including Aboriginal, and immigrant origins can profoundly affect people's lives and that of their families. Scrolling down through the past of Canadian families to present day allows us to examine how diverse families have always been and how the various waves of immigration have transformed our familial landscape into one of cultural diversity. We also see how the European conquest of the Aboriginal lands have resulted in tragedies and oppression and have had negative effects on families that are felt to this day. This chapter is divided into two sections: The first focuses on the past while the second discusses the current diversity of Canadian families.

CANADIAN FAMILIES OF THE PAST

This section begins with a description of the structure and lives of families in the three founding nations of Canada: the First Nations, the French, and the British. It also discusses the family life of a small but important black community early on in Canada and, after 1867, the later large-scale immigration to western Canada of Chinese and Europeans with more diverse origins.

Early First Nations Families

When Europeans *officially* "discovered" the Americas in the 1490s, Aboriginal people in what is now Canada numbered well over 500,000. The most densely populated areas were in the woodlands along the St. Lawrence River and the Great Lakes and in the forests and coastal regions of future British Columbia. The nations in these regions were both hunter-gatherers and horticulturalists. They lived in settled villages and engaged in some trade. In the other regions, especially in the Prairies, the north, and the Maritimes, Aboriginal nations were almost exclusively hunter-gatherers and followed a nomadic existence because of the need to pursue migratory game. There were more than 300 First Nations in North America by the 1490s, with unique histories, cultures, languages, laws, and various levels of economic complexity. Some lived peacefully with neighbouring nations while others were more warfare oriented. Their spirituality and sense of the sacred was well developed and attuned to the cosmos and their natural environment (Paper, 2012).

Before the European arrival, the First Nations were political, social, and cultural entities built around kinship. Some nations, such as the Pacheenaht on Vancouver Island, were **patrilineal**—that is, they recognized descent and inheritance through the father's line. Others, such as the Iroquois in the St. Lawrence Valley, were **matrilineal**, whereby descent and inheritance flowed through the mother's line. Nonetheless, the basic social unit of all First Nations was the extended family within bands, clans, tribes, and nations. These families were communal, and they shared responsibilities and resources—everything from childrearing to food. Two contrasting examples of First Nations are provided, but we always have to keep in mind that we know next to nothing about these nations' histories before the conquest.

Plains Cree and Nadouek Families

The Plains Cree were a nomadic people, and their society tended to be patriarchal and patrilineal. Families united to form a band in order to better protect themselves against attack and to facilitate communal hunting (Mandelbaum, 1979). Varying in size from 80 to 250 persons, bands normally comprised a male chief, his parents, brothers and their families, plus other families that may or may not have been related

(Binnema, 1996). Informal councils composed of male members advised a chief, and band unity was provided by the chief's prestige and power (Christensen, 2000). Yet, while band leadership rested on consensus-building among families, membership was not fixed (Binnema, 2001). For instance, if individual disputes occurred, young men could join another band, perhaps even marrying within it. If a band as a whole encountered difficulties, say the death of the chief, entire families could leave and unite with relatives in other bands (McLeod, 2000).

The type of economy structured gender roles. Men hunted, later cared for horses (after they were introduced), and served as warriors in defending the band and its territory (Friesen, 1999). Women reared children, prepared food, and made clothing and domestic implements. The band provided for needy members, especially the elderly and widows who could not hunt, and older people were at times adopted by younger families. Orphans and boys whose families were in difficult situations could live with the families of the chief or other men of high rank. They were then considered members of these families, and in return for work, were given food and clothing. Like the other male children, they received instruction in hunting and warfare; female children were taught the domestic skills needed for band survival.

In contrast to the Cree, the Iroquois or Nadouek were a group of several settled nations, with territories extending from Quebec to southern Ontario and northern New York state. By the beginning of the 14th century, they had embarked on intensive agriculture. Their tribes were matrilocal and matrilineal: Women owned all property and determined kinship (Danvers, 2001). Therefore, when marrying, a man moved in with his wife's family and, when children were born, they became members of their mother's clan. All clan members were responsible for childrearing. Nadouek settlements were defensive fortifications and contained a series of longhouses, one for each clan, which were often more than 100 feet long; these settlements served as the political and economic centres of each tribe. The Iroquois had to abandon their settlements periodically, either because their farmland ceased to be productive or in order to improve their defensive position.

It was these two elements of social survival—producing food and maintaining defence—that saw gendered divisions of labour among the Iroquois. In terms of food production, since women possessed clan land, they worked the fields that produced crops such as corn, and organized community life (Magee, 2008, 2011). Men hunted and fished, and warfare was their principal vocation (Recht, 1997). But warring societies require political organization. Given the matrilineal nature of Iroquois society, women chose the male leaders from amongst warriors in the settlements. Women of high status were consulted on matters of war (Magee, 2008, 2011). In fact, they were often the instigators of war and had the power to veto male decisions in this respect. They also made the weapons used in warfare as well as the warriors' food supplies. Family life in Iroquois society, therefore, was based on the implicit concept of gender equality, with men and women each having a range of specific responsibilities and rights (Brandáo, 2003; Engelbrecht, 2003). When the individual Nadouek nations coalesced into the Iroquois League, influential clan mothers continued this tradition by determining their nation's representatives within the governing council of the league (Fenton, 1998).

Families of New France

European and Native Precursors

It is difficult to evaluate the changes that might have taken place among eastern Native nations before the official "discovery" date of 1534. By 1000 AD, Scandinavians had seasonal settlements in what is now Newfoundland, at Anse aux Meadows. John Cabot had been to Newfoundland in 1498. Breton fishers had been exploiting cod stocks along the coast all the way to Cape Breton in Nova Scotia, where they had carried out exchanges with the Mi'kmaq, including down the coast of Maine in 1524 (Trudel, 1973). Although the Mi'kmaq still exist in several Maritime provinces (Critchley et al., 2007), these sporadic contacts with northern Europeans could already have resulted in some degree of *métissage** and in epidemics of influenza and chicken pox, for instance, for which the Native peoples had no immunity. As a result, their **demographic profile** might already have deteriorated via imported diseases and, later, loss of territories and food sources (Northcott and Wilson, 2008:25), as happened to the Beothuk of Newfoundland, who were extinct as a nation by the mid-1850s.

It was not until Jacques Cartier came to Gaspé in 1534 that the first regular trading took place with the Mi'kmaqs and Iroquois; in fact, it is these same Iroquois who helped Cartier push his discoveries to Quebec. After Roberval and Cartier's failure in 1541–43, only Basques, Breton, and Norman fishers continued yearly trips to the eastern regions and initiated the fur trade. Iron objects seemed to have been bartered all the way to Huron territories in what is now Ontario. When Champlain arrived in 1603, most of the villages that Cartier had encountered were gone; Algonquins and Montagnais nations had replaced the Iroquois along the St. Lawrence—in itself an indication of profound demographic changes as well as conflicts between the tribes. By the 1620s, some tribes had already noticed an increase in mortality as their contact with the French intensified. They were being decimated by disease. While the Aboriginal tribes in these areas and even beyond were adopting some European habits and objects including tools, clothing, food (such as bread), alcohol, and armaments, a great deal of their ways of living also penetrated the early colonial culture and allowed it to survive (Bumsted, 2010). This includes indigenous food, tobacco, forced germination of seeds, clothing better suited to the harsh winter climate, as well as means of transportation such as toboggans and canoes.

What kind of family structure did the French bring? As Thornton (2005) has well documented, northern Europeans had, well before the 1600s, developed an emphasis on individualism and the **nuclear family** in their own households (Ruggles and Heggeness, 2008). In northern Europe, including northern France, couples married in their twenties because of the necessity of establishing a separate household—a very modern situation already (Ruggles, 2009, 2010). As well, most young people were fairly autonomous in terms of choosing a mate—even though parents among the nobility still arranged marriages. But for the remainder of the population, affection and companionship were already important elements of courtship and marriage, perhaps since the 1300s. *In summary, the northern European family was already adapted to the future requirements of* *industrialization and may have contributed to its rapid ascent in northern Europe, particularly in England.*

Settlement and Colonial Families

The territory rediscovered by Jacques Cartier in 1535 and then by Champlain in 1603 did not become part of France's overseas empire until 1608, when an expedition of 28 men officially established the colony of New France at what is now Quebec City. Only eight survived the harsh winter conditions (Cartier, 2008). After many failed attempts, it was only in 1618 that the settlement at Quebec City started holding, with vegetables and other crops being grown. And it was only in 1642, more than a century after Jacques Cartier, that a settlement in Montreal was undertaken. Parallel to these developments was the establishment of British and French communities in Newfoundland and Labrador early in the 17th century: The colony of Newfoundland already had more settlements than Quebec. In contrast, the British colonies in what was to become the U.S. as well as the Spanish colonies in Mexico and South America were already thriving and widely exporting New World goods (Mann, 2011).

These very slow beginnings were due both to France's lack of interest in settling Canada and the difficulties that the harsh climate imposed on the few French would-be colonizers. As well, these differences stemmed in great part from capitalist changes in agricultural practices (land enclosure, for instance) which led to a surplus agricultural population in Great Britain. As Roberta Hamilton points out, between 1620 and 1642, 80,000 English citizens, or two percent of the population, left their country (1988:32). In contrast, the French agricultural system kept its citizens on the nobility's and the Church's lands. By 1715, the European population of New France totaled 20,000 habitants while the future U.S. already had 434,000 colonists (Bumsted, 2010:125).

The first French-Canadian colonists were **fur traders**, or *coureurs de bois*, who constructed a frontier society while confronting many difficulties: extreme weather, conflict with the Iroquois, and later on intermittent warfare against the English colonies for the control of the fur trade. Until the mid-1600s, there were very few European women in New France. The 1665–66 census indicated that there were 2,034 males and only 1,181 females, including children (Cartier, 2008). In addition to the fur trade, French male colonists were involved in military service and administration. A significant number took First Nations women as wives—called *les femmes du pays*—in unions outside of the Church (Dickason, 2002). These women played an important role in the early development of New France. Not only were their domestic skills key to survival, but their experience with skinning animals and preserving fur pelts, their knowledge of First Nations languages, and their peoples' traditions as traders all contributed to the growth of the fur trade (Jamieson, 1986).

However, the nature of French Canada's economy and society changed over time and this affected these families and particularly women's role: The fur trade began to weaken, and perhaps more importantly, intermarriage between French colonists and First Nations women declined. The Roman Catholic Church encouraged colonists to marry Métis women—those of mixed French and First Nations ancestry—and, later, white women. Between 1667 and 1673, at the request of the first intendant, Jean Talon, France sent almost 1,000 young women, 800 of whom were called *les filles du roi* (the King's daughters), to the colony to marry bachelor settlers (Cartier, 2008). The majority of these women were poor but all received a dowry from the Crown. Although most early colony women married, they adopted a wide range of roles. Some became merchants and administrators while others and their daughters founded religious institutions and even became missionaries (Clio Collective, 1987:49). Up to this point, colonial women had considerable freedom and latitude—far more than their sisters in Europe.

Later in the 1700s, however, four major events combined to relegate women to more specialized female roles and promote family life even more prominently than it was in France itself. The first event was economic and pertained to the declining importance of the fur trade and the coinciding **rise of agriculture**. Although women retained some freedom, large families became essential for the settlement of communities because farm life requires numerous workers. And, as French women had been scarce for many decades, a trend toward early age at marriage was established, in contrast to later ages in France at the time (Bumsted, 2010:129). Under French law, a *seigneur*—akin to France's minor nobility—owned the land, and tenant farmers worked it. The number of land concessions from the Crown worked by a tenant family depended on the number of sons a couple had.

The second event was a strategic consideration: Government policy promoted **large families** to strengthen the colony against British advances (Krull, 2003). Rather than encouraging massive immigration from France, the French Crown promoted high fertility to increase its colonial population. Women's options for economic security were quickly reduced to either marrying or entering the convent, although many continued in various trades (Joël, 2012). In 1666, there were only 3,215 Europeans but by 1763, when the English regime began in Canada, 70,000 French-speaking people lived in North America (Beaujot and McQuillan, 1982). They descended from only about 10,000 French immigrants, who traveled to North America over a 150-year period. This growth constituted an extraordinary rate of natural population increase.

The third event influencing women's role and family life concerned the expanding authority of the **Catholic Church**. As farming communities and parishes increased, the Church gained more power and influence over the colonial population. By controlling education, for instance, the Church developed a gender-specific curriculum: Girls were taught to be good wives, mothers, and servants of the Church. Although also instructed to serve the Church, boys were tutored in the ways of the world. The Church played a major role in implementing the Crown's pronatal agenda (Krull and Trovato, 2003a).

The fourth event, a peace settlement with the Iroquois in 1701, produced a more secure agrarian society. With the family as the base of this society, continued population growth remained the order of the day. Couples in New France kept marrying at a much younger age than elsewhere (Beaujot and McQuillan, 1982). This tendency was reinforced by government policies that gave monetary rewards to females who married before the age of 16 and males before 20. Other policies to strengthen people's desire to have large families included monetary rewards to couples with at least 10 legitimate children. Marriage was viewed as a natural state that all colonists would eventually enter and in which they would remain until their death.

Early colonial families shared several characteristics such as sex-segregated roles, pronatalist attitudes, a neolocal nuclear household, freedom in marital selection (but with parental approval), and extended kinship (Nett, 1993:102). These values and the agrarian framework of the new society continued well into the 20th century and may have contributed to slow down industrialization in what is now Quebec compared to the emerging American states south of the border.

Families during British Colonial Rule

Before Britain's conquest of Quebec in 1759–1760, the British colonial presence in what is now the United States had surpassed the French in terms of both wealth and population. Although the original purpose for Britain's presence mirrored that of France—commercial pursuits centring largely on the fur trade—its demographic superiority lay with London's policy of populating its Empire by massive emigration from the British Isles (Games, 1999). Entire families were a large part of this migration. After the American Revolution of 1776–1782, the British presence in North America remained through control of Quebec and Newfoundland/Labrador, the loyalist colonies in the other Maritime provinces, and Upper Canada or modern southern Ontario.

Families in Upper Canada and the Maritimes

Families in Upper Canada and the Maritimes during the period of British colonial rule, which lasted until 1867, were different from their counterparts in Quebec. Given their greater population, these British colonies experienced a relatively faster urbanization, a more developed capitalist system, and a more rapid industrialization than in Quebec—reflecting parallel developments in England and later in France (Acemoglu and Robinson, 2012; Weber, 1905). Major towns emerged: Halifax, York (now Toronto), Kingston, and Fredericton, among others. **Social stratification** solidified along classes of merchants, professionals, artisans, farmers, and labourers. Moreover, also reflecting British society, an aristocratic element was introduced when British noblemen and their families came to Canada to govern, lead the army and navy, and establish estates. A distinction arose between nuclear families and households: Households included domestic workers, servants, and labourers and their families who worked for and were supported by the patriarch's family (Hoffman and Taylor, 1996). In all classes in the colonies, therefore, there was an intimate connection between family life and production: "The household was the centre around which resources, labour, and consumption were balanced" (Tilly and Scott, 2001:78).

British families in Upper Canada and the Maritimes were nuclear ones built around English Christian principles (MacDonald, 1990; Potter-MacKinnon, 1993). There was no central religious power equivalent to the Roman Catholic Church in Quebec: The several Protestant religious authorities included Anglicans, Methodists, Quakers, Puritans, and Presbyterians. Christian notions that fathers and husbands owned property and were responsible for subservient children and wives underpinned this colonial society. Having custody of their families' moral character as well as their economic well-being, men often worked outside the home. More importantly, British common law gave legal rights to men as the heads of their families. Women were restricted to the home as cooks, cleaners, and caregivers for their children and, sometimes, for elderly parents. But they could take a leading role within households (Smith and

Sullivan, 1995). On a husband's death, for example, widows could inherit land and manage their families' interests on their own. Divorce in Upper Canada was only possible after 1839, but when it occurred, men received better treatment from the law, including custody of their children (Johnson, 1994).

Within the working class, children were crucial for the economic survival of families. After receiving rudimentary education, they worked to help support the family (McClare, 1997). Most working-class boys learned farming, logging, and, in the Maritime colonies, fishing, while others apprenticed in trades such as carpentry and blacksmithing. Within the upper classes, male children had access to good schooling, including university, to prepare for the professions and government. With some exceptions (den Boggende, 1997), upper-class females received a general education that prepared them to take their place in society (Errington, 1995). At lower levels, girls entered domestic service as young as 10 years old, and remained there until they either became financially independent or married. Overall, children only married when their contribution to the family was no longer essential; this translated into the age of marriage being higher in Upper Canada and the Maritimes than in Quebec (Krull and Trovato, 2003b). For very poor families, who had no home and no income, begging was not uncommon (Hoffman and Taylor, 1996). Charity from well-to-do families rather than from the government helped less fortunate ones.

Quebec Families under British Rule

In the period between the British conquest of Quebec (1763) and Confederation (1867), when Upper Canada, Quebec, and the Maritime colonies (except Newfoundland and Labrador) joined to form an independent Canada, the Québécois continued to develop a distinct society with the family at its core (Berthet, 1992). The British could not afford the troops that would have been necessary for a cultural conquest. Therefore, to keep their new French-speaking colony stable, the British let the Québécois use their language, put no strictures on the Roman Catholic Church, and allowed French civil law to remain. The result was that, beneath the English political and economic domination of Quebec, a Catholic, agrarian, and French-speaking society continued to exist as before, and became very homogeneous.

Marriage in French Canada not only remained as the natural state for every colonist, it was seen as essential for the survival of Quebec's distinct culture and society (Krull and Trovato, 2003b). Of course, some women and men chose not to or failed to marry. They generally stayed with their families and, in the case of older daughters, often remained to care for elderly parents. Others entered religious orders and, until the 1960s, most large Québécois families were proud to have a priest or a nun among their children. French-speaking government officials and the Church promoted family growth and more sons were needed to open new territories farther north. Divorce remained extremely rare, as family solidarity was more important than marital happiness. In this way, the nature of Quebec families did not change despite the British conquest. The established pattern of marrying at an early age continued along with large families. But these large families also required many skills and types of manual labours in this pre-industrial society. Thus, a greater de facto diversification of the role of many women existed than was allowed by the Church's teachings and despite their limited legal rights (Joël, 2012).

Montreal became one of Canada's major industrial cities, with a growing immigrant population from Europe seeking employment. But the majority of Québécois in the 19th century lived outside of Montreal. Because Quebec's population was expanding, its best farmland was occupied, and the British had commercial monopoly, some Québécois saw the possibility of a better life for their families outside of the Canadian colonies: Québécois families began moving south to find jobs in industries. Indeed, 900,000 Québécois settled in the U.S., from Maine to Michigan, between 1840 and 1940 (Lavoie, 1981) and many belonged to what came to be called transnational families (Hareven, 2000:64).

First Nations Families under French and British Rule

Contact with both British and French societies continued to bring great changes to First Nations and their families, which became more fragile in the face of increasing European supremacy. At first, the contacts had saved the French colonists, who learned to adapt to the harsh climate from the Native peoples (Bumsted, 2010). There was a level of equity for some decades and this frequently occurred as well when hard-working *coureurs de bois* cohabited with Aboriginal women who, along with their villages, proved to be very helpful to the French. Later, it was largely the progeny of such *métissage* (hence the nation of Métis) that contributed to the expansion of trade in the north and Manitoba (Van Kirk, 1992). But this mutually advantageous state of affairs did not last. Eventually, throughout the decades, close to 3,000 Aboriginals were enslaved. Fur traders often exchanged alcohol and arms, along with new foods, and these created an economic dependency amongst Aboriginal people on the French and later the British colonizers—in addition to implanting alcoholism. As well, Aboriginal tribes were often pitted against one another. To these problems was then added racism that led to the calculated plans by both the French and British colonial governments and Christian missionaries to eradicate First Nations' culture by assimilating them (Fiske and Johnny, 2003:182).

The European educational system played a key role in colonizing Aboriginal culture. The Jesuits in Quebec opened schools to educate Aboriginal children about religion and French culture. The British did the same and, by the end of the colonial period and the early years of Confederation, every region in Canada had **residential schools** for Aboriginal children (Harrison and Friesen, 2004), with the Métis situation being somewhat less clear-cut (Chartrand et al., 2006). Children, now wearing uniforms, were alienated from their families and stripped of all identifiers of Aboriginal culture. They were forced to take Christian names and forbidden to speak their mother tongue. One Aboriginal woman recalls that:

> *"When I got into school, everything changed for me all at once. My parents didn't have a say any more in the way my life went. When I came in off the land, the people with any type of authority were Qallunaat [non-Aboriginal]. . . . They treated us like we belonged to them, not to our parents. . . . They taught us a new culture, a different culture from our own, they taught us that we have to live like the white people. We had to become like the white people."* (Emberley, 2001:61)

Courtesy of Buffalo History Museum, used by permission

First Nations families were extended and often shared a common dwelling in which all the generations lived in close and constant proximity. This communal life meant that all family members were responsible for the rearing of children. They formed an effective community.

Many children were assaulted. Thus, the residential schools have had lasting negative consequences both for the individuals who attended them and their families (Barman, 2003). "Generations of depression, alcoholism, suicide, and family breakdown are the legacy of such traumatic experiences and are described as the 'residential school syndrome' by native people themselves" (Chartrand and McKay, 2006). The First Nations people were treated as unruly children and the government as the benevolent father (Chartrand et al., 2006). Beginning in 1870, a series of *Indian Act*s reinforced the concept of the British nuclear family model by forcing First Nations to change their traditional family structures (Carter, 2008). These changes ranged from "marriage practices, adoptions, and residence rights to an inability to bequeath property according to established custom" (Fiske and Johnny, 2003:183). With the help of the Church, the Europeans adopted a strategy of biological and cultural assimilation of Native peoples (Das Gupta, 2000:150). As well, their traditional economies were destroyed.

In subsequent chapters of this text, we often refer to Natives, First Nations, or Aboriginals. However, these concepts may be misleading at times because, with the *Indian Act* of 1876, the government then enshrined the term "Indians" to refer to those who were so registered at the time. They are also called "Status or Treaty Indians," and generally refer to those who live on reserves. (This term is currently being extended to be more inclusive.) Others who are equally Indian were not part of this legal category. Basically, Aboriginal people include Indians, Métis, and Inuit and are enshrined as such in the Canadian Constitution (Frideres, 2011).

Early Black-Canadian Families

First Nations families were not the only ones whose family structures and social institutions were affected by the cultural imperatives of the Europeans. Even before the conquest of Quebec by the British, a black community lived in what is now Canada. Slavery, which until then had been practised only toward some Aboriginal tribes, was not widespread in France but was in its colonies and was legalized in 1709. Black Africans were brought to New France after 1650 to serve as house servants and general labourers for the French religious, military, aristocratic, and commercial elite (Trudel, 1973; Walker, 1980). Taken from their homes and families in West Africa, only a rudimentary family life was possible for them because their owners determined almost all facets of their lives, as was the case for slave families in the southern U.S. (Gaspar and Hine, 1999). Slavery was curtailed in Upper Canada in 1793 by legislation making it illegal to bring people into the colony to become slaves—although slavery itself was not abolished. As a result, a large number of slaves fled to parts of the U.S. where slavery did not exist (Cooper, 2011). The British Parliament did not pass the *Slavery Abolition Act* until 1833.

The second stage of black immigration began when a mixture of free blacks arrived along with the more than 2,000 slaves who came north after the American Revolution of 1776–83, particularly into Nova Scotia and New Brunswick (Gleason et al., 2011:69). The free blacks were Loyalists and the slaves belonged to white Loyalists who fled the new United States. The third stage was as a result of the same *Act* of 1793 which stated that foreign slaves arriving in Canada would be free. Thereafter began the Underground Railroad—particularly after the American War of 1812, fugitives arrived in Upper Canada (Cooper, 2011).

As occurred in New France, the institution of slavery severely weakened the structure of the family among slaves in Upper Canada and the Maritimes as, legally, blacks had no marital or parental rights (Nicholson, 1994). For their part, Loyalist blacks and former American slaves who reached Canada encountered racial discrimination and social prejudice (Winks, 2000). In one example, Loyalist blacks, compared to Loyalist whites in Nova Scotia, received few land grants after coming north, and whatever land was granted was marginal at best (Calliste, 2003). In another example, in Ontario, although official policy after 1833 was to treat blacks as free citizens equal with whites before the law, they encountered general hostility from white officialdom, even though there was a strong abolitionist movement in Ontario before the American Civil War (Martin, 1974; Stouffer, 1992).

Given their lesser economic status, black husbands and wives commonly worked outside the home, as labourers and domestic servants. Consequently, there was a reliance on the extended family to help in childrearing through a tradition of taking relatives and others who were destitute into their homes; they could help with domestic chores or could earn money. There was a reverence for elder blacks who could also join households to help themselves and the family with which they lived (Dunaway, 2003). In this context, older blacks would have adoptive titles such as "Aunt" or "Uncle" to show that they were part of these extended families. Black Loyalist households could include neighbours, orphans, members of the local church, the widows or widowers of friends, and so on (Walker, 1976). Importantly, given that black men could not always find employment, when black wives and mothers worked in domestic service and other areas at the lower end of the economy, their unemployed husbands stayed home, minded the children, and did what they could to keep their families together (Calliste, 2003).

A more communal way of life emerged for black Canadians in which bonds of kinship became extremely important for their physical and spiritual survival as an identifiable minority. In some places, both in Upper Canada and, later, when western Canada was being settled, entire black communities were founded. Amber Valley in Alberta was such a community, established in 1911 by 90 black families from Oklahoma. The problem was that the white majority was prejudiced against black rural settlers, so that not every effort by blacks to build a family life in Canada was successful (Shephard, 1997). In other places, such as the Africville area of Halifax, black urban communities evolved as a result of both segregation and black leaders' efforts to organize themselves for mutual assistance, property ownership, and education (Clairmont and Magill, 1999). Black women also played a significant role in these efforts to reinforce their communities by strengthening the family (Fingard, 1992; Yee, 1994). A distinctive black family structure and culture had emerged in Canada by the early part of the 20th century.

Families during Industrialization and the Settling of the West

The 19th century was a period of industrialization for parts of Canada, chiefly Upper Canada and the Maritimes. In this context, **urbanization** was also a new element of social and economic development; it affected the family and brought new **social constructs**.* As this was occurring during the high point of the Victorian period, middle-class notions of women as being naturally endowed to provide the moral education of their children and to nurture their sensitivities became widespread (Hoffman and Taylor, 1996:41–91; Van Die, 2005). In the realm of men, no matter their class, the demands of employment took them increasingly from home. There was a heavy emphasis on masculinity (Moss, 1998). The result was that, in cities, the division of labour within marriage became even more differentiated, especially within the middle classes, and gender roles overlapped less. At the working class level, however, both in Montreal and Toronto, women constituted over a third of the labour force in the new industries (Prentice et al., 1988)—all the while being responsible for what Arlie Hochschild (1989) later called the "second shift" at home.

Childhood: A New Social Construct in Context

By the 1840s, the concept of *childhood* began to emerge; urban social reformers became concerned about childhood employment in dangerous and unsanitary conditions, such as in mines (McIntosh, 2003). Reflecting new European ideas that children were actually innocent beings who needed to be protected and educated, laws were passed to restrict child labour and allow for better educational opportunities. But as this new perspective on childhood developed—and no doubt led slowly to the improvement of the life conditions of many children—treatment of certain categories of children did not follow this new trend. The very poor, the homeless, and those of "unsuitable" ethnic background (Irish, for instance) did not benefit from this new climate (Strong-Boag, 2006:18–19). Apart from the mistreatment of Aboriginal children, one childhood topic that is rarely mentioned in sociology chapters on the history of families is that of the **"Home Children"** (2009; Parr, 2003).

Well over 100,000 children, from a few months old to 18 years of age, were sent to Canada from the British Isles between 1869 and the late 1930s (Ontario Heritage Foundation, 1997); approximately 10 percent of the Canadian population descends from them. Who were these children? They were the poor. Some were taken off the streets while the majority came from workhouses that could no longer afford to keep them. Others had been in reformatories, generally for minor thefts, while still others came from various "homes" of philanthropic institutions (BIFHSGO, 2010). They were not generally orphans but poverty had prevented their parents from caring for them. Both the Canadian and British governments supported this immigration

In poor households, children contributed to their families' economic survival well into the 20th century. Many Home Children laboured heavily, especially in rural areas. Thus, the social reconstruction of children's roles did not reach all social classes or groups of children simultaneously or equally.

Library of Congress Prints and Photographs Division [LC-DIG-ncle-00753]

program. It reduced British welfare costs and provided apprentices in Canada as well as adoptions by interested families for the children younger than 10 (Neff, 1996). After 1925, only children who had completed their education in Britain and had reached the age of 14 could be brought to Canada (BIFHSGO, 2010).

Many of these children found a better life in Canada but probably many more were maltreated, abused, and exploited (Strong-Boag, 2006). Many were placed on farms (Parr, 1994). Often, they were no better than slaves and had to sleep in cold barns with the animals, had no shoes, and were isolated (Thompson, 2010). They had been taken away from their own families and cut from their roots and identities. Although many served with the Canadian and British Forces during both World Wars, many of their descendants are still trying to find their parents', grandparents', and even great-grandparents' roots and are discovering distant relatives in the process.

The Beginning of Family Ethnic and Religious Diversity

By the middle of the 19th century, what is now western Canada was a vast area where a small number of white persons, principally British and French, and Chinese men engaged in trade with First Nations and were beginning to settle British Columbia. Métis were particularly numerous, the result of two hundred years of *métissage* with traders and explorers. The Aboriginal population represented a threat to the British colonial culture. In addition, after Confederation in 1867, the new federal government decided that the western regions of Canada should be populated as quickly as possible to counteract U.S. expansion westwards and to ensure Canada's sovereignty over its territory—basically, a territory that belonged to the Aboriginals.

A transcontinental railway was begun in the 1870s to link the west with the eastern regions. There was a conscious effort by Ottawa to encourage white immigration from Europe to populate the west.

But, as the west was being settled, the government was concerned about the continuation of British Protestant culture and morality. Hence, a multitude of pressures were placed on women so that they remained dependent, at least under marriage—for instance, they could not become homesteaders without a husband. For men, mixing with Aboriginal women became frowned upon. Monogamous marriage was imposed to counteract both the Mormon immigrants as well as the polygamous practices among some of the Aboriginals. Divorce was not allowed, which prevented women, particularly Native, who were deserted from remarrying and receiving support for the care of their children (Carter, 2008:285).

Thus, unlike the Maritimes and Upper Canada, which were populated almost exclusively by British immigrants (English, Scottish, and Irish) along with a small group of blacks, and Quebec, which contained a relatively homogeneous francophone Catholic population, the Canadian west came to be settled by increasing numbers of new Canadians arriving from more diverse parts of Europe along with a significant Chinese population brought to work on the railway. As the railway pushed westwards, groups of Swedes, Norwegians, Germans, Dutch, Ukrainians, Italians, and other nationalities settled in the west, including a good number of Home Children and Québécois in search of opportunities (Farnam, 1998; Gagnon, 1994; Stambrook and Hryniuk, 2000). These new ethnic groups also brought with them a greater diversity of religion, particularly of Protestantism (Scott, 2012).

Initially, these new Canadians created an agrarian society that was supported by small towns and villages (Butada, 2005). Men tended the land and herds; women were responsible for domestic chores and childrearing. Yet, women's roles could overlap a great deal with those of men, especially when fathers had to labour away from home for many months (Trussell and Shaw, 2007). In other words, as is still the case today, role "reversals" occurred, more often among women. In the early period of settlement, access to education was limited. Hence, male children helped their fathers as soon as they were physically able; female children acquired domestic skills from their mothers. Adolescent and adult children often worked in other households to help their own families financially. Once schooling was available, children had a few years of learning before working on the family farm or ranch. Communities evolved rather quickly, as groups of immigrants with the same ethnic background or even from the same region of Europe settled close together (Bennett and Seena, 1995; Voisey, 1987).

Within a generation of the railway being built, industrialization emerged in a few cities like Winnipeg and Edmonton, and urbanization resulted in a host of smaller towns like Brandon, Prince Albert, and Red Deer. As a result, very small Jewish congregations began to spread from Montreal and Toronto to Winnipeg, for instance (Robinson, 2012). As well, social stratification in urban areas continued to take hold: Western urban families began to experience different levels of education, labour, and social status. As time passed, groups of immigrants from the same places in Europe—for instance, Italian immigrants in Calgary and Polish ones in Edmonton—began to live in particular parts of these urban areas (Aliaga, 1994; Lukasiewicz, 2002).

Although British political and social custom dominated, large-scale immigration in western Canada (and that of Canada as a whole) began transforming it into a multicultural society with a variety of ethnicities. During this process, Aboriginal societies were further marginalized into reserves, colonialized, and deprived of their religious, cultural, and familial traditions in residential schools, among other practices. Prejudice against mixed marriages had grown. Métis in Manitoba, who were not yet known by that name, were being dispossessed of their lands by European settlers and were strongly discriminated against, often being called half-breeds or *bois-brulés* (burnt wood—Butala, 2005). The dispossession of Métis and other Aboriginals led many to move to Saskatchewan, Alberta, and British Columbia. Discrimination against Métis was racially based but was also the result of Protestants' hate of the French-speaking Canadians and Catholicism. As a result, Manitoba went from a majority of French speakers to having, by 1892, only 7 percent of its population that was francophone (Butala, 2005:93).

From the mid to the late 19th century, Chinese men and a few women settled chiefly in British Columbia and the Prairies. They were referred to as "sojourners" because they did not intend to remain permanently in this country. Their purpose was to supplement their families' incomes in their home countries: Married sojourners were prohibited from bringing their spouses and children to Canada (Dua, 2011). They worked in railway- and road-building, in the lumber industry, and in mining, to name a few of their generally dangerous and low-paying jobs. Many others, in Saskatchewan and Manitoba, operated restaurants (Marshall, 2011). Asian female sojourners worked as domestics (Das Gupta, 2000). The Chinese faced discrimination from the moment they arrived. In 1885, to limit their immigration, the government imposed a head tax of $50 on each Chinese entering the country. The head tax was raised to $100 in 1902 and to $500 in 1903. In 1923, the federal government passed the *Chinese Immigration Act*, also known as the "Chinese Exclusion Act": Until its annulment in 1947, it barred new Chinese immigrants. Further, all Chinese in Canada, including those born here, had to register with the authorities and a great deal of discrimination occurred at all levels (e.g., Stanley, 2003). For instance, they could not practise many of the professions, hold public office, or vote.

For their part, Japanese Canadians, who had begun arriving in 1877 and settling mainly in British Columbia, were evacuated from coastal towns in 1942 after Japans surprise attack on Pearl Harbor. They were sent to internment camps. After the war, many were deported to Japan or sent to Ontario. Later, their "resettlement" was accompanied by stereotyping, discrimination, and general social maltreatment and exclusion (Roy, 2007). It was only in 1947 that they were granted permission to move freely across the country.

By 1947, the injustice of these policies began to be called into question, especially since Chinese Canadians had served in the Canadian armed forces during the Second World War and had fought against the Japanese. By the early 1950s, Canadians of Chinese, Japanese, and Indian ancestry were given the right to vote in federal and provincial elections and were allowed to work in professional fields heretofore closed to them. With the passage of the 1967 *Immigration Act*, the Chinese, Japanese, Indians, and others such as Filipinos received the same rights as other groups of immigrants and began to reunify their families in Canada (Roy, 2007). However, because of their different experience during the war and because of diverging political and economic developments in China and Japan, very few Japanese thereafter emigrated to Canada while the contrary occurred among Chinese and Indians. For their part, people of Muslim faith arrived much more slowly so that they numbered only around 3,000 by 1951 (Zine, 2008:5). But, by the end of the 20th century, Muslims were the largest non-Christian religious group, even surpassing those of Jewish origin. By 2001, 2 percent or 579,640 Canadians were Muslim (Zine, 2008) from the Middle East, Asia, Turkey, and the Balkans as well as Africa. They are even more numerous today as a result of American and Canadian military interventions (Hussain and Scott, 2012).

CURRENT DIVERSITY OF CANADIAN FAMILIES

Between 2006 and 2011, approximately 1.6 million people migrated to Canada (Statistics Canada, 2013a). Asia was the main source of immigrants during these five years (60 percent) and the share of immigrants from Africa, Caribbean countries, Central and South America increased slightly. Over 6.2 million Canadian residents identified themselves as a member of a visible minority group or 19.1 percent of the total population in 2011. The Philippines were the leading source of new citizens and constituted 13 percent of all newcomers, followed by China and then India. The other top countries of newcomers' birth were the United States, Pakistan, the United Kingdom, Iran, South Korea, Colombia, and Mexico. Thus, by 2011, over 1.3 million Canadians were of Chinese origins, over 1 million were from India, close to 950,000 were of black identities, and over 580,000 were Filipino. A majority of these new Canadians have settled in Ontario and British Columbia, and most of those who went to Quebec are in the Montreal area. Thus, the cultural diversity of Canada has substantially expanded recently. The new wave of immigration has also contributed to the religious diversity of Canadian society, particularly with a rapid increase in the Muslim population as well as a greater proportion of Hindus and Sikhs. In this section, we complete the overview of the development of families' structure, culture, and conditions of life in Canada by examining current trends and outcomes in family diversity. We return to Aboriginal and Québécois families—the original two groups of founding families. We then return to black families before examining more recent families, including Chinese and Indian.

Aboriginal Families

In the 2011 census, over 1.4 million Canadians, or about 4.3 percent, identified themselves as Aboriginal persons. Of these, over 851,000 were First Nations (or 61 percent of all Aboriginals), 451,000 were Métis, and more than 60,000 were Inuit (Statistics Canada, 2013a). As we see later in Family Research 2.1, adding multiple identities gave us a total of over 1.6 million Aboriginals in 2006, or 5 percent of the Canadian population. This is a huge change over just 10 years ago, perhaps due to an increased tendency to identify as Aboriginal as a result of a renewed pride in their unique heritage and the fact that more reserves have participated in this census (see

Anne-Marie Ambert

First Nations families are, on average, larger and younger than other families in Canada. In Aboriginal communities, many of the childrearing functions fulfilled by parents in Canadian society at large are shared with relatives, including older children. Sibling influence may be even more important on Aboriginal reserves compared with its importance in society at large—a hypothesis that remains to be tested.

also Lawrence, 2004; Naumann, 2008). As well, children born to an Aboriginal parent and a non-Aboriginal one now tend to identify as Aboriginal (Robitaille et al., 2010). **High fertility rates** also contribute; although these rates have declined over the past four decades, they still remain much higher than the Canadian average of 1.6 children per woman in 2008 (Statistics Canada, 2011d). The Inuit have the highest fertility rate, with an average of 3.4 children per woman, followed by Status Indians with 2.8 children, the Métis with 2.4 children, and non-Status Indians with 2.0 children (Beaujot and Kerr, 2004). As a result of this higher birth rate, the **median*** age of the Aboriginal population is 28 years versus 41 for the remainder of Canada (Statistics Canada, 2013b).

Some provinces have a higher proportion of Aboriginals in their population. For instance, while Ontario has the largest number of Aboriginals, they represent less than 2 percent of the population. However, they constitute close to 16 percent of Saskatchewan and Manitoba (Statistics Canada, 2011a). Approximately 58 percent of Aboriginals who are registered as Status Indians live on one of the 2,284 **reserves** throughout the country. Reserves are lands that have been set aside by the Canadian government explicitly for Aboriginal peoples (Harrison and Friesen, 2004:228). The primary unit of First Nations social structure is the **band,** which originally described small cultural and linguistic groups who either lived together or came together at various times of the year (Harrison and Friesen, 2004). In more recent times, a band refers to an administrative unit that operates under the *Indian Act* of 1876. There are currently 621 bands in Canada (Frideres, 2000).

We have discussed residential schools earlier: The end result has been a legacy of trauma with which the First Nations people are still trying to cope (Grant, 2004; Kirmayer et al., 2007). As James Frideres (2011) so well explains it, with regards to the effects of cultural dislocation,

> *"The establishment of Indian reserves created a loss of territory and lifestyle that had been established in communities and bands. Loss of relationships to their traditional environment was also a severe spiritual and psychological injury. And, finally, to continue the colonization process, Canada attacked the core of their identity—language, family, and spirituality"* (p. 81).

Because they were isolated from their own families, the 150,000 successive students of residential schools were deprived of nurturing and of First Nations familial role models (Das Gupta, 2000). As a result, parenting became more difficult, divorced from traditions, and, consequently, poor parenting skills later developed and subsequently prompted **Children's Aid Services** to remove many children from their families. A 1979 Canadian report on adoption and welfare found that 20 percent of children in state care were Aboriginal, which is a number hugely disproportionate to their share of the Canadian population (Das Gupta, 2000). Today, over 27,000 Aboriginal children are in foster care (Monsebraaten, 2009). Nearly half of all legal wards in British Columbia are First Nations children (Kershaw et al., 2005). Large numbers of Aboriginal children were also taken from their homes and adopted by non-Aboriginal families. "In many cases, children were taken from parents whose only crime was **poverty**—and being aboriginal" (Fournier and Crey, 1997:85). As a result, several Aboriginal communities lost nearly an entire generation (Johnston, 1983). As one woman recalls: "Our family life was shattered after seven of my eight siblings and I were split apart into separate foster homes. We were never again to reunite as a family" (Fournier and Crey, 1997:85). There were so many Aboriginal children adopted out during the 1960s that Patrick Johnston, a researcher for the Canadian Council on Social Development, referred to this mass exodus of children as the "Sixties Scoop." By the late 1970s, one in four Status Indian children could expect to be separated from his or her parents for all or part of childhood. In addition, rates of domestic violence and abuse are extremely high, with women, children, the elderly, and persons with disabilities the most affected (Chartrand and McKay, 2006).

Under the influence of Catholic and Protestant teachings and other cultural pressure, little by little Aboriginal women lost the equality and power they often held in their nation. The 1876 *Indian Act* formally defined "Indian women through their relation to men" (Frideres, 2011:7). However, with Bill C-31 in 1985, women who had lost their status because they had married outside their band had it re-instated. As well, due to their social exclusion, young Aboriginal women are one of the most likely categories of persons to go missing (Kiepal et al., 2012). For instance, between 2005 and 2009, of the 726 homicide cases of women, 292 were identified as non-Aboriginal, 54 as Aboriginal, and 380 as "unknown Aboriginal identity" (Brennan, 2011). After much political pressure, Manitoba finally established the Task Force for Missing and Murdered Women at the end of 2009.

Nonetheless, although many traditional First Nations family structures have ceased to exist, either because of government policies (Carter, 2008) or because of a mass movement from reserves to cities where non-Aboriginals form the majority, the notion "of the caring, effective, extended family, co-extensive with community, continues to be a powerful ideal etched deep in the psyche of Aboriginal people" (Castellano, 2002:16). The importance of the **extended family** in terms of social identity, economic support, and psychological nurturing cannot be overstated. Urban Aboriginals generally remain connected to their kin (UAPS, 2010). Fiske and Johnny (2003) argue that the "importance of family and kin relations takes precedence over all other emotional and social ties in most, if not all, First Nations communities" (p. 182). Their **kin networks** are twice as extensive as those of other Canadians, and they are able to identify more than 50 different familial relationships (Buchignani and Armstrong, 1999). The importance of kin may be one of the reasons why Aboriginal victims of family violence vastly under-report their situation (ANAC and RCMP, 2001). (This topic is addressed at greater length in Chapter 13.)

Within an extended family structure, **elders** tend to be respected and identified as key sources of tradition and wisdom (Buchignani and Armstrong, 1999). Most live with their children or another family member. Elder care is primarily informal, an arrangement which is consistent with traditional values that emphasize familial obligation. Both elder care and visits to elderly family members are generally carried out by women, especially daughters. However, Aboriginal elders face more hardships than other Canadian elders and they suffer a great deal of abuse (Chartrand and McKay, 2006). As well, their income is typically below the poverty line and many support their unemployed children, which means that an extended family lives on less than required for bare subsistence (McPherson, 1998).

Disability rates for Aboriginal seniors are twice the national average, and nursing care facilities on reserves are rare, which forces many to live in nursing homes away from their families and friends. Buchignani and Armstrong (1999) have found that First Nations elders were three times more likely to report their health as "fair" or "less than fair" than other Canadians of comparable age. Similarly, Aboriginals in general, including those living off-reserve, have a poorer health status than other Canadians (Statistics Canada, 2010c). For instance, a 10-year longitudinal study found that Métis and non-Status Indians died prematurely at twice the rate of the rest of the Canadian population while Status Indians died two and a half times more prematurely (Tjepkema et al., 2011a,b).

FAMILY RESEARCH 2.1

Statistics Canada and Ethnic Groups*

Census statistics regarding ethnicities are at times difficult to interpret because the definition of what is a person's ethnicity is a matter of self-definition. As well, the Canadian census allows persons to self-identify with only one group or, if they wish, more than one. Partly as a result of this, the various tables and articles published by Statistics Canada often give *different* numbers depending on the basis of calculation. For instance, we have seen earlier that there are two estimates for the Aboriginal population, ranging from a low of 1.17 million to a high of 1.67 million, depending on the number of self-identities chosen.

For Indians, the total is 962,670 and includes 780,175 with only this identification and another 182,495 with more than one self-identity. For Chinese, the total number is 1,346,510, which includes 1,135,370 with one identification and 211,145 with more than one (Statistics Canada, 2009e). The larger number is generally given but this is not always the case for Aboriginals—perhaps reflecting the greater complexity in the ancestry of Aboriginals due to higher rates of racial mixing historically and currently. Even within one year, in 2011, the census and the National Household Survey gave slightly different numbers.

Over the past few decades, Aboriginals have developed strategies to achieve **self-determination** and self-government. Some have used traditional games, such as gambling, as a means of expanding their economy (Belanger, 2008). The federal government and provinces are currently negotiating various forms of self-government with approximately 90 different indigenous groups including Métis (Hoffman and Robinson, 2010; Saunders, 2011). There have been strong collective efforts to renew traditional knowledge, values, cultural activities, and customs and a determination to take charge of social services and child welfare (Kumar and Janz, 2010). Various healing groups have been formed; some encompass research (e.g., Bopp et al., 2003; Lane, 2002), including some that are specific to the Métis experience (Chartrand et al., 2006). Some reserves in British Columbia have acquired the right to own their homes.

It was not until the 1980s that the last residential school was closed. At that time, the administration of most reserve schools was handed over to Aboriginal school boards (Harrison and Friesen, 2004). First Nations families have demanded the right to teach their children and to develop a curriculum that embraces Aboriginal practices and ways of knowing. Given the importance of language in "the transmission and survival of Aboriginal knowledge and culture," the revival of First Nations language is viewed as pivotal to this process (Harrison and Friesen, 2004). Of the 50 distinct Aboriginal languages known to have once been spoken in Canada, only three are now considered secure: Cree, Inuktitut, and Ojibway. The remaining languages have either disappeared or are spoken by only a few people (Beaujot and Kerr, 2004). Families and schools are cornerstones to the efforts to revive these cultures. About 20 percent of First Nations children aged 2 to 5 are able to understand an Aboriginal language (Statistics Canada, 2010d).

Québécois Families

Since the early 1960s, Quebec society has seen fundamental changes to family life. In 1960, a reformist Liberal government took power and undertook wide-ranging reforms. The economy shifted to one based more on finance and industrialization. Québécois began to replace anglophones in business leadership roles. The French language was used increasingly in the workplace. The power of the Catholic Church was curtailed: Its domination of education was replaced by secular government control and its influence over moral issues, such as the prohibition on divorce, was diminished (Laplante et al., 2006). As well, the Church's political alliance with the conservative political elite was broken. Women's rights were expanded and entrenched: Until then, women had had few property rights, limited access to education beyond primary school (even then concentrating in the domestic sciences), and few legal rights.

Nationalism, pronatalism, and feminism are powerful elements in understanding contemporary Quebec families. Québécois feminists, a relatively small group in 1960, supported the reforms. But by the end of the decade, as Quebec feminists became more organized, the province experienced a second wave of feminism: By 1985, there were more than 300 women's groups involved in political action (Dumont, 1995). Women's roles changed; therefore, so did family life. **Marriage rates** have plummeted since the early 1970s, from 8.2 per 1,000 population in 1971 to only 2.7 in 2001, well below the national average of 5.0 (Girard, 2008). Divorce is now much higher in Quebec than in the rest of Canada. The percentage of never-married individuals at age 50 is almost twice as high in Quebec, and the average age at marriage is one year later (Krull, 2003). Moreover, by 1991, Quebec already had the lowest proportion of married-couple families in all of Canada.

The rapid decline of Quebec's **birth rate** since 1960 clearly changed family structures in the province, as large nuclear families were replaced by smaller ones and many were led by single or cohabiting parents. Québécois society went from exceptionally high reproductive levels—spanning more than 300 years—to fertility rates that have now reached historic lows. This situation has proven problematic in the relations between women's groups and Quebec nationalists. On the one hand, many feminist groups support Quebec nationalism. But nationalists are concerned about the decline of Quebec's francophone population. In their estimation, for Quebec nationalism and the French language to survive, francophone women must produce more babies. However, Québécois women increasingly control their own lives—cohabiting or marrying as they like; pursuing education and careers; gaining financial independence; and limiting their fertility. As one francophone student from Quebec points out:

> "I find that girls here [Ontario] are less independent than at home especially when it comes to becoming mothers. Here they all say they want children but it was not like that at UQAM, many of us didn't want any or [wanted] only one. I have two older sisters and they both put their babies in child care and don't have any problem with this. Here I noticed that women are more hung up about this. . . . They still feel guilty about it. . . . Women also breast-feed longer in Montreal than in Toronto. . . . Anyways . . . I met this guy but I am worried that his family will find me too liberal for them. So that's my problem right now, figuring out where to go."

To push their agendas in the 1980s and 1990s, both Liberal and Parti Québécois provincial governments supported pronatal policies (Ansen, 2000). Financial rewards for women who had children were $500 for a first birth, $1,000 for the second, and $8,000 for the third and for each subsequent birth. Incentives also included a family allowance for all children under 18 years and an additional allowance for children under age six (Baril et al., 2000). Québécois feminists argued that, by advancing pronatal policies, the Quebec government was supporting a "traditional" family structure in which women are valued primarily for their domestic role. Accordingly, the birth rate did not increase and Quebec abandoned its pronatal policies in favour of **pro-family policies** to recognize that people who have children are helping their society.

In 2000, for instance, Quebec introduced a progressive, government-subsidized daycare program for working families, at a cost of only $5 per day per child. With the cost now at $7 per day, the program has a waiting list of up to three years. Yet, because every subsidized daycare in Quebec follows a formal, age-appropriate curriculum that emphasizes school readiness and basic skills such as language, the Canadian Policy Research Network points out that "Quebec is the only province in Canada that has made a commitment to early-childhood education, and not just daycare" (Anderssen and McIlroy, 2004). In addition, the provincial government expanded its provision for parental leave.

Black-Canadian Families

There are important cultural differences among blacks: Those not born in Canada are coming from the Caribbean, the Americas, or Africa. They differ in their history, language, geography, social experiences, family structures, and in their reasons for emigrating (Galloway, 2004). They also differ by religion: While most are Christian, a substantial number of new arrivals from Africa are Muslim. Religiosity is a key element in this international black family culture (Taylor et al., 2004). There are other common experiences shared by black families. For instance, most black-Canadian parents believe that the community is important and tend to "share the African proverbial saying that it takes the whole community to educate a child. While parents believe that individual rights are important, they also think they should be matched with a strong sense of social responsibility" (Dei, 1993:47). Unfortunately, few studies exist on Canadian black families and given their longstanding presence in this country, this lack of research illustrates their marginality (Calliste, 2003).

The number of black families in Canada dramatically increased after racial barriers were removed from immigration laws in the 1960s. During the 1970s and 1980s, the majority of black immigrants came from the Caribbean, South America, and Central America; since 1990, the proportion of black immigrants arriving from Africa has increased. Forty-three percent of black persons are Canada born (Statistics Canada, 2009c, 2013a); of the foreign born

- 26 percent come from Jamaica
- 15 percent from Haiti
- 20 percent from several African countries
- 12 percent from other Caribbean nations

Blacks, who represent 2.5 percent of the Canadian population, constitute the third largest non-white minority group with close to 950,000 persons (Statistics

Black-Canadian families have a varied cultural and social heritage. They also include a wide range of family structures and patterns, which have constituted adaptive strategies that have allowed them to survive in rather difficult environments.

Image Source Plus/Alamy

Canada, 2013a). Cultural factors retained by black immigrants when they come to this country, as well as racism and structural inequalities, have played some part in the evolution of black family patterns and coping strategies. For instance, despite their increasing numbers, black families continue to be disadvantaged. Blacks experience unemployment and income inequality more than any other minority group (Calliste, 2003; Galloway, 2004). Statistics Canada (2004h) pointed out that Canadian-born blacks between the ages of 24 and 54 earned on average $7,500 less per year than other Canadians with the same education. A black student indirectly recalls how her economic problems tainted her relationship with her parents when she was 10 to 14 years of age:

> "We all had a hard time together mainly because our parents couldn't cope with us three children. We weren't bad or anything of the sort but we lived in a cramped apartment near a subsidized project and there were kids, kids, kids everywhere. We had a lot of fun some days but my parents didn't. They were trying to raise us well but the other kids we were always hanging around with would have none of it and their parents weren't always the best either, they'd let them stay out late at night, go wherever, invade and control the hallways, parking lots, you name it. They were up to no good but my sister, brother and myself couldn't appreciate that our parents were trying to protect us from this mayhem. I resented my parents but at the same time I loved them and we had the only father on the block and that made us special also."

Black families have tighter connections to their extended kin (Gosa and Alexander, 2007) and perhaps higher expectations of help. Middle-class black students often mentioned in their autobiographies that they had poor relatives and even siblings who were unemployed, out of money, and even criminal. These relatives, who as one woman put it, "have a sense of entitlement," were often draining these students' familial resources—situations rarely mentioned by other students (Heflin and Pattillo, 2006).

Low socioeconomic status and few employment opportunities contribute to family breakdown. Black spouses, especially in working-class families, are more likely to be separated or divorced and less likely to be formally married, a situation also found in the U.S. and throughout the Caribbean region. Conflicts pertaining to money frequently arise as an issue explaining this racial disparity (Bryant et al., 2008). As a result of disadvantaged economic circumstances, blacks place less importance on marriage as a context for childbearing (see Chapter 8). However, upper-income blacks are more likely to marry before having children, and this class difference also holds in the Caribbean (Barrow, 1996). The high divorce rate and the higher tendency for black women to have nonmarital births have resulted in many black families being headed by a woman: Black children are approximately three times more likely than other Canadian children to be living in a low-income, single-parent family (Chapter 8). Also contributing to low marriage rates is an **imbalance in the sex ratio*** of potential mates available. There are more black women of marriageable age in Canada than black men, primarily the result of earlier policies that admitted large numbers of black women as domestics and the greater tendency among black men to date interracially and to enter into interracial unions than is the case for black women (Calliste, 2003; Clarke, 2011; Harknett, 2008).

Moreover, black female domestics were also denied reproductive freedom in that they were not allowed to marry or have children without facing deportation, a restriction that did not apply to white immigrant women. However, a sizeable proportion of these domestic workers from Caribbean countries already had had one or more children who were left behind, generally in the care of grandmothers, thus forming **transnational families**, well before this concept became widely used. These grandmothers raised and loved these small children. Many were sponsored by their mothers and arrived in large Canadian cities, particularly Toronto and Montreal, at times in winter, to live with a mother they had barely known. This mother may have had a live-in boyfriend or another child. This situation is well expressed by a student:

"The most painful part of my life was when I had to leave my grandmother in Jamaica and come here to my mother I had seen only a few times in ten years. I didn't know her and I hated her and I refused to do anything she asked. . . . Even to this day we aren't close but at least I can feel for her terrible situation." [This student's brother is now in a penitentiary.]

These immigrant children have great difficulties adjusting to life in a high-density, low-income neighbourhood where gangs at times rule. As a result, male black youth are over-represented in jails and are more likely than others to be the victim of homicides (Rankin and Winsa, 2013). Similarly, a greater proportion of black children have a father who is incarcerated (Johnson and Easterling, 2012). Despite all these problems caused by systemic forces, the fact that most of these families find ways of thriving is testament to their resilience and adaptive ability.

Chinese-Canadian Families

Marriage and Fertility in China

For almost 2,000 years, China's family life was shaped by Confucianism. Marriage partners were chosen based on family needs and values rather than on attraction and love (Engels, 1995). It was common practice for parents to negotiate a marriage contract when their children were young; some children were betrothed before they were born. The groom's family was expected to pay a **bride price** and the bride's family was to provide a **dowry**. The Chinese family was patriarchal and overwhelmingly favoured sons. Lineages were very important elements of social organization (Zhao and Guo, 2010). Prior to the founding of the People's Republic of China in 1949, women were barred from participating in public life, had few employment opportunities, and 90 percent were mostly illiterate (SCIO, 2000). It was not uncommon for poor families to sell daughters into servitude to pay the bride price for a son's wedding.

Families underwent tremendous changes in 1949. The communist government passed a marriage law preventing, among others, arranged and coerced marriages. Monogamy became the norm. Child betrothal was abolished; men had to be 22 years old and women 20 years before a marriage could be contracted (SCIO, 2000). However, China was still plagued by its considerable and rapidly growing population. Even though contraceptive technology was officially approved in 1954, fertility rates remained high. In 1970, women were having an average of six children (Zhao and

Guo, 2010). To promote modernization, the Chinese government began a family planning program in the early 1970s (Fong, 2002). The one-child-per-family policy followed a decade later.

The implementation of the **one-child policy** varied by region and over time (Xinran, 2010). For example, great resistance to the policy emerged in the country-side because rural parents depended on their children, especially sons, to work on farms and support them in old age. In the 1980s, the government revised the policy so rural couples could have two children but urban couples were still restricted to one child. These various policies were enforced at the provincial level with rewards and punishments. Pregnant women having an approved birth received free obstetric care and could obtain better housing, extra food rations, and cash subsidies as an incentive to have no further children. However, couples who had an unapproved birth not only paid for their prenatal care, they also faced substantial fines, usually ranging from 20 to 50 percent of a family's annual income. Women were subjected to a number of intrusive enforcement tactics, including coercive sterilization programs and mandatory IUD insertions and abortions.

These policies had unexpected negative effects. For example, Doherty et al. (2001) found that women who had an unapproved birth, and thus were not eligible for free obstetric care, were more at risk of prenatal complications and even maternal death than women who had approved births. As well, the policies did not diminish the tra-ditional preference for sons over daughters, and unusually low numbers of female babies were born and survived in comparison to male babies (Guilmoto, 2009). A normal **sex ratio** at birth is 105 boys for every 100 girls. But, currently, in China, there are 120.5 males for every 100 females—112 in Hong Kong and 109.6 in Taiwan. This imbalance is the result of **selective abortion** of female fetuses (**female feticide***) following ultrasound tests (Chen and Li, 2013). In the past, female infanti-cide, parents' refusal to register daughters, and abandonment or neglect of daughters were taking place (Zhu et al., 2009).

Two years after implementing the one-child policy, fertility decreased dramati-cally to two children per woman and, by 1991, less than two children (Zhao and Guo, 2010). A Chinese woman now has on average 1.5 to 1.8 children (Morgan et al., 2009). Chinese families today, especially in urban areas, tend toward greater gender equality and have become neolocal and bilineal. In eastern cities, such as Beijing and Shanghai, son preference is diminishing and daughters help their elderly parents (Fong, 2002). Nevertheless, the preference for male children has not entirely disappeared, especially in rural areas (Murphy et al., 2011). However, with continu-ing economic and social development, China's sex ratio imbalance may slowly disap-pear, as has been the case in South Korea (Das Gupta et al., 2009). But, the fact remains that many Chinese and Indian immigrants to the U.S. and Canada continue this practice as do many among the richest classes in China and India—including physicians who have access to ultrasound (Hvistendhal, 2011).

Chinese Families in Canada

Chinese Canadians currently represent Canada's largest non-white group: Over 1.3 million Canadians, or 4 percent of the population, 72 percent of whom live in Vancouver and Toronto (Statistics Canada, 2013a). But despite a long history in Canada, family formation by Chinese immigrants has only taken place over the past five decades—after the passage of the *Immigration Act* of 1967. The majority of Chinese immigrants tended to settle in the same areas as other Chinese Canadians. This produced a series of Chinatowns with shops, restaurants, and other cultural and social elements of life.

As the Chinese-Canadian population grew, it transplanted a number of traditions from China, Taiwan, and Singapore into its Canadian communities, including the dominance of patriarchy, extended families, and social stratification* based on wealth (Burney, 1995). However, three-generation households are no longer a dominant Chinese-Canadian family structure (Yasuda et al., 2011). Couples tend to live near extended family members rather than with them. There is still a strong family support network, particularly in child care and assistance in housework (Man, 2001). Two Chinese-Canadian students describe how these social networks maintain cultural identity and help parents reinforce traditional values in their children:

> *"I live in a big house in Toronto with my parents, and my grandparents live in a nearby condo and I have all in all six uncles and aunts who live around and in Markham. So it's easy for us to remain Chinese and my grandparents never have to speak English. They might as well be in Hong Kong for all I know. . . . Sometimes though it's hard because I'd like to be more Canadian but there is so much pressure to be and marry within our group, I feel like I am being choked and I'd like to move to Vancouver later but then who would babysit for me?"*

> *"My peers' values have always been similar to those of my family's because I have always hung around with other Asians. Living in Chinatown has made my life easier. . . . We are different but I do not think that we ever cared much because there always were so many of us."*

As pointed out by the first student, without their extended families, women may encounter problems with child care and household maintenance, which are considered the wives' responsibility. Man (2001) reports from her study on Hong Kong female immigrants to Canada that "the physical spread of Canadian cities, and the lack of transportation systems in suburbia—where most of the Hong Kong immigrants reside—heighten children's dependency on their mothers, intensifying women's workloads. Consequently, some of them experience an intensification of traditional roles, unequal distribution of household labour, and gender and sexual oppression in the home" (p. 434). Moreover, she found that most Chinese women linked power to the ability to manage and control every aspect of family life, and thus, to relinquish control is to relinquish power or to lose face. Chinese women are reluctant to ask their husbands for help, even though they are less traditional than men with respect to gender roles and family hierarchy (Tang and Dion, 1999).

Chinese-Canadian family relationships are, for the most part, based on the notion of filial piety: respect, obedience to one's parents, reverence for and assistance to the elders in the communities. This helping behaviour is reciprocal, as parents often assist their adult children financially and with child care. When one or both parents are not proficient in English, young Chinese immigrants are often faced with having to link the two cultures by taking on the role of **cultural brokers**. This role entails serving as translators for their parents, which often requires accompanying them as they take care of their daily needs, such as shopping and paying bills.

Chinese-Canadian parents tend to be indulgent until their children reach school age, although many remain authoritative* (Cheah et al., 2009)—not to be confused with authoritarian*. Then, children may fall under stricter control, although the level of parental supervision varies greatly. Chinese-Canadian adolescents state that their parents want to choose careers for them more often than is the case for other Canadian adolescents. Moreover, a large majority of Chinese parents expect their children to go to university, whereas fewer other Canadian parents have such expectations. Overall, Chinese-Canadian parents have so far been quite successful at helping their children retain their values (Su and Costigan, 2009). For instance, Chinese youths are generally more conservative sexually. Adolescents of Chinese origin are slow to shift their expectations toward the North American model of early autonomy because of the effectiveness of the family in transmitting its values (Liu et al., 2005).

Indo-Canadian Families

At the beginning of the 20th century, there were about 1,000 Hindus in Canada (DeVries et al., 2010). Sikhs began migrating to serve as manual labourers in mills, even though they were not welcome as citizens in British Columbia and were isolated. Most were male (Nayar, 2010). Once the racial barriers in Canada's immigration policies were lifted in the 1960s, Asians immigrated in greater numbers, especially Indians, who now number more than one million, or about 2.9 percent of the Canadian population (Statistics Canada, 2013a). For their part, Pakistanis, Iranians, and Afghans arrived in larger numbers in the 1980s and after (Moghissi et al., 2009). The roles and status of family members are well defined and understood within the ideal model of the Indian family structure, which is extended and patrilocal (Fuller and Narasimhan, 2008)—even though about half of families are already nuclear in India (Niranjan et al., 2005). Roles and status are challenged when members of extended families move to Canada and must live as nuclear families—although many still live in three-generational households. For many Indian and other Asian

First- and second-generation Indian families have assimilated into the Canadian economy while at the same time retaining many elements of their culture. This is particularly evident at weddings where couples begin life within the rituals of their culture.

© Joel Benard/Masterfile

and Middle Eastern immigrant families, economic survival depends on the wife taking on paid employment. This process not only challenges established gender roles, it accounts for increased conflict between many husbands and wives. However, many Indian wives are happy and feel free because they no longer fall under the control of their **husband's mothers** who are very powerful. When asked about her current happiness, an Indo-Canadian student conveyed anguish over her mother's situation:

"At this stage of my life I am not the happiest. I would like to leave my parents' home because it is really not their home, it's my grandparents' and it is too painful for me to see how badly my grandmother treats my mother as [if] she is her slave and my father lets her do it. . . . She even treats my father badly [she prefers the student's uncle who still lives in India]. I don't understand that my father accepts this because he owns his home and he paid for his parents to come here and my mother worked hard helping him do this. It hurts me so much that I want to run away and take my mother with me."

Let's look at the cultural heritage that Indian families bring with them. "Love-marriages" have been legal since 1872, and, although still rare (Derne, 2008), can occur even in villages (Ahearn, 2001). But, overall, **arranged marriages** still predominate in India (Mody, 2002). There are strict criteria used to determine an appropriate partner for one's child. For example, the future bride and groom need to be matched in terms of caste position, socioeconomic status, age, education, and of course, religion. Emphasis is placed on social compatibility and duty to parents and ancestors rather than on individual compatibility and personal desires for love and intimacy. Indeed, Muslims, Hindus, and Sikhs view the obligation to marry within the group as essential (Mody, 2002).

When Indian families, whether Hindu, Sikh, or Muslim—as well as Muslims from other parts of Asia and the Middle East—migrate to Canada, they are exposed to a social construction of marriage that emphasizes romantic love and companionship. Two results can follow. First, many established couples experience marital strain, at least as perceived by their children. As one woman explains in her autobiography:

"I would rate my parents' marital satisfaction differently, with my father's being high because he has what he needs which is a traditional Indian marriage while my mother is so lonely for just a bit of attention from him . . . and also because she sees that her cousins who came here before get along better and have a good relationship. It's very hard on my mother and it will be terrible when my father's mother eventually moves here from India to be with us."

Second, most Indo-Canadian female university students still undergo some form of arranged marriage—and some even expect to be sent to the U.S. for this purpose; others are still married against their will during trips to India. In England, the Foreign Office's **Forced Marriage Unit** received 1,600 such reports in 2008 and intervened in 420 cases (Aulakh, 2009). In fact, in the Punjab city of Ludhiana, each year several hundred cases of brides abandoned by husbands abroad are registered. "Canada-based families are said to be among the worst offenders," with many husbands living in the Toronto area (Westhead and Aulakh, 2009). But, overall, most women will have a greater say than would have been the case a decade ago (Zaidi and Shuraydi, 2002). One married woman student was introduced to her future husband,

> " . . . But my mother made it clear to me, him, and my father that I had to like him. So he visited me at my home several times and I really liked him; he was so nice and brought me and my mother little gifts. I asked him all kinds of questions. Then, after several weeks, we went out with my brother who left us alone most of the time, we held hands at the movies and he even asked my brother if he could kiss me and my brother said 'go for it' and here I am, married, and pretty happy. . . . I think that when arranged marriages work out, they're great because your parents do all the preliminary work for you. It's a great tradition to this extent."

The parent-child relationship is considered the most intimate and fulfilling familial relationship. **Motherhood** is a key source of *power* for Indian women, as it is among Muslims. According to Kohler Riessman (2000), a child solidifies a wife's often fragile bond with her spouse in an arranged marriage and improves her status in the joint family and larger community; and with a child, she can eventually become a mother-in-law. Moreover, women rely on their children, particularly on their sons, to support them in old age. Indeed, preference for male children exists in many parts of India, especially the Punjab and Rajasthan, where **sex ratios** in the population are 123.8 and 120.7, respectively (Das Gupta et al., 2009; Guilmoto, 2009). In the well-to-do classes, selective abortion takes place (Nolen, 2011). Among the poorer, female malnutrition, non-vaccination, and non-treated illnesses before age five produce an excess of female mortality (Oster, 2009). As well, parents seek less prenatal care when a girl is expected (Bharadwaj and Lakdawala, 2013). Two problems exacerbate the favouritism for male children: first, a dowry, which, although legally abolished, is still paid to the future husband's family; and second, the huge costs of wedding ceremonies—which can last for several days— and which families have to bear to enhance their status. When the bride price is unpaid or too low, many brides are abused and even maimed by their in-laws' families; others are pushed into suicide so that the husband can find another bride with better means.

The parent-child role among Indo-Canadians has also undergone major changes (Nayar, 2004). Although first-generation immigrants have strong expectations that their children will uphold the tradition of arranged marriages, these wishes are often challenged by children who are raised in a culture that devalues such marriages. Zaidi and Shuraydi (2002) found a definite "cultural" generation gap between the family values of second-generation Muslim Pakistani immigrant women and their parents, who typically favour arranged marriages: "This non-conformity to arranged marriages creates a mood of uncertainty for many females as they feel confused, uncertain, and torn between their own thoughts and their parents' belief system" (p. 512). Yet, as we have seen, many other young adults feel comfortable within this cultural perspective (Porter, 2003), particularly when their opinion is considered (Netting, 2006). Arranged marriages are no longer the norm among children of Muslim immigrants to France and Germany. But they remain common among Pakistanis and Indians in Great Britain. Furthermore, because of differences in gender roles, young Muslim men's ability to experience freedom in leisure activities and in the development of their goals is easier and may be more universal than is the case for young Muslim women (Tirone and Sweatman, 2011).

Although other Asian women have made advances such as being able to pursue post-secondary education and seek a career, it is not always easy. For instance, Talbani and Hasanali (2000) found that second-generation Asians tend to adapt to Canadian material culture but "find it difficult to negotiate between cultural control and individual freedom" (p. 625–626). Among Muslim immigrants, however, there may also be issues of others' reaction to "Islamism" that confronts them (Jamil and Rousseau, 2012; Moghissi et al., 2009; Yax-Fraser, 2011). But just as Chinese-Canadian families continue to adapt to Canadian society, so too do other Asian ones, such as Filipinos (Coloma et al., 2012). Indeed, by 2010, the Philippines had surpassed China and India as a source of immigrants to Canada (Friesen, 2011). And the result will probably be the same—finding a balance whereby the family as the core of various ethnic identities will change but not be destroyed and their Muslim, Hindu, or Sikh heritage will remain, albeit perhaps transformed by the Canadian sociolegal landscape and, in turn, contribute to diversify it.

CONCLUSIONS: EVOLVING CANADIAN FAMILIES IN DIVERSITY

Territorial conquests, cultural contacts, colonialism, and economic development all have a major impact on the structure of families as well as on gender roles and general family responsibilities. Prior to contact with the French and the British, Aboriginal families were complex social and economic institutions that allowed for survival in a difficult land. Contact with the colonizers destroyed many of these cultures and family systems. For their part, the British and French brought their own forms of neolocal family structure and adapted them to Canada as conquest, modernization, and industrialization brought economic and social transformations requiring change. The settlement of the Prairies and the West diversified families as other people from Europe and Asia arrived to populate this vast region of the country.

Thus, the family, a crucial institution of Canadian cultural heritage, includes many structures and systems of roles related to the various ethnic, religious, and immigrant groups composing this society. Therefore, being a member of a First Nations family, or a Québécois family, or a black or a Jewish or a Muslim family has a different meaning, connotations, and identities for its members than those of being a member of an Indo-Canadian or Chinese-Canadian or Filipino-Canadian family. However, it is key to recall that all these families show a great deal of variation *within their own groups,* depending on their region of origin as well as on the length of time they or their ancestors have lived in Canada. No group is totally homogeneous and this makes for even greater diversity of family life.

Summary

1. Aboriginal families have historically been distinguished by communal living and the practice of sharing responsibilities and resources. The Plains Cree and Nadouek families are described.

2. There had been contacts between northern European fishers/explorers and Aboriginal peoples before 1534. These contacts altered the demographic profile of Aboriginals. For their part, northern European families had long been nuclear.

3. The first settlers from France were immensely helped by Aboriginals in the fur trade and in terms of sheer survival. Inter-marriages were common. Later, European nuclear families had increasing importance in the development of colonial New France. For economic (agriculture), religious, cultural, and social reasons, marriage became the norm and large families were encouraged and predominated.

4. Colonial British Canada—Upper Canada and the Maritimes—quickly evolved from a preindustrial agricultural economy to a capitalist industrial one and social stratification solidified. Children's work was important. Under British rule, Quebec continued as a culturally and demographically separate society.

5. Both French and British colonial governments—and the government of Canada after 1867—worked to assimilate First Nations into the dominant European society. The consequences are discussed.

6. Black Canadians developed a more communal and extended family life by the early 20th century—an amalgamation of their West African traditions that survived slavery, and newer ones that derived from living in French and then British Canada.

7. The 19th century witnessed industrialization and modernization for parts of Canada, chiefly Upper Canada and the Maritimes. Along with urbanization, these economic changes affected the family in many domains.

8. The development of western Canada brought new European immigrants: Germans, Ukrainians, Italians, and others. The vast majority of new Canadians brought with them family cultures derived from their various homelands. However, Chinese immigrants were long prohibited from bringing their families. The case of "Home Children" is discussed.

9. Since Confederation, immigrants increasingly came from Asia, Africa, Latin America, and the Caribbean. More recently, immigrants have come mainly from Asia and Africa.

10. First Nations are the fastest growing group in Canada. The extended family remains an important emotional and social foundation for them even though it has been severely affected by residential schools, the loss of their territories, and life on reserves.

11. In the 1960s, Quebec's family structure was transformed and women's rights were expanded. The Québécois government has worked to strengthen family life by introducing innovative policies.

12. Blacks now represent the third-largest visible minority group in Canada. Their diversity and shared situation is discussed.

13. In terms of cross-cultural perspectives on family, the People's Republic of China provides an important case study showing how demographic policy can influence family structure. Canadian-Chinese families are then presented.

14. In India, arranged marriages continue to be the norm for both Hindus and Muslims. Indo-Canadian families have made some compromises in terms of gender roles and arranged marriages are perhaps more open.

15. Families have evolved since the advent of the colony and have continued to adapt and to diversify according to their origins. Diversity also exists within cultural groups.

Analytical Questions

1. What accounts for the differences in family structures found between early Iroquois and Plains Cree people?

2. What can explain the development of communal and extended family life among black Canadians by the early 20th century?

3. How is childhood affected by and linked to the concept of industrialization and modernization? And how does this relate to theories of social constructionism discussed in the previous chapter?

4. How has racism influenced government policies historically in Canada? Include all affected cultural groups.

5. How can you analyze the implications of such cultural heritage as arranged marriages, forced marriages, and imbalanced sex ratios?

6. Choose two theoretical perspectives from Chapter 1 and use them to explain a set of historical developments in terms of Canadian families.

CHAPTER 3

Contemporary Changes in Family Life

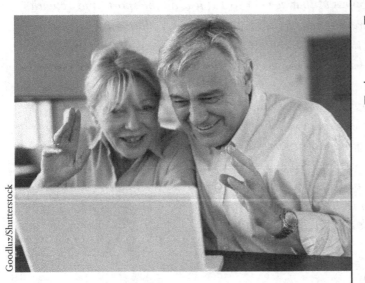

Goodluz/Shutterstock

OUTLINE

Has the Family Lost Its Relevance?
Functions That Have Remained with the Family
New Responsibilities Imposed upon Families
Additional Responsibilities Taken on by Some Families
An Overabundance of Family Responsibilities

Families and Couples Living Apart
Transnational Families
Military Families
Couples Living Apart (LAT)

The Audiovisual/Social Media and Family Life
Television: A Historical Overview
The Continued Effects of the Audiovisual Media: The Internet and Cellular Phone
The Issue of Sociability in Family Life
The Issue of Violence vs. Prosocial Behaviour
The Issue of Consumerism and Lifestyle
The Issue of Sexuality
The Issue of Education

Conclusions: The Family as a "Private" Institution Subsidizes the Economy

Summary
Analytical Questions

"Right now I am not so sure that I want to have children because I am afraid that I couldn't handle everything that we have to do for children nowadays. I can't imagine having to do what my mother has done and is still doing with me and my brothers, taking us here and there, parents' nights at school, us always sneaking behind their [parents'] back and actually doing things that could be considered dangerous or could ruin our reputation or could get us into a lot of trouble for a very long time."

"What made me the happiest at that age [11 to 14] was all the sports and activities I was in. My parents were running like crazy trying to meet all of our sports and arts schedules but I had the greatest time. It was exciting, I was never home. (But now my parents admit that they were burdened and were glad when it was over.)"

"The hardest month of my life happened during the winter when I was 13 when I got ganged up on by the guys in my hockey team after a game in the locker room because I had scored in our net. They hit me with sticks and one stomped on me with his skate. . . . I was cut, bruised and had some cracked bones and spent a painful month at home and that was the end of my hockey career. This episode was also painful for my entire family not excluding that my mother had to stay home from her work to put me back together!"

"I don't know how my parents can stand us because we are never home and when we are we are always in our rooms on the computer or watching television or doing video games and when they talk to us we grunt and just keep doing what we're doing. My parents really don't have a life as parents that they can brag to their friends about and I admit that I should feel guilty and I do at times but the whole bunch of us we're addicted to television and video games and it's so much more fun than parents. . . . [In 10 years] I guess I won't have much to show for myself. . . and my relationship with my parents will be gone and I will regret it but it will be too late because I will have grown into some kind of media freak." [This was written before the advent of Facebook and smartphones.]

The structure and dynamics of family life have evolved considerably over the centuries; yet, certain trends, which appear to be recent, were already in evidence in the 19th century and early in the 20th century (Nett, 1981; 1993). For instance, before the anomalous post-war years from 1945 to 1960, fertility had long begun a slow decline in most societies of the western world. Further, single-parent families had always existed because life expectancy was low: Children were often orphaned. Remarriage and stepparenting were common. Female labour had been widespread in previous centuries, although it generally took place within the household economy. Some of these trends, such as lower fertility and later age at marriage, were briefly reversed following the Second World War—and these few years are the "golden" yardstick by which we tend to compare current families to those of the past. Yet, this "good old past" was an anomaly in the long history of families.

Then, the years following the 1950s witnessed important changes in families. For instance, as the economy and technology evolved, so did the nature of people's employment—including that of women. Further, certain aspects of family structure have exhibited a dramatic transformation: Divorce, cohabitation, births to single mothers, same-sex-parent, and transnational families, as well as adult children remaining or returning home have all increased substantially and have transformed the profile of families. The cultural context within which families live has been altered by information technology.

Concepts such as "traditional," and "new" or "alternative" forms of families are labels that reflect our value system (Thornton, 2005). They are relatively meaningless because what we consider to be the traditional families of the 1950s were actually an alternative to what had just preceded that decade. Labeling prevents us from focusing on the multiple functions that all families fulfill. For instance, cohabiting-parent families are "alternatives"; yet, they fulfill "traditional" family responsibilities. Similarly, same-sex-parent families are "new" forms; yet, they also fulfill traditional family obligations: They all raise their children, love them, and integrate them to the best of their ability within the society in which they live.

Thus, in this chapter, I begin by examining the misleading and much heralded family "decline"—in other words, the family is becoming obsolete because other institutions are replacing it. Is this so? Then, we will discuss three circumstances that shape how a growing minority of families live: transnational families, military families, and couples living apart. This discussion will be followed by the examination of current historical changes that are taking place in our society with regard to the audiovisual/social media. I will look into the impact of certain aspects of these media on family life and child socialization.

HAS THE FAMILY LOST ITS RELEVANCE?

There is no doubt that the family has lost some of its responsibilities *if we compare today's situation with that of the preindustrial period.* As Hareven (1994a) puts it, in those days "the family not only reared children but also served as workshop, a school, a church, and a welfare agency. Preindustrial families meshed closely with the community and carried a variety of public responsibilities within the larger society." But many of the functions that the family has lost in western societies, such as training apprentices, were tied to a specific type of economic and technological tradition that vanished long ago. Thus, these familial functions are no longer necessary for the survival of society and for the integration of family members into society.

However, what is often overlooked—and is the focus of this section—is that *the family as an institution has acquired other responsibilities*. It is also recapturing some "traditional" ones because the social safety net and social policies fail society's most vulnerable members, particularly children, the elderly, and the mentally, emotionally, as well as physically disabled or challenged (Luxton, 1997, 2006a). Above all, the family as an institution has become more specialized in certain domains. These situations are well illustrated in the quotes opening this chapter.

Functions That Have Remained with the Family

1. It is often said that the family has lost its **reproductive function** because, until recently, births generally took place within wedlock. However, wedlock is a marital status rather than a family. As we have seen in Chapter 1, a married couple is not a family until the two spouses have their first child. Similarly, a woman's nonmarital sexual reproduction serves as the foundation to a family form: the mother-headed nuclear family. Understandably, the single-mother form of nuclear family is at times more fragile and at a greater risk of being unable to fulfill its obligations as adequately as those headed by two parents (Chapter 8). Therefore, while it is true that a large proportion of children are born to single parents and to cohabiting couples, this does not change anything in terms of families' reproductive role. The family will lose its reproductive function only when children are conceived, then cut away from their parents, and raised separately in special institutions. Actually, were such a point to be reached, the family as we understand it would disappear because it would lose its intergenerational dimension and all the other functions that flow from it.

2. The **socialization** or sociocultural reproduction of children still begins within the family. While other institutions soon complement parents or even take over their role, particularly child care centres and schools, parents are still children's most important agents of socialization until mid-adolescence. Even with adolescents, parents often are able to counterbalance negative peer and media influences when they exist.

3. The **economic** role of the family is still salient. True, the family no longer is the prime unit of production that it used to be. But all the unpaid *work* that takes place at home, mainly by women (housework, child care, elder care), constitutes economic activities—even if not the ones that a male political world values—in what is called **social reproduction*** (Bezanson and Luxton, 2006). As well, families contribute to the formation of future workers and taxpayers. Thus, families affect a society's level of productivity (Bogenschneider and Corbett, 2010). Feminists have consistently pointed this out (Gazso, 2010). Many families, particularly those on farms and owners of small enterprises, still form a unit of production: They train, employ, and pay their members. In addition, many persons now do paid work from home. Neither should one forget that the family has remained the key unit of consumption and, as such, is a prime mover of the market economy.

4. The family continues to meet its members' needs for physical security. Families still provide **shelter,** attend to basic nutritional needs, and ensure physical **health** according to their means. With the drastic cuts in the health care system, families are called upon to expand their role in these domains (FSAT, 2004). Indeed, post-surgical patients are now released prematurely, as often are birthed mothers and seniors who cannot find a place in a long-term care facility.

5. The family confers to its members their place within the social stratification* system, at least until children are on their own. This is referred to as the **status function.** That is, young members of a family belong to their parents' socioeconomic group—or to their grandparents'. Thus, the reproduction of the class system begins within the family, although Canada experiences a great deal of downward and upward **social mobility*** of adult children compared to their own parents (Corak, 1998). Further, the family contributes to the reproduction of the **religious and ethnic status** of a group, through socialization practices and the structure of opportunities available to its members in a racialized society.

6. The family still serves as an agency of psychological stabilization and provides a sense of identity and **belongingness,** particularly for its children. For instance, a French study found that 86 percent of adults mention their family when asked what defines them (Housseaux, 2003). It follows that the family fulfills many **affective functions.** It is within its boundaries that the young child learns to love and be loved, where attachment first develops, where trust is built. The family is one of the prime movers in **personality development** for children and adults alike. However, the family shares this function with a person's genetic background and with other social entities such as schools, work, as well as the peer group. When adults become parents, their personality development continues as they extend themselves into this new role.

New Responsibilities Imposed upon Families

Not only has the family retained some of the responsibilities it has fulfilled throughout centuries past, but it also has acquired many new ones, most of which are actually performed in great part by women, especially *mothers* and *daughters*. In other words, responsibilities related to social reproduction have increased.

1. Parents have become the coordinators of the education and the services that their children receive from various institutions (Coontz, 2000). Thus, the family has acquired the function of **coordination** or **management:** Parents must make the extra-familial environment (whether schools, child care, or the media) accessible to and safe for their children. They must also interpret these contexts to their children within the perspective of their values. Further, the various institutions and services available to children, especially schools, make great demands on parents' time, and even more so on mothers. Parents, for instance, have to monitor and help in their children's intellectual development, and this includes homework (Mandell and Sweet, 2004). In turn, because of a longer lifespan, when elderly parents become frail, children must manage the care they receive. All in all, the function of **caring** is acquiring new facets.

2. The family has now been charged with the responsibility of policing what its children and youth access on television, the Internet, their cell phone, the social media, and what they want to buy (Moscovitch, 2007). Thus, parents have to filter out noxious influences, whether in terms of consumerism, individualism, violence, or exploitative sexual content, which the media unleash upon everyone (Ybarra et al., 2009). This in itself is a very onerous role for which most adults are ill prepared, receive little social support, and create parent-child tension (Evans et al., 2011). Contemporary parents have to be vigilant on all fronts of a vastly expanding web of social media, in addition to the remaining printed media. Thus, the role of **agency of social control** that the family has always fulfilled has vastly expanded in terms of the cultural territory covered. Indeed, the family boundaries are far more affected by external sources than used to be the case even 20 years ago, hence requiring greater adult vigilance in view of the fact that the messages children, adolescents, and young adults receive may conflict with those imparted by parents—particularly immigrant parents (Yax-Fraser, 2011).

3. By the same token, the family prevents the fragmentation of its young members' lives that would unavoidably occur in view of the numerous and often conflicting sources of socialization to which children are subjected. As Hays (1996) puts it, "the more the larger world becomes impersonal, competitive, and individualistic and the more the logic of that world invades the world of intimate relationships, the more intensive child rearing becomes" (p. 175). The family serves as an **agency of integration** at the personal and social levels. This family function is particularly important in view of the *surfeit of choices* and alternatives that the consumer market economy and an urbanized society present (Bumpass, 2001). The family serves as a *lone* anchor because, in the past, this responsibility was generally shouldered with the help of the parish, village, or neighbours. This role of integration is particularly important in situations of immigration when the family serves as a mediating group between the individual and society (Cottrell and VanderPlaat, 2011:268).

4. The responsibilities related to **caring** may have increased rather than decreased. Not only are there fewer adult family members present in many families (one versus two parents), but there are also too few middle-aged persons to care both for the growing cohort of elderly and of the young whose adolescence has lengthened. Thus, as governments fail to provide alternatives, family members have to offer a larger combination of services to their more fragile kin, particularly as longevity increases. They are often supported by hired female caretakers or domestic help (Arat-Koç, 2011). We return to this point in the last chapter of this text.

5. Indeed, a significant number of families provide the entire **special care** needed by their intellectually, emotionally, or physically disabled or challenged children and, in many cases, frail elderly parents. Thus, the family is again becoming a **welfare agency**, as was the case in the "old" days. However, currently, the family is rather isolated in this role while, in the past, it might have received more help from the community. Further, contemporary advances in nutrition, sanitary conditions, and medicine have increased the longevity and survival rates of the

weakest. As a result, families have been forced to be the main caretakers or supervisors of the help that these relatives in precarious health receive—and women do a great proportion of this work (Mandell and Wilson, 2011; Mitchell, 2004).

Additional Responsibilities Taken on by Some Families

1. Many families fulfill additional functions for their members, depending on their means, social class, racial/ethnic membership, religion, as well as citizenship status. For instance, some families remain a centre of worship and religious education while others provide at-home schooling. Still others continue to serve as a centre of leisure activities, both for their children and adult members. Amish families are a good example in this respect (Hostetler, 1993); until very recently, extended families also fulfilled this function in Newfoundland and in Inuit rural communities.

2. Immigrant families serve important functions for their members, as many subsidize the immigration of their kin and support their resettlement to Canada. Others send remittances to their relatives in their home country and contribute not only to the sustenance but also to the economic survival of entire societies. Cases in point are the Philippines, Vietnam, Cuba, Romania, and Moldova.

3. Transnational families as well as military families with members posted abroad face additional responsibilities. Indeed, they may have to work much harder than other families at keeping their units' "togetherness" and sense of cohesion when one or more members are across the world. Communication becomes more salient with the advent of cell phones, computers, and tablets. Even long-distance face-to-face communication with Skype acquires a new dimension. At the same time, these technological developments in modes of communication allow for an increase in the number of such families who then work very hard at remaining together or even raising their children transnationally (Arat-Koç, 2011). Cases in point are Filipina mothers who may be raising others' children in Canada, the United States, or even Saudi Arabia. Similarly, Caribbean mothers who move to Canada and Great Britain to work in households or in the service industries can perhaps now mother more smoothly from a distance, if not easily, via Skype for instance.

An Overabundance of Family Responsibilities

In short, while Canadian families in general are not always a haven and many are far from perfect, the responsibilities that they shoulder cover an amazing range of personal, social, cultural, and economic needs. And families do so, particularly mothers, with far fewer moral and social resources than was the case in the past, when communities were more cohesive and there was greater value consensus. As imperfect and, at times, limping as it is, *the family still does more and better than any other social institution for its members,* particularly its children and youth (Bogenschneider and Corbett, 2010). Thus, the fact is not that families have become obsolete or irrelevant. The contrary has actually happened: As seen above, families have become burdened with new functions foisted upon them by technology, consumerism, and urbanization (Castaneda, 2002), as well as by governmental cuts to health care, child care, and at-home help to seniors and persons with various disabilities (Luxton, 2006b; Mandell and Wilson, 2011). *Hence, one can only be concerned about families' burden rather than obsolescence when discussing roles or responsibilities.*

Across the world, cultures emphasize familial obligations and mutual support far more than is the case here (Kagitçibasi, 2007; Shweder et al., 2006). *Is it not possible that this dismissal of family responsibilities simply provides a rationale for inactivity on the part of our political systems in terms of better supporting individual families?* As Ravanera and McQuillan (2006) aptly put it, "All of society benefits when families work well. Thus, it is in our collective interest to find ways to support families in achieving their goals" (p. 10). Another source of concern over this alleged decline in family functions is probably the result of an analytical and social policy misunderstanding: It results from equating *individual* families' inability or failure to shoulder certain responsibilities with a loss of functions by the family as an **institution**. People correctly observe that more children are problematic, unhappy, and in foster care than was the case 50 years ago. But the error begins when this is seen as a failure of individual families rather than of society as a whole and, particularly, our economic system.

The new social structure based on the market economy, a culture of individualism, unbridled profit motive, information technology, and the retrenchment of social policies has bestowed upon the family a new set of responsibilities (Wall, 2004). It is therefore not surprising if more individual families fail at these than in the past: Families are more unstable structurally, are more isolated socially, and are less well supported by other institutions at the cultural, economic, and political levels. Thus, too great a proportion of our families are ill equipped to fulfill their obligations, particularly in terms of supervising, guiding, and educating their youth and caring for their elders. Economic deprivation, segregation, social stigmatization and isolation, singlehood, and members' personal deficiencies are among the elements that prevent individual families from fulfilling their responsibilities adequately. A political economy perspective suggests that most of these are socially driven problems, not family-produced ones.

The structural conclusion one arrives at is that the family as an institution certainly requires far more assistance from other institutions to fulfill its numerous functions adequately. Were more assistance forthcoming at the institutional family level, that is, for all families, most individual families would benefit and fewer would fail in this respect. Political institutions have failed to create social policies favourable to families of all types, as well as policies protecting families and their members, particularly children, against the potentially harmful impacts of technology and the globalization of the economy (Chapter 4). We could think here in terms of the structure of the workweek and the workplace, the relative lack of child care centres, the lack of assistance for elder care, and the noxious contents of the media. But we can also think in terms of failure to more adequately assist near-poor and poor families and, soon, we will be mentioning policy failures to protect the natural environment in which families live (Gore, 2006; Suzuki and Taylor, 2009). We can conclude from the above that, if the family as an institution is under attack, it is from the road-blocks created by the materialistic economic forces of society that prevent families from shouldering their obligations.

FAMILIES AND COUPLES LIVING APART

Another very contemporary situation returns us to a topic initially raised in Chapter 1 when presenting various family types. Thus, in this section, we focus on transnational families, military families, and couples living apart—all part of the diversity in family structure, however temporary these situations are for some.

Transnational Families

These are "families that live some or most of the time separated from each other, yet hold together and create something that can be seen as a feeling of collective welfare and unity, namely 'familyhood,' even across national borders" (Bryceson and Vuorela, 2002:3). Globalization has had a tremendous impact on migration and family structures: With more international trade and exchange as well as easier and more affordable transportation, international boundaries have become blurred (Nesteruk, 2013). Many men and women now cross nation-state boundaries to live and work as easily as they once traveled to different cities in the same country. As a result, transnational families, although not a new phenomenon, have become more commonplace in recent times (Hareven, 2000:64). But, as Beaujot and Kerr (2004) point out, "There are winners and losers in globalization, and the glaring disparities in standards of living around the world are themselves a leading cause of migration" (p. 98). Consequently, the experiences of transnational families vary by ethnicity, gender, country of origin, and occupational class. For instance, "guest workers" on a two-year visa to work for an industry or a farm, who may number over 300,000 in Canada currently, certainly experience a transnational family life that does not compare to that of an educated executive on leave to Dubai or Hong Kong. These low-skilled and low-paid workers often become "illegals" after losing their job and have more difficulty supporting their children back home. Then, as illegal workers, they are further exploited (Contenta and Monsebraaten, 2009). Another example is the large number of children in rural China left behind by one or both parents who migrate to distant eastern cities in search of work. These children are often disadvantaged, as a result, in terms of health and school behaviours (Wen and Lin, 2012). Their parents, of rural origins, are discriminated against in urban centres (*The Economist*, 2013).

Another phenomenon is that of Korean families in which mothers and children migrate to Canada for an English education while the fathers remain in Korea—what are called *Kirogi* or "wild-geese" families. These mothers gain some independence; as well, in contrast to the past, the families spend daily time together transnationally via the Internet so that fathers actually spend more time with their children than before, albeit virtually so (Jeong and Bélanger, 2012). In the same vein, Waters (2002) was particularly interested in the experiences of Taiwanese and Hong Kong "astronaut" wives, immigrant women whose husbands, within a few months after their arrival, returned to their country of origin to work. For the most part, Chinese and Taiwanese astronaut families in Vancouver and Toronto are of higher social class. According to Waters (2002), such families exemplify "the ways in which social relationships can operate over significant distance, spanning national borders, and reducing the importance of face-to-face context in personal interaction" (p. 118). Thus, current trends in transnational families find children increasingly separated from one of their parents. Traditionally, the father is away and the mother raises the children alone.

However, the global market economy has also resulted in an increase in female-headed transnational families where the mother works in a country different from where some or all of her children reside (Arat-Koç, 2011; Dreby, 2010). Indeed, economically advanced countries continue to demand low-wage female domestics, cleaners in condos and hospitals, and caretakers, as well as nannies from less fortunate countries. This trend in transnational mothering has disrupted the notion of family in one place. But often overlooked are the detrimental effects of mothering one's children from a distance, a situation often forced on migrant **domestic workers** with children, particularly Filipinas and women from Caribbean nations. In the absence of their mothers, children of transnational women are generally raised by their grandmothers. When these children are reunited with their mothers, they often resent her authority and her absence, not wanting to obey a mother they have never met or have rarely seen. A student who was reunited with her transnational mother explains:

> *"What was the hardest at that age [10–14] was leaving my grandmother behind in Jamaica. I had been so excited about living with my mother. . . . I had seen her only three times since she left when I was 4. . . . She really was like a stranger and she was so busy. . . . I thought she had money but we had to live in a poor place, real tough kids that I can see now were bad but for me they were exciting because life with my mother and her boyfriend was no fun. I paid no heed to her and him and I skipped school. . . . I missed my grandmother and I wanted her here but she had to help with my other cousins over there."*

As Dreby (2010) has shown for Mexican transnational families, fathers can still fulfill their traditional role as providers from afar. However, such is not the case for mothers whose role is more scripted toward being caretakers so that their children's expectations are different, resulting in guilt and moral sanction from their offspring. As we see in Chapter 10, another aspect of transnational family life is the relationship between adult children who have migrated to North America and their elderly parents remaining in the home country (Sun, 2012). We hear a great deal about such families from Asia but one also has to consider those of Eastern European origins for whom a strong mutual reliance between generations exists, which was particularly functional under the difficulties of past communist regimes (Nesteruk, 2013).

Military Families

Military nuclear families often become transnational, albeit temporarily. In 2011, apart from single men and women, there were over 57,000 conjugal units in the Canadian Forces and 75 percent of these had children, for a total of over 64,000 children under the age of 18 (DND, 2012). All army personnel are members of families, whether their parents' families with whom they may still have been living when they were recruited or their spouses and children. The Canadian Forces (CF) are involved in many peacekeeping operations throughout the world. It is when army personnel are mobilized abroad, especially in war zones, such as Afghanistan at the time that this text was written in 2013, that the impact on their families is the greatest. Currently, being a soldier posted in Afghanistan is a high-risk occupation, mainly because of improvised explosive devices that maim and kill so many soldiers and civilians. Therefore, the soldiers are affected in a dire way. In addition, many return home suffering from post-traumatic stress disorder (PTSD), serious injuries, and amputations. PTSD has been related to a lower quality in many of the aspects of the spousal relationship when soldiers return from deployment (Allen et al., 2010). Soldiers' PTSD is also related to higher levels of distress among spouses (Renshaw et al., 2011). As a result, families, including parents, care for these young adults with comparatively little support from the government (Chung, 2010).

Families are also affected because they are separated from their loved one, are worried, and their daily routines are changed. Indeed, Sudom (2010) reports that about 70 percent of spouses have experienced the deployment of their military partner at least once. Even very young children develop fears of what could happen to the parent who is deployed abroad and this type of parental absence is related to anxiety and even behavioural problems (Booth et al., 2007; Card et al., 2011; Dekel and Goldblatt, 2008). Adolescents report signs of depression, stress, and "short fuse" in their at-home parent while the other is away. When the parent returns, adjustment difficulties include reintegrating the parent into the daily routine and helping with his or her difficulties in recognizing the changes that have occurred in the children during the parent's absence (Huebner and Mancini, 2005). It is assumed that repeated separations are more disruptive of family life (Orthner and Rose, 2009).

What coping mechanisms do these families use? What are their main sources of support? Apart from a few researchers, the Canadian and American armed forces themselves are also conducting some basic research. Both forces recognize the importance of their personnel's families and their websites offer support resources for them. The Canadian Forces (2008) state that "spouses play a vital role in promoting the well-being, readiness and performance of military members and their ability to carry out missions." Given this, "it is crucial to understand how families maintain or enhance resiliency during and after military deployments and separation."

The CF are trying to keep track of stressors involved and factors that could mitigate or exacerbate these outcomes. For its part, the U.S. military has found that remarried parents with children from a previous union encounter more family problems in part because the children may have a wider range of adaptations to make than other children. Yet, these same families were the most likely to be satisfied with military resources and support and willing to re-enlist (Adler-Baeder et al., 2005). They were also happier in the military than couples in their first marriages: A more mature outlook to couple life is advanced as the main reason for this finding. Through these internal studies, military officials have concluded that more resources in mental health and better access to medical care were key areas that needed attention.

The military profession brings two negative economic realities for families. First, it is important to recall that the armed forces everywhere are an institution with the most complete and all-encompassing set of norms—and it is a very stratified institution. It is often a total environment, especially when families are posted abroad or live on a military base (Harrison and Laliberté, 1994). As such, spouses and children often become extensions of the personnel and the army. This has the potential for creating many problems, especially for female spouses who may not be able to exercise their own profession. Second, salaries for recruits are low and often the spouse left behind or relocated has difficulty finding employment: Fewer than 50 percent of spouses have full-time employment (Dursun and Sudom, 2009). As a result, army families are often disadvantaged economically compared to others. The average recruit is generally a young person, often just out of high school, and consequently with no savings or resources, and may have a young spouse and small children. Army couples often have children at a younger age than persons in other occupational categories (Lundquist and Smith, 2005). Because of their youth, these families are doubly disadvantaged at the economic level (Uecker and Stokes, 2008). As well, younger persons may have more difficulties adapting than older persons with more life experience (Adler-Baeder et al., 2005). This is why accessibility to quality child care is so important (MacDermid et al., 2004). Despite the fact that one often hears that military couples are at higher risk for divorce, Karney et al. (2012) explored this question by comparing the marital status of the American civilian population to that of military personnel. Controlling for a variety of key variables, they found that service members are much more likely to be married than others but are *not* more likely to be divorced. This said, rates of divorce, particularly among women soldiers, have recently increased in the U.S. military (Teachman and Tedrow, 2008).

A topic that is salient on the CF website is family violence, particularly spousal abuse, because it is an issue against which the army has taken a strong official stand with its Family Violence Action Plan (Herrington, 2009). It is pointed out, in these analyses, that certain aspects of military life make it more difficult to cope with spousal violence than is the case in the population at large (Harrison, 2006). These difficulties include "victims' economic dependency on their CF spouses, frequent postings, an unfamiliar and closed environment [on army bases], peculiarities of Married Quarters neighbourhoods, and, in some cases, language disadvantages" (Herrington, 2009). But the best predictor of spousal abuse in the army is a history of such before entering the military. However, in recent years, rates of spousal abuse have diminished in the military as has been the case in the remainder of the population. For its part, child abuse in the military is more likely to occur with younger than older parents (Booth et al., 2007). It may also be more frequent during periods of transition in times of deployment (Huebner et al., 2009).

Another topic on which there is relatively little research in the life course of CF families is the transition back to civilian life. Over 53 percent of the transitioning personnel have been in the Canadian Forces for at least 20 years. Overall, Thompson et al. (2011) have found that a quarter of the transitions are very difficult. One would want to know how this meshes with spousal and familial relationships and what are the familial, personal, and military factors contributing to a smoother transition. The gender of the released or retiring person would be a key variable in this respect, as would be a background of trauma (Campbell and Renshaw, 2012). Ray and Forchuk (2011) have listened to the problems experienced by homeless veterans in several large Canadian cities. This preliminary work indicates that they lack institutional support, especially from the military, and insufficient attention is paid to problems of alcohol and other drug abuse or addiction.

Couples Living Apart (LAT)

Couples who live apart together (LAT) maintain separate households, may or may not be married (Borrell and Karlsson, 2002), and some may be simply "dating." In 2011, 7 percent of Canadian adults lived in LAT unions (Statistics Canada, 2013c). Although most (57 percent) belonged to the 20- to 29-year-old age bracket, another 11 percent were found among those older than 50 (Milan and Peters, 2003). Others are professionals whose careers cannot be accommodated within the same geographical area. LATs are also becoming more common in some Asian countries, particularly Japan where 70 percent of women involved in these unions are still living with their parents (Jones, 2007).

According to Statistics Canada (2013c), about 42 percent of LAT couples lead this lifestyle because they are constrained by circumstances such as financial or studies-related issues. Work requirements are more often cited by middle-aged LATs. Others mention the need to retain their independence. Levin and Trost (1999) found that nearly half of these persons expected eventually to live with their partner, but only a minority of those older than 50 held such expectations (Bawin-Legrow and Gauthier, 2001). For the older and widowed, this arrangement protects their children's inheritance. They may prefer to retain their own residence and ways of living.

Persons who choose this lifestyle hold less traditional ideas concerning the importance of having long-term relationships than either married or cohabiting persons (Milan and Peters, 2003). Unfortunately, the studies do not tell us what proportion, even though small, of such couples are actually married to each other—closely resembling what has often been referred to as "commuter marriages." When young couples have to be separated for work reasons, they may choose to cohabit rather than marry, at least for the duration of the separation period (Binstock and Thornton, 2003).

This phenomenon of extra-residential unions is widely found in the Caribbean region as an adaptive response to the socioeconomic conditions that require women to head households with very little or no economic support from their co-progenitors (Barrow, 1996). In Canada, LATs are found across all income levels but especially more so among those who earn less than average. Unfortunately, studies of LATs do not include couples with children in which one of the spouses lives with the children separately abroad and become transnational families, as is the case for some Korean and Taiwanese families in Canada (Noh et al., 2012).

THE AUDIOVISUAL/SOCIAL MEDIA AND FAMILY LIFE

Perhaps one of the most salient historical developments for society, its families, and their children has occurred relatively recently. It first resides in the introduction of the audiovisual media, particularly television in the mid 1950s and, later, video games,

The black American politician, Jesse Jackson, has called television "the third parent." It would be interesting to know whether children build more connections among themselves within a family via videos, television programs they share, the social media, or face-to-face activities they engage in together.

Anne-Marie Ambert

the Internet, and now smart cellular phones to the cultural landscape, along with the new social media of texting, messaging, Facebook, Twitter, Instagram, and other new ones that will already be available when this book appears. This is what has been called by Manuel Castells (2010), *"the rise of the networked society"* which, as we see in the next chapter, has given rise to a new type of economy. It also is changing interpersonal relationships and how people think. Major events are now experienced and socially constructed through the prism of these media, whether it is the news, sports, talk shows, "reality" shows, sitcoms, social networking, or "tweets." As well, the proliferation in Canada of television channels, radio frequencies, and the Internet has allowed for the expansion of programming in many languages, whether Mandarin, Cantonese, Punjabi, Russian, Persian, Spanish, or Italian and several others. As a result, new immigrants can keep up with the culture of their countries of origin as well as news. In fact, aged immigrants who arrive here under family reunification programs and do not speak English or French can function very well in terms of leisure activities—not to omit religion, shopping, and even neighbourliness as there are many ethnic villages in Canadian cities and suburbs.

Television: A Historical Overview

In 1951, there were 90,000 television sets in Canadian homes, all receiving American programming. Three months after the advent of the CBC in 1952, this number grew to 224,000 sets (Gorman, 1997). Television represented a mode of "family entertainment" that was to prove radically different from anything in the past. It had no historical precedent in terms of its ability to inform, influence, and structure daily life. Between 1951 and 1955, nearly two-thirds of the nation's homes acquired a television set. By 1960, almost 90 percent had at least one set and, at that point, the average person watched television about five hours a day. By the 1960s, television had replaced the piano in family rooms and "TV dinners" (the precursor to prepared food) appeared in grocery stores.

The first television show geared to children, *Howdy Doody*, ran from 1947 to 1960, and with it, the debate about the effect of television on children began and has continued to this day. The debate has not, however, been accompanied to the same extent by discussions over the impact of television on adults and on family life, although the research done for advertising and marketing firms indicates strong media effects on adults' beliefs, lifestyles, approach to medication, as well as on family life. *Howdy Doody* also marked the beginning of the impact of audiovisual **advertising** on children.

Sesame Street, which began in 1969, presented a revolutionary format, and is still widely watched by the nation's small children. This program emphasizes the acceptance of ethnic differences, as well as values of cooperation and environmentalism. It is devoid of commercialism, violence, and sex. Its goal is to provide skills to help prepare children for school, and research has shown that children from varied backgrounds do learn by watching it (Christakis, 2009). *Sesame Street* complements parents' role as educators and does not conflict with family values.

Situation comedies, or **sitcoms**, began early in the 1950s; they were generally family shows, such as *Leave It to Beaver*. These shows were based on the socioeconomic realities of the post-war decade and represented the ideal American family at the time: white, middle-class, with a working father, and a stay-at-home mother. The program offered a perspective on family life from a child's point of view. Not only did *Leave It to Beaver* become a cultural icon in later decades when American and Canadian families had changed from the idealized type of the 1950s, but it also set the stage for the nostalgia of what Stephanie Coontz called *The Way We Never Were* (1992).

Soap operas had long been a staple of radio programming in Quebec. Therefore, it is not surprising that television adopted this genre early on in the 1950s in Quebec, with programs focusing on family relationships in small communities, as in the very popular *Les Belles Histoires des Pays d'En Haut* set in the early 1900s. As the decades went by, the shows began focusing on single adults, particularly in the workplace, and included more women in new roles. The U.S. Commission on Civil Rights (1977) found that, in the period between 1969 and 1972, almost one-half of the female characters portrayed on television were married, yet fewer than one-third of the males were. At about the same time, McNeil (1975) revealed that 74 percent of the female interactions on television took place within the context of problems associated with romance and family, compared to only 18 percent of male interactions. Later on, *The Cosby Show*, running from 1984 to 1992, represented yet another milestone, as it introduced a black family headed by two professional parents. The family came closer to approximating a two-paycheque family than any other show had done. In the mid-1980s, it was still quite unusual to think of a black family as well-to-do. It was probably the first sitcom with which black families could identify, at least in terms of race if not necessarily lifestyle. Then, the *Fresh Prince of Bel-Air* followed a similar format, but within an even more affluent and "hip" context. Other more recent sitcoms, such as the *Little Mosque on the Prairie*, have become more inclusive in terms of ethnic and cultural diversity, and even environments. Others are giving a salient role to men as nurturing fathers, and even gays and lesbians.

Then, problematic aspects of family life started to be reflected and often overblown in the many **talk shows** that began appearing in the mid- to late-1980s, such as *The Oprah Winfrey Show* and later *Dr. Phil*. Many of these programs place the spotlight on the self-disclosure of problems, from weight to sexual infidelity, attempted suicide, drug addiction, and incest.

Television changed family leisure patterns: As people watched it, less time became available for reading and the development of skills, such as musical abilities, creative play, and for family entertainment that might involve all the members (whether dancing, singing, playing card games, or just visiting). Early studies summarized by Andreasen (1994) indicate that, by 1952 in large cities, a great proportion of families reported regularly eating with the television on, which meant less interpersonal exchange during dinner. Families with a television set went to bed later, talked less, and often ate separately while watching different programs at different times—trends that are even more pronounced now (Moscovitch, 2007) because of the Internet and smart phones.

Today, children and particularly middle-class adolescents have their own personal entertainment centres in their bedrooms or in their pockets. In the U.S., low-income children are even more likely than others to have this equipment in their bedrooms, except for the Internet, and they read less. Overall, only a proportion of children report having **rules** set by parents about their use of what they see or do and time spent with media. For instance, Rideout et al. (2010) found that 64 percent of 8- to 10-year-olds had rules set by parents, but in only 38 percent of these cases did parents enforce them. Parents with a high level of education tend to restrict television or cell phones more during mealtimes and to have more rules concerning use, especially for small children; their children also read more. Yet, already a decade ago, 25 percent of elementary school children and 50 percent of high-school students reported that they had email accounts of which their parents were unaware (Taylor, 2002).

Family members who view television together find the experience more pleasant than when they watch it alone. Unfortunately, in a good proportion of families, television is on most of the time, even when no one is watching, and especially during **meals**. Now even cell phones are on the table and eagerly scrutinized during meals. This limits familial conversations (Kirkorian et al., 2009). Nearly all students today have grown up with television, video games, the Internet, and cell phones. Few know what family life is without these media. For most, the low level of time currently spent talking and sitting in the den or in the backyard just enjoying one another's company seems normal. As well, more and more youth access the media through their cell phones and laptop computers. When parents control access, children spend less time with these media than their peers.

The Continued Effects of the Audiovisual Media: The Internet and Cellular Phone

A contemporary and much debated issue is the role that the media play in the development of children's attitudes and behaviours (Bakan, 2011; Garbarino, 2006). Some contend that the media have no effect—even though, as we have seen, it does have an impact on adults. Further, it is illogical to deny that violent or sex-suffused media have no effect, while at the same time accepting the fact that the tobacco industry's ads foster smoking among adolescents. Why would companies invest so many billions in advertising if it had no effect? Observing how children and even some adults dress in imitation of their favourite stars provides a clear indication that the *media create needs and a reality*, while reinforcing stereotypes of ideal feminine body types and of a tough masculinity (Abu-Laban and McDaniel, 2004; Malszecki and Cavar, 2004). As well, there are fears in some quarters that accepting research results pointing to the media in the causality chain of children's problematic behaviours might lead to censorship. Lawyers for the media industry are particularly active in promoting this fear. This is a **political economy issue**: The media constitute a very powerful and increasingly interconnected industry and lobby. For instance, many news magazines, newspapers, and now web pages are owned by mega conglomerates that include television stations, cable networks, and film and music companies. Thus, the media can easily prevent the wide dissemination of research results that could be damaging to their image—and to their bottom line (Bushman and Anderson 2001).

In the following sections, we focus on the role that the audiovisual and social media may play in various aspects of family life and child development. We can be concerned about the unknown consequences for young adults and particularly children and adolescents of presenting themselves and their lives to a larger than normal circle of family and friends via Facebook and related outlets. Many parents now even create Facebook pages for their school-age children or, yet, the children do it themselves. In terms of symbolic interactionism, *children and adolescents now put their own lives on a **stage** and manipulate their self-presentations to fit a circle of what are consumers of their own lives*. Every adolescent can now be on a stage. What does this do to children's development to have their **fabricated selves** on stage and how, at such a young age, can they differentiate between their real selves, as they evolve, and these reflections of themselves? For instance, there are reasonable contentions that social media such as Facebook increase narcissism (Twenge and Campbell, 2010). Research has yet to catch up on the effects of such cultural developments: One would need longitudinal studies of children raised with these social media and compare them with children raised without these media. Not to be omitted here are issues of health: All these media are used in a sitting or lying position and children do not get enough physical exercise (Luneau, 2013). In fact, the Kaiser Family Foundation has reported that American children spend an average of 10.5 hours a day on various media which leads to very little physical activity (Rideout et al., 2010). In 2010, they also found that children of parents with less education spent 90 minutes more on digital devices because their parents are more powerless to stop it. It is probably because of their lower socioeconomic status that black and Hispanic children spend four hours more a day on media than other children. For all children, media exposure has greatly increased, by one hour daily, in less than six years. These researchers also found that *heavy* media users were less happy with their lives, got along less well with their parents, "got into trouble more," and had lower grades in school, even after controlling for race and socioeconomic status (Rideout et al., 2010).

The Issue of Sociability in Family Life

The new "reality" shows, whether *Dancing with the Stars* or *Canadian Idol*, place the spotlight on competition rather than cooperation. Many, including *Survivor*, are based on voting others out, exclusion, and **competition**. Values of altruism are out of the question. A great deal of **bullying** takes place in these shows at a time when this problem is widespread in schools and is being exacerbated by the public aspects of Facebook and cell phones, even resulting in teen suicide—what is called **cyberbullying.*** Furthermore, a majority of the shows that small children watch contain social aggression (Pearce, 2012). Thus, apart from the fact that the media cut down the time that a young person spends on *face-to-face* sociability, both in and out of the family, the little research devoted to how these media can foster sociability and human relations within the family is very embryonic and almost exclusively relies on self-reports (Williams and Merten, 2011),

On the positive side, since the 2000s, many parents and grandparents take advantage of email, Facebook, and now Skype and texting to keep in touch with relatives and their children in college, and teenagers exchange messages with their classmates after school—and, less positively, even during class time! As well, some parents use the Internet in order to find information about various aspects of family life, including parenting (Keown, 2009). These media can also break senior citizens' social isolation when they are place-bound (Clark, 2001). Still, in 2010–11, only 35 percent of parents surveyed felt that "technology keeps my family closer together" while only 23 percent of 18- to 24-years-olds agreed that it helped them have a better relationship with their parents (VIF, 2012c). So, on the one hand, technology improves the number of contacts within the family, but too much technology reduces **intimacy** and relational closeness (Williams and Merten, 2011).

Large-scale Canadian data analyzed by Williams (2001a) over 10 years ago clearly indicate that a good minority of people cut down on visiting or talking with family (14 percent) and friends (13 percent) because of the time they spend on the Internet—when it was not as used and developed as it now is. In 2010, Canadians spent less time socializing with friends and relatives than in 1998 (Statistics Canada, 2011b). Heavy Internet users are even more likely to reduce time interacting with family—and, perhaps, so do heavy cell phone users? After comparing the results of the 1998 and the 2000 General Social Surveys, Williams concluded that Internet users spend about 48 fewer minutes per day in social contact with others in their households, but spend about 72 minutes more in contact with people outside their households. This would probably be even more so now since the advent of Facebook, texting, and tweeting, all of which can be very time consuming.

Internet use is even more **individualistically oriented** than television viewing. It follows that extensive Internet exposure by family members, often in their own separate bedrooms/studies, or while out with others, may contribute to lack of interaction and a loss of communication skills. In fact, parents and children's cyber worlds diverge widely. For instance, while a majority of parents say that they talk to their children about the children's Internet activities, only 24 percent of children report the same. Furthermore, 83 percent are alone when they go online (Taylor, 2002).

The next few years will indicate the direction the social media are taking culturally and the type of use family members make of these. But when we include all the modes of electronic communication in the possession of all family members and the incessant recourse to them many make (particularly cell phones), we may well be "too connected" in general—but, one might fear, less so with our family in terms of *face-to-face interaction* (Williams and Merten, 2011). In fact, there is a great deal of social pressure pushing individuals to use their cell phones more. For instance, the Pew Internet and American Life Project (PewIALP, 2012) found that 39 percent of cell phone owners have received complaints to the effect that they do not respond promptly to phone calls or text messages and 33 percent were told that they do not check their phone frequently enough. Keeping in mind that in the fall of 2012, 85 percent of American adults aged 18 and older had a cell or smart phone, this represents a great deal of collective pressure. Indeed, 67 percent of these persons do check their phones regularly and even 44 percent sleep with it so as not to miss a call or an update during the night—and this, in times of an epidemic of insomnia! The younger people are, the more likely they are to engage in such behaviours.

How often do we observe mothers or fathers pushing a baby in a stroller or walking with a small child while being entirely absorbed in a cell phone conversation? These parents miss out on the possibility of a quiet moment of interaction with their child. As well, how often can we observe entire peer groups of youths in subway cars or on the street, fresh out of school, all interacting with their cell phones, texting friends who are elsewhere while ignoring friends who are with them? Does this enhance or decrease the ability to verbally and emotionally connect with peers? Even young couples eating together at restaurants spend a large amount of time on their cells, hence diminishing the intimacy of the moment. This said, there are clear indications that Internet-type technologies, particularly in the form of interactive videos, programs on small computers and tablets can help children with autism, both in terms of learning, modulating their behaviours, and in facilitating relationships (Wright et al., 2011).

The Issue of Violence vs. Prosocial Behaviour

The average child has witnessed well over 8,000 murders on television by the end of elementary school. In the U.S., the National Television Violence Study (1998) found that over 40 percent of violent acts are perpetrated by "good" characters—thus glamorizing violence—and over 55 percent of victims of violence show little pain or suffering, thus desensitizing people to its true effects (Donnerstein and Linz, 1995). The rate of violent crimes in the U.S. and other western countries rose dramatically after 1965, coinciding with the coming of age of the first generation of children raised with television (Bushman and Huesmann, 2001).

In the 1980s, researchers began harvesting the results of **longitudinal studies** (see Family Research 3.1). They found that young adults tended to act more aggressively when they had watched more violence as eight-year-olds or as adolescents (Johnson et al., 2002). The link between adult aggressiveness and childhood viewing of violence on TV was even stronger than it had been at age eight. Boys who had not been aggressive at age eight but had watched more violence had become more aggressive young adults than a similar group of non-aggressive boys who had watched fewer episodes of violence (Bushman and Huesmann, 2006). Studies of more recent cohorts have shown that television violence now affects American girls' level of aggressiveness

Experimenting with Real-Life Situations to Determine Causality

In the fall of 1973, a study on the effect of television on children was initiated by creatively exploiting a naturally occurring social situation: At that time, a Canadian town, renamed Notel, was to receive television transmission for the first time. Notel was not isolated but was located in a valley, which prevented transmission. A nearby town, called Unitel, had already been receiving one Canadian channel for seven years, and a third town, called Multitel, had been receiving several U.S. channels in addition to a Canadian one for about 15 years. Notel (no television) became the experimental town; Unitel (one channel) and Multitel (several channels) became the two control towns.

In Phase 1, in 1973, students in Grades 4 and 7 from the three towns were tested on a wide range of behaviours and skills. In a longitudinal design, they were retested two years later (Phase 2), in Grades 6 and 9, to measure the effects of television. In order to rule out maturation or growing-up influences, additional students in Grades 4 and 7 were also included in Phase 2. The children in the town that had received television two years earlier showed a substantial increase in aggressiveness that was not observed among the youngsters in the other town (Joy et al., 1986). They also exhibited a sharp increase in sex-role stereotyping (Kimball, 1986). It is regrettable that similar experiments were not carried out more systematically before and after the advent of Facebook and texting in groups of children and parents to see the effect of these social media on time spent in face-to-face interaction, distractibility, quality of peer interaction, and parental work load, among many facets of life that could be logically affected.

as well (Huesmann et al., 2003). Other studies continue to show that exposure to TV is an independent contributing risk for aggressive behaviours in children as young as three years old (Manganello and Taylor, 2009).

Even when it is a predilection for aggressiveness that leads children to select media violence, this violence then leads to aggressiveness (Manganello and Taylor, 2009). Although exposure to violent television and videos is not the main factor in the etiology of aggressiveness, it is part of the **enabling environment** for problematic behaviours (Garbarino, 1999). Viewing violence may teach children that conflict can be resolved only with verbal or physical aggressiveness. It may also be related to the development of a lower threshold for frustration and a higher level of narcissism (Twenge and Campbell, 2010) so that children tolerate irritants and contradictions less easily and react to them more explosively. As well, exposure to violence may desensitize viewers to the severity of its consequences, so that even killing can appear routine (Cantor and Nathanson, 2001).

In fact, killing is often the goal in **video games**: Children learn aggressive techniques such as how to punch, kick, and kill. Indeed, a link has also been found between this interactive media and aggressive thoughts and behaviours (Anderson et al., 2004), as well as increased aggressive behaviour problems among 6- to 12-year-old boys (Hofferth, 2010). However, the research on the effect of video games still has to include longitudinal studies, although one short-term longitudinal study did find that children who played violent video games became more aggressive later in the school year (Anderson et al., 2007). Future research would need to separate the effect of violence on television from that on videos and the Internet, not exactly a small task today (Wartella et al., 2004). As Funk et al. (2000) point out, at the very least, playing violent video games will not improve children's overall behaviour, although it may improve their visual-manual coordination. Others point out that it can enhance problem solving and cooperation (Adachi and Willoughby, 2013).

Several studies have also shown that positive thoughts and behaviours can follow when contents are prosocial. First, listening to prosocial lyrics increases empathy and positive behaviour (Greitemeyer, 2009). Second, prosocial video games increase willingness to cooperate, to intervene when someone is harassed, and to be more willing to devote time to help (Gentile et al., 2009; Greitemeyer and Osswald, 2010). These studies even conclude that the effects of video games, whether aggression or positive behaviour, may be more powerful than those of television: "Video games teach whatever concepts are repeatedly rehearsed within them" (Buckley and Anderson, 2006:366). One should not omit in this discussion the issue of bullying which is enhanced and made more lethal by **cyberbullying** (Scheeler, 2012). O'Keefe and Clarke-Pearson (2011) conclude their review of the research on the impact of social media thusly: "Social media sites allow teens to accomplish online many of the tasks that are important to them offline: staying connected with friends and family, making new friends, sharing pictures, and exchanging ideas" (p. 803). Yet, as they point out later in their article, using social media becomes a risk more often than adults realize.

Another related issue that society faces, often within the context of families, occurs both on the sports fields and especially on television: **violence in sports** (Coakley and Donnelly, 2004). This issue is salient because about 54 percent of children aged 5 to 14 regularly participate in organized sport activities, including 25 percent who play hockey (Kremarik, 2000b). In Canada, the problem centres on hockey violence—among professional players, among children on competitive teams, often by parents against coaches or other parents, and even in situations where parents encourage their sons to "beat up" opposing team members. In Newfoundland, the Minor Hockey League officials have required parents of all players, in 2012, to take a course on acceptable behaviour at the rink (Wallace, 2012). At any rate, the constructs of masculinity as related to violence are evident in the culture of sports (Burstyn, 1999; Malszecki and Cavar, 2004).

In addition, in the U.S., the off-field behaviour of professional football and basketball celebrities is a concern: Many players have been arrested for criminal behaviours, including rape and murder. Too many have been implicated in fatal traffic and boating accidents, while others father children in an assembly line fashion! A July 18, 2003, *Toronto Star* article proclaims, "Bad boys of the NBA." Violence in sports is a problem that plagues the entire society. It is promoted by the mass media because it "sells." Overall, a climate of violence, when it exists, is certainly not an ideal one within which to form relationships and raise children (Garbarino, 2006).

The Issue of Consumerism and Lifestyle

The advertising industry spends over $12 billion a year marketing directly to children, who see over 40,000 ads a year on television alone (Moscovitch, 2007).

Further, pop stars promote lifestyles (clothing, for instance) that preteens and adolescents try to emulate. Thus, mass culture creates **false needs**, which then contribute to less prosocial attitudes and even behaviours, both among parents and children. The American Psychological Association's Task Force on Advertising and Children points out that "advertising might trigger materialistic attitudes by teaching children to measure personal worth by the products they own" (Dittman, 2002).

Children learn how to dress and to behave according to this clothes-related self-presentation from the media (Quart, 2003). When ads, pop stars, and words in song lyrics promote premature sexiness in children, for instance, one should study how this inappropriate socialization might affect their sexual behaviour a few years later. One might also want to know if clothing styles promoted by certain popular entertainers relate to difficult behaviours down the road. In other words, there is no research on how children's consumer behaviours may be linked to the development of problematic or positive behaviours. As Seiter (1993) points out concerning the mass-media targeting of children, "A distinctive, peer-oriented consumer culture now intervenes in the relationship of parents and children, and that intervention begins for many children as early as two years of age" (p. 193).

Whenever experts give conferences on issues of media effect, they unavoidably remind parents that they have to exercise control over what children view, and that they should discuss potentially detrimental programs with children. The entertainment industry follows suit and shamelessly places the entire responsibility on parents' shoulders—*one additional family responsibility*. How this responsibility affects parents and their relationship with their children is not addressed. At least one observational study has shown that, in a supermarket, 65 percent of all parents' refusals to buy food items advertised on TV resulted instantly in parent-child conflict or arguments (Atkin, 1978). I have often observed children having screaming fits in these contexts. One can only wonder about the level of conflict that takes place in the privacy of the home when parents attempt to curtail TV viewing, video games, and especially Internet use, including texting (Evans et al., 2011).

The Issue of Sexuality

One also has to consider the impact of the media's sexual contents (Mitchell et al., 2001). For instance, Lowry and Towles (1989) compared the sexual content in soap operas in 1979 and 1987: There were more episodes depicting sexual behaviours per hour in 1987 than in 1979. The U.S. Kaiser Family Foundation (2003) also found that 64 percent of 1,123 randomly selected programs contained sexual material in 2002: 14 percent included sexual intercourse, up from 7 percent only four years earlier. Nearly all soap operas and movies had sexual content, as did a majority of sitcoms, dramas, and talk shows. Greenberg and Busselle (1996) found that the average number of sexual incidents in soap operas increased from 3.7 per hour in 1983 to 5.0 in 1994—and one can imagine what it is now. Lowry and Towles (1989) concluded that the 1987 contents gave the following messages:

> *"Nonmarital sex is the most exciting; spontaneous sex is very romantic, especially between unmarried persons; it carries no consequences such as unplanned pregnancy and sexually transmitted infections (STIs), which are rampant among some teen groups; all unmarried people engage in sex, often with several partners."*

Chandra et al. (2008) have reported that young teens who watch many programs that include sexual content have a greater risk of pregnancy later. Others have found that sexual content relates to earlier sexual activities in some groups of teens (Brown et al., 2006). In Brazil, the country's famed soap operas or novellas that broadcast nationally "have pushed the limits of permissiveness" in the 1990s. Reboucas (2002) links this observation to the fact that, by the late 1990s, the age of first sexual intercourse had declined: Of adolescents who had ever had sex, 40 percent had had intercourse before reaching the age of 14. Of these, 64 percent originated from single-parent families.

The new genre of "reality" shows that began in 2003, such as *Temptation Island, The Bachelor, The Bachelorette,* and *EX-treme Dating,* promotes sexuality, infidelity, lack of commitment, and superficiality in the selection of partners. Not only do these shows promote values that have been found to relate to low marital quality and high divorce rates, they do not represent reality. One can only wonder how adolescents are affected by such portrayals, whether in terms of expectations, attitudes, or behaviours in their own dating relationships. As may be the case for the effect of violence, the effect of sexuality on television may already have reached its saturation point, at least among adolescents, because American high-school students initiated sexual intercourse in 2001 at a later age than in 1991 (U.S. Department of Health and Human Services, 2002).

Second, it is estimated that there are tens of thousands of websites throughout the world with pedophiliac and pornographic content. The exploitation of children becomes more widespread because the Internet is not easily policed. In a survey, a quarter of children aged 9 to 17 reported that they intentionally entered porn sites, while 53 percent have ended up on such a site by accident (Taylor, 2002). This is hardly surprising if one considers that pornography constituted at least 7 percent of the 3.3 billion web pages indexed by Google in 2003 (Paul, 2004). Further, chat rooms that are preyed upon by pedophiles are a danger to children that parents have to monitor (Wolak et al., 2008). As well, adult pornographic, racist, and hate websites are so easily accessible by children and adolescents that some schools have had to monitor closely their students' use of the Internet during class time.

More recently, sexting has been presenting a new risk for children and youth even when they only send such a message or photo to a friend or two. Too often, these photos are shared and spread within a group: This then may lead to ridicule, a loss of reputation, bullying, as well as sexual exploitation (O'Keefe and Clarke-Pearson, 2011). When these sexually explicit photos appear on Facebook, they may lead later to difficulties in the world of employment.

The Issue of Education

A study on the association between media exposure (TV and radio only) across 48 developing countries has found a link to more contraceptive use and lower fertility (Westoff and Koffman, 2011). This association was found simply for time spent and did not even examine the contents watched or heard. Therefore, the media can be very helpful. In western countries, children and adults also use media presentations as a source of information. However, here, TV and the Internet have become what the critical sociologist Habermas (1987) called an insulating expertise that splits children and adults from "the context of everyday practice" (p. 16) and leads to cultural impoverishment. On the one hand, children are active social actors and participate in the reconstruction of the messages they receive from the media. However, they can make a realistic reconstruction only to the extent that the real world around them, particularly their families, their peers, and schools, offers them this possibility. Yet, not all children benefit from such healthy environments (Garbarino, 2006). In fact, perhaps 25 percent of children do not have a home/peer/school environment that can counterbalance the negative effects of the media on their attitudes and behaviours.

While parents watch television and videos, they often include their babies: This begins when the infants are three months of age in about 40 percent of babies and this premature exposure has been related to delays in speech development (Tanimura et al., 2007). The American Academy of Pediatrics (2011), after an exhaustive review of the literature, has concluded that the audiovisual media have potentially negative effects on children younger than three (particularly in terms of language development and active time spent with parents) and *no* known positive effect—despite advertising to the contrary. In fact, many parents use videos specifically made and advertised to enhance infants' intellectual and verbal development when, in reality, they may actually delay it. There are suggestions that television, videos, and cell phones may contribute to hyperactivity (Christakis, 2009).

While the Internet, tablets, and cell phones now displace television to a great extent, they also take away from time spent on homework and studying. A study of university students revealed that 21 percent felt that their Internet use and computer games had affected their academic performance (CACUSS, 2013). An American survey of first-year university students revealed that, during their last high-school year, they had spent less time on homework and studies and more on surfing the net (HERI, 2003). In 2008, 70 percent of boys and 58 percent of girls exceeded the two-hour-a-day limit of time spent on television, video games, and the Internet that is considered healthy (CIW, 2010). In 2009, 32 percent of male high-school students in Ontario played video games daily (Paglia-Boak et al., 2010).

Children aged 9 to 17 report spending 38 percent of their online time on homework—while their parents' perception is that 68 percent of their children's time is so spent (Taylor, 2002)! Children's favourite online activities include downloading music and emailing, as well as visiting chat rooms and texting. Facebook use is widespread and a great proportion of adolescents openly display their own risky behaviours, whether violence or sexuality (Moreno et al., 2009). Others upload school fights, rapes, and incidents of bullying onto YouTube.

Therefore, as is the case with television, the Internet also contains dangers. For instance, it is far from an unmitigated blessing in terms of providing reliable information, because information is generally mixed with advertising. It is often difficult to assess the origin and accuracy of the material presented on websites. Erroneous and misleading information is too frequently presented. As well, the constant use of the Internet is changing the way youth process information, evaluate it, and use this technology to replace traditional skills while, at the same time, new skills are not compensating for this loss (Levey, 2009). Constant exposure to and use of these media combined, such as the constant texting, *may influence the brain structure*. At the very least, these activities take time and *may in part well explain why so many students are stressed out*, even at the high school level. One can also be concerned that the time itself spent with the new media may place at risk the continuation of the artistic cultural heritage that is so obvious in provinces such as Quebec and Newfoundland/Labrador and among the Inuit.

CONCLUSIONS: THE FAMILY AS A "PRIVATE" INSTITUTION SUBSIDIZES THE ECONOMY

The research presented in this chapter does not support the pessimistic view of a general family decline and loss of relevance. Rather, the research supports pessimism concerning *individual* families' ability to fulfill their ever-increasing social reproduction-related responsibilities adequately, particularly that of the socialization of children and the care of its elder and fragile members. On the one hand, the family as an *institution* is highly valued and demands are placed on it in terms of its responsibilities in ever-expanding domains. But, on the other hand, this exacting sociocultural context generally fails to provide individual families with equivalent moral support and practical as well as financial help that could allow them to shoulder their social reproduction responsibilities (Bezanson and Luxton, 2006).

For instance, society is choosing to embrace information technology and market forces as values and as a way of life. Political economy theories suggest that there are high costs to such a choice and families bear a disproportionate burden in this respect, especially those that are marginalized by poverty, segregation, and lack of access to the new types of jobs. As Blank (1997) phrases it, given that our society "has chosen a market-oriented economy, it has a responsibility to those who cannot survive in the market on their own" (p. 198). This responsibility should not be displaced onto families. Unfortunately, this is exactly what is happening in the ever-widening gap between the rich and the rest (Stiglitz, 2012).

As Hewlett and West (1998) point out, too many **conservatives** fail to recognize the ways in which *market values are destroying families and family values*. For their part, too many on the **liberal** side, with their emphasis on rights and freedoms, "fail to understand that we need to rein in untrammeled individualism if we are to recreate the values that nurture family life" (p. 34). The family is the cornerstone of society because it reproduces, nurtures, and socializes society's future workers, citizens, taxpayers, and leaders. Thus, *a private institution subsidizes an entire society*. When families "fail," largely due to income and cultural causes within the same society, such families produce society's future unemployed poor, welfare recipients, and even criminals. In other words, what happens within the family affects the entire society. But, above all, the economic, political, and cultural agenda of society have a far greater impact on its families. Still, there is an incessant feedback dynamic between the private and the public spheres of life—between the family and society at large. However, more socialistic societies such as Finland, Sweden, and Norway have made different political value choices and have kept social inequalities at a lower level with a more equitable redistribution of resources. They consequently are able to offer more options to families with children and seniors for their care and they protect the unemployed more adequately. Thus, their individual families are less likely to fail because the *institution* of the family itself is better protected by the state.

In most western societies, the family is a small and relatively isolated unit in terms of the mediocre support it receives while being much affected by its environment. In recent decades, this cultural and socioeconomic environment has broadened considerably because of globalization and a more pervasive as well as **intrusive technology**. At the dawn of the new millennium, families experience change at a rapid pace, are contextualized in a larger world, but receive relatively fewer resources in terms of instrumental and effective moral support. Empowering families, no matter their structure, is one of the key social challenges of the 21st century.

Summary

1. Although the family has lost a few historical functions, it has gained a number of new ones. Its main responsibilities are described. In fact, there is an overabundance of family responsibilities created by a lack of social support and political investment in the institution itself.

2. Globalization has made transnational families more numerous and diverse than in the past, both ethnically and economically. Military families face particular challenges that deserve more research in Canada. Couples choosing to live apart together (LAT) are a fairly new phenomenon in Canada and also exist in some Caribbean nations.

3. An important historical development took place at the cultural level between 1951 and 1955, as nearly two-thirds of the nation's homes acquired a TV set. A historical overview of the trends in television programming highlights the changes in the content of programs as the decades went by.

4. Family life and leisure continued to evolve with the introduction of the Internet and cell phones. Various issues pertaining to family life and child development are reviewed as families are affected by the contents of the media and the time devoted to these media.

5. Feminist political economy sociologists are generally concerned that certain types of family structure are not sufficiently supported by the economy and the polity and cannot fulfill their many responsibilities related to social reproduction.

Analytical Questions

1. Now that you have completed this chapter, revisit Analytical Question 1 in Chapter 1: What more can you say?

2. Can you think of additional responsibilities that families shoulder in Canada, and especially in other countries?

3. Are military families a new development historically and cross-culturally?

4. Do television and the Internet reflect reality or do they create a reality? What is the role of advertising in this respect?

5. Write down a hypothetical time diary that would illustrate your family life on a daily basis this coming week, were you without television, Internet, and cell phones.

6. Write down how you would describe your family life to a researcher. Then, write how you would present it on Facebook. Which theoretical perspective would explain discrepancies, if any?

7. Which theory or theories best explain the lack of support that families receive within the context of the responsibilities that families shoulder in our society?

CHAPTER 4

Effects of Economic Changes and Inequalities on Families

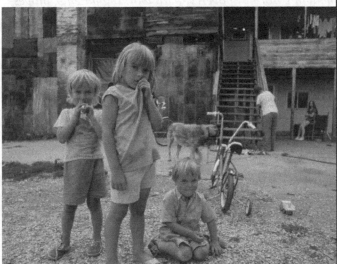

Nathan Benn/Corbis

OUTLINE

Overview of Economic Changes

Effects of Economic Changes on Families
The Rise of Feminine Employment and the Dual-Income Family
Domestic Division of Labour along Gender Lines
Economic Realities and Changing Family Time
The Rise of Consumerism in Family Life

Family Poverty

Sources of Family Poverty
Current Structural Sources of Poverty
Difficulties Encountered by Recent Immigrants as Risks for Poverty
Sociohistorical Sources of Poverty
Sociopersonal Sources of Poverty
Divorce and Break-Ups as Risks for Poverty
Births to Single Women and Father Absence as Risks for Poverty

Consequences of Family Poverty
For Mothers
For Fathers
For Children

Conclusions: The Costs of Family Poverty

Summary
Analytical Questions

"In 10 years from now I will be either a lawyer or a doctor. I want to make money, lots of it. That's my primary goal."

"In 10 years I hope to be out of this noisy apartment building and live in a modest house in the countryside. I hope to have travelled a bit and especially help my mother and sister out of here. I would want my mother to stay home and not to have to worry about money for the first time in her life."

"Right now my big problem is lack of money, nothing new here but now that I am getting close to becoming a teacher and having a bit for myself for the first time in my life, I can't stand it any longer!"

"This autobiography is going to be rather boring. I have lived the typical 'American dream' or should I say 'Canadian'? Born to poverty, hard working parents, moves to better neighbourhoods and now our dream come true: a big house on a street with other big houses."

"My father is a lawyer and when I turned 10 my mother became a stock broker. . . . We've always lived in the same lovely neighbourhood in a fairly large home with lots of trees and flowers, in two homes actually because my parents at some point decided to have a house with a two-level foyer with French doors and matching staircase."

"At that age [10 to 14] all I can remember is being hungry most of the time but especially by the end of each month and never having something special or nice that belonged to me. I don't have one pleasant memory."

In the preceding quotes, we hear from students who want to become doctors or lawyers because their dreams include a lot of money, students who simply want to have just enough for a decent life, students who suffered from the deprivations and fears of poverty, and others who lived in affluence. As these quotes begin to illustrate, economic circumstances and the economic system in which people live affect all facets of their lives and of their families' lives. Without some understanding of the economy, we cannot fully grasp the sources of the recent family transformations that are discussed in this book. The decades of the 1970s through the 2010s are characterized by an economy that has been radically transformed by information technology, which in turn has contributed to globalization. There is a historical parallel between the Industrial Revolution, which came to Canada in the 19th century, as discussed in

Chapter 2, and the ongoing technological revolution: In terms of political economy theories, both have created new employment-related environments, new modes of exploitation of labour, and a new set of economic realities (Marx, 1867). In turn, both have changed the sociopolitical landscape to serve the interests of the new ruling classes (Bartels, 2008; Stiglitz, 2012). All of these changes have had an impact on families' lives and roles.

OVERVIEW OF ECONOMIC CHANGES

We now live in what is called the postindustrial economy. It is characterized by **information technology**, high finances, including "paper" speculation (the stock market), and the predominance of the service sector. The economy is no longer organized along regional or even national lines; rather, it is international or global. This phenomenon is referred to as the **globalization of the economy** and is driven by corporations operating throughout the world. In order to increase their profits, corporations move manufacturing, call centres, and IT services around the globe, depending on the availability of cheap labour—thus pitting national labour forces, especially the less skilled, against one another (Marx, 1867). It is a world of mergers and acquisitions, speculation, and of restructuring and downsizing for the benefit of the few (Moen and Roehling, 2005). Instead of investing in businesses that produce goods and services and, by the same token, provide jobs to citizens, the banking and investment sectors simply concentrate on making money (Lin and Tomaskovic-Devey, 2013; Martin, 2011). In the process, they destroy productive and even profitable companies, lay off workers, and ruin pension plans (Livesey, 2012). National economies are thus at the mercy of these unchecked predatory market forces—thanks to deregulation—and worldwide financial fluctuations more than ever before (Coburn, 2010). This was very apparent in the recent 2008–09 recession largely generated by a lack of controls over the stock market and investment sectors which led to risky borrowing that originated in the U.S.

Corporations, hungry for **profit** for their shareholders and their CEOs, dictate trade and commercial laws as well as who will work, where, at what wage, and under what conditions (Brenna, 2012). Therefore, globalization and various free trade agreements have important consequences for families: Governments now have more difficulties stepping in to improve the economic opportunities of a disadvantaged neighbourhood or of an area that is threatened by plant closure, for instance (Langille, 2009). As well, powerful financial companies are too connected with the American government. For instance, two of Goldman Sachs' past four leaders have served as head of the U.S. Treasury. Even worldwide, a majority of countries' finance officials attending G-8 meetings have been former Goldman Sachs men. Furthermore, not only are nearly half of all members of the U.S. Congress millionaires but, in 2010, 37 percent "of the newly out-of-office members of Congress went to work for lobbying firms or clients" (Hayes, 2012:151). As well, the interests of the moneyed classes are given more weight by legislators than are those of the more disadvantaged citizens (Bartels, 2008; Langille, 2009). All of these factors prevent decisions from being taken in the best interest of the general public rather than speculators.

Until the 1970s, some of the largest Canadian employers were industries producing materials and goods such as steel and cars. Manufacturers provided well-paying entry-level jobs, employment security, and, later on, under the push of unions, benefit packages as well as pension plans to young workers fresh out of high school. These industries hired large numbers of youths, often immigrants. With such jobs, youths, especially males, could marry and support a family. After the 1970s, as technology progressed, fewer low-skilled workers were needed. Plant closures, downsizing, relocation, and imports from abroad, particularly Asia, followed and the proportion of the labour force working in manufacturing declined, subsequently leading to higher unemployment (Kollmeyer and Pichler, 2013), particularly among youths aged 15 to 24. The rates of youth unemployment have increased in recent years (14.3 percent in Canada), especially in some European countries where it is as high as 30 percent (Bernard, 2013). In 1951, 27 percent of jobs were in **manufacturing,** but this number had already plummeted to 15 percent by 1995. All of these and other factors began to restrict working-class individuals'—particularly young men's—ability to earn decent wages and secure a job during certain periods, such as the early 1990s, the early 2000s, and then 2008–10 (Sum et al., 2011). In the 2008–09 recession, some of the feminine domains such as health, education, and service sectors sustained fewer losses than the more masculine manufacturing, mining, farming, and even oil sectors. This situation is placing a strain on men's traditional role as breadwinners and is contributing to the delay in conjugal union formation and in the reduction in fertility across the western world, topics that will be discussed in subsequent chapters (Kotkin, 2012). Despite the increase in two-earner couples, families are not much better off financially than they were in the 1960s (FSAT, 2004). In fact, currently, couples aged 25 to 34 have an income equivalent to those in the late 1970s while various costs have mounted, particularly housing (Kershaw and Anderson, 2011).

Also, by the late 1970s, another phenomenon was occurring that changed the entire employment profile: The **service sector** expanded, a large segment of which offered only low-paying and part-time jobs—for example in the restaurant, hotel, and retail industries. These jobs constituted only 18 percent of the labour market in 1951 but employed 37 percent by 1995. Furthermore, in the face of a more competitive and high-tech economy and the requirements of corporations' shareholders, many jobs have been downsized into **part-time positions** and contracts, what Duffy and Pupo call "bad" jobs (2011). These are less secure, less well paid, and do not provide any health or pension benefits—and ultimately contribute to poverty.

Inequality is growing in Canada as it is in most countries of the world—even in communist ones such as China and Russia. In other words, the **gap between the rich and the poor** in terms of **wealth** (assets such as real estate, stocks, and savings accounts) has increased (Brenna, 2012)—and this gap favours the more educated (Chen et al., 2011; Frenette et al., 2007). For instance, in 1982, the reported **median*** income of the top one percent of income-tax filers was $191,600 or seven times higher than the $28,000 median for the remainder of the Canadian population. By 2010, their median income was 10 times higher than the stagnant $28,400 of other Canadian tax filers (Statistics Canada, 2013a, e). The CEOs of Canada's 100 most important publicly-listed corporations earned 189 times more than the average worker (Mackenzie, 2012a).

Not only are the rich getting richer, but the middle class is losing ground (Sauvé, 2009b). The hollowing out of the middle class is of great consequence because, as Mackenzie (2012b) puts it, "it has been the glue that binds," and it allows people "to remain connected to one another in fluid social relationships" across social classes. It is the turntable of social mobility* for families. Demographic trends have contributed to strengthening this gap because it is also related to marital status—married couples have more assets (Ozawa and Lee, 2006). It is also related to the fact that marriages increasingly consist of two high-earning or two low-earning spouses (Schwartz, 2010a). As well, children of the affluent are far more likely to live with both parents, which means intact family assets are at their disposal. And, among affluent house-holds, both spouses are likely to have a university degree. The financial sector fami-lies and individuals have particularly benefited from recent economic changes (Hayes, 2012). We tend to see Canada as a fairly equalitarian society, yet the concentration of wealth and power is very high (Livesey, 2012).

One has also to consider the role of social policies: The income tax system in Canada (as well as in the United States) has increasingly favoured the rich over the others. Not only have the richest one percent in Canada seen their income rise sub-stantially since the 1980s but, at the same time, the tax system has lowered their tax rate (Yalnizyan, 2010). In 1948, a person earning $250,000 would have been taxed at an 80 percent rate. Today, such a person is taxed at 43 percent. Since 1948, sev-eral tax brackets have been eliminated so that, for those earning more than $126,000, there is now only one tax bracket and rate—even though today, there is quite a dif-ference between an income of $125,000 and one of $500,000, one million, or more. For instance, Yalnizyan points out that the average yearly *income* for this one per-cent group is $405,000—and their *wealth* is vast.

As well, the **debt** load of Canadians has increased substantially so that, by 2012, the ratio of debt to disposable income had reached 163 percent. One result is that less well-off families have more difficulties repaying their debts and securing home equity and a higher number of bankruptcies ensue. This is particularly so for single parents (Sauvé, 2012:22). With flat-lined incomes in the past two decades, young families have seen the cost of housing grow by 76 percent across Canada between 1976 and 2010—by 149 percent in British Columbia and 93 percent in Quebec (Kershaw and Anderson, 2011). Tuition fees are increasing much faster than inflation (Statistics Canada, 2012i), in great part because the government's contribution per student has fallen to $11,600 a year down from a high of $22,400 in the 1970s (Davidson, 2012). As a result, student loans delay young people's ability to repay debts and accumulate assets (Luong, 2010). In turn, about 35 percent of parents will need to delay their own retirement in order to help their children financially (CIBC, 2013).

EFFECTS OF ECONOMIC CHANGES ON FAMILIES

Throughout the world, the economic changes combining globalization and information technology have greatly affected the relations between the genders as well as families, including family structure, lifestyle, and dynamics. To begin with, in the already affluent societies of Europe, North America, Australia, and New Zealand, the new economy presents a less secure employment and financial environment for families than was the case in the 1950s and 1960s when the manufacture of goods predominated. It is a more demanding economic environment, particularly for youth (Bernard, 2013). Among the consequences are the increase in maternal employment and two-income families, the "time crunch," the rise of a consumerist culture, and the lengthening of youths' dependence on parents—the latter discussed in Chapter 10. Other consequences such as delayed couple formation and fertility are discussed in Chapters 7 and 8 (Duffy and Pupo, 2011). Some of these consequences are actually strategies that families actively develop in order to control their environment (Hareven, 2000:77ff).

The Rise of Feminine Employment and the Dual-Income Family

Since 1980, women's participation in the *formal* labour force has substantially increased across the world. For instance, it is now over 60 percent in Sub-Saharan Africa, the world's poorest area—although women continue to earn less than men everywhere (World Bank, 2012). In Canada, by 2011, 81 percent of childless women under the age of 55 were employed as were 73 percent of women with children at home compared to only 47 percent in 1980 (*Canada Year Book*, 2012). In Table 4.1, we present the overall employment rates from 1980 to 2011 by age of youngest child still at home: Mothers' labour participation has increased at each child age level. This has given rise to an increase in **two-income families**. Currently, *without the earning of the second worker, the number of families living in poverty would double.* Indeed, in two-parent families, mothers' wages have become increasingly important and now account for 41 percent of total family earnings (Statistics Canada, 2009f). This percentage is, however, much lower when there are children below the age of six. By 2008, 29 percent of wives earned more than their husbands, up from only 11 percent in 1987: They are the "primary earners" in their families, and many earn twice as much as their husbands (Statistics Canada, 2010e).

But this "glorious" fact should not let us forget that, although the **wage gap** between male and female workers has narrowed, women who are *employed full-time* still earn 72 percent of what men earn (Drolet, 2010). This is a fairly

TABLE 4.1	**Percentages of Mothers Aged 55 and Younger Who Are Employed by Age of Youngest Child at Home in 1980, 1990, 2000, and 2011**			
	Youngest child is 0–2	Youngest child is 3–5	Youngest child is 6–16	No children at home
1980	37	45	53.5	65
1990	53	59.5	70	73.5
2000	60	67	74	76
2011	64.5	70	79	81

Source: Published by authority of the Minister responsible for Statistics Canada. © Minister of Industry, 2012. All rights reserved. Use of this publication is governed by the Statistics Canada Open Licence Agreement. Catalogue no. 11-402-X, Frequency: Annual, ISSN 0068-8142, Ottawa.

universal phenomenon, even among the very educated and the younger cohorts*. The reasons are manifold but can be subsumed under the rubric of gender inequality in a masculine social order. Labour by women and feminine employment activities continue to be devalued (England, 2010). Women still tend to occupy positions that are less well remunerated in the service sectors (such as retail salespersons, cashiers, and babysitters). But even for jobs that require a great deal of education, there is a "glass ceiling." Other women earn less because 27 percent of them work part-time compared to only 12 percent of men (Drolet, 2010): Women constitute 70 percent of all part-time employees (Lindsay, 2006). Of note is the fact that a third would prefer full-time jobs. As well, hourly wages of women with children is 12 percent lower than wages of childless women and this gap widens: By the time mothers are 40 years old, they earn 21 percent less than childless women (Statistics Canada, 2009g). A German study has also found that both mothers' child care and housework contribute to the wage gap, but mainly for those who spend more than two hours a day in housework (Kühhirt and Ludwig, 2012; see also World Bank, 2012).

Studies have found that women who **delay childbirth** by at least one year past the average age at first birth for their cohorts earn higher salaries—up to 17 percent higher. Postponing a first birth is even more important among younger cohorts of women, in part because of the types of careers now open to them. As Drolet (2003) points out, "wage growth and promotion opportunities are substantial early in one's career" (p. 21). Women who delay childbirth are more flexible for career moves, additional training, and may also be inherently more career oriented than women who begin childbearing earlier. As well, career interruptions of more than three years have a great impact on mothers' wages; by age 40, such women earn close to 30 percent less than other mothers and childless women (Statistics Canada, 2009g; also, Staff and Mortimer, 2012). We know that, in Canada, 90 percent of mothers and 26 percent of fathers take a leave of absence after the arrival of a child (Findlay and Kohen, 2012). In Quebec, the percentages are 99 and 76, respectively. Generally, paternity leaves are much briefer and, thus, less likely to affect a father's work. Other mothers interrupt their work cycle for a substantial period of time, thus delaying promotions and salary increases (Damaske, 2011).

Thus, the traditional gender division of labour and of income, with women earning less, remains in the new economy (Statistics Canada, 2009h). This **detrimental feminine wage** and labour situation contributes to poverty in single-mother families and in low-income families in which two salaries are necessary. Further, feminine inequality in wages, education, employment, and political participation, especially in poorer parts of the world such as in Africa and Asia, has many societal consequences: It lowers food productivity among farmers, reduces the availability of a qualified work force, diminishes children's human capital, especially health, and may increase political corruption (World Bank, 2012).

At another level, 30 percent of men and 28 percent of women engage in **shift work;** they report higher levels of work-related stress and work overload. This is even more so for women than men (Williams, 2008). As well, both men and women on evening shifts report more relationship problems with their spouses and lower well-being than those with daytime employment (Davis et al., 2008; Shields, 2003).

Another study has found that children whose parents have nonstandard work schedules have more social and emotional difficulties, in part as a result of lower parental well-being and less effective parenting (Strazdins et al., 2006).

Recourse to women's labour for family survival is a recurrent theme in history (Bradbury, 2000; Parr, 2000). Not only did women (and children) fully participate in the family economy in past centuries, but in the 19th century, many low-income families already had (needed) two or more incomes (Bradbury, 1996; Parr, 1980). What is now unprecedented is that the majority of women of all classes work for wages while children no longer do; also unprecedented is the combination of economic and cultural forces driving feminine employment. In many two-parent families, two wages have become a necessity because of a rise in economic instability and consumer expectations. As husbands' salaries plunge or as they lose their jobs, wives increase their own labour market participation (Morissette and Hou, 2008). Further, higher divorce and single parenting rates make it necessary for divorced and unmarried mothers to be employed.

But feminine employment would have nevertheless grown despite these economic necessities, although perhaps to a lesser extent. Indeed, the 1970s wave of the women's movement has led to the liberalization of attitudes concerning women's roles in society. This cultural change has allowed women to enter the labour force in greater numbers and to penetrate occupational fields that had been traditionally masculine, such as law, medicine, and the physical sciences. One should, however, consider that a proportion of women still choose and enjoy being homemakers and full-time parents and have minimal aspirations as far as paid employment is concerned. There is a lack of attention in feminist theories to this aspect of many women's condition, as we have tended to focus on paid employment (Marks, 2004). One could as easily see that many men might also want to become full-time fathers were they socialized within this perspective. In fact, there is a small but noticeable trend in this direction, especially when fathers are unemployed, or when mothers earn substantially more and paying for child care would be too expensive.

Domestic Division of Labour along Gender Lines

As we have just seen, a majority of mothers, even those with very young children, are gainfully employed. Paradoxically, this shift toward maternal employment has occurred at a time when the requirements of care for small children have become more labour intensive and the pressure on women as mothers has mounted (Hays, 1996). The net result is what sociologist Arlie Hochschild has, in 1989, called *The Second Shift*. That is, although society has become more accepting of women's status and role in the workplace, this development has not been accompanied by a similarly liberating one on the domestic front (Damaske, 2011)—and this topic is further discussed in Chapter 9 from a relationship perspective. In the "second shift," women come home from work to work even more. After picking up children at the daycare centre or at the sitter's, they cook and serve dinner, prepare lunches for the next day, perhaps do laundry, and help the children with their homework and bedtime (Hochschild, 1997). Women's key role in social reproduction* has not proportionally decreased (Bezanson and Luxton, 2006).

TABLE 4.2	Housework by Men and Women for 1986 Compared with 2005	
	1986	2005
% of men who do housework daily	54%	69%
% of women who do housework daily	90%	90%
# of hours of housework (for men who do any)	2.1 hours	2.5 hours
# of hours of housework (for women who do any)	4.8 hours	4.3 hours

Source: Marshall, 2006, Statistics Canada; Table adapted by Ambert with permission from Statistics Canada.

In Table 4.2, we see that women do more housework than men, although masculine participation has increased. Not shown is the fact that there is a similar pattern for child care (Ornstein and Stalker, 2013; Raley et al., 2012). Wives who are not in the labour force do more housework than other wives, and wives employed part-time do more than wives employed full-time. The scenario that comes closest to equality in terms of housework is when the husband is not in the labour force but his wife is employed full-time. When both spouses are employed full-time, wives still do more child care and housework than husbands (Moen and Roehling, 2005). Yet, Raley et al. (2012) have also found that fathers do more actual physical care of children and care for them alone when their wives' relative earnings are higher—even though the total time fathers spend is still lower than mothers'. They also found that, generally, fathers spend more "fun" time with their children than mothers do. As well, shift work by both parents results in more paternal child care (Täht and Mills, 2012). Overall, married fathers have more leisure time per day than married and single mothers also employed full-time (Saxbe et al., 2011). One consequence of this overload is that women take more time off work for family reasons other than maternity. In fact, in 2000, married women with children took 12 days off versus one day for married men with children and four for single-parent women, because employed mothers are more time stressed than fathers (Marshall, 2006).

An important gap in the literature is the lack of widespread research on **children's contributions** to household tasks and child care—including self-care as well as the care of disabled parents or siblings (Owen, 2010). Not only do we need to know how much work children do and what they do, but how easy or difficult it is for parents to obtain their cooperation in this respect. For instance, only 4 out of 10 teens do some housework daily, for about one hour (Statistics Canada, 2008g). Further, well over 10 percent of husband-wife households employ some domestic help (Statistics Canada, 2003d), particularly when wives' incomes constitute a greater share of the joint income and house size is larger (Palameta, 2003). In fact, 43 percent of households with income of $160,000 and over hire **domestic help** (Macdonald, 2010; Marshall, 2006). Domestics and nannies, who are usually immigrant women, contribute to alleviating better-off women's own domestic burdens and time squeeze. Hence, they participate in the gendered division of household labour, both in the host family and in theirs back home (Ehrenreich and Hochschild, 2002; Parrēnas, 2002).

Employed mothers, whether married or single, have little time for themselves, are overworked and stressed, frequently worry about their children, and often feel guilty, even more so when child care arrangements are not optimal or when their children are alone at home after school or in the company of problematic peers. Overall, there are both negative and positive work/family spillovers, but these differ depending on each family's context. A national survey reveals that fathers and mothers in two-parent families are happier at home than at work, but divorce often reverses this trend (Kiecolt, 2003). However, for women who shoulder most of the burden at home, paid work outside is often less stressful than housework and childrearing (Larson and Richards, 1994). It is, nevertheless, quite possible that the *ideological devaluation of housework* in recent decades has contributed to the fact that it is now generally viewed as stressful and as something that everyone prefers to avoid (Zimmerman, 2003).

Economic Realities and Changing Family Time

When both parents, and especially mothers, have demanding hours, less time is available for personal needs, as well as family and couple interaction (Clark, 2002). However, when adults feel that their work environment provides flexibility, they benefit from a more favourable work-family balance (Hill et al., 2001). As well, when children's activities outside school are regimented into a variety of lessons and sports, they have less time for spontaneous play—even though these structured activities may be favourably related to cognitive development (Hofferth and Sandberg, 2001). Further, information technology has spawned "gadgets" such as smart phones, to which adults and children are tethered, and which occupy a great deal of their time in interaction with other persons, often to the detriment of face-to-face interactions with family members.

Thus, another effect of economic changes on families consists of what is called the **time crunch**: Too many activities are crammed into too few hours, as illustrated in the example below (CIW, 2010).

> *"This suburban family consists of two parents, aged 35 (husband) and 33 (wife), both professionals in large brokerage firms, and two boys of three and six years of age. The family rises at 6:00 a.m. The parents alternate taking the boys to the daycare centre where they arrive at 7:00 a.m. From there, Glenn, the oldest, is picked up by minivan at 8:45 and brought to a nearby school, where he is in grade 1. The parents take turns fetching the children at 6:00 p.m. at the daycare, where Glenn has been since 3:15, after another ride in the minivan. Once a week, a taxi drives him to music classes after school and returns him to the centre. One parent takes the hungry children home and promptly serves them supper; the other parent arrives at 7:00 p.m., equally hungry and tired. The children are in bed at 8:00, quite exhausted by then.*

Saturday morning, the father takes the boys for swimming lessons; the mother takes them for skating lessons in the afternoon. Sunday is spent going to church, shopping, and visiting with friends and relatives. Both parents are intelligent, attractive, and sociable. The boys get along well and play together in the few hours of unstructured time they have. They are apparently intelligent. However, Glenn's report card indicates that his verbal skills are below his grade level. His visiting grandmother explains that this is due to the fact that the children are always in the company of other children and are rarely alone with adults who, at any rate, are obviously of no interest to the child-oriented boys. The boys basically spend only two hours daily with their parents who are all the while busily catching up with housework activities. Little conversation takes place. Life is fast paced."[†]

Parental time pressure in two-income families is related to depression but much less so for well-to-do parents (Roxburgh, 2012) who may be more secure in the fact that their children are still well taken care of. Duxbury and Higgins (2012) also report that employees who are economically better off appear to be more able to cope with the demands of time, perhaps because they are more able to purchase services. The use of the Statistics Canada Time Crunch Instrument has revealed that 23 percent of parents of children under the age of six are "highly time-stressed"; 68 percent feel that they do not spend enough quality time with their children (Invest in Kids, 2002). The U.S. Bureau of the Census has estimated that, between 1960 and 1986, parental time available to children has diminished by 10 hours per week for whites and 12 for blacks (Fuchs, 1990). The phenomenon of "latchkey" children comes to mind here, as well as of older siblings taking care of a younger one after school (Riley and Steinberg, 2004). Not only do parents work more hours, but the average Canadian now spends 1 hour per day commuting to and from work (Statistics Canada, 2013f).

In 2005, the average worker was spending 45 minutes less with his or her family during weekdays compared to 20 years earlier. In part, this is due to the fact that Canadians work longer hours than two decades ago (Duxbury and Higgins, 2012). These data are very solid because they are based, not on retrospective information, but on time journals provided in the General Social Survey on Time Use (Statistics Canada, 2007c). Other researchers have found that adolescents now spend an average of three hours a day alone at home (Schneider et al., 2000). Only 35 percent of 15- to 17-year-olds eat a meal with their parents on a typical day (CIW, 2010). As well, another study found that, "In low and high income households, parents report spending under 5 minutes a day reading or talking with their children and less than 20 minutes a day playing with them" (Williams, 2002:10).

However, while total parental time has diminished in two-parent families, time per child may have increased—because there are fewer children (Wolff, 2001). Other research indicates that parents of small children (five and younger) spend more time with them than was the case in 1960 (Gauthier et al., 2004). Therefore, when considering studies of parental time with children, one has to look at the age of the child. Still, overall, mothers have been able to balance their hours with children by doing less housework, having less leisure, and having fewer children (Schor, 2001). Both mothers and fathers would prefer to have more family time. It is difficult, however,

[†]*Source:* Courtesy of Anne-Marie Ambert.

to know if the children themselves feel deprived of "family time." High-income families may be even more affected than low-income families in patterns of time consumption. Parents with a higher income work at least six hours more per week than those on a low income (Williams, 2002). As an illustration of this time squeeze, let's hear what another young professional couple, with both spouses employed full-time, said when interviewed:

> *"The spouses in their early thirties both complained during their separate interviews that they had "no time for each other; it's even difficult to put some sex in our lives because we are always on the run" [wife]. For his part, the husband felt that his wife "could work fewer hours; that way, it would be easier to arrange our schedules so that we can take some time out for our relationship." He did not mention that he could also work fewer hours, a realistic possibility, given that he stayed at the office daily until 8 p.m. This was an affluent couple with extremely high material expectations—costly expectations. In contrast to the other couples interviewed, this couple was not concerned about having practically no time for their four-year-old son. Fortunately, the little boy appeared to be good-natured and easily contented. He made no demands during the two hours I spent at his home and he occupied himself peacefully."*

The Rise of Consumerism in Family Life

One reason families now need larger incomes resides in the rise of consumerism fuelled by advertising and television programming, which all contribute to a sense of relative deprivation (Easterbrook, 2003). New "needs" are created by advertisers, whether for clothes, smart phones, computers, tablets, entertainment units (DVD players, large flat-screen TVs), or more cars per family. Children are particularly rewarding "targets" of such advertising and play a very active role as consumers, often as a result of peer pressure (Cook, 2004). As well, the size of houses has increased substantially and their price has skyrocketed, and these large spaces have to be furnished. In contrast, there are indications that parents who encourage their children to have a savings account are, by the same token, helping them in terms of math achievement (Elliott et al., 2010)—perhaps as a result of the positive effect of delayed gratification on intellectual development. Conversely, it would be important to know what happens later to children and adolescents who are given large allowances and credit cards.

Family members often develop a sense of identity in part related to their possessions (Côté, 2000). Further, consumerism—looking at catalogues and online displays, going to malls, searching for items in mega stores or online—takes time. This time could be used for other family activities; thus, consumerist activities may compound the time crunch felt by parents. Long ago, the sociologist Thorsten Veblen (1899) developed the concept of **conspicuous consumption**: In other words, families acquire possessions that are visible (conspicuous) and give them a certain status. However, technology and fashion change so rapidly in this new century that families have to keep upgrading their possessions to reflect their affluence or to have what others have. It is somewhat surprising that contemporary sociologists of the family have paid little attention to these processes and dynamics of market forces. As Daly

(2003) points out, we have given little "attention to understanding how spending behaviours and consumer goods are the basis for the construction of meaning in the everyday experience of family life" (p. 778).

FAMILY POVERTY

Canada is an advanced society technologically; yet poverty, even if diminished—but higher again as a result of the 2008–2009 recession—has persisted, particularly among the working poor. The **working poor** are those whose wages are too low to raise their family above the poverty line determined by the government (Raphael, 2011). As Mary Cornish (2012) puts it, a "living wage" should be a human right because, when wages are minimal, many families become or remain poor, despite the fact that both parents may be employed. In 2009, 1.6 million Canadians aged 25 to 64 lived in low-income *employed* families—with at least one earner—or 9 percent of the population, compared to 1.2 million low-income but *un*employed families or 7 percent of that age group (Luong, 2011). *Therefore, more poor families are employed than are not.* The low-income employed group was somewhat better educated (18 percent even had a university degree); earned $10,000 more; had a few assets, but also had more debts, primarily because of mortgage payments; had basic savings for the unexpected; and scored higher on a number of health variables than the unemployed. Part-time work and minimum-wage jobs are largely responsible for the condition of the working poor.

Statistics Canada calculates a "Market Basket Measure" based on a formula that includes the cost of food, clothes, shelter, and transportation for each region. This formula tells us how much, in theory, a family needs to earn in order to meet its basic needs: Families who earn less are considered disadvantaged, thus the concept of "living below the poverty line," or LICOs, which stands for low-income cut-offs. In 2007, the following poverty lines were established for Canada's major cities for a family of four, from most to least expensive cities to live in (HRSD, 2009):

Vancouver	$31,768	St. John's	28,544
Toronto	31,729	Winnipeg	27,256
Calgary	30,951	Saint John	27,202
Charlottetown	30,527	Regina	26,835
Halifax	29,761	Montreal	26,560

Although the percentage of persons in poverty in general had dropped from 15 percent in 2000 to 9.4 percent in 2007, one can see that poverty touches a large proportion of the Canadian population at one time or another in their **lifespan** (Campaign 2000, 2010). Between 2002 and 2007, *20 percent of Canadians experienced at least one year of low income and 8 percent at least three years* (Food Banks Canada, 2009). For instance, *27.8 percent of all children below age 13 had been poor at least once.* In addition, nearly 10 percent of children had experienced persistent poverty between 2002 and 2007 (HRSD, 2009).

Statistical Cautionary Remarks

Poverty percentages may differ depending on which income is used: before income tax or after income tax. Poverty rates are higher before taxes because disadvantaged families receive tax credits after they file their returns. These credits reduce the proportion of persons in poverty. In 2008, for instance, without the income transfers, 25 percent of children would have lived in poverty rather than the 9 percent actual figure after income tax (Campaign 2000, 2010:7).

Especially at high risk for poverty are children who live in mother-headed families, who are Aboriginal, or belong to recently immigrated families, particularly minority ones. For instance, while 9.1 percent of Canadian children were poor in 2008, fully 36 percent of Native children were and so were 41 percent of children of immigrant parents (Campaign 2000, 2010). In 2007, well over 40 percent of children in mother-headed families were poor compared to only 11 percent among children living in a couple family (Statistics Canada, 2009j). To these statistics, one must add at least another 10 to 15 percent of families and children who hover precariously above the threshold. These vulnerable families constitute the **near poor** (Morissette, 2002). Any crisis can send them tumbling below the poverty level—crises such as a dental emergency, the need for prescription medicine, the birth of an additional child, or the loss of even one of the many part-time jobs these families may hold. At least one-third of all families have no liquid assets and cannot survive even a modest spell of unemployment (Ratcliffe and Vinopal, 2009).

Another aspect of poverty is its **depth**—that is, how deep down below the poverty line families are. For instance, in 1999, half of all one-parent families with one child who were poor had incomes of $10,000 or less—this is called deep poverty (United Way, 2001). The profile is similar for recent years. In Toronto, an additional $15,000 would be needed on average to lift poor families with children out of poverty (FSAT, 2004). As a result, most disadvantaged families cannot afford some of the basics of life, such as food. As well, fewer low-income families can afford certain expenditures that provide social, cultural, as well as material capital for families—as indicated in Table 4.3. This table shows the differences in lifestyle between the well-to-do and the poor.

SOURCES OF FAMILY POVERTY

The sources of family poverty differ depending on the economic and political level of societies. Currently, because of their very large populations, the emerging economies of China and India still hold half of the world's poor (*The Economist,* 2013). For its part, Sub-Saharan Africa contains a third of the world's poor (Summer, 2012). These

TABLE 4.3	**Percentages of Households Purchasing Certain Goods and Services by Income Level, 2005**

Goods & Services	Income Levels		
	Poorest Fifth	Middle Fifth	Richest Fifth
Children's summer camps	1	6	16
Own vacation homes	2	7	18
Dental insurance plan	2	8	11
Attend live sports events	6	17	34
Accident & disability insurance	4	13	21
Buy sports & athletic equipment	11	36	58
Books & other reading material	25	52	75

Source: Adapted with permission from R. Sauvé. Table commissioned by R. Sauvé, 2008, from Statistics Canada's Survey of Household Spending.

societies also have very high levels of internal inequalities, with extremely rich people at the top and extremely poor people at the bottom—and a taxation system (or no tax system at all) that does not redistribute any wealth, as is done to some extent in western societies. Many of the poorest societies are **failed states*** (Afghanistan and many African countries). Famines and droughts regularly occur, often as a result of civil wars, along with displacement of populations, corruption, and lack of democracy and civil rights. What poverty has in common cross-culturally is that it is a **political issue**—in short, it results from the choices that people at the top make (Brenna, 2012; Kharas and Rogerson, 2012). It is an issue of inequality, power, and political control over wealth and labour (Marx, 1867).

Why are there so many disadvantaged families amidst affluence in countries such as Canada? At the risk of oversimplifying what is a highly complex issue, the sources of poverty in technologically advanced societies fall into three categories: First are the systemic, or structural, sources at the societal level, largely stemming from a lack of redistribution of riches controlled by the powerful. Second, originating from these are causes that are rooted in the historic treatment of some groups, or sociohistoric sources, and, thirdly, the personal sources. Structural and sociohistoric refer to overall social conditions, whereas personal refers to particular status situations rather than attributes and behaviours of the poor. The personal sources are generally fostered by the large-scale socioeconomic or structural causes that generate both the personal sources of poverty and poverty itself. If the economic, historical, and social causes of poverty were eliminated, the personal sources, while not vanishing entirely, would be radically reduced, as is the case in Holland and Scandinavian countries and to some extent in France. *What these countries share is a political will to redistribute resources more equitably*—although the current economic depression is leading to a deterioration of these societies' social safety nets.

Current Structural Sources of Poverty

In Canada and the U.S., poverty is the result of an unequal distribution of resources among families rather than an overall lack of riches (Ambert, 1998): *It is strictly a political choice that protects the interests of the rich at the expense of the rest of the society* (Marx, 1867; Stiglitz, 2012). As we have seen, the gap between rich and poor families has widened in the past two decades. The following structural aspects of the organization of our society constitute the major causes of family poverty:

- the loss of employment due to the restructuring of the labour market, such as companies relocating jobs "offshore"—that is, to other countries where salaries are low;
- cutbacks in health care and downloading of care onto families (Luxton, 2006a; Mandell and Wilson, 2011);
- the destruction of well-functioning and productive companies by executives in hostile take-overs, in order to increase their gains, with the consequent loss of large numbers of jobs, whether Nortel or Stelco in Canada, or more recently, Hostess in the U.S.;
- "welfare for the rich" whereby very high earners pay taxes that are relatively low in comparison to those of more equitable countries such as Sweden and Denmark where poverty is less common;
- the lack of creation of green industries that would open employment opportunities to replace the loss of manufacturing jobs;
- low-paying and part-time jobs, especially among women and minority groups, and the lack of a subsidy for minimum wages. In 2009, *19 percent of workers earned less than $12 per hour* (Campaign 2000, 2010);
- the timidity of our governments (federal, provincial, and municipal) that fail to improve infrastructures that would create jobs for the present *and* the future;
- the greed of some unions in terms of overtime for the "haves" that prevents institutions and companies from hiring additional persons or helping the "have-nots";
- but the fact that fewer workers are unionized also creates problems for low-paid workers;
- pay inequity by gender (women are paid less than men for comparable job qualifications) and overall inequality;
- insufficient social benefits for families and social reproduction work.

Difficulties Encountered by Recent Immigrants as Risks for Poverty

In general, recent immigrant families have more difficulties making ends meet than older immigrants and Canada-born persons of the same educational level or even with a higher education. There are four general reasons for this. First and foremost at the societal level is the fact that recent immigrants arrive in an economy that has changed drastically in terms of labour market opportunities, as explained at the outset of this chapter. Second and third, recent immigrants suffer more from social exclusion (perhaps related to **racism**), particularly on the labour market, and therefore have higher unemployment rates, with some exceptions (Curry-Stevens, 2009:53–54; Galabuzi, 2009). For instance, in 2011, adult Filipino immigrants had the highest employment rate, at 85.6 percent, higher than the 83 percent rate for Canadian-born persons and well above the 73 percent rate for Asian-born individuals and the 70 percent of African-born immigrants (Statistics Canada, 2012d). In 2006, recent immigrants with a B.A. had an **unemployment** rate of 11.4 percent, much greater than that of Canadian-born persons with a B.A. (Statistics Canada, 2007a). As well, immigrant persons aged 15 to 24 had even greater rates at 17 percent compared to 11 percent among Canadian-born youth. Recent immigrant women have a higher unemployment rate at 13 percent: The intersection of their race and gender may place more restrictions on their paths in a racialized and still masculine society (Chui, 2011; Galabuzi, 2006; Topen, 2011). Further, foreign workers on temporary permits are frequently exploited by employers, particularly in industries such as cleaning, hospitality, retail, and construction (Monsebraaten, 2011). They even earn less than other immigrants for the same work (Thomas, 2010). Immigrants on temporary work permits are not generally included in poverty studies although they constitute 1 percent of all full-time workers in Canada. They may get wages that are lower than the legal minimum or not get paid at all. They may not be able to complain to authorities because of language difficulties or for fear of being deported or being retaliated against by their employers. Some may leave the employer and go "underground," in effect becoming illegal immigrants.

The fourth source of economic liability for recent immigrants resides in **language difficulties** (and also explains in part the above sources). Immigrants who speak neither English nor French or who use neither in their work not only earn less but they also have higher unemployment rates (Boyd and Cao, 2009; Chun and Cheong, 2011). As indicated by Statistics Canada (2009k), such persons are less able "to convert their educational qualifications into higher earnings." This problem can also be reinforced by the fact that recent immigrants who arrive here as adults and settle in **ethnic enclaves** earn lower incomes than warranted by their educational levels (Li, 2008; Warman, 2007).

Finally, although more educated on average than the remainder of the Canadian population (because of Immigration Canada's point system), immigrants who have earned their degrees abroad before arriving have higher unemployment and lower salaries than comparable Canadians (Fong and Cao, 2009). In other words, the **accreditation system** is prejudicial and disadvantages more recent immigrants, *especially those from non-European countries* (Ferrer and Riddell, 2008; Li, 2008; Tastsoglou, 2011). As well, the lack of "Canadian experience" in their résumé is another barrier. All of these factors combined lead to lower income and greater difficulties in adjustment for the entire family.

For instance, recently I met a 40-year-old concierge working in a high-rise condo, earning about $13/hour, who was supporting his wife and sons while his wife was doing her accreditation years to return to the profession she had had in a Middle Eastern country: a physician. This man then left his low-paying job because it was his turn to be supported while he studied for his accreditation: He also had been a physician in his country. In two other buildings, an engineer from an African country is employed as a superintendent, and a former university professor from a South Asian country does the paperwork and answers the phone for a management company.

There are indications that upward social mobility takes place, via a Canadian university education, among the second generation. However, this is not so much the case for blacks (who have very high rates of poverty and single parenting, as seen in subsequent chapters). This is also less the case for Filipinos, even though their labour rate participation is very high (Abada et al., 2009).

Sociohistorical Sources of Poverty

The sociohistorical sources of poverty are those that have occurred during the history of Canada and have resulted in such inequities that their effects are still felt today. The most salient and painful ones pertain to the centuries of cruel attempts at the social exclusion and cultural genocide of Aboriginals, deprivation of territories, and nefarious effects of contacts with Europeans—as described in Chapter 2. Indeed, currently, poverty is probably the most evident social problem facing many Aboriginal families who tend to have the lowest living standard of any other group in the country (CCPA, 2009). Using the same index used by the United Nations Development Program, which consistently ranks Canada as one of the best places to live in the world, Beavon and Cooke (2003) found that persons designated as "Status Indian" and living on reserves would be ranked seventy-ninth.

Canadian Aboriginal peoples suffer from high unemployment rates, substandard housing conditions, and inadequate health care and educational services, which result in their having the lowest education, income, and health levels in the country (Frideres, 2011). Although Aboriginals constitute only 3.8 to 5 percent of the population, they constituted 12 percent of those assisted by food banks in 2008 and 2009 (Food Banks Canada, 2009:7). They have significantly higher infant mortality rates and substantially lower life expectancies (Harrison and Friesen, 2004; Tjepkema and Wilkinson, 2011). Because of poverty, lack of employment opportunities, and generations of family breakdown caused by the residential school system, the suicide rate among Aboriginal peoples is, on average, between two to seven times that of the national population. Other serious problems include alcoholism, substance abuse (even among children), and delinquency, including, more recently, the formation of criminal gangs in some communities. Hunger, especially among children, is an issue, particularly in distant areas such as Nunavut (Egeland et al., 2010). Aboriginal men and women constitute a disproportionate share of prison inmates (Statistics Canada, 2005b). And, as we see in Chapter 13, domestic violence is widespread.

Such deeply ingrained problems cannot be remedied within a few years as their solution would involve a thoughtful and open-minded reconsideration of the reserve system and of the role of some chiefs and bands in the finances of their group (Popplewell, 2010). Other solutions might include the creation of employment opportunities near reserves and Native villages as well as programs of monetary incentives for youths and their mothers based on school attendance and delayed childbearing (programs that are being tested in a few large Canadian and American cities).

Sociopersonal Sources of Poverty

The sociopersonal sources of family poverty are generally the ones favoured for discussion by the public, the media, and policy-makers. These sources imply that individuals who bear certain demographic characteristics, such as single mothers, are

The working poor include families in which both parents are employed in low paying jobs. One parent may even hold two jobs. These families are hovering precariously, just one slippery step above the poverty level. This situation is even worse in the U.S., where these families rarely have health insurance.

responsible for their poverty and for all the consequences flowing from it. An emphasis on the strictly personal aspect of these sources of poverty too often precludes a consideration of the larger socioeconomic causes of poverty and conveniently excuses the lack of political change to remedy the situation. This is why, in decades of budgetary restraint, welfare programs for mothers with dependent children are popular targets of suspicion and cuts: Welfare policies are gendered (Vosko, 2002).

Divorce and Break-Ups as Risks for Poverty

Divorce is a direct source of poverty or near poverty for women and children, although a sizeable proportion of divorces are themselves caused by economic hardship (Amato and Previti, 2004; Frenette and Picot, 2003:15). Indeed, families under economic pressure are more likely to experience negative interactions, spousal conflict, domestic violence, and child abuse. Any of these problems can lead to divorce and break-ups, as more extensively discussed in Chapter 12. Once separation takes place, the mother and child unit becomes even poorer, even though mothers' earnings generally increase (Tamborini et al., 2012). Rotermann (2007a) found that, within two years after a separation/divorce, 43 percent of women had experienced a decrease in household income as had 15 percent of men. In contrast, 29 percent of men and only 9 percent of women had experienced an increase. After divorce, women are more likely to go on welfare (Frenette and Picot, 2003). Although the sex of the person is not specified, 4 percent of all bankruptcies are the result of a marriage breakdown (Sauvé, 2009a).

For women who were comfortably middle class before divorce and who fall into poverty after, this situation usually is transitory. They are generally able to lift themselves out of poverty, after several months to a few years, through employment, their parents' help, fathers' child support, and especially remarriage and cohabitation. Nevertheless, lone-parent families (separated or other) tend to have a high debt load (Hurst, 2011).

Births to Single Women and Father Absence as Risks for Poverty

Single parenting more often than not stems from poverty and leads to poverty (Singh et al., 2001; Thomas and Sawhill, 2005). This is particularly so for teen births (*Hamilton Spectator,* 2011). Single-mother poverty exists in all western societies (Brady and Burroway, 2012). As we descend the socioeconomic ladder, the number of births to unpartnered women increases noticeably—and the same is evident for the males who coproduce these children (Guzzo and Furstenberg, 2007a; Manlove et al., 2008a).

Following Wilson's (1987) example, American demographers have studied the impact of men's and women's wages on marriage formation for all races. They found that both men's and women's marriage rates rise with each additional thousand dollars that men earn. In addition, men's wealth is particularly important in the formation of marital unions (Schneider, 2011). Poverty is not the only source of nonmarital births because most single women and men who are poor do not have children. However, disadvantaged adolescents who hold low educational and vocational expectations are more likely to engage in risky behaviours leading to pregnancy (Clark et al., 2006). They may also feel that they have little to lose by engaging in unprotected sex that might lead to pregnancy. As England et al. (2011) point out, "Individuals are unlikely to avoid early, unintended births without a belief in their own efficacy and substantial self-regulation" (p. 42). This attitude is well expressed by a student:

> *"I am 28 and had my son at 16. At the time I was fed up with school and my mother and I didn't care to work and I thought the baby would be fun to have. I didn't go out of my way to have one but I certainly took no precautions. . . . It didn't end up being the rose garden I had wanted. . . . I was on welfare for many years . . . and bored. I went back to school at 23 and it has been a struggle."*

For many impoverished young women, having a baby alone may be the only form of social status they can look forward to. Motherhood provides an important source of satisfaction and self-esteem when economic opportunities do not exist. Disadvantaged young fathers' own social standing among peers may also benefit and they frequently have additional babies from different "baby mothers" (Guzzo and Furstenberg, 2007a). From the individual point of view of the young mother, it makes short-term sense to have a child alone because there are relatively few males who could marry her and help support her child, particularly if she is black (see Chapter 7). Further, in the short term, lone motherhood makes relatively little economic difference in the life of an already impoverished teenager or young woman. But once she has a child, her maternity entrenches her poverty or makes it last longer, and her chances of marrying decrease. Such mothers also spend more time on welfare than divorced mothers do (Cooke, 2009). Single parents have a 16 percent probability of being poor for at least four years, compared to 3.5 percent for couples with children (Morissette and Zhang, 2001). And, even more recently, the Canadian National Longitudinal Survey of Children and Youth has shown that 43 percent of children aged two to five years who were in poverty in 1994–95 were still disadvantaged eight years later (Statistics Canada, 2005a). In the future, it may become more difficult for such young women and their children to exit poverty, because of the educational requirements of the new economy, lack of child care facilities, and lower social assistance payments (Little, 2011).

As well, when the putative fathers are equally disadvantaged educationally, there is little chance that they will contribute significantly to support the children. Thus, single parenting makes no sense for the child who is born in poverty or who becomes at higher risk of poverty. Even when his or her mother exits poverty two to six years later, these few years represent a sizeable proportion of a young child's life (Morissette and Zhang, 2001)—and early poverty is most detrimental to later educational and occupational outcomes. Indeed, whether children in single-mother families have divorced or never-married parents, two salient facts emerge. First, these children are much more likely to be poor than those who live with both parents (Bogenschneider and Corbett, 2010). Second, having a single mother who is a member of an ethnic minority places children at an extraordinary risk for poverty because of discrimination (Statistics Canada, 2009j). As well, single mothers, even when not poor, are less likely to accumulate net assets (Morissette, 2002). Thus, one can be concerned that the near future will result in a larger proportion of poor elderly women who have been single mothers most of their lives and have never received any support from the men who coproduced their children.

This said, older single mothers have lower rates of poverty than in the past because more of them have post-secondary education than in previous decades (Myles and Picot, 2006). For their part, Menaghan and Parcel (1995) find that single mothers who are employed in well-paid occupations provide their children with a home environment equivalent to that available in similar two-parent families. Unfortunately, among the never-married, these mothers are the exception, unless they had their first child later in life, were able to accumulate both social and financial resources, or had a supportive coprogenitor.

CONSEQUENCES OF FAMILY POVERTY

Poverty creates malfunctions and stressors at the community and societal levels. It is costly to a society, both in the short and long terms, as early poverty may follow people into adulthood and old age (Gilmour, 2012; Raphael, 2011; Shippee et al., 2012). For instance, Briggs and Lee (2012) estimate that poverty in Alberta costs several billion dollars a year. This includes costs of forgone earnings, crime, ill health, and the cost of children who grew up in poverty but could not escape and have since become low-income adults. Dauvergne (2012) puts the costs of the *adult* correctional system in Canada to about $4.1 billion in 2010–11. These costs, and many others, are most evident among Aboriginals who live on reserves or in the disadvantaged neighbourhoods of many of our large cities. Not only do these communities have a very low level of well-being but, as the years go by, they will increasingly be different from other Canadian communities economically (Frideres, 2011:124).

Poverty contributes to isolating people socially; for instance, low-income Canadians are much less likely to participate in community activities or to say that they trust other people than are other Canadians (Statistics Canada, 2004l). Put differently, poverty deprives communities and families of social capital. It also deprives them of food. Food Banks Canada (2009) reports that in March 2009 alone, nearly 800,000 Canadian residents walked into a food bank seeking help, which was an increase of 18 percent over March 2008—a result of the recession. The following provinces had the largest increases: Alberta saw a 61 percent increase; Nova Scotia a 20 percent one; Ontario, 19 percent; Manitoba, 18 percent, British Columbia, 15 percent; and New Brunswick a 14 percent increase. In Alberta and Saskatchewan, over 40 percent of those who were assisted were children.

Overall, Food Banks Canada (2009) estimates that at least 2.7 million persons will experience what they politely call "household food insecurity" during the year (p. 13).

This is nearly 9 percent of the population. In all provinces, between 32 percent (in Alberta) and 71 percent (in Newfoundland and Labrador) of those who approach food banks are on social assistance, indicating that government assistance is insufficient. It may not be surprising, therefore, that low income is related both to poorer health and a lower life expectancy (McIntosh et al., 2009) and this is particularly so among people with Aboriginal ancestry whose life expectancy is much lower than that of the rest of Canadians (Tjepkema and Wilkins, 2011). Egeland et al. (2010) reported, for instance, that 25 percent of all Inuit children in 16 Nunavut communities were in a situation of severe food insecurity. These children had to skip meals, went hungry, and in 60 percent of these cases did not eat for an entire day. Overall, children of immigrants and of racialized families are also at risk (Campaign 2000, 2010). In a nutshell, poverty creates stressors which then increase distress among mothers and fathers (Orpana et al., 2009). But poverty affects mothers, fathers, and children differently, in part because of gender roles (mothers versus fathers) and in part because of life stage: Children are affected early in their life course, whereas fathers and mothers are affected as adults, although many had also been poor as children.

For Mothers

Impoverished mothers who live in neighbourhoods with a high concentration of poverty, especially when criminality is added, are particularly vulnerable to failure as mothers because the circumstances under which they raise their children are simply unfair. Their ability to supervise their children is undermined by the conditions imposed by poverty. They often have recourse to harsh parenting, which leads to further behaviour problems in their children (Scaramella et al., 2008). In view of this situation, it is not the elevated rates of negative child outcomes that are surprising, but the fact that they are not higher. That so many of these mothers' children grow up to be decent citizens is a tribute both to the resilience of some children and to their mothers' extraordinary diligence and devotion.

These mothers, who are both poor *and* live in low-income areas, are deprived of the resources that a middle-class woman takes for granted in raising her children. In addition, they often lack credibility in their children's eyes, due to their poverty and, in some cases, due to their never-married status, as described by the following student:

> *"What made me the most unhappy between ages 10 and 14 is the conscious struggle I went through because of my mom* [who had her first child nonmaritally at age 18]. *I loved her but didn't pay her any respect and obedience and my brother didn't* [either]. *We had big mouths and we knew that we could get away with murder because what could she do all alone with us? . . . I got pregnant twice and had two abortions before I turned 17. I felt guilty about my mom but I wanted to have fun. . . . My brother had babies . . . and did time. . . . At 18 I finally got my act together probably because my mom was a good woman, she worked so hard and she wanted me to get an education. I wanted the respect she never got and I am no unwed mother, I tell you."*

As Cook and Fine (1995:132) note, low-income mothers have few childrearing options and cannot afford to make errors. In many neighbourhoods, they have to be more strict and vigilant because "errors" lead to delinquency, drug addiction and trafficking, early pregnancy, and even death. Therefore, success in socialization goals is seen in terms of "sheltering their children from the pitfalls of self-destruction, such as drugs, crime and cyclical government dependency" (Arnold, 1995:145). Loftier goals, such as the development of children's verbal and reading skills, are a luxury in such environments. The basic tasks of feeding, housing, and shielding their children, and especially their adolescents, from danger are at the forefront of these mothers' thoughts and energy. When Alisha, a student, was small, her mother emigrated from Jamaica to Baltimore, where Alisha and her two younger brothers joined her. Alisha was then 10 years old and was 13 when the family relocated to Toronto. In both cities, they lived in poor neighbourhoods. She recalls her life in the Baltimore "ghetto":

> "In the morning, we were often late for school and I had to get my brothers ready because my mother had left a long time ago; she had to commute to her job. . . . After school, we'd go back home minding our own business and careful to stay away from the older boys as my mother had told us to do. We'd get something to eat and then watch TV and my mother would come home around 8:00. When it was dark in the winter months we used to be real afraid alone and sometimes Jamal would disobey and leave the apartment and get into trouble with the boys down the hall. I was so scared that my mother would blame me. . . . During weekends my mother would take us grocery shopping and then we'd stay home. We didn't have friends because my mother was afraid that we'd run with the wrong crowd. . . . We were not doing well at school and when we got to Toronto we were put back two years. I was so lonely in Baltimore . . . my mother was no fun to be with because she was real strict with us because she was afraid we'd go wrong or we'd get killed."

As they become single parents, many women and their coprogenitors perpetuate and even create poverty. But this occurs more in countries that have very limited profamily and prochild social policies. For example, in countries such as Finland, single mothers' poverty rates are not much higher than that of married mothers. Why? First, Finland and other European countries provide adequate subsidies and child care arrangements that allow mothers to be employed, whatever their marital status. A second reason why the poverty rate in single-mother families is not much higher in some countries is that most first-time single mothers are older: Rates of single teen childbearing are very low, thus further reducing the potential for poverty.

For Fathers

The effects of poverty on men as fathers have been less extensively studied than those on mothers, in great part because fathers are often absent in indigent families. Fathers are affected by poverty differently, depending on the place they occupy in their families of procreation. In this respect, at least four categories of economically disadvantaged fathers exist:

1. fathers who are part of two-parent families and are gainfully employed (their salaries are low and they may have to combine two jobs, or their work is seasonal)

2. unemployed fathers in two-parent families

3. separated or divorced fathers with minimal income or who are unemployed
4. men who have fathered children and do not reside with them, who are either unemployed or earn inadequate wages

The first two categories of fathers are the most negatively affected by poverty, particularly when they are unemployed. They experience a great deal of pressure, even if only from within themselves, to support their family more adequately. They may be working two jobs, in itself a source of stress and a potential for ill health. Society defines fathers as the chief breadwinners and this assigned role can be a heavy psychological burden on the shoulders of a disadvantaged man (Edin et al., 2011). His self-esteem may be badly bruised; he may feel that he has little control over his life or that he is failing his children and spouse. In stark contrast, a man who earns a decent income is proud of his ability to support his family and his psychological health is positively affected (Schindler, 2010).

For a married or cohabiting man, unemployment becomes a source of friction, general tension, and irritability between the two spouses. Men feel diminished, experience psychological duress due to their unacceptable status and their humiliating and fruitless job searches, and may react more abrasively and withdraw emotionally from their wives or partners. These behaviours may undermine the spousal relationship and contribute to conjugal instability. Wives and partners may become resentful of their lack of financial resources and, when employed, may complain that they are shouldering the entire family's economic burden.

For their part, divorced or separated fathers who are too poor to contribute child support may distance themselves from their children. Their ex-wives may also prevent these men from seeing their children, either because they fail to support them or they are a "bad example" or a "bad influence." They are "deadbeat dads." Others were abusive before. As for those men who have fathered children nonmaritally, do not live with them, and are too poor to support them (which may well be a majority of adolescent mothers' boyfriends), very little is known as to how poverty affects them as fathers.

For Children

Child poverty denies human beings the chance of developing adequately and securely from the very beginning of their lives. It often prevents children from accessing their society's cultural capital (Bourdieu, 1977) and may substantially reduce their human and social capital (Coleman, 1990a). In contrast, children raised in higher-socioeconomic status (SES) families have more opportunities to activate their positive genetic potential (Tucker-Drob and Harden, 2012; Wickrama and O'Neal, 2013). Their family background allows them access to a wider range of experiences, including higher education (Foley, 2012). As well, parents with a higher educational level tend to spend more time with their children, especially in terms of activities related to intellectual development (Monna and Gauthier, 2008). However, not all children are affected in the same way and, in fact, despite the high risk factor that it creates, most poor families are resilient. Thus, how children are affected is contingent upon a **combination of factors**, including characteristics of the child, the family, the environment, and especially the length and timing of poverty (Conger et al., 2010; Schnittker, 2008).

Mounting evidence shows that, in terms of IQ development and school achievement, the most devastating impact occurs when children begin life in poverty. Thus, **early child poverty** is the most detrimental in terms of a child's future adult status in society (Duncan, G. J., 2010). This is in great part because homes that are disadvantaged are more likely to be less stimulating cognitively (Eamon, 2002). Also, the accompanying stressors of poverty lead to higher levels of cortisol, which, in turn, is related to a less well-developed executive function, already by age three (Blair et al., 2011; Tough, 2012). **Persistent** poverty, particularly when it begins early, is also related to negative life course outcomes (Wagmiller et al., 2006). Young children who live in persistent economic hardship are more at risk of developing several problems, particularly at the cognitive and behavioural levels, than those whose poverty is temporary (NICHD, 2005). In turn, the latter have more problems than children who have never experienced disadvantage. Early disadvantage tends to be related to higher levels of antisocial behaviour when a child is small and this high level persists when they are 12 to 13 years old. Antisocial behaviour remains higher on average than that of children who were never poor (Strohschein, 2005). Sawhill et al. (2012) describe how, in the growing up cycle, children from disadvantaged families fall behind *at every stage*—unless repeated interventions take place. These children are less likely to be ready for school at age five, to achieve core academic and social competencies at the end of elementary school, to graduate from high school with decent grades and no involvement with crime or teen pregnancy, and to graduate from college or university or achieve the equivalent income in their twenties.

Children who experience poverty at any point are three times more likely to be poor as adults than children who have never been disadvantaged, and are also more likely to earn less—even when the economy is flourishing. *It is estimated that 20 to 25 percent of children from poor families will also experience poverty in adulthood* (Ivanova, 2011). That is, the consequences of child poverty and its attendant misfortunes may far outlast the initial period of poverty and may be lifelong. The **depth of poverty** also exerts a dramatic effect on children's abilities and performance: Children in families with an income that is 50 percent below the poverty level are at a great disadvantage. Overall, children born into indigence or who are poor for many of their formative years *are denied the opportunity to actualize their abilities*, to receive a good education, often to live in a safe neighbourhood, and even to be fed adequately (McIntyre et al., 2002). In turn, these cumulative disadvantages can later produce deficits in employment and health well into adulthood: Malnutrition and stress caused by poverty imperil health and well-being in midlife and old age, and ultimately reduce life expectancy (Evans, 2004). Characteristics of the environment, such as a detrimental neighbourhood (high crime rate and proportion of poor families, pollution), quality of schools, presence of antisocial peers, as well as racial/ethnic segregation of disadvantaged minorities are also key factors and are discussed in the next chapters.

Family characteristics such as family structure (one versus two parents), parental education and mental health, and functioning such as warmth and parental monitoring of child's activities, particularly during adolescence, are also key elements that mediate the effect of poverty on children. At their negative level (e.g., low maternal education and lack of parental supervision), all of these variables represent risk

National Longitudinal Survey of Children and Youth (NLSCY)

This ongoing large-scale research program has already begun to give us a deeper knowledge of the role that poverty plays in a child's developing life. The NLSCY has been conducted by Statistics Canada and Human Resources Development Canada every two years since 1994/95. It follows a representative sample of thousands of children aged newborn to 11, in all provinces and territories, into adulthood. In each family, the person considered most knowledgeable about the child answers a set of questions designed to provide socioeconomic and general health information about himself or herself, the spouse or partners, and the child, including the child's health, general development, and social environment. When the children were 10 to 13, both parents and children provided information. At older ages, children answered questions themselves. Were the data for all these family members analyzed jointly, much information could be gathered on families rather than just on individuals.

factors: The greater the number of risk factors accompanying poverty, the more negative the effect. At their positive level, variables such as maternal warmth and stimulating activities offer resilience against the potential negative effects of poverty (Kim-Cohen et al., 2004). As well, when disadvantaged mothers have to increase their work hours, children, particularly adolescent sons who become less supervised, may suffer negative consequences in terms of their school behaviours (Gennetian et al., 2008). There is some evidence that poorer parents who have mental health problems and stressors are more likely to have a difficult spousal relationship (Maisel and Karney, 2012), a factor that would place a further burden on children. As well, economically strained families experience a greater effect of sibling delinquency on a younger brother or sister (Low, 2012).

Child characteristics also have to be considered. Any problematic child characteristic, such as low birth weight, deficient cognitive abilities, or difficult temperament and hyperactivity can combine with poverty to produce additional negative effects for the child, both currently and in the future (Ambert, 1998). In contrast, a similarly frail child raised in an economically secure family generally has a more positive life course (McLoyd, 1998). As well, children with qualities such as a more outgoing temperament are less affected by deprivation (Kim-Cohen et al., 2004).

The most visible and consistent deficit related to poverty is that disadvantaged children, on average, have lower IQs, academic skills, and school achievement, and have more behavioural problems than non-poor children (Willms, 2002b; Boyle and Lipman, 2002). On average, therefore, poor children repeat grades, drop out of school, and become unemployed or enter dead-end jobs more often than children who have never been poor. Thus, one can see why it is so important to prevent early childhood poverty, both for the short and long term. A recent longitudinal Canadian study illustrated how low income affected adolescents' chances of going to university, which was not so much because of the high tuition fees as generally believed.

Rather, the reason rested in a peer group with little interest in schooling, lower academic performance in high school, lower marks, and lower parental expectations than is the case among higher-income youths (Statistics Canada, 2007b).

Disadvantaged children have more frequent accidents than other children because their surroundings are less safe and they are less well supervised. This is particularly so in areas with a high concentration of disadvantaged Aboriginal residents (Oliver and Kohen, 2012). Poor children are also less healthy and witness violence at home more often (Moss, 2004). As well, their mental health problems far outstrip those of other children (Carey, 2001) and they are more often identified by teachers than other children for behavioural problems, and this difference remains substantial and is confirmed across the world. In a nutshell, the study of the effects of poverty on children combines elements of life course perspectives and behaviour genetics within a framework of political economy theories. The political choices made by the powerful to serve the interests of the owners of corporations create a web of disadvantages for children who end up in poverty—a web from which it is very difficult to extricate oneself from an early age on.

CONCLUSIONS: THE COSTS OF FAMILY POVERTY

Family poverty in Canada largely stems from the increasing gap between the very rich and others, an unprecedented concentration of corporate power, and the policies that result (Brenna, 2012). When all the consequences (both short term and long term) of family poverty are considered, it becomes obvious that it is much more economically advantageous for a society to invest in families and children to prevent child and adult poverty—a topic to which we return in the last chapter of this book. Otherwise, society has to keep paying throughout the decades for poverty's multiple, recurring consequences. This means that subsequent generations will pay for the current societal neglect of poor children. They will pay in terms of remedial schooling, health care, mental hospitals, juvenile courts, prisons, drug rehabilitation programs, and, later on, unemployment and medical care in old age—to name only a few of the long-term economic costs on society of child poverty (Bogenschneider and Corbett, 2010). Not to omit here the fact that children, especially those of single mothers who are unsupported by their coprogenitors, too often repeat the parental pattern of poverty in their own adult lives (Scaramella et al., 2008).

Today, people live in an era in which the economy, broadly defined, dominates society and is probably one of the most determining features of family life, along with gender, although people are rarely conscious of this effect as they go about their daily activities at home. The economy, its accompanying technology, and an ideology allowing a minority to control social policies determine job and income availability, which, in turn, have an impact on family life and even family formation and structure (Coburn, 2010; Marx, 1867). These same larger, structural forces contribute to poverty, which then creates a fertile ground upon which personal sources of poverty (such as divorce and single parenting) can grow. In turn, the personal sources of poverty reinforce the effect of the larger economic forces that cruelly bear down upon the poor. When detrimental neighbourhoods are added to this cauldron of forces, there is, on the one hand, a potent recipe for an enormous range of familial problems, and, on the other hand, an even wider range of familial resilience, survival, and success against all odds, but at an *unfair* price.

Summary

1. Economic and technological developments have contributed to the current profile of families. As a result of the changes in the economy, the gap between poor and rich families has widened.

2. The effects of economic changes on families are discussed with a focus on increase in feminine employment and two-income families, changing family time, and the rise of consumerism in family life.

3. The structural and sociohistorical sources of family poverty are reviewed, with special attention devoted to the difficulties encountered by recent immigrants and poverty among Aboriginals. The two main sociopersonal sources of family poverty are also discussed: divorce and the formation of families by single women with absent fathers.

4. The consequences of poverty are presented separately for society, mothers, fathers, and children.

5. The consequences of poverty for children are more numerous and more severe depending on several situations.

6. It would be economically advantageous for society to eliminate poverty.

Analytical Questions

1. LeVine (1990) states, "Although we take justifiable pride in the advanced technology . . . that provide(s) our high standard of living, our reliance on these external systems makes us incomplete persons in terms of adaptive competence" related to the environment in comparison to many African nations. Does such a statement still apply today? Justify your answer based on the state of our current technology.

2. Given the structural economic forces discussed at the beginning of the chapter, what could the government do for the future of our country in these domains so that families are not further burdened?

3. Analyze the two-way relationship between poverty and the formation of families by single mothers.

4. Above all, what role do men play in this economic causality path?

5. Within the family itself, how can parents alleviate the negative effects of poverty on their children?

6. What social policies would prevent family and child poverty?

CHAPTER 5

Impacts of Neighbourhoods and Housing Conditions on Family Life: Contexts of Social Inequalities

OUTLINE

Affluent Neighbourhoods

Low-Income Neighbourhoods
  When Social Problems Are Added
  Risk Factors for Children in Low-Income
    Areas
    *The Risk of Inadequate Mainstream
      Socialization*
    *The Risk of Inadequate Supervision
      and Protection*
    *Well-Functioning Families in Low-
      Income Areas*

Ethnicity and Race in Neighbourhoods

Homeless Families
  The Sources of Homelessness
  The Effects of Homelessness on Mothers
    and Children

Rural Areas and Family Life
  Farm Families
    Kinship and Gender Roles
    *Farm Families' Adaptation to
      Economic Crises*
  Vacation Areas

Families' Housing Conditions and Variety
  Condos: The New Trend
  Mobile Homes
  Family Privacy and Overcrowding

Residential Mobility

Conclusions: Neighbourhoods and
Housing as Contexts

Summary
Analytical Questions

Mark Richards/PhotoEdit

"We lived in three different places since my birth moving each time to a bigger better house. The first was a rented semi-detached that I lived in until I was 5, then we moved to a semi-detached we owned on a better street also downtown and then we moved to where we are now when I was 12 in our own house with three bathrooms and a big yard."

"My parents bought a three story semi-detached house downtown one year before I was born and we still live in the same house today. My family occupied only two rooms, a kitchen and a washroom. Every other room in the house was rented [to pay for the mortgage]. In four years, we started taking up more rooms for ourselves."

"I grew up on a farm that we still own. We could see the neighbours' farmhouses but we could not see the neighbours themselves. Except for the road turning into a near highway with more traffic coming through, nothing has changed much. Some neighbours have died and some farms have been sold but we know everyone even though we do not see them often. I like the feeling of community and I miss it here where I live during the school year. Everyone is in a rush and no one knows who lives where."

"My family has always lived in a two-bedroom apartment except that we have not lived in the same one all the time. I think we have lived in eight different ones. According to my mother we have moved because we were evicted once, we couldn't afford the rent. Then the other times we moved because the neighbours were either too noisy or too rough or too criminal. Now that we are older we are thinking of buying a townhouse just north of here [beginning of a middle-class suburb]."

Housing and neighbourhoods constitute a family's first immediate context. As the students' quotes well illustrate, families' economic conditions and lifestyles are expressed through their dwellings and surroundings. Families' daily lives—and, in turn, their children's opportunities, health, and behaviour—are affected by these surroundings. From this perspective, Chapter 5 continues the discussion on social inequality broached in the previous chapter and informed by political economy theories. Although rarely encountered in family textbooks, the study of neighbourhood effects on families is a domain of sociological inquiry with a long tradition. This tradition has recently been renewed and has become particularly visible in studies by researchers for Statistics Canada and in sociologically oriented sections of child development publications. It is a field inspired by the Chicago School of Sociology

(Park and Burgess, 1925) and by current concerns about the socioeconomic difficulties families encounter in American inner cities—problems that are replicated to some extent in many Canadian cities (Kohen et al., 2002a). In this chapter, the discussion is extended to an entire spectrum of families' housing conditions.

What is important to remember is that social inequalities have increased at the neighbourhood level. More and more, neighbourhoods are divided between the haves and the have-nots and some cities, such as Montreal, Toronto, Winnipeg, Calgary, and Edmonton, as well as Vancouver, are losing their middle class (Chen et al., 2011). Even suburbs are becoming polarized. For instance, the Peel region east and north of Toronto is experiencing an erosion of its middle class (Mendleson, 2013). Instead, now, a majority of top income tax filers live in these very same cities (Statistics Canada, 2013a). Hulchanski (2011) predicts that by 2025, 59 percent of Toronto will be populated by low-income families and individuals (versus only 19 percent in 1970) and 21 percent by high earners (versus 15 percent in 1970). For its part, the middle class that constituted 66 percent of Toronto in 1970 will be a mere 20 percent—hence social polarization.

As Reardon and Bischoff (2011) explain, there are two consequences for society and the poor themselves of intense income segregation. First, low-income families are not able to take advantage of local schools, parks, and even health services in which affluent communities invest. Second, because high-income residents then have few social contacts with low-income families, they will be less willing to support investing in city-wide services that would benefit all, such as roads, utilities, parks, services, and cultural amenities. All of these factors contribute to depriving the poor of social and cultural capital and help explain why their health is better when they live in integrated areas where services are of higher quality (Greenberg and Normandin, 2011). Segregation in low-income enclaves is one of the reasons why already disadvantaged persons in such areas have poorer health outcomes. Recent research has even found that, on average, their cognitive functioning between the ages of 55 to 65 years old is negatively affected (Aneshensel et al., 2011).

Another aspect of neighbourhoods that has changed is that many families, especially in middle-class and affluent areas, now opt to enroll their children in supervised activities after school, rather than allow them free play time on the streets of their neighbourhoods. In the past, children had the potential of turning a set of streets into a community because they played outside and established links between families, as described by this student who grew up in the 1970s:

> "I also remember how much fun I used to have playing on our street. When my family moved into our house, the housing area was new and just starting to develop and many young families also moved into the area. The street was full of kids in the same age group, and we would get together and play games such as hide-and-seek, and almost everyone would play. . . . As I now realize today, it was the kids of this age group which linked our street together, and as we got older we spent less and less time with each other."

Consequently, children's role as informal community organizers and links between families may have eroded (Torres, 2009). The advent of video games, the Internet, and cell phones, along with television, has changed children's patterns of play and social interactions. Provincially, families living in the Maritimes and Saskatchewan have the most interaction with neighbours, while Québécois have by far the least (Kremarik, 2000a). In the Maritimes, there is a greater community spirit which also contributes to life satisfaction (Helliwell and Barrington-Leigh, 2010). In contrast, Québécois are less likely than other Canadians to engage in community activities (Jones, 2000). They also feel less connected to their local community (Shields and Tremblay, 2005).

AFFLUENT NEIGHBOURHOODS

While there are many studies comparing families in low-income neighbourhoods to those in average or middle-class areas, very little information exists on family life itself in affluent or upscale neighbourhoods. As Marks (2000:613) points out, affluent families are part of **family diversity**, yet they are rarely studied (Luxton, 2006a). Rather, they tend to be positively stereotyped in view of their economic and social capital advantages or, yet, to be analyzed as the oppressing class—which may have again become a reality at the one percent level. The very rich congregate in some areas where they are sheltered from the realities of other social classes. One can think here of "Halifax's south end, Montreal's Westmount, Rockliffe Park in Ottawa, Forest Hill, Rosedale and the Bridle Path in Toronto, Tuxedo in Winnipeg, Calgary's Upper Mount Royal and West Vancouver" (Livesey, 2012:20).

In well-to-do areas, a majority of households hold assets in the form of real estate, stocks, bonds, and businesses. They own or manage a majority of the means of production in society. Their heads are heirs, investors, and top executives of large corporations (at the upper-upper class level). Others are bankers, successful stockbrokers, highly educated persons in the top echelons of the civil service, as well as owners of smaller private corporations (at the lower-upper class level). The neighbourhoods of the affluent are also home to scholars, physicians, lawyers, and entertainers at the upper-middle-class level. These families together account for about 15 percent of the population. Thus, one has to emphasize the fact that the rich are a heterogeneous group of families and that their family dynamics will be related to the lifestyle they adopt and the degree to which they emphasize values that are, or are not, purely materialistic and competitive.

However, in this group of affluent families are parents who, above all, value social and material success. The pressure to work, acquire, and consume depletes their energies to the detriment of interpersonal relationships. These parents are over involved in high-paying jobs. As a result, they have very little time for their children and are minimally involved in their upbringing, so that the children feel isolated (Luthar and Becker, 2002). Further, they are teaching values that are materialistic and competitive. Children are put on a "treadmill" of acquisitiveness and they measure their sense of self by what they have (Tough, 2012). Because these well-to-do areas are more "private" and there is a greater distance between houses, children and parents are also less likely to exchange services with friends or to feel connected to a social community in their neighbourhood (Myers, 2000). They may experience a lower level of social solidarity (Durkheim, 1893). However, adolescents whose parents are not disproportionately invested in materialistic and status-related rewards should, one can hypothesize, have a higher level of social conformity, lower anxiety, and feel more connected to family and community than the other group of adolescents (Kasser, 2002). But at the adult level, studies of physical and mental health show a positive correlation between neighbourhood income and well-being (Diener and Biswas-Diener, 2002).

The few studies that have appeared on families who live in affluent neighbourhoods are American and focused on young adolescents living in suburbs. As Luthar (2003) points out, we do not know if these results apply in all regions and to adolescents who live in affluent neighbourhoods within cities. Luthar and Becker (2002) have found that a higher proportion of these affluent suburban teens suffer from anxiety and depression, and use alcohol, marijuana, and other illicit drugs more than disadvantaged inner-city students do. They are also less supervised in their home, as young as age 10 to 12, perhaps because parents rely on the relative safety of their neighbourhoods (Luthar, 2003; Tough, 2012). Thus, a segment of relatively affluent adolescents spends their time in cars, at various "hot spots," or partying with drugs in otherwise empty homes, and even engages in gang activities leading to break-ins and thefts. Hence, one should not err in the direction of attaching an aura of superiority to a district simply on the basis of material affluence and lack of visible street criminality. An affluent neighbourhood is not automatically a "good" one in which to raise children. Obviously, family studies would benefit from an injection of research on affluent families, both in rural and urban Canadian neighbourhoods.

LOW-INCOME NEIGHBOURHOODS

An area is defined as low-income when at least *one of every five households, or 20 percent, fall under the poverty level* (Statistics Canada, 2004a). Thus, not all disadvantaged persons live in a low-income area. Overall, low-income areas have a detrimental effect on family life and on individuals' opportunities, even when families are well functioning or are not poor (e.g., Duncan, L., 2010; Xu et al., 2009). In Montreal, Toronto, and Vancouver, low-income families moving into a low-income neighbourhood tend to remain locked in for an average of five years (Frenette et al., 2004; Statistics Canada, 2004a). Families that are started in these disadvantaged areas may remain in them even longer. For their part, Natives on reserves are generally locked in poverty. Indeed, 96 of the "bottom 100" Canadian communities are First Nations (Popplewell, 2010). This is called "Canada's Third World" and the Native situation in these poor communities is frequently flagged by the United Nations. We know that poverty relates to poorer health outcomes. Whatever health statistics we examine, neighbourhoods with high proportions of Aboriginals, including reserves, generally have the highest rates of premature deaths, illness, alcohol use, childhood substance abuse, as well as suicide (e.g., Oliver et al., 2012). Poverty combines with a long tradition of discrimination, exclusion, and cultural genocide, as seen in Chapter 2, to create such results.

When Social Problems Are Added

Often, but not always, low-income areas suffer from visible cues indicating the breakdown of social order (Ross and Mirowsky, 2009)—cues such littering, graffiti, loitering, harassment, crime, and even violence. As indicated in Family Research 5.1, residents perceive this situation (Callahan et al., 2011). Generally, many of these neighbourhoods experience a *multiple* concentration of disadvantages, each feeding on the other: poverty, deteriorated housing, violent criminality, as well as drug trafficking, and single-parent households with absent fathers (Pougnet et al., 2012). The predominant factor related to high rates of violent crime in cities across Canada, as is the case in the U.S. and European countries, is low income, that is, when a high proportion of residents living in a neighbourhood are disadvantaged (Charron, 2009; Fitzgerald et al., 2004; Savoie, 2008).

Sociologist Robert Sampson and colleagues (2002) suggest that social disorganization follows when a community is no longer able to maintain **social control** or to supervise youth peer groups. For instance, both in Montreal and Regina, neighbourhoods with a high proportion of youth and low income show higher crime rates (Savoie et al., 2006; Wallace et al., 2006). Often, these areas also include the families of men and women who are or have been incarcerated, which is another problem given the high rates of recidivism (Johnson and Easterling, 2012). As well, the concentration of female-headed households not only means that children may be less well monitored when their sole parent is employed, but also that large numbers of unattached young males roam the district with few responsibilities and too much free

---

FAMILY RESEARCH 5.1

Measuring Respondents' Perception of Problems in Their Neighbourhoods

Ross and Mirowsky (1999) designed a 15-item scale to measure respondents' perception of neighbourhood problems. Respondents are given statements and indicate the extent to which they agree with them. Examples are:

- Vandalism is common in my neighbourhood.
- There is too much drug use in my neighbourhood.
- There is a lot of crime in my neighbourhood.
- In my neighbourhood, people watch out for each other.
- People in my neighbourhood take good care of their houses and apartments.

For each question on this and similar surveys, respondents are given choices ranging from "totally agree" to "totally disagree." This is what one calls "close-ended" questions.

Each response is scored so that computers can make calculations, just as in multiple-choice questions on a test. For instance, totally agree = 5, and totally disagree = 1, if the scale is a 5-point scale. Some scales range from 1 to 7 while others have choices from only 1 to 3. A larger range allows respondents to give answers that are closer to their feelings. With only three choices, respondents are very restricted in the choice of answers, and this may introduce a bias in the results—i.e., the results may not be as valid.

time on their hands. A heavy concentration of out-of-school and unemployed young males generally precludes effective social control of their activities and those of male children who grow up imitating them. Toronto has several such areas (Powell and Rankin, 2012), which, unfortunately, make the news on practically a daily basis. "Mayhem's ground zero," hails the *Toronto Star* (Doolittle, 2009). Turf wars between rival gangs have resulted in successive murders in several cities.

These young males, neither responsive to their mothers' demands nor to their children's needs, are the most important element of community disorganization (see Luster and Oh, 2001). Their perceptions of women are often of dominance and are suffused with exploitative attitudes (Fleury and Fernet, 2012). The absence of responsible adult males in households often leads to the perception of women and children as more accessible targets for victimization. Such areas undermine trust among neighbours and often lower family cohesion, all of which increase controlling behaviour on the part of parents, at the expense of children's psychological heath (White and Roosa, 2012). However, generally, adolescents are less supervised and become easier recruits for delinquency. As seen later in Chapter 10, there is a correlation* between low supervision and delinquency. This is illustrated in Figure 5.1 on the following page. (The purpose of Figure 5.1 is to allow the reader to visualize what correlations look like.) In some areas of Toronto, for instance, youth gangs kill a shocking number of other males of their own race—assured that the numerous eyewitnesses to their crimes will not report them to the police out of fear of retaliation: This is a reversed form of social control. The *Toronto Star*'s Moira Welsh (2006) captures well this situation:

> *"Some of their* [youth's] *mothers work 14-hour days and when their sons say they are at the Boys and Girls Club playing basketball, they believe them."* Later on in her text, an underground arms dealer admits being afraid of his young

FIGURE 5.1

Correlation between Adult Supervision and Number of Delinquent Acts

Each dot represents an adolescent who is placed on the diagram depending on how many delinquent acts he or she reports and how well supervised he or she is by adults (parents, teachers, neighbours, etc.). When the dots fall in a well-ordered pattern, as in Panel A, this is an indication that a good correlation exists. The straighter the line, the higher the correlation. However, in Panel B, there is no correlation because there is no pattern: The dots are scattered, which means that there is no relationship between level of adult supervision and self-reported delinquent acts. Panel A describes reality (more or less), while Panel B is presented only to illustrate what a lack of correlation looks like.

clients: *"These kids aren't very smart and they're not afraid of getting caught. It's like they think they're in a movie. . . . Boys in their early teens get power by being so vicious that brutal men fear them."*

As a result, there is a culture of silence that pervades entire neighbourhoods because no one wants to be caught "snitching" (Kirk and Papachristos, 2011). Violence continues and more mothers' children die. These same young men, by the time they are 21, often have one to three small children by different "baby mothers." There are indications, however, that a good school, even in a detrimental neighbourhood, can deflect some of these problems (Chapter 6).

These residents' physical and mental health is poorer on average (Curtis et al., 2004; Hou and Myles, 2004; Kim, 2010). Their life expectancy is five years lower for men and 1.6 years lower for women than in the highest-income areas (Wilkins et al., 2002). This deficit in life expectancy is especially salient among Aboriginals (Maxim et al., 2003). As well, violence in disadvantaged areas is related to early reproductive behaviour in both genders and lower rates of school completion (Harding, 2010). Neighbourhood disorder produces noxious results on residents' health (Hill et al., 2005).

Despite all the dire statistics and the mediatic visibility of gangs and gun violence, and its growing social inequality, Toronto is, as of 2011, the third safest city in Canada after Guelph and Quebec City, and is followed by Ottawa and Barrie, both in Ontario. The top five cities with the most crime are, first, Regina, followed by Saskatoon, Thunder Bay, Winnipeg, and Kelowna (Jackson and Whittington, 2012).

Risk Factors for Children in Low-Income Areas

The wording of this subtitle is important: "Risk factors" mean that there is a higher probability that problems will arise for families in low-income areas than in other areas (Nathers and Rivers, 2006). But, as indicated in the title of two books, *Good Kids from Bad Neighbourhoods* (Elliott et al., 2006) and *City Survivors* (Power, 2007), it certainly does not imply that the majority of families are malfunctioning or yet "pathological." Nevertheless, parents in these areas are aware of these risks, for only 35 percent of Canadians with low income agree that their neighbourhood is an excellent place in which to raise their children. In contrast, a majority of middle-class and affluent families have a positive image of their neighbourhood in this respect (Peters, 2002).

For those who are trapped in an area with a high rate of criminality, often violent, and especially those who live in a high-rise where gangs rule, the dangers are real, and parents can become helpless. In some cases, there may be selection processes that have taken place so that a certain number of less well-functioning parents drift to these areas (Boyle et al., 2007). In such cases, children experience heightened risk factors: from their parents, from their own predispositions, from the area, from the peer group, and from the interaction between all these variables. Children who are exposed to violence in their neighbourhood are more likely to develop conduct problems later (McCabe et al., 2005) and their parents are more likely to feel depressed (Kim, J., 2010). When mothers feel that their neighbourhood is dangerous, even toddlers can be affected as these mothers' parenting often becomes harsher, which increases the little ones' level of anxiety and probability of problems (Callahan et al., 2011).

The Risk of Inadequate Mainstream Socialization

Thus, one can see how children in neighbourhoods that are both poor and beset by social problems, especially when their parents are also poor, may be less adequately socialized; that is, many may not be taught the social skills needed in the workplace or in their personal lives, or general habits expected in mainstream society (Wilson, 1996). For instance, even when their families' socioeconomic status (SES) is taken into account, children as young as four and five years of age who live in poor neighbourhoods have lower verbal skills and more behavioural problems than children whose neighbours are more comfortable financially (Kohen et al., 2002a). A good-natured student from a very deprived family and neighbourhood describes the difficulties she encountered in Grade 1 when she went to a religious school out of her area. This touching quote well illustrates a young child's own resilience, maturity, and ability to plan strategically to overcome disadvantage:

> *"Going to school for the first time was supposed to be a wonderful experience and I had so much looked forward to it: At last I was going to have something special that my four younger brothers and sisters didn't have. But things turned out differently than expected. . . . I was always late in the morning because my parents never got us up on time and we were too tired because we had watched TV late, even the babies. Then I would often fall asleep at my desk so that I missed out on a lot of things and most of the children seemed to know what to do and I didn't and I didn't know what to ask my parents to buy for me and they had other things on their minds anyways; for them my being at school was just one fewer child in the house but as far as the rest was concerned they were hopeless. Then I dressed differently than the other children or my clothes were dirty because we didn't have a washing machine in the apartment and my mother had to go to the laundromat. . . . I tried to fit in by copying the other children's behaviours and even watching what their parents did for them when they picked them up. Slowly by the end of Grade 1 I had learned my way around school in terms of expected behaviour and I've wanted to be a teacher ever since."*

Where large housing developments are located, and fear and mistrust reign, parents cannot establish links among themselves and collectively monitor the whereabouts and activities of one another's children (Chung and Steinberg, 2006; Ross and Mirowsky, 2009). Thus, parents in such areas are deprived of adequate power of supervision over their children and even good parenting practices may not prevent child antisocial behaviours (Simons et al., 2002). Indeed, studies have shown that community adversity affects adolescents' mental health; in some cases, a favourable family environment cannot even compensate for the negative impact of the neighbourhood (Wickrama and Bryant, 2003). Already in 1995, Steinberg and colleagues pointed out that parenting is "more than the individualistic process that contemporary society makes it out to be." It is a group phenomenon. **Collective efficacy** refers to those social ties within the community that facilitate the collective supervision and socialization of children concerning shared norms and behaviours (Odgers et al.,

2009; Sampson et al., 1999). This also overlaps with the concept of the **effective** or **caring community** (Bould, 2004). In such a community, parents are involved in school activities, supervise their children's behaviour and associations, and get acquainted with other children's parents (Coleman and Hoffer, 1987:7).

Kupersmidt and colleagues (1995) compared children with familial vulnerabilities living in relatively low SES areas to similar children living in somewhat more affluent neighbourhoods. They found that the latter neighbourhoods served as a protective shield against the development of aggression in high-risk children. These areas do not tolerate street and school aggressiveness. Therefore, children are less likely to associate with difficult peers so that inadequate parental supervision is not as detrimental as it would be in a low-income area. Thus, it seems that a certain percentage (a **critical mass***) of low-income neighbours increases the risk for behavioural problems, subsequent school difficulties, and children's lower achievement (Sastry and Pebley, 2010). In contrast, a critical mass of affluent neighbours raises a child's chances of completing high school and developing a better sense of self-efficacy (Dupéré et al., 2012). Low-income neighbourhoods begin producing a negative effect on the development of a child's IQ by age three, above and beyond the family environment (Klebanov et al., 1998). In a nutshell, there is a larger concentration of negative child outcomes in low-income areas (Mather and Rivers, 2006; Katz et al., 2001; Ludwig et al., 2001).

The Risk of Inadequate Supervision and Protection

It is apparent, then, that many poor children in unsafe areas are at risk of not being as adequately supervised as children in other neighbourhoods (Clampet-Lundquist et al., 2011). They may have peers who belong to gangs that largely escape the supervision of responsible adults. In addition, adolescent boys often affiliate themselves with older peers for protection, which may serve to further socialize them into antisocial activities (Harding, 2009). Moreover, as mentioned, these neighbourhoods are also disproportionately populated by single-parent families, and the children are less well monitored (Fischer, 1993), particularly when mothers' educational level is low (Quane and Rankin, 1998). Single mothers are frequently beset by problems that worry them, thus taking away attention and time that could be devoted to their children. However, as emphasized earlier, supervision by parents in individual families may no longer be a sufficient element (Baumer and South, 2001). Rather, it is a collective level of supervision that is necessary (Sampson, 1997).

Finally, children and adolescents who live in areas of poverty are more at risk of being inadequately protected; many mothers feel powerless in controlling teen daughters whose deviant peers are at the centre of their lives (McDonald and Armstrong, 2001). Lack of collective supervision leaves children free to roam buildings and streets that are unsafe. It also allows them to be prey to negative opportunities that may be too difficult to resist, particularly because they are exposed to peers who may engage in deviant activities. These children are not sufficiently protected from bullying, sexual abuse, substance abuse, delinquency, and early pregnancy—especially when one considers that, when prison inmates are released, many return to their low-income areas and contribute to its disorder (DeFina and Hannon, 2010).

Well-Functioning Families in Low-Income Areas

The focus of research and social policies is on poor families and their problems; consequently, very little is known about the majority of families that succeed despite all the risks surrounding their lives. High levels of parental monitoring are particularly protective for children in poor neighbourhoods that are beset by social problems (Pettit et al., 1999). These families try to protect their children from the negative influences that pervade their area. Their tasks are numerous—they have to keep their adolescents in school and ensure that they make good grades. This is difficult to achieve in areas with a high dropout rate and the presence of gangs whose lifestyle may appear exciting to a teenager from a good family, "where nothing ever happens." Parents also have to delay or prevent early sexual activity that could lead to premature parenting (Moore and Chase-Lansdale, 2001). Then, they have to shelter their adolescents from the attraction of drugs and criminal activities. They also have to orient their youths toward the job market, a difficult task when many neighbours are unemployed.

How do parents manage? Many succeed only by controlling their children's activities outside the home. They may take them to public libraries, to swimming pools and parks, or to lessons at church. Many children (and even adolescents) are kept at home after school hours and during weekends. Overprotection is necessary to weed out negative influences and physical dangers. Choosing schools away from the neighbourhood is also an adaptive response. Indeed, children and adolescents who are exposed to violence in their area have better mental health outcomes when they perceive receiving moral support from parents and siblings and when they are more attached to their school (Ozer, 2005). In other families, mothers sacrifice their own needs for companionship (see Burton and Jarrett, 2000). A student describes his reaction to his parents' efforts to keep him safe in a high-risk area:

> "At the time I didn't appreciate having to be home early and not going in the schoolyard to play ball with the other guys. My parents were afraid that I would get into drugs, that I would get a girl pregnant and whatever. I don't know if any of this would have happened but I know that it did happen to most of my old buddies so now I can appreciate their devotion and the fact that they put up with the fuss I stirred up."

Some of these parents help organize support groups, crime prevention patrols, and other constructive activities in their immediate neighbourhood. Already in 1994, Furstenberg et al. appropriately wrote of the "supermotivation" that such parents, often single mothers, need in order to protect their children and to create opportunities for them. Overall, neighbourhoods constitute contexts for families and children: These negative areas constitute incredible forces, largely via peer groups, which dilute familial resources* and capital, hence effect. Deleterious areas amplify and reinforce vulnerabilities (Dupéré et al., 2008; Kohen et al., 2008).

ETHNICITY AND RACE IN NEIGHBOURHOODS

Often, immigrant families settle in areas where they feel comfortable at first, which may mean neighbourhoods that "contain a relatively large number of people from the same ethnic background" (Murdie and Teixeira, 2003:137). According to Statistics

Canada, the number of neighbourhoods that are largely populated by non-white groups has increased from a mere six in 1981 to 254 in 2001. A *"visible-minority neighbourhood"* is so defined by Statistics Canada *when more than 30 percent of the population is from a particular group other than white or Aboriginal* (Hou and Picot, 2004). Such an area is more likely to exhibit minority concentration, which is not the same as ethnic diversity (Hou and Wu, 2009).

More than 60 percent of these neighbourhoods are Chinese, primarily in Toronto and Vancouver. Nearly a third are South Asian, and only 13 percent are primarily black. Blacks are often less segregated from whites—which is a reversal of what takes place in the U.S. (Kim, 2009). Perhaps one reason why black families are less concentrated geographically is that the black population in Canada is more fragmented than are other non-white minority groups: It is fragmented by language, culture, social class, and geographic origins (Owasu, 1999). For their part, Aboriginal families are found in higher concentration in Winnipeg, Regina, Saskatoon, and Edmonton where they tend to live in low-income neighbourhoods (Binda, 2001; CCPA, 2009).

However, in Vancouver, Toronto, and Montreal (cities containing the majority of recent immigrants), black families are also more likely to live in neighbourhoods with a low SES and higher rates of criminality. Hou and Milan (2003) have actually found that neighbourhoods that have larger proportions of blacks are characterized by lower SES and, with growing social inequalities in general, this racial association with low income has increased. This phenomenon has also been observed for Southeast Asians in Toronto and Vancouver. However, when black families' income rises and, especially when they buy a home, they generally exit minority neighbourhoods (Myles and Hou, 2004). In contrast, among the Chinese, home ownership leads to the formation of ethnic enclaves with access to good schools, as has been the case for Italians and Jews (Balakrishnan et al., 2005).

This situation was predicted by Logan et al. (2002), who foresaw that segregation *by choice* would become more prevalent among ethnic groups with high levels of capital. These enclaves are often in suburbs, especially around Vancouver and Toronto. However, these tendencies do not (yet) result in racial segregation as it exists in the U.S., for instance; rather, what we have is segregation by income first (Balakrishnan et al., 2005). The lower incidence of residential segregation of blacks than that of Chinese may be one of the reasons why blacks have high rates of interracial unions compared to Chinese Canadians (Milan and Hamm, 2004).

HOMELESS FAMILIES

The number of homeless people, particularly families, has increased greatly, especially since the late 1990s following welfare cuts and increases in rents. In 2010, there were over 150,000 homeless Canadians (Salvation Army, 2011)—about 65,000 of whom were youth (Goldstein et al., 2011). Currently, in Toronto, each night, over 5,000 persons are homeless: About 90 percent sleep in 64 shelters (Chiu et al., 2009), and over 300 children are born to homeless women each year (Ogilvie, 2010). In many western cities, Aboriginals are overrepresented (Calgary Homeless Foundation, 2012).

The Sources of Homelessness

The homeless are the most destitute among the poor. A majority have either been poor all their lives or poised at the margin of poverty, and as many as a third suffer from mental illness (Salvation Army, 2011). However, this may not necessarily apply to the homeless who are recent immigrants as the latter may actually have fewer problems than others (Chiu et al., 2009). Families are homeless because of a lack of affordable housing. They can no longer pay rent and are evicted while others have left their homes because of domestic violence, family breakdown, or mental illness and addiction.

Among adolescents, running away is a contributing factor to homelessness, although many, particularly among immigrants, simply have no one (Chiu et al., 2009). Runaways often have been maltreated and generally have a conflictual relationship with their parents, although the latter does not unavoidably involve bad parenting (Shane, 1996:5). As Winland et al. (2011) point out, "Canadian responses to youth homelessness typically problematize family relations and generally do not help youth to re-engage with family members." Many youths from foster care also run away or are left homeless (Goldstein et al., 2011). Neighbourhood victimization, school suspension, and delinquency are also precursors, particularly among females (Tyler and Bersani, 2008). Whatever the causality, homeless youths' mental health is more precarious (Taylor et al., 2004) and they experience more problems with their parents (Collins, 2010), as well as far more drug use, than at-home youth (Mallett et al., 2005). They are often victimized, assaulted, and live in a very insecure environment (Huey, 2012). But compared to the other homeless, youths do not uniformly originate from the disadvantaged class, although a majority do. A student from an affluent and educated family describes her former street life after she was "kicked out" by parents who had, until then, tolerated all her drug- and sex-related activities:

> "I went and stayed at various friends' houses. I continued this for some weeks, but I soon ran out of friends. When one lives nowhere, on the street, one loses common ground with one's old companions. They want to talk about things they've done or seen. You're more concerned with basics. A shower for the first time in days. Some socks. Perhaps eating or actually washing your clothes. Frankly, you turn into a bum. 'Hey, what's happening man? Like, can I have your clothes, shoes, underwear, food, money, cigarettes? Cool! Blankets! Like, I've been sleeping in this stairwell, you know. It's not so bad, ya don't get caught or nothin, ya just gotta get out before the mall opens in the morning. Ya got a smoke?' . . . I spent nine months as a street kid. My experiences were, for the most part, fun. I think this is partly because I knew that I could always go home. I still don't know why I kept it up for so long. . . . It's a complete subculture and many kids simply don't want to leave even if they do have somewhere to go."

In addition to poverty, mental illness, disabilities, and addictions contribute to continuing homelessness once it has begun (Chiu et al., 2009). The John Howard Society of Toronto (2010) has found that about 33 percent of those in jails will go to shelters upon discharge. Imprisonment increases the risk for homelessness and vice versa. In the case of youth, those with fewer behavioural problems when leaving home or who decrease their problems are more likely to feel closer to their parents (Milburn et al., 2005). Parents who try to protect their homeless young adults often experience high levels of stress as a result (Polgar and North, 2009). A great proportion of homeless adults have never married; most others are either separated or divorced. Most have no relatives or even friends who can take them in during hard times, possibly because their own families are equally poor or because they have lost touch with them. The magnitude of the personal problems many suffer from may have worn out their welcome with their families or depleted the support the homeless person could receive from them. It is also possible that many of their families are equally maladapted. At the very least, the personal problems of many of the homeless certainly prevent their reintegration into society at large. They are, also, particularly very young Aboriginal women, more likely to become missing persons (Kiepal et al., 2012).

Psychiatric problems as well as various addictions are endemic and contribute to social isolation. Moreover, the decades-old deinstitutionalization of people with mental illness, without the safety net of community care that had been promised by politicians, has exacerbated the problem: Too many families are unable to shelter and care for their relatives with serious mental illness. Domestic violence is also often a cause of homelessness for women and their children, and may serve to isolate them from at least a part of their family. In fact, homeless mothers often have a long history of victimization. Once homeless, a mother's mental health easily deteriorates. In other words, homelessness is a risk factor for emotional disorder and general ill health (Carey, 2004). Nevertheless, many mothers develop coping mechanisms in order to keep their young families together and reduce the effect of the daily stressors they encounter.

The Effects of Homelessness on Mothers and Children

Most children who are homeless live in shelters with their mothers. As many of these women have been abused and/or suffer from emotional problems, their children are doubly affected (Gewirtz et al., 2009). Once in shelters, mothers encounter many difficulties in fulfilling their parental role. For instance, they no longer have control over the daily routine of their family life, whether it is bedtime or other rituals. They may, however, receive practical help as well as recourse to mental health agencies. Mothers often report a sense of becoming closer to their children while in the shelter. A woman student on welfare describes her experience:

> *"The most painful event in my life occurred two years ago after my husband left me with my two preschoolers. I became very depressed, didn't do much of anything and ended up evicted. I had no family here and we ended up in a shelter. I got even more depressed, was briefly hospitalized, my children were in foster care, and back into the shelter where I finally bounced back or else I was going to lose the children. A social worker helped me find a job and daycare and then a small apartment. But it had been a nightmare: we couldn't sleep, the children were totally out of it and went berserk, it was awful."*

In order to separate the effects of homelessness from those of poverty, studies have compared homeless children in shelters to disadvantaged children who live in their own home (e.g., Schteingart et al., 1995). The two consistent disadvantages of homelessness reside in health and education. In terms of **health**, homeless children are ill more often than other poor children. Their incidence of respiratory infections is especially elevated as a result of crowded conditions and the sharing of inadequate sanitary facilities. One can also presume that noise, overcrowding, and parents' distress depress children's immune systems so that they easily catch viruses.

The second domain in which homeless children are at a particular disadvantage is **schooling**. Their disadvantage in this domain stems from a variety of interlocking causes: They change schools, are sick more frequently than other children, and have higher rates of absenteeism. The crowded conditions in which they live are not conducive to homework, and may even deprive them of sufficient sleep. Their parents may be too distressed or emotionally unbalanced to help and guide them. Older children may not want to go to school because they fear the ridicule of peers who, even though poor themselves, at least can claim a permanent address. Frequent school changes isolate homeless children socially, lead to disengagement from school, and even to falling in with a crowd of antisocial peers. Moreover, schools are unprepared to address these children's multiple problems as many of them have been in at least two different shelters.

RURAL AREAS AND FAMILY LIFE

The rural population (farm and non-farm) is decreasing and accounted for 19.7 percent of the Canadian population in the 2006 census. The farm population itself included only 2.2 percent of all Canadians or just over 684,000—although these percentages are higher in the Prairies, particularly Manitoba where the population is 35 percent rural and 11.5 percent farm. There were 229,000 farms in Canada in 2006, half of which were family operated (Statistics Canada, 2008d). The lives of rural families have undergone substantial change in recent decades because of increased proximity to urban areas, technological development, and economic uncertainty. In some regions, particularly when rural life involves the seasonal fishing or lumber industries, young people migrate to larger cities, thus leaving many rural communities populated by seniors and middle-aged householders. This phenomenon is especially relevant to Newfoundland and Labrador, where fully 42 percent of the population is rural, largely coastal.

In other cases, rural areas grow into towns or suburbs and become populated by young families who have recently moved to a new housing subdivision: Fathers and mothers commute to work in the nearest city or even metropolitan area, sometimes an hour or more each way, in order to remain in their towns where housing and land prices are lower and where they feel that it is easier to raise a family away from the hectic pace of the big cities (Statistics Canada, 2011c). Rural areas offer families a better chance of being members of a true community. Indeed, in rural communities over 50 percent of individuals know all their neighbours versus only 16 percent in cities (Statistics Canada, 2005c). Greater social cohesion may offer family members advantages from which urbanites do not benefit. However, rural areas are not devoid of problems such as drugs, delinquency, and homelessness (Edwards et al., 2009).

Of course, many rural residents make their living without relying on nearby cities. However, when rural family members lose their jobs, it is more difficult for them than for urbanites to find another occupation at reasonably close proximity. This stems in part from the fact that rural areas are less diversified at the economic level: They contain a higher proportion of blue-collar workers than do urban zones. White-collar workers with more education tend to move out of rural areas so that this selective out-migration reduces the diversity of human resources available to all rural families. In areas with fewer than 5,000 persons, young people, especially women, leave home much earlier than other youth (Beaupré et al., 2008). There are fewer alternatives in rural areas, including health services and care of the elderly (Morris, 2004).

Farm Families

Farm families constitute a tiny minority of the total population, even though they feed the entire country and many other parts of the world as well. Farm productivity increased tremendously in the 20th century: In 1946, about 1.2 million Canadians worked on farms as a main job while only 346,205 did so in 2001, and even fewer in 2006, down to 327,055 (Statistics Canada, 2008c)—a 5.5 percent decrease in just five years. In 1931, one in every three Canadians lived on a farm; by 2006, only one out of every 46 did (Statistics Canada, 2008e). In some parts of Canada, especially near expanding suburbs that form a ring around large cities and metropolitan areas, farmland is rapidly disappearing. This creates a multiplicity of problems in terms of lack of preservation of the environment, availability of fresh produce, and general well-being, not to omit a cultural loss because farm families are part of our **diversity** (Josey, 2008).

Children growing up on farms are not only more involved in the family's economy, but when small, they also benefit from the lessons of the natural environment and helpful relationships with neighbouring families.

alekuwka83/Fotolia

As well, the median* age of farm operators has increased to 52 and 50, respectively, for men and women: 40.7 percent are 55 and older. The **aging** of the farm population is particularly evident in British Columbia where 13.5 percent of farm operators are over 65. Such numbers have deep implications for the well-being and care of senior couples and elderly widowed persons in rural areas, as they may not necessarily have adult children living in close proximity.

Farmers are far from being a homogeneous category as they vary in terms of their economic circumstances: Some are tenants and others are migrant workers; some own small acreage and are struggling financially, and others are involved in large-scale agribusiness and ranching. Moreover, there are differences in the farming lifestyle, depending on the crops produced—from grain to cattle in the Prairies and the west, to fruit, vegetables, and wine-grapes in southern Ontario, to dairy products in Quebec, Ontario, and Newfoundland (Coyne, 2011).

The level of technology utilized also determines the daily activities of farm families, from the Amish and Mennonites, who often do not have recourse to fuel- or electricity-propelled machinery, to others in which computers dictate levels of feed, fertilizers, and pesticides. Farm families also vary with respect to their degree of isolation. Many farms cluster along well-traveled rural roads, yet others are more remote and connect with neighbours in their area only via long drives, a ferry, the telephone, and for a few, the Internet and cellphone.

Kinship and Gender Roles

Although nearly 28 percent of all farm operators are women, farm families tend to be patrilineally oriented because property is generally acquired via a son's inheritance—in fact, his parents frequently live nearby. Consequently, although grandparents play a more salient role in rural families than in urban ones, paternal grandparents are particularly important (King et al., 2004). This is in contrast to the urban situation where maternal grandparents play a larger role. The trajectory of inheritance is a long one across the two generations and involves decades of shared familial work, which leads both to family cohesiveness and stress (Froese, 2012). This situation can become problematic when middle-aged parents begin to think about their wills. If they decide the inheritance should favour the son who is interested in farming, then the bulk or even the entirety of the estate has to go to him if he is to survive at all economically. Perhaps very little can be passed on to the other children—a situation that may create sibling conflict later on in life (Froese, 2012; Taylor and Norris, 2000).

Despite the hazards of farming, Swisher and colleagues (1998) found that marital and familial conflict was less frequently reported by farm men than non-farm men in Iowa. However, when conflict exists, it is particularly detrimental because farm families are units of production. Thus, conflict threatens the normal pattern of subsistence, employment, and kinship interdependence. Non-farmers, in contrast, establish more obligations based on friendship and can escape, to some extent, from the negative impact of family conflict. The potential for conflict and the experience of stress is especially great for a daughter-in-law in multi-generation farm families. This is more so when she feels left out of decision making and perceives her relationship with either of her in-laws as deficient.

Farm machinery does not require as much physical strength to operate as before, thus many wives work in the fields and even prefer this lifestyle to staying home. However, wives are more likely to be fully involved on vegetable farms, on those that have a mixture of crops and livestock, and on organic farms than on those where mechanization is very heavy and intensive crop production exists—perhaps a matter of gender roles (Hall, 2007). Children raised on farms are initiated in the use of large machinery early in life. It is not uncommon for 12- to 15-year-old boys to drive combines alongside their fathers in the fields—even though they do not qualify for a driver's license.

Farm couples devote more time to their livelihood than do other Canadians—as much as 108 hours a week on large dairy farms. Couples share their long hours, but husbands put far more time on farm work while wives do a much larger share of the housework. This division of labour, however, is more egalitarian on small than on large farms. As well, when young children are present, wives do somewhat fewer hours of farm work but much more housework than their husbands or than wives without young children (Silver, 2001).

One aspect of the lives of family farms that is not much discussed are those 40,000 seasonal workers from Mexico and the Caribbean who come yearly for several months to Canada on a special permit to work on farms. Most are men who leave a wife and children at home and about three percent are women, generally single mothers who also leave children behind in the care of others (Preibisch, 2012). Their lives here are difficult, with many health risks, poor living conditions, and social isolation. It would be worthwhile to study their family lives from the perspectives of the spouses and children back home.

Farm Families' Adaptation to Economic Crises

One of the reasons for the increasingly small numbers of farmers, apart from the incessant work required and the costs of fertilizers and equipment, is that farm income is rather unpredictable, depending as it does on weather conditions here and around the world. Farm families also depend on subsidies, quotas, and crop insurance—which all tend to favour agribusiness and large farms. Surprisingly, farm incomes have increased recently in several provinces (Statistics Canada, 2012d). Still, by 2006, 48 percent of farm operators held a second job. At the lowest farm income level, 60 percent did so (Statistics Canada, 2009m). In fact, more and more farmers have a job other than farming as their primary employment—a situation with a long history in Canada, as evidenced, for instance, with Nova Scotia's shipyard communities in the 19th century (McCann, 1999) and Saskatchewan's homesteaders (Rollings-Magnusson, 2008). These jobs often took fathers away for long months, thus enlarging women's role (and increasing their work) in their home and community (Trussell and Shaw, 2007). In order to respond to economic and environmental challenges, many farmers are diversifying into new crops, new products and livestock (llamas, for instance), and even on-farm processing of produce (Bessant, 2006). These entrepreneurs tend to be families that are more attached to their farm and where both spouses see their agricultural work as their main occupation and branching out may be a way of retaining family members in full-time farming (Barbieri et al., 2008).

Mothers who have to seek off-farm employment not only benefit their families financially but they also gain personal and occupational skills as well as making new social contacts. However, most miss their previous lifestyle and long to return to work alongside their husbands. In some families, even adolescents increase their off-farm employment hours or leave school and take a job in order to help the family financially or to be self-supporting, thus minimizing family expenditures. In other families, both boys and girls increase their on-farm economic activities or work for relatives. A student explains how her contribution to her family's economic survival as an adolescent had shaped her sense of self:

> *"Between the ages of 10 to 14 I recall being very happy because I really felt that I was important in my family. I helped my mother with cow milking before I went to school and we enjoyed each other's company. After school, I helped my father feeding the same cows and cleaning up. It was dirty work but it was meaningful because we all had to pitch in as we were afraid to lose the farm."*

Vacation Areas

Many rural areas near lakes, rivers, oceans, or skiing facilities have been transformed into vacation spots for urbanites while still serving as a primary home for regular residents. Thus, cottages, condos, hobby farms, or other forms of rural property develop where city families can choose their lifestyle and replenish their relationships, as described by a student:

> *"I was especially happy there* [at the cottage] *because my family was always around, and there was a certain air of freedom that we could not find anywhere else. This is probably due to the fact that the cabin had no electricity or hot or cold running water. So essentially we were roughing it. We received water from a manual pump in the kitchen, and we got light from oil lamps and warmth from blankets and each other. We never knew or cared what time it was or what anyone else was doing, just as long as our little world was happy, and we only had guests on the rare occasion. It seemed like a different world because we were the only ones* [in the area] *with no means of communication, such as telephone, radio, television, or close neighbours to rely on. . . . For instance, we counted on catching fish at least three dinners of the week, so it became a matter of survival."*

This quote is interesting from yet another perspective: It illustrates the lifestyle contrasts that may exist between urban families on vacations and neighbouring rural families. The former at times embrace a temporary frugal lifestyle, whereas the latter often have to struggle to avoid it. In many areas, rural families make a living by offering goods and services to these tourists and cottagers.

Ownership of a second residence in the countryside is generally related to a higher income and some level of wealth. About 7 percent of Canadian households own a vacation home. Of these, only 26 percent are owned by married families with children. However, many other children and adults have free access to such homes via their grandparents or other relatives (Kremarik, 2002). Others rent cottages or condo units. It would be interesting to study the organization of family time and dynamics as families shift from urban residence to vacation home. This is yet another element of family life for which no research exists.

FAMILIES' HOUSING CONDITIONS AND VARIETY

In this section, we look at the quality of the interiors in which families live. Not only are families affected by their neighbourhood surroundings, but their functioning is also related to the size of the lodging, the state of its maintenance, the personal space it allows, how close it is to other buildings, the level of noise, and its costs (Bryant, 2009). For instance, the state of **maintenance** or deterioration of a dwelling can have an impact on family atmosphere as well as on health. The houses and apartments in which low-income families live may be poorly ventilated in the summer and inadequately heated in the winter, and the plumbing may have so deteriorated that leaks frequently happen. Such situations occur mainly in rental and social housing and in poor neighbourhoods, thus further adding to the diminished state of well-being of the disadvantaged. As well, in many cities, dilapidated housing is one of the correlates of higher crime rates. In France, it also correlates with higher feminine mortality—either because women in poor health can only afford this type of housing or because of the general impact of this housing and area on their health (Mejer and Robert-Bobée, 2003).

Overall, the burden of **housing costs** has increased since the 1970s and then even more after the 1990s, both in terms of rental and of ownership. There are serious concerns about affordability if and when interest rates go up. This housing burden is particularly heavy for single-mother, minority families with three or more children, and Natives (Tjepkema et al., 2011a:Table a). *Two-thirds of Canadians own their home*; ownership is most common in the Maritime and Prairie regions (about 75 percent), while Quebec has the lowest rate at 58 percent (Lefebvre, 2003). Before the Second World War, ownership hovered around 45 percent. The Canadian rate of ownership is similar to that of the U.S., lower than that of Ireland and Spain, and higher than that of France and Germany.

Home ownership tends to be the rule among top-earning families, but what is of particular significance among the more affluent is that ownership occurs early on in family formation and remains stable thereafter. Young couples coming from high-income families are often helped by their parents. (This is referred to as the intergenerational transmission of wealth.) In contrast, home ownership occurs later in the family life cycle among other social groups, including the middle class. For instance, in 2006, 77 percent of higher-income persons aged 20 to 34 were homeowners. In fact, 94 percent of high-income couples aged 20 to 34 with children owned their home, which is a large increase from 1971 when only 65 percent of such couples were homeowners. As well, 60 percent of single young adults with high incomes were owners compared to only 13 percent in 1971 (*Canada Year Book*, 2011). Thus, the importance of home ownership has increased as a cultural value and investment but is more attainable with higher incomes. Of high-income persons aged 55 to 64, 90 percent were homeowners but among low-income ones, only 55 percent were.

Thus, at the higher-income levels, children grow up in homes that are owned by their parents, whereas children in other families reach this goal at a later age or never. *What is important to recall here is that home ownership inequality has increased.* In 1971, among young persons, 31 percent of those with lower incomes owned their homes compared to 38 percent among top earners—not a huge difference. But, by 2006, only 19 percent of low-income young persons were homeowners versus 77 percent of the same-age top earners (Hou, 2010). *Thus, low-income persons are much less likely to be homeowners now than in 1971 while top earners are more likely to be so—reflecting the increasing gap between rich and poor* discussed in Chapter 4, even among young adults. In addition, we know that renters have, on average, a lower income than owners and more are poor. In 2008–09, 87 percent of those who had recourse to a food bank lived in rented accommodations (Food Banks Canada, 2009:8).

Further, the **size** of the family home has been increasing steadily at a time when the number of persons living in the average household has decreased from 3.7 persons in 1971 to 3 in 2000 (Statistics Canada, 2002b). Between 1951 and 1996, homes passed from having 5.3 rooms to 6.1 rooms and even the most modest new homes now have two and even three bathrooms. Currently, among the well-to-do, particularly the new rich, the tendency is to build homes with over 4,000 square feet. This phenomenon is often referred to as the "mansionization" of housing; others call them "monster" homes or McMansions.

Currently, very little is known about how family space contributes to increasing or eroding intimacy as well as parents' ability to socialize their children. There is less sharing of familial space (Clark, 2002), a factor that may contribute to feelings of isolation (Pappano, 2001). Researchers might focus on how families who live in large dwellings (where each member has his or her own separate suite, often on different floors) develop mechanisms that contribute to family cohesiveness and interaction as opposed to isolation and interpersonal distance. Such families may have more clearly delineated boundaries within their system than others: The parents on one side and each child separately on the other side.

Condos: The New Trend

Condominiums (or strata in B.C.) have existed for several decades in North America (and in Europe before this, with different names). But it was only in the late 1990s that this mode of housing really became more prevalent in Canada as a result of climbing prices of detached homes, immigration, and lack of available space in large cities. This is an ecologically friendly form of housing in the sense that 300 households can live vertically where, before, only 10 might have. But it is also a way for the government to shift some of its civic responsibilities onto individual owners (Kern, 2010). Owners then acquire an additional layer of governance with boards of directors that too often turn them into second-class owners. This said, condo living may be ideal for extended families that do not want to live together but would want to be close to one another: Indeed, I am aware of several instances where an adult couple lives on one floor and their aged parents live on another or in an adjacent building.

Unfortunately, there is no information on family life in condos as it is not a topic that has been researched—perhaps because this is not a lifestyle that university professors generally choose! Even Statistics Canada cannot tell us how many people or households live in condos because such residents fall under the rubric of "apartment" or "multi-unit" dwellers. But in Ontario, over one million persons are condo dwellers. Interestingly, contrary to detached homes, the size of condo apartments is shrinking: In 2000, the average size of a resale condo in the Toronto area was 1,052 square feet, whereas it was 749 for new units in 2011 (*Toronto Star*, 2011b). Thus, more and more singles live in condos, some as tiny as 300 square feet or the size of a bedroom. Some condo residents may be owners while others are tenants of owners who live elsewhere, whether in the same city, in Canada, or abroad. For instance, in some areas of Toronto, over 60 percent of condo residents are tenants. There are concerns that some of these condos may become "towers of poverty" or *vertical poverty*. In 1981, about 30 percent of low-income families rented in a high-rise. By 2006, this had increased to 43 percent (Baluja, 2011). For non-resident owners, condos are simply an investment. In certain cities, such as Toronto and Vancouver, a great proportion of absentee condo owners are from China, Taiwan, South Korea, Russia, and Iran.

It is regrettable that, with one exception (Kern, 2010), researchers, especially urban sociologists, are missing out on the opportunity of studying basic issues of family life in condos—and such issues abound as can be gleaned via letters posted on a Canadian website providing information for condo owners. *This is another example of research lagging behind new realities.* Sociologists would want to know what adaptations or constraints does condo living require of couples and parents? What are specific family issues that arise, if any? Are condo dwellers less or more inclined to participate in neighbourhood, school, and other civic activities that would provide social capital to children and parents alike? How do condos facilitate immigrant families' integration to Canadian life in view of the close proximity of neighbours compared to other type of housing? This is only a sample of the questions that sociologists and psychologists could address.

Mobile Homes

At the other extreme of housing diversity are mobile homes, which, in 1996, represented about 1 percent of private dwellings. Although 57 percent are located in rural areas, others can be found in small cities and towns (Kremarik and Williams, 2001). Mobile homes are more likely than other dwellings to house smaller families, single people, and seniors. Families living in such homes have on average a lower income and over half of the adults have not completed high school (MacTavish, 2007). In fact, mobile homes are convenient for lower-income families because they are less expensive to acquire and cost less to heat, for instance. As well, such homes can be relatively roomy (Ladurantaye, 2010).

However, dwellers often lack sources of community support and may be marginalized (Notter et al., 2008). Their homes are built less solidly and require more repairs and maintenance than other dwellings; as well, they are more hazardous during stormy weather. As a result, a larger proportion of mobile homes are in poorer condition than other types of residences, although new developments are well maintained (Ladurantaye, 2010). Well over 300,000 Canadians live in mobile homes; however, there is no research on family life and community dynamics in this alternative type of residence. Some harbour resilience while others shelter domestic abuse, child maltreatment, and elder abandonment (Notter et al., 2008).

Family Privacy and Overcrowding

Family privacy is both a characteristic within the family itself and a situation of the family toward the rest of the world (Coontz, 2000:284). Family life is much less public than it used to be when homes were designed with front porches, for instance. Now, the family has retreated inside or to the backyard. Families have become more individuated*, as individualism is closely related to the concept of privacy. Technological change has contributed to the notion of privacy. For instance, air conditioning (the windows of the house are closed); few, if any, trips to the laundromat (most homes have washers and dryers); and even a reduction in neighbourhood grocery shopping (as online shopping increases in popularity and as many families shop in larger malls or superstores where they go by car). All these factors have enhanced privacy and separation from one's immediate neighbourhood.

As reviewed by Berardo (1998), family privacy allows couples to resolve their problems without external pressure. It serves to protect family members against the pressures of the external world. In this sense, privacy functions as a buffer as well as a protection. In contrast, public exposure and revelations are probably some of the elements that contribute to the rapid and successive divorces and repartnerings often occurring among film, sports, and entertainment personalities. On the other side of the coin, privacy also means that abuse and neglect can go on for extended periods of time without external detection and/or intervention. Therefore, privacy can camouflage problems and prevent victims from seeking help, as is the case in some instances of elder abuse.

Overcrowding is the opposite of privacy and is often, but not always, a result of poverty (Rizk, 2003) and the lot of renters rather than owners (Engeland et al., 2005). It is not generally a valued state, so that Canadian-born or raised families do not accept it as a fact of life and may find it highly stressful. Therefore, when too many family members congregate in too little space, the following is likely to happen. First, parents may not be able to spend time alone; the level and quality of their communication and intimacy may suffer. Second, personal hygiene may become problematic when the facilities have to accommodate too many persons. Third, contagious illnesses, such as colds and flu, may spread more easily in families living in cramped quarters, so that work or school days are frequently missed. Moreover, neither children nor adults may get enough sleep; as a result, their physical and mental health may be affected. Fourth, the noise level may distract children and prevent them from doing schoolwork, particularly when the television is on at all times in the small dwelling. (Here, one can see that technology exacerbates the impact of our ideological preference for private space.) Children with an attention deficit disorder may be particularly affected in this context.

Finally, family members unwittingly compete for scarce space so that conflict may arise; in some families, siblings may quarrel more, parents may yell at them and tell them to "shut up," and the atmosphere is one of exasperation. Particularly affected both by overcrowding and dilapidated housing are Aboriginal families, especially those living on reserves (Tjepkema et al., 2011a). For instance, in 2006, 28 percent of First Nations people lived in homes that needed major repairs—including 44 percent of those on reserves—compared to only 7 percent of the non-Aboriginal population (Gionet, 2009). As well, 44 percent of recent immigrant households have to live in housing that both needs repairs and is too small (Engeland et al., 2005).

Nevertheless, some families do cope well in cramped quarters. These are often immigrants who were used to very little space in their home country because of weather, culture, war, or poverty. In fact, their crowded situation in Canada may be an improvement over what they had at home. Others came from high-density areas, such as Hong Kong, where small apartments are the norm, or Cuba or Moscow, where several families may share a few rooms. Again, these new Canadians may adapt well to this situation as it compares favourably to what they left behind and, at any rate, they expect to do better in the near future. Tolerance of overcrowding therefore depends on cultural norms and the family's stage in the life course.

RESIDENTIAL MOBILITY

Between 2001 and 2006, 41 percent of the total population had moved. Half of these moves took place within the same municipality (Statistics Canada, 2007d). Turcotte and Vezina (2010) show that 14 percent of persons between the ages of 25 and 44 in Toronto, Montreal, and Vancouver had moved from the core city to the periphery between 2001 and 2006 because they had become parents. Over 1.5 million Canadians moved in 2004 alone (Statistics Canada, 2005d). However, Canadian mobility is a historical fact, not a new phenomenon: The frequency of residential moves within and out of Canada in the past has been underestimated (Lavoie, 1981; Stott, 2006; Van Die, 2005). Some provinces, particularly Newfoundland/Labrador, have had historically high rates of outmigration, both to the U.S. and Ontario, as well as Alberta more recently, because of the degradation of the fishing industry and the seasonal nature of the work available to young people. In contrast, Europeans change residence far less frequently.

Moving from one home to another and, particularly for children who are already in school, from one neighbourhood to another, is an important transition in a family's life. It does require adjustment. Further, a family move does not benefit its members equally (Audas and McDonald, 2004). Several studies have documented that the number of moves experienced by children and adolescents correlates with lower school achievement and lower rates of high school completion, and even with behavioural problems and early sexuality (see South et al., 2005). This may be related to the fact that school-age children in separating and divorcing families move the most. By 2006, for instance, 57 percent of Canadians who were in a separated family had moved within the past five years as had 45 percent in divorced families compared to 34 percent for those in married families (Statistics Canada, 2007d). Thus, children of separating parents are already at risk of poor school performance and, by moving, acquire another risk. When divorced families relocate, they tend to go from being owners to renters because their economic situation has deteriorated. Consequently, the adjustment that children and adolescents have to make may be too demanding: They incur four losses simultaneously—their old family structure, their school, their former peer group, and their house. As well, adolescents' friendship networks also suffer (South and Haynie, 2004). They may have difficulties integrating themselves into existing peer groups. As a result, they may be attracted to new peers who are more delinquent, thus accounting in part for their higher rates of delinquency and violence (Haynie and South, 2005).

Adjustment may be particularly difficult when a move leads to an unstable neighbourhood where the social control of youths is largely nonexistent. In such contexts, an adolescent from a family that has just suffered a break-up may be particularly susceptible to opportunities for delinquency. School performance suffers with mobility, but this impact applies more to one- than to two-parent families. Children in one-parent or stepparent families seem to suffer from any mobility (Tucker et al., 1998). The reason is that such families face more adjustments and have less social capital that can be devoted to children to counterbalance the potentially negative impact of moving. A male student describes part of this dilemma:

> "The most painful thing that happened to me was when I had to move. I lost all my friends and had to leave my school but the worst ... was coming to a new school with new kids. They aren't very nice in Grade 6 if you don't wear the same clothes as them or have as much money, etc. This was truly one of the hardest periods of my life. I remember going into the cafeteria at lunch and having to sit by myself or with some other losers who were in the same position as me. I was bothered and picked on by a lot of people because I was small and it took me a long time to adjust to my situation. Of course I eventually made friends but I never quite made it with the people who I most wanted to be friends with."

(As an aside, it is interesting to note that the student labeled other children in the same situation as "losers." This evaluation reflects cultural norms of what is entailed in being successful in one's peer group.)

When a family relocates in order to enhance a father's position on the job market, the mother may not benefit. She may actually have to abandon her own job, and if the move takes the family to another province or even to the U.S., she may lose her social support network. Nevertheless, spouses who move because of the relocation of the chief breadwinner generally experience wage growth (Audas and McDonald, 2004). But children have to adjust. Elder's (1995) developmental or life course theory offers a new perspective on this situation. What is an advantage for the father or mother becomes a dislocation in the children's lives: The two generational stages in the life course of a family do not mesh and the goals of one are incompatible with the needs of the other. However, this disparity in the life-course timing of the family members can be mitigated in several ways. Husbands or wives can compensate to some extent for their spouses' loss of social support, and may even accept a promotion requiring relocation only after their spouses have also found a new job. Because of "prevailing labor market inequality and gender ideology" (Shauman, 2010:390), it is still rare that a family moves to meet a wife's career opportunities, but it happens.

As far as children are concerned, a harmonious home as well as the continued or even increased involvement of both parents in their lives is an important stabilizing element. Mothers' involvement helps, but the combined paternal and maternal involvement mitigates the disruptive effects of mobility on children more effectively. When only one parent is involved, the social capital from which children can draw on may not be sufficient during a transition period. When neither parent is involved, because of financial or career pressures or because of personal problems, children are at high risk of failing to integrate themselves in a positive way in their new neighbourhood and school.

CONCLUSIONS: NEIGHBOURHOODS AND HOUSING AS CONTEXTS

This chapter reinforces and extends the findings presented in Chapters 3 and 4 on ethnic and economic inequalities. In a nutshell, particularly via the sections on disadvantaged neighbourhoods and homelessness, this chapter is also informed by political economy theories as well as rational theories, the latter in terms of the development of capital in children and the role of the effective community (or lack thereof) in child outcomes. We also saw how disadvantaged neighbourhoods present a context in which children may be at risk of not fulfilling their positive genetic inheritance. Further, neighbourhood structure and housing conditions not only have an impact on people's lives, particularly on children's opportunities, but also reflect a society's values concerning social diversity. Finally, this chapter also serves as a link between the chapter on economic inequalities and the next one on education and religion, two institutions that constitute additional contexts influencing family life—in some cases, limiting family members' opportunities and, in other cases, enhancing them.

Summary

1. Neighbourhoods constitute families' first immediate, external context. Urban areas vary widely, ranging from metropolises to small towns, and include a great variety of suburbs. The types of families residing in these various areas differ by social class, race, and household composition.

2. Affluent neighbourhoods are described with an emphasis on the fact that little research exists on families who are well-to-do. Neighbourhoods that are poor and to which social problems are added present several risk factors for children.

3. Disadvantaged areas nevertheless contain a high proportion of families that function well and are resilient. But the tasks facing parents of successful children are enormous, as parents have to be far more vigilant than similar parents in middle-class areas.

4. Canadian minority groups are not as segregated as they are in the U.S., particularly blacks. However, Chinese families are becoming more segregated by choice.

5. Entire families have joined the ranks of the homeless and are generally found in shelters. The key forces leading to homelessness are

discussed as is family life in shelters. Compared to poor children living at home, homeless children have more health- and school-related problems.

6. Rural areas vary in their settings and in the employment opportunities they offer to families. Farm families are now in the minority and many are severely stressed economically. Today, most farm couples combine off-farm work with farming to make ends meet. Rural areas also contain vacation neighbourhoods for city families, another topic on which little research exists.

7. The state of maintenance of a dwelling can have an impact on family atmosphere and health. Three types of housing trends are discussed: mansionization, condo dwelling, and mobile homes. Privacy and overcrowding are also considered.

8. Family residential mobility is discussed along with its consequences for family members within the life course.

9. Neighbourhood structure and housing conditions affect families' lives and reflect society's values concerning social diversity and reflect social inequalities.

Analytical Questions

1. How can the theme of the effective community help determine social policies that could improve the lives of children and parents living in high-poverty areas where social problems may exist?

2. How different are well-functioning families living in high-risk areas compared to those living in middle-class neighbourhoods?

3. Given what you have read in this chapter, is the building of "social" housing developments in certain areas of town a good social policy? (Support your answer with the help of research results.) If your answer is no, what might be a better solution?

4. Suggest at least three research questions that are lacking concerning rural families and housing conditions in general.

5. Draw up a correlation diagram showing a relationship between numbers of moves in young adults' past lives and school achievement.

CHAPTER 6

Roles of Educational Institutions and Religious Participation in Family Life

Monkey Business/Fotolia

OUTLINE

The Educational System: An Overview

Child Care: Quality and Outcomes
  The Effects of Child Care on Children
  Early Childhood Education for Children
    in Low-Income Families
  The Effects of Child Care on Parents

Schools and Families
  Parental Involvement
    *Parents' Higher Social Class and
      Involvement*
    *Barriers to Low-Income Parents'
      Involvement*
  Family-School Compatibility
  Schools and Antisocial Behaviour
  Minority-Group, Immigrant, and
    Aboriginal Children

Private Education
  Private Schools
  Home Schooling

Religious Participation and Family Life

The Role Played by Religiosity
in Family Life
  Religiosity Correlates with Well-Being
  Religiosity Scaffolds the Parental Role
  Religiosity Relates to Marital Quality
    and Stability
  Limitations of Religion for
    Nonconventional Families

Conclusions: The Balancing Act of Family
Responsibilities

Summary
Analytical Questions

Roles of Educational Institutions and Religious Participation in Family Life

"Between the ages of 14 to 18 the hardest part was school, school, school. I was not a good student, not motivated and a shit disturber, it seems I did my best to be the worst. . . . I ended up suffering for this and dropped out and [moved] back in at my parents' pleadings so that I was still in high school at age 20. . . . It wasn't all my fault because the school was the pits, the teachers didn't care, they just gossiped about their divorces and whatever and the students were more or less like me so we all deserved each other except that our parents didn't deserve this and it took them four years after that to convince me to go to a community college from where I enrolled here."

"High school was my best experience, better than my friends because my teachers were supportive and I got involved in about 10 clubs and participated in various contests and won and my parents were proud of me. It was an exciting time for all of us because both my parents volunteered, my father as a coach, and my mother helped organize many school functions. They were well liked by all the teachers and even the students and it was just great, I felt at home everywhere I went."

"For sure the cornerstone of all my values and of my life for that matter is my faith in God. We're very religious by today's standards in the younger generation and at times I used to be teased by kids in high school about it so I like the freedom of university life in this respect. The only problem is that university life says nothing about religion. I haven't had a single prof in sociology who even went so far as to say a single word about it."

"I get along reasonably well with my parents now that they accept my lack of interest in religion and a few other deviances on my part. But I've never been religiously inclined and I don't feel I miss out on anything."

Education and religion are key cultural and social institutions* that have an impact on family life. In view of the salient role that education plays in children's outcomes, it will not surprise the reader to learn that students' autobiographies contained a great deal of material about their experience with the school system. In fact, schools are the second most frequently mentioned source of past misery, after peers—and they are not often referred to as a key source of happiness. For its part, religion plays a dominant role in the lives of only a minority of students. For the majority, it is a matter of membership and general beliefs rather than active participation. However, in recent years, more and more of my students have come from Asian and Middle

Eastern countries; these Hindu, Sikh, and Muslim students mention religion as a central theme in their lives more often than most other students. In this chapter, the focus is on religiosity rather than religion per se, in order to link this with the lived experience of families.

THE EDUCATIONAL SYSTEM: AN OVERVIEW

Although schools existed over 2,000 years ago in ancient Greece and Rome and later in China and Japan, they were the prerogative of a select group. The remainder of the child population worked alongside adults. In Western Europe and North America, primary school attendance became compulsory between 1840 and 1890. Middle-class children were the first to benefit, whereas working-class and rural parents had some difficulty adjusting their economic circumstances to the loss of their children's labour and wages. Therefore, several decades elapsed, well into the first part of the 20th century, before mass schooling spread to all social classes equally. Quebec lagged particularly in this respect because of its rural economy. For instance, in 1891, the census revealed that 41 percent of the Quebec population was illiterate compared to 18 percent of the Ontario population.

Yet, the first infant school and the first daycare opened in Montreal in 1828 and 1858 respectively; all were charitable organizations for poor children. In English Canada, the first child care facility opened in Toronto in 1857 (Prochner, 2000). From the 1920s to the 1950s, the focus of early education was on children's emotional and social development, while from the 1960s until now, the focus shifted to intellectual development. Currently, the emphasis of governments regarding early education is on preparing children from disadvantaged families for a schooling system that is becoming more and more oriented toward a global, technological labour market (Pitt, 2002).

In essence, the educational system pursues family goals of gender-role differentiation and of the social integration of children in society and particularly its economy (Reynolds, 2004). In other societies, particularly Muslim ones, schools emphasize religious scriptures and children's integration into the faith of the country. Overall, children are now more **age segregated** in supervisory settings (Coakley and Donnelly, 2004). At the middle-class level, their lives have become more structured, **organized**, regimented, less spontaneous and free ranging than in the past (Perry and Doherty, 2005). Therefore, children's time is rationalized and institutionalized in order to increase their safety and prepare them for the growing rationalization of postmodern life (Boekhoven, 2009). As well, children spend less time within the folds of the family and are increasingly "serviced" by other adults and institutions (Hareven, 2000): Thus, families become underconnected, especially across the generations (Uhlenberg, 2009). Within this analytical framework, educational institutions are **institutions of exclusion**, even exclusion of children from their parents' world, largely to suit the needs of the economy (Côté and Allahar, 2006; Schlegel, 2003). In turn, as mentioned earlier, parents have to manage and integrate the role of these institutions.

Thus, in modern economies, not only are children segregated into age groups, they are also especially segregated from many of the activities carried out by their parents. As Coontz (2000:290) points out, while youth today are more excluded from productive roles, they are paradoxically much more fully involved in **consumer roles**. This age segregation is promoted by consumerism and is often self-chosen and reinforced by the peer culture that has evolved along age lines. In contrast, children living in the small villages and rural areas of Africa and many Asian countries are fully integrated in the life of the community and in their parents' world, including work that is basically familial. Children learn their adult roles by imitating their parents as they help them, even though they attend the village school. Moreover, these children play in mixed-age groups, the 6-year-olds or 10-year-olds watching over the babies collectively (Hewlett and Lamb, 2005).

In Canada, the majority of children now begin school earlier than they did 30 years ago. Currently, most attend kindergarten, and a substantial proportion participates in preschool programs. Moreover, about a third of preschool children whose parents are employed are in daycare centres, some as young as six weeks old. Therefore, the educational function traditionally assigned to families has been taken over by institutions at younger ages. However, parents have to manage and integrate the role of these institutions at a time when they have other time constraints in their own lives. Parents have to do far more planning than was the case in the 1960s, for instance (Sweet and Anisef, 2005).

CHILD CARE: QUALITY AND OUTCOMES

Child care generally refers to the care given to a child by a person other than his or her primary caregiver—and the primary caregiver is usually defined as the mother (see Chapter 1). Overall, Canada suffers from a lack of government-funded child care facilities, and waiting lists are very long, especially for subsidized and regulated care. Further, Canada does not have a national strategy for early childhood education and care (Campaign 2000, 2010). Quebec has the best system of inexpensive daycare but there are not enough places to meet the demand, as indicated in Table 6.1: In 2012, only 20.5 percent of all young children could be accommodated in **regulated** child care in Canada and 22.5 percent of those aged zero to five in regulated centre-based care (Friendly et al., 2013). As well, in most provinces, the proportion of for-profit child care centres is increasing—and these are more likely to be accessible only to higher-income families. On the positive side, the number of child care centres on reserves has increased.

We already know that 70 percent of mothers with a child aged three to five are working, so we see the inadequacy of this situation (*Canada Year Book*, 2012). Parents have recourse to a variety of other child care arrangements, from alternating shifts between mothers and fathers to non-regulated care in another individual's home or care by relatives, especially grandmothers, or a nanny or at-home sitter. For instance, about 50 percent of all off-reserve Aboriginal children who are in care are in a centre (Findley and Kohen, 2011). Young children who have a *multiplicity* of non-parental child care arrangements tend to have more behavioural problems (Morissey, 2009): It is probably too difficult for them to adapt to a variety of rules that are often inconsistent. Compared to the 1960s, proportionally more children are

TABLE 6.1	Percentage of Children Aged 0–12 and 0–5 for Whom There Was a Form of Regulated Child Care Space in 2012	

	Aged 0 to 12*	Aged 0 to 5**
Canada	20.5%	22.5%
Newfoundland / Labrador	11.2	18.9
New Brunswick	22.9	30.7
Prince Edward Island	20.8	46.5
Nova Scotia	15.1	23.9
Quebec	37.4	36.3
Ontario	15.4	20.8
Manitoba	16.3	20.5
Saskatchewan	7.6	11.5
Alberta	19.8	19.9
British Columbia	18.0	24.6
Northwest Territories	n/a	n/a
Nunavut	11.8	20.8
Yukon	26.8	28.6

*Regulated child care spaces
**Regulated full or part-time centre-based child care spaces
Source: Adapted with permission from Friendly, Halfon, Beach, and Forer, 2013, Tables 12 and 13, pp. 66 and 67.

in centres than with female relatives, because the latter tend to be employed. As well, affluent families are the least likely to choose care by relatives.

Child care of **high quality** includes a low child-to-caregiver ratio allowing for more adult-child interaction (Schipper et al., 2006). The availability of activities, toys, and educational materials, as well as space, are other indicators of quality. Nutritious food and an age-appropriate structuring of daily activities, including naps, are other important elements. More and more, an integrated educational component is a requisite of a good child care system. But particularly important are caregivers' qualifications (Mashburn et al., 2008). We should consider staff's low salaries as an indicator of quality: Low salaries lead to high turnover rates, thus instability in children's lives. In Canada and the U.S., caregivers' salaries are much lower than those in Europe, and their turnover rate consequently is around 40 percent per year. In 2006, the **median*** full-time salary of early childhood educators was $25,100 and $27,366 for those with the ECE credential (Beach et al., 2009). These are low salaries for persons who take care of our children—this country's most important investment. In Canada, non-profit centres generally provide better quality child care, and have better trained staff and lower turnover (Friendly, 2000). Caretakers who are more adequately trained and are satisfied with their working conditions provide a more optimum environment for children (White and Mill, 2000).

The Effects of Child Care on Children

Poor-quality care has been related to child disadvantages in the domains of cognition and language, as well as social and emotional adjustment, as found in follow-up studies of children after they have begun school (Belsky et al., 2007; McCartney et al., 2010). Unfortunately, research on the effect of nonfamilial care on children has until now largely failed to take **family characteristics** into consideration. It is entirely possible that some of what are believed to be negative consequences of day-care centres are actually results of other activities the children are involved in at home or of certain family characteristics, such as a mother's low educational level or a detrimental housing situation (NICHD, 2004; Watamura et al., 2011). Naturally, to some extent, parents choose or are forced to accept a quality of care corresponding to some of their own characteristics, including income (Kohen et al., 2002b). But this is less the case in Quebec than in other provinces because of indirect subsidies.

In studies that have controlled for family variables, the quality of daycare centres still produces a small but evident difference in terms of language and cognitive development (McCartney et al., 1997). In a longitudinal, multi-stage study by NICHD (2006), higher quality child care was related to advantages in cognitive, language, and preschool outcomes at several points and better socioemotional and peer outcomes at some ages. Also found were more negative behaviours, more teacher-child conflicts, and more peer problems at some ages for those who had spent more time per week in care (also Fram et al., 2012). Several studies find that children in daycare centres are more self-confident, assertive, expressive, and helpful, as well as less timid in new situations than children in other types of care. But other studies also report that many of the children in nonmaternal care are less polite, agreeable, and compliant with mothers' or teachers' requests, and more irritable, aggressive, and boisterous (Belsky et al., 2007; NICHD, 2006). These results are particularly evident for children who have been placed in care when very small and spend long hours in this setting. By age 15, these children still have a somewhat higher score on externalizing problems (Lowe Vandell et al., 2010). However, a restructuring of daycare educational ideologies that would foster cooperation, responsibility, and engagement with the natural environment might redress the situation (Maccoby and Lewis, 2003). The NICHD group thus concludes that parents should be supported, quality child care centres encouraged, and that *one should reduce the amount of time that children spend in care.* On the positive side, more hours in care for the entire cohort could lead to higher levels of learning in grade school even with only slightly more advanced cognitive and language skills. However, on the negative side, such classrooms could also be more difficult to manage because of a higher level of undesirable social behaviours. Still, *children from disadvantaged home environments do benefit* from the compensatory influence of good-quality child care (Watamura et al., 2011).

A review of large-scale studies of hundreds of centres that was carried out in the U.S., Bermuda, Sweden, and Holland concludes that children from disadvantaged homes, for whom quality child care programs may supply missing elements in their lives, benefit from quality daycare, particularly in terms of school achievement later on and fewer behavioural problems (Votruba-Drzal et al., 2004, 2010). However, as seen earlier, small children who have too much **peer contact** or spend too many hours

Good child care centres are a society's investment in its work force, the stability of families, and in the future of their children. Child care that is affordable contributes to parents' and children's well-being. It also contributes to job creation and satisfaction. Quality child care centres are thus functional for families, children, and the economy.

Anne-Marie Ambert

with a large group of peers may develop more externalizing problems (McCartney et al., 2010). Children who have too little adult attention early in their lives may be at a deficit in terms of social adjustment, especially when they are more socially fearful by nature (Watamura et al., 2003). We already know from other studies on large family size that such children are at a disadvantage in terms of language skills and intellectual development (Marks, 2006). Overall, the long-term effects of parenting seem to predominate over those of nonparental care (Belsky et al., 2007). There is nevertheless one important question that is still being debated: Are children who are in daycare for over 30 hours a week from an early age less influenced by parents' teachings and other family characteristics than children who are in care for fewer hours?

Early Childhood Education for Children in Low-Income Families

Children from low-income families are often unprepared when they enter Grade 1 and consequently fall behind at each subsequent level. Many such children repeat grades and then drop out of school to join the ranks of the unemployed and underpaid. Programs such as Head Start, which was created in the U.S. in 1965, raise the level of disadvantaged children's school readiness (Dearing et al., 2009). Much of the research on this topic is American, but its results apply to the Canadian situation. Indeed, expanding early childhood education for all families and also with the purpose of helping disadvantaged children should be a key element in all provinces. Further, an Aboriginal Head Start program was initiated in 1995 for northern and urban communities and was expanded to include reserves in 1998 (Goulet et al., 2001; Mayfield, 2001). By 2002, 16 percent of six-year-old Aboriginal children had attended a preschool program locally developed to meet the culture and the needs of the community (RCAP, 1996; Statistics Canada, 2004k). The following conclusions about children who have participated in Head Start or similar programs are distilled from the research of Brooks-Gunn (2003), Love et al. (2005), Lowe Vandell et al. (2010), Nisbett et al. (2012), and Raver et al. (2011):

1. Children experience a short-term boost in IQ scores that may last for a few years.
2. Once they are in Grade 1, these students do better than comparable students not previously enrolled in Head Start.
3. Only a small group is eventually placed in remedial "special education."
4. Only about one-fifth are eventually retained in a grade, compared to one-third of a control group that did not attend Head Start.
5. Positive effects on cognition and school achievement are still evident at age 15.
6. More Head Start children graduate from high school.
7. More of these children are eventually employed than those children in the control group.
8. Children show an improvement in family interaction, health, and nutritional status, as well as socioemotional adjustment.

Some of the above results may in part be related to the fact that quality Head Start programs generally provide positive parent-teacher contact that encourages mothers to help their children remain motivated and to read to them, for instance (Raikes et al., 2006). Moreover, some of these programs have reduced abuse and neglect over the children's life span to age 17 (Reynolds and Robertson, 2003), perhaps because they increase low-income mothers' sensitivity to their children (Nomaguchi and DeMaris, 2013). When children arrive in Grade 1 free of major behavioural problems and language difficulties, not only are they more attentive in class and better able to learn but they also impress their teachers and peers more favourably. *Teachers, in turn, expect more of them,* and these higher expectations carry through the rest of their school years, *even though their initial IQ gain eventually disappears.* As Entwisle and colleagues (1997) remind us, "It is key to realize that only modestly better achievement in the first couple of grades might be enough for children to avoid retention or Special Education" (p. 18).

Children's reading proficiency begins early and this advantage carries over into post-secondary education (Statistics Canada, 2006a, 2011e). The precursors of school readiness are already established between the ages of three to five (Statistics Canada, 2006b). For example, nine-year-old children whose scores are high in math, vocabulary, and attention span already had developed these skills by age five (Statistics Canada, 2009n). Most experts now agree that disadvantaged children who are segregated in poor neighbourhoods would do far better if they were to start preschool as early as possible, even at age two. They also agree that such an early intervention should extend through grade school to build on the initial progress and to involve other aspects of these families' lives (Reynolds and Temple, 1998). Such an extension would prevent the loss of early gains, a situation that currently occurs as a result of the low-quality school environments in which disadvantaged children find themselves after Head Start. What is needed is a program such as "Beyond 3:30," which was initiated by the Toronto Community Foundation, whereby children stay in school until their parents return while engaging in interesting activities and receiving remedial help (Daubs, 2009). However, one problem that arises for low-skilled children in low-income centres is that they are surrounded by other small children who have equally low language skills, a factor that probably diminishes the potential gains (Justice et al., 2011).

Overall, Head Start programs are an excellent **investment for a society** that has a large pool of disadvantaged families (Rushowy, 2004). It is an investment in education, in children's present and future, in families, and in a society's economy. In as much as such programs are both remedial and preventive, they are cost effective and save taxpayers enormous burdens in the long run, in terms of lower rates of delinquency, unemployment, ill health, and even adult criminality (Bogenschneider and Corbett, 2010). In Quebec, by 2008, Fortin et al. (2011) have documented how child care has increased women's employment and provincial productivity; it also added $717 million in additional revenue to the federal government. In Chicago, child-parent centres from ages 3 to 9 have been found to produce economic benefits that exceed their costs with increased earnings by age 26 and tax revenues as well as averted criminal justice systems outlays (Reynolds et al., 2011).

The Effects of Child Care on Parents

Child care should also be studied in terms of its effects on parents, particularly on their well-being. Care that is too expensive reduces parents' well-being as well as that of the entire family: If too great a proportion of the domestic budget goes into child care, it depletes resources that could be utilized for other aspects of family life, such as better housing, nutrition, and leisure activities. Furthermore, expensive daycare may prevent some parents from having a second child, or, when a second baby arrives, one of the two parents (generally the mother) may be forced to leave her employment. Thus, indirectly, via the expenses required, inadequate social provisions for affordable child care may reduce parental well-being and even fertility—hence the importance of inexpensive child care in Quebec. As well, in the north, lack of child care in community colleges prevents Aboriginal women from pursuing post-secondary education, another aspect of family well-being (Bonnycastle and Prentice, 2011).

There is a second path via which child care can lessen parental well-being: Low-quality care not only has a negative impact on children's development, but parents worry about their child as they attend to their job during the day (Erdwins et al., 2001). Mothers especially may feel insecure and guilty. In other instances, the child is well cared for, but by relatives or sitters who exact a psychological price from parents, particularly mothers, by being intrusive or quarrelsome. Also, parents may feel that their child needs more attention, but they may be afraid of antagonizing relatives by making additional requests.

Thus, child care availability, affordability, and quality are key ingredients in parents' well-being. From an economic perspective, quality and affordable child care increases productivity, lowers employee stress and absenteeism, and offers a wider pool of potential workers. It also contributes to a healthier family situation. When both parents can be employed because they have access to quality child care, this contributes to preventing poverty. Thus, child care is especially important for young single mothers, both in terms of jobs and as an educational tool in the care of their children. As well, care for children with special needs is essential, including for their parents' well-being in all social classes, with an emphasis on vulnerable families. Hence, child care availability and quality should be a prime target of social policies directed at improving family life and the future work force—although one has to emphasize the fact that nonfamilial child care is a necessary correlate of the type of economy we live in. But it is not a universal need.

SCHOOLS AND FAMILIES

Schools and families are intersecting environments in the unfolding lives of children and contribute to the reproduction of a society's cultural capital and class structure (Bourdieu, 1984; Marx, 1867). For one, schools constitute a key context for child development and family relations. In turn, family characteristics, such as their socio-economic status (SES) and religion, dictate to some extent the type of school children attend. From the perspective of rational theory, schools that serve as an effective community can add resilience to a child whose family is experiencing a stressful situation, such as divorce (Leon, 2003). Schools that create a prosocial environment contribute to children's health and behavioural outcomes (Ma and Zhang, 2002; Nisbett et al., 2012; Tough, 2012). Other key school variables are fair and consistent discipline, safety, extracurricular programs to encourage physical activity, school commitment, and parental involvement. Smaller class size is also important for younger children (Chetty et al., 2011).

Teachers play an important role in children's lives. Children who have more experienced teachers early on in life do better as adults on some socioeconomic dimensions (Chetty et al., 2011). Positive teacher-child relationships are an important element in a child's school success and in the prevention of aggressiveness and victimization (Brendgen et al., 2011; Maldonado-Carrēno and Votruba-Dzarl, 2011). Teachers may counterbalance or exacerbate negative familial environments (Forehand et al., 2002). In terms of motivation and behaviours at school, good and supportive teachers can be even more influential than parents (Wentzel, 2002). More studies are needed to see which type of school social capital can be beneficial to children, and at what age, over and above the social capital available from their parents (Dufur et al., 2008). In normal situations, the more schooling children receive, the larger their cognitive growth. Years of schooling tend to increase IQ levels, and absence from a good school for a prolonged period results in lower scores (Nisbett et al., 2012). Further—and to pursue a theme just discussed—in terms of social capital, when the number of pupils is too high and/or the teachers are indifferent, children from homes with less capital become particularly at risk developmentally (Parcel et al., 2010). This may be especially so for immigrant adolescents whose command of English or French is not yet fully developed (Anisef and Kilbride, 2003).

Vulnerable children who attend schools with relatively few difficult students are less likely to associate with peers who reinforce their own negative tendencies: Their opportunities for negative behaviours are reduced (Cleveland and Wiebe, 2003). But the contrary may happen when there is an aggregate of more aggressive **peers** as it affects the classroom climate (Thomas et al., 2011). For instance, female teens who attend schools with a large percentage of disadvantaged students are more likely to become pregnant than if they attend a school with a different SES profile (Manlove et al., 2002). As well, when a school is predominantly populated by students from single-parent families, children's test scores are significantly reduced, largely a function of poverty (Bankston and Caldas, 1998). For their part, children from female-headed families who attend a school where most peers have two parents, and have therefore more resources, are positively affected in their test scores. In contrast, children from two-parent families who attend a school where most families are headed by lone mothers do less well in test scores (Pong, 1998).

In the following subsections, we investigate family variables that promote or impede school success: parental involvement, social class, family-school compatibility, antisocial behaviour, and minority-group status. These variables largely derive from social inequalities by class and race that permeate all global market economies, whether capitalist or communist. As such, these variables are informed by political economy theories and link with the two previous chapters.

Parental Involvement

Parental involvement in education is related to children's achievement and fewer behavioural problems (Nokali et al., 2010). It is a key concern of teachers who expect parents to support them and to prepare children for school. In Aboriginal communities, it is recommended that schools involve Elders and other members as well as parents to ensure cultural continuity (Goulet et al., 2001). But the concept of parental involvement implies that it rests solely on parents' motivation. Yet, there are several elements that either encourage or discourage parents from being involved, such as teachers' attitudes and mothers' workload (Pena, 2000).

Parents can involve themselves directly in school activities—for instance, by volunteering or being on parent committees in Islamic schools (Zine, 2008). They can also closely follow their children's education from home by showing interest, maintaining high expectations, and supervising homework (Mandell and Sweet, 2004). In this respect, maternal supportiveness has been found to be even more effective than paternal in terms of fostering school readiness among *young* children (Martin et al., 2010). Overall, parental participation and empowerment is related to children's school performance and interpersonal relationships (Ma and Zhang, 2002—see Family Research 6.1). All in all, parents can have a positive effect on raising their children's school achievement, as well as educational expectations and personal aspirations.

However, once school and family background characteristics and child's prior academic achievement are taken into account, parental involvement's effect is not significant in terms of cognitive development. But parental involvement prevents behavioural problems "when they volunteer at school, help children with homework, and check their children's homework" (Domina, 2005:245). In other words, parental involvement is not the panacea for all problems as it is often promoted.

How to Study Parental Involvement

Ma and Zhang (2002) used the 1998 data from the Canadian Cross-National Survey on Health Behaviours in School-Aged Children (HBSC) to examine the effects of some aspects of school experience on health and behaviours of students enrolled in Grades 6 to 10. About 10,000 students participated in the survey during school time. Health behaviours were measured with questions pertaining to the use of drugs, recent medical treatments and injuries, exercise habits, hygiene, and eating patterns. Other questions addressed interpersonal relationships, self-esteem, and the ability to make new friends.

For its part, parental involvement was measured by the following statements:

- If I have problems at school, my parent(s) are ready to help me.
- My parents are willing to come to school to talk to teachers.
- My parents encourage me to do well at school.

Other statements pertained to the quality of the child-parent relationship:

- My parents understand me.
- My parents expect too much of me.
- I have a lot of arguments with my parents.
- What my parents think of me is important.

Parents' Higher Social Class and Involvement

Building on Coleman's (1988) **theory of resources,** Lareau (2011) demonstrates how parents' social class equips them with an unequal set of resources that can differentially affect their ability to be involved in their children's education. Her sample included black and white families at the upper-middle-class executive or professional level. These parents have the competence to help when their children encounter difficulties with the curriculum. They feel self-confident with teachers and do not hesitate to request changes that could benefit their children or to question teachers' decisions. At the negative level, it is not uncommon for such parents to flatly reject teachers' suggestions concerning children's behavioural difficulties. This situation is described by a student teacher who is doing her practicum in a new upper-middle-class neighbourhood where parents are upwardly mobile and are extremely busy with their careers:

> "Right now I can't wait to get out of that school because some of these parents aren't used to money and what comes with it and they treat you as if you were their maids. Most kids are fine but we have a few bad apples and the parents are high on denial, perhaps because they are never home to see what's wrong with their precious children. There's nothing that their Danny Boy or whoever can do wrong, yet the boy is a regular delinquent. Oh no, he doesn't steal, how dare we complain, accuse him of this! More or less they tell us to learn manners, which they don't even have themselves. It ruins your life as a teacher."

In their own social networks, upper-middle-class parents often have access to professionals, such as psychologists and other teachers whom they can consult on school matters. These parents are also better equipped to meet teachers' requests, because they have more material and cultural resources at their disposal (Bourdieu, 1977; Jaeger, 2009). They can provide their children with educational supplies, computers, tutors, art or music lessons, and even summer camps (Ertl, 2000; Nisbett et al., 2012). Lareau (2011) mentions that these parents often bring work home from the office that expands children's horizons, gives them some preparation for the adult world of employment, and may serve as an incentive for homework. One student explains this:

> *"I've always wanted to be a family doctor because my father sells pharmaceuticals to them and he used to bring his samples home to show us at dinner time and it was very educational. But at a later time my mother returned to school to get her advanced degree in social work and the cases she'd talk about at home started to fascinate me. So I figured that I could be a social worker in a hospital context because I like both areas. So that's what I am studying for."*

Educated parents are also more likely to read to their children and spend time with them, although this frequency is much lower when mothers are employed full-time and as children get older (Cook and Willms, 2002). Above all, middle-class parents engage in a process of **concerted cultivation** (Lareau, 2011). That is, they deliberately stimulate the development of their children's cognitive and social skills by fostering larger vocabularies, familiarity with abstract concepts, and negotiating abilities. They enroll their children in an array of organized activities. (Indeed, both Aboriginal and other Canadian children who participate in extracurricular activities do better in school and in their relations with friends—Statistics Canada, 2004k). All of this gives children an advantage with institutional representatives, raises their sense of entitlement, and transmits habits that will be useful for higher education and on the individualistic, competitive labour market later on (Knighton and Mirza, 2002). In contrast, in working-class and disadvantaged families, children experience a socialization pattern that includes more free time, clear boundaries between parents and children, parental directives, a simpler speech pattern, and lower expectations of personal entitlement—what Lareau (2011) calls "natural growth."

This concerted education, although American in origins, can be observed in educated families of most ethnic groups in North America. However, because a smaller proportion of blacks and Aboriginals are middle class, as is the case for other Aboriginal groups elsewhere, this parenting style is less often encountered among them. This places children at a disadvantage in schools—but not necessarily in their personal relationships. For instance, Baker (2001:45) points out that Samoan children in New Zealand are disadvantaged by the school system because they are taught at home not to question their elders, and their learning style is of the "passive" type. In contrast, the process of concerted education stems from the individualistic and competitive nature of North American middle-class education in particular and places additional demands on mothers, as seen in Chapter 1 (Pitt, 2002; Wall, 2004). *It is in itself an ideology supported by the technological and capitalist infrastructure of society.* Yet, it is not widely practised in Europe's most economically advanced countries where parents rely on a more casual transmission of their culture and depend more on their country's school system, as is the case in France and Germany.

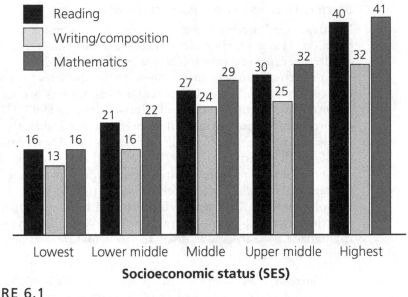

FIGURE 6.1

Percentages of Children Ranked Near the Top of Their Class by Their Teachers (by SES)

Source: Human Resources Development Canada and Statistics Canada, National Longitudinal Survey of Children and Youth, 1994–95; Lipps and Frank, 1997.

As indicated in Figure 6.1, children from families of higher SES do better in reading, writing, and mathematics (Lipps and Frank, 1997). In Toronto, children in gifted programs disproportionately come from higher-status families (TDSB, 2013). These observations hold internationally (Willms, 2002b). As well, university attendance is still related to social class (Knighton and Mirza, 2002). Thus, inequalities in achievement continue over the life course (Anisef et al., 2000; Pallas, 2002). Further, children who attend schools with a greater percentage of students from higher SES backgrounds do better academically (Frempong and Willms, 2002).

Pong (1998) found that, at the group level, high parental participation in educational activities alleviated the economic deficit by providing a positive community effect on the school and its students. Students did better when parents' participation was high, in general, even though their own individual parents may not have been involved. The same findings applied for the extent to which parents were acquainted with one another. When parents knew many other parents, they served as sources of information and reinforcement for one another. This helped them create a positive climate within the school for the benefit of all students. These results support Coleman's (1988) *theory of social capital and the positive effect of an effective community above and beyond a family's social class and structure.* However, Crosnoe (2004) found that there is overlap between social capital available in families and schools: Students who receive more emotional support from their parents then benefit more from the socioemotional resources of school.

Barriers to Low-Income Parents' Involvement

Disadvantaged parents often value education as much as their wealthier counterparts do. However, they may have low achievement expectations for their own children because several problems stand in their and their children's way that prevent the actualization of their values. These obstacles then lower their aspirations. Indeed, studies indicate that parental expectations are key predictors of school achievement, starting in Grade 1. Entwisle et al. (1997:93) point out that *raising* **parents' expectations** could affect performance indirectly for several years after Grade 1. As we have seen, programs such as Head Start often lift parents' expectations, which in turn contributes to their children's success. Disadvantaged parents encounter several problems that prevent them from actualizing their high value for education. First, they often lack the skills to help their children when they have school problems. This was well illustrated by a student describing her Grade 1 experience in the previous chapter (p. 129). Second, they often feel intimidated or stigmatized by teachers, as discussed by a mature and already well-educated student on welfare:

> *"Currently, one of my worries is my daughter's school, rather, her teachers. They know that I am a single mother on welfare and it does not matter to them consequently that I have as much and even more education than they have. I can't talk to them, any of them, because they have subtle ways of putting me down, of making me feel that I am not a competent parent and person because I am poor. I wanted to get them involved in making sure that the children spell correctly . . . well, what a mistake because they can't spell themselves! But, of course, I am the problem: I am poor. Who am I? How can I have an opinion about my daughter's education, least of all spelling?"*

Third, teachers make more frequent requests for involvement from disadvantaged parents, but these requests are often negative, in part because poor children have more learning or behavioural problems. In fact, when children's grades are low, parents have more contact with the school. Otherwise, low-income parents attend parent-teacher conferences far less frequently. Often, lack of child care prevents them from doing so. Others may not have a flexible work schedule that would allow them to participate in school activities such as volunteering, which would give them the opportunity to become informally acquainted with teachers and other parents. Such activities would, in turn, give their children an advantage within the system—an "inside track." Aboriginal parents too often feel out of place and do not feel welcome by teachers (Poonwassie, 2001).

A fourth aspect of a family's low position in the class system that affects parents' expectations and children's education resides in the fact that, when these parents want to help their children with school work, they often meet resistance because the youngsters lack confidence in their competence. A female student, reminiscing on her own experience growing up in a disadvantaged family, makes this point:

> *"When I look back on that period what I regret the most is the way I treated my mother; just because we were poor I felt that she was not as good as other mothers and whenever she'd try to help me with homework, I'd turn to her and give her my most despising look. Not only [did] I hurt her a lot and made her feel*

useless as a mother but I made her feel worthless as a person because even then she was more educated than I am now especially when it comes down to writing proper sentences."

A male student recalls how his negative view of his mother as a woman deprived him of much needed help:

"I always refused my mother's help with my homework because I felt that as a woman she didn't know much of anything. I was a guys' guy and always resisted any suggestion for improvement from my mother and I felt that it was her fault that we were poor and that if she had been any brighter, my father would not have left her . . . . Now I see how much better off I would have been with a better attitude."

However, the gendered division of labour and child care that focuses on mothers presents a serious roadblock in parental involvement, although it may be slowly changing as fathers are becoming more involved in their children's education. Still, the intensive mothering that society and schools now expect cannot easily be fulfilled by women on low incomes who may be struggling to simply feed their children (Hays, 1996). *The child as a project* (a social construct serving a type of economy) is often out of these mothers' reach, their best intentions notwithstanding (Wall, 2004).

Family-School Compatibility

Although Canada is a multicultural society, the structure of its economy rests on skills and education. Children are more successful at school and better adjusted to its requirements when family life is similar to the skill set required by the school system (Roche and Ghazarian, 2012). Children in families that have a **schedule**—where they eat breakfast, where rules are followed, and where educational activities are encouraged—are more easily integrated into the school system. Households with no employed adults are less likely to provide such a structure. In homes where everyone gets up whenever he or she wants, does not dress until later or not at all, eats meals whenever hungry, watches unlimited hours of television, and where reading material is absent, daily life is a world apart from school routine and goals. Children from these families may experience more difficulty fitting in at school, as well as have more trouble learning, because the two lifestyles clash. (See the student's quote on p. 129.)

Several researchers have emphasized the differences that exist between children of diverse social classes in terms of **summer activities**. Middle-class children benefit from summer activities that are compatible with school routine. For instance, many attend special camps. In contrast, disadvantaged children often spend their vacations in pursuits that increase their distance from what is required for school performance. A knowledge vacuum is created and they have more difficulty in readapting themselves to school work and routine once classes resume. Not surprisingly, these children lose a few points on the IQ scale as well as on tests of mathematical ability and reading skills during vacations (Brown, 2012). A student inadvertently explains this linkage:

"What I like best to remember at this age [11–14] was my summer camps. I used to go to these camps that were basically for gifted children and we did a lot of

science experiments and maths along with the usual crafts & physical activities. . . . And when it was time to go back to school I always did better than the others, my science project was ready and I had more time to play hockey so I was not put down as a geek. I also liked showing off to my parents with everything I had learned and they were proud of me. All of this has helped me to this day."

Entwisle and colleagues (1997) tested children and examined their school grades at the beginning, middle, and end of the school year. They found that, although disadvantaged children begin the school year with lower scores and less knowledge than those from more affluent families, they gain as much proportionately. In other words, some of the yearly difference in test scores between poor children and children of higher SES is caused by summer loss for the former. A student describes her frustration:

"I hated school because the other kids were so much more advanced than me, they'd come back to school with all kinds of stories about their summer activities and camps and special classes and they'd be rearing to go while I had spent all my summer watching TV babysitting and it'd take me until Christmas until I'd be caught up with the others, well some of the others. I was always last and later I had to take summer school to help my grades. It's been tough because I didn't have the same opportunities that the other students had."

Schools and Antisocial Behaviour

But there is another aspect of school/family compatibility that has to be taken into consideration. It resides in the fact that a substantial proportion of youth criminality occurs on school grounds. In fact, 27 percent of violent crimes involving youth and 20 percent of drug offences occur on school property in large cities (Savoie et al., 2006). Thus, schools can be an area where deviance-training takes place (Snyder et al., 2008), especially when there is a large number of difficult students in classrooms (Janosz et al., 2013). A student inadvertently sheds some light on this situation:

"Right now what's most stressful to me is my kid bro, he's 16 and more than a handful and my mom doesn't see it this way because he brings in money and I can't believe that my mom doesn't see where it comes from [drugs]. He also got a gun that goes down well in his baggy pants, he's a real delinquent but I think my mom's afraid of him and to tell the truth I am too. He brings his gun to school and he's going to hurt someone some day. He got a girl he gives bling-bling [to], she loves him, it sickens me because one day she be left with kids and him dead. So the school cant do a thing, he skips most of it, but he a real bad influence and the teachers are afraid of him. So he's the king of the castle until he ends dead. I know lotsa mothers like my mom that sort of know that their boy is packing and in shit but they're afraid of them and they get food on the table and bling-bling around their neck, ya know such a 'good son.' He treats me bad and my mom too."

School is also the place where bullying begins. In Ontario, about 13 percent of high-school students are worried about being harmed or threatened at school—and more so in Toronto (Paglia-Boak et al., 2010). This may become more prominent and more inescapable because it now is amplified with smart phones, Facebook, and other forthcoming media. Thus, bullying at school no longer stays there: It follows students home in the form of **cyberbullying***.

Many studies have found that a school climate, "the feel" of a school as perceived by teachers and students, is related to children's behavioural outcomes (Lawrence, 2007). Schools with a more engaged and interested staff have lower rates of students' problems; in contrast, a school that feels less safe or has a lot of vandalism will have higher rates of student behavioural problems (Gottfredson et al., 2005). In a study by Fitzgerald (2009), school social capital and school disorder were measured and compared to rates of students' self-reported delinquency. They found that Toronto schools that had the least **social capital** (low student attachment, low teacher involvement, fewer activities) had rates of violent delinquency that were 53 percent higher than in schools with the highest level of social capital.

Students' own characteristics as well as those of their families also predicted violent behaviour, as described by the student above. But similar students attending schools with low disorder and high social capital are much less likely to become offenders (Fitzgerald, 2009). Therefore, good schools, attentive parents, and secure neighbourhoods all combine to reduce difficult behaviours and, together, constitute a tripartite zone of **effective**, collective socialization. However, one can also see that the sudden influx of a critical mass of difficult teens in a previously good school can demoralize teachers, lower social capital, and "contaminate" more fragile students:

> *"I'd describe myself as not so happy, about 2 [out of 5]. My placement is at that same high school where I graduated just four years ago and although it was not as good in the last two years, I don't recognize it. The students have no attention span, a whole bunch of them disrupt classes, talk out of turn, laugh at you, intimidate you. I heard that a lot are delinquent and there is certainly drugs going on, but the worst part is that some of the really good teachers we had have retired early because they could not cope with this; some of the new ones that have arrived have 'adjusted' and couldn't care less, and the few other good ones left don't smile anymore, they are like scared and scurrying around, totally discouraged. I am totally discouraged myself because I know that I couldn't cope with this; I don't want to be a parole officer!"*

Minority-Group, Immigrant, and Aboriginal Children

Family and school compatibility may be particularly challenging for minority-group children. For instance, a study of 15-year-olds' reading achievement in five provinces shows that those who attend the French school system in English-speaking provinces have much lower scores than those who attend the English school system (majority language). In provinces that are predominantly English speaking or mixed, French-speaking children often attend schools that are of lower academic quality than their English counterparts, except in large cities. Moreover, many of these francophone children live in a family that may no longer be technically fluent in their French language (Statistics Canada, 2004e). As well, the TDSB (2013) found that disadvantaged minority children, particularly black, are overrepresented in special education programs and among students labeled with behavioural issues—particularly among males. Thus, black children often lag behind their peers in terms of academic achievement; same-race mentoring may be particularly helpful in promoting educational attainment among underprivileged black high-schoolers (Hurd et al., 2012).

For their part, immigrant adolescents who arrive without sufficient Canadian language skills often acquire them more rapidly than do their parents and may have to act as cultural brokers or translators for them (Anisef and Kilbride, 2003). One of the consequences of this situation is that, while these parents generally hold high educational aspirations for their children, they are not in a position to become involved with the school system or to help their adolescents with homework, even though they may be highly educated themselves (Yax-Fraser, 2011). Further, the Anisef and Kilbride study group encountered immigrant youths who resisted conformity to "the culture, values, and established norms of the mainstream society" as coping mechanisms (2003:245). The end result is often conflict with parents and failure at school. This may be compounded by the fact that parents are struggling to make ends meet and are unable to be as supportive as they might have been in their country of origin. However, here as well, immigrant parents' economic means, own level of education, language skills, and high expectations all combine to facilitate school achievement. From the perspective of parents, the school system also contributes to "Canadianize" children more rapidly than is the case for parents, both in terms of language and culture. This situation often makes parents feel that they are losing control of their family situation, that their parenting practices are not valued and recognized as valid. They may also feel that children are informed about their own rights but with "little explanation of their responsibility to be respectful to their parents' teachings and to the guidance of school teachers" (Yax-Fraser, 2011:315).

In terms of Aboriginal students, there is an embryonic attempt at integrating their culture within mainstream teacher education (Vetter and Blimkie, 2011). Above all, village- or band-controlled schools value Aboriginal children's culture more and understand their family dynamics better. For instance, Wall and Madak (1991) have found that high-schoolers who attended tribal schools reported that their teachers and parents held higher educational aspirations for them than did Natives who attended regular public schools. In the latter case, cultural heritage may be substantially diluted and staff may lack an understanding of Natives' family processes. These two factors combine to place children at a disadvantage in terms of school achievement. As well, the fact that Aboriginal languages are still being lost in these schools remains a major problem in the cultural continuity of families (Nicholas, 2001). A reverse problem exists when a Native language is taught at school but parents no longer speak it (Paupanekis and Westfall, 2001).

Further, family characteristics (parents' education, employment, and marital status) do not necessarily have the same impact on school success on reserves as they do off reserves and in the population at large (Ward, 1998). Reserve Native parenting style is less supervisory than is the case in the rest of society, because it is their custom to rely on assistance from their **extended kin** or community for child supervision. For these parents, then, how well their children do in school may depend more on the social capital the community makes available to children than their own socialization practices. As well, many Native parents have been alienated from their education and that of their children because of historical factors, and would need to be reintegrated into the educational system (Poonwassie, 2001). This reintegration is particularly important for Natives who live off reserves, especially in cities such as Winnipeg where they are concentrated in disadvantaged areas and may no longer benefit from the support of their original community.

Ideally, when an Aboriginal village controls the school, parents and other community members can voice their concerns and have a greater impact on the curriculum. When a school has a very high proportion of Native students, the students are more likely to participate in extracurricular activities and to develop an attachment to the school. Both variables, in turn, may improve learning and prevent drop out, which is an enormous problem among Aboriginals (Hunter, 2011). However, in some cities, students are often placed in classes for "special needs" children, which in effect pathologizes their history of discrimination (Binda, 2001). This situation prevents Native families from accumulating human capital that could be passed on to the next generation and allow them to become integrated at the economic level. As well, there are several, albeit yet insufficient, programs to help Aboriginal high-school students pursue their education into post-secondary training and university; for example, the Aboriginal Students Links program in North Bay, Ontario, and the Model School at the University of Winnipeg (MacQueen, 2011). Shawn Atleo, national chief of the Assembly of First Nations, reported that "If we were to close the education and the labour market gap, in one generation it could result in $400 billion output to the Canadian economy and $115 billion in saved government expenditures" (MacQueen, 2011:74). Despite the emphasis on village schools, First Nations children who live off reserve and attend regular schools were reported by their parents to be doing as well (or as poorly in a small group) as other Canadian children age 4 to 14. A majority of these First Nations parents agreed (90 percent) that their child's school provided sufficient information on their child's progress, attendance, and behaviour (Statistics Canada, 2009a).

PRIVATE EDUCATION

We look at two different alternatives in children's education: private schools and home schooling. Both are institutions that may be related to a more effective community and, particularly for private schools, may constitute a more powerful collective socialization environment, and bring more closure to children's socialization process (Bourdieu, 1977; Coleman and Hoffer, 1987). Hence, these forms of education may be better able to reflect parents' socialization goals than is the case in the general school system.

Private Schools

Semi-private institutions include public schools that are religious in nature, such as the public Catholic school system in many provinces. Then, there are also schools that are sponsored by religious groups—whether Jewish, Mennonite, Sikh, Muslim, or Mormon—that do not receive taxpayers' subsidies (Seljak, 2005; Zine, 2008).

Bibby (2009) also found that students attending Sikh, Muslim, and other non-Christian schools would be less likely to live in Canada if they had a choice, which may bring complications in terms of integration into their new country later on. Next are private schools that focus on academics and are a means for certain families to raise their children within an exclusive environment. CAIS (2009) reports 81 such independent schools in Canada with an enrolment of 40,813 students and a teaching staff of 4,863. Students who attend these schools tend to have higher occupational and social class outcomes later on than students in public schools. This result remains even after family selection factors are controlled (Brewer et al., 1999). These schools contribute to the solidification of the upper classes and, indirectly, to the reinforcement of social inequalities (Khan, 2010). However, they may help social mobility for students whose families are low income. A third type of school, often called the alternative school, serves children whose parents are ideologically opposed to certain tenets of mass schooling (i.e., competitiveness, individualism), children who have not adapted to regular schools because of behavioural, emotional, or intellectual challenges, or, yet, children with careers. Some of these alternative schools are publicly funded to meet certain students' needs while others are entirely private.

Parents expect that private schools will pass on their values as well as their lifestyles to their children, whether religion- or class-inspired. From this perspective, such schools serve as an **extension of the family** far more than public schools can:

> *"I had a wonderful adolescence! My parents put me in this wonderful private school in Grade 7 and I just bloomed. It was like one very large family that sheltered us from the bullies we had had at the public school. I was a nerd and there certainly was no problem with this at this school. I was actually encouraged to read, explore new fields, ask questions, and tag-along [with] the teachers. We were all nerdy and it was just great. Both boys and girls were like that so that even dating was not a problem even though the teachers and our parents all made us understand that this was a stage of life that could wait. So we waited. We did not have to conform to the 'peer culture' (some Culture!) at other schools. We never envied them and all of us grew up to be very well rounded, sociable, and athletic nerds. If we had gone on to public high schools, we would have grown up screwed up or most of us would have given up being intelligent just to fit in."*

The staff of a private school are hired on the basis of academic qualifications and indirectly on how well they conform to the school's ideology, which in turn reflects parental ideology. The compatibility between the two is particularly evident in the preceding student quote. Parents and teachers encouraged their adolescents along similar lines of intellectual, moral, and social development. Bibby (2009) has found that students in religious schools hold ideas and values that diverge on some dimensions from those held by other youth. They are less likely to be tolerant of homosexuality, uphold honesty and hard work more, and are more concerned about world poverty.

Home Schooling

Home schooling is where the worlds of children and parents are most intertwined. Parents who resort to home schooling are reacting against the quality, philosophy, structure, and functioning of the formal educational system. Others, especially in the

U.S., home-school for religious and moral reasons, while many are responding to what they perceive to be dangerous peer influences (Smith, 1993). Home schooling is currently considered somewhat unusual. Yet, when one examines human history, home education has always prevailed until recently.

Both in Canada and the U.S., home schooling has been growing each year. The timing of this growth is somewhat paradoxical: It occurs while most families have two wage earners. Yet, most home teachers are mothers, so that they in effect have to forgo paid employment. In 2000–2001, there were between 60,000 and 95,000 registered home-schoolers in Canada (Ray, 2001). Over 60 percent are elementary-school students. In Ontario, only 8 percent are high-schoolers compared to 45 percent in Alberta and Saskatchewan. In the U.S., there are approximately two million home-schooled children (Murphy, 2012).

Home-schooling parents do not generally function in a vacuum (Brabant et al., 2004). To begin with, every province supervises home-schoolers for compliance with the *Education Act*—although some parents fail to register their children with their local school board. In some provinces, students can use public school libraries and other resources. Both in Canada and the U.S., national, state, and provincial organizations exist for the purpose of offering instrumental and moral support to families involved. One can think here of the Nova Scotia and the Alberta Home Education Associations and the Ontario Federation of Teaching Parents. Similarly, several relevant magazines are published; jointly, they probably reach most home-schooling parents.

Objections to home schooling, especially by the educational establishment, largely fall into three broad categories: (1) worries that the education provided may not meet national standards, (2) concerns that "zealot" parents may brainwash their children ideologically and religiously, and that (3) children will lack peer contact, will not develop appropriate social skills, and may become socially isolated.

In order to examine the validity of the first objection, Brabant et al. (2004) and Mayberry et al. (1995) have summarized the social profile of the parents of home-schooled children in Quebec and the U.S., respectively. The majority are white and tend to engage in occupations at the professional and technical level more than is the case nationally. The educational level is quite high, especially in Quebec. On average, the familial income is higher, situating them at the middle- to upper-middle-class level. Overall, these parents are educationally qualified, even though they have not generally been trained as teachers. What probably counts for children's achievement in home schooling is parents' unusually high involvement and motivation. The children perform at the national average and frequently exceed it on standard tests. Many accelerate while being home schooled and enter higher education at a younger age. The only home-schooled student I ever had explains her experience. Although it is on the idyllic side, it nevertheless makes interesting points:

> "I never attended school until I entered university. [When] my younger brother . . . left to do his last two years at a private school, I came here . . . my parents are researchers and we lived up north in the bush really and both my parents wanted their career and neither wanted to go at it alone and be separated. We partnered with a private school when I was in Grade 6 and they sent us video tapes of two classrooms so we could see other children and we sent them tapes of our lives

here and talked about our lives and did questions and answers from both sides and we visited the school each January and some came here to visit us on field trips. We made friends like that and still have them. We learned a lot and our parents were great teachers and also used us as assistants so we would grow up to be socially responsible. We were all crazy about books and came back from our annual January trips to California and BC with crates of books and also videos. A lot of people were afraid that we would grow up maladjusted but I don't think that there is anything wrong with being 'stuck with your parents' and not having a peer group. Unlike many other children, we had no worries, no anxieties, no fears. We also were very active physically with hiking, canoeing and swimming in wet suits in summer and skiing and skating in winter."

As to whether parents brainwash their offspring and offer them an education that is, for instance, so religiously oriented that it closes the door to children's options in the future, there is no direct research that could answer this critique scientifically. However, it would seem that "brainwashed" children would not do very well on the standard tests they have to take to enter college or that researchers have given them. Yet, we have seen that the contrary happens, although there are certainly exceptions to that rule. Parents themselves have an answer to this objection. They point out that secular humanism taught in public schools does brainwash children into values and beliefs that go against their principles (Gorder, 1996).

In terms of growing up socially inept and isolated, as well as emotionally malad-justed, the tests that have been carried out indicate normal development. However, it can be argued on the basis of other material presented in this chapter that *the potential for maladjustment exists for too many children who attend regular schools.* As we will see in Chapter 13, studies unanimously indicate that children are often bullied and victimized by peers. These statistics and experiences actually lead many parents to begin home schooling. Children who are home schooled generally have at least one sibling. They also meet peers who are in similar circumstances; they know children in the neighbourhood and many participate in extracurricular activities, such as sports teams and Scouts, which put them in frequent contact with regularly schooled peers. At the high school level, many home-schooled teens have jobs like other youths. Overall, although home schooling is unusual, it does not appear to produce negative effects, and perhaps quite the opposite occurs (Rothermel, 2000). Unfortunately, we have no research on how home schooling affects family relationships and the parental couple's happiness.

RELIGIOUS PARTICIPATION AND FAMILY LIFE

Religion constitutes one of the most important cultural domains in most societies and has been recognized as such by early sociologists, such as Durkheim (1897, 1912) and Weber (1905). Historically, it has been a key factor in shaping policies regarding family life, labour, and poverty (Lam, 2011; van Kersbergen and Manow, 2009). In Canada, religion still plays an important role in the lives of a substantial proportion of families, even though its institutional role and moral authority have declined, as is the case in most western societies (Bibby, 2002). Its impact on family life is therefore likely to be more obvious among the observant, hence the focus on religiosity. New arrivals to Canada, particularly Buddhists, Catholics, Hindus, Sikhs, and Muslims, are often very religious (WIN-Gallup, 2013; Clark and Schellenberg, 2006). Family studies do not yet adequately reflect this reality (Biles and Ibrahim, 2005). As is the case in Europe, new immigrants' level of religiosity may contrast with that of the remainder of the citizens (Westoff and Frejka, 2007; Zine, 2008).

In the 2011 National Household Survey, over two-thirds of Canada's population reported being affiliated with a Christian religion, with Roman Catholics predominating (Statistics Canada, 2013a). For their part, Muslims constituted 3.2 percent of the population, Hindus 1.5 percent, Sikhs 1.4 percent, Buddhists 1.1 percent, and Jews 1.0 percent. In addition, 24 percent wrote that they had no religious affiliation, up from 16.5 percent a decade earlier. Most Buddhists and persons with no religious affiliation who have arrived since 2006 came from China while Pakistan was the main source for Muslims.

The Christian population is older than the more recent arrivals. The **median** ages for each religion is as follows:

Roman Catholics	**43 years of age**
Anglicans	51
United Church	52
Muslims	29
Sikhs	33
Hindus	34

In a large survey of 57 countries, 59 percent of the world population defined themselves as religious, 23 percent as not religious, and 13 percent as atheists. The least religious countries were China, Japan, the Czech Republic, and France—these countries also had the highest proportions of atheists. The most religious were Ghana (90 percent), Nigeria, Peru, and Brazil. In comparison, Canada was 46 percent religious (its percentage lowered by Quebec, as we see below) and the U.S. was at 60 percent, in both cases a decline of about 10 percent since 2005 (WIN-Gallup, 2013). But both Canada and the U.S. had a relatively low percentage of respondents who declared themselves atheists: 9 and 5 percent respectively. One has to keep in mind the phrasing of the question: "Irrespective of whether you attend a place of worship or not, would you say you are a religious person, not a religious person, or a convinced atheist?" In other words, the options were rather radical, but revealing nevertheless with such a large sample.

How is the importance of religion to a family or to some of its members measured? A great deal of controversy revolves around this matter, as one can well imagine, because religiosity is difficult to define or measure and so, especially, is spirituality. Religiosity is more community focused and organized, with specific beliefs, while spirituality is more subjective and personal (Koenig et al., 2001). The two may be related but one does not necessarily follow the other (Taylor et al., 2004). In this chapter, the focus is on the *communal aspect*.

The most obvious and commonly used **indicator*** of religiosity is attendance at religious services (see Family Research 6.2). Generally, phone, Internet, or door-to-door surveys ask questions such as: "Did you, yourself, happen to attend church, mosque, or synagogue in the last seven days?" This is actually a Gallup survey question (Smith, 1998). (However, Canadian Social Surveys now include the word "meetings"—Statistics Canada, 2004l.) The first problem with these and similar questions resides in how well they reflect the increasing religious diversity in Canada.

For instance, among Hindus, religious ritual is often focused on the home and in a variety of practices; thus the question asked will fail to tap their level of religiosity, even though they have multi-use temples, particularly in British Columbia and the Toronto area. For their part, Sikhs' religious life is focused on their temples or gurdwaras (Banerjee and Coward, 2005), as is the case among Muslims with mosques and community centres (Hussain and Scott, 2012). Further, for many, attendance at temple or mosque functions *may be more a matter of maintaining their culture and of networking within their ethnic group than being religiously observant* (DeVries et al., 2010; Kim, P.G., 2010). Tapping into Chinese religiosity is even more complex (Marshall, 2011): It focuses in the home, temples, festivals, and Chinatowns—and many are Buddhists while others are Christians. As Lai et al. (2005) point out, "since Chinese religion is so completely intertwined with daily life, culture, and family, one could argue that the many Chinatowns are themselves the most accessible public expression of Chinese religion in Canada" (p. 100). It is very important to add that many of the temples, mosques, gurdwaras, and ethnic Christian churches also serve as "Sunday" schools or, yet, have full-time schools teaching a curriculum that is more sensitive to various groups' religious beliefs, ethnic customs, and languages (DeVries et al., 2010). These institutions, therefore, fulfill many educational functions

FAMILY RESEARCH 6.2

What Can Be Done with a Question on Religiosity?

Statistics Canada conducts an annual General Social Survey from a sample of 10,000 Canadians. Since 1985, two questions about religion have been included. One question concerns religious affiliation and the other pertains to religiosity, that is, the frequency of attendance at religious services or meetings. Clark (1998) first controlled for or took into account income, family structure, education, age, sex, and employment because it is well known that these variables are related to various aspects of well-being. Then, with these controls in the background, the researchers still found that persons who attend religious services or meetings weekly are half less likely to feel stressed and 1.5 times more likely to have a very happy marital relationship than those

who do not attend religious services at all. Weekly attendees' marriages are also far more likely to last. Overall, weekly attendees hold more conventional family values and adopt better health practices.

It would be interesting to break down the results by religious affiliation, given that Canada is such a diverse society: Would these results apply equally well for Chinese religion, Hindus, Sikhs, Buddhists, or Muslims? As well, there are more indicators of religiosity that could be included, such as frequency of reading religious books, watching/listening to religious television/radio, and prayers (Atkins and Kessel, 2008; Taylor et al., 2004). Would these make any difference in terms of family life?

TABLE 6.2	**Change in Religious Attendance by Place of Birth in the Three Largest CMAs*: Percentages of Those Who Attend at Least Once a Month***		
	1989–1993	1999–2001	Difference
Montreal			
Canadian-born	26%	17%	–9%
Born outside Canada	44	40	–4
Toronto			
Canadian-born	31	28	–3
Born outside Canada	44	50	+6
Vancouver			
Canadian-born	19	21	+2
Born outside Canada	35	39	+4

Source: Adapted from Statistics Canada, General Social Survey; Clark, 2003.

* population includes those aged 15 and over

for children and their families. They may, in addition, serve political purposes and are often used to fight racism (Nayar, 2010). It is also possible that, among immigrants and second-generation Canadians, religious congregations that are built along ethnic lines may "hinder broad social cohesion at the same time that they cushion the individuals and families who join them from the trials and tribulations of a culturally pluralistic society" (Baker, 2010:181). This would be especially the case when these communities also provide schools.

In 2005, about 21 percent of the adult Canadian population attended religious services on a *weekly* basis, down from about 67 percent in 1946 (Lindsay, 2008). In 2008, 31 percent of women and 26 percent of men attended religious services at least once a month (Statistics Canada, 2010a). The monthly rate in the U.S. is 45 percent, thus much higher. In Canada, there are regional as well as immigration-related differences. Monthly attendance ranges from 53 percent in Prince Edward Island to 36 percent in Ontario and 25 percent in Quebec and British Columbia. Table 6.2 illustrates the fact that attendance has declined among the Canadian-born but has increased among immigrants, except in Quebec—probably as a result of the strong secular effect of that province or a selection effect among future immigrants themselves. The increase of religious attendance among immigrants may stem from a change in the countries of origin of immigrants (Chapter 2). More Filipinos attend Catholic churches, as is the case in Toronto. In addition, mosques as well as Hindu and Sikh temples have been erected during the past decade and facilitate attendance (McDonough and Hoodfar, 2005). In terms of giving money to charities and volunteering time, Canadians tend to give more of both to religious organizations (Grona, 2009). Further, individuals who are more religious give more to charitable organizations than those who are not religious at all—several thousand dollars more yearly (MacQueen, 2012; Turcotte, 2012).

Considering all the religious indicators together, but particularly attendance at services, women are more religious than men, the older more than the younger, "conservative" Protestants more than "liberal" Protestants, and the married more than the single and divorced (Presser and Stinson, 1998). In the U.S., black families attend religious services and participate in other religious activities far more frequently than do white families, except Latinos (Aldous and Ganey, 1999). There is a greater mixture of secular and religious functions in the black community.

THE ROLE PLAYED BY RELIGIOSITY IN FAMILY LIFE

Parents transmit their beliefs to their children by their teachings and their example. Attendance at church, synagogue, temple, or mosque constitutes a powerful socialization context (Pearce and Thornton, 2007). We can then ask if religious participation fulfills any role in family life besides the transmission of beliefs and related behaviours. What does religiosity do for the family and its members? Religious beliefs can be analyzed as a form of capital—**religious capital** as Iannaccone (1990) calls it—from which families can, in theory, draw cohesion as well as strength. Participating in a congregation may constitute a form of **social capital** in the guise of informal networks of social support (Petts, 2012). The following discussion is based on studies of Christians and to some extent Jews. I would hypothesize that the research described below applies equally well to other religions (Hirji, 2012), but with differences pertaining to matters related to gender roles and marital quality (see Bramadat and Seljak, 2005). The issue of **cultural capital** may even be more salient in other religions, especially for recent immigrant families, depending on their historical background and country of origin (see Daneshpour, 2013).

Religiosity Correlates with Well-Being

A substantial body of literature indicates that religious involvement and strength of beliefs are related to general feelings of good self-assessed health, even in European countries (Huijts and Kraaykamp, 2011), as well as psychological well-being and lower adult mortality (Hummer et al., 1999). This benefit may manifest itself as early as adolescence (Crosnoe and Elder, 2002). Religiosity provides internal coherence; it serves as an explanatory platform that enables persons to make sense of everyday life and its adversities. It offers guiding principles of action, and makes people less individualistic and more duty bound. It serves as an internal and external **agency of social control** (Durkheim, 1897); hence, religious commitment lowers health risks such as alcoholism, drug addiction, and precocious sexual activity, and may serve to prevent depression and anxiety (Ellison et al., 2009).

In fact, religiosity is related to children's prosocial behaviours (Bartowski et al., 2008). It may deter drug use and delinquent behaviour among adolescents, in part because religious adolescents are less likely to associate with peers who use drugs (Johnson et al., 2001). Adolescents who are more religious view delinquent actions as morally unacceptable and tend to select a peer group with a similar commitment. As a result, their level of delinquency is lower than that of non-religious adolescents, hence facilitating parental socialization (Simons et al., 2004). Other studies show that private religious practice among adolescents, or the degree to which their religion is internalized, is related to fewer behavioural problems in environments in which violence is often witnessed and victimization occurs (Pearce et al., 2003). Finally, let's mention the many studies indicating that family religiosity is related to a later age of onset of sexual behaviours among adolescents (Manlove et al., 2008b).

Religious participation contributes to extend a family's social network and sources of social support. Frequent churchgoers have somewhat larger social networks than others and enjoy more frequent person-to-person contacts. They are also more involved in their community (Jones, 2000). They receive more help and report feeling cared for and valued. Therefore, religious participation becomes an important social resource for families (Bramadat and Seljak, 2005). This is expressed by a student below:

> *"My mother is a concern to me at this stage because she is 65 and widowed and unemployed* [but not poor]. *But I think that her church activities and all the friendships she's made there help her a lot and will sustain her for some years to come. Sometimes I even go with her because I like meeting all these people of all ages. Anyway, my mother says that religion keeps her in good health and she is far from being a zealot."*

Religiosity Scaffolds the Parental Role

Religious beliefs strengthen parents' involvement with their children, even when the latter become particularly difficult and stressful. Pearce and Axinn (1998) surmise that "exposure to religious themes such as tolerance, patience, and unconditional love" through religious activities constitutes a resource that helps parents and children maintain a good relationship (p. 824). Parent-child similarity in religiosity strengthens the bond between the two, particularly with boys (Kim-Spoon et al., 2012). Some studies indicate that, especially among African Americans who are disadvantaged, religious parents use fewer coercive methods with their children than non-religious parents (Wiley et al., 2002). Overall, research shows that religious mothers experience a higher quality of relationship with their children (Pearce and Axinn, 1998), and that religious fathers, whether married or divorced, are more involved parents (King, 2003b). In turn, children, even small ones, are less likely to display behavioural problems.

In a study of five European countries, Gans et al. (2009) found that religious individuals were more likely to engage in supportive behaviours toward elderly parents. Regarding single mothers, Petts (2012) concludes that religious participation encourages them "to engage in parenting practices that promote positive child development" (p. 251). Adolescent mothers who attend church services have been found to be less abusive and had children with fewer internalizing and externalizing problems by age 10—as religiosity increased social support and served as a protective factor (Carothers et al., 2005). But it is possible that a genetic selection process occurs as well to explain this correlation.

Worshipping together constitutes a form of social capital. Religious participation can also be the basis of an effective community, which contributes to child and adolescent socialization, and buttresses the parental role.

Myrleen Ferguson Cate/PhotoEdit

Following a **family developmental perspective**, Stolzenberg et al. (1995) demonstrate that people often become more religious with age. But the addition of children to the family unit further enhances this increase in religious participation (Nock, 1998b). In contrast, as childless married adults age, their religious participation does not increase to any great extent. One explanation may be that adults with children seek religious membership and participation in order to become better anchored in the community and as a means of social support in their parenting role. Along this line of reasoning, another student projects a greater role for religion later in her life:

> *"Right now I don't go to church often but I intend to become active again as soon as I have children, just as my parents did. I think that a bit of religion is very helpful to children: it teaches them values other than what they see on TV. The few times I go to church I am always struck by how civilized people behave and it gives you a warm feeling of humanity."*

One could perhaps speculate that many parents need religion nowadays in order to feel more secure in their role in a very demanding and confusing world. Religion may serve as a compensatory mechanism for the blaming and disempowerment they receive from so many quarters. Wilcox (2002) concludes: "The irony is that religious institutions, generally taken to be carriers of more traditional mores, seem to be showing some success" in fostering paternal involvement in times of change (p. 791). Parents may also use religion as an agent of socialization and as a source of support for their children. In this respect, it is interesting to note that Canadian youths leave home significantly earlier when they never attended religious services as teenagers (Beaupré et al., 2008).

Religiosity Relates to Marital Quality and Stability

Adults who declare a religious affiliation are more likely to see marriage as a lifetime commitment than adults who profess no religious affiliation (Stanley et al., 2004). New research in Canada also indicates that this may apply to Muslim couples, particularly men (Moghissi et al., 2009:79) This may extend to same-sex couples (Oswald et al., 2008). Couples who hold beliefs that are more religious experience higher conjugal satisfaction and quality (Lichter and Carmalt, 2009; Treas and Giesen, 2000; Tremblay et al., 2002). They are also less likely to engage in extramarital sex. Couples who regularly attend church together have a lower rate of divorce than those who attend infrequently or not at all (Fincham and Beach, 2010; Provencher et al., 2006). However, couples in which only one spouse attends are even more likely to divorce than couples who never attend (Vaaler et al., 2009)—especially when it is only the wife who attends (Schramm et al., 2012). The latter finding can probably be explained in terms of religious similarity, or homogamy, described in Chapter 7: Couples who differ in religious matters have one potentially large source of conflict. In contrast, couples who attend church together benefit from the sharing of a social and spiritual activity that reinforces their solidarity. They may also benefit from exposure to more **altruistic values** than nonchurchgoers, and this would in turn contribute to a less individualistic pattern of marital interaction. A student expresses this sociological observation within the context of his intimate relationship:

> *"My problem right now is that my girlfriend is not religious and this worries me a lot because I know from my parents' experience that sharing beliefs and especially* [going to church] *. . . give a couple a lot in common. Above all I am concerned that my girlfriend may miss out on the importance of values that help keep a marriage together, like learning how to be committed and think in terms of the good of the relationship and not just about your own personal desires."*

Similarly, mutually shared religious beliefs strengthen marital stability—although this factor may be less important in remarriages (Schramm et al., 2012) as religions tend to be pro-marriage rather than pro-divorce. Amato and Rogers (1997) report that frequent church attendance may reduce the likelihood of divorce through a reduction in marital problems. Why would couples who attend church frequently experience fewer marital problems? Their explanation is congruent with the ones just presented. They reason that church attendance, or even shared at-home devotional activities, allow for the internalization and thus acceptance of norms of behaviour that encourage couples to get along (Ellison et al., 2010). They also refer to the social aspect of church attendance: It serves as a **support group** as well as a control group or an effective community. Vaaler et al. (2009), for their part, note that more religious people are less prone to divorce because their level of marital satisfaction is higher, their likelihood of engaging in domestic violence lower, and "they perceive fewer attractive options outside the marriage than their less religious counterparts" (p. 930). As well, parents' religiosity influences adult children's attitudes toward divorce (Kapinus and Pellerin, 2008). The sum of these studies therefore indicates a salutary effect of religiosity on the quality of the marital relationship as well as on the stability of the family unit. This effect is not so obvious in remarriages, perhaps in part because remarried couples are less religious (Schramm et al., 2012).

Limitations of Religion for Nonconventional Families

Organized religions, which *have been culturally developed by men over several millennia or centuries, support gender stratification* (Sered, 1999). It follows that families headed by women and men who are strongly aware of inequalities based on gender may not find spiritual sustenance and stability in religion as much as do other families. Further, most religions frown on nonmarital forms of sexuality, and individuals who regularly attend religious services are less favourable toward nonmarital sex. Depending on the religion, churchgoers may also strongly disapprove of homosexuality.

Therefore, while faith and religiosity are very positive for the faithful's well-being on many levels, they are less so for the well-being of those who engage in nonconventional forms of family life, such as families headed by same-sex couples. Religious communities by and large exclude these couples so that these families are deprived of a powerful instrument of child socialization and a powerful source of family stability. There are indications that many gays and lesbians are deeply religious but fear rejection, as explained in a student autobiography:

> *"My lover and I both come from religious families and this has probably contributed to our mutual attraction. We're basically both moderately religious but we can't go to church. I suppose we could go separately and I could even join the choir . . . and he might volunteer in the child care. But we can't do this because we'd stick out like sore thumbs and we might even be discouraged from participating. We could go with my parents but what if they were ostracized as a result? I'm sure that there must be other gays out there who are religious but Bob and I don't mix much with the gay community because we're a monogamous couple."*

(It is probably not a coincidence that this couple is planning on adopting children; their values are mainstream.)

In many areas, various congregations are opening their community to homosexuals and have been at the forefront of gay rights issues (Rayside and Wilcox, 2011). As well, churches located in downtown areas may be more accepting of diversity than those in suburbs or in rural areas. But overall, one can conclude that religious establishments do not serve the entire spectrum of families equally well, although some congregations are far more proactive than others in this respect. As well, religion is heavily influenced by *regional cultures and even political situations*. For instance, in most countries that are predominantly Muslim, homosexuality is a crime (*The Economist*, 2012b). As well, depending on cultural origins and time periods, Muslim women may dress in an "occidental" or, yet, another manner relevant to their own cultural group, while others wear a head scarf and even the burqa or hijab. As well, political and cultural (and regional) interpretations of the Qur'an have placed the onus of external morality on women's bodies, hence segregation (Clarke, 2003). This responsibility has led to honour killings of daughters, even in Canada.

CONCLUSIONS: THE BALANCING ACT OF FAMILY RESPONSIBILITIES

Children and adolescents attending educational facilities and child care centres come to school from their families and return to their families when the school day is over. Their parents must manage this institutional link and remain vigilant so that the best interest of their child is well served. This is an especially difficult role for families because school systems serve the economies in which they are nestled and economies are currently largely driven by a relentless technological and globalized marketplace. Many families are unable to compete and even survive within the harsh realities of this context.

In particularly deficient schools, parents have to supplement their children's education. As well, when schools harbour a critical mass of antisocial children, parents have to step in, if they can, to protect and even shelter their children. Thus, although schools have taken over some of the duties previously fulfilled by families, schools have also forced an extension of school functions into the home domain. Furthermore, depending on family structure and place within the social class system, schools create a host of demands on parents.

Thus, to return to the discussions in Chapter 3, the educational system often expands family responsibilities and may even burden the family system and, more specifically, mothers. For families that are religiously oriented, however, religion seems to scaffold parents in their socialization role—providing support for the parental role and support for adolescents and youths who wish to lead a life devoid of lifestyle risks. Therefore, at least for religious families, the practice of their faith generally strengthens their ability to fulfill their functions in a society that often provides pressures against this goal.

Summary

1. After parents, schools are a main agent of child socialization. Children today begin school earlier, and for many, this experience includes child care other than parental. The types of non-parental child care available are discussed and the consequences of poor-quality care are related. Child care availability, affordability, and quality are key ingredients in contemporary children's development and in their parents' well-being. The benefits of Head Start programs for disadvantaged children are discussed.

2. Parental involvement in their children's education, parents' social class as a determinant, advantages for children from higher-SES families, and the process of concentrated cultivation are discussed. Other topics are family and school incompatibility, particularly for Aboriginal and immigrant children.

3. Private schools as well as home schooling are presented as systems that parents turn to in order to ensure the passage of their values to their children as well as their educational success.

4. Religion plays an important role in the lives of many Canadian families. The most commonly used indicator of religiosity is church, temple, or mosque attendance.

5. Overall, religious involvement is related to health, psychological well-being, marital stability and happiness, as well as child socialization. Religiosity supports the parental role. However, some religions are less supportive of nontraditional families.

6. While the educational system often increases the responsibilities that families have to fulfill, the religious system may offer a supportive framework for the fulfillment of their responsibilities.

Analytical Questions

1. What would be some methodological difficulties involved in the study of the effect of daycare on child development?

2. Why do you think that school officials and even some researchers are worried about home schooling? (Note: The question is *why* they are worried, not what they are worried about—the answer is not directly in the text.)

3. How could the school system be reformed to meet the needs of families of immigrants as well as low-income families?

4. Religion and especially religiosity are rarely discussed in family textbooks. Why do you think that this is so? (The answer is not directly in the text.)

5. What role does religiosity play in families that are not Christian or Jewish? (You will need to use other sources or your own personal experience/observations to address this question.)

CHAPTER 7

Couple Formation and Sexual Relations

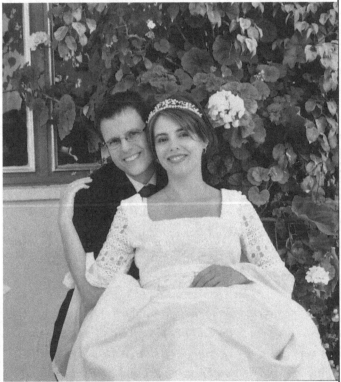

Anne-Marie Ambert

OUTLINE

Dating and Sexual Relationships
Heterosexual and Same-Sex Dating
Interracial Couple Formation
Internet Dating

Date and Partner Selection
Elements in Partner Selection

Cohabitation
Relationship Stability and Reasons for
Entering into Cohabitation
Relationship Aspects
For Older Adults

Heterosexual Marriage

Same-Sex Marriage

Singlehood

Sexual Relations
Adolescent Sexuality
Issues of Control and Consequences
*Early Teen Sexuality and the Role of
Peers*

Sexual Identities and Sexualities
Marital and Cohabitational Sexual
Relations
*Frequency of Sexual Intercourse and
Aging*
*Frequency of Sexual Intercourse and
Relationship Quality*
Extracouple Sexual Relations
Media Portrayals of Infidelity and
Pornography

**Conclusions: The Changing Profile of
Couples and Sexuality**

Summary
Analytical Questions

"The most painful aspect of my life at this age [about 21] is that I don't have a steady boyfriend. I haven't had one in two years and I am worried that life is passing me by."

"I rate myself as very happy . . . . Before I broke up with my boyfriend of two years I had no life. I was entirely wrapped up in a relationship that denied my identity. . . . It's freedom now and time for me to use it to mature."

"I live with my boyfriend and I really like it for now but I worry about the future. I am 23 and want to get married one day but the way I see it, he likes it just fine the way it is and won't want to commit himself to something more serious."

"In 10 years from now I realistically see myself living with a partner but it will not be the one I am with now as you can guess [this lesbian student is currently living with a woman at least 15 years her senior who supports her financially but is very controlling and possessive]. *This relationship has left me with some 'emotional' baggage I have to get rid of before I can contemplate another relationship and I plan on living on my own for some years after school is over."*

"What has made me the most unhappy in the past years has been the gay social scene. I really hated every minute of it. . . . What has made me the most happy in the past year has been getting out of the gay social scene and finding my lover who just feels the way I do. [This student lives with his parents.]

"I am still a virgin and it has its inconvenience socially [popularity]. *. . . I am proud of myself because I have stuck to my principles and my parents' and one day the full discovery of sex will be a very exciting experience to share with my husband. It will add something to our marriage and he will know that I have waited for him."*

This chapter is the first of two in the section on patterns of partnering and family formation. These two chapters combined describe recent developments in couple formation as well as among singles. In turn, we see how these changes are related to other recent demographic developments in the timing of family formation at the nuclear level and, in the case of low fertility or childlessness, result in a major demographic upheaval with far-reaching consequences. The preceding students' quotes reveal how they feel about dating, cohabitation, being partnered, and sexuality—all main topics of this chapter, which starts with the chronological beginning of couples:

Individuals select partners, become couples with various levels of commitment, and initiate sexual relations. Sexual identities as well as infidelities are also discussed.

DATING AND SEXUAL RELATIONSHIPS

Dating was, at the beginning, an American institution* that emerged after the First World War. More recently, it has even expanded at the preadolescent level in the U.S. where researchers seem to accept the ages of 13 and 14 as "developmentally appropriate" for the onset of dating (Longmore et al., 2001)—perhaps an ethnocentric perspective. Dating in itself is now widespread in the western world and accepted in many other countries. When it began, dating was revolutionary because it replaced the traditional *courtship* system as a prelude to marriage: It represented a shift in terms of control over couple formation—from parents to the youths involved. Parental or familial control as well as the cultural necessity of a woman's chastity are the reasons why dating is not an acceptable institution in many parts of the world: Hindu states are examples as especially are Muslim countries, where the family honour often rests on the regulation of women's behaviour (Zine, 2008).

But dating as a social invention has also evolved over time. The period of adolescence has lengthened and age at marriage has been delayed in order to consolidate education and career at the upper and middle echelons. As a result, dating was separated from marriage as a goal: Its purpose became recreational and sexualized. In fact, today some youths, particularly males, are simply more interested in hooking up than in dating (Bogle, 2008; Hamilton and Armstrong, 2009)—although there are indications that these hook-ups* and "friends with benefits"* are far less common than presented in the media. Indeed, most Canadian college students who have had sexual relationships report having had only one sexual partner in the last 12 months (CACUSS, 2013). This said, both men and women who have participated in such relationships identify advantages as well as disadvantages of friends-with-benefits relationships. But women are more likely to hope that this relationship would progress to something more exclusive and romantic, both in Canada and the U.S. (Weaver et al., 2011). Gusarova et al. (2012) also found that a third of women in their sample had had a negative experience versus 19 percent of the men. Women were 3.3 times more likely to want to avoid such relationships in the future.

We need longitudinal studies that would follow students to later adulthood to assess what differentiates those who are willing to have hook-ups and friends with benefits and how these relationships, if at all, affect subsequent attitudes about dating, cohabitation, marriage, and also divorce risks. Indeed, just as non-committed cohabitations are related to higher divorce rates later, one can well wonder how teens and young adults who enter into casual sexual relationships without emotional intimacy, and do so serially or concurrently, will be prepared for future committed and more psychologically intimate relationships (Regnerus and Uecker, 2011). How do these relationships "shape or war against their vision of marriage—or even how marriage might fit in with their other life goals" (p. 170)? *Hook-ups and other casual sexual relationships constitute socialization contexts*. What do they teach? There is even a new word used for those who enter, exit, and enter again into the same sexual relationships at an accelerated pace: *churning* (Halpern-Meekin et al., 2013).

Couples also become sexually involved fairly rapidly now: Sassler et al (2012) have found that one-third of their married and cohabiting respondents had become sexually involved within the first month. They further discovered that the speed of entry into sexuality was later related to lower marital happiness among women but not men, joining Regnerus and Uecker's concerns. Women who had entered marriage without prior cohabitation had more often waited up to six months before becoming sexually involved. These same women were significantly more likely to be happier in their relationship over a wide range of indicators. The researchers concluded that it was entry into cohabitation, via early sexual involvement, that led to poorer marital results. Other youths move in together rather than date.

Heterosexual and Same-Sex Dating

Children as young as age five are at times asked if they have a girlfriend or boyfriend yet. They learn, perhaps too young, that a couple culture pervades North American social life, which later makes it difficult for individuals to feel that they "belong" if they do not have a steady date or partner. Thus, steady dates represent a measure of social and personal predictability and security in a youth's social life. But when concerns about being a couple occur early in a child's life, these concerns may supplant other experiences and sources of self-definition. Not surprisingly, research indicates that young adolescent females who are romantically involved are more vulnerable in the emotional and academic realms than are older adolescents (Brendgen et al., 2002; Joyner and Udry, 2000). Dating often becomes a form of social pressure and a key source of status, although this may be diminishing (Bibby, 2002:180). Dating and, as seen earlier, casual relationships serve the function of socializing youths, both positively and negatively, for the role they will play when they cohabit or marry.

Women tend to invest more in their dating relationship than do men (Sacher and Fine, 1996). This pattern of **gender roles** *in the emotional domain is pursued at all levels of casual and romantic relationships.* This greater female investment stems in part from their socialization, which has taught them to be nurturing and understanding of others (Onyskiw and Hayduk, 2001:382)—not necessarily "bad" qualities but, as they go against the grain of masculine values, this situation places women at a disadvantage. Consequently, females also perceive that they have access to fewer desirable alternatives outside their relationship than do males. Students' autobiographies indicate that this situation exists across social class and ethnicity:

> *"The most painful experience at this stage has occurred three months ago when I broke up with my boyfriend of three years. . . . I should have broken up with him two years ago . . . but I was afraid to be left alone, that I wouldn't be able to go out without a boyfriend, that I couldn't find another one, but now I realize that I have wasted two years of my life, and that's terrifying."*

This perception of a lack of alternatives contributes to reinforcing women's tendency to work harder at relationship maintenance, even if this is to their detriment. Dating interactions are nonegalitarian, at least at the beginning (Laner and

Ventrone, 1998). This pattern is pursued into pre-wedding relationships (Humble, 2003) and spousal relationships, as discussed in Chapter 9. However, in terms of **social exchange theory,** females with the most desirable resources (often defined by males as attractiveness) can "afford" doing less maintenance work, as their alternatives may be more numerous and desirable than those of their date.

It is not yet possible to provide solid information on same-sex dating because little research exists on this topic. To begin with, gay persons are not readily accessible for research purposes (Goldberg et al., 2010). Many shun publicity so as to avoid stigmatization because they constitute a small minority and, among youth, there are still a great deal of anti-gay remarks circulating in schools (Rushowy, 2011; Taylor et al., 2011). Furthermore, there is not always a clear-cut demarcation between homosexual and heterosexual self-identity, particularly among youths, although this also occurs among adults, particularly women (Baute, 2010).

This being said, one can presume that dating may fulfill emotional functions for homosexuals similar to those among heterosexuals (Ronson et al., 2012). Same-sex dating may, however, be difficult in terms of high school popularity as well as social acceptance in colleges and universities located outside key metropolitan areas. The high school environment is often anti-gay, as it is at some universities. As a result, gay youths may be harassed, which in turn can lead to mental health problems. Thus, gay adolescents and young adults, then, might not be able to date as do their heterosexual peers for fear of being socially stigmatized. In many countries of the world, particularly in Russia, the Middle East, and Africa, open homosexuality is actually condemned, particularly in Muslim countries (Pew Research Center, 2013).

Another problem may reside in that young gays may not yet know how to recognize a potential partner or may not have access to enough potential partners to find an appropriate one, while others may rely on sexual minority youth groups to find partners or, yet, on the Internet, which reduces the fear of marginalization (Hillier and Harrison, 2007). Further, for many, "coming out" (revealing their sexual identities) may occur only when they reach adulthood. Older and more mature gays and lesbians may find it easier to begin relationships, especially if they have been out for a long time. Overall, gay men's scripts are more sexually oriented whereas lesbians' are more emotionally oriented (Goldberg et al., 2010).

Interracial Couple Formation

Race and **ethnicity** are usually the first two elements that are considered in partner selection. Even hook-ups largely involve same-race persons, albeit far less so than dating (McClintock, 2010). Although intermarriage (exogamy*) between whites and other groups is now widely accepted at the attitudinal level in Canada, *only 3.9 percent of married and 4.9 percent of cohabiting couples are racially mixed* (Milan et al., 2010). For instance, in the 2006 census, there were 247,600 couples involving a white person with someone who is from another group, or 3.3 percent of all couples; in addition, there were 41,900 couples involving members of two different non-white groups, or 0.6 percent of all couples. (In contrast, 9.8 percent of same-sex couples were mixed.) Japanese Canadians are overwhelmingly intermarried at 60 percent, in part because they are a smaller group and thus have more opportunities of meeting persons who are *not* of their racial background (Milan et al., 2010; Statistics Canada, 2009p). However, mixed unions are proportionately fewer as we ascend the age ladder (Milan, et al., 2010). We present below some rates of intermarriage based on ethnic *origin:*

South Asian	6.8 percent
Chinese	9.5 percent
Filipinos	19.8 percent
Latin American	30.7 percent
black-identified	25.5 percent

It is, however, expected that Asian rates will increase over time (Lee and Boyd, 2008). As well, a much larger proportion of black men than black women who are in unions are in mixed ones—in fact, in 2006, 41 percent of all *unions* in which there was one black person were interracial, the majority of whom were black men (Milan et al., 2010). The same situation occurs in the U.S. where black women are the "least inter-married" group (*The Economist*, 2011a). This creates a serious imbalance for black women, what has been called the **"new marriage squeeze"** (Crowder and Tolnay, 2000). In fact, when American black women date interracially, they are often "has-sled" by other blacks, which Karazin and Littlejohn (2012) equate as a throwback to slavery. A study of college-educated black women shows how they are disadvantaged in terms of dating, not only because of a lack of potential black partners with a similar level of education but, also, because non-black men do not tend to dater black women, especially educated ones (Clarke, 2011). Black women, when students, are also con-cerned about black men's reluctance to commit themselves to exclusive relationships (McClintock, 2010): "Even black men who nominally commit to one woman" are far more likely than white men "to have others on the side" (*The Economist*, 2011a). Both in Canada and the U.S., black/white unions are far more common in casual hook-ups and simple dating than in cohabitation and especially marriage (Batson et al., 2006). Such unions are also less stable. A black student expresses her frustration:

> *"My older sister is tall and slim and has great features and she just married a nice black guy and our parents are so proud of her. I admit, they're a lovely couple but this leaves me nowhere because I don't have her looks and I haven't met a decent black guy who isn't interested in just sex (and I apologize for being so crude but I guess I'm really angry) or white girls. They seem to think that black girls are there just to make kids for them. . . . I'm not bold enough to look at white guys and I'm afraid that if I got a white boyfriend his family and friends would be very disappointed and this would reflect badly on our relationship. Lots of my girlfriends are in the same spot but it doesn't make me feel any better. I don't think that people understand this."*

As well, in the U.S., middle-class black women college students are less accepting of cohabitation than are low-income black women and even white women of their class (Willoughby and Carroll, 2012).

As the number of Canadians who belong to minority groups increases, interracial marriages will also increase over the years, as has been the case in Great Britain (*The Economist*, 2012a). Indeed, Kalbach (2000) has found that, at least for ethnicity, the Canadian-born have higher exogamy rates than the foreign-born. Further, white interethnic marriages are the norm rather than the exception among Canadian-born groups from northern and western Europe. In general, however, intermarriages involve partners who, except for race or ethnicity, are very similar in terms of religion, education, lifestyle, and values (Yancey, 2002).

Internet Dating

Internet dating has greatly increased recently and seems to be widely accepted. By 2009, about 20 percent of heterosexual couples and 60 percent of same-sex couples had met online. About 25 percent of Canadians "have tried Internet dating and 16 percent have had sex with someone they met online" (Engelhart, 2013:46). What is written here about this new phenomenon is tentative because it is too soon to expect extensive and *reliable* research to have been carried out in this domain. There is a proliferation of Internet sites for the purpose of meeting dates, sexual partners for all types of casual and committed relationships, and marital partners. There are ethnic and religious sites, sites where parents can try to match their children with others from their group, same-sex sites, sites pertaining to match people with certain conditions, such as HIV. Internet dating, chat rooms, and now "apps" that show who is available for a date on the street where we are walking all contribute to enlarging both the structure and the meaning of dating itself.

There are several important issues that require urgent research, even though this approach to relationship formation is evolving rapidly (Wilson, 2009). For instance, when one meets someone in person rather than on the Internet, a chain of dynamics begins: A face-to-face interaction develops, and one can immediately "test" certain realities, such as physical appearance, voice, facial expressions, and general demeanour. Online, in contrast, one starts with a description that may or may not be accurate, even when pictures are attached—*a great deal of deceptive self-advertising takes place*. Then, emails may be exchanged, additional pictures may follow, a phone call may result. The face-to-face interaction arrives only after one has already developed an impression, formed an image, of the other, and even after an online relationship has progressed.

A second difference is that Internet and "speed dating" involve a multiplicity of potential partners; it is akin to a buffet as opposed to a sit-down dinner! What does it do to a person to have access to so many potential contacts? Does it take a shorter or a longer time to concentrate on one person, to commit to one person? Do Internet daters run the risk of never committing themselves to a relationship? And how solid is this commitment when one knows that there are so many others "out there" that one could try? Is there not the possibility that we may end by no longer seeing commitment as a value? Yet, studies have shown that it is one of the key ingredients in good and lasting marriages. Do new Internet partners go through the same phases of acquaintanceship and attachment as others do when they meet face to face? A study quoted by Englehart (2013) found that the average length of a courtship before marriage had been 18.5 months when the first contact took place online compared to 42 months for those that began in person. Are the relationships as successful, as happy, as long? Do they result more in cohabitations or in marriages? These are only a few of the questions that could be studied. On another sociological level, one can also ask whether there are social class and ethnic differences between Internet daters and non-Internet daters.

DATE AND PARTNER SELECTION

Dates and now hook-ups as well as friends with benefits are at first largely selected from schools, neighbourhoods, part-time work sites, and social clubs to which adolescents or their parents belong. Parents, siblings, and their friends may also constitute a source of dates, particularly in some religions or ethnicities among whom marriage within the group is preferred. Overall, **propinquity**, or physical proximity, is the first rule that explains how adolescents choose dates and, later on, partners. In young adulthood, proximal availability continues to be an important factor, but its scope broadens to include the worlds of higher education, employment, and volunteer work (see Belot and Francesconi, 2013). Thus, the new phenomenon of Internet dating defies the first rule of partner selection.

As they age, adults generally become more selective and the pool of eligible dates narrows because each individual then tries to select only certain types of persons (Sassler, 2010). This is called **assortative mating***, which refers to choosing a date or partner on the basis of certain traits. When two persons choose each other on the basis of some elements of similarity, this is called **homogamy***. The term **endogamy*** is used when people hook up, date, cohabit, and marry *within their own status group or with persons who are similar to them in terms of basic social characteristics.* Homogamy leads to compatibility of interests, values, and lifestyle. Endogamy and homogamy make sense because similarity of lifestyle, values, and interests gives couples a larger pool of experiences they can share and activities they can engage in together. It strengthens mutual feelings, "we-ness," and companionship—key elements in modern relationships—and lowers the risk of divorce (Kalmijn et al., 2005).

Elements in Partner Selection

We have already discussed race and ethnicity as the first two elements that are considered in partner selection. **Social class**, or socioeconomic status (SES) endogamy, as well as educational endogamy, is also widespread. This is partly explained by the fact that the proximity factor is driven by parents' social class, which dictates where children live and which schools they attend (Nelson and Robinson, 2002). Even at work, people are attracted to one another because of common interests and shared topics of conversation that are partly related to their class-linked resources, including education and leisure activities. When the partners are discrepant, the more common scenario involves a woman in a relationship with a man of higher income, although this may be changing.

In terms of **education** alone, there is an even greater trend than 30 years ago toward homogamy, especially among the university educated (Hou and Myles, 2008). Inasmuch as higher education is related to better salaries, as seen in Chapter 4, educational similarity at the top contributes to the increasing gap between the rich and the others. However, in terms of gender, men are more advantaged than women in this respect because 68 percent of university-educated men marry homogamously but only 53 percent of similar women do (Hou and Myles, 2007). One has to keep in mind here that men and women with university degrees are still a minority in Canada, although the number of degrees is increasing among younger cohorts. First marriages are more homogamous than subsequent ones (Schwartz and Mare, 2012). As well, cohabitants, whether in Quebec or in the rest of Canada and the U.S., have a lower level of educational homogamy (Hamplova and Le Bourdais, 2008; Martin and Hou, 2010; Schwartz, 2010b).

Religious endogamy is more important in some groups, especially Sikhs, Hindus, and Muslims, than among Protestant, Catholic, and even Jewish groups. Statistics Canada (2006c) reports that people who are highly religious, are older, or are immigrant and belong to communities that are religiously homogeneous, are less likely to marry someone of another religion. In 1981, 15 percent of couples were interreligious and, by 2001, 19 percent were—not a huge increase. Nearly half of these unions were between Catholics and Protestants which are the two largest religious groups in Canada. Sikhs, Hindus, and Muslims have the lowest interreligious marriage rate and it is even lower now than it was in 1981 when fewer persons of these religions lived in Canada. Muslims who marry out represented 4 percent of couples in which there was one Muslim spouse. About 17 percent of couples in which there was one Jewish person were interreligious in 2001, up from 9 percent in 1981. However, substantial proportions of these marriages are remarriages. Religious similarity is related to marital quality but less so than a generation ago and less so for remarriages (Myers, 2006; Schramm et al., 2012).

A preference for **age** similarity also exists. In over half of couples, the spouses are no more than three years apart while 24 percent have a spouse who is four to six years older. However, when there is an age difference, norms favour an "older man–younger woman" situation: While 36 percent of Canadian couples include a male who is older by three years, only 6 percent of couples include a woman who is more than three years older than the man (Boyd and Li, 2003). When men marry at an older age, or remarry, they usually do so to women considerably younger than they (Wu et al., 2000). The **age gap** increases with subsequent remarriages. Thus, the older men are at marriage, the larger the age difference (England and McClintock, 2009). Because there is a double standard of aging, men are generally less receptive than women to the idea of marrying someone older than they (Buss et al., 2001), and they value good looks in women when seeking a partner (Abu-Laban and McDaniel, 2004). Overall, large age differences tend to be found more often among the foreign-born, non-white minorities, cohabitations rather than marriages, and lower-income groups (Boyd and Li, 2003).

The principle of homogamy or assortative matching *is somewhat less important among same-sex couples* (Jepsen and Jepsen, 2002). Homosexuals are nonconformists in at least one area of their lives—their sexuality. This may well lead them to be nontraditional in other domains, including the criteria that dictate choice of partners. Further, as a minority, they may have to cast a wider net than do heterosexuals because suitable mates may not be readily available. Thus, because of necessity or rejection from their ethnic group, gays and lesbians who belong to minority groups have high rates of interethnic and interracial partnering (Milan et al., 2010).

The qualities that men and women seek in a partner have been converging in recent decades, although males still value **physical appearance** more than women (Buss et al., 2001; Carmalt et al., 2008). In a study of newlyweds, both spouses behaved more negatively toward each other when they had rated the wives to be less attractive than the husbands (McNulty et al., 2008). Physical attractiveness is a more important element of mate selection among males (Fisman et al., 2006). Hence, partner selection among gay men may be more influenced by physical appearance than is the case among lesbian women. There is, in fact, a certain obsession about "partner-shopping . . . for Mr. Right only if he is also Mr. Buff—muscled and perfectly toned" (DeAngelis, 2002). This theme is developed by the gay student quoted at the outset of this chapter and pursued by another below:

> *"What was so hard for me is that I am not Mr. America, I am small framed and . . . I look a bit older so that I don't appeal to males who are looking for a well built body and especially an adolescent type. I am not particularly sexy. I am just a plain guy with plain habits and the bar and club scene was very hard on me. Another problem is that I am not the promiscuous type and there is no way, but no way, that a gay guy is able to find a partner if he is not willing to do a lot of compromising in this respect. Maybe things will be better when guys like me can meet partners in a more normal environment like at school or whatever. Maybe then the gay scene will evolve from muscles and flesh (the meat market) to personalities and feelings."*

In contrast, many lesbians are less concerned about femininity and general appearance (Krakauer and Rose, 2002). Therefore, the principles guiding partner selection may differ for male and female homosexuals.

COHABITATION

Cohabitation is referred to as a *common-law union* in Canada. After two to three years of coresidence, the partners are as legally protected as are married couples in terms of health care insurance, other financial aspects (not in Quebec), but not residence ownership. As indicated in Table 7.1, the proportion of all couples living common-law is far higher in Quebec than it is in other provinces. But, overall, a higher proportion of Canadians now choose common-law rather than marriage as a *first* union (Le Bourdais et al., 2000).

A cross-cultural perspective on family structure compares the prevalence of cohabiting couples in various western countries with Sweden as a baseline: This country has a longer history of consensual unions. Table 7.1 shows that *Quebec has an even higher proportion of cohabiting couples than Sweden and Norway.* When Quebec is excluded, only 13 percent of Canadian couples are common-law. Hence, the cohabitation rate for the rest of Canada more closely resembles the American rate than the Quebec one (Kerr et al., 2006). Further, the phenomenon is mainly a Quebec one rather than a francophone one (Belleau, 2007): Francophones in other provinces have cohabitation rates similar to those of the rest of the population (Laplante et al., 2006; Laplante, 2006). Neither is it a French phenomenon because, in France, the percentage of cohabiting couples is lower than that of Quebec and French cohabiting couples are more likely to marry subsequently than Quebeckers (Prioux, 2012). In general, Québécois marry even less than people in France: In 2001, France had the same marriage rate as that of Canada at 5.0 per 1,000 population compared to 2.7 for Quebec (Girard, 2008). Reasons that are generally given for

TABLE 7.1 | **Proportion of Couples that are Cohabitational in Canada, the Provinces and Territories, and Selected Other Countries**

Country or Province	As % of All Couples	Year
CANADA	**19.5**	2011
Canada without Quebec	**13.0**	2010
Newfoundland/Labrador	15.1	2011
Prince Edward Island	13.1	2011
Nova Scotia	17.0	2011
New Brunswick	18.8	2011
Quebec	**37.2**	2011
Ontario	12.8	2011
Manitoba	14.0	2011
Saskatchewan	14.7	2011
Alberta	15.5	2011
British Columbia	14.9	2011
Yukon	30.9	2011
Northwest Territories	35.9	2011
Nunavut	44.4	2011
France	**28.2**	2010
Sweden	**29.0**	2010
Norway	31.0	2010
Russia	17.0	2010

Source: St-Amour, 2012; Wiik et al., 2012; Statistics Canada, 2012a.

Quebec's low marital rates include a reaction to centuries of dominance by the Church's teachings on nuptiality, chastity before marriage, and high fertility.

Further, when studying Canadians' attitudes to living common-law, the 2001 General Social Survey found that those most willing are young people aged 15 to 25, francophones, and the non-religious (Milan, 2003). Within each of these categories, there is a substantial **gender difference:** As reflected in Figure 7.1, women are much less willing than men (Belleau, 2007). In some Latin American countries, where consensual unions now constitute about 50 percent of unions, highly educated women are less often found in such unions than in marriage (Esteve et al., 2012). When educated women have children, they tend to be married. Cohabitations are more likely to result in marriage when the male partner has economic resources (Smock and Manning, 1997). In Canada, 64 percent of women with a university degree have a husband with the same level of education compared to 48 percent of similar women who are cohabiting (Martin and Hou, 2010).

There also has been a rise in serial cohabitations, that is, having multiple cohabiting relationships—often of short duration (Lichter et al., 2010). Although serial cohabitations are concentrated among the disadvantaged, particularly those who have children as adolescents, this is nevertheless a phenomenon which is spreading and is replacing serial dating. At least in the short term, in the life course of young couples, cohabitation is delaying marriage because cohabitants are less likely to be actively searching for a marital partner than others. However, among young adults aged 20 to 29, the proportion of those who are *neither* cohabiting *nor* married has increased. *This means that fewer adults are living in unions than in the past*; therefore, it is not only cohabitation that is delaying marriage but also a **longer period of singlehood,** as discussed in a subsequent section.

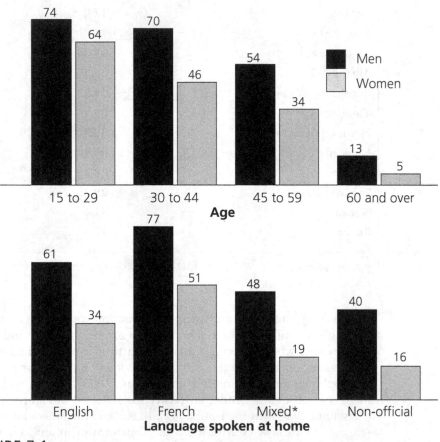

FIGURE 7.1

Percentages of Canadians Who Are Willing to Live Common-Law by Age and Language

Source: Statistics Canada, General Social Survey, 2001; Milan, 2003.
*Mixed refers to any combination of English/French and/or unofficial language.

Relationship Stability and Reasons for Entering into Cohabitation

Some individuals choose cohabitation because it requires, in their opinion, less sexual faithfulness than marriage (Bibby, 2004). Further, fewer cohabitants than married persons feel that it is very important to have a lasting relationship to achieve a happy life (Milan and Peters, 2003). Overall, the **role demands** of cohabitation are weaker than those for marriage. In other words, it is easier to enter into a cohabitational than a marital relationship because it is *less institutionalized**. For the same reason, it is easier to dissolve because there are fewer barriers against dissolution—whether legal, economic, or social—than is the case for marriage. Research is needed on same-sex cohabitation, particularly now that same-sex marriage is legal in so many countries.

In the 1990s and early 2000s, more than 50 percent of all cohabitations ended in dissolution within five years (Milan, 2000), a phenomenon that is also noted in Latin American countries. In North America, instability even increased in the past decades, in great part because fewer such unions result in marriage than in the past (Bumpass and Lu, 2000). Thus, cohabitations are not as stable as marriages—and this is true in all western societies (Wu, 2000). Further, they tend to dissolve more rapidly (Provencher et al., 2006). Cohabiting couples are less tolerant of differences between them than are married couples (Hohmann-Marriott, 2006). They also have more conflict (Marcussen, 2005). As well, fewer cohabitants who break up attempt reconciliation than married couples do (Binstock and Thornton, 2003).

However, in a society such as Sweden where cohabitations are more **institutionalized**, such unions last longer, and their quality is generally close to that of married couples (Wiik et al., 2012). This is also the case for Quebec compared to the rest of Canada. It is estimated that 55 percent of Quebec women aged 30 to 39 who opted for cohabitation as a first union go through a separation, compared to 66 percent among women in the other provinces (Turcotte, 2002). Nevertheless, no matter how one looks at these numbers, they are far higher than the 30 percent Canadian divorce rate after five years of marriage. But, as the population ages, it is expected that cohabitation will become more stable.

Furthermore, cohabitations are not a homogeneous category, so that stability depends in part on the reasons why a couple cohabits, on commitment, and how quickly the relationship is transformed into a marriage (Poortman and Mills, 2012). The term "stability" includes cohabitations that last and others that are transformed into a lasting marriage. The latter are forming a smaller proportion of all cohabitations than before in Canada. For instance, in the 1970s, about 50 percent of cohabitants went on to marry their partner within five years. This compares to only about 30 percent in the early 1990s. Today, couples do not need to be concerned about marriage as the "next step." In fact, probably fewer than half of couples begin their union with marital intentions (Guzzo, 2009a). In Quebec, cohabitation is more a substitute than a prelude to marriage (Belleau, 2007). In the U.S., women with a B.A. or more are much less likely to have had two or more cohabitations than those with less education (U.S. Department of Health and Human Services, 2010).

A large proportion of young couples who cohabit now begin living together rather quickly after the onset of dating, with little thought of permanency and least of all of marriage. As some say, "it just happened" (Stanley and Rhoades, 2009). One would expect very high rates of eventual dissolution, as a short acquaintance is a precursor to divorce among the married. It may well be that instability is in the very nature of casual and/or **rapid-onset cohabitations**, which are more akin to "glorified" *dating* than to other types of cohabitations. Unfortunately, they may also be more painful and complicated to end than dating is, and this may be why many simply "slide" into marriage. More research is needed to define the various characteristics and trajectories of types of cohabitations, including those that are entered into as a precursor to marriage.

Sexual availability motivates many persons to cohabit rather than to continue dating (Willoughby and Carroll, 2012). A woman student expressed this in her autobiography:

> *"Right now I'd rate myself as being fairly unhappy and it's because I have found out that my boyfriend I live with lives with me just so that he can have sex that he knows is safe.... That means that I have wasted the past 18 months of my life that I could have better spent looking for a better guy and also one that would have accepted me as a whole person and not just as a sex machine.... Now I have to think about ending this relationship but it's hard you know because I am really attached to him."*

Living together also results when one or the other dater is looking for an apartment (Sassler, 2004). Cohabiting is then a form of savings: Sharing an apartment is less expensive than maintaining two separate ones. Adults who divorce may also find similar economic advantages in cohabitation, especially in view of the fact that many divorced men have to support a child who lives elsewhere. It is a matter of convenience and **economies of scale**, even though cohabitants are more likely than married couples to keep money separately, especially when one or the other has previously divorced (Heimdal and Houseknecht, 2003). Young couples who are engaged often find cohabitation similarly convenient for financial reasons, as described by a student:

> *"We're getting married this summer and we're both looking forward to it. We've lived together for one year because we could not afford the wedding and we felt that paying for one apartment as opposed to two would help us financially for when we get married. I would not however have lived with him had we not been engaged. That's a good way to get burned."*

Relationship Aspects

As we see later, cohabitants have more frequent sexual intercourse than married couples (Yabiku and Gager, 2009). In part, this is because cohabitations are of shorter duration and the frequency of sex is generally higher earlier on in unions of any type. This result may also stem from the nature of cohabitation itself: These relationships are more individualistic and may be more invested in sexuality, while marriages may be more characterized by a greater general commitment. Indeed, although low sexual frequency is related to union dissolution, it is more so among cohabitants than married couples (Yabiku and Gager, 2009). Although married spouses are usually happier with their relationships than are cohabitants, when cohabitants plan to marry, the quality of their relationship is not much different from that of a married couple that has been together for the same duration. In Quebec, couples who cohabit for several years are more similar to married ones in terms of relationship satisfaction—which suggests that more studies should be carried out on couples who have been together for many years (Lachance-Grzela and Bouchard, 2009).

Cohabitational couples may feel freer to invent their relationships outside the mould of traditional expectations and gender roles. Yet, recent studies are not unanimous: Some do find a more equal **division of labour** within cohabitation than within marriage while others do not. Generally, young cohabiting women do less housework than married ones and young cohabiting men do more than married men (Davis et al., 2007). But women who do more housework also tend to continue doing so after marriage, which has led Kuperberg (2012) to conclude that women or couples who are more gender traditional will be more likely to marry rather than remain as cohabitants. Matters may be different in countries such as Sweden that have higher gender equality.

There is also evidence that entry into cohabitation does not provide the same protective benefits against depression as does entry into a marriage (Lamb et al., 2003). However, overall, Wu et al. (2004) did not find significant health disadvantages related to cohabitation nor in terms of social engagement (Schimmele and Wu, 2011). But entry into cohabitation heightens a woman's risk of physical abuse (Brzozowski and Brazeau, 2008; Sev'er, 2002) and even spousal homicide (Ogrodnik, 2009). Kenney and McLanahan (2006) have found that there is more conjugal violence among cohabitants than among married spouses. This is probably because cohabitants who are violent are less likely to be selected into marriage while married persons who suffer from violence are more likely to divorce. As a result, the married population has a lower rate of conjugal violence than the cohabiting population.

Cohabitants are **less faithful** to their partners sexually than married persons, even after controlling for personal values regarding extramarital sex (Treas and Giesen, 2000). This may be one of the reasons, among many others, why serial cohabitation has become more frequent (Lichter et al., 2010). Cohabiting men below age 50 especially are often less committed to their relationship and partner than are married men (Stanley et al., 2004). This sentiment is expressed by a divorced man during an interview and by his former cohabiting partner at a follow up, and then by a student in her autobiography:

> *"No, I don't know if I'll get married* [to the woman he lives with]. . . . *Right now I am not even sure that she's the right woman for me so that I prefer to take it easy; I have a wait-and-see attitude at this point."* At the follow-up interview two years later, this couple had separated. He was casual about it, but the woman was very upset: *"He should just have dated me, I mean, you don't start living with someone if you don't love them . . . it's dishonest. It's even worse because I have two small children. I mean, it's not a game you play with children."*

> *"I have lived with two different guys and that's it! No more! It's always the same thing: We just play at being married because they don't want to do anything except play. They couldn't get married because . . . the usual line is 'I'm not ready for such a commitment.'"*

What these quotes, as well as one of the chapter's openers (with the recurring themes of "play" and lack of commitment), well illustrate is that cohabitation can serve to delay commitment and give a longer time lead during which to find a better alternative—more among men than women (Rhoades et al., 2012). Many cohabitants, perhaps more male than female, remain in a **permanent state of availability**. Among individuals aged 18 to 55 in eight European countries, Wiik et al. (2012) found that cohabitants more often had breakup plans and were less satisfied with their relationships than married individuals. In other words, they are still "playing the field." In terms of exchange theory, the committed partner has less power because the relationship is more important to him or her than it is to the partner who has less invested. As a result, the partner with more invested is unhappy, may feel depressed, harbour regrets, and feel more insecure and less in control of his or her life (Brown, 2002). Furthermore, in view of the fact that marriage is still the most valued conjugal state in our society, one partner often wishes to transform the cohabitation into a marriage. Therefore, cohabitation may be problematic for many young and middle-age adults, particularly women, as expressed by yet another student:

> *"I would rate myself low on happiness currently because I have lived with my boyfriend for two years against my parents' wishes* [after one year of dating] *and when we talk of marriage, he always says that we're too young for this, he is 29 and I am 25. Or he'll say, you know, marriage is 'serious business' and this makes me feel that he sees what we have as being of a lower quality. I love him and we're well suited but I'm afraid that he'll leave me if I put a deadline for marriage. But how long can I wait? I think that women are getting short changed when they agree to live together."*

In fact, women who cohabit *serially* are at high risk of never marrying and, if they do, of divorcing (Lichter and Qian, 2008; Sassler, 2010). On the other hand, there are indications that young people who wish to marry do not view cohabitation outside a committed relationship as favourably as young persons who have no clear marital plans (Willoughby and Carroll, 2012). Nevertheless, as cohabitation becomes better accepted and more institutionalized, committed cohabitation is likely to become more similar to marriage in terms of its benefits. It should then also become a more stable relationship. Indeed, the new research, although not unanimous, is finding results in that direction. Further, a more widespread and institutionalized cohabitation will be less likely to lead to instability when cohabitants marry, particularly when they had marital plans before starting to live together (Manning and Cohen, 2012). Overall, as time passes, the factor of social selection of the more advantaged into marriage rather than cohabitation will nearly disappear as greater proportions of couples cohabit.

For Older Adults

For older adults, cohabitation may carry far fewer risks than it does for younger adults, and it is not generally related to economic disadvantage as it is among too many young couples (Vespa, 2012). For those who are widowed or divorced, cohabitation may be more advantageous psychologically and in terms of relationship satisfaction and quality (Brown and Kawamura, 2010; Hansen et al., 2007; Wu, 2000). It then becomes an alternative to marriage, a relationship in its own right with a similar level of commitment and a low frequency of separation (to Brown, S. L. et al., 2012). In fact, King and Scott (2005) have found that *older cohabitants have higher levels of relationship quality than younger cohabitants.* In later life, the double standard of commitment that often exists among young and middle-aged cohabitants may disappear entirely because, in terms of exchange theory, males may need a partner as much as or even more than females—especially after age 60. Hence, older males are likely to be more committed than younger males because they need a spouse more: For instance, after widowhood, older men do not adapt easily to the loss of their wives and are more helpless than are widowed women.

Men generally benefit highly from living with a partner (Cooney and Dunne, 2001). In comparison, widowed and divorced women in later life are often hesitant to relinquish their newly acquired independence or to replace a deceased spouse whom they loved. They may also be afraid that a marriage will soon return them to the role of nurse for an ailing husband. Such women may welcome a new form of partnership and may find cohabitation functional. Indeed, cohabiting partners provide less care than married spouses do (Noël-Miller, 2011). Others may actually look for an emotional and sexual relationship that does not involve the sharing of a dwelling—thus maintaining their independence. The economic benefits of cohabitation over remarriage may be even more important among the older generation: It offers the advantage of economies of scale while, at the same time, it may allow the partners to protect their respective children's inheritances.

HETEROSEXUAL MARRIAGE

As indicated in Figure 7.2, the yearly rate of marriage per 1,000 population has diminished substantially since 1941, its peak year. This is due in part to the low marriage rates in Quebec; in part because a proportion of persons are living alone or cohabiting and will never marry; and also because the aging of the population means that fewer people of marriageable age are present. Quebec has a large population and its low marriage rate, 2.9 in 2007, contributes to reducing the overall Canadian rate (Girard, 2008:64). As seen in Figure 7.2, the rate was 4.7 in Canada, from a high of 6.0 for PEI, 5.2 for Ontario, 5.6 for Alberta, 4.9 and 5.0 for Manitoba and Saskatchewan respectively. The rate at which Quebec singles marry is nearly half that of Canada, France, Sweden, and Italy. Marriage rates are especially high in the U.S., at 6.8, down from 8.2 in 2000 (CDC, 2012). The American rates have gone down mainly among low-income groups (Trail and Karney, 2012).

Marriage, particularly a good and equitable marriage, carries many benefits for the spouses. It is, above all, highly beneficial to children, whether it is equitable or not between the parents. There is a school of thought whose proponents argue that what is important is not family structure (one versus two, married versus cohabiting parents), but healthy **family processes**. It is certainly true that positive family dynamics explain a large part of children's positive outcomes; however, the fact remains that *healthy dynamics are more likely to occur in married families or perhaps long-term cohabitational families.* As well, even though unachievable for many poor

FIGURE 7.2

Marriage Rates per 1,000 Population, 1921–2003

Source: Statistics Canada, Selected Marriage Statistics 1921–1990. Cat. 82-552. *Canadian Social Trends*, 68, 2003, p. 27; Statistics Canada, 2007e.

women, marriage carries high positive symbolic value (Edin and Kefalas, 2005). For instance, the 2011 General Social Survey found that 42 percent of cohabitants in stepfamilies wanted to marry—as proof of love, commitment, and to make the relationship official (Vézina, 2012:6).

Both married men and women, compared to men and women in any of the other marital status categories, do better in the domains of health, well-being, and longevity. In addition, entry into and stability of marriage reduce risky health behaviours (Green et al., 2012; Martikainen et al., 2005). Married persons have lower rates of emotional problems, are healthier physically, and live longer (Coombs, 1991). In a study of 17 western countries and Japan, Stack and Eshleman (1998) have found that being married is 3.4 times more closely tied to happiness than is cohabitation. Their results indicate that marriage, rather than cohabitation, increases both financial and health satisfaction, which in turn increase happiness. (See, also, Bierman et al., 2006.) As well, a genetically informed study found that marriage, more than cohabitation, was causally associated with a reduction in externalizing or behavioural problems (Horn et al., 2012). For the time being, the educated tend to choose marriage more than the less educated (Schoen and Cheng, 2006). Moreover, married adults are more likely to maintain a healthy lifestyle than nonmarried adults. The former eat at home more, stay out late less, use alcohol and illegal drugs less, and are better organized to take care of their basic needs (Bachman et al., 1997). A cohesive marriage is an important social resource and brings an *informal element of social control* into the lives of individuals. This may be the reason why married people drink less than cohabitants (Horwitz and Raskin White, 1998).

Some literature indicates that marriage may be more advantageous to men than to women—even though younger women want it more than men (England, 2000). Health has generally been used as the key indicator. There is a larger difference between the scores of well-being of married men compared to divorced and never-married men than there is among similar women, although the male gap has narrowed (Liu and Umberson, 2008). Why would marriage benefit women less? To begin with, once children arrive, women have more responsibilities than men, particularly when both spouses are employed, and they suffer from more work interruptions than men. Therefore, for many women, marriage becomes a mixed blessing. However, for both genders, the self-rated health of the divorced, separated, and widowed has worsened in the recent past and it may have worsened more for women than men, although women still cope better in this respect (Liu and Umberson, 2008).

Marriage formation, happiness, and stability are important elements in the social organization of western societies: They contribute to couples' well-being and productivity as well as to their children's positive outcomes, both currently and in the long term.

Anne-Marie Ambert

In a study of 27 countries, Lee (2012) found that married women's life happiness was higher than that of cohabiting women. But this was so only in countries that were more religiously traditional. In a study of premature mortality in Denmark, however, Drefahl (2012) was unable to disentangle causal effects from selection effects of the *lower* mortality they found among the higher-SES cohabitants compared to married individuals. There is a lack of studies on the relative responsibilities of cohabitants who have children. The quotes presented earlier highlight problems of emotional security, powerlessness, and unhappiness among young cohabiting women who were not engaged to their partner. There were clear indications in these quotes that the benefits of cohabitation are also gender specific among the young: They may favour males even more than marriage does and this may well be more so when children are present. However, the following hypotheses deserve to be tested: Women may be as advantaged by cohabitation as men in cultures where the phenomenon is more widespread, such as

Quebec, Sweden, or Norway. We also saw that both genders are equally advantaged when they cohabit later in life after a divorce or widowhood and after children from previous unions have become independent. Such advantages are not likely to exist, however, among groups for whom cohabitation is not sanctioned, such as people of Hindu or Muslim faith.

The **quality of the relationship** is an important determinant of well-being. All in all, marriage is beneficial to adults, but a troublesome marriage negates some or all of these benefits, particularly for women. Second, the benefits accrued in marriage and cohabitation may differ for men and women depending on the domains studied—emotional well-being, physical health, happiness, or security. Finally, the benefits of marriage depend on the time or cohort period that serves as a context for marriage. For example, more recent cohorts of women seem to benefit from marriage less than preceding cohorts, and this would be especially so for career women. But, here again, one has to consider the dimensions of personality and life that are measured in these studies because it is possible that *more recent cohorts of researchers* favour some aspects of life (i.e., independence) over others. Financially, marriage and committed cohabitions are advantageous to both genders, so long as they last.

SAME-SEX MARRIAGE

Same-sex marriage is discussed separately because it is such a recent phenomenon that there is too little research, particularly longitudinally, on the many aspects of its relationship quality, happiness, stability, benefits, and effects of and on children compared to heterosexual marriage. In 2000, Parliament enacted the *Modernization of Benefits and Obligations Act* which extended benefits and obligations to common-law couples, be they of opposite sex or the same sex. In 2001, the Netherlands became the first country to legalize same-sex marriage and was followed by Belgium in 2003. British Columbia and Ontario did so in 2003, and Canada followed suit, as have several other countries since. It was only in 2013 that France followed suit after much debate and huge public demonstrations.

The 2006 census enumerated 45,345 same-sex couples of which 16.5 percent were married (Statistics Canada, 2007h). The 2011 census revealed 64,575 same-sex couples of which 32.6 percent were married—a doubling in just five years (Statistics Canada, 2012a). Same-sex couples are more likely to be male than female, whether they are married or cohabiting. As well, a greater proportion are younger than among heterosexual couples. Because of the recency of the social and political acceptability of this situation, only a very small proportion of same-sex couples are older than 65 compared to 17.8 percent of heterosexual couples (Statistics Canada, 2012a).

Marriage is defined as a sexual, economic, social, and emotional partnership involving obligations as well as rights. Commitment is a key aspect of the institution and so is fidelity. Some gay groups are ideologically committed to "open contracts"—that is, a relationship that includes extramarital outlets (Sullivan, 1995). This is a contradiction in terms because marriage is, by definition, a committed and exclusive relationship. Thus, it could be argued that homosexuals who intend to marry share a commitment to monogamy and fidelity. It would also be important that a similar cultural consensus concerning the unacceptability of same-sex extramarital infidelities emerge in the public at large. Otherwise, a **double standard** would develop: one for heterosexual marriage and one for gay marriage. Same-sex cohabitations, particularly male, are much less stable in England than are opposite-sex cohabitations and marriages (Lau, 2012). It remains to be seen if same-sex marriages are more stable. There are indications that same-sex couples who choose to marry are more committed and have been together for longer (Fingerhut and Maisel, 2010). This said, Green (2010) has found that 40 percent of female and 60 percent of male same-sex spouses do not believe that marriage always needs to be monogamous. Nearly half of males had arrived at an explicit agreement of non-monogamy in their marriage. However, as reported by Goldberg et al. (2010:23), more recent cohorts may value monogamy more. Thus, it remains to be seen how future generations of same-sex spouses will view and construct their relationships. As well, we need to know more about lesbian patterns in this respect. It would also be very important to know how and if non-monogamy remains after children arrive to same-sex unions and what effect non-monogamy can have on the same-sex family unit and its children. Finally, there might be a difference in the divorce rate of monogamous and explicitly non-monogamous couples—and this difference could go in either direction. Further, one study has found no difference in relationship quality between monogamous and non-monogamous gay couples (Parsons et al., 2012). Marriage has often been seen "as a way of overcoming stigma and gaining greater recognition and legitimacy for same-sex couples" (Ocobock, 2013:202). Yet, perhaps depending on where these couples live, marriage may also result in renewed experiences of family rejection. Although this needs to be confirmed, marriage in Canada may provide more positive effects than in the U.S. where opposition has been more strident (MacIntosh and Andruff, 2010). However, a majority of gay couples who were waiting for the legalization of marriage in their state anticipated greater security and permanency (Shulman et al., 2012).

SINGLEHOOD

The single status includes never-married, divorced, and widowed persons who do not live in a union. From 1981 to 2011, the proportion of 20- to 29-year-old Canadians *living in a union of any type decreased* from 52 percent to 31 percent (Statistics Canada, 2012b). For young men, it decreased from 44.7 percent to 25.2 percent. For young women, the drop was from 59 percent to 36.5 percent. The difference between males and females reflects the fact that young women enter into unions earlier. Another way of looking at this situation is that the 2011 census revealed that 27.6 percent of Canadian households were one-person ones—and this proportion increases with age. The proportion is the same in the U.S. whereas, for example, in Sweden nearly half of households have just one resident (Klinenberg, 2012:3213).

Some of these Canadian singles have already been in a union that did not work out; however, most are delaying their entry into a first union, be it cohabitational or marital. At the same time, more persons than before will never marry, whether this is intended on their part or "accidental," that is, related to unfavourable economic conditions, insufficient supply of affordable housing, or lack of suitable partners (Kotkin, 2012). Further, this phenomenon is international, with the exception of African countries south of the Sahara. Jones and Gubhaju (2009) have estimated that up to 25 percent of all East Asian women will still be single by age 50. For instance, in 2010, one-third of Japanese women reaching the age of 30 were still single and so were about 20 percent of those reaching the age of 40. Kotkin (2012:3) reports that the sociologist Mika Toyota predicts that, by 2030, about a third of Japanese males may still be unmarried by age 50. In fact, the percentage of sexually active female university students has fallen precipitously from 60 percent in 2005 to 47 percent in 2011 (Kotkin, 2012:27). In the United Arab Emirates, about 60 percent of women over 30 are still unmarried, up from 20 percent in 1995—in great part because of the high bride price or *mahr* (Soffen, nd). These are unprecedented developments because these numbers are eight times higher than in 1960 and two times higher than in 2000.

A longer period of singlehood results from the necessity of pursuing an advanced education, establishing oneself in the employment sector, and getting settled economically (Beaujot and Bélanger, 2001)—all of which take a longer time than was the case 20 years ago. As well, the new economic situation has created more joblessness among men than women so that more and more men are now less good marital prospects from a woman's perspective, reducing both sexes' tendency to marry (Bolick, 2011). Further, the household division of labour still favours males, which may also reduce women's incentive to marry, particularly in Asia (Kotkin, 2012). Thus, a prolonged period of singlehood before a first marital transition is becoming the norm and is a choice for many. For other persons, including a proportion of young women who give birth nonmaritally, as well as minority women who are poor, singlehood may be imposed by demographic circumstances, such as scarcity of eligible partners within one's age group, social class, or race. Others are older widowed or divorced individuals, particularly women who, because of better health and the unavailability of potential mates, live alone.

Urbanization has contributed to making the single life a more viable option; singles were both more isolated and visible socially when society was largely rural. (In the 17th and 18th centuries, single persons were discouraged from living alone.) In a city, in contrast, singles are less visible because they are far more numerous, and this lowers the potential for isolation. They have access to a larger and more varied social network. The availability of a range of food- and household-related commercial services has also facilitated single life.

Economic independence for a segment of women, especially the well educated and the professional, is another structural/historical factor making singlehood a more accessible alternative than in the past. As well, the postponement of marriage and the high divorce rates contribute to making the single status more fluid and less socially stigmatized than used to be the case. The greater acceptance of sexuality outside of marriage is also a factor that facilitates remaining single, or, at the very least, postponing union formation. The possibility of giving birth nonmaritally or of adopting a child as a single person are also enabling factors. As well, the trend among young adults of remaining in their parents' home fosters single life and delays marriage, a phenomenon also observed in Japan (Raymo, 2003).

Statistics Canada has found that persons between the ages of 25 and 64 who live alone have smaller social networks than those living in a couple: These singles have fewer close ties with relatives and fewer acquaintances. But they have a similar number of close friends and are more frequently in contact with them than those who live in a couple. The singles are also more likely to say that there are not enough people to whom they feel close; those living in a couple feel that they have many people they can rely on in times of need and also have more persons they trust entirely. Finally, those living alone more often have a feeling of social loneliness than those in couples (Vézina, 2011). These results indicate that, just as living in a couple has economies of scale, it also doubles the opportunities for acquaintances and family relationships. Divorced, widowed, and never-married singles also have higher mortality rates than cohabiting and married persons, even after accounting for socioeconomic variables (Liu and Reczek, 2012). But it is expected that, with cultural and social changes, single persons will become as advantaged as married ones in terms of health, happiness, and general quality of life, at least in western countries.

SEXUAL RELATIONS

The focus of studies on sex has been on measuring attitudes toward premarital and extramarital sexual intercourse and frequency of intercourse. Measuring the frequency of sexual intercourse alone may represent a **masculine bias** in the research as it may misrepresent the level of sexuality among heterosexual and lesbian couples (Patterson, 2000; Rothblum, 2002). There is more to sexuality than penetration: Mutual masturbation, kissing, and caressing are important elements of sexuality and affectivity among couples. *Thus, the incidence of sexuality in general is likely to be far higher among some groups than depicted in the statistics on intercourse.*

The study of sexuality is influenced by **social constructs** (Marshall, 2011). To begin with, sexuality is a prime concern in western countries, as illustrated by the contents of audio-visual media, advertisements, online material, literature, as well as magazines and newspapers. People from non-western cultures and especially previous centuries might well view our focus as an obsession. Sex, especially in the form of intercourse, has come to be defined as a primary need. While it is indeed a basic human instinct, its absence in a person's life cannot be equated with the consequences of being deprived of air, food, or light.

Attitudes about nonmarital sex have become more permissive. Bibby and Posterski (2000) found a gender difference both among adults and adolescents concerning the propriety of having sex before marriage. While the majority of adolescents (82 percent) agree that sex before marriage is acceptable when people love each other, this acceptance declines to 48 percent among females and 68 percent among males when "people like each other" (Bibby, 2001). Only 5 percent of females but 20 percent of males approve of sex on a first date. This **gender divide** means that many young women actually have sex at a time when they are not emotionally ready for it, as explained by a woman student:

"I got conned into having sex when I look back on my first experience [age 16]. . . . [H]e told me all the things he knew I wanted to hear, but none were true . . . and

I felt really cheap after . . . plus it was very, very painful, you know, I cried out and it was humiliating. . . . I lied and told my friends it had been great but I stayed away from guys for a year after that."

Adolescent Sexuality

We do not have precise information as to the median* age when young Canadians begin having **sexual intercourse**, but looking at the following statistics, one could venture the age of 18. In a national survey, Rotermann (2008) reports that, in 2005, about 33 percent of 15- to 17-year-olds had had intercourse as had about 66 percent of 18- and 19-year-olds. Another national survey of over 10,000 students in Grades 7, 9, and 11 carried out in 2002–03 presents similar results, as detailed in Table 7.2. These are lower percentages for females than in 1997 (Rotermann, 2008). The proportion of teens who had had intercourse before age 15 also fell from 12 to 8 percent between 1997 and 2011 (Rotermann, 2012). (A similar decline has been noted in the U.S.) In 2009/2010, 68 percent of 18- to 19-year-olds and 86 percent of 20- to 24-year-olds had had intercourse (Rotermann, 2012).

Among those who had intercourse in Grade 9 (23 percent of all males and 19 percent of all females), fully 40 percent of these males and 29 percent of these females had had three or more partners. Rotermann found that 33 percent had had

---

TABLE 7.2 **Description of High Schoolers' Dating and Sexual Activities for Grades 9 and 11, for Males and Females, in Percentages**

	Grade 9		Grade 11	
	M	F	M	F
No. of boy/girlfriends past year:				
None	42%	37%	38%	32%
One	26	30	36	40
Two+	32	34	28	27
Ever had intercourse	23	19	40	46
If yes: No. of intercourse partners:				
One	45	53	43	54
Two	15	19	21	18
Three+	40	29	36	28
Reason for **not** having had intercourse: not yet ready	29	40	12	30
Ever had oral sex	32	28	53	52

Source: Boyce et al., 2006. Adapted from Tables 3, 5, 6, 7, and 8.

more than one, *with males reporting multiple partners more often*. In other words, some 15-year-old youths are quite experienced: They constitute over 10 percent of all adolescents their age. It would be paramount to have more information on this group, which is at risk for many problems, including STIs. Adolescents who have **multiple partners** and do not practise safe sex tend to consume alcohol more and have lower school achievement and a more difficult parent-child relationship. They are also less likely to receive a great deal of supervision; permissive maternal attitudes about sexuality are equally related to having multiple partners (Miller et al., 1999). In a Toronto survey that was not representative, 3 percent of the teens had experienced their first sexual intercourse by age 13 (Pole and Flicker, 2010). Homma et al. (2012) found that between 2 and 3 percent of adolescents in rural schools in Canada who have ever used alcohol, marijuana, or other drugs, both males and females, have exchanged sex for substances—a lower proportion than what is generally encountered among homeless youth. Impulsivity as a character trait was a key factor in this exchange. Transactional sex, even of children younger than 10, is fairly common in countries beset by civil wars where a culture of violence coexists with poverty. Boys and girls are left unprotected by their families or encouraged into prostitution to obtain essential items (Aubert and Holder, 2013). One can think here of Syrian refugees in Jordan currently, of certain parts of Colombia, and many parts of Africa.

As seen in Table 7.2, in both Grades 9 and 11, a greater proportion of students had had **oral sex** than intercourse. In the U.S., it is estimated that 65 percent of males and females aged 15 to 24 have had oral sex—and 25 percent had oral sex before vaginal intercourse—numbers that were very similar to those of Canadian college and university students (CACUSS, 2013). In contrast, a few decades ago, oral sex was considered a more intimate step to take and generally followed intercourse. Indeed, the recreational or "fun" aspect of sexuality, as opposed to the relationship aspect, is often one of the highlights of early teen parties. In 1980, an older student wrote:

"Today I am upset because my 12-year-old daughter went to a party this weekend and the spin the bottle game found her in a closet with the target boy masturbating each other. The reason I found out was the telltale semen on her dress. When I was her age, we'd spin the bottle and kiss. Things have changed and I am very, very concerned about what this does to these children's frame of mind when time comes to get into a real relationship."

Over twenty years later, in 2004, a female student wrote on the same theme:

"My 13-year-old sister tells me everything because she thinks I'm cool. She was supposed to go to a sleepover at some girlfriend's house but they ended up at this boy's party, her age, not supervised and they drank quite a lot and then spinned the bottle among other things and each girl had to suck the boy's you-know-what. She thought it was both hilarious, mature, and 'yukkie.' It's her first sexual experience and I don't think it's a good start and I am very worried about her."

Spin-the-bottle is a "game" with a content that has been evolving over the decades toward a purely genitalia focus among some early teens.

Are Results on Teen Sexuality Valid?

You may ask, especially if you belong to a cultural group that does not allow early adolescent dating (Zaidi and Shuraydi, 2002; Zine, 2008), if these research results are "for real"? In other words, is it a sample that represents the entire population of Canadian adolescents? And was that study well carried out? First, let's recall that Rotermann's results in 2012 were essentially the same as those in Table 7.2. Second, the Boyce et al. sample is a very large one: The study was carried out in a representative stratified sample of schools, and the methods are entirely credible. "Active parental/guardian consent was obtained for all study participants. The students were guaranteed anonymity and sealed their surveys in individual envelopes for return to the researchers" (Boyce et al, 2006:60). As you can imagine, nearly 20 percent of students did not return the parental consent, nearly 9 percent were absent on that day, and 5 percent refused to participate, so that there was a response rate of 67.7 percent—which is very good, *if it is representative.*

However, Alberta and British Columbia did not participate and neither did private and religious schools, whether Muslim, Jewish, or Catholic. It is difficult to ascertain how this might have affected the results. As well, it is possible that the 25 percent who refused to participate or whose parents refused may have been very different: These students might have come from families where parents objected to this study on moral and religious grounds—which might have excluded from the study adolescents whose parents have a different set of values and who, as a result, were delaying sexual activities until later or marriage. If the latter were the case, then the actual proportions of adolescents having oral sex and intercourse would be lower, which may well be the case.

Not shown in Table 7.2 is the fact that, in Grade 7, the proportion of students who reported having had *no steady* girlfriend/boyfriend for the past year (42 percent of males and 46 percent of females) is fairly close to that of ninth graders. However, 18 and 15 percent of the seventh graders reported having had three or more "steadies," which is higher than older students. The authors conclude that "adolescent relationships have been characterized as serially monogamous and of short duration" (Boyce et al., 2006). There is a complementary explanation. It may be that many seventh graders may include as a "steady" a peer they have a crush on, or one who regularly talks with them or walks home with them, something that an older student would simply describe as a friend:

> "I was nuts about this girl in my class . . . I lived for the moment she would look at me. . . . She was this big thing in my life and I was crushed when she started walking home with another boy. It was puppy love for me and all of this was more in my mind than real."

> "What made me the most happy between the ages of 11 and 14 was this 'boyfriend' I had in Grade 6. He and I used to be on the same school bus and after a while he started to sit with me. I was in heaven! He was soooo cute, at least I thought so. Everyone called us an 'item' but we never even talked on the phone

or go out together but having a 'boyfriend' certainly raised my status among my classmates. Now I can't even remember how it ended."

In fact, in their autobiographies, I rarely encountered students who mentioned having had a steady boyfriend or girlfriend by Grade 7. This generally occurred, when it did, one to three years later. In contrast, students recalled word-for-word "how it had ended" with real boyfriends or girlfriends. They always mentioned this as having been the most, or one of the most, painful aspects of their lives at ages 15 to 19 or even older.

Issues of Control and Consequences

Simply mentioning when first sexual intercourse takes place camouflages an important reality: the degree of **voluntariness** and desire for the experience. In the Boyce et al. (2006) study, 17 percent of females in Grade 9 and 28 percent in Grade 11 had been pressured into sex, while the percentages for males were 7.7 and 11 percent. There is also a great deal of difference by gender in the quality of the experience at first intercourse among adolescents. In part, this may stem from the fact that sexuality is more goal oriented toward intercourse—and rather quickly—which is more a male than a female vision of sexuality, as mentioned earlier. While males describe their first intercourse as exciting and satisfying, more females report fear, anxiety, embarrassment, and even guilt.

For many adolescents, sexuality is a positive experience. And, overall, mental health issues arise only in certain contexts. Therefore, several variables have to be taken into consideration when evaluating the impact of adolescent sexuality. Ann Meier (2007) has found that when adolescents are sexually active and others are aware of it, a relationship breakdown can be very embarrassing and humiliating. This can, as a result, affect their mental health, particularly when the relationship was not a committed one: Sex without commitment may induce greater regrets among girls than boys. In fact, females in the Boyce et al. (2006) study were more likely than boys to give "love for the person" as the reason for having had first intercourse: 39 percent of Grade 11 males compared to 60 percent of the females.

In a country as diverse religiously and culturally as Canada is, one should carefully consider the possibility that, for youths whose parents are recent immigrants from countries that segregate the sexes, engaging in adolescent sexuality may carry negative consequences in terms of guilt, relationships with peers and parents, and difficulties finding a mate later. In fact, a young woman's life could be in danger as a result of the shame she could bring to her family (honour killings) or she could be "shipped back home" and forced into an arranged marriage. It should be noted that, for Canadians in general, persons who have had a high number of sexual partners are not considered as desirable dates and partners (Garcia, 2006).

One problem concerning sex among adolescents is the high rate of sexually transmitted infections, particularly for those who begin intercourse by age 13 (Rotermann, 2005). Let's just take one instance: chlamydia, an infection that does not have overt symptoms and generally goes undetected but can lead to infertility or tubal pregnancy. Although its incidence has decreased over the years, young women aged 15 to 19 are far more likely to contract this disease than their older counterparts (Health

Canada, 2000). Overall, STIs are very common among teens (Tu et al., 2009). Hence, an important aspect of adolescent and youth sexuality is the use of condoms. Statistics Canada found that both in 2003 and 2010, condom use for those aged 15 to 24 was higher among males (73 percent) than females (63 percent). As well, condom use declined with age: It was 80 percent among sexually active 15- to 17-year-olds but 63 percent among those aged 20 to 24 years, probably because the older age group is more likely to be in a monogamous relationship (Rotermann, 2012).

Early Teen Sexuality and the Role of Peers

Besides gender, the following variables contribute to a later sexual initiation: higher parental social class, two-parent family, fewer family transitions, school achievement, and religiosity (Brauner-Otto and Axinn, 2010; Mendle et al., 2009). Parental caring and monitoring are key elements (Longmore et al., 2009). Both high-quality parent-child relations and less permissive parental attitude toward early sexuality delay initiation. Early puberty is also related to earlier sexual involvement (Cavanagh, 2011). Among girls, engaging in sports is related to postponement of sexual activities (Manlove et al., 2002). In contrast, teens who engage in risky behaviours such as alcohol and drug use and who have been sexually abused are more likely to begin sexual intercourse at a younger age than other teens (McKay, 2005). Even smoking is related to earlier sexual initiation (Garriguet, 2005). There are two trajectories in the explanation of these links. One is the selection process: Students who smoke, drink, or do drugs are more likely to be at least somewhat different than others who do not in terms of willingness to go against certain rules and this may, for many, include sex. The second trajectory concerns the fact that both alcohol and drugs lower inhibitions and can easily lead to unplanned sex. Garriguet (2005) reported that girls whose self-concept was weak at ages 12 and 13 were more likely than those with a strong self-concept to have had intercourse by age 14 or 15 while the opposite was true for boys! The latter's early age was more related to low income and a poor relationship with parents.

Some of these factors continue to exert an influence among college and university-age groups. For instance, religious attendance is significantly related to lower rates of sexual intercourse among nonmarried students (Uecker, 2008). It is also related to a lower number of sexual partners (Barkan, 2006). Muslim adolescents are also more likely to have lower rates of sexual intercourse (Pole and Flicker, 2010). As well, patterns of sexuality and relationships initiated during adolescence are precursors to behaviours in young adulthood. For instance, casual sex in adolescence is related to cohabitation rather than marriage later (Raley et al., 2007).

Were it not for general **peer pressure** and, in many instances, rape or psychological coercion, perhaps a majority of young women would initiate oral sex and sexual intercourse later than they currently do. Even some males obviously feel pressured as well as "left out":

> *"I always felt left out in high school just because I didn't get laid. I was the only guy still a virgin at graduation.* [This was probably his perception based on peer boasting rather than a fact, or else his 'crowd' included very sexually active peers.] *The counsellor told me there was nothing to worry about and he was right but to a 16-year-old that's not what you want to hear."*

Several studies indicate that a student's peer group is a key ingredient in *early* sexual initiation. The Boyce et al. (2006) study shows that very few students who think that their friends have *not* had sex report having had intercourse themselves. However, when most of their friends are perceived to have had sex, then they themselves also report having had intercourse. This is quite a "correlation" indicating a peer influence or a choice of peers based on similar values and behaviours. Sieving et al. (2006) found the same results in a longitudinal study: High-schoolers who perceived that they would gain their friends' respect by having sex themselves were also more likely to have initiated intercourse in the 9 to 18 months that elapsed between two interviews. (See, also, Boyce et al., 2008.)

As well, sixth to eighth graders who have a boyfriend/girlfriend initiate intercourse earlier. Young teen girls who have a boyfriend who is six or more years older than they are have a higher chance of beginning intercourse, of being more active sexually, and of acquiring an STI than other girls with a same-age boyfriend (Kaestle et al., 2002; Marin et al., 2006; Ryan et al., 2008). Therefore, parents and schools who are able to convince young adolescents to postpone dating are, by the same token, helping them delay intercourse and attendant risks at that young age. This would require that an effective community exists in schools because students' perceptions of their peers' sexual experience is such an important element (Hampton et al., 2005). Families' and schools' social capital may also play a different role for male and female students (Smylie et al., 2006). Similarly, keeping boys away from gangs would be helpful even from the perspective of sexuality as gang members' sexuality tends to be more exploitative (Fleury and Fernet, 2012). From what I have gathered throughout the years from the autobiographies, delayed dating would also be a relief to students who feel left out when they do not date while their peers do or are perceived to be so doing. Many students could recall that, in order to enhance their status within their peer groups, they invented stories of dates, sex, "pot," and later "rave" weekends, from Grade 6 through the end of high school.

> *"I was convinced that I was the only one in my class who didn't have sex, so I made up all kinds of stories and this was easy for me to do because we had a cottage and we went there nearly every weekend and no one could check. I have had pictures of me with some girls on the ski slope to prove everything but these girls were just children of my parents' friends."*

> *"All the girls in my class had sex so of course I said that I had it too except that it was all a bunch of lies because I was well supervised by my parents and they were good at communicating with me why I should wait and do things that were more enriching at that stage of my life ... the funny thing about this is that a couple of my friends told me years later that they were still virgins and that they had lied as well so we all felt so happy to know that we were not the only ones [not having had sex] and now looking back on all of this trauma, I suspect that most of our friends and classmates were making up similar stories and this means that we were all living in a fantasy world that didn't exist except that we were creating this world together, one big deception that is so hurtful and throws so many kids to the wolves so to speak and they are not ready for this."*

In other words, a **collective delusion** often takes place. And this delusion of a perceived, but not real, situation still affects many students even in university.

For instance, in the 2013 CACUSS study of college and university students, a great proportion perceive a far greater use of various drugs by others than they themselves use.

SEXUAL IDENTITIES AND SEXUALITIES

Sexuality may be somewhat more fluid, both in terms of identity and practices, than heretofore realized, and because of cultural changes toward acceptance of diversity (Baute, 2010). Based on the fact that younger Norwegians are less attached to "fixed identity structures, more so among women than men," Andersson et al. (2006:81) ask how **homosexuals** should be identified: Should respondents be asked how they identify themselves or is it better to measure sexual practice? For instance, at some point in their life course, but not necessarily throughout their entire adult years, a number of persons identify as homosexual. With three large American data sets, Black et al. (2000) estimate that possibly as many as 30 percent of gay men and 46 percent of lesbian women are or have been married heterosexually. Similar results have been obtained in Sweden and Norway (Andersson et al., 2006). In fact, until now, a good proportion of lesbians, especially those older than 30, have discovered their identity later in life (Morris et al., 2001). Some may identify as bisexual and many do not engage in genital sex (Rothblum, 2002).

In a 2004 survey of Canadians aged 18 to 59, 1.3 percent of men and 0.7 percent of women considered themselves to be homosexual. As well, 0.9 percent of women self-identified as bisexual versus 0.6 percent among men (Statistics Canada, 2004n). In a 2013 survey of Canadian college students, 2.5 percent reported being gay or lesbian, and 4.2 bisexual (CACUSS, 2013). In the U.S., the carefully designed studies carried out by Laumann et al. (1994) indicate that 2.8 percent of men identify as gay and 1.4 percent of women identify as lesbian. In 2006, 1.5 percent of young adults identified as homosexual and 1.55 as bisexual (Meier et al., 2009). In terms of *behaviours*, these figures are similar to the rates for men and women who have exclusively same-sex relationships: 3 percent for men and 1.6 percent for women. In the Black et al. (2000) analyses, 4.7 percent of men and 3.5 percent of women had had at least one same-sex experience since age 18. But only 2.5 percent of men and 1.4 percent of women had engaged in *exclusively* same-sex activities over the year preceding the survey. In the U.S in 2002, about 3.3 percent of women and men reported having had sex with a same-sex person in the previous year (Butler, 2005).

All these numbers are presented to document the fact that, whether one uses self-identity or behaviours as a measure, homosexuality is a minority phenomenon. Lesbians and gays at times appear to be more numerous than they are because they disproportionately live in large metropolitan areas in most countries (Andersson et al., 2006). In Canada, this means Vancouver, Toronto, and Montreal (Statistics Canada, 2007h). This concentration gives them higher social visibility, allows them to advocate for equality, and gives them media exposure. Furthermore, there is a tendency among homophobic persons to exaggerate the size of the homosexual population in order to sustain their "worst-fear" scenarios and prejudices. And, among some homosexuals, there is a tendency to inflate the numbers for political and social purposes. Hence, many misleading "facts" abound.

This being said, a number of individuals identify as **bisexual**, but there is little research on their family lives (Biblarz and Savci, 2010). Some have sex both with men and women while others have sex only with persons of their own sex or even with the opposite sex. Bisexuality is an identity and, especially, a practice that has far more complex ramifications and risks, including a vulnerability to HIV and STIs (Engler et al., 2005; Pole and Flicker, 2010). In the Boyce et al. (2006) study of high schools, about 5 percent of female and 2.5 percent of male students reported some attraction to the same sex or both sexes, or about one such student in each classroom.

Perhaps as many as one-third of all teens in some groups experience sexual violence before reaching adulthood (Saewyc et al., 2008a). But teens who are gay, lesbian, or bisexual are more at risk of being stigmatized, less well protected sexually, more often violated and physically abused, both currently and as children (Balsam et al., 2005). The younger they are when their sexual identity develops, the higher the rates of victimization (Corliss et al., 2009). A surprising result is that such young females have much higher rates of pregnancy (Saewyc et al., 2008b). Many of these teens have more partners and begin sex even younger than others; they are thus at greater risk for a multiplicity of problems, in great part because they have little adult guidance in this respect.

More recently, the term **transgendered** has been used to refer to individuals who are born into one sex but, from very early in their lives, have never felt comfortable in this designation. They may, later on, receive hormonal and even surgical treatment in order to be reassigned to the other sex (Staley, 2011). On March 13, 2010, CNN presented one such case in a documentary entitled *She Was Named Steven*. Several transgendered persons have been or are still married to an opposite-sex persons (that is, to a person of the sex other than the one they were born into or raised into). Transgender is not the equivalent of cross-dressing, which may be an occasional lifestyle that people of one sex engage in for entertainment or personal gratification. Overall, there is practically no research on transgendered persons and their family conditions (Biblarz and Savci, 2010). But their lives are more difficult than those of other sexual minorities and, in school, they are more discriminated against (Taylor and Peter, 2011). As well, a recent Ontario survey found that they experience a great deal of employment inequality: Many are unemployed or earn much less than other equivalent persons (Wolkowicz, 2011).

Marital and Cohabitational Sexual Relations

Interestingly enough, conjugal sex is not as popular a topic of research as is sex outside of marriage! The few studies on marital sexuality tend to focus on the following questions: How often do couples have intercourse? What factors differentiate those with a high frequency compared to those with a low frequency?

Frequency of Sexual Intercourse and Aging

There is agreement that the frequency of sexual intercourse in marriage diminishes with age (Karraker and DeLamater, 2013). This downward trend is illustrated below in averages provided by Call et al. (1995):

19 to 24 years of age	11.7 times per month
30 to 34 years of age	8.5 times per month
50 to 54 years of age	5.5 times per month
65 to 69 years of age	2.4 times per month

But Call and colleagues caution the reader that averages are not the best measure of couples' sexual activity after age 50. This is because couples who stop having sex depress the overall average. For instance, for respondents older than age 75, the average stands at about once a month (Karraker and DeLamater, 2013). But when only those who have sexual intercourse are considered, the average rises to three times a month.

The question to address here, however, is how to untangle the effect of age from that of marital duration. In other words, as couples age, so does their marriage and habituation could be a factor reducing frequency. Call et al. (1995) have done the calculations to answer this question. First, they found that age is the main variable, particularly for men (Karraker and DeLamater, 2013). However, marital duration, health, and remarriage are all independently associated with sexual activity or inactivity. Indeed, they found that 53 percent of the respondents aged 75 to 85 had been sexually inactive in the past year. Second, if habituation has any effect at all, it occurs early in the marriage. That is, couples' frequency of sex was highest during the first two years of marriage, regardless of age. After two years, or what is called the **honeymoon period**, the frequency of sex declined sharply. The researchers explained that, if habituation kept producing an effect, sex would then keep diminishing in frequency as the marriage continued, which is not the case.

The same phenomenon is observed in remarriages. *The frequency of sexual intercourse is high at the beginning of the relationship, no matter the age,* and drops after the initial period. After that, it becomes a matter of age rather than length of marriage. Generally, couples who are younger at marriage or remarriage have a higher frequency of sexual intercourse than couples who are older. Couples aged 70 to 86 interviewed by Lodge and Umberson (2012) emphasize emotional intimacy over sex as they aged. It is possible that, in a few years, this section will be rewritten to include references to the effect of sexual enhancement pills such as Viagra on older couples' sexual lives—what Marshall (2011) calls the medicalization of sexual health. We are beginning to hear anecdotes from lawyers who are seeing more divorces stemming from older men who have discovered "the fountain of youth," "trespassed into younger pastures," and discarded what are for them less attractive wives.

Laumann and colleagues (1994), Call et al. (1995), and Yabiku and Gager (2009) find that cohabiting couples have sexual intercourse much more often than married couples. For instance, Laumann and colleagues report that only about 7 percent of married men mentioned having sex four or more times a week compared to nearly 19 percent of cohabiting men. The women's reports were similar. The reader may then perhaps conclude that, at least as far as sex is concerned, cohabitation is more enjoyable. Is it?

Unfortunately, most cohabiting unions tend to last, at best, for the same duration of time as the honeymoon period in marriage (Milan, 2000). Therefore, it is entirely possible that a higher frequency of sex among cohabitants simply reflects the fact that they are mainly honeymooners. When the couple remains happy together, most then go on to marriage and, at least at the beginning, may maintain a higher frequency of sex. So far, there have not been sufficient numbers of cohabiting couples at older ages whose relationships have remained intact for 10 to 25 years to compare them to married couples of the same age. However, it appears that sex plays a more important role in cohabitation than it does in marriage and constitutes a larger part of the mutual attraction (Yakibu and Gager, 2009). Nevertheless, the frequency of sexual intercourse may also diminish with age among cohabitants who remain together. Longitudinal research is needed in this domain, comparing couples consisting of two men, two women, and heterosexual partners (Patterson, 2000).

Frequency of Sexual Intercourse and Relationship Quality

Couples with a higher frequency of sexuality experience a happier relationship and greater conjugal stability (Yabiku and Gager, 2009), although this is not the key element in marital satisfaction and stability (Dzara, 2010). The more vital couples are, the more likely they are to remain interested in each other, and this interest generalizes to the sexual aspect of their relationship. Couples who get along better and share a higher level of companionship are inclined to be more physically affectionate, which leads to a desire and opportunity for sexual activities. Another complementary process is also at play: Having intercourse leads to a greater satisfaction with the marriage and the partner. Sex is a valued activity, and when it is satisfying, it increases a person's sense of well-being and appreciation. The partners feel rewarded. In contrast, when frequency diminishes too much or sex becomes less pleasant, the overall relationship may be negatively affected. As well, when a couple quarrels a great deal or is more distant, this in turn depresses marital satisfaction and contributes to a decrease in sexual activity. One actually encounters both processes when studying how divorced couples' marriages deteriorated. One woman put it this way about her ex-husband in my study on divorce/remarriage:

> "He always wanted sex more than I did and he was always mortally offended that I didn't. But he was always so mean to me otherwise that I had developed a sense of physical, you know, I felt repulsed at the thought of even touching him. I mean, you can't just separate the two. He used to call me a cold bitch, frigid, and that explained it all [her lack of interest in sex] in his mind. But, you know, my husband [remarriage] will tell you that I am a very physical woman [laughs]. If someone, your husband, is wonderful to you, it goes without saying that sex comes easily."

The next respondent, also remarried, is explaining why he stayed so long with his ex-wife even though he did not like her much:

> "Don't take me wrong here, I am not a pervert [we both laugh] but sex is the answer. We didn't get along well at all and didn't share much, but our sex life was great. It's difficult to explain but it was a nice release at the end of a hard day at work and even at home. That's why I stayed: I had a lot to lose here."

Extracouple Sexual Relations

Generally, no matter the type of union they are in, males engage in extracouple sex more than women, as indicated in the percentages provided by Blumstein and

Schwartz (1990). The respondents were men and women who reported at least one instance of extrapartner sexuality:

Husbands	11 percent
Wives	9 percent
Male cohabitants	25 percent
Female cohabitants	22 percent
Gay unions	79 percent
Lesbian unions	19 percent

In the 1994 study by Laumann and colleagues, the results were essentially similar. Of those who were married, 94 percent had been monogamous compared to 75 percent of the cohabitants. More recently, Whisman et al. (2007) report an annual rate of infidelity of about 2 percent among the married. In 2005, Allen et al. reported rates of *ever* having had extramarital sex at 11 to 15 percent for women and 22 to 25 percent for men, but this included persons who had been divorced as well as married ones. In addition, we know that over recent decades there has been an increase in infidelity, particularly among older men and the younger cohort aged 18 to 25 (Fincham and Beach, 2010).

This said, there is general agreement in the various reliable sources of statistics and several salient conclusions emerge. First, heterosexual men and women are more faithful than homosexual men are. Second, among gay unions, men are less monogamous whereas lesbian women are more. And third, married spouses have the lowest rate of infidelities. Cohabiting couples are far less monogamous than married ones, but there is little difference between men and women (Treas and Giesen, 2000). In fact, in the U.S., attitudes toward extramarital affairs have become less accepting in recent decades (Thornton and Young-DeMarco, 2001). There is actually a great deal of consensus among western countries that extramarital infidelities are unacceptable. For instance, Swedes, who are very liberal in other domains of sexuality, nearly unanimously disapprove of conjugal infidelities: 96 percent compared to 94 percent among Americans (Widmer et al., 1998). In 2009, 85 percent of Canadians disapproved of marital infidelity (MacQueen, 2009). It is generally agreed that marital infidelities are highly traumatic for the other spouse; yet, not all couples divorce after he or she learns of it. Many factors enter into play to help a couple overcome the trauma, including the value the relationship has, commitment, forgiveness, social support, counselling, and changing couple dynamics (Abramson et al., 2012).

Media Portrayals of Infidelity and Pornography

The least that can be said is that married couples are *more sexually faithful than portrayed in the media*. This stems in great part from the fact that many commercial enterprises catering to various sex trades/businesses want to promote the idea that "everyone is doing it," that "infidelity is natural" to make **money**. This media bias also stems from the other fact that **media "personalities"**—generally actors, some sports figures, entertainment persons—are far more likely than the remainder of the population to have extramarital affairs and to divorce; as well, television soap characters portray such behaviours along with multiple marriage breakups. A new outlet for infidelities now resides in online dating services, especially those catering to extramarital affairs.

Douthat (2008) asks the question whether "pornography is adultery?" Some research indicates that spouses who are unfaithful are three times more likely to have viewed Internet pornography than others who have not been unfaithful—which rather contradicts those who promote the idea that pornography and infidelities "save marriages" by providing a sexual outlet. As well, online pornography is far more watched by males than females at all age levels, including student populations (Douthat, 2008). Pornography is a billion-dollar industry, constituting a vast market, largely exploitative of women. Pornography may raise expectations in terms of performance and may frustrate couples who fail to meet these "standards." It may create a sense of relative deprivation within relationships and dull the senses to simple acts of sexuality short of "acrobatics." Yucel and Gassanov (2010) have indeed found that pornography consumption reduces sexual satisfaction in marriage. There are various research questions that arise in how porn contents can affect people's expectations regarding sexuality, emotionality, and faithfulness once in a committed relationship (Fincham and Beach, 2010:639). Noor Javed (2013) quotes scholars who are concerned about the potentially negative impact of pornography on teens' current and future relationships.

CONCLUSIONS: THE CHANGING PROFILE OF COUPLES AND SEXUALITY

The past three decades have brought about changes in cultural attitudes and practices concerning sexuality and couple formation. Despite these many changes, marriage is still the preferred type of union, especially among heterosexual women. Gays' recourse to this institution in part confirms its desirability and its symbolic value. This said, we have also seen that casual sexual relationships, such as hook-ups and friends with benefits, are becoming more common—although there are no reliable statistics on this topic and the incidence may be exaggerated. We also know that delaying union formation as well as cohabitations that are entered into without commitment are becoming more common. Therefore, more research is needed to understand how these casual encounters may serve as a socialization context leading to values and habits that go against commitment and may, therefore, preface even more unstable cohabitations and marriages in the near future.

Changing trends are not equally shared by all ethnic or religious groups in Canada, especially among recent arrivals whose cultures still emphasize marriage and restrict sexuality within its boundaries, particularly for women. One can particularly think here of Muslims, Sikhs, Hindus, and Catholic Filipinos. Thus, the new "lifestyle alternatives" practised by so many Canadian-born citizens constitute a difficult environment for others who prefer to wait until the right person comes along and for immigrants from different cultural backgrounds, and especially for their children. Textbooks that emphasize the changing aspects of family life in Canada may inadvertently misrepresent reality—when "changing" refers only to liberalization and individualization, rather than cultural diversity (other values, religion) under our large Canadian roof.

Summary

1. Dating as an institution originated in the U.S. and replaced traditional courtship. Women tend to invest more in their dating relationship than men do. Same-sex dating, interracial couple formation, and Internet dating are presented, as are more casual sexual relationships.

2. The choice of heterosexual dates (and later, partners) at first follows rules of propinquity. Assortative mating becomes more prominent later on, and the term homogamy is used to refer to couples who are similar to each other in some group characteristics.

3. Cohabitation has increased in Canada from 6 percent of all couples in 1981 to 13 percent in 2010; however, the largest increase took place in Quebec. Women are less favourable than men to cohabitation. The heterogeneity of cohabitation is discussed.

4. Marriage is discussed as an institution in the lives of men and women.

5. Same-sex marriage became legal in Canada in 2004 and is discussed.

6. Singlehood is presented cross-culturally.

7. Issues of gender are first introduced regarding sexuality. The study of adolescent sexual relations largely centres on factors related to onset, delayed initiation into sexual intercourse, multiple partners, and oral sex. Variables that contribute to later sexual initiation are discussed. The role of peers is emphasized. There are degrees of voluntariness and desire in the experience.

8. Homosexual and bisexual identities are discussed as well as transgendered situations.

9. Frequency of sexuality within a marriage or a remarriage is discussed. Cohabiting couples experience higher rates of sexual intercourse. Frequency of sexual activity is related to marital happiness. Contrary to myths, a majority of married couples are sexually faithful. Extramarital infidelity is presented in terms of differences between men and women, cohabiting and married couples, heterosexual and homosexual couples.

10. The role of the media and pornography is mentioned as well as how these can affect conjugal relationships.

11. The new changes in couple formation are not shared equally by all ethnic or religious groups in Canada, especially among recent arrivals. One can wonder about the consequences of an increase in casual sexual relationships.

Analytical Questions

1. What makes dating an American institution even at this point in time?

2. Cohabitation has increased in Canada. Yet, as we see in Figure 7.1, there is a large difference by gender in terms of willingness to live common-law. What are the implications of these two seemingly contradictory trends?

3. If you were entirely free to choose your own union type, which would you prefer: cohabitation or marriage? Examine the reasons behind your choice.

4. Why is singlehood becoming more frequent than in past decades?

5. Does same-sex marriage endanger the institution of marriage, as some people think?

6. Discuss the notion that sexuality is a largely male construct in our society.

7. Give two examples of "facts" that are actually social constructs.

8. If this chapter were written in a Hindu or Muslim country, how different would it be?

CHAPTER 8

Patterns of Family Formation and Planning

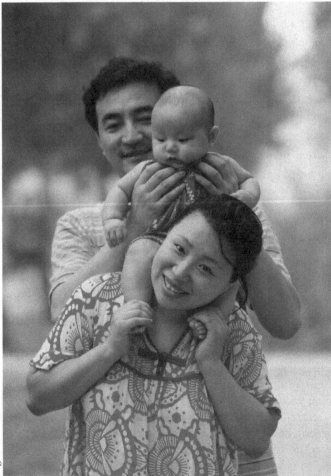

ping hat/Fotolia

OUTLINE

Overview of Family Structure

Family Formation via Marriage

Family Formation via Cohabitation

Same-Sex-Parent Family Formation

Family Formation by Single Parents
  Family Formation by Adolescent
    Mothers
    The Structure of Adolescent Parenting
  Multi-Partnered Fertility and Responsible
    Parenthood
  Children Born to Single Mothers

Delayed Parenthood

Family Planning, Births, and Fertility
  Births and Fertility
  Infertility and Childlessness by Choice
  Abortion

Reproductive Alternatives
  Donor Insemination
  In Vitro Fertilization and Transplantation
  Surrogate Mothers

Family Formation via Adoption
  The Social Construction of Adoption
  Adopted Children's Development
    *The "Real" Child–"Real" Parents
      Dilemma*
  The Diversity of Adoption
    Stepchild Adoption
    *Transracial and Transnational
      Adoption*
    *Open Adoption and Opening
      Adoption Records*
    Reunions with Birth Parents

Foster Families: Family Restructuring

Conclusions: Family Formation
Alternatives in Context

Summary
Analytical Questions

"I come from a single-parent family and I wouldn't recommend it to anyone. My poor mom had too much of a hard time raising us three all alone, with no help and no respect from anyone."

"My father left my mother before I even knew he existed so that I haven't missed out on much. The only drawback is that we weren't very well off, but outside of this I often think that I may just end up a single mother too one day if the right man doesn't come along. Beats not having children and besides I am very much like my mother and I would do very well thank you."

"I had an abortion two years ago and that was rather draining emotionally because it would have been nice to have had the baby, but it would also have ruined my plans for school and perhaps getting married. So now I am thankful for it."

"Abortion is much easier than birth control." [from a student who had had three abortions]

"I hope to have had two children by then [in 10 years]. *I guess it would be too much to think of having three because I'll need to keep my job."*

"I don't see children on the horizon. I've got too many plans for my life and all that I can fit in there is a wife to share these projects with. Children are too time consuming nowadays."

These students' reflections on some aspects of family structure and planning set the tone for this chapter in which we look at family formation, including alternative modes such as adoption and recourse to reproductive technologies. Family formation has different starting points: marriage and cohabitation (including same-sex) as well as single parenthood. Although adults and couples are present in this chapter, the focus is on children's well-being *within the various alternatives for family formation*. This chapter also analyzes the current nearly-universal decrease in fertility, a phenomenon that has no historical precedent and will have many repercussions for the economy, the care of the older generations, and perhaps even children themselves.

OVERVIEW OF FAMILY STRUCTURE

The 2011 census indicates that the proportion of families comprised of a mother, father, and at least one dependent child has continued to decline while other forms of family structure are increasing. This parallels the steep decline in marriage rates in the 1990s described in the previous chapter. This decline is in part driven by the exceptionally low rate of marriage in Quebec, which had dropped to 2.9 per 1,000 population by 2007, compared to 6.9 in 1980 (Girard, 2008). In Table 8.1, we see that married-couple families constituted 67 percent of all families in 2011. This is down from 83 percent in 1981—a substantial change. At the same time, the proportion of cohabiting families increased from 5.6 percent in 1981 to 16.7 percent in 2011. The proportion of one-parent families remained stable. *In Quebec, only 51.9 percent of families fall into the married category, the lowest rate for all provinces.* However, the less populated Nunavut, Yukon, and Northwest Territories also have low rates of families headed by married couples, perhaps as a result of the greater poverty of these regions as well as cultural dislocation inherited from the past among Aboriginals. In terms of ethnicity, 26.5 percent of all black census families were single parents. Less than 9 percent of Filipino, Korean, Japanese, and Arab families were single-parent; less than 5 percent of Chinese, Pakistani, and Punjabi families were so.

Looked at from a **child focus**, in 2011, 63 percent of children below the age of 15 lived with married parents (compared to 81 percent in 1981), 16.3 percent lived with common-law parents (versus 4.5 percent in 1981), while 19.3 percent lived with one parent versus 12 percent in 1981 (Statistics Canada, 2008h, 2012a). First Nations and Métis children were far more likely to live in a one-parent family: 37 and 31 percent, respectively (Gionet, 2009). But these rates are dwarfed by those of

TABLE 8.1	**Distribution of Canadian Families by Marital Status and Provinces/ Territories, 2011 Census**		
	% Married	% Cohabiting	% One-Parent
Canada	67.0	16.7	16.3
Newfoundland and Labrador	71.7	12.9	15.3
Prince Edward Island	72.7	11.2	16.1
Nova Scotia	68.5	14.2	17.3
New Brunswick	67.9	16.0	16.1
Quebec	**51.9**	**31.5**	**16.6**
Ontario	72.3	10.9	16.7
Manitoba	71.0	11.9	17.1
Saskatchewan	71.1	12.5	16.4
Alberta	72.0	13.6	14.5
British Columbia	71.7	13.0	15.3
Yukon	**54.4**	**25.1**	**20.5**
Northwest Territories	**50.0**	**28.7**	**21.3**
Nunavut	**39.1**	**32.7**	**28.2**

Source: Statistics Canada, 2012a (Table 2); adapted from Statistics Canada.

children of Somalian and Caribbean ancestry: 52 percent of Somali, 51 percent of Jamaican, 44 percent of Haitian, and 41 percent of Trinidadian and Tobagan-ancestry children lived in single-parent families in 2006 (Mata, 2011).

Overall, because of a decline in fertility and the aging of the population, there was a decline in the proportion of **couples with children** at home—whatever the marital status. In 2001, 43 percent of all census families were couples with children at home compared to 39.2 percent ten years later in 2011 (Statistics Canada, 2012a). In other words, now more couples have no children at home than in the past: They are either childless or have had fewer children and these children have all left home.

FAMILY FORMATION VIA MARRIAGE

In Chapter 4, we saw that children living with their married parents have the lowest poverty rate. In Chapter 12, the effect of parental divorce and remarriage will be studied. The overall conclusion from these cumulative sources of information is that *children benefit more unequivocally than adults from their parents' marriage.* But, children who experience a conflictual parental marriage benefit less than children living with a well-balanced single parent. However, highly conflictual marriages generally do not last long because of the acceptability of divorce as a solution to marital problems. At any rate, even among those who divorce, at best one-third have highly conflictual marriages and many of those are childless. Therefore, *a relatively small proportion of marriages are detrimental to children and an even smaller proportion of divorces are beneficial to them.* Conflict aside, even when parents do not judge their marriage to be the happiest, children still benefit from it. *What is important to children above all else is* **family stability** and the care they receive from their parents— not whether their parents are madly in love with each other. The latter is an adult western perspective.

In a society with a nuclear family system, children who have **two parents**— whether biological or adoptive, whether of the same or opposite sex—are at an advantage because they have two rather than one person invested in their well-being, responsible for them, and acting as authority figures. Two (or three or four—Stacey, 2011) parents provide a greater repertoire of behaviours, attitudes, and knowledge from which children can draw and learn. In James Coleman's theory, two (or more) parents constitute a greater source of social capital, which then translates into more human capital for the children. With two parents, children have an alternative when the other has less time, is ill, or is otherwise preoccupied. Two parents can also provide moral support to each other in their coparental* duties, and this benefits children. Children also benefit from marriage in terms of economic security, health, supervision, school achievement, emotional stability, prosocial behaviour, and later on as adults, in terms of work (Langille et al., 2003; Schmeer, 2011). Infant mortality is lower in married families, and this advantage is even found in Scandinavian countries, where there is less poverty among single mothers and where cohabitation is more institutionalized than it is in Canada (Oyen et al., 1997).

Inasmuch as the institution of marriage contributes to the emotional stability and overall well-being of adults and children, it becomes *an institution beneficial to society.* It produces a great deal of **social capital** and serves as an **agency of social** control. For instance, children in two-parent families on average get more education and are less often on welfare. Later on, they pay more taxes. Proportionally more children from married families are successfully socialized (Bachman et al., 2012). As well, women who are married have a higher fertility rate than those who are cohabiting. This is particularly important in terms of the fertility rate in Quebec where women cohabit more than in the rest of Canada: Canadian women are married for 15 of their 35 reproductive years versus only 10 in Quebec. As well, "women who married first are thus more likely to spend a larger number of their fertile years in a union, compared to women who formed a common-law union first" (Bélanger et al., 2010:369). In this respect, marriage contributes to society's future both in terms of the biological reproduction and social reproduction of tomorrow's citizens.

FAMILY FORMATION VIA COHABITATION

Family formation through cohabitation occurs when a couple cohabits before or just after the birth of their child; or when a mother begins cohabitation before or after the birth of a child with a man who is not the biological father. In other cases, cohabitation occurs as a form of repartnering after a conjugal dissolution. A large proportion of cohabitations involve children (Seltzer, 2000). As seen earlier, in 2011, 16.3 percent of Canadian children aged 0 to 14 lived in common-law households—including in Quebec, where over 30 percent lived in such households. When Quebec is excluded, the Canadian rate falls to 8.2 percent of children. In many cases, however, one of the two spouses is the child's stepparent.

Cohabiting couples with their own children have a higher level of stability and are more likely to marry. However, even children whose parents cohabit will experience more **instability** than those whose parents marry before they are born (Smock and Greenland, 2010), and this holds true in most countries, including Sweden, Norway, and the U.S. (Osborne et al., 2007), but may not apply to same-sex parents (Stacey, 2011). It was found that 60 percent of children born to cohabiting parents had experienced family disruption by age 10, compared to 14 percent of those children whose parents had not cohabited (Marcil-Gratton, 1998). Overall, children are more likely to experience a parental divorce when their parents began their union as cohabitants or when a single mother cohabits and then marries. In some families, there is a "revolving door" situation, whereby serial partners succeed one another over the years. In a nutshell, children born to cohabiting parents are not at a large advantage compared to those in one-parent families, especially when a mother cohabits with a man who is not the children's father. As cohabitations become more institutionalized, they will become more stable and perhaps as beneficial to children as marriage is.

Results are contradictory as to whether children living with their own parents have fewer or more behavioural and emotional problems depending on whether the parents are married or cohabiting (Brown, 2002; Manning, 2002). Brown (2004) has documented more problems among adolescents whose biological parents are cohabiting (see, also, Bachman et al., 2012). However, much of the literature on children in cohabitations is complicated by the fact that perhaps a majority, when they are adolescents, have a stepparent and have been part of a familial transition (Bumpass and Lu, 2000). Manning and Lamb (2003) have found that *family instability rather than structure* is a more important factor for adolescents' well-being. More research is needed on small children whose mothers cohabit with a man who is not the biological father. These couples are generally quite young and often disadvantaged. Unemployment is common. Such mothers are in a precarious situation both conjugally and economically (Brown, 2002). In some instances, the mothers themselves enter into these unions for short-term benefits and do not commit themselves to marry a man whose economic situation is unstable. In other instances, the mothers are the most committed partner but they are in a weaker bargaining position because they have a child who does not belong to the partner.

The potential instability of these women's unions and the uncertainty of the level of support they receive result in stressors that can disrupt their parenting activities (Beck et al., 2010). The mother's partner is not as likely to compensate for this neglect as a married father or even stepfather might do because the partner's attachment to the children is often low. Physical abuse is also more likely and girls are at risk of being sexually abused; this is especially so in homes where males are transient. In instances where the mother is obviously sexually active with a series of men, the transmission of poverty, early pregnancy, and behavioural problems may become an intergenerational characteristic of these families. A student dramatically explains this:

> *"What made me the most unhappy at this age [0 to 5] is the same for all the other ages to this day. You see, we never lived with our fathers* [her two siblings have two different fathers] *for long and the men my mother lived with took from us the time and attention my mother could have given us without them. Sometimes, they even took the money too.... I remember the times when my little brother's dad used to reject me and my other brother because we weren't his.... This* [other] *man beat us up and my mother when he drank.... We had to move often because my mother would get a bad reputation so we had to change school. I never had friends.... This was the year* [14] *when I ran away and lived in a shelter and where I got my first break in life.... My two brothers got their first 'breaks' with the police ... they both have babies, not me."*

After divorce, cohabitation instead of remarriage may bring in a less involved stepparent (Manning and Lamb, 2003). Further, when a divorced father cohabits, he visits his children less often than a father who is remarried. This may be less evident in Quebec and in countries where cohabitation after divorce is more prevalent and more institutionalized. Nevertheless, at this time in North America, cohabitation is not a situation that signals investment in children as much as does marriage, although there are many exceptions. Commitment and stability are at the core of children's needs; yet, in too many cohabitations, these two requirements are absent, which may have consequences well into adulthood (Teachman, 2003). As well, commitment in a parental relationship is an important value that is transferred to children and may affect their own subsequent relationships (Ryan et al., 2009:950).

SAME-SEX-PARENT FAMILY FORMATION

In 2011, there were 64,575 same-sex couples in Canada or 0.8 percent of all couples—they were twice as numerous as in the 2001 census (Statistics Canada, 2012a). Only 9.4 percent had at least one child at home, as a parent or stepparent.

In fact, nearly half of all same-sex couples with children are stepfamilies. A greater proportion of these children live with a female couple: 16.5 percent of female same-sex couples had a child at home compared to only 3.4 percent of male couples—perhaps reflecting the reproductive difficulties of male couples. These numbers omit lesbians, gays, and bisexuals who are single and have a child living with them—these figures are counted among single-parent families. As well, these numbers omit gays and lesbians who are married heterosexually and have a child at home, as well as those whose heterosexual ex-spouse has custody of their children following a divorce. Thus, overall, the 2008 U.S. General Social Survey found that 19 percent of gay and bisexual men and 49 percent of lesbians and bisexual women have had a child (Gates, 2011).

Society would benefit if all family types were equally supported. Children in same-sex-parent families need stability and security, as do other children, in order to grow up to become fully functional members of society.

Therefore, until now, a majority of children in same-sex couples were born to a mother-father unit that ended in divorce and the lesbian or gay parent obtained custody. A similar situation exists in Sweden and Norway (Andersson et al., 2006). Thus, a majority of these children have another parent who is heterosexual. There are instances when both partners bring children from previous relationships. These situations are similar to those of stepparenting among heterosexuals, but they may also differ depending on whether the children came from a heterosexual marriage or from another same-sex union.

The focus on *educated* same-sex couples in research—because of easier accessibility—*has failed to capture the heterogeneity of same-sex parent families in terms of social class and race*. In a U.S. study, 47 percent of same-sex couples with no high school education are raising children versus only 15 percent of those with a graduate degree. More startling is the fact that 20 percent of children raised by same-sex couples are living in poverty, which is twice the rate of other children. Yet, children with homosexual parents grow up as healthily as those of heterosexual ones (Veldorale-Brogan and Cooley, 2011). Furthermore, while 16 percent of white same-sex couples are raising children, 40 percent of black same-sex couples are, as well as 28 percent of Latinos (Gates, 2011). However, one has to keep in mind that both black and Latino same-sex couples constitute a very small minority because of a lower acceptance of homosexuality, particularly male, within these two ethnic groups.

More and more lesbian couples give birth via donor insemination or adopt. In order to share motherhood more equally, one can donate a fertilized egg to the other partner who will carry it to term (Dondorp et al., 2010). More gay couples also adopt. In the U.S., particularly California, several have had recourse to surrogate mothers. Same-sex couples who have a child together, rather than from a previous heterosexual union, have to do far more **planning** than heterosexual couples, both before and after a child's arrival (Stacey, 2011). They may, for instance, arrange for a cooperative childrearing environment with another homosexual couple of the opposite sex via donor insemination, an arrangement that allows children to have parents of both sexes and a larger kin group. In lesbian couples where one of the two women has given birth, the biological mother typically assumes greater responsibility for the care of the child and at first enjoys a closer relationship with this child than the co-mother (Bos et al., 2007). Other studies show an equivalent attachment to both mothers as the child ages (Goldberg et al., 2008). Upon the arrival of a child, lesbian and gay couples experience transition issues in their relationships equivalent to those of heterosexual couples (Biblarz and Savci, 2010; Goldberg et al., 2010). Some research shows that they receive less support from friends who are not planning on having children and more from their families (DeMino et al., 2007)—which used to be the contrary in the past when families had difficulties accepting their adult children's homosexuality.

Studies of planned families of *lesbian* couples indicate that their children are as well adjusted as children in heterosexual families (Bos et al., 2008; DeMino et al., 2007). The same result applies to children raised by solo lesbian mothers (Golombok and Badger, 2010). Indeed, in a follow-up study of lesbian couples who had used a fertility clinic, the 10-year-old children were receiving as much affection and discipline from each mother—as perceived both by the children and parents—compared to a heterosexual sample (Vanfraussen et al., 2003). Another study comparing lesbian and heterosexual mothers, some single, some in couples, found no difference in children's development around age seven, even though all had been produced by donor insemination—which is certainly an additional complication in a child's self-definition (Chan et al., 1998). Overall, as parents, lesbian mothers are similar to heterosexual mothers; it is not their sexual orientation that emerges as an important variable but their **identity as mothers** (Bos et al., 2007). Similar results have been obtained for children adopted in gay/lesbian homes (Averett et al., 2009). Healthy family processes are key to children's well-being, whether in same-sex or heterosexual families (Strohschein, 2010).

Tasker and Golombok (1995, 1997) initiated a longitudinal study comparing children of *single* lesbian mothers and heterosexual mothers. The children were, on average, 9 1/2 years old, and were re-interviewed 14 years later. The young adults with a lesbian mother reported a better relationship with her and with her partner than did young adults whose mother was heterosexual and brought in a stepfather. The children of lesbians even had a better relationship with their fathers, probably because a mother's female partner does not compete with a father. However, a divorce between two same-sex parents may be as difficult as that between two heterosexuals, a topic that deserves research.

Children with experiences of homophobia are more distressed (Gartrell et al., 2005), and this is far more common in schools than expected in Canada (Taylor et al., 2011). They have more behavioural problems, as a result, especially in the U.S. compared to countries where there is a greater acceptance of lesbigay relationships (Bos et al., 2008). These children are often teased by peers and shunned by their peers' parents, and thus their lives may be more stressful (Morris et al., 2001:151). Yet they do not seem to grow up disadvantaged emotionally and may even possess certain strengths of character such as tolerance of diversity, empathy, and contentment (Gartrell et al., 2005; Goldberg, 2007; Patterson, 2000). However, other evidence points to difficulties experienced by adolescents who feel embarrassed by their parents' homosexuality, a situation which will be attenuated in later cohorts (DeAngelis, 2002).

Children of homosexual parents usually adopt heterosexual identities (Veldorale-Brogan and Cooley, 2011). Nevertheless, young people raised in same-sex-parent families are more tolerant of same-sex experimentation, and they develop a homosexual identity more often than do children in other families—whether heredity and learning are interrelated causal factors is impossible to evaluate at this point (Stacey and Biblarz, 2001). Tasker and Golombok (1995) found that, when mothers had had more lesbian partners and were more open about their sexuality when the children were young, there was a greater likelihood that, as young adults, these children would have a homosexual identity. *However, we do not know to what extent a mother's serial same-sex relationships pose developmental problems similar to those found among children whose heterosexual mothers have had serial relationships, particularly multiple cohabitations* (Dunifon and Kowaleski-Jones, 2002). As Potter's (2012) study clearly indicates, the cumulative number of family transitions is a key element missing in research on same-sex-parent families. Overall, much research remains to be done on same-sex parenting, both separately and in comparison to other families, as well as with more representative samples. For instance, researchers have avoided studying same-sex families where the children were also homosexually identified, in part because of difficulties in locating random samples and, in part, perhaps, to protect such children and families from further stigma (Goldberg, 2010).

FAMILY FORMATION BY SINGLE PARENTS

Single parents can be female or male and are of interest to sociologists because the cultural values of most societies dictate that children should have two parents rather than one. Second, families that deviate from this norm often differ from two-parent families in other ways as well, especially in economic circumstances (England et al., 2011; Gazso, 2012; Wu and Schimmele, 2003). But contrary to what is often believed, *single-parent families do not represent a new phenomenon* (Nett, 1993). In 1941, for instance, they accounted for 14 percent of all families. In the past, because life expectancy was shorter, large proportions of children lost one parent and then another to death. What has changed over time is the **composition** of such families: By the 1970s, a majority of these families had divorced rather than widowed parents. As the years went by, a larger proportion of nonmarital one-parent families occurred as sexuality outside marriage became more acceptable and as single mothers increasingly kept their babies rather than have them adopted.

The number of **births** to unmarried mothers has increased continuously since 1921, when only 2 percent of all Canadian births were outside marriage. This number reached 5 percent of all *births* by the end of the Second World War, nine percent in 1971, 14 percent in 1981, and 27 percent in 1991 (Belle and McQuillan,

1994). There were over 1.4 million single-parent families in 2006, or 16 percent of all families with dependent children (refer to Table 8.1). *A majority are headed by a female parent, generally a divorced one.* In Canada, 25 percent are headed by a single woman as a result of a nonmarital birth, compared to 35 percent in the U.S.

When a single mother is employed, not only is she the sole wage earner for herself and her child, she is also far more likely than a male worker to earn a low salary and to fall behind in her loan and housing payments (Pyper, 2002). She generally earns less than an employed divorced mother, even though the latter does not earn as much, on average, as a male breadwinner. Therefore, the economic disadvantage of women in general is especially detrimental to single mothers' families, both divorced and never married, but particularly the latter.

However, not all these families suffer from adversities, and a proportion do not differ from two-parent families in any meaningful way. The main problem with the generic concept of "single parenting" is that it actually is a **gendered** one because women, not men, give birth. Further, from a feminist political theory perspective, it is single women, not men, who engage in social reproduction-related activities, particularly caring work, and have the ensuing financial responsibility (Little, 2011; Luxton, 2006a). They are blamed by society for their poverty and their children's problems—and by the welfare system in particular (Ambert, 2006; Gazso, 2012). This is related to what has been called the "feminization of poverty" (Brady and Kall, 2008). Older single mothers and fathers by choice, however, are rarely studied. They represent a select group of more educated or more motivated women and men: Their children are generally positively affected (Golombok and Badger, 2010; Jadva et al., 2009a).

Family Formation by Adolescent Mothers

The U.S. birth rate for single teen mothers has been and still is much higher than the Canadian one. Americans more than Canadians have held a moral and social problems-oriented discourse on this issue. Overall, adolescent pregnancy is sociologically relevant, particularly in terms of developmental and political economy theories, because it occurs very early in the life course and, as such, is increasingly non-normative in our societies. It is "off time" in terms of the acceptable time frame for family formation and has economic repercussions. Teen pregnancies, live births, and abortions have *declined* in the past two decades and, in all cases, the rates are higher for adolescents aged 18 and 19 than for younger ones. In Canada in 1996, there were 22 births per 1,000 women aged 15 to 19 versus 14 in 2007. This compares to the low Swedish rates of 7.7 and 5.7 for those years, and the high American rates of 53.5 in 1996 and 31.9 in 2010 (Hamilton et al., 2012; McKay and Barrett, 2010). Births to single teen mothers *have never represented more than 20 percent of nonconjugal Canadian births*. Looked at differently, in 2009, the percentage of births to teen mothers constituted approximately 3 percent of all births in Quebec, Ontario, and British Columbia but were more than 20 percent of those in Nunavut (VIF, 2012b). Below are the teen birth rates per 1,000 women aged 15 to 19 for the year 2007 in Canada (Statistics Canada, 2009s):

For Canada as a whole	14.0 births per 1,000 teens
Newfoundland and Labrador	17.0
Prince Edward Island	17.0
Nova Scotia	16.5
New Brunswick	19.8
Quebec	9.7
Ontario	10.8
Manitoba	31.9
Saskatchewan	35.2
Alberta	20.9
British Columbia	10.7
Northwest Territories	35.7
Nunavut	116.7

Quebec, British Columbia, and Ontario have particularly low teen birth rates, in part because of urbanization and the availability of contraception and abortion. Since 1974, the proportion of teens choosing or being able to access an abortion has climbed steadily, while the proportion of those giving birth has declined accordingly. Teen mothers are now less likely than in the past to have subsequent children while still so young. Those who do are highly concentrated in low-income neighbourhoods, particularly among Aboriginals and blacks (Guzzo and Furstenberg, 2007b; Rotermann, 2007b).

The Structure of Adolescent Parenting

In 1974, only 10 percent of teens who gave birth were single, but now about 80 percent are and it is this fact that led to the concept of "teen" pregnancy. Thus, "teen" pregnancy and births are **historically grounded social constructs,** and are a concern for policy-makers (Bonell, 2004). The causes and consequences of adolescent motherhood are similar in all western countries and the structure of this motherhood—generally associated with poverty (Chapter 4)—contains the seeds of disadvantage, often for several years (*Hamilton Spectator*, 2011). It is difficult in our society to be both an adolescent and a mother or a father. Adolescence is socially constructed as a period during which children acquire rights and independence as well as formal education, whereas motherhood involves assuming responsibilities and being tied down. The two may conflict to the girl's detriment, but particularly to the infant's disadvantage, and this is often problematic for the entire kin group, especially for teens' mothers and siblings (East and Jacobson, 2000), as illustrated in the following quote from a resilient student:

> *"My sister had her first baby at 15, the second at 16, and the third at 18. She 'loves' babies but we've always had to take care of them and now she lives in our*

basement. I really resent her because sometimes I have to write a paper and there are these babies that I have to babysit. And now guess what, my brother's girl-friend is pregnant too and she's only 17. My mother should have never set a precedent by helping my sister."

Many young mothers at first bask in the sun of family attention and love for the baby, peer support or curiosity, as well as the young father's temporary interest. For many, the baby represents someone who will love them unconditionally. The transition to motherhood is overlaid with the usual transitions that adolescents in this society make as they become more independent from their parents. Teen mothers thus experience a double transition. But it is more likely that many adolescent mothers had long emancipated themselves from their parents and had done this earlier than comparable girls who led a more normative life course. This premature disaffection from parental authority may actually have been one of the immediate causes of their becoming sexually active and pregnant. As well, when these young women have many friends who also have babies, they are more likely to have subsequent children (Raneri and Wiemann, 2007).

Further, because they initiate life course transitions early, adolescent mothers are more likely than older mothers to experience multiple transitions, such as successive cohabitations and separations (Luong, 2008). These transitions make lives, especially those of small children, less stable and more vulnerable—a situation that too often becomes intergenerational (East et al., 2007). Little is known about how women who mother on their own most of their lives and then become **single grand-mothers** experience their personal development, identity, health, and old age (Kasper et al., 2008).

There are several paths to adulthood among adolescent mothers (Oxford et al., 2005). Those who complete high school and, especially, those who go on to pursue some post-secondary education are not much different from other mothers when they reach their thirties. Luong (2008) suggests that other resources and **characteristics** of these young mothers may account for their education and ability to support themselves and remain out of poverty. In contrast, Serbin and colleagues (1998) report from Montreal that childhood aggressiveness is related to early pregnancy and dropping out of school. Before having a baby, adolescent mothers average more instances of suspensions, truancy, drug use, and fighting in school than other adolescent girls—which may be related to the mothers' own genetic predispositions interacting with their early disadvantaged environment (Reiss et al., 2009). Among poor teens, psychological distress is also related to a pregnancy (Mollborn and Morning-star, 2009). Thus, single parenting is part of a non-normative life course for a number of adolescents who were problematic children long before becoming pregnant (Woodward et al., 2001). Even though these adolescents are still antisocial and impulsive, as are many of the fathers, they now have the responsibility of a helpless baby and some will have additional children from other partners (Guzzo and Furstenberg, 2007a). The **babies' fathers** often have a background similar to that of the young mothers. Pougnet et al. (2012) have found that French-speaking fathers in a low-income area of Montreal who are absent tend to have children who replicate this pattern of absentee fatherhood two decades later.

Multi-Partnered Fertility and Responsible Parenthood

In this section, we focus on heterosexual men and women who are *unmarried* and have children with more than one partner. This type of family formation is related to disadvantage (Manlove et al., 2008a). For instance, in the U.S., of the men who are deeply below the poverty line, 27 percent of whites and 37 percent of blacks have had children with at least two women, and 16 percent of these same black men with three or more partners (Evenhouse and Reilly, 2012). Guzzo and Furstenberg (2007a) have calculated, for the U.S., that one out of six poor black men aged 34 to 45 have had a child from three or more different women—a pattern of "serial" fatherhood. As well, most alarming is the fact that recent cohorts transition from one birth with one mother to another mother more quickly and at a higher rate than in the past (Manlove et al., 2008a). Cancian et al. (2011) found that, by age 10, 60 percent of first-born children of single mothers have had a half-sibling on their mother's side, which means that they are also likely to have one or more on their father's side. These children tend to have young and low-income mothers. Multi-partner fertility is belatedly receiving research attention south of the border (e.g., Sinkewicz and Garfinkell, 2009); it has been found to reduce the likelihood of marriage and social support from family and friends (Harknett and Knab, 2007). Moffitt et al. (2002) found that *young men who are highly antisocial* produce nearly three times the percentage of babies than do more prosocial young men by the time they reach the age of 26. Woodward et al. (2006) have obtained similar information about young fathers (and mothers) in New Zealand. Fathers with a history of incarceration—and thus of social exclusion from mainstream society—are more than twice as likely to have had children by two or more partners (Carlson and Furstenberg, 2006). For these young men, the practice and meaning of fatherhood is very different from that of other fathers. They are less likely to spend time with their children and some of these children are more at risk (Bronte-Tinkew et al., 2009). Thus, children of such family structure are less likely to spend time with their own father or receive support, and it is also more difficult for the partners to coparent. These factors may lead to more problems among the children (Bronte-Tinkew et al., 2009). In turn, the complexity of the situation and the resulting parenting stress and child difficulties may lead to maternal depression which, in turn, may lead to more such births (Turney and Carlson, 2011).

Children Born to Single Mothers

Poverty, especially when it is intergenerational, is one of the key causes of single motherhood that is related to deficits in children. Therefore, general consequences for children born to single mothers overlap with the effects of poverty (Chapter 4). However, the consequences for children of having a single mother depend greatly on:

- socioeconomic environment: quality of neighbourhood (Chapter 5), availability of good daycare centres (Chapter 6), access to health care, and relevant social policies (Chapter 14)
- mother's characteristics: age, education, income, mental health, maturity, social conformity, social support, and access to social services

- parenting quality: warmth, involvement, supervision, expectations
- father's characteristics: age, number of other children elsewhere, contribution, involvement, and relationship with mother (Shook et al., 2010)
- child's characteristics: birth weight, health, abilities, temperament, and parity

On average, children of single mothers are more likely than children living with both parents to exhibit behavioural problems including hyperactivity, aggressiveness, fighting, and hostility, especially when the mother was an adolescent (Pogarsky et al., 2006). They are also more at risk of becoming young offenders (Willms, 2002b; Zeman and Bressan, 2008) and of repeating this pattern of family structure (Hofferth and Goldscheider, 2010). Emotionally, they are more at risk of suffering from depression, anxiety, and other disorders, as well as having relationship problems, in part due to their difficult behaviours. On average, they do less well in school and repeat grades more often. Adults who have spent part of their childhood in a single-mother-headed family are more likely to have a child nonmaritally, particularly during adolescence, to have achieved lower educational levels, to be unemployed, and to do less well economically than those adults who have spent their entire childhood in a two-parent family. They are also at greater risk of having a criminal record for violent and serious property offences and to have marital problems and divorce.

Outcomes for the children of adolescent mothers are more negative than those for children of older mothers (Letourneau et al., 2007). This also holds true for Inuit children, for instance (Guèvremont and Kohen, 2013). In turn, outcomes for the babies of difficult teen mothers are more negative than for the babies of conforming mothers (Stevens-Simon et al., 2001), as explained by a mature student:

> *"I had my only child when I turned 17 and although I had a lot of support from my mother our family situation became precarious because I was too young and saw my son as a doll that I could leave behind when I went out with my friends or at other times I would take him out with me at all hours. The friends I had were not very good... .The clincher in all of this is that I didn't nurture my son, he had no regular life and became hyperactive and out of control by age 2. He was no longer a live doll and I often resented him. He is now 13 and the problems are endless... . I have no life because of him ... [but] when he was small he had no life and no luck because I was an irresponsible adolescent who only wanted to have a good time."*

Thus, difficult adolescent mothers are often unable to meet even basic child needs and use harsher parenting techniques (Berlin et al., 2009:1416; Lee, 2009), particularly when the child was not wanted (East et al., 2012). As a consequence, their small children are more frequently brought to hospital emergency rooms because of injuries that suggest both neglect and abuse (Serbin et al., 1996).

However, some previously difficult teens change for the better after the birth of their child. But they may have much catching up to do in terms of acquiring habits necessary for the survival of a young parental unit. The corollary is that parenting by older and well-balanced adolescents is less detrimental for all involved and may actually be based on a rational decision. Adolescent mothers' educational level is the best predictor of small children's outcomes (Clark, 1999; Serbin et al., 1998). As already mentioned, young mothers who are able to remain in school and continue on to higher education probably possess other positive characteristics—such as maturity and emotional stability—that are also helpful in their parental role. It would be interesting to know the characteristics of children's fathers that are helpful in promoting better outcomes.

As well, studies in behaviour genetics contribute to explaining the linkages between adolescents' early sexuality, early childbirth, and their children's subsequent behavioural difficulties. Indeed, there are indications that certain genes, which are also related to problematic and antisocial behaviours, at least create a frailty in some of the resulting children. This frailty then interacts with a disadvantaged socioeconomic environment to result both in difficult behaviours and early sexuality, which then lead to early childbearing, and in turn to the new children's own vulnerabilities (Mendle et al., 2009)—and the intergenerational transmission of poverty and early parenthood. In other words, an environment of poverty would affect more negatively those children with frail genetic predispositions inherited from their difficult young parents—hence the necessity of early intervention to prevent another cycle of poverty and problems. This is an example of a situation where we can visualize the many linkages between political economy theories, family development perspectives, and behaviour genetics.

DELAYED PARENTHOOD

Family developmental theories also inform the subject of delayed parenthood, particularly within a historical context (Elder, 1995; Hareven, 2000). Indeed, the age at *first* birth is increasing in Canada and in many countries of the world: By 2006, it had reached 30 years or higher in many countries (Ram, 2010). In Canada, it is 27.7 years for women—28.5 in Ontario and British Columbia (Statistics Canada, 2004i). As well, the proportion of women who have their first child at age 30 and over has increased spectacularly: They represented nearly half of first births in 2006 compared to 24 percent a decade earlier. Births to women aged 35 and over represented 11 percent of all first births versus only 4 percent in 1987 (Statistics Canada, 2008h). Still in 2006, 9 percent of the women aged 40 to 44 were mothers of at least one child aged 0 to 4 versus 4.3 percent in 1986 (Vézina and Turcotte, 2009).

Overall, fertility declines with age and women underestimate the power of the biological clock (MacDougall et al., 2013). As a result, couples in which the woman is 35 or older are the most likely to seek help for conception, probably one in seven (Bushnik et al., 2012b). Male fertility also declines with age and, in addition, **paternal age** is related to various negative genetic mutations and conditions in children, such as autism, dyslexia, schizophrenia, as well as odds of miscarriage (Callaway, 2012; Kingston, 2013). Late-timing mothers also are more likely to suffer from hypertension during pregnancy, to have a caesarean section, to have a child with Down syndrome, and 17 percent of their children are born pre-term compared with 11 percent of other children (Statistics Canada, 2008h). Older mothers are also more likely to have recourse to fertility treatment and, consequently, to have multiple births.

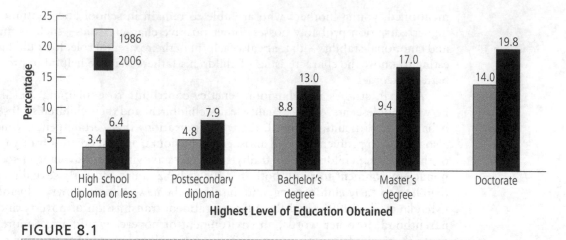

FIGURE 8.1

Proportion of Women 40- to 44-Years Old Who Were Mothers of Young Children, by Educational Level, 1986 and 2006

Source: Statistics Canada, censuses of populations 1986 and 2006. From Statistics Canada; Vézina and Turcotte, 2009.

As indicated in Figure 8.1, women who give birth for the first time after age 40 are, on average, more educated—and this higher educational level is one of the contributing factors to delayed parenthood (Rajulton and Ravanera, 2006a). In turn, having delayed parenthood is what has allowed many women to acquire more education, a more solid economic future, and, possibly, a better marriage (Casad et al., 2012). Delaying women are more likely to be urban, immigrant, and professional, incurring another delay for career formation (Toronto and Vancouver have the highest rates). They have higher incomes (Vézina and Turcotte, 2009). Naturally, a delay in the transition to marriage also accounts for later parenting (Jones, 2007). In turn, both are a prelude to lower fertility (Edmonston et al., 2010).

Overall, the results generally indicate a lower level of parenting stress, greater nurturing, and fewer interparental childrearing conflicts among older than younger first-time parents (Cebello et al., 2004). In 1995, Heath had already found the same positive results of late parenting and included that late-timing fathers are more nurturing and hold higher behavioural expectations for their children than young fathers. Late-timing fathers are often more positive about their role, more involved, and more satisfied with their marital relationship. Older parents often feel more competent, and their self-esteem is less tied to the vagaries of parenting. Greater personal maturity during the transition to parenthood implies a more stabilized sense of self, one that is less easily bruised by "failures" in the exercise of the parenting role. Older parents offer more material and social capital to their children as well as a more stable marital union (Lockhead, 2000; Powell et al., 2006).

As illustrated in Figure 1.1 (Chapter 1), delayed parenthood decreases the number of generations present in a family. One also has to consider that many of the postponed first births may be so for only one of the two spouses: One of them may already have had children from a previous relationship.

FAMILY PLANNING, BIRTHS, AND FERTILITY

Family planning refers to individuals' or couples' decisions concerning the number and spacing of children they desire. Family planning still remains particularly problematic for adolescent women whose first intercourse is not voluntary. People's intentions change over time, depending on circumstances such as health, finances, and work requirements. Only 7 percent of Canadians aged 20 to 34 do not intend to have children (Stobert and Kemeny, 2003): 12 percent of those who have no religious affiliation wish to remain childless. Men generally want to have slightly fewer children than women—2.28 versus 2.46. The **desired fertility** is therefore higher than the **achieved** one, as indicated below. Many individuals are unable to achieve their ideal family size because of financial problems, instability in conjugal relationship, and the difficulty of linking production with reproduction, particularly social (Beaujot, 2004; Beaujot and Muhammad, 2006; Luxton, 2006a). Couples who have reached the goal of one son and one daughter stop childbearing more often than those who have two children of the same sex, especially female. For example, some couples with two or three girls "try one more time" in order to have a son. Or, yet, as is the case in China and particularly India, they have recourse to sex-selective abortion until they have a son (Ram, 2012).

Births and Fertility

Fertility or birth rates refer to the number of births per 1,000 women during their fertile years (ages 15 to 44). The **total fertility** rate, which is an estimate, *refers to the lifetime average number of children per woman.* Currently, it stands at **1.68** in Canada (for 2008), which is well below the 2.1 children needed per woman for population replacement (Statistics Canada, 2011d). Rates are the lowest in British Columbia at 1.51, highest in Nunavut at 2.98 and Saskatchewan at 2.05. Aboriginal women have a much higher fertility rate: 3.4 among the Inuit, 2.8 among Natives who are Status Indians, 2.4 among the Métis, and 2.0 among non-Status Indians (Beaujot and Kerr, 2004). Women who have their first child when they are younger than 25 years old are the most likely to have a third one. Those who are over 30 when their first child is born are the least likely to have a third one. Thus, smaller family size is in part related to a greater proportion of women than before waiting until later to have their first child (Edmonston et al., 2010). It is also related to early entry into cohabitation rather than marriage and to repeated conjugal disruptions (Bélanger et al., 2010; St-Amour, 2012a). However, *among women who have at least one child, the average number of children was 2.4 in 2003.* While over half of women currently aged 65 to 69 have had three children, fewer than a quarter of women in the 35 to 39 age group have (Bélanger and Oikawa, 1999). In 2010, only 13.8 percent of all births in Canada were a woman's third child.

Family size began declining after the 1880s, as illustrated in Figure 8.2, and stood at 4.6 children in 1901, down to 3.5 by 1921, then dropped further to 2.6 in

FIGURE 8.2

Total Fertility Rate per 1,000 Women Aged 15 to 64, 1851–2008

Sources: Milan, 2000; Statistics Canada, 2004i; Statistics Canada, 2011e. Adapted from Statistics Canada.

1937 during the Great Depression (Milan, 2000). This decline continued throughout the decades, only to reverse temporarily during the **baby boom** of the late 1940s and 1950s. Indeed, after the Second World War, there was a sharp increase in fertility, in part because of the social and economic optimism then generated. This increase was also fuelled by a return home of soldiers and young women who had been employed during the war. Thereafter, the downward trend resumed and has continued to this day with an upturn after 2000, in part because the 25 to 34 age group has been increasing in terms of first births during this decade (Beaupré and Cloutier, 2007). However, the uncertain economic situation that followed the 2008 recession seems to have had an impact in Canada and internationally.

In the past decade or so, most European nations and economically advanced Asian societies have experienced fertility rates below the 2.1 replacement value needed to maintain a population (Kotkin, 2012). There has also been a rebound in some by 2006, but recent economic developments are hurting Europeans and again stalling fertility, as is the case in the U.S.: The American rate was 2.1 in 2006—the exception in the western world—but, by 2011, had fallen to 1.89 (Hamilton et al., 2012). The drop was particularly substantial among immigrant women (Livingston and Cohn, 2012). Several European nations have a rate at or below 1.4: Spain, Greece, Austria, Germany, Italy, and Russia. As well, the more economically advanced Asian countries have had very low fertility rates for a decade now and

China for over two decades (Zhao and Guo, 2010): Japan, 1.25; South Korea, 1.08; Taiwan, 1.12; Singapore, 1.25; and Hong Kong, 0.97. Even Vietnam's rate is at an all-time low at 1.89. China's fertility rate is around 1.5 to 1.8 and is even lower in some cities such as Shanghai where it is at 0.7. As well, Latin American rates have dropped drastically since 1980. For instance, Brazil's fertility is now 1.9 from 4.3 while, overall, South America is at 2.3. Africa south of the Sahara is one of the exceptions as the continent's fertility still averages 5.10—which is lower than in the late 1970s when it stood at 6.69. Both Pakistan's and Afghanistan's rates are still very high at 6.07 and 7.19 respectively, while both India and Bangladesh have seen a substantial decline to 2.72 and 2.38 each (Kotkin, 2012; Morgan et al., 2009).

These very low fertility rates are a result of the combination of post-industrialization, urbanization, and individualism, all of which in turn lead to higher female education and labour force participation, later age at marriage and at first birth, and increased singlehood (Jones, 2007; Kotkin, 2012; Krull and Trovato, 2003a). Parents respond to the economic situation by increasing the number of wage earners in their family unit and decreasing childrearing costs because the social reproduction of each child becomes too onerous without proper supportive social policies. Children are less useful to the family unit than in the past and more costly in industrialized and technological societies (Ram, 2010). As Charton and Lapierre-Adamcyk write (2010:373), "The present-day family needs fewer children to realize parents' projects and self-fulfillment." As a result of this demographic change, there are fewer children in Canada. In 1971, children and persons younger than age 24 constituted 48 percent of the population versus 29.9 in 2010 (*Canada Year Book*, 2011). As a further result, there are proportionally more seniors than before and the population is aging. In contrast, families tend to be larger in horticultural and agricultural societies, such as in Africa, or in the countryside more than in the urban zones of these societies. Agrarian children contribute to the familial economy in ways that are often substantial, as is the case in Afghanistan. In these same societies, large families, particularly those with many sons, are a source of masculine pride.

Infertility and Childlessness by Choice

Involuntary infertility, or the inability to conceive, affects approximately 15 percent of all couples (Bushnik et al., 2012a). Although precise statistics do not exist for Canada, this trend is largely the result of delayed childbearing among current cohorts who then have difficulty conceiving when they finally try to do so during their less fertile reproductive years. In Canada, infertility rates among women go from 7 percent between the ages of 18–24 to 10.8 percent for the ages between 30 and 34 years and 14.3 percent for those 40 to 44 (VIF, 2012a). *Fertility also declines among men* (Kingston, 2013). Women are generally more affected than men emotionally because, until now, the onus has been placed on their reproductive role. It is only recently that medicine has discovered that men are equally implicated and **male infertility** is now widely recognized. Men may be infertile for many reasons: Some do not produce sperm or not enough, or the sperm's mobility or concentration is too low; in other cases, the quality of the sperm is compromised. Infertility can be genetic or related to stress, including heat stress in the scrotum region, or environmental (pollutants, for instance), and can also result from obesity or other health reasons. There are indications that semen concentration is diminishing in some countries (Rolland et al., 2013).

In terms of **voluntary childlessness**, it is difficult to know at which point in their life course women, or couples, reach the decision to remain childless, which is certainly facilitated by the recognition that women can occupy roles other than that of mother (Wu and MacNeill, 2002). Thus the same sociocultural factors that have lowered fertility are implicated in childlessness by choice. Women and couples who choose this alternative tend to have higher incomes (Smock and Greenland, 2010). Bélanger et al. (2010) have estimated that 27 percent of women in Quebec will remain childless compared to 24 percent in the rest of Canada. Although childless couples are more likely to divorce, controlling for number of years in a marriage, they experience greater marital satisfaction on some dimensions of their relationship than do parenting couples (Twenge et al., 2003). Childless couples retain a more egalitarian division of household labour, for, as we see in Chapter 9, the transition to parenthood leads to more traditional roles between husbands and wives. A couple alone has far less housework and does not have a schedule revolving around children. Consequently, the spouses do not have to renegotiate the terms of their relationship concerning who does what after the arrival of the first child, as is the case among couples who form a family. Childless couples have more freedom for work and leisure and fewer economic constraints. Their sexuality may be more spontaneously expressed. Their life choices as individuals are more numerous. As for the effect of being childless at older ages, it largely depends on attitudes (Allen and Wiles, 2013).

Nevertheless, whether individuals or couples are childless by choice (careers, lifestyle issues) or by circumstances (infertility, lack of suitable partners, generally poor economic conditions, health issues, lack of affordable housing, unfavourable gender division of labour) or limit their fertility to one or two children, the fact remains that the impact on society is very severe. Indeed, the results of prolonged low fertility after a large baby boom cohort are an aging population, a reduced labour force, and a crisis in caring for children with disabilities as well as the frail elderly (Mandell and Wilson, 2011). Another result is a reduced economic development—all social trends for the near future that are discussed in the last chapter. On the positive side, population decline may also lower humanity's pressure on the environment. But one can also wonder if the quasi absence of children in some Asian countries *does not change the culture of reproduction, particularly social reproduction, and may not reduce its appeal entirely* (Christiansen, 2013). As well, it remains to be seen what the other cultural impacts of small families, of an aging society, and lower population density will be on lifestyles, intergenerational values, the sacredness of life, respect for elders, and human development, as well as gender roles.

Abortion

Induced abortion is an extreme form of birth control and occurs after other methods have failed or because no precautions were taken. Abortions are also constitutive of the gendered aspect of reproduction. Similarly, women are overrepresented in contraceptive measures, from the pill to the IUD. Even sterilization is a gendered division of fertility work in some countries when ideals of masculinity too often excuse men from vasectomies, which are a rather benign procedure medically in contrast to women's tubal ligations, which are a more complex procedure (Bertotti, 2013).

In 1969 in Canada, a law was passed allowing abortions to be performed by a qualified medical practitioner in a hospital after approval by a Therapeutic Abortion Committee. In 1988, the Supreme Court gave women more freedom in this domain. Abortion clinics outside of hospitals existed only in Quebec (initiated by Dr. Henry Morgentaler) but, by 1995, other clinics were in existence in all the other provinces. In the U.S., therapeutic abortions became legal in 1973, with the famous *Roe v. Wade* case. But this issue has remained mired in political minefields and emotional rhetoric in the U.S. where it is still being restricted at the state level. However, the fact that abortion is legal does not necessarily make it equally accessible in all parts of Canada. For instance, it is still not available in many rural and northern regions, where women have to travel long distances for this purpose (Peritz, 2010).

Abortion rates increased dramatically after 1969, then dropped and stabilized at a lower level in the early 1980s, and increased again after the 1988 Supreme Court decision. Between 1990 and 2001, the rate rose slowly from 14.6 to 15.6 per 1,000 women aged 15 to 44 years and then declined to 13.0 by 2006 (Statistics Canada, 2004f, 2009r). The Territories, Nunavut, and Quebec had the highest abortion rates in 2006. In terms of age, the rates are as follows per 1,000 women:

Under 15	1.2 per 1,000 women
15 to 19	14.2
20 to 24	**25.8**
25 to 29	18.7
30 to 34	12.6
35 to 39	8.2
40 and older	2.9

Abortion to adolescents constitute fewer than 20 percent of all abortions in Canada and have declined from 22.1 abortions per 1,000 teens in 1996 to 14.2 in 2006 (McKay and Barnett, 2010). Overall, abortion rates have declined worldwide: Fewer unintended pregnancies are occurring because of contraception availability. However, unsafe abortions are not declining and are still one of the five major causes of maternal deaths (York, 2012). But there are also countries where abortions are used routinely, more or less replacing birth control measures. For instance, in Armenia, Azerbaijan, and Georgia (former Soviet countries), women have on average three abortions in their lifetime (Sedgh et al., 2007)—and these countries are now using it to prevent births of female babies (Hvistendahl, 2011). In Canada, about 35 percent of abortions are repeat procedures, generally a second one, compared to about 48 percent in the U.S. (Fisher et al., 2005). A history of physical or sexual abuse by a male partner is associated with repeat abortions as is a higher tendency to be nonmarried, with more children, and a member of a non-white group.

The decision to terminate an unwanted pregnancy, while not lightly made, rarely leads to serious and lasting psychological distress, as expressed by a student:

"My boyfriend didn't want a baby so I had an abortion and I really hated myself for it eventually. . . . But he had said that no man should be forced to be a father

*against his will and that one day I'd ask for support when he couldn't afford it
or the child would bounce up and sue him.... So it broke up the relationship. ...
Now with hindsight I know I am better off all around."*

When abortion is accompanied by a great deal of lasting distress, there generally are
preexisting emotional problems. In fact, among adolescents, the long-term consequences of childbearing are more detrimental than those of abortion (Fergusson et al.,
2007). Further, children who were unintended at times suffer from negative outcomes and may receive less parental investment than intended children (Barber and
East, 2009; Hummer et al., 2004). Other parents consciously compensate by lavish-
ing resources and love on these "unexpected gifts," as explained by a student:

*"I am an 'accident' of birth and I arrived when my last older sister was 19 and
my parents thought that my mother who was then 45 couldn't get pregnant.
After a period of shock and readjustment to their plans of living happily in an
empty nest home, my parents were overjoyed, felt that they had been given a
new start in life, and gave me so much love and attention that I was even spoiled
compared to what the older ones had received but I am glad that they [older
siblings] thought that this was a hoot."*

This being said, however, it is quite likely that abortion can result in lasting distress when the woman's moral beliefs, or those of her family, are opposed to it.
Therefore, abortion is both a matter of conscience and practicality. But the matter of
conscience is often both ignored in research and over-emphasized among politically
conservative groups.

Another problem resides in that abortion is often used as a measure of **sex selection** and, nearly always, the aborted fetus is female—**female feticide***. This occurs
particularly in India and China and is one of the reasons why the **sex ratio*** is so high
in these countries (Gaudin, 2011). The practice also occurs in North America, among
the same groups, but on a lower scale. Still, the use of ultrasound is widespread and
in areas of the Greater Toronto Area, the birth ratio favours sons, particularly in
families from the Punjab (Aulakh, 2009). This has led to suggestions that the sex of
a child should not be divulged (Kale, 2012; Ogilvie and Aulakh, 2012). Already in
1994, India passed a law prohibiting the use of prenatal diagnostic techniques to
determine the sex of the fetus. Fines and even imprisonment were included, but none
of this is working. In fact, the most highly educated families with the most resources
have recourse more often to these technologies, particularly in the most economically
advantaged states such as Punjab and Delhi (Aulakh, 2013; Ram, 2012). However,
positive governmental and institutional interventions in Tamil Nadu have begun to
reduce the sex ratio in that region of India (Srinivasan and Bedi, 2013).

REPRODUCTIVE ALTERNATIVES

For women and men who are infertile, medical advances now offer a wide range of
reproductive alternatives generally labeled "reproductive technologies." The issues
surrounding these technologies are sociologically interesting (Spar, 2010). First, for
medical researchers, biologists, and geneticists, discoveries represent progress as well
as a source of income. However, governments are not given a chance to evaluate the

social merits of these discoveries before they are implemented. Second, critics argue that children may become commodities themselves, made to order in a catalogue. Third, better-off women, men, and couples are advantaged in this process (Goldberg, 2010). Finally, there is the issue of rights: These technologies are creating children who will have needs and rights separate from the wishes of their parents (McWhinnie, 2001). *These children are created specifically so that persons can become parents.*

Donor Insemination

Donor insemination is a relatively simple and accepted procedure that was practised by the end of the 19th century. Newer techniques exist, such as intracytoplasmic sperm injection or ICSI. ICSI is more successful because semen does not always contain sperm and the clinic may be able to extract it from the father (mother's spouse). In any case, donor insemination generally requires that a woman take hormones to promote ovulation. Although sperm donors are occasionally friends or relatives, organized donor insemination now predominates: Males donate their sperm to a physician or to a sperm bank. In this instance, the husband is not the biological father; he is technically the social father and, in lesbian couples, only one of the two mothers is the biological parent (Chabot and Ames, 2004). Prospective parents can also request "designer" sperm by choosing a donor with certain characteristics, such as high IQ.

Should parents divulge to the child his or her biological background? After all, only one parent is not biological and this factor can easily be kept secret. Indications are that most heterosexual parents do not tell their child about his or her different genetic origins (Brewaeys et al., 2005)—as is the case in the estimated 5 to 8 percent of children who are the result of an extramarital "slip" (McWhinnie, 2001). Unfortunately, many parents confide in other people and this creates the risk of the child learning about it from another source (Golombok et al., 2002). Therefore, several European countries have legislated children's right to know the donor after age 18. At the same time, these donors are protected against any legal and financial duty toward child and mother and are not obligated to meet the child. However, this law has had the effect of substantially reducing the number of sperm donors (Janssens, 2006).

As well, one can wonder about multiple donations by the same man within a narrow geographic area. The possibility exists, however remote, that two half-siblings of the opposite sex could meet and have a child who may then suffer from a birth defect. In France, only two or three donations per man are cautiously allowed.

In Vitro Fertilization and Transplantation

Another step in reproductive technologies occurred in Great Britain in 1978 with the birth of the first test-tube baby, Louise Brown. Her mother's egg was fertilized in vitro (in a test tube) by her father's sperm, and was then implanted into her mother's womb. Other kinds of IVF then followed, each involving a degree of biological distancing and pushing the boundaries of the "nature" of parenthood:

- The mother's egg is externally fertilized by donor sperm and then transplanted into her uterus. The birth mother is the biological mother, whereas her spouse is the social father.

- A donor's egg is fertilized by the father's sperm and then transplanted into the wife's uterus. The wife becomes a nonbiological birth and social mother to her husband's and donor's biological child.
- A donor's egg is fertilized by a donor's sperm and transplanted into the birth mother's uterus. Neither the birth mother nor the birth father are biological parents. They are very similar to adoptive parents, except that the mother has carried the baby and given birth.

The last technique has recently been applied for women over age 55; one birth mother in India was 72 years old. These cases have raised many questions concerning the future of a child who may be left orphaned at a young age. But it has been pointed out that older men often have children without encountering social disapproval; older women, the argument goes, are discriminated against simply on the basis of their gender.

The rate of success of both ICSI and IVF is increasing but is still relatively low, and many mothers discontinue treatment because of stress, financial problems, and health issues (Rajkhowa et al., 2006). As well, IVF and ICSI carry risks of premature delivery, miscarriage, multiple births, low birth weight, and a small risk of birth defects even to single infants (Bonduelle et al., 2005; Hansen et al., 2005; Ombelet et al., 2006). In turn, low birth weight is associated with an increased risk of cerebral palsy and developmental delay (Stromberg et al., 2002). However, other studies attribute these differences, not to the treatment, but to pre-term births (Middelburg et al., 2008). But the highest risk is that of **multiple births** which result in more stillbirths and postnatal death (Sullivan et al., 2012). One can recall here the "Octo-Mom" of 2009 fame whose physician transplanted too many embryos. Indeed, because implantation frequently fails, there is a higher chance of pregnancy when two or more embryos are transplanted. Sweden, for instance, allows only one transfer in order to decrease maternal and child health risks associated with multiple births. Quebec also recommends only one embryo transfer.

Lesbian couples generally use IVF. The same donor may be used for both women. In other cases, one woman can carry to term the other's fertilized embryo. These approaches are used to reinforce genetic bonds and equalize the situation of motherhood.

Deborah Davis/PhotoEdit

Parents who search for their children's donor and half-siblings generally report a positive experience (Freeman et al., 2009). Couples wishing to delay parenthood or when one is to have radiation therapy can freeze their embryos so that they may have children of their genetic background when they are in their late thirties or early forties—a relatively safe procedure (Pelkonen et al., 2010). However, there have already been cases in France and the U.S. of the death and divorce of the potential parents and legal issues arose (Ciccarelli and Ciccarelli, 2005): Who has the right to these embryos? Overall, resulting children's psychological and social development seems to be proceeding well (Golombok et al., 2002). This is especially so when informed earlier rather than later of their origins (Jadva et al., 2009b). As well, both with donor insemination and egg donation, the father-child relationship developed normally (Casey et al, 2013).

Surrogate Mothers

A surrogate mother is a woman who carries a baby to term and relinquishes the child to the married couple or, more rarely, gay couple who contracts with her, generally for medical expenses and a fee to compensate for her time. However, following the *Assisted Human Reproduction Act* of 2004, payments other than medical expenses are not allowed in Canada. Further, it is illegal in certain countries, particularly France, and resulting children may be denied citizenship when parents go abroad for this procedure. Traditionally, the surrogate is inseminated with the father's sperm: Therefore, these women are actually biologically related to the child. This is called **genetic surrogacy**. Other surrogates carry a woman's ovum fertilized by either the father or a donor: This is called **gestational surrogacy**. These two situations can carry vastly different consequences for all parties concerned, both legally and emotionally (Ciccarelli and Ciccarelli, 2005).

Surrogates develop "constructive coping mechanisms towards the baby following delivery, thereby minimizing any potential feelings of loss at relinquishment" (van den Akker, 2007). Being well treated by the intended parents is key to surrogacy. However, it was also found that surrogates receive less social support, including from their parents and partners. It is suggested that everyone would benefit if these women received more social support during and after the pregnancy. A British study found that many intended parents and children remained in amicable contact with the surrogates, although these contacts diminish over time (Jadva et al., 2012). At this early stage of research, there are no indications that small children, intended parents, and their relationships are negatively affected by this type of family formation and contacts (Golombok et al., 2006, 2007).

Attitudes toward this phenomenon are not entirely positive in the population at large (van den Akker, 2007). This alternative can be analyzed from feminist political economy perspectives: Couples or gay men who avail themselves of a surrogate's services are unavoidably well off financially, whereas the surrogate is usually of modest to average means, albeit not poor (Ciccarelli and Beckman, 2005). Europeans turn to former Soviet countries for surrogacy, particularly Ukraine where they have special institutions for this purpose and where the practice is well accepted as it presents many economic advantages. Others turn to India where medicine is advanced and the costs are lower. Thus, there is a social class gap between the parties involved, and this is seen as exploitative. Feminists point out that this "rent-a-womb" arrangement exploits women and uses their bodies, although until now, another woman (the mother) has benefited.

However, there have been many cases of a mother carrying her daughter's baby because the daughter had no uterus or could not carry a baby to term, or of sisters doing the same, including here in Canada. In South Africa, for example, a mother carried all her daughter's children; in other words, she gave birth to her three grandchildren. In 2005, a surrogate in the U.S. gave birth to quintuplets and declined the agreed-upon payment so as to help the parents financially. The motives in these cases are purely altruistic. Therefore, although surrogacy is questionable from some analytical frameworks, it can also be analyzed from an altruistic perspective (Bahr and Bahr, 2001). Many surrogates describe their act as a gift to another woman.

FAMILY FORMATION VIA ADOPTION

The main difference between children who are the result of assisted reproduction and those who are adopted is that the former are created to provide children for people, generally couples. In contrast, adopted children already exist but their parents are unable to care for them. In all cases, however, children's needs are the same. In the late 1990s, 1.2 percent of Canadian children under 12 years of age had been adopted (VIF, 2002). In the U.S., 2.5 percent of all children under 18 are adopted (Adoption Council of Canada, 2003). However, we have no information on the proportion of the entire Canadian population that is adopted—the estimate is around 2 percent—nor how many children are adopted each year. But we do know that Ontario alone has about 150,000 adoption registrations (Beaute, 2009). Although many adoptions involve adults who are already related to the child, the focus here is on *non-kin adoption* because the issues that surround it allow for a deeper sociological analysis of family formation within a social constructionist perspective.

The Social Construction of Adoption

Adoption is found in all cultures, at times known as child "borrowing" (Arnett, 2008; Miller, 2005:183). A great deal of child "transfers" between households occurs among Aboriginal families and communities where need arises—what is called custom adoption (Strong-Boag, 2006). It is very frequent in Caribbean nations, for instance (Rawlins, 2002). In Africa, it often takes the form of child fosterage to a kin's family for educational advantage (Twum-Danso Imoh, 2012). It also was frequent in China in the past for the survival of lineages (Zhao and Guo, 2010). In North America and other societies of European origin, family is equated with biology and this cultural bias leads to ambivalence concerning adoption—even though, in general, a majority of Canadians and Americans express favourable views toward adoption in public opinion surveys (Miall and March, 2005). Yet, adoption is now rarely offered as an option to young single women who have an unplanned pregnancy.

In more recent years, advances in the fields of **genetics** and **medicine** have given rise to a "genetic consciousness" that reinforces negative stereotypes of adoption. What Lebner (2000) includes under the rubric of medicalization and geneticization of our life stories—of our medical risks based on our parents' histories—increases adoptive parents' anxieties when they do not have a full account of their adopted children's background. Yet, these anxieties are only rarely justified because, for the majority of human beings, the environment is far more influential than genes in the domain of health. Further, very soon, a person's own genetic profile will be mapped regularly for preventive medicine and treatment purposes.

Biological motherhood is often considered superior to adoptive motherhood, even by a few feminists (Chesler, 1989). This alliance of biology with feminism presents an anomalous situation at the ideological level because feminist theories generally reject gender roles based on biological constraints (Rothman, 1989). We have all heard the well-known feminist slogan that "biology is not destiny." Arlene Skolnick (1998) rightly criticizes this "new biologism" as a cultural phenomenon with policy implications. As well, Rothman (1989) points out that "we can recognize and appreciate the genetic tie without making it the determining connection" (p. 39).

The more recent development of **reunions** of adopted children with their birth mothers well illustrates the theme of the social construction of adoption. Search-movement activists have depicted the psychological need to search as a universal one, although not every adoptee has this need and will feel "incomplete" without a reunion (Wegar, 1997). What "incomplete" entails is also a social construction but it is **compelling imagery**: It has high value in current psychology. This need is packaged within other very modern themes such as "the need to find oneself," freedom, choice, human rights, and the presumed personal problems and "repression" of those who do not search. It is a need that has been created by our culture and then has become real and quite salient in many adoptees' lives. *But the recognition of the social construct aspect of this phenomenon is not synonymous with shrugging the **created need** aside.* Bartholet (1993) points out that the search movement has inadvertently contributed to stigmatize adult adoptees who are not interested in finding their birth parents. This is well illustrated in a student's autobiography—she had been adopted along with her non-biological siblings:

> *"Last year ... my sister [age 19] was reunited with her birth mother.... The school counsellor had put it in her head that she'd feel 'whole' only after she was able 'to make peace with her past.' Lisa and me had long arguments over this because we were both adopted within a month of our birth and I said, 'What past? Our past is here.'.... I have had parents practically from Day One and I don't see what finding a woman who is supposed to be my mother just because I got a set of genes from her and she carried me would do for me.... So my sister located her birth mother and she doesn't look a thing like her and the woman is not sure who the father is on top of it all ... my sister is still recovering from the shock of these discoveries and she even thinks that the Children's Aid located the 'wrong mother' because she has it in her mind that she should have looked just like her."*

Adopted Children's Development

Therefore, because of this need, one should really expect adopted children to develop many problems of a serious nature, in addition to the fact that more adopted children have various disabilities—12 percent versus 5 percent among biological children. Yet, difference in adjustment between adopted and non-adopted persons are generally non-existent or small (for reviews, see Miller, 2005; Sharma et al., 1998). However, several studies have also indicated that adopted **adolescents** have slightly more problems and conflict with parents than non-adopted ones (Miller et al., 2000). Rueter and colleagues (2009) observed interactions in various types of adoptive and biological families and did not find that parents interacted differently with their adolescents; rather, on average, the adopted adolescents themselves were more conflictual.

The deficits and strengths that are found largely depend on the methodology used, the type of adopted children in the sample, the comparison group, and the outcomes measured. For instance, adoptive mothers report more child problems, whereas adoptive fathers' and adopted children's reports are more similar to those in biological families (Lansford et al., 2001). But, overall, adoptees and their parents do not show any deficit that would warrant concern (van Ijzendoorn et al., 2005). This may be in part related to the fact that parents of adopted children are generally of higher SES and tend to seek health care and preventive interventions more often than do other parents (Bramlett et al., 2007; Nisbett et al., 2012). In fact, children adopted in higher-SES families tend to develop intellectually much better than their biological siblings who are not adopted and better than anticipated when their genetic background places them at risk (Nisbett et al., 2012; Reiss et al., 2009). Two studies of young adult adoptees concluded that whatever differences existed between them and non-adopted adults were small; as well, these differences were not identical in both studies (Feigelman, 1997; Smyer et al., 1998). Borders et al. (2000) focused on adoptees who ranged from 35 to 55 years of age compared to a similar group of non-adopted adults. Both groups were experiencing their adult years similarly, but adoptees had a slightly lower level of self-esteem and a slightly higher level of depression—perhaps due to the past social contexts of adoption. One study has shown that adopted children fare equally well across a variety of family structures—whether they are only children, have younger or older adopted siblings, or have younger or older biological siblings (Brodzinski and Brodzinski, 1992). However, adoptions of multiple siblings have a higher rate of failure (Smith et al., 2006).

Parents often experience more stress when they adopt **older children** (Tornello et al., 2011): Older children frequently have special needs or suffer from problems related to difficulties in their original families and/or foster placements (Selwyn et al., 2006). They may also have had more problematic parents than children adopted at birth and thus have inherited more difficult predispositions (Miller et al., 2000). Therefore, older children who are adopted bring with them genetic, emotional, and contextual baggage that may make it more difficult to form an attachment to their adoptive parents and to be parented successfully. One problem that is encountered is ARND or alcohol-related neurodevelopmental disorder and, at a more severe level, FASD or fetal alcohol spectrum disorder, which are caused by alcohol drinking during pregnancy (Buxton, 2004).

Overall, adopted children experience a wide range of outcomes and adjustment in life, as do non-adopted children. But, although adopted children generally feel as loved and as accepted by their parents as non-adopted children, their peers and even adults often openly express doubts to them on this topic and so do the media (Leon, 2002). This situation is similar to that of children of gay and lesbian parents who become more distressed after they encounter questions about their type of family (e.g., Gartrell et al., 2005; Taylor et al., 2011).

The "Real" Child–"Real" Parents Dilemma

An adopted respondent in March's (1995a) study said that outside the family, people *"never believe that your adoptive parents love you like their parents love them. Because you aren't biological"* (p. 656). One of my students recalls returning home one day quite distressed and asking her mother, *"Is it true that you can't love me as much because I am adopted?"* Another student reported that, upon learning she was adopted, her peer on the school bus shrieked, *"Oh, you poor poor child! You don't have any real parents."* Another student recalled the following causality chain:

> *"When I was 6 one day I proudly told one of my friends that I was adopted. To me, this had been a source of joy because I had always been told by my parents how much they had wanted me... . My little friend didn't say much and with hindsight I gather that she probably didn't know what I was talking about. The next day she and another girl turned around me in a funny way and my friend finally said, 'My mom feels sorry for you.' I was puzzled and asked why. 'Because you're 'dopted [sic] and you don't have real parents. You're not their real little girl and you don't look like them.' I didn't understand any of this at first but it sounded awful and I started bawling out and the teacher had to call my mother to come and console me. It did the trick but I never thereafter talked about being adopted to any other child until I was in university. It didn't change my feelings about my situation at home but this incident definitely made me feel different, more socially anxious, and less self-assured."*

This theme of not being a "real" child and not having "real" parents is an excellent example of the **social construction of adoption** and is a recurring one in the autobiographies of students who have been adopted and in the emails sent in 2006 as a result of an online paper. As a woman who is both an adoptee and the adoptive mother of two children, now young adults, explains:

> *"... peers being tactless and thinking that adopted children are not 'real' too often happened to my daughter but not so much to my son because I think that boys are so busy playing games and being active that they don't have time for this nonsense."*

This stigmatization is discriminatory and may constitute a heavy mental burden on adoptees (Leon, 2002). Children are especially vulnerable to what their peers think. If their peers present them with questionable notions of their adoptive status, then these children are at risk emotionally. *This may explain why, in some studies, adolescence is the time when adopted children begin to show a higher rate of behavioural problems compared to other children* (Miller et al., 2000). A mother with an adopted daughter and a biological son recalls that:

> *"when both children were in the school system, it became known that one was adopted and the other 'real' or one was ... 'not natural.' Our daughter* [who up to that point had delighted in having a little brother] *was devastated ... she changed in a very short time: she became teary, moody, sensitive, touchy, and later on rebellious ... and felt like the 'fifth wheel in this family.'"*

For other children, the fact that their adoptive status is questioned by peers and significant persons in their lives may push them to rebel against their parents. One of many adopted adults who mentioned this put it this way:

> *"The way I see it, society provides adopted children with loopholes or excuses that may encourage them to become maladjusted without taking any responsibility for their attitude themselves... . In order to excuse my own behavior, I*

started ... diminishing the benefits of their values and ways of living (after all, they [her parents] were successful and I was becoming an asshole), and just saying in effect, well, I am becoming myself and if you don't like it, just shove off."

Adoptive parents are more likely to be white, older, educated, and to have a higher income than biological parents. Whether same-sex or heterosexual, they invest more resources in their children, including economic, social, or interactional, than do biological parents (Hamilton et al., 2007). These resources constitute a positive environment that explains why some genetically at-risk adoptees often progress very well (Reiss et al., 2009). At least one study has found that the transition to parenthood was easier for adoptive than for biological parents (Cebello et al., 2004). A birth mother concluded her email by saying that:

"the best solution is to embrace the adoptive parents ... because they have loved and raised and paid for this child ... I did cringe when I saw this 60 Minutes segment of a girl being reunited with her birth mother and the poor real [adoptive] mother was just an onlooker and it was a love story between girl and birth mother . . ."

The Diversity of Adoption

Stepchild Adoption

We do not have information about stepchild adoption in Canada. Although there are a few similarities between regular adoptions and adoptions by a stepparent, there are important differences as well as motives specific to each situation. The main reasons for step-adoptions after divorce reside in a desire to be a "regular" family, to legitimize the roles and relationships within the reconstituted family, and to sever the ties with the nonresidential parent, particularly when the latter does not contribute child support, is uninvolved with the child, or the child has never known him or her (Marsiglio, 2004). The nonresidential parent either consents to the adoption or the case can go to court. A judge will rule in favour of the adoption only if the nonresidential parent is deemed unfit or if it is in the child's best interest to sever the relationship. A better model might be that of the *British Children Act* of 1987, whereby stepparents can have responsibilities for children without obliterating noncustodial parents' responsibilities and rights. The long-term consequences of stepchild adoption have yet to be studied but are certainly related to the initial age of the child at adoption (Schwartz and Finley, 2006).

Transracial and Transnational Adoption

We do not have solid information on transracial adoption in Canada but the U.S. 2000 census indicates that 17 percent of adoptions are transracial (Adoption Council of Canada, 2003). Overall, there is absolutely no indication in the American and British research that black children adopted in a middle-class environment by white or biracial parents turn out differently as adults than those adopted in comparable black families (Butler-Sweet, 2011). In fact, they gain substantially at the educational level (Nisbett et al., 2012). Vroegh (1997) reports from a longitudinal study that, by adolescence, these children are still well adjusted and enjoy a high level of self-esteem—as is the case for children born to interracial couples (Tatum, 1999). Most interracially adopted black children grow up identifying as black, and most parents conscientiously promote their children's African-American heritage (Vroegh, 1997). This does not prevent them, however, from at times feeling out of place in a totally white environment and without a role model of the other racial group.

In Canada, the adoption of Native children by non-Native parents has been and continues to be an issue, in great part because cultural genocide indeed took place in the recent past as it did in the U.S. However, in the U.S., the First Nations represent a smaller proportion of the population than in Canada and are less visible politically so that this topic is less researched. But, again, we do not have statistics on trans-adoptions of Native children in Canada. Currently, the numbers seem to be relatively small—despite the large number of these children in foster care.

As the number of young children available via foster care and especially private agencies declined, international adoptions increased. For instance, Canadians adopted 2,127 children abroad in 2009 (*Canada Year Book*, 2012:60). Quebec and Ontario are the provinces with the most transnational adoptions (Ouellette and Belleau, 2001). There has been a preponderance of girls over boys: 68 percent and 32 percent respectively (Adoption Council of Canada, 2003). This sex ratio imbalance in part stems from the fact that adoptions from China peaked at 53 percent of international adoptions in 2005 and plummeted to 22 percent in 2009. The U.S. constituted 12 percent of our international adoptions followed by 8 percent for Ethiopia, Vietnam, and Haiti (*Canada Year Book*, 2012:61). In China, most of the available children are female because of the one-child family policy and preference for male children (Dorow, 2006; Xinran, 2010).

However, adoption of children who had been very deprived in their country of origin often leads to stressful parenting, especially when behavioural problems emerge (Judge, 2003). Older age at adoption and pre-adoption adversity are related to lower levels of adjustment later, including in a sample of Chinese little girls adopted by Americans (Tan, 2009). Age and deprivation among East European adoptees have also been related both to improvement and persistence or even development of problems (Beckett et al., 2006; Welsh and Viana, 2012). Yet, overall, international adoptees experience only slightly more emotional and behavioural problems than other children (Juffer and van Ijzendoorm, 2005).

But international adoptions represent a political and economic situation of inequality and lack of resources in the home countries, and a position of economic superiority among the host countries (Bartholet, 2010). It can also lead to exploitative situations whereby disadvantaged parents lose their children permanently, as occurs occasionally in Haiti and several African countries, out of need and misunderstanding of procedures and their life-long consequences.

Open Adoption and Opening Adoption Records

In the past century, adoption largely meant that a child's past was erased (Strong-Boag, 2006). The trends are toward opening the process of ongoing and future adoptions as well as opening the records of past adoptions with vetoes for persons who do not want to be found, as has been done in Ontario on June 1, 2009. Reports from several countries indicate that privacy is rarely invaded, which has been a fear expressed by some adoptees and birth parents (Carp, 2008).

Adoptions are categorized along a continuum ranging from confidential to mediated and then to fully disclosed (Faulkner and Madden, 2012). Confidential adoptions provide anonymity but generally disclose parents' backgrounds. In the mediated category, the adoption agency may transmit pictures, letters, and gifts, or even arrange meetings between parents without full identification. In the fully disclosed category, both parties know each other's identity and may meet. Many single mothers now relinquish their infant only under circumstances that allow them greater control over the adoption process and even access to the child. At the extreme continuum of openness, biological parents more or less enter the adoptive parents' family system as they exchange regular visits and participate in decision-making concerning their child's health.

Studies on the outcomes of open adoption are still embryonic, but, overall, many indicate that most of the adoptive and biological parents are satisfied with their relationship with one another (Grotevant et al., 2008; Ge et al., 2008). However, semi-open (or mediated) adoptions might be more functional than fully open ones. For instance, in fully open cases, many adoptive parents reported feeling burdened by meetings with birth parents. Berry et al. (1998) and Frasch et al. (2000) noted that, in nearly half of the open adoptions, the level of contact between the two families had decreased after four years. Openness does not threaten adoptive parents' sense of entitlement to parenthood. Rather, it generally strengthens it. Adoptive mothers find it more difficult than fathers. Gay and lesbian couples have the easiest time navigating open adoptions. Gay men receive the message that children need a mother figure in their lives. Also, they do not feel threatened in their identity as parents as is at times the case among heterosexual adoptive mothers (Stacey, 2011). As one respondent in Goldberg et al.'s (2011) study said, "So, I have no issue knowing that Janice is her mother. But if her father was part of the equation, if he was still present, I would have a much bigger issue. I wouldn't want to compete with another man" (p. 513). For their part, lesbian couples are also somewhat more accepting of open adoptions because they are already used to the notion that there can be more than one mother.

The concept of boundary ambiguity leads to the possibility of problems when children are attached to two sets of parents, as is the case in foster families (Leathers, 2003), or when children have been adopted at older ages (Logan and Smith, 2005). Kohler et al. (2002) concluded that adolescent "preoccupation with adoption is not an inherent outcome of confidential adoptions" (p. 100). Further, studies have found no difference on measures of child adjustment between open and confidential adoptions or between physical versus letter contact with birth relatives (Neil, 2009). As well, adoptive parents and children are more likely to be in contact with birth parents in private adoptions than in adoptions from the foster care system, in part because of concerns for the children of the type of birth parents involved and their often more difficult circumstances (Faulkner and Madden, 2012). For instance, 68 percent of parents in private adoptions had had contact with birth parents versus 39 percent for those who had adopted from the foster care system.

Reunions with Birth Parents

Today, search for birth parents or biological siblings is legally encouraged and records are more accessible than in the past. Mothers and daughters are the most common searchers. This **gender difference** may be the result of women being more biologically involved in reproduction and birthing and because women are socialized to be more nurturant and family oriented than males. In some instances, young women search for their birth parents only after they have become mothers themselves. Others do after their parents' divorce (Tieman, 2008). Similarly, **birth fathers** are less commonly involved (Passmore and Feeney, 2009). They are often not known and more difficult to locate, in great part because only a small fraction of the past adoption records list a father's name (Beaute, 2009).

The few existing studies on the topic of reunion indicate that a majority of adoptees who have been reunited with their biological family see this as a positive experience (March, 1995a), although March (1995b) also documents many cases of rejection. In most instances, the adoptee acquires a stronger sense of being their adoptive parents' child and, although at times apprehensive at first, adoptive parents are generally at peace with the situation. Even birth fathers recognize the adoptive fathers as the real one (Passmore and Chipuer, 2009). However, a mismatch between the respective motivations and expectations of the two parties may develop over time, especially when there are vast differences between adoptees and birth parents (Passmore and Feeney, 2009), as experienced by a birth mother who had adopted her four stepchildren and was then reunited with her birth daughter:

> *"After several long weekend visits, matters started spoiling. It was obvious that she wanted all my and my husband's attention ... so she started sniping at the* [adolescent] *children, at talking against them, at trying to make alliances with one against the others ... having temper tantrums."*

Another reunited birth mother had a different perspective and felt that her daughter was too attached to her adoptive parents: *"I feel used because she has found me and now she knows her background... . All I am for her is a background, a piece of information."*

More recent research has included reunions initiated by birth mothers and various effects on adoptive parents (Petta and Steed, 2005). One should also mention that it is very difficult to study birth mothers and their families. As a result, only those who search or who are reunited can be studied. As well, adoptees who do not search are usually not studied either, which certainly biases the results. As a last note I will mention that no research exists that would describe and explain the impacts of reunions on the spouses and children as well as families of birth parents.

FOSTER FAMILIES: FAMILY RESTRUCTURING

Fostering is really a form of family restructuring rather than family formation and it is much more common than adoption. The number of children in need of foster care far exceeds the availability of suitable families. In 2011, there were 47,885 foster children reported in the Canadian census—the majority of whom were under 15 (Statistics Canada, 2012a). The largest proportions of foster children are in Manitoba, Northwest Territories, Nunavut, and Yukon. However, the Adoption Council of Canada put the number at about 80,000—with 30,000 available for adoption. In the U.S., well over 524,000 children are in the foster care system at any point in time in comparison to about 200,000 in the 1980s; of those, about 120,000 are awaiting an adoption that may never come (Ross, 2006).

There are three main problems preventing adoption of older foster-care children. The first is that people prefer to adopt small children. Second, biological parents refuse to let go, even after years. And, thirdly, couples who might adopt, particularly foster parents, are deterred because of financial reasons (Duncan, 2013). In this respect, it is less expensive for the government to provide a subsidy to these families; otherwise, keeping a Crown ward in care costs over $30,000 a year (Monsebraaten, 2012)—and the results are not very good. It is further suggested that Crown wards who reach 18 be helped to age 25 so that they can continue their education rather than end up homeless or on very low incomes and chronically unemployed later.

Poverty is the main reason why children end up in foster care and this is especially relevant for First Nations children who are disproportionately represented in the system (Fluke et al., 2010). In fact, in 2011, nearly four percent of all Aboriginal children aged 14 and under were in foster care versus 0.3 of non-Aboriginal children (Statistics Canada, 2013b). Along with poverty, homelessness is a prominent factor (Zlotnick, 2009). Most other reasons, such as parental incarceration, drug and alcohol addiction as well as mental illness, child abuse and neglect and domestic violence, also have poverty in the background. Children with fetal alcohol spectrum disorder or FASD (Dej, 2011) or who need special attention because of delinquent behaviours are also prominent in the system. Therefore, it is not surprising that children who have been in foster care and group homes generally have more negative outcomes than other children, particularly in terms of delinquency, mental health, and adult criminality (Lawrence et al., 2006; Viner and Taylor, 2005). A meta-analysis showed that adopted children, particularly those adopted at older ages, have more learning problems at school than others (van Ijzendoorn et al., 2005). However, these children did better than those left in foster care, including biological siblings who were not adopted. Adolescents and young adults who are later incarcerated too often suffer from FASD, a situation that is only beginning to be recognized. Indeed, foster care children are a select group (Berger et al., 2009): These children were neglected or abused in their families and the placement represents an additional dislocation (Harden, 2004).

There is little research on children's and parents' lived experience with foster care. Some children call their foster parents "Mom" and "Dad," whereas their biological parents may be referred to by name or as the "other mother." Some foster children believe that they are much better off than in their parents' homes and are even grateful to have been removed from the home when they were small. Others rebel against their foster family and the fact of being in foster care (Whiting and Lee, 2003). Length of care brings greater closeness and a sense of identity with the foster family. On the other hand, regular contact and hopes of reunification with the natural family decrease closeness with foster parents (Leathers, 2003; Moyers et al., 2006). Children who are to be reunited with their original families do better when their parents visit them regularly (McWey and Mullis, 2004). In the U.S., slightly over half of children are reunited with their parents; however, nearly a third eventually return to foster care, often within one year (Connell et al., 2009; Wulczyn, 2004). Children who had suffered from severe neglect are likely to come from more dysfunctional families and are less often reunited (Barber and Delfabbro, 2009): Such children are less likely to be successfully reintegrated with their family of origin than physically maltreated children, even though they are younger (Bundy-Fazioli et al., 2009; Marquis et al., 2008).

Foster care does not always work out well and for a variety of reasons, including the scarcity of homes, low payments, the lack of support, training, and supervision received by foster parents, as well as children's age and past difficulties, abuse, and neglect (Eggertsen, 2008). A proportion of foster care parents are violent at one time or another as a result of frustration and many more report having been aggressed by the youth in their care (Ringstad, 2009). Foster care within the extended family may result in less dislocation for children and mothers and may demand less adaptation from children (Lawrence et al., 2006; Metzger, 2008). However, relatives and, especially, grandparents, are generally not as well compensated financially or emotionally supported and this may create severe stressors. Finally, there is very little social support for youth leaving foster care upon or before legal maturity (Collins et al., 2008; Kaplan et al., 2009).

CONCLUSIONS: FAMILY FORMATION ALTERNATIVES IN CONTEXT

The evidence points to marriage and *committed* cohabitation as being the current optimal forms of family formation for children and, to some extent, adults. Overall, one can conclude that what is the best combination for the healthy development of any child is having two parents who are committed to each other and especially to the child, who have access to some resources and support, and with whom the child enjoys a warm relationship (Strohschein, 2010). As well, the research is unanimous to the effect that married fathers invest far more in their children than either cohabiting or single fathers (Cooksey and Craig, 1998; Gallagher, 2010). An exception are gay fathers who parent by themselves or with another man (Mallon, 2005; Stacey, 2011).

What about single mothering? *Under the current economic and political system*, absolutely nothing in the extensive research literature recommends solo motherhood for adolescents and adults alike. For established and mature adults, however, single parenthood may well be a positive alternative for parent and child. This alternative is socially advantageous when an adult adopts a child who would not otherwise have a family. A feminist political economy analysis suggests that women (and men) should not have to depend on marriage and should have the option of forming one-parent families that function well and contribute to society's social capital (Coontz, 2000). Thus, **single parenting** could become a far better alternative for children and adults in the future under the following circumstances:

1. If young males were socialized to be nurturing and equally responsible for their offspring, then even children in single-mother families would have two parents invested in them and supporting them (Marsiglio and Roy, 2012).

2. If women earned incomes equal to those of men, then the poverty rate of families headed by women would diminish substantially, and so would children's problems.

3. If social reproduction was valued by society and if what is now unpaid work was remunerated, mothers and their children would have more options.

4. Once all these conditions are in place, delaying childbearing until attainment of greater maturity would be the last necessary ingredient to making single parenting more functional for children and their parents than it currently is.

Thus, overall, while much of the research literature documents the disadvantages that single mothering *on average* brings, disadvantages are not inevitable (Ruspini, 2000). Rather, they are tied to the economic structure of our societies, thus to deprivation, lack of a supportive community, and the culture of feminine inequality that pervades all domains of life (Vosko, 2002). Nevertheless, I would be derelict in my duties as a researcher were I to romanticize single parenting as an alternative to free women from conjugal life—for, indeed, as a few feminists have pointed out, women end up paying the price, not society nor the fathers (Folbre, 1994; Walby, 1997).

Single-mothering and, to a lesser extent, cohabitational parenting currently present a risk element for women and their children, especially within the context of poverty. *Ultimately, family processes are more important than family structure for child outcomes. But the point bears being reemphasized: Positive family processes are more likely to be found in committed conjugal structures, whether heterosexual or gay.*

On another level, individuals and couples now have the option of regulating the number of children they have, which is a form of social progress. However, we have seen and will further see in Chapter 14 that what is good for individuals is a problem for societies because their population is not replenishing itself sufficiently to support older generations and even the economy. This low fertility, particularly in Asia and some European countries, may dilute family values and affect the entire culture. Christiansen (2013) ponders why a society such as Japan is not concerned about the "human, social, and cultural capital lost" (p. 19). He asks, "What happens to a culture when fewer people have the opportunity to care for children?"

Summary

1. Recent changes in family structure in Canada include a decrease in marriage and increases in cohabitational families. A longer period of singlehood and more cohabitation among young cohorts are delaying marriage.

2. The role of marriage as an institution for children and society is discussed.

3. Cohabitations involving children have increased. The role of cohabitation for children is examined, especially when a mother cohabits with a man who is not their father.

4. So far, most children who are raised in same-sex-parent families were born in a mother-father family where divorce occurred. But more and more, same-sex couples are having children by donor insemination and adoption. Overall, the results indicate that the public's concern for these children is unwarranted.

5. Nonmarital fertility has increased dramatically since the 1960s. Although one-parent families are not a new phenomenon, their composition has changed over time and most are now the result of divorce. Nonmarital teen births have increased and then stabilized at a lower rate. The life course and background of adolescent mothers and fathers are studied.

Children born to single mothers tend to be the most disadvantaged in their outcomes, but much depends on a key set of variables.

6. There has been a general decrease in fertility in all industrialized countries, and Canada's current fertility rate of 1.66 is no exception.

7. As the age at first birth is increasing, a greater proportion of first births are to women aged 35 to 45.

8. Childlessness by choice has also increased while abortion rates have declined. Abortion for sex selection is discussed.

9. New reproductive technologies are detailed.

10. The social construction of adoption as an alternative form of family formation is pre-sented. The literature on the consequences of adoption for children is discussed.

11. Stepchild adoption and transracial adoption are presented.

12. The following are detailed: open adoption, reunions of adopted children with birth parent, and foster children along with their outcomes.

13. Currently, marriage is the pattern of family formation that is in the best interest of children. Single parenting could become a more appropriate alternative with cultural and economic changes at the systemic level. The societal consequences of low fertility are discussed.

Analytical Questions

1. It is said in the media that cohabitation is replacing marriage. Discuss the pros and cons of such a statement.

2. Some often believe that, for children, cohabitation and single parenting are equivalent modes of family life to that of parents' marriage. Yet, the research literature across the world points to a different conclusion. How can you reconcile these two perspectives?

3. Children in same-sex-parent families fare as well as other children, contrary to what many people think. Explain why this is so. (The answers are not necessarily *all* in the text.)

4. The teen birth rate was far higher in the 1950s than it currently is. How can this be, given the statistics presented in the text?

5. Currently, the Canadian fertility rate stands at 1.66, while the American one has just recently fallen to 1.8 from 2.1. This is a relatively large difference. What factors can explain it?

6. Using social constructionism, discuss the "nature" of parenthood within the context of adoption and reproductive alternatives.

7. What do feminist political economy perspectives bring to the analysis of some of the contents of this chapter?

CHAPTER 9

Spousal Relationships

David Hanover/Stockbyte/Getty images

OUTLINE

Types of Marriage and How They Change
The Vital and Total Relationships
The Devitalized Relationship
The Congenial Relationship
The Conflict-Habituated Relationship
The Congenial Reproductive-Familial
  Relationship
The Cultural Reproductive-Familial
  Relationship
Marriages Evolve Over Time

Aspects of Spousal Relationships
Marital Happiness, Satisfaction, and
  Success
Communication Issues
Partner Conflict and Problems
Marital Quality through the Decades
The Next Time Around: Remarriage
The Conjugal Relationship in Later Life

Division of Labour and Inequality
A Classification of the Domestic Division
  of Labour
The Effect on Marital Quality: Overview
  of Recent Changes
Division of Labour in Remarriages with
  Stepchildren

The Silent Division of Labour: Emotional Work

Same-Sex-Couple Relationships

The Effect of Children on the Couple Relationship

The Effect of the Parental Relationship on Children
Conjugal Quality Fosters Supportive
  Parenting
The Role of Learning and Personality
Genes and Within-Family Environment
The Larger Environment Affects
  Marriage and Childrearing

Conclusions: Definitions of Relationship Quality Are Culture Specific

Summary
Analytical Questions

"Right now, I'd rate myself as somewhat unhappy despite the fact that I just got married, which is what I wanted to do most in my life. It's just that marriage is so different than dating and becoming engaged. We used to do things together, special things, and had all the time in the world to talk. Now we're married and it's just like things are all settled for my husband; he has to work. I work, and I am finishing school and there's no time for the nice things in a relationship. Last year we were equally busy but he could find the time. I know that I may be too romantic and that I have to get used to this, but it is so disappointing."

"The past two years have certainly been the happiest of my life and mainly because I got married and even though I felt I was too young at the time it's the best decision I ever made. It's just the little things that make me happy like when I come home and he has the supper ready for me because he knows I have had a hard day and he knows that I am not used to cooking on a regular basis. What I like best probably is that we have so much to talk about, and we still talk about loving each other after two years but now we're also seriously planning the future as in having children. I can tell him that I am afraid to be cooped up in the house with two kids and no one to talk to and he takes it seriously and he says we'll have to find a way to keep me working and him doing a lot of fathering."

These two women students are at the beginning of their marriages and are of the same age—around 24 years old. Yet, their experience, level of happiness, and the extent to which their conjugal **expectations** are met are entirely different. In their autobiographies, they are fairly similar on many personal aspects, such as personality and values. They have, however, married young men with radically different conceptions of conjugal life. As a social category, men are more powerful agents of the construction of reality than women. This systemic advantage, as we see in this chapter, carries into intimate relationships.

Throughout the last half of the 20th century, the relationship between spouses became far more diverse than it used to be. To begin with, the explosion of divorce on the familial scene has meant that marital stability can no longer be taken for granted. Couples now enter marriage with a less secure feeling of permanency than was the case in the past. Second, the massive re-entry of women on the labour market has resulted in more complex feminine expectations and often more complex forms of masculine cooperation or resistance in terms of the household division of labour. Couples now have to negotiate who does what at various stages of family development, and this situation can result in a tense relationship. Third, couples' expectations of marriage concerning love, sexuality, and companionship have heightened. More is demanded of marriage in terms of relationship than in the past, while, at the same time, couples may be less patient when their expectations are not met (Amato et al., 2007). *The cultural focus of marriage as an institution has shifted toward an individualistic axis emphasizing needs and gratification;* yet, this has not translated into happier marriages. Rather, what is often overlooked is that **commitment** to marriage as an institution is still a key source of marital happiness and stability (Wilcox and Nock, 2006). In this respect, couples in which one of the spouses develops a serious medical illness, such as multiple sclerosis (MS) or brain tumours, present an informative situation. Indeed, a study by a group of physicians has found that women who had such a condition were much more likely to be abandoned by their spouse than male patients. This was particularly so when the marriage was 15 years or less compared to longer-lasting ones that were on average over 20 years of duration (Glantz et al., 2009). The patients who became separated, in turn, had poorer outcomes: They used more antidepressants, participated in fewer clinical trials, were more frequently hospitalized, and less likely to die at home.

The relationship between spouses has also become more **diverse** for the simple reason that it now includes more categories of couples. Today, the term *spouse* has been extended to all couples involved in living-together relationships, whether cohabitants, same-sex couples, or remarried couples. Despite this diversity, marriage is still the predominant demographic basis of family formation. Even though couples are now delaying marriage, a majority of Canadians, if not necessarily Québécois, still expect to marry at least once. This demographic reality, combined with the fact that comparatively more research has been carried out in the past on the marital relationship than on any other form of partner relationship, means that a majority of the pages of this chapter are devoted to heterosexual marriage. However, it should be noted that ideological trends in research are such that we are currently in a cycle where less research is published on the marital relationship than needed to keep up with changes that may be occurring. For instance, one might want to know about the impact of the omnipresence of media such as cell phones, texting, tweeting, and Facebook in the lives of couples.

Finally, it should be pointed out that, perhaps following the individualistic values of the past decades, research on the spousal relationship has been carried out mainly within an individualistic and psychological perspective, with too great an emphasis on conflict and perceived satisfaction, as opposed to other processes, such as altruism, commitment, or complementariness (Fincham et al., 2007b). As well, the research in general fails to situate couples within their familial, social, and cultural contexts, something which we try to remedy (Karney and Bradbury, 2005).

TYPES OF MARRIAGE AND HOW THEY CHANGE

I wanted to begin this chapter with an overall classification of marital relationships, but I could not find recent in-depth studies of marriage types. Rather, I noted three methodological trends in the research on marriage and married life. First, usually sociologists do not themselves interview or even observe couples but have recourse to large-scale surveys designed by other researchers. (This is called "secondary analysis" on p. 30.) Second, these surveys, dominated by multiple-choice questions, do not provide sufficiently complete descriptions, and generally focus on only one of the two spouses. The result is that research on marriage (and on other areas of family life, for that matter) tends to present isolated bits and pieces rather than overall, holistic perspectives. Third, as already indicated, most of the studies reach only one of the spouses or, when both are interviewed, they are not linked to each other in the results but, rather, males and females are analyzed separately as two groups. Consequently, the *couple* perspective is lacking (see Sanford, 2010).

In 1965, using a qualitative approach, John Cuber and Peggy Haroff proposed a typology derived from in-depth interviews with 107 men and 104 women who had been married *for at least 10 years* and had never considered divorcing. The five types of marriage derived from the interview material were named on the basis of their central and distinguishing themes. They represent different configurations taken by the couples' relationships. This typology still applies today in *western* countries and can probably be extended to cohabitational couples as well as same-sex couples. Research is needed in these domains. Further, the influx of immigrants from countries that are more patriarchal and, in other cases, where marriage is less a matter of companionship than a matter-of-fact relationship for reproductive and economic purposes requires that sixth and seventh types be added. I have taken the liberty of calling these the "congenial reproductive-familial relationship" and the "cultural reproductive-familial relationship."

The Vital and Total Relationships

The essence of a vital relationship is sharing and togetherness. Couples value their relationship, regularly discuss it, and when alone, often think about it. When they encounter conflict, they resolve it rapidly and move on. Differences are settled easily, even though with much discussion, but without insults or humiliating put-downs, as would take place among the conflict-habituated couples. This type of marriage comes close to conforming to Canadians' perception of an ideal marriage. But when a vital relationship moves to a less involved one, such a marriage may become intolerable to one or both partners, even though it may still be a far better marriage than average. Divorce, rather than adjustment, may follow. The vital marriage probably typifies the first years of a great proportion of western marriages as well as many marriages that are past the childrearing years. For others, it lasts into the older years (Dush and Taylor, 2012). In other words, it is not only a type of marriage but, for many couples, it represents a *stage* in their relationship: the honeymoon.

For their part, couples in a **total** relationship form a minority and are the "stuff of novels." They are in many ways similar to the vital couples—the main difference being that there is more sharing at the intellectual and psychological levels, and more discussions taking place for the sake of sharing their interests verbally as well as physically. In many instances, the couples have professional interests in common and help each other, attend conventions together, and confer on a wide range of issues. Whereas vital couples retain their individual existences, total couples melt into the same existence, like identical twins. The French call these couples *fusionnels*. These couples' sexual relationship is very important and is expressed in a multitude of settings and forms. Total couples define each other as lovers and best friends. Despite this, some do divorce because they have very high romantic and companionable standards. Experiencing less than what they have had, often after two or three decades, is not tolerable.

The Devitalized Relationship

In a devitalized relationship, the spouses had been deeply in love early on in their marriage, had enjoyed their sex lives, and had shared much together. Over time, the relationship lost its original "shine" and vitality. Now these couples simply take each other for granted but conflict is rare. Most of the time spent together is a matter of duty, to fulfill parental roles, to present a united front to the world, and to take care of each other's careers. These couples are often exemplary parents.

The relationship continues because of their commonly shared duties as well as the absence of conflict. There generally are other rewarding aspects in their lives, in which they invest much. They celebrate anniversaries and appreciate each other as parents or as workers. Some hold values that supersede that of individual happiness and they respect marriage as an institution. Cuber and Haroff found this type of marriage to be common in their sample and may today constitute a proportion of all marriages of long duration.

However, these couples are susceptible to divorce because this type of marriage is considered less than ideal in our culture and the lack of positive affect takes a toll. It is a breach of romantic expectations of marital bliss. The risk of divorce is particularly high in view of the fact that these couples have, in the past, experienced greater companionship and pleasure in each other's presence. They are able to make comparisons with what they had before so that expectations for a happier relationship can arise and strain the status quo. Such expectations can also lead to extramarital affairs which may, or may not, lead to divorce—and, here, the cultural context may be very important in terms of the acceptance of such transgressions.

The Congenial Relationship

The congenial relationship may be quite similar to the devitalized relationship, with the exception that these couples do not have an early exciting past that has been hollowed out through the years. They harbour deep affection and especially respect for each other and are not disillusioned as are the devitalized couples. In fact, they are quite *comfortable* with their situation. They emphasize what they share, such as their total agreement on a variety of political or religious issues, or the fact that they have similar leisure interests, parenting goals, and social network.

These couples' dating lives were generally uneventful, and a strong element of level-headedness rather than passionate love was at the basis of their decision to marry. For them, marriage is a secure platform from which to explore and develop other deep and even passionate interests, whether in parenting, politics, careers, or even volunteer work. Compatibility of background is important. Many of these spouses believe that society is placing too much emphasis on sex and passionate love. Although some of these marriages end in divorce, the risk is not high because this marriage fulfills many culturally acceptable functions for the spouses and their families and across cultures. These unions may also be cemented by strong principles and these couples may rate their marital happiness quite highly. Contentment may be a good adjective for this category in the older years.

The Conflict-Habituated Relationship

The main characteristics of the conflict-habituated union are tension and unresolved conflict, some of which is overt and appears in the form of nagging, quarrelling, and excessive teasing. The spouses seem to argue for the sake of it. When on their best behaviour, these couples are polite, particularly in the company of others. But they do not conceal their differences from their children and, during the interviews, emphasized their incompatibility and how tense they were in each other's presence. Many of these couples had already been conflictual at the dating stage. What holds their marriage together may be force of habit, lack of alternatives, and the fact that the spouses have personalities that are combative or have been so chiselled by the relationship that they might have difficulty adjusting to a more peaceful situation were they to divorce. In other cases, they cannot afford to divorce because of poverty or shared wealth and/or social position. This category can include marriages in which spousal abuse occurs, and this is discussed in Chapter 13.

Among young couples today, this type of marriage is more conflictual than conflict-habituated because conflicted relationships are likely to end soon. Even in the Cuber and Haroff sample, this type of marriage was not the most frequently encountered. Today, it might cover well over 10 percent of long-term marriages. This is not a marital interaction that is valued in Canada, although it is far more acceptable in other cultures, especially when people appreciate arguing for the sake of it and when a "macho" code of conduct encourages marital spats in public, especially at the expense of women.

The Congenial Reproductive-Familial Relationship

The congenial reproductive-familial relationship is added to the Cuber and Haroff typology to include marriages that are *more or less* **arranged**—that is, with the adult children's participation—and do not become emotionally intimate but are cordial. This type can, to some extent, also cover those marriages that are not arranged but have been encouraged for familial, rational, or social reasons rather than for romantic purposes. Cordial reproductive-familial marriages are characterized by a focus on tradition or practicalities rather than on romanticism and affectionate companionship. The spouses tend to lead largely separate lives: Wives take care of the children and spend their leisure time with other women, often kin, although they may also be employed. Men are the breadwinners and their family's representatives in the community at large, and they spend their leisure time with other men. The extended family system is generally important and family visits usually result in men and women sitting and conversing separately.

Although such marriages may not play the emotional role they do in western societies, it would be wrong to assume that the relationship between husbands and wives in India or other similar countries is unavoidably weak or lacks in companionable values, at least at the ideal level (Orsini, 2007; Zysk, 2002). The spouses interact with each other for sexual purposes but with a minimum of romanticism involved, although a degree of affection exists. Wives are faithful sexually while men may or may not be. Spouses also have long conversations when alone or in the presence of their children. These conversations are cordial, may involve a great deal of mutual respect, may be supportive, but their focus tends to be on matters related to the family, children, business, jobs, and forthcoming celebrations. These conversations may involve discussions of the relationship and the functioning of the household.

The Cultural Reproductive-Familial Relationship

This type of marriage is similar in structure to the previous one, but it has differences in terms of gender segregation and power. These marriages are **arranged** or even **forced** according to cultural norms with the matter of feelings being totally left aside. This is the union of a man and a woman that links two families together and where patriarchal, social, and cultural considerations are paramount. The couples spend no time alone together, except for sleep, generally live with at least the husband's family, and the importance of the relationship is within the kin context. These couples are even more gender segregated than the previous type and women are rarely employed in non-familial work. Family honour is paramount. Such marriages may be polygamous. These unions are at very high risk for wife abuse and this abuse may be culturally sanctioned. These marriages are imports to Canada from western and southern Asia, the Middle East, and North Africa. Except for moving into the conflict-habituated or the congenial-reproductive categories, they are much less likely than the previous type to move into another category of relationship.

Marriages Evolve over Time

The types of marriage described above are not necessarily cast in stone: Marital and cohabitational relationships evolve over time. Marital quality often diminishes and then rebounds later to some extent; yet some couples have a much higher level of happiness at the outset than others so that the consequences of this decreasing quality has different meanings and effects for different couples (Umberson et al., 2005). Most middle-class couples probably begin at the vital stage, but a proportion rapidly become conflictual or devitalized. At that point, marital satisfaction plummets and divorce rates soar. In today's cultural climate, only a minority of marriages survive constant conflict. The others make a conscious effort to change or seek counselling. Semi-arranged marriages, for their part, may also evolve into a congenial or even a vital relationship or they may degenerate into a conflict-habituated one, often very early on. Divorce may also follow. Marriages that are more or less forcibly arranged have far fewer opportunities for positive transformation. Yet many become congenial and even loving. But, as an option, divorce requested by a woman may lead to difficult consequences because of the cultural context of patriarchy in the groups.

A devitalized marriage can also become a conflictual one over the years. At any point during these sequences, the marriage may break down, particularly when conflict and abuse occur, or when better alternatives present themselves. However, another change that may occur throughout the years consists in a revitalization of the marriage after childrearing is completed. This is illustrated in the following student quote. She had described how the burdens of parenting and jobs had dulled her parents' marriage during her adolescence:

> *"Since then, my parents' happiness with their marital situation has been steadily rising. The business is great and my father's working less hours, Mary [a problematic adolescent] has a job, and I'm in college. They're happy with the whole family in general and they're like best friends. They're always getting all dressed up and they go out here, there, and everywhere. In fact, as I'm writing this down, they're on their way to Florida for a two-week vacation—both from work and us kids. They're as close as a couple could be and are celebrating their 26th anniversary this year. They've made a lot of plans for the near future and they seem very happy and excited about it. Neither would be whole without the other."*

ASPECTS OF SPOUSAL RELATIONSHIPS

Spousal relationships involve elements of happiness or disaffection, communication, as well as potential for conflict and conjugal problems. These elements have a three-fold developmental dimension. First, they can be studied throughout the lifespan of a *couple* well into the later years. Second, within a person's lifespan, marriages can succeed one another so that the sequencing of marital types, division of labour, commitment, and marital happiness constitute an important research theme. Third, marital quality can be studied by *cohort*—that is, among couples born and raised in different decades who, consequently, may have different expectations (Amato et al., 2003). Other important aspects of the marital relationship, such as **commitment**, altruism, and forgiveness, receive little attention (Fincham et al., 2007a)—reflecting the values of western researchers in the last half of the 20th century. Indeed, there are suggestions that commitment may prove to be as important a variable as marital happiness, for instance, in the study of marital quality (Amato et al., 2007). Future research may well find that commitment drives marital happiness and success. There is a cultural aspect to the various elements just mentioned but, so far, researchers have been westerners. Therefore, again, the cross-cultural perspective is lacking, although this is slowly changing as researchers from East Asia as well as India are publishing in North America (e.g., Williamson et al., 2012). It is possible that some of the elements just described are not relevant in other cultures while there may be other elements of marital relationships that are paramount. However, at the same time, many cultures are becoming westernized in this domain, especially among the more educated classes, as is the case in China, South Korea, and India (Derne, 2008; Fuller and Narasimhan, 2008; Orsini, 2007). As well, we need more research on the transformations that occur among immigrant couples originating from these countries, as well as Muslim areas, such as Pakistan or Iran (Shirpak et al., 2011).

Marital Happiness, Satisfaction, and Success

The concepts of marital happiness, satisfaction, and success have been very popular in the North American marriage literature ever since Burgess and Locke began their studies in the mid-1940s (Burgess et al., 1963). The goal of this research is to define what a successful marriage is and compare the characteristics of couples who are satisfied and happy with those of couples who are not. These various concepts are often used interchangeably, but there are different meanings attached to them. Marital happiness is an emotional state and is totally subjective and individual. In contrast, marital adjustment and success, while also subjective, depend much more on how the persons in the dyad perceive how they have achieved their goals, how well they communicate, and how companionable their relationship is (see Family Research 9.1). *What makes for a happy marriage changes with the centuries and even the decades* as couples' expectations evolve under various cultural influences that provide different **social constructions** of the conjugal relationship. As already pointed out, the emphasis on marital happiness as the foundation of a union is rather unique to western countries. In most societies, the notion itself does not even exist.

A researcher by the name of Loveless, as paraphrased in Carroll and colleagues (2005), has identified three types of marital happiness. One is hedonistic and pertains to the satisfaction of desires. The second is individualistic and pertains to individuals' goals. The third is altruistic: The needs of the other are a primary concern and happiness occurs as a result of fulfillment of this goal. It is also posited that a focus on the first two types of marital gratification to the detriment of the altruistic one prevents researchers from focusing on marriage "as a social institution that involves important social, intergenerational, and public dimensions" (Carroll et al., 2005:277). The strictly individualistic view on marriage prevents an analysis of the shared aspects of marriage and of its role in society.

FAMILY RESEARCH 9.1

How Is Marital Adjustment Measured?

Several measuring instruments have been devised to quantify marital adjustment and satisfaction. These instruments are generally called *scales* and are used during phone, Internet, and face-to-face surveys designed to evaluate a couple's or even a family's functioning. Among the best-known is Spanier's Dyadic Adjustment Scale, which can be used for couples in general (see Spanier, 1976). The scale contains 32 close-ended questions testing for dyadic satisfaction and happiness, dyadic cohesion (shared activities and communication), dyadic consensus or perceived level of agreement, and perceived agreement on demonstration of affection, including sexuality.

Examples of questions are:

- How often do you kiss your mate?
- How often do you confide in your mate?
- How often do you work together on a project?
- How often do you quarrel?

The methodological issue to be addressed in this type of research is how one would measure marital satisfaction in cultures where husbands and wives lead largely separate lives and where romantic love is not the norm, even though it may happen.

Overall, studying marital happiness is a complex undertaking, for it depends on a multitude of variables and it is impossible to include even most of them in research. *The variables that help individuals achieve marital happiness can be found at several levels.* Some, including economic situations, are derived from the social context and may help explain the lower marital satisfaction among blacks, who, on average, are less economically advantaged (Aldous and Ganey, 1999; Broman, 2005). Yet, cultural origins are also important because black cultures attribute different values to marriage as well as behaviour (Mitchell, 2010). For instance, Caribbean women living in the U.S. have a higher level of marital satisfaction than African-American women (Bryant et al., 2008). Mid-life Canadians born in Canada but with immigrant parents report higher marital happiness than those born abroad, suggesting a certain cultural adaptation (Mitchell, 2010). Other variables are psychological and involve personality characteristics, communication styles, and coping mechanisms. For instance, Miller et al. (2003) noted that being expressive toward one's spouse (the "love" word) promotes marital satisfaction: Expressiveness leads spouses to engage in affectionate behaviours and to interpret their partner's behaviour in a favourable light. Persons who remain unhappily married over many years develop lower levels of overall happiness and life satisfaction as well as lower self-esteem and health. In fact, people in low-quality marriages do less well on these indicators* than those who divorce and remarry and even divorce and remain single (Hawkins and Booth, 2005). In contrast, marital happiness increases well-being over time.

One can study what types of couples are happy together and what contributes to their dyadic satisfaction and even success. **Longitudinal studies***   indicate to what extent marital happiness at Time 1 predicts happiness at Time 2 and what has happened in the interval to explain change or stability. Currently, researchers are able to predict with reasonable accuracy which relationships will end in divorce and to verify this prediction with a follow-up study of the couples. We do know that marital happiness diminishes after the "honeymoon" period among some couples (Mitnick et al., 2009). However, Dush et al. (2008) have also found that couples who begin with a very high level of marital happiness experience a less steep decline over a 20-year period. Many couples remain very happy. As Lavner and Bradbury (2010:1182) point out, "growing disenchantment in marriage does not appear to be inherent to marriage itself in the manner implied by the honeymoon-is-over effect but is instead confined to subgroups of spouses." Overall, at any point in time, only about 20 percent of marriages are unhappy. However, commitment to the spouse and to marriage as an institution may be better predictors of marital quality and stability than marital satisfaction (Wilcox and Nock, 2006).

Communication Issues

Communication is a key component of the conjugal relationship. When couples who have been married for 50 years or more are asked the reasons behind their successful marriage, they unavoidably include "good communication" in their explanation. The quality of communication depends largely on its regularity, predictability, thoughtfulness, sharing characteristic, as well as how well spouses listen to each other. Spouses who are satisfied with their relationships tend to talk with each other about everything, share their thoughts, feelings, and hopes. They enjoy listening to the other and are attentive to the other. Perhaps one of the reasons why women's marital quality is on average lower than that of their spouse is that husbands often communicate less about personal matters and are less interested in these issues—the gendered emotional work mentioned earlier. As a result, women want more companionable communication (Heyman et al., 2009). Positive communication is related to satisfaction in all cultures, as indicated in a cross-cultural study that included Pakistan (Rehman and Holtzworth-Munroe, 2007).

However, there are also signs that inadequate communication may at times be the result rather than the cause of marital distress: Carroll et al. (2006), for instance, have found that negotiation skills are effective only when they are grounded in love and consideration for the spouse—and, they add, commitment to the relationship. They conclude:

> *"This distinction calls for therapists and educators to carefully assess whether difficulties in communication are the result of a deficit in the ability to negotiate or in the ability to love on the part of one or both of the spouses. . . . For example, without sustained commitment to one's spouse and marriage, communication skills are likely to falter as a basis for long-term marriage, and without the virtue of justice or fairness, marital problem-solving skills can descend into businesslike negotiations between two self-interested parties"* (p. 1029).

As we have seen, women are more invested in their marital and parental relationships than men. In their role of emotional workers, wives are more involved in problem resolution. For all these reasons, wives are generally less satisfied with their current and past marriages than husbands, a situation that is also found in a study of Afghan, Iranian, and Pakistani immigrants in Canada (Moghissi et al., 2009:67). But more to the point here, wives are compelled to make more demands and express more dissatisfaction to their husbands than the reverse and are therefore in the unpleasant position of initiating more conflict. For their part, men are more likely to withdraw (Christensen et al., 2006). Thus, in terms of quality of communication, women can be more negative than men because they are emotionally more threatened in view of their greater investment in the relationship.

Partner Conflict and Problems

Researchers evaluate the frequency of spousal conflict via self-reports and, at times, observations in homes or in a laboratory. They also investigate the mechanisms used by couples to resolve their conflicts. They have often categorized conflict behaviours as destructive, constructive, or withdrawal (Birditt et al., 2010). The research shows that same-sex and opposite-sex couples engage in similar conflict-resolution mechanisms (Kurdek, 1994). All report a relatively low level of conflict. Lesbian women report using more constructive conflict-resolution styles. They also mention making greater effort to resolve conflict, perhaps because, as women, they have been socialized to be attuned to a partner's distress more than is the case among other couples that include at least one man (Metz et al., 1994). In this chapter, the focus is on conflict in general.

Marital conflict arises from issues pertaining to the division of labour, communication, lack of attention to each other, finances, sex, children, and leisure time. Finances involve not only how money is spent but who controls it as well as who earns it. When it exists as an issue for a couple, money becomes a pervasive and recurring source of conflict (Papp et al., 2009). Overall, difficult economic situations are related to conjugal conflict among both cohabiting and married young couples (Hardie and Lucas, 2010). Debt is problematic because it prevents couples from achieving some of their projects and expectations (Dew, 2008). As well, on average, the presence of children increases the frequency of disagreements (Hatch and Bulcroft, 2004).

There is substantial evidence that a genetic component is involved in conflict via personality, temperament, and emotional lability (Harden et al., 2007). Thus, styles of conflict resolution appear to form during the first year of marriage (Schneewind and Gerhard, 2002). Constructive outcomes occur when the communication of the dissatisfaction results in a better understanding of each other's feelings with a mutual search for a solution, including compromise. Egalitarian couples tend to be more responsive to each other's disclosure of dissatisfaction and are more likely to engage in mutually satisfactory solutions. Less egalitarian couples are more likely to avoid discussing their dissatisfaction, particularly with the division of labour. As well, conflicts are least likely to be resolved constructively when, for instance, the husband withdraws from the interaction and thus maintains the status quo: **Conflict avoidance** or withdrawal does not resolve problems and may decrease marital happiness (Christensen et al., 2006). However, were a researcher to ask these "avoiding" couples about conflict, the answer might be that little exists—compared to what the researcher would find among couples containing at least one egalitarian spouse. Thus, a lack of reported conflict in this case simply refers to overt conflict; such couples may actually have a very high level of what could be called covert or simmering conflict, as described by a divorced woman:

"My ex-husband always said to whoever would be present that we never had problems or quarrels. That's true, we never fought verbally and certainly not physically. But we could never talk about our disagreements and problems. As soon as I'd mention something, he'd smile, or laugh, or joke and walk away. He just left and things just kept getting bottled up; I mean we couldn't talk about money, about sex, about going out or not, his mother, nothing. Sure, we had no quarrels, we had no communication."

Forgiveness is a mechanism of conflict resolution that is rarely studied (Fincham et al., 2007a). It seems to help in providing closure, prevents negative conflict resolution strategies, and enhances self-regulation (Braithwaite et al., 2011). However, McNulty (2008) has found that it is functional only when it is followed by a change in the misbehaving spouse. Indeed, some spouses continue misbehaving after being forgiven, which results in higher tension in the forgiving spouse—leading McNulty to conclude that spouses should not forgive the constantly misbehaving partner. Empathy is another component residing in individual partners that may prevent conflict (Cohen et al., 2012).

Marital problems are more encompassing than conflict. However, the two overlap in the sense that disagreements and conflict constitute one type of problem reported by spouses. As is the case for the division of labour, there is a **gendered aspect** to marital problems: Wives report problems more than husbands and say that more problems are created by their husbands, both during marriage and after divorce. Further, marital problems affect women's health more negatively than they do men's, although both men's and women's health suffers as a result of marital strain (Hetherington, 2003; Umberson et al., 2006). Not surprisingly, the quality of relationships in wives' own family of origin may have a greater effect on their perception of marital quality (Sabatelli and Bartle-Haring, 2003).

Marital Quality through the Decades

The quality of marriages may have declined, at least since 1969. In 1991, sociologist Norval Glenn first showed that the proportion of people reporting their marriages to be very happy had declined between 1973 and 1988. This finding was unexpected because divorce rates had increased during the same period. One would think that the surviving marriages would be happier than in the past when unhappy couples were forced to stay together. A complementary study carried out by Amato et al. (2003) used data gathered previously through two national phone surveys of couples 55 years of age or younger, one survey in 1980 and the other in 2000—and this was before the advent of the ubiquitous presence of smartphones.

Members of the 2000 survey reported less marital interaction, more conflict and problems in their marriage, but marital happiness and divorce proneness remained constant. Generally, there was greater conflict and less interaction when both spouses were employed and when there were small children at home. There was also more conflict when the spouses had fewer economic resources and the marriage had been preceded by cohabitation. The researchers concluded that *the lives of husbands and wives are becoming more separate* and couples are less likely to share activities such as eating meals, shopping, working on projects around the house, visiting friends, and going out for leisure activities (Amato et al., 2003:19).

The Next Time Around: Remarriage

Remarriages are as happy as first marriages, once duration is taken into consideration (Ganong and Coleman, 1994). Yet, remarriages end in divorce more than first marriages. How can this paradox be explained? First, Kurdek (1990) has found that marital satisfaction decreased more in remarriages than in first marriages. Booth and Edwards (1992) suggest that it takes less deterioration in marital quality to precipitate a divorce among remarried than married couples.

Second, in a remarriage, the spouses enter the union with more emotional baggage than in a first one. Their previous union may have raised or depressed their expectations and it may have made them more or less tolerant when expectations are not met (see Chapter 12). So far, the higher re-divorce rate suggests that couples are less tolerant the second time around. Remarried spouses may be less willing to cope with what are considered by others to be smaller disappointments;

these disappointments then bring ideas of divorce that might not occur so rapidly in a young couple who has never had to contemplate divorce. Obviously, there are processes involved in the second marital relationship that bring about a dissolution more readily than the first time around. Consequently, remarriages that are successful may require a deeper commitment and a conscious effort to avoid the downward spiralling trend. A re-evaluation of what is and is not important in life is required, as expressed by a remarried man during his interview:

> *"I came to the conclusion that if marriage is to be successful, both partners have to work at it or at least spend time enjoying it. I had to rework my priorities and . . . I had to learn to give in a bit. Point of fact, my wife is very similar to my first wife and the reason is obvious: My first wife was fine. It's just that we failed to live our married lives. Now my career's less important, my marriage more. . . . It's a shame that it took a divorce to come to this realization."*

Further, re-divorces occur even more rapidly than first divorces. This rapid breakup may reflect the inability of many remarried spouses to establish a satisfying relationship very early on because of the complications of the structural factors involved. The presence of stepchildren, ex-spouses, and ex-in-laws represents for some couples a force that diverts their attention from the task of building their relationship and hampers their ability to invest in the dyad. A man reflects a similar perspective when trying to evaluate the quality of his remarriage during an interview:

> *"I think it's very difficult to start a remarriage on the right footing even with the best of intentions. There's always someone ready to make you trip over, especially her children. I find it hard to commit to this relationship—and I love her deeply, don't take me wrong here—because her children are so hostile. I can't separate them from her; they come in a package deal. One minute we're happy and I feel that I belong and the next minute they come in, throw stuff around, just ignore me, and it's so awkward."*

Thus, when studying remarried couples' conjugal quality, it would be important to distinguish between those who have dependent stepchildren and those who were childless when they remarried. The latter have a much lower divorce risk.

The Conjugal Relationship in Later Life

In this section, we focus on couples who have been married to each other since young adulthood. In other words, we are addressing the topic of marital longevity. Although a proportion of older couples live a conflict-habituated or a devitalized relationship, on average, they experience relatively high levels of marital satisfaction, with a great deal of closeness and little conflict. At this point in time, it is difficult to determine if this elevated level of happiness in later years is the result of the **U-curve phenomenon** or if it is a matter of cohort. The U-curve refers to those studies that have found a dip in the quality of marriages during the childrearing years, followed by an upward trend after children's late adolescence. Such studies imply that the quality of a marriage varies during a couple's life course and is particularly affected by the negative aspects of parenting—these aspects may be less prominent in societies that offer more child care support to parents and when the parental role does not predominate over the conjugal one, as is the case in France. So if the U-curve applies, higher marital satisfaction in later years could reflect relief from the stress of active parenting without adequate social support as well as work-related problems.

In terms of a **cohort effect**, older couples who married 40 to 70 years ago began their relationship in a social climate that emphasized more mutuality or duty rather than personal gratification in marriage. These couples may have had lower expectations to begin with in terms of what marriage could do for them, focusing instead on what they could do for the relationship. They may, as a result, have been happier maritally. More recent longitudinal research also indicates that couples who believe in lifelong marriage and in sharing decision making are more likely to have low conflict and a happy long-term marriage (Dush and Taylor, 2012). Rather than being mutually exclusive, it is likely that both the U-curve and the cohort effect are implicated in the longitudinal dynamics of marital quality.

At retirement, 78 percent of Canadians are still living in a couple (Hébert and Uriarte-Landa, 2012). **Retirement** presents both opportunities and potential strains on the conjugal relationship (Szinovacz and Davey, 2005). On the one hand, it can result in an identity crisis, particularly among men (McDaniel, 2009). On the other hand, it reduces the pressure of commitments related to work, as well as time constraints. Couples can then engage in more activities together and make plans that cannot be derailed because of role conflicts. However, leisure activities can become one of the most contentious issues among older couples (Henry et al., 2005). Increased togetherness may be stressful for some, particularly when their entire lives had revolved around parenting and working, and their relationship had become hollow. They may have too much time on their hands and too little to say to each other, and thus some divorces occur at this stage. Many wives dread the day their husbands retire because "he won't know what to do with himself and I'll lose my freedom."

When both spouses live into old age, one of the two may become frail. Physical impairment, such as difficulties walking, does not diminish closeness between the spouses. But a spouse's **cognitive impairment** lowers the degree of closeness, as perceived by the caregiving spouse (Boylestein and Hayes, 2012). This spouse also perceives that his or her efforts are less effective. Cognitive disabilities—such as dementia and Alzheimer's disease—bring changes in personality and behaviours that break the pattern of the relationship. In addition, the caregiving spouse becomes more socially isolated because of the demands of his or her new role. A distressed caregiving spouse's health, including memory, may be affected (Mackenzie et al., 2009). It is then more difficult to cope with the conflicts engendered by the new dependency, such as when the afflicted spouse criticizes the efforts of the other, refuses the help offered, or even becomes aggressive. This is more likely to be the reaction of chronically ill husbands (Calasanti, 2004). In contrast, when the frail spouse is supportive of the partner's efforts, the caregiver feels more efficient, less stressed, and is more satisfied with the caretaker role. Similarly, when levels of marital happiness were higher, activity limitations are much less likely to result in negativity on the part of each spouse (Roper and Yorgason, 2009).

DIVISION OF LABOUR AND INEQUALITY

One very important aspect in the spousal relationship is the household and child care division of labour as well as its perceived equity, an element that was lacking in Cuber and Haroff's typology. When they did their research, gender roles and the domestic division of labour had not yet become salient social concerns. These themes were soon to become far more discussed under the convergence of two western trends occurring in the 1970s: the influence of feminism and the massive re-entry of wives into the employment market, thus placing into question the division of labour that had prevailed up to that point. The domestic division of labour is a perfect example of a microsociological phenomenon (here, domesticity) that is closely related to societal ones, in this instance, the social stratification by gender that pervades society's organization, including the work environment (Doucet, 2009).

A Classification of the Domestic Division of Labour

I have derived a classification of the division of labour between spouses from the sum of the research carried out on this topic. The domestic division of labour involves two elements: who does what and who is responsible for planning or management—in other words, chores and responsibilities or availability. *This classification is based on behaviours rather than attitudes because far more couples believe in an egalitarian system than practise it.* In other instances, daily necessities force couples to share child care equally, yet this egalitarian practice is not necessarily accompanied by egalitarian beliefs, particularly by husbands. Thus, the gap between attitudes and behaviours makes it preferable to focus on the latter.

The Egalitarian, Nongendered Division of Labour

In the egalitarian, nongendered division of labour, both spouses or partners are employed and participate equally in all aspects of the functioning of the household and in the care of the children. They may grocery shop and cook together, or they may alternate, the husband cooking one week and the wife the next. They may dress the children, get them ready for school, help them with breakfast, and so on together, or they may alternate—one week the father does morning duties while the mother does evening duties. If researchers went into such a household, the hours done by each parent on chores and responsibilities would add up to near identical totals.

Although many childless couples fit this description, fewer couples with children do. The arrival of the first child is generally the structural element that contributes to a shift in the spousal division of labour toward the other end of the continuum (Bianchi et al., 2006). However, this is slowly changing in many western countries (Dribe and Stanfors, 2009). That said, when it is generally the mother who takes a parental leave, this further entrenches the gendering of caring and working (Beaujot, 2000). But paternity leaves, which are becoming more frequent, probably contribute to consolidating the egalitarian division of labour, especially in Quebec (Ravanera et al., 2009).

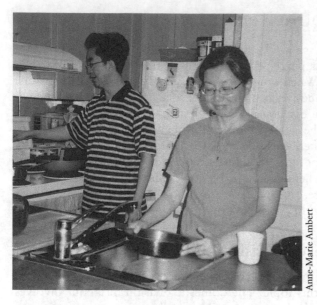

Anne-Marie Ambert

When both spouses are employed, couples with a companionable marriage are more likely to share equally in terms of housework. In turn, equal sharing of work and responsibilities reinforces mutual feelings of satisfaction and companionship.

The Equitable but Gendered Division of Labour

The equitable but gendered division of labour involves a similar number of hours of work (paid and unpaid) and child care but each spouse does different tasks largely based on what is considered appropriately male or female by this couple. For instance, the father may take care of the outside of the house, and he may cook and do the dishes, but the mother does the cleaning and the child care and buys the groceries. They may both visit with their children's teachers; however, the father participates in coaching while the mother is responsible for sick days.

Researchers observing such a family would again arrive at a comparable number of hours for each spouse, but they would note that fathers and mothers generally engage in different tasks and have different responsibilities. Despite increasing trends in this direction, still relatively few families fit this description. Although gendered, this division of labour is deemed fair by employed mothers, even those who earn high salaries, because what is important to them is that *fathers participate equitably*.

The Specialist Division of Labour: Equitable and Inequitable

The specialist division of labour may be gendered or not and may be equitable or not: It resides in the recognition that one of the two spouses is better at cooking, while the other is more enthusiastic about cleaning or doing the laundry. One spouse or the other is better at putting the children to bed, while the other is more competent at supervising or helping with homework. In other words, things get done by the partner who is defined by the other or who self-identifies as the most qualified for the job. Some tasks may be occasionally shared or rotated depending on who is present when the necessity arises. Researchers studying such families may come up with two vastly different sets of results. In one group of families, both spouses spend the same number of hours on their different tasks. This would be an equitable specialist situation, and is often encountered in lesbian- and gay-headed families (Goldberg et al., 2012; Green, 2010).

In the other group of families, one spouse has specialized in minor chores (e.g., washing the car and taking out the garbage) so that the other is left doing everything else on a daily basis. The other could be the wife or the husband, depending perhaps on which spouse earns the most or has the most power in the relationship (Goldberg et al., 2012). Here we see the beginning of inequity and of the potential for dissatisfaction by the spouse who carries most of the burden, generally the wife.

The Husband-Helper Division of Labour

The husband-helper takes *no* responsibility to ensure that dinner is ready, that a babysitter is available, that the children do their homework, and so on. The mother takes all the responsibilities and remains on a permanent state of availability for these duties. In some cases, it can be the reverse and it is the wife who is the helper, particularly if her job is demanding or if she has more power in the relationship. But the scenario that typifies so many Canadian families sees the wife attending to most of the chores and child care responsibilities with some husbandly help. The mother's total number of hours devoted to child care and house chores will constitute 60 to 90 percent, and the father's will constitute the balance, after the work the children may do is factored in (Hofferth and Sandberg, 2001). This is why mothers in general have less free time than fathers (Sayer, 2005).

This division of labour typifies situations where the wife is not employed, as well as cases of dual-earner couples. In families where the wife is employed, the husband's help is often perceived as fair because she feels that he appreciates her role by offering to pitch in. Husbands of unemployed wives may, however, find their own help very generous and less fair. Thus, fairness in this respect is defined in a gendered way. When there is a discrepancy in perceptions, husbands' beliefs and perceptions are more likely to affect wives' perceptions than the reverse (Wilkie et al., 1998:592)—a reflection of the greater masculine power in society at large. Husbands can generally choose the timing of their help, but wives are more bound to a schedule of tasks that have to be performed on a daily basis. Fathers often choose activities they like. This may be why Larson and Richards (1994) have found that mothers' moods are at their lowest when they engage in housework. In contrast, fathers often feel relaxed and cheerful.

The Complete and Delegated Divisions of Labour

With the *complete division of labour*, the mother does nearly everything and the father either watches television, tinkers with his car, or has a beer with his buddies after work. More often than not, the wife is unemployed or holds a part-time job. This division of labour is becoming less frequent but still occurs, particularly at the working-class level. It also characterizes many families that have emigrated from countries where gender roles are patriarchal and the relationships are reproductive-familial.

For its part, the *delegated (and paid) division of labour* is a phenomenon observed among affluent families that can afford a housekeeper, a nanny, or even a gardener—introducing a social class issue within the household context. Although neither spouse actually does the work, and child care consists of engaging in leisure activities with the children and visiting their teachers, the wife is usually responsible for finding, hiring, training, and keeping the help, what Macdonald (2010) has called the "performance of class via gender and through mothering" or housework (p. 204). The wife may or may not be gainfully employed. When she is not, she engages in extensive community and volunteer work, organizes her husband's social activities, travels, and spends time shopping. It should be added that there is little research that looks at couple and family dynamics when a low-wage female employee contributes her labour to the household or takes care of the children in her home (Macdonald, 2010).

The Effect on Marital Quality: Overview of Recent Changes

When all these types of division of labour are considered, the husband-helper and the specialized division of labour are probably still the most common ones now (see Ravanera et al., 2009). Whether the mother is married, divorced, part of a stepfamily, or single, she does most of the housework and child care (Coltrane, 2000)—and she does so even when both spouses are employed, although perhaps less so in Quebec where cohabitation predominates. Further, unless they belong to the egalitarian, equitable, or specialist categories, fathers devote little mental energy to worrying about household and children's daily needs or planning activities for them.

In the 1950s and even in the early 1960s, middle-class wives' employment contributed to reducing marital satisfaction, especially among husbands, because it was then an infrequent and unusual phenomenon (Burke and Weir, 1976). Changes in gender roles at the cultural level had not yet occurred. In those days, there was no social support available to wives engaged in paid work. For their part, husbands suffered a lowered sense of self-worth because wife employment often signalled that husbands earned too little and could not support their families. By the 1980s, a cultural shift had occurred spearheaded by feminism, particularly among women, so that employed wives, especially highly educated ones, were more satisfied with their marriages than housewives (Houseknecht and Macke, 1981). In contrast, husbands who held conventional beliefs about the division of labour and preferred to see wives at home reported lower levels of marital happiness when their wives were employed and earned high salaries (Perry-Jenkins and Crouter, 1990). Although economic necessity is currently still one of the main reasons why mothers work for pay, it is today a culturally recognized fact that two paycheques are necessary. Therefore, husbands do not generally feel diminished by their wives' employment, as used to be the case 40 to 50 years ago. Most take it for granted and are as proud of their wives' achievements as wives are of their husbands'.

At the same time, researchers began to focus on the perception of fairness in the division of labour as it relates to marital happiness. In the 1990s, wives who were employed full-time were less satisfied than their husbands and than other wives concerning the equity of the work-family balance (White, 1999). At the close of the 20th century, researchers were observing a correlation* between marital satisfaction and the perception that the division of labour at home *and* at work is fair. In women's overall evaluation of the quality of their marriage, the division of labour at home is much more important, whereas the division of labour at work is considered more frequently by husbands (Wilkie et al., 1998). Perceptions of inequity reduce marital happiness and may lead to divorce, particularly when commitment is low (Frisco and Williams, 2004). In a recent British study, mothers who felt that their husbands participated in the care of their small children were happier in their marriage, while the fathers were also positively affected but only after the child reached age three (Schober, 2012). An American study of two surveys from 1980 and 2000 has shown that, as husbands' share of housework increased, husbands reported less marital happiness and wives more (Amato et al., 2003). Yet, there is also evidence that it is not egalitarian beliefs and practices per se that make a huge difference in marital happiness, but emotional love and commitment to marriage and each other (Wilcox and Nock, 2006).

Still, the division of domestic and paid work has positive and negative effects on marital satisfaction for both spouses: The effects are still stronger for wives than husbands because equity, as perceived by women, is not reached (Dew and Wilcox, 2011). Finally, more longitudinal studies are needed because the division of labour changes over time within couples (Lam et al., 2012b). Dush et al. (2008) have found that western couples who remain highly satisfied with their marriage over time are also the ones who are the most likely to change by becoming increasingly equitable.

Division of Labour in Remarriages with Stepchildren

With stepchildren present, the division of labour may constitute a more salient aspect of the spousal relationship. Stepchildren who visit often cause an enormous amount of work to stepmothers in terms of cooking and cleaning. In some reconstituted families, fathers tend to contribute more. But in many others, the father simply entertains his visiting children, or he leaves with them after lunch for an outing while his wife inherits a load of dirty dishes. The following is a quote from a woman reminiscing about the problems created by visiting stepchildren in her previous (second) marriage:

> *"His kids kept coming here because he didn't want to visit them at their place, of course, because he hated his ex-wife. We had six kids here at times and his are the rough type; after they'd gone, the whole house was a mess for us to clean and the fridge was empty and I had to pay."*

This theme of inequity recurred throughout my interviews with stepmothers and was often exacerbated by complaints from the children's mother to the father, which he then passed along. Some mothers complained that the children had not slept enough, had not been well fed, or had watched too much television while at their father's place. The stepmother felt targeted because, after all, she was the one responsible for the smooth functioning of the household.

> *"I feel like a glorified babysitter. I mean, she brings her boys here so that she can have a nice weekend of rest and go out. It's nice for her but I get nothing out of this except work, work, and more work, and the boys order me around like a slave."* [Their father?] *"Oh, he's so afraid of having further problems with her or that the boys won't want to visit that he says nothing. He pretends it's not there."* [This stepmother did not intend to *"stick around much longer."*]

In short, the matter of the division of labour seemed to bring in a great deal of conflict among these couples who had been together for only a few months or years at most. The wife's feelings of inequity may have been greater than in a first marriage with her own children: In a remarriage, the wife is labouring for another woman's children—those of the ex-wife. It would be important to study what develops in this respect when the reconstituted family adds a new shared child.

THE SILENT DIVISION OF LABOUR: EMOTIONAL WORK

Another aspect to the division of labour resides in that, generally, women do more caring as well as emotional or "love" work than men (McDaniel, 2009). Most exceptions to this rule would be found among the vital and total couples. We have seen in Chapter 7 that girls and women who date invest more emotionally in the relationship. They work harder at maintaining it, they initiate more conversations about the relationship, they express their love more often, they divulge more of themselves to their partner in order to show him their commitment, and they plan more of their activities together than he does, often including their wedding ceremonies (Humble, 2003). This pattern continues during cohabitation or marriage. We see in subsequent chapters that females nurture their relationship with their parents, siblings, children, and grandchildren more than males. Thus, all in all, whatever the familial roles they assume, from the time they are very young, females are socialized to become the **kin-keepers**, the expressive partners, and the **emotional workers** (Erickson, 2005). Were they to be differently socialized, society would lose out because, at this point in time, there are no indications that males are ready to step in and compensate.

According to Hochschild, in *The Managed Heart* (1983), "emotion work" is capital or an asset that women exchange for security in a relationship. In *subordinate* positions, the role occupants tend to rely on is emotional capital. There are couples where the husband is subordinate because he wanted the marriage more than she or because she has more alternatives than he. This analysis fits the **exchange theories** outlined in Chapter 1. In general, women have fewer alternatives, either because their maternal investment restricts their ability to work or to find other partners, or because there are many other women competitors "on the market." In other cases, women are disadvantaged because of the double standard of aging: Note in Chapter 12 the tendency for men to remarry women younger than their previous wives.

Wives are not necessarily more invested in the stability of their marriage than husbands, but they are more invested in its *quality maintenance*. This differential investment is a source of insecurity for women, thus of subordination. It is also a source of marital discontent. Men are not as observant as their wives are concerning the quality of their relationship. They tend to take it for granted, because they are not the emotional worker. However, women get more intrinsic rewards from these relationships—again a matter of gender-role socialization. For instance, Larson and Richards (1994) observed that wives' moods are more positive when they are with their husbands. Husbands' moods are also more positive when with their wives, but less so. As well, a husband's mood affects a wife's mood far more than the reverse. Indeed, other studies show that women are more affected than husbands by marital processes and their spouse's behaviours and mental health (e.g., Du Rocher Schudlich et al., 2004; Kiecolt-Glaser and Newton, 2001; Stimpson et al., 2006). When spouses arrive home unhappy from stressors at work, it is the husband who is more likely to transmit this state of mind to his wife (who is more attuned to his feelings and more dependent on them), than is the case when the wife returns home unhappy. If a husband has any argument at work, this increases substantially the probability that he will have an argument with his wife later on, although both spouses' work stress spills over into their home life (Story and Repetti, 2006). In her autobiography, a mature student explains how deeply affected she is by this situation:

> *"The only reason that I take one course each year is that it gives me something to escape to when my husband comes home in a bad mood because of pressure at work. . . . He wants all of us to feel it or to suffer with him; he takes it out on us. But the few times that I have done this, he laughed it off and walked out. It's so unfair* [when husband ignores wife's bad mood]. *I just hop in my car and come to the library to work on my paper. If I stayed home and went downstairs to type he would follow me and manage to pick a fight."*

SAME-SEX-COUPLE RELATIONSHIPS

Research on the quality of the dyadic relationship among married and cohabiting same-sex partners is scant, and much of what exists is flawed methodologically. To begin with, it is difficult to draw large random samples of same-sex couples (Goldberg, 2010). Therefore, most of the studies on same-sex couples have been small and many have relied on self-selection (i.e., researchers have placed ads in gay/lesbian newsletters and clubs to solicit couples' cooperation). Obviously, such an approach draws samples that are not representative and disproportionately include relatively educated couples who maintain links to the homosexual community, may be activists, are white, and are fairly young (Chapter 8). Moreover, gays and lesbians have suffered from stigmatization and may not wish to share the intimate details of their lives with researchers for fear of being further victimized or categorized. As a result, only couples who are happy together may respond to such ads.

In a large American sample, Kurdek (2008) compared cohabiting gay/lesbian and heterosexual couples with married heterosexual couples, some childless, some with children, and found that all of these relationships worked in similar ways (Kurdek, 2008). Gay couples reported more autonomy from each other in terms of activities, friendships, and decision making than heterosexual married dyads. Lesbian couples reported more intimacy, autonomy, and equality than heterosexual dyads. (However, the researcher did not present comparisons between gay and lesbian couples.) Both gay and lesbian couples had higher rates of dissolution than heterosexual ones. In countries such as Canada where same-sex marriage is legalized, it would be important to compare those couples who married to a group of similar same-sex couples who are cohabiting to see if the married ones will stay together longer—as is the case among heterosexual couples.

In the domain of conflict, Kurdek (1994) compared gay, lesbian, and heterosexual couples and found little difference in the rank order of frequency of conflict in six global areas: power, social issues, personal flaws, distrust, intimacy, and personal distance. Issues pertaining to intimacy and power were the most frequent sources of conflict among all three types of couples. This is interesting in itself because it indicates that *problems related to power are not entirely explainable in terms of gender roles or the patriarchal order, for they exist in same-sex couples as well.* For all three types of couples, conflict over intimacy and power was more related to either partner's lower satisfaction with the relationship than other sources of conflict. During the one-year duration of this study, conflict over power was the most predictive of later relationship deterioration. These findings are in agreement with those of other researchers for married heterosexual couples. Overall, as herein indicated and as seen in other chapters, there are more similarities than differences in the way homosexual and heterosexual couples live their relationships: The structure and requirements of daily life place similar demands on them.

THE EFFECT OF CHILDREN ON THE COUPLE RELATIONSHIP

Children transform a couple into a family with a lesser focus on the couple and more on the parenting role (Dew and Wilcox, 2011). In fact, parenting couples, whether heterosexual or homosexual, spend very little time together without their children (Campos et al., 2009; Goldberg, 2010). Unplanned births decrease marital satisfaction the most (Lawrence et al., 2008); as well, a child's poor health reduces the probability of parents staying together (Reichman et al., 2004). The division of labour becomes less egalitarian after the birth of a first child (Bianchi et al., 2006). As a result, mothers are more affected by children than are fathers. Among lesbian couples, the biological mother is often the one who does more physical care, although many share equally. Gay new parents are also more likely to be sharing care equally (Goldberg, 2010). In addition, the simple fact that some infants cry at night has an impact on how parents relate to each other (Meijer and van den Wittenboer, 2007). Children who show a great deal of negativity affect the parental relationship (Schermerhorn et al., 2007). It is also possible that, in remarriage, stepchildren's behavioural problems influence couples more negatively than is the case for shared children (Jenkins et al., 2005b).

All of the above notwithstanding, this research has largely been done in western societies where the culture of romantic marriage predominates (Ghandour and Perry-Jenkins, 2008). If we think of cultures where marriages of the reproductive-familial type discussed earlier predominate, a child's arrival may have an extremely positive effect on the level of happiness and personal security of married women. Indeed, among Muslims, Hindus, and Sikhs, marriage still is a familial relationship, an exchange between two families, with the purpose of producing at least one child, preferably a son. The romantic aspect of the relationship is usually not considered but the marital relationship may actually be more positive after the birth of a child. The new mother may derive happiness from her husband's approval as well as from her new status in her family and, especially, his family when the system is patriarchal. Given our diverse Canadian population, we should be able to do research that considers culture, religion, and immigrant generation as key variables. In fact, Wilcox and Dew (2011) did find that religiousness played a part in protecting new mothers from a decline in marital satisfaction among Christians. It would be interesting to study this link in other religions.

Few researchers have examined the effect of parenting satisfaction on marital happiness when the children are older. Sociologists Rogers and White (1998) found reciprocal effects between marital happiness and parenting satisfaction, both for mothers and fathers. (Parenting satisfaction was defined as parents' satisfaction with their relationship with their children.) They conclude that "success in one family role primes an individual for success in other family roles . . . parents may include their own success as parents as one component of their marital evaluation" (p. 305). Not unexpectedly, when couples have conflict over raising their adolescents, this translates into a decrease in marital satisfaction over time (Cui and Donnellan, 2009). Generally, there is a decrease in love and marital happiness, especially among wives, when children pass through adolescence (Whiteman et al., 2007). However, many studies have shown this to begin in the early years of parenthood and rebounds to occur after children go to school (Keizer and Schenk, 2012). Particularly difficult for the parental relationship are problems encountered when a grown child suffers from a psychological disability (Hartley et al., 2012).

Thus, within a transactional perspective, children affect their parents' relationship (Ambert, 2001). Indeed, most studies show a decrease in marital happiness after the birth of a first child and during the childrearing years—particularly for wives (Dew and Wilcox, 2011). However, one can ask if this change comes from the parental transition alone or simply the effect of time on marriage because we know that many couples' happiness diminishes after the first few years of marriage (Mitnick et al., 2009), particularly among women (Keizer and Schenk, 2012). It seems that both variables interact because parenting has also been found to carry more costs for marital quality among *younger* couples (Umberson et al., 2005). In fact, Kurdek (2008) may have provided the answer when he found that couples' relationship quality declines rapidly and then levels off. However, couples who had become parents saw yet another period of decline. This said, it seems that the transition to parenthood intensifies preexisting relationship problems. It would be important to know how a couple's level of commitment to each other helps negotiate this transition (Kluwer, 2010). As well, although leisure time together and happiness may decline among some new parents, those couples who started from higher levels are still happier than those who were at lower levels of shared leisure and marital happiness before the birth (Perry-Jenkins and Claxton, 2011).

THE EFFECT OF THE PARENTAL RELATIONSHIP ON CHILDREN

Researchers are particularly interested in finding a theoretical explanation for the observed link between the quality of parents' relationship and children's well-being. So far, the research has focused on **parental conflict**. This emphasis is understandable in view of the fact that inter-parental conflict diminishes the quality of parenting (Fosco and Grych, 2010). Overall, children who live with openly conflictual parents are often less well adjusted than other children, including those in well-functioning single-parent families. Very young children are affected differently by parental conflict, through their perception (Ablow et al., 2009): For instance, they may perceive that the conflict is their "fault" and that they are to blame, which may translate into internalizing problems (Jenkins et al., 2005b). Marital hostility is related to adolescents' internalizing and behavioural problems via various psychological mechanisms

Anne-Marie Ambert

The quality of the spousal relationship is one of several key ingredients in a child's development. Parents in a secure and happy relationship transmit similar feelings to their children. Such parents are also more likely to agree in terms of socialization goals, thus again benefiting their children. Therefore, a child's home environment depends in great part on his or her parents' relationship.

such as self-blame and emotional dysregulation (Buehler et al., 2007). Marital discord has also been shown to affect mothers' parenting and adolescents' academic outcomes in urbanized Taiwan (Lee et al., 2011). Overall, children are more disturbed when the content of the conflict pertains to them. For instance, parents who openly fight about their children upset them more than if they are quarrelling about money. But attentive and warm parenting can mitigate the potentially negative effect of marital conflict (Kaczynski et al., 2006).

Parental disagreement by itself does not affect children negatively (Cummings and Davies, 2010). In fact, children can learn functional ways of solving human problems by listening to their parents iron out their difficulties in a cooperative manner. However, constant disagreement that is left unresolved or that simmers as well as continued parental conflict of the hostile type lead to negative effects on children and can result in a lower quality of parent-child relationship in adulthood (Schudlich et al., 2011; Yu et al., 2010). Children exposed to repeated hostility between parents fail to learn adaptive modes of conflict resolution.

But, as Fincham (1998:551) correctly remarks, there is more to a marriage than absence of conflict. For instance, in a unique study comparing married and cohabiting couples, Carlson et al. (2011) have found that a supportive marital relationship is related to good parenting among parents of small children. When they reached age three, the good quality of the couple relationship was even more important for fathers than mothers who were cohabiting rather than married. When parents enjoy a good marriage or cohabitation, the mother's relationship with her small child is warmer and she is more nurturing. Fathering is even more affected than mothering by the quality of the union. All in all, when parents get along well and support each other, children exhibit far fewer behavioural difficulties than they do when parents are in a conflictual marital situation. The advantage extends to adolescence and adulthood (Hetherington, 2003). Further, a happy parental relationship is related to greater parent-child affection and consensus. Longitudinally, adolescents' negative behaviours tend to increase or decrease after a change in their parents' marital problems (Cui et al., 2005).

Several complementary explanations exist for the correlation between the quality of parents' relationship and their children's outcomes. These are illustrated in Figure 9.1 and discussed in the following sections. But before we examine them, it is important to mention that such a correlation may not be so evident in cultures where

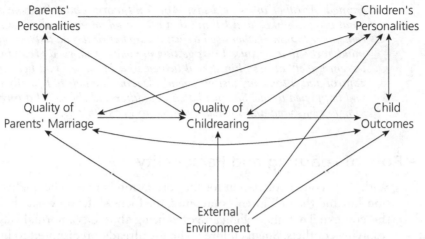

FIGURE 9.1

Variables Explaining the Correlation between the Quality of Parents' Relationship and Child Outcomes

reproductive-familial marriage is the norm—that is, where fathers and mothers, men and women, live largely separate lives; where the marital interaction might revolve around patriarchal authority and kin relationship; and where the relationship is an institutional one rather than one that is largely personal. It is not known what effect, if any, the quality of the marital interaction has on child development or on parenting in these societies, or in Canada, in these types of marriage.

Conjugal Quality Fosters Supportive Parenting

The most frequently mentioned explanation is that the supported and loved mother and father live in a warm environment that translates into a close and attentive relationship with their child (arrow from left to centre and then to right in Figure 9.1). In contrast, when conflict exists, parents are stressed, feel unappreciated, and may be less able to transfer loving feelings to their child. Childrearing is disrupted and parents agree less with each other in terms of child care. It becomes more difficult to use authoritative* socialization practices (Schoppe-Sullivan et al., 2007). In contrast, a good marital adjustment is related to more effective coparenting (Bonds and Gondoli, 2007). Fathers need mothers' support even more than mothers do, even in other cultures (Taylor et al., 2012). Parents' hostility toward each other often results in harsh parenting and rejecting behaviour toward children. As well, parents may become so absorbed in their marital problems that they are less available to their children (Sturge-Apple et al., 2006). In some cases, parents use their children to get at each other, as had occurred to a student who, in his self-description, grew up to be "out of control":

> *"I was more attached to my father because I always turned to him when my mother said no and he usually said yes so that I always ended up doing what I*

wanted. At other times he'd say, 'Ah, don't worry about her, she doesn't know what boys are like,' and I think that after a while my mother gave up on me. I remember that my father used to just ignore her or would tell her off and I didn't mind at the time because I was getting my way. It worked great during my adolescence, well, at first, but then it turned sour because I had become way out of control and it took my last girlfriend's leaving me before I finally realized what had happened to me. She just hated my father and she said I'd turn out just like him as a husband and she wasn't going to live with this."

The Role of Learning and Personality

With the second explanation for the correlation between the quality of parents' relationship and their children's outcomes, the focus shifts on what children can learn in this context: That quarrelling and even being abused is a normal way of living and of resolving conflicts. Small children who are already predisposed to hyperactivity, nervousness, or aggression may be especially vulnerable to parental conflict; they may be particularly susceptible to acquiring maladaptive behaviours by observing and modelling their parents' conflictual interaction.

This leads us to the third explanation that resides in assumptions about personality and temperament, as shown at the top of Figure 9.1 (Ganiban et al., 2009): A conflictual marriage may arise because the two parents have problematic personalities, are difficult to get along with, do not like to compromise, or are aggressive. Even if only one of the two parents is so, the marriage is likely to be unstable. As well, when parents are too anxious, they may miss out on some cues from each other or their children (Bar-Haim et al., 2007). Further, if a mother is impatient, irritable, and has little tolerance for frustration, she may exhibit these patterns in her parenting practices, and the same holds true for the father. This would explain why, in conflictual marriages, the parent-child relationship is less warm and more erratic and why the babies and children in these families experience more adjustment difficulties, anxiety, and behavioural problems. In contrast, in a peaceful and supportive marriage, there is a strong chance that the parents' personalities are conducive to good relationships, and the child's environment is accordingly regulated (Papp et al., 2004). On the other side of the equation, parental conflict, which can be negative even for infants, affects them differently depending on the infants' own emotionality (Pauli-Pott and Beckman, 2007). Thus, the child's temperament has to be considered as well as adolescents' own emotional and cognitive styles (Buehler et al., 2007).

Genes and Within-Family Environment

The fourth and complementary explanation flows from the preceding one. It resides in joint genetic and environmental considerations. Parents who are aggressive, have little tolerance for frustration, are impatient, or are not easy to get along with will not only interact less positively with their children but they will also be less supportive (Trentacosta and Shaw, 2008), and they may well pass at least some of these characteristics via genetic inheritance to their children (Zuckerman, 2005). The result is that some of these babies may themselves be more fussy and irritable. Later, they may become more oppositional, hyperactive, and aggressive than children born to parents who are warm, patient, and cooperative, and who consequently have a stable relationship. In other words, kinship by biology brings some similarities (and differences) caused by genetic factors (Harden et al., 2007).

As well, each person in a family constitutes part of the others' within-family environment. Thus, the behavioural manifestations of parental characteristics become part of the children's environment, both as childrearing styles and as marital styles (Rutter, 2002). At the negative level, children's own behavioural manifestations of their partly inherited traits, such as hyperactivity and aggressiveness, elicit a negative reaction from parents. This reaction then also becomes part of the children's environment. These partly genetically driven environments interact with one another and result in inadequate parent-child relationships as well as negative child outcomes or adjustment.

The Larger Environment Affects Marriage and Childrearing

Finally, as shown in the lower part of Figure 9.1, marriages and childrearing can be strained by the environment imposed upon a family—poverty and neighbourhoods come to mind here as they have been discussed in previous chapters. Parents having to work in another country, as is the case for many Filipino families, is another instance (Harper and Martin, 2013). Children's personalities and outcomes may be indirectly affected by these environmental strains. Further, as they age, children whose parents have a conflictual marriage may be more at the mercy of deleterious neighbourhood, school, and peer influences. A student unwittingly puts her finger on this chain of circumstances when she points out the following:

> "I stayed home as little as I could between the ages of 10 and 18 because my parents weren't easy to get along with and were fighting all the time, more my father than my mother, and a lot of the time they'd get mad at me or yell at me or it would upset me to see my mother cry. My parents were too busy fighting and maybe it was a relief for them when I was out so that I was on the streets most of the time by [age] 10. Of course, I got into all kinds of trouble but they became aware of little of it and I ran around with much older children. . . . I think that all of this affected my personality because I am somewhat difficult to be with and I don't put up with much. I don't know if I got that from my parents [genes] or because I ran around [with] peers who were like that or because the teachers gave me a hard time (after I gave them a hard time), I don't know. But the fact is that I'd like to have a nice relationship with a male but it's an uphill battle because I tend to fly off the handle."

CONCLUSIONS: DEFINITIONS OF RELATIONSHIP QUALITY ARE CULTURE SPECIFIC

A spousal relationship consists of several dimensions, from the affective level to its power-sharing aspect. Some of these dimensions tend to be given a greater emphasis in different cultures, at different historical periods, and, within each couple, at different times in their life course. For instance, the romantic or love aspect considered so important in North America is not even taken into consideration in many countries of the world. In other countries, love often develops among a proportion of married couples, but it is not an aspect of marriage deemed necessary. The sexual satisfaction dimension was not given much emphasis in this country 100 years ago, particularly for women. Sex was certainly not something openly discussed concerning marriage. In western countries, romantic love may be considered far more important at the beginning of a couple's relationship, for instance, and so may sexual satisfaction. As time goes by and as the relationship develops, these domains may become less salient than value consensus, shared activities, the division of labour, and parenting.

Culture is a key factor in teaching men and women what to expect of marriage and in determining what constitutes a satisfying conjugal relationship. As culture changes, so do cultural definitions of marital happiness to some extent. Currently, the media are a key source of cultural definitions, including books written by experts and articles in popular magazines, as well as what is depicted in films, on television (particularly talk shows), and the Internet.

The media largely focus on heterosexual dating, cohabiting, and marriage. Thus, the general public inherits the cultural representations that depict ideal partner relationships mainly as opposite-sex couples. Yet, we have learned that there is a great deal of overlap between what makes a homosexual and a heterosexual couple satisfied with their respective relationships. In other words, there is much similarity between gay, lesbian, and heterosexual couples. It would be interesting to gain a better understanding of how and from where homosexuals develop expectations concerning relationship satisfaction in view of the fact that they grow up in a predominantly heterosexual culture.

Summary

1. The Cuber and Haroff typology of couples married for at least 10 years is used and expanded to represent the Canadian multicultural situation.

2. The spousal division of labour includes not only who does what in the household and in child care but also who is responsible for what. A classification is suggested.

3. The effect of this unequal division of labour on marital quality seems to have changed during the last decades of the 20th century along with the evolution of the cultural and economic climate concerning the employment of women. The spousal division of labour becomes a particularly thorny issue for stepmothers of live-in or frequently visiting stepchildren. An important aspect of the spousal division of labour resides in emotional work.

4. The concepts of marital happiness, satisfaction, and success are defined and differentiated. The quality of marriages may have been declining since the 1970s as a result of changes in the social context of marriage.

5. Same- and opposite-sex couples engage in similar types of conflict and conflict-resolution mechanisms. Sources of conflict are discussed. Wives are generally less satisfied than husbands and perceive more problems.

6. Older couples experience relatively high levels of marital satisfaction. Qualities that sustain long-term unions are detailed. The relationship is altered when one spouse becomes challenged, particularly at the cognitive level.

7. The study of the relationship among same-sex couples is still in its infancy and requires methodological refinements.

8. Children have an impact on the parental relationship and the parental relationship affects children's development.

9. Culture is a key factor in teaching men and women what to expect in marriage and in determining their level of happiness.

Analytical Questions

1. Why did Cuber and Haroff study couples who had been married for a long time rather than newly married ones to arrive at a typology of marriages?

2. Considering the classification of the domestic division of labour, what can be concluded on the basis of exchange theory? (A return to Chapter 1 may help in answering this question.)

3. Which explanation do you prefer for the correlation between the quality of parents' marriage and their children's outcomes? Justify your choice.

4. How does culture play a role in the definition of what constitutes marital happiness? You may want to reexamine Chapter 2.

CHAPTER 10

The Parent-Child Relationship and Child Socialization

Anne-Marie Ambert

OUTLINE

Parents' Socialization Practices: Reflections of the Economic Environment
Authoritative and Authoritarian Parenting
"No-Nonsense" Parenting
Permissive and Uninvolved Parenting
Wavering-Negotiating Parenting
The Question of What Constitutes "Proper" Parenting
Determinants of Parents' Socialization Practices
Contextual and Cultural Determinants
Parents' Personalities and Adaptation to Children

The Parent-Adolescent Relationship
The Social Construction of Adolescence
How Do Parents and Adolescents Get Along?
Cultural Determinants of Parental Influence
The Role of Peers in the Parent-Adolescent Relationship

The Relationship between Parents and Adult Children
When the Child Is a Young Adult
When the Child Is a Mature Adult
Parents Help Their Adult Children
Adult Children Help Their Elderly Parents

An Extension of Parenting: Grandparents
Grandparents Who Raise Grandchildren

The Death of Adults' Parents

Conclusions: Life Course, Economy, and Personality in the Parent-Child Relationship

Summary
Analytical Questions

If you stay a while in the nursery of a hospital maternity ward, you will see that each newborn is different from the very beginning of life. For instance, you may see Lucia, who cries constantly, even when picked up, and who is agitated and resists feeding. In the next crib, Jack is a total contrast: He sleeps contentedly, nurses avidly, and cries but stops as soon as he is fed or changed. A third baby, Latitia, is small, quiet, does not cry, sleeps most of the time, and drinks little milk.

Each baby needs different types of care. Baby Lucia requires more attention because she calls for more of it with her cries (what is called a child-driven stimulus). In contrast, Baby Jack demands little attention and is easy: All he needs is to be fed, changed, and cuddled. Jack's parents have more free time and feel competent because it seems to them that everything they do for him is rewarded with success. From the beginning of his life, Jack and his parents establish a smooth relationship that is likely to continue in the future.

Lucia's temperament presents at the outset the potential for problems. Her parents may feel less competent and more tense, especially if she is their first child. If they are poor and experience marital conflict, Lucia may constitute an additional challenge. Her parents' reactions may not always be positive because they are already frazzled by other preoccupations. As a result, she might grow up with less positive interactions and may not find interpersonal relations as rewarding as Jack will.

For her part, Baby Latitia arouses her caregivers' concern because of her low birth weight and minimal appetite. At the same time, her parents are likely to feel comfortable because she is an easy baby. If fed regularly, she will eventually thrive and will not make too many demands on them. But when a mother does not know much about infant care, a neonate such as tiny Latitia may deteriorate and waste away because she may not cry enough to indicate that she is hungry.

Our three fictive newborns illustrate some of the mechanisms at the origin of the parent-child relationship, which is herein studied in its historical context and within a combined interactional-transactional, behaviour genetics, and life course perspective (Hareven, 2000). What emerges from these vignettes are **interactions** or transactions (Clark et al., 2000). On a basic level, each baby has different needs to which parents (generally mothers) respond; this means that infants unwittingly initiate many of the parental gestures that form the cornerstone of the relationship. For instance, a baby who cries constantly may elicit fewer positive reactions from his or her parents. In turn, this reaction depends on parents' gender, personalities, perceptions, and life circumstances (Crockenberg and Leerkes, 2003). Then, these reactions (being fed, changed, cuddled, or discouragingly ignored) become part of the babies' environment and contribute to the shaping of subsequent behaviours and, later on, their attitudes and beliefs as well as relationships with siblings (Jenkins et al., 2005a).

A small child who is blessed with positive characteristics, such as having a good attention span and low impulsivity, finds it easier to comply with parents' requests as he or she internalizes cultural rules and norms more easily. In turn, this child requires less supervision and less repetition, and receives fewer negative reactions from his or her parents. Such children may form stronger attachment to their parents, both as a result of their personalities and of the way parents react to them. This **attachment** then further reinforces their willingness and ability to be socialized. Thus, within the interactional and transactional as well as behaviour genetics perspectives, parents and children interact with and influence one another's behaviours and attitudes (Leve et al., 2010a; Natsuaki et al., 2009). Utilizing the Canadian National Longitudinal Survey of Children and Youth, Elgar et al. (2003) found that maternal depression and children's behavioural problems interacted, one worsening the other over time in a bidirectional pattern. Small children with a negative temperament made it more difficult for parents to coparent* together (Yaman et al., 2010).

Thus, from the very beginning, children contribute to the way their parents see them and treat them—albeit unwittingly so. Children, and even more so adolescents, contribute to the formation of their environment and of their own development (Lam et al., 2012a). In other words, **children are coproducers** of their own development (Huh et al., 2006). They are co-agents in their socialization process: As we see in Chapter 11, children's and parents' genetic background may be nearly as important as parenting (Horwitz and Neiderhiser, 2011; Rutter, 2002). Second, these interactions between parents and children become part of the children's environment (Ambert, 2001). Third, these interactions are in turn affected and shaped by sociostructural variables (Bronfenbrenner, 1979; Lewis, 1997). These include the number of children and adults in the family, the family's economic situation, and how society defines children, good parenting, as well as motherhood and fatherhood—social constructionism.

The level of **adaptation** required of parents in general, particularly by very young couples after the birth or adoption of a baby, is underestimated (McDaniel and Teti, 2012). The simple shift from that of being a couple or one individual to becoming a family with a tiny infant is not without inherent problems—particularly for very young parents. In addition, I would hypothesize that the transition to parenthood is probably more difficult for current cohorts of new parents than was the case 40 years ago. Now, because of low fertility rates, many adults have never been close to a baby intimately before they have their own while, in the past, larger families and earlier births offered many role models. As well, one can wonder what the impact on new parents is of living in a city that is largely childless, as is the case in some cities of Japan, China, and Singapore, and where mothers are consequently enjoying their parenting role less (Christiansen, 2013). Further, as we saw in Chapter 1, the intensification of parenting at the middle-class level presents to new parents all manners of requirements in terms of what they have to do and not do (Hays, 1996). The list is long and not always obvious (Wall, 2009).

PARENTS' SOCIALIZATION PRACTICES: REFLECTIONS OF THE ECONOMIC ENVIRONMENT

Socialization is a lifelong process, even though we focus on its childhood and adolescent stages in this text. In addition, it is a process that takes place within many contexts, as we have seen in earlier chapters, particularly educational institutions including day care centres, as well as religious and leisure activities, especially those involving the new media of communication. Socialization practices are methods by which parents ensure child understanding of and eventual internalization of society's rules (Lansford et al., 2009). *Socialization practices are culture-specific as well as specific to the historical stage in which we live.* In the western world, professionals dictate standards by which parents, and especially mothers, should interact with their children. This is part of current trends to standardize and rationalize lives in a postmodern economy, with emphasis on individualism and the development of qualities such as independence, self-sufficiency, and academic achievement (Ambert, 1994b; Wall, 2004). These parenting goals are spreading in Asia as well (Sriram and Sandhu, 2013; Xu and Yeung, 2013). Until now, parents in most developing countries have emphasized socioemotional rather than cognitive activities with their children (Bornstein and Putnick, 2012). Thus, parenting practices and parent-child interactions are **social constructs** (Arnett, 2008) that are class related (Fox, 2006) and often contribute to mothers' oppression (Badinter, 2010). North American societies stress "democratic rather than authoritarian relations, including autonomy, psychological well-being, and emotional expressiveness" as the ideal (Pyke, 2000:241). These values and constructs are shared by family theorists and clinicians alike and often make it difficult for many immigrant children to value their own family's style of interaction, which they see as deficient compared to the model presented to them by television, books, and the Internet (Pyke, 2000).

Much of the vast literature on parents' socialization practices purports to link proper ways of parenting causally to positive child outcomes. This literature generally ignores the role of genes, the dynamics of the interactional perspective, the social construction of motherhood, fatherhood, and childhood, as well as whether both parents have similar or different socialization practices. The coparenting aspect is neglected here although it is becoming more frequently studied in terms of father involvement, cooperation, and support of each other as parents (e.g., Ranson, 2010; Riina and McHale, 2012; Szabó et al., 2012). Further, there is little research on "character" and moral or ethical outcomes of children (Anderssen, 2011; Brooks, 2001; Tough, 2012). In other words, the research does not address the **moral context** of our society. Indeed, morality is a domain that is strangely absent from sociological inquiry. Political economy theories would suggest that also absent is any discussion of the fact that socialization practices support the values of the technological capitalist system (Nadesan, 2002) and its attendant class system (Marx, 1867). Parents' choices are heavily dictated by corporations' actions (Bakan, 2011).

Overall, *researchers' and clinicians' focus on childrearing practices has been on the form they take—not the contents*. The question has been how the practices (form) are related to children's outcomes. But, within each set of practices, parents can be teaching their children different lessons and passing on different values. One has many opportunities to observe children and parents in various public spheres such as stores, streets, near schools, playgrounds, planes, restaurants, hotels, as well as beaches. In North America, particularly in affluent neighbourhoods, most children receive very little guidance from their parents in public. One rarely hears "no, you can't do this because people around you need some quiet." Or, "no, don't touch this with your dirty hands because the waitress is going to have to clean it again, it's not fair to her, she has a lot of work to do." Too many parents seem to be afraid to give their children the message that they have to think of *others*. There is very little **altruism** or even basic **consideration for others**, particularly among indulgent parents of the wavering-negotiating style discussed later. Thus, childrearing practices, in terms of contents, now reflect the requirements of our capitalist society or market economy (Marx, 1867). In order for our children to become consumers, they have to be somewhat materialistic, individualistic, demanding, and with a low tolerance for frustration. They have to become the centre of their world. Hence, North American and western parenting styles and contents, which are spreading abroad, contrast with those of societies which are agrarian, and particularly hunters-gatherers, especially in Africa (Bledsoe and Souv, 2011; LeVine, 1990).

In the presentation that follows, we begin with Baumrind's (1967) initial typology of parents' socialization practices: authoritative, authoritarian, and permissive styles of parenting. This typology is expanded to meet criteria of cultural diversity.

Authoritative and Authoritarian Parenting

Parents who are authoritative* combine warmth, respect for their children's individuality, and psychological autonomy with monitoring of their activities and whereabouts (Gray and Steinberg, 1999). They are firm, yet loving, involved, and make demands for age-appropriate behaviours (Baumrind, 1990). Such parents explain to their children the reasons behind their demands and the consequences of not complying. They insist on obedience and then follow through with enforcement of rules and appropriate punishment. Reasonable punishment, when necessary, increases the effectiveness of reasoning for small children. It may increase their ability to internalize rules of behaviour so that, when older, they will no longer need to be punished (Larzelere et al., 1998).

Warmth and monitoring have been correlated with successful child and adolescent outcomes in all types of family structures in Canada, the U.S., and other western countries. More specifically, **monitoring** is related to lower rates of risky sexual activities among adolescents, fewer behaviour problems among early adolescents, and higher academic achievement. Overall, teens whose activities and peers are monitored by their parents are *much* less likely to engage in violent activities than others (Fitzgerald, 2009, 2010). In general, supervision is related to much lower delinquency rates (Statistics Canada, 2007i). Thus, the authoritative pattern correlates the most with good adjustment on all dimensions of development, but its various components (psychological autonomy, monitoring, parental knowledge, warmth, and involvement) contribute in unique and independent ways to diverse child outcomes (Gray and Steinberg, 1999).

However, parental monitoring is often affected when adolescents' problematic and delinquent behaviours increase (Laird et al., 2003). Thus, within an interactional perspective, authoritative parenting cannot prevent all problems, as illustrated here in a male student's autobiography:

> "I had continued to do drugs through Grade 9 and managed to keep a decent average in school. Pete's, John's and my parents had been comparing incidents and behavioural changes for a little while and finally figured that we were doing drugs. The straw that broke the camel's back was when Pete's mother found drugs in his room. . . . Pete admitted everything, including my participation. What followed was what was most painful to me and that was reality. I had hurt my family, my reputation, and who knows what else during my drug times and now I had to deal with all of this. Firstly, my parents sat down and talked to me. They were crying and told me I was not allowed to see any of those people again, that I was grounded, that I would be much more accountable now, and that I would improve my marks in school to meet my potential."

In this incident, the parents could not detect drug use that was taking place behind their backs. But vigilance, communication with other parents, and then a firm but loving stand contributed to the adolescent's redress—along with his cooperative personality. Thus, again, one sees the interaction between parental efforts, child characteristics, and an effective community. This has led Kerr and Stattin (2003) to advance that it is actually an adolescent's willingness to disclose information to parents that allows them to be authoritative. As well, adolescents' difficult behaviours can discourage parents from engaging and monitoring them (Huh et al., 2006). Still, parental monitoring and control remain important components of adolescents' behaviours (Barnes et al., 2006; Fletcher et al., 2004).

What predominates in the **authoritarian*** parenting style is the dimension of control, restriction, and, at the extreme, coercion. This style is often met, particularly among fathers rather than mothers, in some immigrant groups (Bledsoe and Souv, 2011; Tyyskä, 2003). Other authoritarian parents are characterized by inconsistency. They are arbitrary and erratic; they tell their children what to do and punish severely and indiscriminately, or they threaten, then harshly punish one day, but fail to follow through the next day. They "order" this and that without explaining why. They are often quick with slaps. They "natter" a lot. This type of discipline is not as effective because children can take advantage of its inconsistencies; it neither stimulates the development of self-control nor does it respect children as persons (Stevenson, 1999). This style of childrearing is not so effective for most North American adolescents, perhaps in part because it is not socially constructed as suitable within the broad cultural context. In fact, it may contribute to difficult behaviours (Joussemet et al., 2008). However, restriction and control are very important factors of childrearing in many non-western countries (Bledsoe and Souv, 2011).

"No-Nonsense" Parenting

If Baumrind rewrote her typology today, she would probably include a socialization practice that falls between the authoritative and the authoritarian: no-nonsense parenting. This style is higher on control than in the authoritative pattern but also involves more warmth and nurturance than is the case in the authoritarian style (Kagitçibasi, 2007). As Nelson (2010) calls it, it is "parenting with limits." In this style, parents are the parents rather than their children's friends. We see this type of parenting in two contexts: First, it occurs across the world in societies where control is viewed as guidance (Steinberg et al., 1992). But it is not as well documented, except in some anthropological studies (e.g., LeVine, 1990). For instance, it is currently much discussed regarding Chinese parents because many have immigrated to North America. Second, it is often observed among black Canadians and Americans as well as in Caribbean samples.

This no-nonsense pattern, first described in an ethnographic study by Young in 1974, can also represent an "adaptation to contexts that are more dangerous" (Brody and Flor, 1998:813); it signals to the child that the parent is vigilant and cares. So far, studies have found that this style of parenting promotes black children's sense of competence and regulation, and results in lower rates of detrimental behaviours and attitudes (Brody and Murry, 2001). This style of parenting is related to black teenagers' better school outcomes and taking personal responsibility—even though these adolescents may find that their parents "hassle" them (Spencer et al., 1996).

Permissive and Uninvolved Parenting

Permissive parents place very few maturity demands on their children, who can behave very much as they wish. Such parents do not actively socialize their children, because they fail to set rules concerning school, behaviour at home, or activities with peers. Neither do they supervise their children. Permissiveness can be combined with either a high level of warmth and acceptance or with disinterest and even rejection.

The well-known developmentalist Urie Bronfenbrenner already pointed out in 1985 that parental permissiveness has more negative consequences than authoritarianism in times when there is cultural and social instability. In such a fluid context, norms of behaviour change rapidly, and a child needs far more guidance than in times when the entire community agrees on what constitutes proper and moral behaviour. Today, there are more dangers that confront adolescents than was the case even 15 years ago. Consequently, "premature emancipation is perhaps a greater threat to mature identity formation than delayed separation from family attachments" (Baumrind (1991:114–5).

A perfect example of permissive but warm parenting is described by a student whose parents were both professionals. She had initiated sexual intercourse at age 12, had had two abortions, had been "stoned" throughout high school, had sold drugs, and had lived on the streets by choice—all experiences she recalled fondly. Her parents allowed drug use and sex at home and finally bought her a condominium to give her more freedom while she was a drugged teenager:

> *"We were allowed to toke in the house and grow pot plants in the basement. . . . My parents were completely straight, but extremely liberal. They allowed all manner of goings on. . . . School at this point was a joke. I was stoned every single day. . . . From age 15 to 18 I simply didn't have any notably painful experiences. This was partly because I was constantly stoned and partly because I was having such an adventurous life."*

The two students quoted in this section shared one problem: drugs. But the two sets of parents' and offspring's reactions to this problem are dramatically opposite and the results are entirely different. These different outcomes and student appraisals of their situations are not caused just by their parents' socialization practices. They are also the result of environmental factors that both parents and adolescents created as well as of the interaction between parents' and adolescents' shared genetic predispositions (Leve et al., 2010b). In these autobiographies, one detects some similarities of character traits that each set of parents and their adolescent share. The male adolescent and his parents are more duty bound and emotionally connected. As a young man, he describes himself as cooperative and stable. The female adolescent and her parents are less tied to conventions, less emotionally involved, as well as more individualistic and gratification oriented. As a young woman, she describes herself as unstable, "depressed," and "highly critical" of other people's ways of living.

Subsequent to Baumrind's description of permissive childrearing, another style of parenting was added: uninvolved parents (Maccoby and Martin, 1983). Such parents are either permissive and indifferent or permissive and rejecting. They do not pay much attention to their offspring and do not fulfill their socialization function. Low parental control and rejection are the opposite of support and monitoring and they are a combination that has been consistently related to a host of negative outcomes, including delinquency (Steinberg et al., 2006). Teens raised in such a context tolerate frustration poorly and are more likely than others to be underachievers. They lack emotional control and long-term goals as well as purpose in life. At one extreme, such parents are called **neglectful**: Chao and Willms (2002) refer to them as irresponsible. Others are **abusive**.

Wavering-Negotiating Parenting

There may yet be at least one other type of parenting style that has not been discussed by researchers. It overlaps somewhat with the permissive, and is herein tentatively called the *wavering-negotiating* pattern. Parents who exhibit this style do not guide their children, even their toddlers, or make demands of them. Rather, they *consult* with their children about every step they undertake, even when the child is very small. When the parents make suggestions, they change them as soon as the child objects or disagrees. Such parents never punish but are very involved and loving. Here are two examples I recently observed:

The mother and a two-year-old boy are getting in line at one of the checkout counters of a large food store. **M:** *You want to follow the lady?* **B:** *No, no, want to leave!* **M:** *If you wait a minute, you'll get to ride the conveyor belt.* **B:** *Want a candy bar.* **M:** *OK, what about this one?* **B:** *No, this one.* **M:** *OK, now let's follow the lady.* **B:** *Want belt right away* [stamps foot]. **M:** *Ask the lady* [me] *if she can push her cart.* The conversation went on like this for the approximately three minutes I stood at the checkout counter. When I turned around to leave, the child was on the conveyor belt, to the clerk's obvious dismay.

The mother of a four-year-old girl is trying to buy a blouse in a department store. **G:** *It's ugly, I don't like it.* **M:** *Of course, honey, you're right, but I really* *don't need a pretty one.* **G:** *This one is nicer* [grabs one from the rack. Note that she is eating ice cream that is running down her hands]. **M:** *All right, I'll try it on if you want.* **G:** *No, I'm tired, I want to see the dollies.* **M:** *All right, sweetie, let's go and see the dollies.* The mother patiently follows.

In all the numerous instances when this pattern of interaction was observed, the mothers appeared well educated and upper-middle class (Nelson, 2010). Mother-child negotiating went on for extended periods and the mothers unavoidably lost each round with a weary smile or sigh. The children never appeared satisfied and, when the mothers finally drew the line somewhere, several of the children threw loud temper tantrums—all in public places and some even kicked and slapped their mothers. These observations are anecdotal, but it is my guess that if researchers carried out systematic observations in large food stores and malls in certain upper-middle-class metropolitan areas, they would encounter this pattern regularly. This is not a pattern that less advantaged parents can afford because it would be too disruptive to their lives: As so many researchers point out, working-class parents, poor parents, and parents living in subsistence economies focus on the primary tasks of sheltering, feeding, clothing, and teaching basic skills and values to their children (Lareau, 2011; LeVine, 2010). Misbehaviour and negotiations are "luxuries" that only better-off families can afford, and these children will become, first of all, individualistic, demanding, easily frustrated—a good preparation for their role as consumers.

The Question of What Constitutes "Proper" Parenting

A particularly sensitive issue when discussing impoverished families as well as families from other cultures is the matter of what constitutes "proper" childrearing practices: the **social construction of proper parenting**. In North America, good parenting is synonymous with the authoritative style with decreasing control as adolescents age (Keijsers et al., 2009). This approach is endorsed by professionals, especially psychologists and social workers, as well as child advocates. However, "What may be experienced by adolescents as parental intrusiveness in some cultural groups may be experienced as concern in others" (Steinberg et al., 1992:729)—which returns us to no-nonsense parenting discussed earlier. When peers are problematic, more controlling measures are adaptive and act as a deterrent to detrimental behaviours. *Therefore, one needs to evaluate "proper" parenting practices within the context in which they are applied.* Rather than value independence and creativity in their children, minority mothers frequently value obedience and respect for authority—as is the case in most countries of the world. The valuation of independence and creativity is a **western phenomenon**, a consequence of education, relative affluence, capitalism, and safe environments (Arnett, 2008). In these respects, let's read what Cottrell and VanderPlaat (2011) write about problems that immigrant parents and their adolescents are more likely to confront than is the case among Canadian-born families:

> "First, the construction of adolescence in Canada and its accompanying social script is . . . often at odds with that prescribed by their [immigrants'] cultural heritage. Second, this social script is strongly reinforced by a cultural milieu wherein attributes such as independence, self-sufficiency, decision-making,

sexual awareness, and relationship formation are encouraged as important dimensions of adolescent socialization . . . Third, the institutional emphasis on and support for child protection and child rights in Canada adds to the perception that in situations of conflict between parents and their teens the latter have greater legal standing and institutional recourse than their parents. Hence, the playing field upon which the struggles between parents and teens take place is by no means equal" (p. 291–2). (See, also, Bledsoe and Sow, 2011; Yax-Fraser, 2011:315.)

There is a related debate among the public as to whether physical or corporal punishment is acceptable. So far, North Americans still largely practise it in small doses (Barnett et al., 2005; Bibby, 2004; Durrat et al., 2003). Research documents a relationship between **corporal punishment** and low self-esteem, delinquency, aggressiveness, depression, and other problems, both during childhood and later on in life (Gershoff et al., 2012; Straus, 2008). However, this research corpus has several limitations. The first rests in a failure to differentiate harsh from mild corporal punishment accompanied with reasoning (Lansford et al., 2012; Lynch et al., 2006). The second limitation stems from the fact that most studies are not longitudinal: It is possible that troubled young adults recall their parents' behaviours more negatively than they were in reality and this cannot be verified unless the study is longitudinal. However, McLoyd and Smith (2002) have found a longitudinal increase in behavioural problems among children who had been spanked. But this increase nearly disappeared in situations of high maternal support of the child and disappeared with mild spanking (also, Berlin et al., 2009; Lansford et al., 2012). Unfortunately, as they point out, "our measure does not reflect the extent to which spanking episodes are or are not preceded by the use of reason to gain the child's compliance" (McLoyd and Smith, 2002:52). Thus, the third limitation of this research is that it rarely inquires about the *remainder* of the parents' socialization practices or the broader parenting context. For instance, spanking out of frustration is more detrimental than reasoned spanking (Berlin et al., 2009). A life course perspective suggests that some of the adults were difficult children: Parents of children with behavioural difficulties generally try more disciplinary methods of all kinds, including reasoning, grounding, withdrawal of privileges, and then spanking. Thus, parents may have been responding, albeit inappropriately, to children who were already problematic and are still so as adults. In fact, early child externalizing problems elicit more spanking (Gershoff et al., 2012).

Finally, this research does not tell us whether children perceive the punishment as a sign of parental rejection or concern. Indeed, in English-speaking western countries, physical punishment is harmful psychologically when the child perceives it as a form of parental rejection or when the overall parent-child relationship is negative (Foshee et al., 2005:339; Larzelere et al., 1998). It is also harmful for adolescents in general (Lansford et al., 2009).

In summary, it is unlikely that *occasional, fair, and light* (a tap on the bottom) corporal punishment of young children in itself causes the ills with which it has been associated. Nevertheless, even light physical punishment is not a parenting practice that is appropriate on a *regular* basis or at all (Straus, 2008): It is certainly detrimental for adolescents and children younger than two—particularly when they have difficult temperaments (Berlin et al., 2009; Mulvaney and Mebert, 2007). Young children tend to be more aggressive and less prosocial when their parents are punitive (Statistics Canada, 2005a). **Harsh physical punishment** is dangerous because it is unfairly painful, and is likely to be perceived as an act of rejection and aggressiveness by the victims (Lynch et al., 2006). It may also provide children with an example of a violent style of interaction. There is a subset of parents who use harsh discipline to the exclusion of other approaches (Lansford et al., 2009). Further, physically punishing children who tend to be negative and at genetic risk for aggressive behaviour is likely to intensify their detrimental predispositions (Horwitz and Neiderhiser, 2011; Reiss et al., 2009). Several European countries have now made it illegal while, in Canada, a recent Supreme Court decision upheld parents' rights to fair corporal punishment, as spelled out in Section 43 of the *Criminal Code*. But the Court set some guidelines, including the danger of hitting the head or a child younger than two. This is important because perhaps as many as 40 percent of parents of infants under the age of one do use some physical punishment (Invest in Kids, 2002).

Determinants of Parents' Socialization Practices

How do parents develop their socialization practices (Belsky et al., 2009)? What influences them to adopt one approach over another? Three types of influences come to mind. They are complementary rather than mutually exclusive, and interact with one another: contextual and cultural influences, parents' personalities, and adaptation to their children's personalities and behaviours. Parents' genes affect some of their socialization practices to some extent via personality traits (Burt et al., 2005).

Contextual and Cultural Determinants

Parents' beliefs about the proper ways of raising children are important determinants (Berlin et al., 2009:1416). These beliefs are culturally influenced and depend on which constructs of children predominate. For instance, in the Republic of the Congo, Bofi farmers and Bofi foragers share a same language and general geographic area but operate within two very different economic systems. They hold diverging values concerning children (obedience and control among the farmers; independence and nurturing among the foragers). Consequently, they respond differently to children and child outcomes also differ (Fouts et al., 2005). Beliefs also often originate from the way parents were themselves raised (Bailey et al., 2009), and the extent to which the country of origin is patriarchal (Tyyskä, 2003).

Childrearing practices can become ineffective or harsh because of environmentally induced stressors such as poverty, unemployment, marital conflict, and divorce. These stress-inducing circumstances tend to disrupt parental practices and make parents less responsive to children's needs. Stress experienced by mothers because of marital problems, domestic violence, or economic hardship often leads to a more erratic, punishing, and disciplinary relationship with their children (Graham et al., 2012). Lenton (1990) suggests that harsher disciplinary practices "are explained by insufficient resources and because parents may also experience an erosion of their authority" (p. 173). Thus, the quality of childrearing may change over the life course, not simply in response to the different needs of growing children but also as a consequence of evolving contextual factors.

Parents with amicable personalities and who enjoy a supportive relationship with each other are more likely to use appropriate socialization practices.

It would be interesting to know how parental practices change in transnational families where one parent is left with the children. For instance, Filipino fathers who go to work abroad to support their families influence their children's mothers' level of stress and parenting warmth via the frequency of their contacts and the size and regularity of their remittances (Harper and Martin, 2013). Such families constitute interesting contexts and real-life experiments with which to study child socialization. Similarly, one could use the context of economic and cultural change currently happening in Vietnam to see how it is altering paternal practices and parenting values that have so far been very much influenced by Vietnam's Confucian heritage (Jayakody and Phuong, 2013).

Parents' Personalities and Adaptation to Children

Parents' personalities constitute the second key element determining how they raise their children (Ganiban et al., 2009). For instance, a wide range of adult personality characteristics can lead to authoritative parenting (Denissen et al., 2009): Parents who are patient, calm, and affectionate, have a sense of humour, or are businesslike may be more inclined to use authoritative or even no-nonsense techniques. In turn, constructive parenting is maintained across generations because of the offspring's positive adjustment that follows (Kerr et al., 2009). On the other hand, think of a man who is easily frustrated, impatient, and impulsive. Such a man is more likely to become a harsh, rejecting, and perhaps abusive parent. There is then a good chance that his children will show some of these partly genetically influenced traits (DeGarmo, 2010). Their irritating behaviours trigger bouts of impulsive punishing, especially when he is under stress (Reiss et al., 2009). Poor parenting results to a certain extent from parents' difficult personalities and lack of empathy.

A third factor influencing parents' socialization practices is suggested by the interactional perspective: Even if they do not always do so consciously, parents adapt their practices to fit their children's behaviours, personalities, and abilities (Lam et al., 2012a; Keijsers et al., 2009). Several studies document this process of adaptation (Huh et al., 2006; Pettit et al., 2007). In 1985, Tarver-Behring and Barkley showed that, when hyperactive children were successfully treated with the drug methylphenidate, or Ritalin, their hyperactivity diminished substantially, and mothers became less controlling. Similar reactions have been observed among teachers (Whalen et al., 1980). In other studies, mothers of cooperative children and mothers of oppositional children were experimentally paired with a difficult child (not their own) and then with a cooperative child (not their own). Both types of mothers exhibited more controlling and intrusive behaviour with the oppositional child than with the cooperative one (Brunk and Henggeler, 1984). In other words, adults may adapt their parenting practices to children's behaviours, or adolescents may determine them (Kerr and Stattin, 2003), as illustrated by this student:

> *"I was not an easy child to raise and I think that in the balance of things I had a bigger influence on how my parents raised me than they had on me because I was for ever changing and going through phases of this and that, and I can't imagine that my parents could even figure this out."*

Pursuing this interactional line of reasoning, one can see that children and adolescents may influence their parents to become coercive or rejecting, even if they do so unwittingly (Simons et al., 2002). Parents may actually monitor children with behaviour problems more closely than they do children without these problems. Yet, as Simons et al. (1994) point out, "rebellious, antisocial children often punish parental efforts to monitor and discipline while reinforcing parental withdrawal and deviance" (p. 359). Early oppositional and defiant behaviours undermine later parenting practices and nurturance (Huh et al., 2006). In turn, diminished parenting can lead to affiliation with deviant peers and delinquency. It is difficult to monitor the whereabouts of an adolescent who is extremely oppositional (Moilanen et al., 2009). It can be said that children coproduce the parental socialization practices of which they are the beneficiaries or the victims (Lansford et al., 2009). Thus, this transmission stems both from genetic and environmental factors as well as their combination (Kovan et al., 2009), including situations of social inequalities (Wickrama and O'Neal, 2013). Nevertheless, parenting generally affects child behaviours more than child behaviours detrimentally affect certain aspects of parenting, at least until mid adolescence (Scaramella et al., 2002).

THE PARENT-ADOLESCENT RELATIONSHIP

The parent-adolescent relationship is influenced not only by the social construction of parenthood but also by societal definitions of what adolescence is (Arnett, 2001). In this section, we also examine the limits and contexts of parental influence on adolescents.

The Social Construction of Adolescence

Much research has been devoted to parent-adolescent conflict. In contrast, harmony is much less emphasized in western research. This interest in conflict derives in part from old-fashioned western notions that portray adolescence as being necessarily a period of turbulence—the idea of "storm and stress." At the beginning of the 20th century, the psychologist Stanley Hall was at the origin of this perspective on adolescence as a naturally turbulent stage. Sigmund Freud, who was very influential, reinforced this idea that adolescence is unavoidably a period during which all youths undergo emotional turmoil. Were this textbook written in Africa or in parts of Asia, this discussion on adolescence would either be absent or have a totally different focus (Arnett, 2008).

The beginning of adolescence is generally determined by the onset of puberty—that is, hormonal changes and the development of primary and secondary sexual characteristics. This transition exists in all cultures, even though the age of onset varies depending on life conditions, such as nutrition. *It is important to underscore that this period of physiological puberty does not give rise to an identical psychological and social puberty throughout the world* (Schlegel and Barry, 1991). But, despite the fact that the "storm and stress" ideology concerning adolescence does not apply universally, it still remains a widely held belief that influences reality: Some students confessed to using it to their advantage:

> *"Between the ages of 12 and 16 I was the worst for my parents because we were adolescents and we all felt as did our teachers and psychologists that it was natural for us to go through this bad period so we felt all justified in all our bad behaviors and our parents had to put up and shut up because what can you say when psychologists agree with your children? Now looking back on this I truly feel ashamed of what I put my parents through because it was all so avoidable and especially not necessary; it was actually parent-cruelty."*

The famed anthropologist Margaret Mead (1928) was the first to document the fact that the problematic type of adolescence, which has become common in most western countries, is a cultural rather than a biological entity. At that time, her research was going against the grain of prevailing social constructions. But in the last four decades, most qualified specialists have reached the same conclusion. "Teenagehood" is a **historical phenomenon** (Modell and Goodman, 1990). Historians Kett (1977) and Demos (1971) have placed the invention of adolescence as a social category between 1890 and 1920—after most middle-class youngsters were pushed out of the labour market and into the school system, separated from the adult world of which they had until then been part (Côté and Allahar, 1994). Adolescent crisis is in great part created by the type of environment that has evolved in most western countries—not by the nature of adolescence in general (Tyyskä, 2001).

The old ideology has recently resurfaced via a new issue: That of adolescent brain structure and function. Here again, one has to recall that experience, activities, and responsibilities contribute to brain formation—brain formation is not only a biological phenomenon but a cultural one as well (Sercombe, 2009). Therefore, brain development during adolescence may well differ cross-culturally and historically in terms of its timing and the areas that are favoured, perhaps in part depending on the level of social responsibility young persons shoulder or are sheltered from.

How Do Parents and Adolescents Get Along?

As stated earlier, much of the literature on the parent-adolescent relationship focuses on conflict, which generally pertains to daily routines rather than key value issues. North American adolescents report more conflict than do their parents. Naturalistic studies based on day-to-day reports, such as the one described in Family Research 10.1, show higher levels of daily tension than survey questionnaires do (Larson and Richards, 1994). This information finds resonance in students' autobiographies: Approximately one-third recalled experiencing a psychologically and socially painful adolescence that put a strain on their relationship with their parents. Another third described this period as a happy one both for themselves and their parents; the remaining third recalled an adolescence that included happy as well as unhappy periods. *A majority of the adolescents' sources of unhappiness were located at the peer-group level.* This was followed by school problems, and much farther down in the hierarchy of stressors were problems with parents. Interpersonal difficulties experienced with parents tended to have resulted from the adolescents' state of mind and transgressions and particularly from peer-driven stressors (Keijsers et al., 2009). Yet another key aspect of what leads to good relationships between adolescents and their parents is that of personality traits such as agreeableness. As well, Denissen et al. (2009) have found that the effect of adolescent personality increases with age. One should not omit the fact that an adolescent's behaviour problems can have a very negative impact on parents. Coley et al. (2011) have even found that they can limit disadvantaged mothers' employment success.

The absence of conflict over controversial topics such as sex and drugs most likely means that, although parents and adolescents differ in attitudes about them, they do not discuss these issues. In turn, this prevents parents from properly advising their children (Keijsers et al., 2009). In Canada, only 8 percent of adolescents turn to parents for guidance about sex (Bibby and Posterski, 2000:172), although this takes place much more often among immigrant Muslim teenagers, such as Iranian, Pakistani, or Afghan, particularly female (Moghissi et al., 2009:121). Another explanation is that parents and adolescents spend very little time together. While parents' and adolescents' reports on time spent together are somewhat at odds, both mention spending only a few minutes each day talking (Larson and Richards, 1994). In fact, only a minority of adolescents share a meal with their parents on a typical day (CIW, 2010). Yet, family dinners have also been found to promote positive adolescent-parent communication (Fulkerson et al., 2010; Offer, 2013).

Larson and Richards (1994) report that adolescents experience less conflict with their fathers than their **mothers**, partly because mothers interact more with them concerning the basics of their daily lives. The division of household labour based on gender places mothers at a disadvantage over fathers in this respect. In this vein, Collins (1990) reviews studies illustrating that, when a mother interrupts her adolescent during a discussion, the youngster subsequently interrupts her even more, but does not do so for the father. Yet, all studies indicate that adolescents are closer to their mother than their father, confide in her more, and seek her advice more (Nomaguchi, 2008).

Immigrant parents and children encounter greater *potential* for conflict, particularly in areas where they may be very "different" from other children, and when children rebel or fail to "fit into" the structures provided (Jaya and Porter, 2011). Areas of great concern for immigrant parents focus on gender roles, relationships, and sexuality (Cottrell and VanderPlaat, 2011). It is difficult to know whether these parent-child differences lead to conflicts and whether these conflicts

Naturalistic Self-Reporting: Daily Activities

In a study conducted by Larson and Richards (1994), adolescents and their parents were asked to carry a pager for one week. (Now, such research is done via cell phones.) When beeped, each completed a report indicating what they were doing, where and with whom they were, as well as their thoughts and emotional state at the time of each signal. They were beeped once at random within every two-hour block of time between 7:30 a.m. and 9:30 p.m. This method was called the Experience Sampling Method. Adolescents were sampled from the fifth through ninth grades of a middle- and working-class Chicago suburb. In addition, parents and adolescents filled out many questionnaires about themselves and their family life.

This combination of methods allowed the researchers to study daily activities and accompanying moods of all the family members individually. But above all, it allowed them to compare how each family member felt in the company of the others and how each felt while engaging in various activities together or separately, whether at school, work, home, with peers or coworkers. The researchers could also obtain on-the-spot reports of conflict, contentment, or boredom while family members were together. They could also, for instance, compare how each reported on the same conflict.

caused by their immigration situation are fewer in areas with high heterogeneity such as Toronto or in more homogeneous areas, such as the Maritime provinces, for instance.

One domain of the parent-adolescent relationship that is still unexplored pertains to children and adolescents who become **caregivers**. Their parent, sibling, or grandparent may be chronically ill, have a serious disability, a debilitating emotional problem, addiction, or even a developmental delay. In a Vancouver survey, Charles et al. (2012) have estimated that 12 percent of youths are in a caregiving role. The demands of this role often isolate these youths and force them to grow up rapidly. The situation may be stigmatizing, especially when it pertains to a condition that leads a parent or a sibling to behave in inappropriate ways, as a student well illustrates in her autobiography:

> "When I look back on these years what was totally devastating is that my mother was an alcoholic and even worse than that she was a drunk. She started drinking after my father left and went down rapidly so that by age 14, I had to feed us, sort of clean the house and at first my brother helped with the outside but then he also left to live with our father and neither bothered to help me. I was left all alone with this drunk, and I could no longer have friends over because it was more than embarrassing as my mother was often on the floor with a bottle. . . . I tried to get rid of all the booze but this was even more dangerous because she'd get in the car to buy more. I was desperate and asked a kind elderly neighbor to haul the car away to her own garage and hide it. . . . After months of begging by the time I was 16, my mother got treatment for her alcoholism . . . things started looking up but she was very messed up, ashamed and abandoned . . . but it gave

me a bit of slack to go out some, catch up with my school work. . . . I am OK but my mother never will. After that up to now, she's lost her way as a mother, she has only me, my brother never recognizes her."

This student exhibits all the negative consequences of young caregiving without support: no parent-child reciprocity, shame, isolation, lack of recognition of her role, even by her own family, becoming the parent of her parent rather than simply caregiving (Charles et al., 2012). Another student recalls how the worst years of her life occurred when, at age 15, her mother was diagnosed with a severe case of MS (multiple sclerosis) that prevented her from even moving about. She was so debilitated that she could barely feed herself. In this case also, the father left but did not take with him the little sister, aged 6, nor did he help. Therefore, the 15-year-old had to take care both of her sister and her mother. However, one soon notes below that the mother remained the parent and gave a great deal of moral support to the caregiving daughter.

"At that point my mother suggested that I should go on with my school and get my little sister ready for school but we didn't have much money. My mother had some good friends that took turn cooking for us and their husbands took care of the lawn and that sort of man stuff. My mother was able to talk to us a lot and read stories to my little sister and we watched TV together and she encouraged me to go on sleepovers at friends' places. But it was a lot of work in the house and helping my mom get dressed and bathed, even with all that help and it was so hurtful to see my mother so sick, but she was so supportive of me and so thankful and I learned so much out of this, it gave me a good feeling of contribution to my family life and to this day my little sister looks up to me and I have been able to prevent her from getting into stupid things with her friends last year so I feel good about this except that my mom will never be her good old self again but at least she functions well and is a great role model to me."

Cultural Determinants of Parental Influence

Parental influence or the ability to socialize children and affect their outcomes is a much discussed topic these days, particularly with regard to adolescents. But parental effectiveness does not operate within a vacuum: It is circumscribed by society and the child outcomes it values. Family relationships take place within a distinct cultural context, at a given historical period, and under specific economic conditions (Hareven, 1994a, 1994b). As a general rule, the extent of parents' influence on their children, particularly on their adolescents, varies according to these prevailing sociohistorical conditions (Bronfenbrenner, 1989). In other words, there are **historical eras** or *time periods when it is easier for parents to influence their youngsters and others when it is far more difficult to do so.*

Families' social and cultural contexts have altered drastically and with an extreme rapidity that has no precedent in history. The environment is now controlled by information technology, including the **audiovisual media**. The workplace, schools, homes, and leisure activities have all been affected by these changes and the evolution of the value systems that generally accompanies such transitions. Parents have had to adapt their role within this new context and raise their children accordingly, although much of this adaptation takes place unconsciously (Alwin, 1990). Often, as seen in Chapter 3, the contents of media do not support parental efforts and may even undermine their moral and practical teachings. In contrast, religion, which generally supports parents and upholds their moral authority, used to be a more powerful influence than it is now throughout all regions and social classes. Thus, parents have lost a degree of legitimacy through these two changes alone. For their part, in western societies, children react to their parents according to what they learn through their environment, including their peer group and the messages they receive from the media as well as from professionals. As a result, children's and adolescents' receptivity to parental socialization efforts has evolved: Some no longer see their parents as legitimate sources of information or even of authority for their behaviours.

As society evolves, it places a premium on certain specific human outcomes. Thus, parents are emphasizing autonomy and self-reliance in their socialization practices both because of **society's value orientation** toward individuality and because parents who are employed need more self-reliant children (Rossi and Rossi, 1990)— thus the influence of our competitive economic system: Mainstream technological society also values the development of self-esteem and educational achievement (Daly, 2004). Although all of these outcomes are, to some extent, affected by parents, these outcomes are particularly influenced by peer interaction, the school situation, and the media. In contrast, a few decades ago, the development of politeness, obedience, conformity, service to others, and patriotism were given more importance in the socialization of children (Alwin, 2001), as they still are among many immigrant parents (Cottrell and VanderPlaat, 2011). These outcomes are more culturally influenced; they are thus subject to direct teaching and example and are more amenable to parental socialization. Therefore, parents were more influential in these respects than is the case for outcomes that are more personality driven, such as self-esteem and the ability to be independent.

The Role of Peers in the Parent-Adolescent Relationship

At the outset of this section, it should be pointed out that the importance of the peer group in children's and particularly adolescents' lives is greater in cultures that are individualistic and emphasize independence from the family, as is the case in North America and in some western societies (Schwarz et al., 2012). Second, today's western parents have less control than in the past over whom their child associates with after a certain age—especially whom they associate with on their smartphones and on the Internet. *Peers now contribute to parental isolation.* The phenomenon of age-segregated peer groups is typical of only North America and Europe (Schlegel, 2003). It is not a universal situation but more one stemming from urbanization combined with modern education (Arnett, 2008). In North America, particularly, the peer group may support parental teachings, but it may also conflict with parents' values and, as children pass into adolescence, peers' norms begin producing a much greater effect (Masten et al., 2009). The problematic aspects of this phenomenon are particularly salient for immigrant parents (Cottrell and VanderPlaat, 2011). Overall, children's socialization is considerably easier when peers and parents agree, and is difficult, at best, when fundamental value contradictions exist between the two systems (Drew et al., 2010). The greater the similarity between parents' values and those of their children's peers, the lower the level of parent-child conflict.

What parent has not heard, "But all the others are going!," "Everybody is doing it," and "Everybody has one" (Daddis, 2011)? These are powerful and often intimidating messages handed to parents. Thus, each parenting couple and, more and more, each single mother or father has to face what is presented by their child as a normal entitlement among youngsters. This alleged consensus among adolescents allows them to speak with great authority to their parents, because parents are generally more isolated than children when it comes to tactical and moral support. *Adolescent groups and subcultures are much more cohesive and less fragmented for each child than are adult subcultures for each individual parent:* This constitutes a disequilibrium that is detrimental to parents' role. A single mother expresses the situation during an interview in an attempt at understanding how her teenage daughter became delinquent without her noticing it:

> *"My daughter has a lot of friends, some I know, some I don't. They talk on the phone on a daily basis . . . they make plans, they exchange clothes, they cover for each other, they watch each other's back against their parents. . . . New clothes that she wears are borrowed from Mindy and if I ask Mindy, she'll say, 'Don't I got good taste!' If Mindy's mother calls to find out where she is, all I can say is that they went to the movies together. That's what I was told. But they actually went to this boy's place. If Mindy's mother calls about clothes, I say that they exchange a lot while in reality they are all shoplifting. So you see you have to be a very, very clever parent to keep track of all of this and to add it all up together to one conclusion: My child is a shoplifter and she's barely 15 and she's screwing around. But don't think for one minute that I added this up on my own; the police did it for me. These girls just protect each other. Protect for what? They're the ones who need protection against each other."*

The last three sentences of this mother's quote are worth reflecting upon.

Along these lines, Steinberg and colleagues (1995) find that, when adolescents' peers have authoritative parents, the latter contribute to positive developmental outcomes above and beyond the adolescents' own parents' authoritativeness: "We believe that this may be due in part to the higher level of shared social control provided by a network of authoritative parents" (p. 453). Yet, in the preceding quote, the parents are exhibiting all the "symptoms" of being authoritative, but their children's delinquent peer group is far more clever and better organized.

Parent networks can fulfill several functions both for parents and their children (Knoester et al., 2006). When these are school based, they can contribute to a smoother socialization process, norms that are more closely adhered to, and better-informed parents. It is, however, far more difficult for adolescents' parents than for young children's parents to know their children's peers' parents and to form an effective community—at a time when such a context would be the most helpful. As a result, parental knowledge of adolescents' behaviours generally diminishes, particularly when adolescents have high levels of behavioural problems (Moilanen et al., 2009). Problems arise particularly when adolescents have close peers who accept illegal behaviours: These teens are then four times more likely to engage in violent delinquency than others, for instance (Fitzgerald, 2009). There is also the fact that teens who are difficult tend to choose similar peers, which reinforces their problems (Burt et al., 2009)—thus, children's choice of peers is derived in part from their own genetic predispositions (Beaver et al., 2009).

In addition, parents inherit what one student called "the flak," that is, spill-over of peer maltreatment or bullying, and can be blamed by clinicians for these traumas (Ambert, 2001). A student's recollections illustrate this latter phenomenon quite vividly:

> "Up to that age [11 years] I had been quite happy at school but then something happened to me, I stopped growing and I became in no time the shortest and skinniest and soon the pimpliest little runt at my grade level. The other boys used to pick on me, hide my coat, steal my lunches, and would never include me in their games. They'd laugh at me openly and the girls started avoiding me too because it wasn't cool to be seen with the most unpopular boy. . . . You can't imagine how many times my mother had to keep me home because I'd start throwing up. I became scared shitless. . . . my parents had to send me to a psychiatrist and he turned around and blamed them for not being supportive and for whatever else. . . . My parents were sort of being made miserable because of this little runt I was and now by this psychiatrist and to this day they have never blamed me and have always been supportive."

THE RELATIONSHIP BETWEEN PARENTS AND ADULT CHILDREN

There are both continuities and changes in the parent-child relationship throughout the various stages of family development, as well as throughout the life course of each family member.

When the Child Is a Young Adult

In North America, full adulthood has traditionally meant financial independence from parents and the establishment of a separate household, usually with a marital partner. However, this life stage is now postponed because of recent changes in the economy (Côté and Allahar, 2006). Whereas adolescence as a social construct was the invention of the dawn of the 20th century, young adulthood is the creation of the closing of that century (Côté, 2000): The term **"emerging adulthood"** is now frequently used for the 19 to 35 age bracket (Beaujot, 2006). This term signifies a status somewhere between adolescence and full adulthood (Nelson et al., 2007). It is a new stage of life (Hareven, 2000). Young adults remain home (**coresidence**) more often than was the case three decades ago and many remain financially dependent on their parents for a longer period of time (Beaupré et al., 2006; Mitchell, 2000). For Canada as a whole, the number of young adults aged 20 to 29 at home has jumped from 26.9 percent in 1981 to 41.1 percent in 2001 and has since remained stable at **42.3 in 2011**—with young men more likely to live home than young women. Ontario has the highest rate at 50.6 percent while Saskatchewan and Alberta have the lowest rates of young adults living at home—30.6 and 31.4 percent respectively (Statistics Canada, 2012b).

There are also differences between certain census metropolitan areas in 2011 from east to west geographically (Statistics Canada, 2012b):

St. John's	39.2	Kingston	32.4
Saint John	40.2	Oshawa	55.2
Halifax	31.1	Guelph	40.1
Moncton	27.7	Greater Sudbury	38.1
Montreal	40.3	Winnipeg	43.3
Sherbrooke	**25.5**	Regina	33.3
Ottawa-Gatineau	39.2	Saskatoon	27.6
Toronto	**56.3**	Calgary	34.7
Hamilton	53.3	Edmonton	33.1
Thunder Bay	44.8	Vancouver	46.7
Peterborough	38.6	Victoria	28.9
Kitchener	42.2		

This is a widespread phenomenon in the western world (Ruggles and Heggeness, 2008). In fact, rates of young people up to age 34 who are **single** and have never cohabited are extremely high—as high as 55 percent in Italy, most of whom still live at home (Jones, 2007). *This historic context, in turn, postpones parents' transition to the empty nest. It also delays grandparenting.* Young adults whose parents are still together, whose mother is educated, who are close to their parents, leave home on time or later because their parents are better able to help them through higher education (Miller, 2012; Ravanera et al., 2003). Children of immigrant mothers also leave home later (Beaupré et al., 2006). All in all, intense support of young adults is generally helpful, although for parents, the consequences are more mixed (Fingerman et al., 2012a). This is particularly so when young adults are failing to meet certain maturity milestones and are too dependent. "Overparenting," for its part, is related to less satisfying parent-young adult communication: But it results in neither deficits nor advantages in terms of adaptability (Segrin et al., 2012). However, it is difficult to draw solid conclusions because the definitions and measures differ vastly from study to study. It is currently a new area of research that is becoming popular, in part related to anxieties adults and children harbour about success in this type of economically competitive society.

How to explain this new phenomenon? First, young adults stay home because they remain in the educational system longer and this is costly. Luong (2010) has documented how students' debt load prevents them from accumulating assets while still in their twenties. Second, the development of the service economy and the shrinking of the manufacturing base have resulted in an increase in part-time and **low-paying jobs** for young people without higher education—these jobs force them to remain with their parents for financial reasons (Gee et al., 2003). Thus, coresidence enables better transfers of capital from parents to children (Beaujot, 2004). In contrast, children who leave home too early may be disadvantaged, especially over time.

A third reason for the lengthening dependence of young adults, which is rarely mentioned, may be related to the fact that they are increasingly endorsing **consumerist values** (Bibby and Posterski, 2000). What were considered luxuries in previous cohorts—cars, home entertainment systems, computers, and cell phones—have become necessities for current ones, thanks to various marketing strategies that permeate our world (Côté and Allahar, 2006). Consequently, the earnings required to reach such heightened material expectations come later, and in the meantime young adults can afford them only when they remain with their parents. Fourth, in some cities, rents are out of reach for those on low incomes, which makes the parental home comparatively more appealing. This may be one of the reasons why coresidence is so common in some expensive cities, such as Toronto and Vancouver. A result of high costs and longer dependence on parents is that young families are now less able to accumulate assets early on than was the case in the 1980s (Beaujot, 2006:120).

Another change that has occurred in recent decades is that the family may go through **transition reversals**: Approximately one-third of young Canadians aged 20 to 29 have returned home at least once after an initial departure (Billette et al., 2011). The reasons for this include unemployment and other financial problems, or because a relationship has ended (Mitchell and Gee, 1996). This has been referred to as the *revolving-door family* and the "boomerang" children. As Hareven (1994b) points out, whereas in the late 19th century children remained at home to help aging parents or widowed mothers, now "young adult children reside with their parents in order to meet their own needs" (p. 448). As well, coresident children contribute little in terms of housework (Mitchell, 2004). This entire situation represents yet another refutation of the pessimistic point of view of the "decline" of the family. Rather, active parenting is maintained well beyond what used to occur and is even reactivated, often repeatedly, after all the children have left home for the first time. As Mitchell (2004:121) points out, mothers have become the new "unpaid social workers" as the welfare state continues to retrench. However, there is also some evidence that children who leave home later tend to live closer to their parents than earlier leavers and are more likely to provide help to their aging parents (Leopold, 2012).

When the Child Is a Mature Adult

One key aspect of the *life course perspective* is that it brings attention to the development of the relationship over time as both parents and adult children age and as cohorts change (Hareven, 2000; Martin-Matthews, 2000). For instance, only 8 percent of persons born in 1910 still had a surviving parent by the time they had reached age 60. This percentage rose to 16 for those born in 1930 and it is expected to rise to 23 for people aged 60 born in 1960 (Rosenthal, 2000). As well, there is the fact that more elderly women than men live alone, which may be a factor that motivates their children or even nieces and nephews to be in touch with them. But whatever their age, a majority of adults and their parents report having a good relationship and being in contact with one another at least weekly (Ménard and Le Bourdais, 2012). In fact, a study of seven European countries showed increased contact with mothers via cell phones and the Internet (Treas and Gubernskaya, 2012). Generally, the affection that exists between parents and adult children is the chief motivator in continued contact and exchange with parents (Rossi and Rossi, 1990). The more parents and children see one another, the greater affection they have for one another, and vice versa. But the Rossis have found that this reciprocity of affectivity does not always apply to fathers. They concluded that "the motivations for interaction between adult children and their mothers and fathers are different."

Studies tend to present demographic characteristics to explain the quality of the parent-adult child relationship: gender and marital status of parent and child, socio-economic status, geographic distance, and parents' health status and even religiosity (Connidis, 2010; Lin, 2008). One variable that is overlooked, perhaps because this is still a recent phenomenon, is the adult stepchild-stepparent situation (Ménard and Le Bourdais, 2012). The interactional perspective also suggests studies that would look at a child's and a parent's personality characteristics that could affect the relation-ship. From a life course perspective, other researchers believe that, as adult children mature, their values become more similar to those of their parents because they have lived through similar experiences, such as getting married, having children, and shouldering work responsibilities (Rossi and Rossi, 1990).

Parents Help Their Adult Children

In general, parents, especially when they are still in reasonable health, provide a great deal of help to their adult children, including financial (Gee, 2000)—even to their grandchildren (Ploeg, 2003). They are a key resource for adult children with fewer social assets (McIlvane et al., 2007). Parents respond to grown children's needs and problems (Fingerman et al., 2009; Suitor et al., 2006). They provide services such as babysitting, food, clothing, lodging, and gifts in kind as well as cash, and moral sup-port, at least once a month.

Parents often do not or cannot disengage from the problems experienced by their adult children. Parents who have one child with adult problems are lower in well-being. Having one child who is successful in life does not predict well-being but hav-ing several successful children does (Fingerman et al., 2012b). Adult children's problems correlate significantly with depression in the older parents, and some stud-ies find that older parents who have to provide a great deal of help to their children feel more depressed. These parents may be particularly worried over children who fail to achieve a reasonable level of independence (Birditt et al., 2010). In addition, when children have problems, they may receive advice that is not wanted or that they are unwilling or unable to put into practice. One can see that, at the very least, the potential for intergenerational ambivalence is high (Connidis and McMullin, 2002a, b). In contrast, parents offer more companionship to children they perceive to be more successful, perhaps because they have more in common with them (Fingerman et al., 2009). Parents over age 65 who have a coresident child usually receive rela-tively little in terms of household or financial help from that child. In a Dutch study, it was found that a 30- to 40-year-old child's coresidence with a parent was in a majority of the cases dictated by the child's needs (Smits et al., 2010). In the U.S., a majority of single mothers and their children have to live with the mothers' parents at some point because of need (Pilkauskas, 2012). Overall, the research shows that older parents still contribute a great deal to society via helping their families as well as volunteer work (Rajulton and Ravanera, 2006b).

Adult Children Help Their Elderly Parents

When elderly parents become much older, generally after age 80, a proportion experience diminished health as well as mobility limitations. At that point, adult children often become parents' key instrumental and social support resources (Chappell and Funk, 2011; Connidis, 2010). Few adult children actually engage in the physical care of their parents; rather, they help them with groceries, house chores, and visits to physicians (Rosenthal, 2000; Turcotte and Schellenberg, 2007). With shrinking social services and the shift away from institutionalized care, demand for family members to provide care for their elderly parents will increase at the same time that there are few child care facilities as well as institutional help for young adults with challenges—and autism is one of the many. This shortfall of help may be especially problematic for those elderly women who are divorced or have been single all their lives and may have fewer social and material resources at their disposal (Abu-Laban and McDaniel, 2004). Aged lesbian women and gay men without partners also need to be studied in this context.

A popular concept is that of the **sandwich generation**: adults caught between raising their children and caring for frail parents. In reality, only a minority of adults provide care to both generations at the same time (Duxbury et al., 2009; Rosenthal, 2000). However, their numbers will increase because more have children late in life. Family-work role challenges can become as important among the mid generation as it is among younger parents of small children (McDaniel, 2003). Still, one should not downplay the potential for burnout for spouses, generally wives, or daughters who reside with an aged loved one with severe limitations. This situation can be very detrimental to their health. Adult children who help care for a parent are far more stressed when the parent suffers from cognitive-behavioural than physical disabilities (Starrels et al., 1997). In contrast, when the parent's challenges are physical only, the parent-child relationship generally continues to include most of its previous elements. (The same situation occurs when it is a parent who cares for an adult child.)

So far, the research literature has emphasized the stress experienced by adult children, especially daughters, as a result of their role as caregivers of disabled parents. This stress is real and is related to role overload, and more hours result in even greater overload and tension with one's employment (Gordon et al., 2012). In this respect, the concept of **burden** is frequently utilized. This, in itself, is yet another social construct worth analyzing, because it reflects cultural values about intergenerational relations. For instance, *one does not encounter this concept when studying the care that parents give to their children,* even when youth or adult children are quite problematic (Vaughan et al., 2013). Rather, the words "strain" or "stress" are used. The reason is that caring for their children is considered to be part of parents' role—particularly by the state, thus justifying the system's failure to provide adequate support. However, when these same parents age and their health falters, help extended to them by their children is analyzed in terms of burden—when in other societies it is simply a duty or an adult child's role. This is a double standard. For instance, among Chinese, it is part of filial piety (Sun, 2012). However, economic changes and small families have also contributed to new trends: In 2012, the Chinese government had to propose a law demanding that adult children visit their elderly parents more often as more cases of physical abuse, neglect or abandonment, and financial exploitation are regularly reported in the Chinese press. As illustrated in Chapter 2, it is often a male child's role whereas in North America, it is a female child's duty, hence the aspect of **gender inequity** resurfacing once more (McDaniel, 2009).

There is also little research showing the positive side of caring for or helping one's elderly parents (Martin-Matthews, 2001). In this respect, Pruchno et al. (1997) have pointed out the importance of distinguishing between caregiving burden and caregiving satisfaction (Northcott and Wilson, 2008:126). Cranswick (1997) has found that Canadians who help their elderly parents tend to be more positive than negative about this experience, even though a substantial proportion have had to make adjustments in their own lives in order to fulfill this duty, such as sleeping less, changing working hours, and taking fewer vacations. Dupuis and Norris (2001) have found that daughters of parents in long-term care facilities adopt a wide variety of roles/attitudes in this respect and Kemp (2012) has also found that supporting parents who are together in an assisted-living environment includes additional tasks. Robison and colleagues (2009) have shown that negative effects of caregiving largely stem from specific circumstances, in particular low income and lack of community help. Resilience, as Chappell and Dujela (2008) suggest, is a characteristic that deserves more attention as it provides for better adjustment. New research, both in Spain and North America, is also emerging on grandchildren's role when grandparents have dementia (e.g., Celdran et al., 2012; Hamill, 2012).

Daughters are far more likely to become their elderly parents' helpers and caregivers than sons (Michelson and Tepperman, 2003), which returns us to the concept of **social reproduction***** and its social inequities discussed by feminist political economy theorists (Luxton, 2006a; Mandell and Wilson, 2011). The time demands and emotional costs of help are also higher among daughters than sons (Raschick and Ingersoll-Dayton, 2004). However, when a son has the responsibility for his parents, his involvement is as stable as that of a daughter (Martin-Matthews, 2001). Often, his wife assumes this duty or, at the very least, contributes to it. This is an especially important role for Chinese and Taiwanese daughters-in-law (Sun, 2012), even transnationally. The key to receiving help resides in having one daughter, and married couples are more likely to respond to the needs of the wife's parents (Shuey and Hardy, 2003) or, in other cultures such as India, the husband's parents. This situation reflects the fact that women are generally assigned nurturing roles in society and learn to be responsible for the well-being of others from the time they are young (Abu-Laban and McDaniel, 2004). Consequently, parents may also expect more help from their daughters than their sons—although the reverse occurs in many other societies, such as China or Japan.

Starrels and colleagues (1997) have found that elderly parents who receive help from their children tend to reciprocate more with sons than daughters and provide less assistance to daughters than sons. Parents seem to appreciate their sons' caregiving more than their daughters' caregiving, perhaps because sons are still more valued and also because it is taken for granted that daughters are nurturing. It is expected that they will help their elderly parents as part of their feminine role. This gender expectation and the greater reciprocity with or recognition accorded to helpful sons may be reasons why daughters experience more stress than sons in their helping role. In general, *female caretakers received less help than male ones* (McDaniel, 2009).

For their part, elderly parents are happier when they give than when they receive, and they accept help more readily when they can contribute something in return (Lowenstein et al., 2007). However, even this parental help may result in feelings of ambivalence in their mid-generation children, particularly when the relationship was not optimal during childhood (Connidis, 2010; Ingersoll-Dayton et al., 2001; Wilson et al., 2003). When parents require a great deal of support from their children, they are less satisfied with the relationship. In part, this can be explained by the fact that contact with the child is necessitated by the parents' needs rather than by the child's desire to see the parents or by the spontaneity of a visit just to socialize (Silverstein et al., 2010). It is not surprising, therefore, that when older parents are in better health, they report a more positive relationship with their children. Even parents who are in palliative care are concerned about burdening their children (McPherson et al., 2007).

Elderly adults who are **childless** are not less happy or in poorer health than those who have living children, although seniors receive more help when they have children (Kohler et al., 2005). What seems to count for the emotional well-being of the elderly is not whether they have children but the quality of the relationship between them and their progeny (Connidis, 2010). For instance, a warm relationship with adult children may increase parental longevity after widowhood. Childless elderly women generally have an economic advantage over other women their age (Plotnick, 2009). This is not surprising because it costs at least $167,000 to raise a child to age 18 and, in addition, childless women are much less likely to have had to interrupt their work years (Canadian Council on Social Development, 2006).

One issue that needs to be further addressed is how the **migration** of adult children affects elderly parents who are left in the home country or who choose to remain there. As well, how are the cultural requirements of filial piety, which are so strong in societies such as China and Taiwan, affected and transformed by this migration to North America or Australia? Sun (2012) has found that, because physical care is no longer possible, the migrants and their parents transform the concept of filial piety and emphasize its emotional and symbolic aspects. In contrast, when migrant families are poor, adult children send remittances home to help their elders. As Ken Sun (2012) points out, "In this sense, social class is central to understanding how the rules of intergenerational reciprocity are negotiated and transformed within transnational families across the socioeconomic spectrum" (p. 124).

Overall, there is a certain degree of ambivalence in the relationship of adult children to aging parents, and this is especially so among women, toward in-laws, and when the relationship was not optimal during childhood (Connidis, 2010; Wilson et al., 2003). *Basically, in our society, there is a lack of normative support for this intergenerational situation.*

AN EXTENSION OF PARENTING: GRANDPARENTS

In the 19th century, adults who became grandparents for the first time were often still busy raising their younger children. Today, grandparenting tends to be a separate family developmental stage. As age at marriage is delayed, age at first grandparenting is also going up. In 1995, women were becoming grandmothers on average at age 53.6 and men were becoming grandfathers at age 56.8. Currently, 79 percent of all adults aged 65 and over are grandparents and the average grandparent has 4.7 grandchildren (Statistics Canada, 2003f). This is an average that may soon diminish with the reduced birth rate. Indeed, the average 70-year-old grandparent today has 3 to 10 fewer grandchildren than his or her own parents' cohort had. The family tree becomes leaner. Thus, because of longevity, more generations are present in families but with fewer members in each generation. This is called the "bean pole" family because its structure is long and thin (Bengtson, 2001; McPherson, 1998).

The role of grandparents is not rigidly scripted; it is dynamic and fluid (Kemp, 2004; Rosenthal and Gladstone, 2000). It has been qualified as a stabilizing force and as a source of family continuity. Grandmothers have been described as **kin-keepers** and as persons who open the kin system so as to support members in difficulty. The role that grandparents play differs according to their age, health, and ethnic group, as well as the age, gender, and location of their grandchildren. That role may differ for each grandchild; as Mueller and Elder (2003:413) point out, the grandparent-grandchild relationship should be studied within the context of the entire network of family ties.

King and Elder (1995) indicate that the quality of the relationship between grandparent and adult child has a significant impact on the grandparent-grandchild relationship, which may explain why grandchildren are closer to their maternal grandparents (Chappell et al., 2010; Monserud, 2008). Adult children who do not feel close to their parents or who perceive them to be meddlesome are less likely to encourage their children to visit them and to form close bonds with them. Similarly, it is possible that when children feel that their parents are not well treated by their grandparents, they may be reluctant to form close bonds. Parents act as mediators in the grandparent-grandchild relationship. One area of research that should soon be addressed is the family relationships of grandparents who are gay or lesbian (Connidis, 2003b).

More than 60 percent of U.S. grandparents provide care for at least one grandchild on a regular basis (Luo et al., 2012). **They often babysit** while their daughters are at work. African-American grandmothers fill this role even more than their white counterparts, particularly when their daughters are single. However, more grandmothers are now employed themselves, thus precluding extensive babysitting. Some even simultaneously help their older mothers—care work or social reproduction is intergenerational (Mandell and Wilson, 2011). Grandmothers who have several children and

Anne-Marie Ambert

More young grandmothers are employed than in the past. Therefore, it is necessary for research to address the issue of change in their roles, particularly as babysitters, in families where two generations of women who are mothers are now employed simultaneously.

grandchildren have more opportunities to become babysitters. This opportunity increases when a teenage daughter who lives with them has a baby. Grandmothers who simply babysit, and can do so without relinquishing their employment, may even harvest health benefits (Hughes et al., 2007).

Grandparents Who Raise Grandchildren

In 2011, 0.5 percent of all Canadian children were in the care of their grandparents to the exclusion of their own parents, for a total of 30,005 children between the ages of 0 and 14 (Statistics Canada, 2011a). Of course, the real numbers are higher because children aged 14 and over are not included. This is now called the "skip generation" household because no parent generation is present (Milan et al., 2009). Another 239,310 children and a parent also lived with grandparents in an extended family arrangement. All in all, 4.8 percent of all children in this age group share a home with a grandparent—up from 3.8 in 2006—and this occurs particularly among Natives: 8 percent of Aboriginal children are in the care of grandparents or other relatives (Gionet, 2009). In some American states, and particularly among African Americans, over a quarter of children in foster care are living with grandparents, generally a grandmother. In Canada, the numbers are more modest, in part because there are proportionally fewer never-married young mothers, and drug addiction is not as prevalent.

Grandchildren often live with their grandparents because the child's mother suffers from emotional problems and/or addictions, including alcoholism. In half of the cases, mothers suffer from a multiplicity of problems—not to omit the fact that fathers are absent. Obviously, such grandparents are taking charge of children who have lived in deteriorating family circumstances, a situation well described in this student's autobiography:

> "I was raised by my grandparents who took me and my little brother in after my mother flipped after my father left her. We had had a hard life and all I remember about it is that my parents were scary [they were alcoholics]. Anyways we were better off with my grandparents and we knew them because they had often kept us over weekends. . . . Now that we're older it's harder on them in a way because my brother grew up with lots of problems but at least I turned out just fine and this just makes up for it. . . . I love them like my own parents and we owe them everything and I am planning on making a lot of money to take care of them because they are getting on in years."

Generally, grandchildren are thankful for the grandparents' intervention (Dolbin-MacNab and Keiley, 2009). In Canada, grandparents who single-handedly assume the financial responsibility of their grandchildren tend to be younger, healthier, and more educated than grandparents who live with their adult children and grandchildren (Milan and Hamm, 2003). In contrast, in the U.S., those who raise one or more grandchildren tend to be poorer than the average for their age group, more often unemployed, and less educated. In Strawbridge and colleagues' (1997) longitudinal study, many of these grandparents had experienced negative life events in their own past, such as problems with marriages, finances, and health. The life course of many of these caregiving grandparents had differed from that of other grandparents for several decades, probably as a result of poverty. This is an example of how the consequences of poverty carry through the generations—from the grandparents to their children and their grandchildren, and back to the grandparents again.

Being raised by a grandparent is a generally reasonable alternative for children, but it is a more problematic one for the grandparents (Burnette, 1999; Smith and Hancock, 2010). This is especially so when they are middle-aged and are encountering high demands from several generations as well as employment (Sands and Goldberg-Glen, 2000), or when the child care is very demanding. A study in China indicates that grandparental health may deteriorate (Chen and Liu, 2012). In fact, non-retired grandparents who take in a grandchild are far more likely to remain employed (Wang and Marcotte, 2007) and they can now claim EI (Employment Insurance) in Canada. Jendrek (1993) has studied the impact that this caregiving role has on grandparents' lifestyles, especially the changes that grandparents have to bring to their own lives, the dreams they have to postpone or abandon altogether, and the physical and emotional demands that such a role places on them to the detriment of their health (Bachman and Chase-Lansdale, 2005). Support groups now exist for foster grandparents; these groups constitute an indicator of changing times (Beltran, 2001).

THE DEATH OF ADULTS' PARENTS

As they age, parents are transformed into patriarchs and matriarchs. When their health falters, their role vis-à-vis their children changes. A transitory period often occurs during which the elderly parent, generally the mother, may reside in a long-term care facility. At that stage, the older person may renegotiate her sense of self in terms of what it means to be old and healthy, as one adult describes it:

> "My mother is 90 and she is totally dependent for her care as she cannot stand up or walk, has Parkinson's in her hands, is in a wheelchair. But she thinks of herself as healthy because she has no illness, no cancer or heart problem, even though she is on medications. She is happy and accepts her dependency with good grace and considers herself lucky. Ten years ago, she would have felt very sorry for a person in her situation."

Even though middle-aged and young senior adults fully expect their parents to die, this is an event that represents a transition both in their own individual lives and in the life course of their family system (Rossi and Rossi, 1990): The mantle is passed on to the next generation of older adult children who, if they themselves are grandparents, form a new branch of the family, each with the generations that descend from them. The very large family reunions that used to take place around the now deceased generation become smaller gatherings as the grandparent couples or singles head their own extended, but smaller, families separately from those of their siblings.

Compared to the past, children and parents have a longer relationship because of an increase in life expectancy (Connidis, 2010). This means that both generations go through family transitions together or witness each other's transitions more often than in the early 1940s, for instance. A century ago, many parents did not even live long enough to see all their children marry (Martel and Bélanger, 2000). Most now do and even watch their children become parents; an increasing proportion see them become grandparents (Silverstein and Long, 1998). Thus, the relationship is not only longer but it also involves more shared life transitions than in the past.

The end result is that adults, particularly females, have a more extended period of time during which to identify with their parents and delay the rupture of the knot by death than in the past. The death of an elderly parent is equally momentous among all ethnic groups, but is expressed differently by men and women (Umberson, 2003). However, this death was probably a more significant passage in previous centuries when people's life expectancy was much shorter: The first generation left young adults and even dependent children orphaned, and the remaining spouses often quickly remarried, especially fathers.

CONCLUSIONS: LIFE COURSE, ECONOMY, AND PERSONALITY IN THE PARENT-CHILD RELATIONSHIP

The parent-child relationship is best examined within the context of the life course of the two generations involved (Hareven, 2000). Out of the child's relationship with his or her parents is born the adolescent relationship and from both flow the adult child-parent involvement, closeness, or conflict and distancing. In addition, the life course is a road that is paved with both risks and successes, much of which originate from the extra-familial environment. Therefore, social and cultural changes as well as social policies and economic situations can influence both the quality of parenting (which, in turn, influences child socialization and development to some extent), children's behaviours and attitudes, and the parent-child relationship. Some of these social forces include peer groups, the media, as well as economic and cultural requirements that, for instance, currently lead to delays in departure of young adults from the parental home.

We consider the effect of personalities both on the quality of parenting and on the parent-child interaction. Parents' and children's personalities influence their behaviours and their subsequent reactions to one another. Children's personalities influence their familial environment just as do their parents' personalities. Personalities are the result of the interaction between nature and nurture and, in turn, the familial environment is also the result of this interaction between genetic and environmental forces, which are experienced over the generations. The future in the study of the parent-child relationship lies in the recognition of the combination of economic, political, sociocultural, and genetic influences on family members, a line of inquiry continued in Chapter 11.

Summary

1. The beginning of the parent-child relationship is rooted in the intersection between the infant's personality and needs, the parents' reactions to these needs, the feedback between the two levels of personalities and reactions, as well as the familial environment that they create.

2. The main types of parents' socialization practices are discussed as are their multiple sources. In this interactional perspective, children contribute to the development of their parents' socialization style. The matter of what constitutes proper parenting is analyzed as a social construct within its context.

Research on the consequences of corporal punishment is discussed.

3. The parent-adolescent relationship is largely based on social definitions of adolescence. Adolescence is a social construct or a cultural invention rather than an unavoidable and universal period of stress and turmoil. Parent-adolescent conflict is discussed.

4. Eras or time periods as well as the human qualities that are valued within each make it easier or more difficult for parents to influence their adolescents. Currently, the media are a key player in this domain.

5. Children's peers affect their relationship with their parents through the peer group spillover effect, the cross-pressures they place, and the relative solidarity of peer subcultures.

6. The factors influencing the postponement of the passage into full adult independence are presented. Young adults often remain home longer than was the case in the 1980s. Some adult children also return home. Coresidence is discussed. Within the life course perspective, as children age and acquire new roles, the parent-child relationship generally remains strong, particularly with mothers. Several demographic variables contribute to the frequency of interaction. Values, attitudes, and lifestyles may also be important variables.

7. Overall, elderly parents help their adult children substantially. Adult children help their elderly parents who become frail or disabled, but few actually undertake their entire care. The concept of burden is discussed as a social construct. Daughters provide more help, particularly of a personal nature.

8. The grandparent role is not as culturally scripted. Grandmothers are kin-keepers and a substantial number provide some form of care for at least one grandchild on a regular basis. Some grandparents raise grandchildren who are in their custody. There are attendant stressors to this situation.

9. The parent-child relationship has to be examined within the context of the personalities involved and the sociocultural situation in which the family is embedded.

Analytical Questions

1. How is social constructionism utilized in this chapter?
2. What does interactionism help explain in this chapter?
3. Are parents more or less influential in their children's lives than was the case in the 1950s, for instance?
4. Is there a new construction of young adulthood in the making? If yes, what are the consequences on family dynamics?
5. On the whole, which generation of adults, parents or adult children, benefits the most from the other in our type of society?
6. What does the theory of behaviour genetics contribute to explain in this chapter?
7. How can you link some of the contents of this chapter with some in Chapters 5 and 6?

CHAPTER 11

Siblings: Relationships, Nature and Nurture

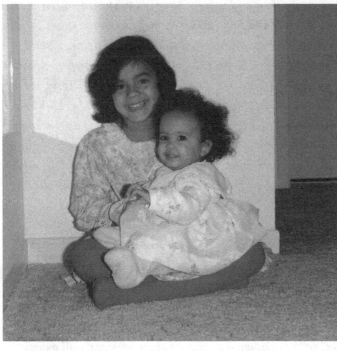

Anne-Marie Ambert

OUTLINE

The Sibling Relationship Begins
Consequences of Family Size
Multiple Births

Child and Adolescent Sibling Relationships
Sibling Influence
Supportive Sibling Relationships

Differential Parental Treatment
Birth Order and Developmental Stage as
Factors
Gender as a Factor
Developmental Impact of Differential
Treatment

Adult and Stepsibling Relationships

Nature and Nurture
How Can Siblings Be So Different?
Twins as Natural Experiments

The Contexts of Parental Influence

Conclusions: Nature and Nurture

Summary
Analytical Questions

At age seven, my family structure became more complex: I inherited four European siblings, whom I had never met, ranging in age from 15 to 21. At the time, I was merely affected by the mixed blessing that such a drastic family restructuring brings to the life of a child and especially that of her 30-year-old mother. I was too little to appreciate how dislocated these fun-loving young people's lives had been. Their mother had died when they were small; my father had left them in the care of two of his sisters and had moved to Canada. When the Second World War arrived, they had to flee to the southwest of France. Finally, two years after the war was over, they emigrated to Canada where they had to lead a more modest middle-class life shared with small siblings, one of whom had yet to be born.

Besides a large age gap, there were then and remain to this day striking differences between my father's two sets of children. For example, only one in the older group became a professional, whereas all of us younger ones did. We "little ones" had several advantages: We had stable lives and an energetic mother, we benefited from stimulating older siblings, and our parents had a very happy marriage. True, we all shared one absent-minded, intellectual father who looked upon all of his children with some sort of "benign" annoyance. Nevertheless, whereas he was absent when the older children were growing up, we in the second group were able to prod him into helping us with our Latin and French homework, in which he would become as involved as we were. This engagement created bonds, stimulated our intellect . . . and led to great marks in school!

Our father had a gift for writing that ran in his family. A strange "coincidence" emerged: We children, so different from one another in terms of personality, life choices, and educational level, share one characteristic—all of us write well; five took up writing as a job in one form or another, and four of these have published books (in three different languages). This peculiar aspect of my adult family profile is certainly responsible for my awareness of the combined impact of environmental and genetic forces on family dynamics and human development. I have no doubt that some of us were born (genetic) with this gift, but we would not have been able to develop it had our parents and the cultural tradition in our family not encouraged us in this direction.

This autobiographical vignette—my own—introduces one of the key aspects of this chapter: the combined effect of the environment, including the familial one, and of genetic inheritance in the development of siblings' life course. Almost 80 percent of Canadians have at least one sibling—although this percentage will diminish over time, as it also does across the world, because of low fertility rates. Still, it is a very important type of familial relationship, which also generally outlasts the parent-child relationship (McDaniel, 2009; McHale et al., 2012).

When children reach adulthood, the sibling relationship in industrialized societies, particularly those of western cultures, becomes discretionary. That is, continuing the relationship is a matter of choice and is secondary to the spousal and parent-child ones. In contrast, in other societies, continuation of the sibling relationship into adulthood is the norm and is of fundamental importance for a family's integration into society at large. Sibling relationships, particularly between two brothers or two sisters, may actually be more consequential than their relationship with a spouse, both at the social and economic level (Ogbomo, 1997). Still, in Canada, most adults perceive that they have obligations toward their siblings (Connidis, 2010).

THE SIBLING RELATIONSHIP BEGINS

The transition to a two-child family is one that parents have to help the first-born negotiate (Kramer and Ramsburg, 2002). Children who are between two and four years of age are particularly affected, because their entire life has been spent as their parents' only child. Children who are older are more competent cognitively and can understand the situation better. Parents may be able to appeal to their sense of being "grown up," as explained by this student:

> "What I like best to remember when I was 5 is the birth of my little sister. I had wanted a brother to play hockey with but you can't be too choosy. What I liked best was that my parents made me feel so important, so grown up to be the big brother. I just loved to take care of her even though the novelty wore off after a while."

Generally, whether the first-born child recognizes it or not, the birth of a second baby transforms his or her life entirely, as well as that of the family as a system. A new set of interactions is created, those between siblings. *Each successive child enters the family at a different moment in its history and contributes to changing its environment* (Zajonc, 2001). Furthermore, the family's economic resources available per person diminish with each new child. However, with the arrival of a second baby, the older child generally has a lower chance of experiencing a parental divorce: Happily married couples are more likely to add another child to their family than couples who are not happy together.

With the arrival of each baby, parents spend more time interacting with their children altogether, but they have less time for each child individually. With a second child, parents can no longer maintain their exclusive relationship with the first-born, a factor that may become paramount in this child's life experience if he or she feels a loss of status as well as affection. The survival requirements of an infant are more urgent and constant than those of an older sibling. As a result, parents give more attention to younger than older children. With the arrival of the second child, the mother-child relationship often becomes less affectionate, particularly if the spacing between the two children is small and the family experiences a reduction in income per person. As a result of all these and other changes, the first-born child occasionally suffers from a variety of problems of adjustment, including anxiety, clinging behaviour, bed-wetting, and even aggressiveness.

The child's reaction to the baby's arrival is largely tailored by his or her personality as well as by the steps that parents undertake to reassure and involve him or her. Dunn (1994) points out that small children who are intense and less adaptable react more negatively to the baby's arrival than children with a sunnier and more content disposition. The former may even protest when the mother pays attention to the infant. The following amusing anecdote from a student portrays this situation:

> *"When my little sister was born, I was three, and when my parents brought her home I asked them to return her to the hospital. I did not like to see all the fuss over this little red faced creature that cried all the time. Then one day, seeing that my parents were not returning her, I tried to wrap her in gift wrapping paper and my mother caught me in the act. It's funny to think of this now because we are best friends and often laugh over it. My sister has had my mother tell this story over and over: She just loves it."*

Such an older child's reaction to the newborn often becomes part of the family culture: It constitutes a story everyone loves to hear.

Additional infants benefit from the experience that parents have acquired with their earlier-born children. Many first-born young adults, looking back on their past, feel that their parents acquired a great deal of skills at their expense:

> *"If I could relive my life, I would have wanted to be the second oldest child in my family. I disliked having to be the first to 'test the waters.' I wish that I had had an older sibling whose errors would have served as warning posts on what lay ahead. . . . I was a learning experience for my parents."*

Obviously, the education that the first-born provides parents, while perhaps to the advantage of subsequent children, is often recalled as an injustice by the older child. During the newborn's first months, the infant's schedule is quite different from that of the older child, especially if the latter is already at school. With four years or more of spacing between the two children, the parents' relationship with the first-born may continue to be exclusive during a portion of the day as the baby sleeps. With this much spacing, each sibling is in a way an only child, and little competition takes place, especially if the older one likes to play at surrogate parenting:

> *"Surely the happiest memory I have of my mid-teens is when my mother announced that she was pregnant. This took a bit to get used to, you know the idea that your parents are 'doing it.' . . . Then the best times arrived with my little sister. Oh how we loved that baby. . . . my mother was happy because she had less work to do as I always volunteered to take care of Kathy. . . . Now Kathy is seven and the brightest kid on the block because we provided her with an adult environment and each one of us in the family taught her different skills. . . . We read to her, made her read when she was three and took her skating, biking, rollerblading, swimming. She became incredibly well coordinated. She is also very sociable because despite all the spoiling she got from us older sisters and our cousins, we still insisted on good manners and no temper tantrums or anything of the sort. She had a whole batch of parents to raise her."*

In terms of educational achievement, children, particularly the eldest one, do less well, on average, when they are closely spaced (Buckles and Munnich, 2012). For instance, parents have less individual time for two children who are close in age, because they essentially follow the same routine. When one child is several years older, however, the two children have different needs at different times and receive more individual attention. The older child is an only child longer and the younger child benefits both from having a sibling who is more developed and from parents who have more time for him or her.

Consequences of Family Size

In terms of number of children, those from large sibling groups generally do not do as well at school, on average, as children from small families (Downey, 2001). Neither do they advance as much professionally later on as do adults coming from smaller families. These results become less salient but nevertheless remain when parents' social class is taken into consideration (Marks, 2006): Even upper-class parents provide fewer resources per child in large families than in small families (Fingerman et al., 2009). The concept used to explain this family size effect is the **dilution of parental resources*** (Downey, 2001). In effect, this means that parents have fewer resources for each child individually, whether in terms of time, attention, and even economic means. In fact, mothers are less individually responsive to their children in larger families (Onyskiw and Hayduk, 2001). Therefore, a large sibling group often dilutes the quality of the home environment available to each child. This occurs even more when children are closely spaced in a large family, because they interact more among themselves and have less adult attention; they also learn less than they would with one or two much older siblings or alone with their parents. Aggressiveness also appears more often in larger families, and children leave home earlier than in smaller families (Beaupré et al., 2006).

But, of course, there are plenty of exceptions to the rule and there are large families, particularly well-to-do ones, where all the children do very well at school or become high achievers in their professions later on. These families may benefit from other resources, such as the help of relatives and the presence of a large community of parents' friends and colleagues who contribute to stimulate children's intellectual development and serve as role models. The extended family increases resources and compensates for the dilution of the resources at the nuclear level. These families, in other words, have more **social capital*** to offer each individual child.

Further, as Zajonc and Mullally (1997) pointedly remark, there are advantages to large family size that are not measured by the research perspectives emphasizing achievement. For instance, it may well be that siblings growing up in a large family are more "affiliative, more affectionate, good leaders, less prone to depression, or otherwise healthier" (Zajonc and Mullally, 1997:697). They may be less individualistic and more cooperative. They are used to sharing everything and adjusting to a far greater number of personalities. They can compromise and overlook frustrating situations. However, the only large-scale study on this topic has not found any family size advantage in terms of sociability and need to be with others (Blake et al., 1991). Downey and Condron (2004) reported that having one or two siblings was positively related to better social skills; additional siblings did not provide more advantage. Finally, it should be pointed out that this research is of western inspiration. Studies in Asian, African, or Latin American countries might yield different results.

On the other side of the equation, it is equally possible that some siblings in a large family suffer from a lack of individual recognition, feel oppressed by the social pressure within their intimate group, and are hampered by a lack of privacy. Such persons may adapt by growing up to be individualistic and may even distance themselves from the family group. However, despite having had less individual attention, there is no indication that adult children from large families are less attached to their parents nor their parents to them than in small families.

Multiple Births

One aspect of the sibling relationship that is not sufficiently understood is the relationship that exists between twins and "multiples." As we see later, twins are much studied but are so within the perspective of behaviour genetics rather than simply as an interest in the relationship itself. Twins who are identical are fairly constant in the population: Dissimilar twins, also called dizygotic or DZ, are more related to heredity, thus can run in families (Hoekstra et al., 2008). *Normally*, twins and higher-order births occur in the population at the rate of 1 or 2 percent: one set of twins per 90 births; one set of triplets per 9,000 births; one set of quadruplets per 500,000 births. However, after 1972, triplet births increased by 156 percent, quadruplets by 386 percent, and higher-order births by 182 percent among white women, who constitute the majority of fertility clinics' clientele. In 1995 alone, 57 American infants were born who were quintuplets or sextuplets, although not all survived.

Women who have recourse to fertility drugs have a 25 percent chance of giving birth to more than one baby. Furthermore, women are more likely to release multiple eggs when they are older. Delaying parenthood consequently causes a rise in the number of multiple births. After the 1997 birth of the McCaughey septuplets, the less publicized 1998 birth of octuplets, and in 2009, the "Octo-Mom," the medical establishment belatedly began considering the ethical ramifications of fertility treatments that allow the release of several ova or the implantation of multiple embryos. These pregnancies place mothers' lives in serious danger.

Nearly all multiple births have two immediate health consequences for infants: The fetuses have to compete for scarce resources in the womb, and a majority of the infants are born **prematurely** because the womb becomes too crowded. Twins therefore have low birth weight, and babies of higher-order births can have extremely low birth weights—as little as or less than half a kilogram. These infants are then at a far higher risk of neonatal death than singletons. The danger period may last several months, during which the infants are kept in neonatal intensive care units. Prematurely born infants are also far more likely than others to suffer from neurological deficits, whether learning disabilities or muscle coordination problems, although most of them make remarkable progress—and most twins and triplets develop well. For parents, twin and multiple births require a far greater adjustment to parenting than does a single birth (Golombok et al., 2007): more time demands; fewer economic resources available per capita; the necessity to seek and accept help, even from total strangers; and more health-related concerns. All of these factors combined

Twins and higher-order births occur more frequently than in the recent past because of fertility treatment and delayed conception. Their relationship and the relationships they have with their parents and other siblings in the family as well as with their peers need to be researched.

Wong Sze Fei/Fotolia

make it imperative that we learn more about the impact that such an event has on the life of an older sibling and on the various sibling relationships that occur in these families compared to those of "regular" ones.

CHILD AND ADOLESCENT SIBLING RELATIONSHIPS

At the personal level, sibling relationships are determined by children's characteristics, their personality similarities and differences, parents' behaviour toward the children, and siblings' perception of such. Given that most of these factors are reasonably stable through each childhood, one can expect a certain degree of stability in the sibling bond. Yet, as children age, relationships can also change (Richmond et al., 2005). As well, the availability of peers as alternate playmates in later childhood and early adolescence is likely to bring change in the sibling relationship. Generally, brothers and sisters whose personalities are compatible or complementary experience greater connectedness than those who are temperamentally incompatible.

Furman and Lanthier (1996) gave personality tests and a relationship questionnaire to 56 triads of mothers and two siblings, one age nine and the other age 11. They found that it was the older child's personality that more strongly affected the distribution of power in the relationship. The dimensions of conscientiousness and agreeableness, particularly in the older child, were strong predictors of harmony and lack of power struggle. Dunn and colleagues (1994) found that older siblings tend to be fairly consistent over time in their behaviour toward their younger brother or sister: Aggressiveness or friendliness persists. This means that, in some families, younger children spend their entire childhood with a friendly and supportive sibling, whereas in others, they are in a relationship that is hostile, disparaging, and physically aggressive. The impact on child development may be substantial, but it is a question that is rarely raised in research, because theories focus on parental rather than **sibling effect**

(McHale et. al., 2012). *It is possible that negative effects that have been attributed to parents and to their harsh or rejecting treatment actually result from the rough handling that a child has received from siblings or from siblings and parents together* (Richmond et al., 2005). Such a possibility makes sense from the perspective of genetics alone: Intolerant and irritable parents may produce some offspring who are like them and may jointly have a negative impact on the sibling who is different from the outset.

In contrast, younger siblings show less stability of behaviour toward their older siblings: They adapt their style of interaction in order to secure the older child's goodwill. The older child does not have to adapt, because it is the younger ones who do. Overall, older siblings tend to be more domineering, and younger ones are forced to be more compliant in the relationship. Putting these variables together, it is therefore not surprising that, in terms of development, the older child usually, but not always, has a stronger effect on the younger one than vice versa (Dunn et al., 1994).

By the time they were 12 or 13 years old, first-born boys in a longitudinal study by Dunn (1996) reported a more distant relationship with their younger siblings than did first-born girls. This difference was, in part, explained as a result of the older boys' growing ties with their peer group. As well, the second-born children were becoming more assertive and more willing to disagree with the older boys, and this in turn contributed to the cooler climate. These pitfalls were less in evidence with older sisters. Indeed, **girls** maintain more intimate bonds with both siblings and peers than do boys (Kim et al., 2006). Thus, females begin at an early age their function of **kin-keepers** and emotional workers, as described in Chapters 9 and 10.

Another interesting aspect in the study of siblings is that they do not perceive their relationship similarly (Whiteman and Christiansen, 2008). Dunn and McGuire (1994:120) mention that only 23 percent of the siblings in their sample reported a degree of closeness similar to that reported by their brother or sister. This discrepancy may be explained by the age and gender differences among siblings. Smaller children may be more susceptible to feeling left out by older siblings who, for their part, may be more involved with peers and largely ignore the younger ones. Girls may find their brothers less supportive, whereas boys may find it "normal" to ignore their sisters who are "just girls."

Sibling Influence

As we have seen in the previous chapter, peers are a powerful source of influence on children and adolescents. In contrast, sibling influence and pressure—as well as sibling abuse—are rarely acknowledged in research (Chapter 13). McHale and Crouter (1996) report that preteens spend 33 percent of their out-of-school hours with siblings versus 13 percent with friends. These numbers alone should predict a great deal of sibling influence. What information do researchers have?

Overall, when an older sibling is competent, the younger one is positively affected (Brody and Murry, 2001). Contrariwise, when an older sibling is aggressive, the other tends to follow suit, even at a very young age (Baillargeon et al., 2002). But this is less likely to happen with pairs of older brothers and younger sisters (Williams et al., 2007). Thus, siblings are important agents of socialization to one another in this

Kablonk Micro/Fotolia

Sibling relationships are more important to each child's well-being and development, particularly the younger one's, than is generally believed. Not enough research has been devoted to the sibling role and influence when children are growing up.

respect, and probably in many others that have yet to be researched. The aggressive interaction style of the older boys in some families trains the younger boys to be equally coercive (Criss and Shaw, 2005). There is a significant level of concordance among boys in a family in terms of delinquency: When one boy is delinquent, there is a good chance that the other one also is. The same has been found for girls (Slomkowski et al., 2001). Further, when one adolescent abuses alcohol, the other is at risk of doing so.

In terms of sexuality, Widmer (1997) reports that older siblings have an effect on the timing of first intercourse among their younger brothers and sisters. Adolescent girls who have a sexually active or childbearing adolescent sister, as well as similar peers, tend to be more sexually active, even when other family variables, such as education, are taken into consideration. East (1999) reasons that a birth to a teenager may make it more difficult for mothers to supervise their younger children, as the grandchild increases the new grandmother's workload. Brothers are even more influential than sisters in the timing of sexual intercourse. When older brothers remain chaste longer, their behaviour may reinforce parental teachings on sexual restraint by giving them validity in the mind of younger siblings. However, East et al. (1993) point out that this fraternal influence is less important than parental attitudes and teachings on this topic. In summary, these results together indicate that older siblings act as **role models** for younger ones (Jenkins-Tucker et al., 2001). As well, the sharing of activities leads to an indirect form of influence. A complementary explanation is that siblings share certain personality characteristics that make them equally vulnerable or equally resilient to life's circumstances.

Sibling influence can be compounded by the sharing of friends. During adolescence, and more in adulthood, siblings' similarity of characteristics seems to increase friendliness and contact as well as the sharing of friends. In turn, frequency of positive contact contributes to an increased resemblance between siblings over the long term, especially with regard to ideas, values, and leisure activities. One would expect that the sharing of a prosocial peer group by siblings enhances their own prosocial behaviours. This, in turn, greatly facilitates parental duties as these prosocial children are probably easier to raise. This network of peers becomes a form of **social capital** to both parents and children. Prosocial peers are also more likely to have authoritative parents; when a group of peers have similarly oriented parents, the burden of supervision is lessened for each individual set of parents, given that they all participate to some degree in the monitoring process. This refers us back to the concepts of the **effective community** and group or collective socialization.

By the same token, when siblings who are already predisposed to deviance share a delinquent or aggressive peer group, this raises the chance that they will commit delinquent acts. Consequently, parents must increasingly monitor such offspring and set more limits on their activities and whereabouts. This demanding level of supervision and alertness may go beyond the abilities of many parents, as indicated in the following passage from a female student's autobiography. It graphically illustrates the family dynamics that may occur during adolescence when siblings are closely spaced, get along well, and encourage one another and peers in activities that parents disapprove of:

> *"The problem with my family at that age is that there were four adolescent children, two boys, two girls, and we actually ran the house. There was nothing that our parents could do to control us. If we wanted some friends over for the night, we'd hide them and my parents would not notice. Anyway, they hated to come in our rooms which were an absolute mess. . . . My brother got a girl pregnant when he was only 15 and my sister became a drug addict at 16. The other two of us turned out all right, which is amazing considering the bad example we got from the other two and the fact that we used to encourage their misbehaviour, side with them, and help them out when in trouble. We had absolutely no solidarity with our parents. It was just among us children, as we were one or two years apart. Our second solidarity was for our friends."*

Supportive Sibling Relationships

The literature on the family is by necessity often oriented toward the study of problems rather than daily dynamics. One of the consequences of this orientation is that there is relatively little research on supportive sibling relationships during childhood and adolescence (Jenkins-Tucker et al., 2001). The major exceptions pertain to brothers and sisters whose parents are conflictual, divorce, or remarry, and to children who have a sibling suffering from a disability. Indeed, sibling support is very important to Canadian children who have disabilities, as most live at home: Parents usually shoulder the responsibility of caring for or coordinating their care well into adulthood. A cooperative sibling can greatly lighten parents' burden; parents often develop particularly warm feelings for that helpful adult child, as illustrated in this situation:

> *"My older sister is retarded and has some heart problems so that my relationship with her is one of role reversal. She is five years older than me but I take care of her a lot to give some breathing space to my parents. When I was a bit younger . . . once in a while our needs clashed with hers or the demands our parents placed on us because of her. She does look normal and my mother often*

asked us to take her out with us to see a movie or something of the sort. Jackie loved it but it was different for us because we wanted to be with our friends and felt unpleasantly 'special.'. . . My parents really appreciate what we do for her and for them because they say that they trust that we will take care of her after they are gone, which is the biggest worry that parents of delayed adult children have. My brother and I will take care of her for sure although thankfully our parents are still young. But I think that of the two of us I may end up having to do most of the caring because I noticed that my brother does less than he used to do—he is a male!"

However, in reality, there is no indication that siblings become the primary caregivers of their disabled brother or sister when parents are no longer able to do so. Many of these disabled individuals have to turn outside the family for help. Seltzer and colleagues (1997) found that adults had a higher level of well-being and a closer relationship with a sibling with a mental delay than a sibling with a mental illness. Siblings, like parents, are affected more negatively by behavioural and attitudinal problems than by intellectual limitations. In other words, adults who experience better psychological well-being are those whose siblings with mental illness are kept at a distance. This also means that the sibling with mental illness receives less support than the one with mental delay, unless the latter also exhibits difficult behaviours. The researchers indicate the necessity of helping "the mentally ill develop less confrontational behaviors with their siblings." Horwitz (1993) also suggests that therapists should encourage adults with emotional problems to develop mutual relationships with their siblings, given that people are more willing to help someone who reciprocates.

During childhood and adolescence, having a brother or sister with special needs or disabilities also carries costs (LeClere and Kowalewski, 1994). The literature is quite unanimous in this respect and the previous student quote illustrates this dilemma (Kilmer et al., 2008). The siblings of special needs children generally get less parental attention because so much is demanded for the care of the affected children. The family can less easily pursue leisure activities than other families, and friends cannot be invited home, lest they disrupt the routine of care. When a sibling with disabilities is aggressive toward the helping child or adolescent, the latter tends to be less well adjusted emotionally.

Overall, among those sibling groups that remain cohesive, mutual support reduces the number of problems experienced when they are exposed to parental conflict. In families with two children, the presence of at least one girl enhances the chance that a cohesive sibling relationship is established (Conger and Conger, 1996). Thus, once again, children's gender is an important variable.

DIFFERENTIAL PARENTAL TREATMENT

As seen earlier, parents treat children differently depending on each child's age. The focus of this section is on children and adolescents. However, differential parental treatment is probably even more common in adulthood. In fact, Suitor and Pillemer (2000) have found that children's personal problems resulting from their own acts, such as drug use or criminality, are related to a weaker bond with parents. Thus, as

Parents' Knowledge of Each Sibling's Daily Activities

Crouter and colleagues (1999) wanted to see if parents would be more aware of the older sibling's or the younger sibling's daily life, and whether this knowledge would depend on the children's sex, personality, as well as parents' employment hours. Letters were sent to the homes of fourth- and fifth-graders in 16 central Pennsylvania school districts. The 203 participating families were headed by two parents with at least two children, and the second sibling had to be younger by one to four years.

In a first step, family members were interviewed at home separately; parents and children also filled out questionnaires. Questions were read aloud when children's literacy skills required it. In a second step, both parents and children were interviewed over the phone on several different evenings during a two- to three-week period. Parents and children were queried about their daily activities. An interesting aspect of this research consisted of questions designed to measure parents' knowledge of their children's activities:

- Did child X have English homework today? What was the assignment?
- Did child X watch TV, videos, or movies at home today? What did he or she watch?
- Did child X have any conflict or disagreement with a friend today? Which friend?
- Was child X outside the home at 4 p.m. today? Where was he or she?

children age and make life choices, differential treatment from parents may become more prevalent, although not necessarily more visible to the children themselves.

The younger child is favoured by both parents in some circumstances, yet the older one is in others. It is not uncommon, either, that by adolescence mothers are closer to one identical twin than the other (Crosnoe and Elder, 2002). Fathers show more interest in sons, particularly first-borns, and in children who have a more expressive personality (Crouter et al., 1999; see Family Research 11.1 for other aspects of this study). Parents who are stressed by poverty or marital conflict or who are depressed are more likely to treat one child less well than the other. Differential treatment can involve chore assignments as well as privileges (Tucker et al., 2003) and differential child behaviours to which parents react (Lam et al., 2012a). There is also some evidence that parents' personalities play at least a small role in differential treatment of siblings (Brown, D. T., et al., 2012).

Birth Order and Developmental Stage as Factors

A longitudinal study showed that mothers treat children in a manner appropriate to each age level, *so that both children are treated similarly at a given age*, yet are treated differently in the *present* because they are of different ages (Dunn et al., 1986; Whiteman et al., 2003). But the correlations between the maternal treatment of the children at the same age are not perfect. This suggests, first, that mothers adapt their behaviour to each child's individuality and developmental rhythm. Second, the later-born child enters the family system at a different point in the **family's life course**. The mother is now a more experienced parent; she may also be busier or more tired when the younger child is two years old than she was when the older one was the same age a few years earlier. This difference in treatment could also be explained by any other factor that may have changed in the child's and mother's lives and environment. For instance, when child B reaches age two, the parents may have separated and the mother may be under more (or less) stress than she was when child A was age two. Her higher or lower level of stress could affect her parenting vis-à-vis the younger child.

To sum up, it seems that mothers tend to treat their children similarly at a given level of child maturity. But they are not necessarily as consistent toward the same child while he or she is growing up because children change with age, and some become easier or more difficult; as well, the parental context evolves. In some families, it is obvious that parents treat their children differently, not simply because of age, but because of birth order: A certain favouritism may exist for a younger child and a more adult relationship with the older one (Suitor and Pillemer, 2007). As well, one offspring may be less adaptive or need more encouragement or structure.

Information concerning parenting consistency during adolescence and later ages is lacking. As children grow older, it is quite possible that parents, or one of the two parents, treat them increasingly differently so as to respond to their developmental needs (Lam et al., 2012a). Children may contribute to this differential treatment as they try to differentiate themselves from their siblings in order to assert their own individuality.

Gender as a Factor

Gender is one of the most important variables in child socialization (Kimmel, 2000). Parents raise boys and girls to assume different roles in society, although families vary in the extent to which they socialize boys and girls differently. Overall, fathers are more likely than mothers to make a distinction between sons and daughters and are generally more involved with sons. In the student autobiographies, parents are reported to be treating sons and daughters increasingly differently as they age. Women students repeatedly complained that adolescent brothers were given much more freedom than they had been allowed at the same age. In some ethnic groups, a slightly older brother or even a younger one chaperones a sister whenever she goes out, especially in the evenings. Causing even more resentment is the fact that these girls have to do more housework, age for age, than their brothers, and some even have to clean up after them:

> "In my family, there are two standards: one for my brother and one for my sister and I. We girls do everything in the house and work to pay for school whereas my brother does nothing and works to pay for his car and dates. I really resent it even though I try to rationalize it this way, that my parents come from a non-Christian background, but it does not erase the unpleasant reality. People who immigrate here should leave behind their unpleasant backgrounds and adapt to what families do here which is by and large to treat boys and girls the same."

> "My brother gets to go out without even telling my parents where he is going. My sister and I have to tell my parents everything, where we are going, what time we will be home and so on."

The more males are valued in a culture, the greater the difference in parental treatment (Papp, 2010). (In fact, in some societies experiencing scarcity, sons are given the best food while daughters go hungry—Oster, 2009.) However, it is possible that, in large families, parents have less time to react to each child's gender and accordingly treat their offspring more similarly than do parents with fewer children. Or, alternatively, they may treat all the boys one way and all the girls another way. In some instances, fathers feel closer to sons and mothers to daughters because they share same-sex interests, aspirations, and chores.

Developmental Impact of Differential Treatment

Volling (1997) makes a distinction between *differential favouritism*, which has negative consequences for family relationships, and *differential discipline*, which is age appropriate. As well, differential parental treatment that does not appear fair to children causes jealousy and resentment on the part of the less favoured child, and may well give rise to feelings of entitlement on the part of the preferred child, who becomes the little king or queen. The less favoured offspring may become more distant or express his or her resentment toward the preferred one (Shanahan, L., et al., 2008). These negative feelings may be the result of justified jealousy or, alternatively, it may be the result of the more difficult personality of the less favoured child, who behaves less pleasantly toward siblings and parents alike. As well, negative feelings on the part of parents may spill over into sibling relationships (Jenkins et al., 2005a). Indeed, favouritism by mothers in childhood results in a weaker sibling bond; this perceived favouritism continues to influence the sibling relationship into adulthood (Shanahan, L., et al., 2008; Siennick, 2013). As Suitor et al. (2009) point out, this demonstrates "continuity in family processes across the life course" (p. 1036).

The sibling who receives the most favourable parental treatment seems to do better than the other (Richmond et al., 2005). Daniels (1987) reports that the sibling who enjoys more affection from the father has more ambitious educational and vocational goals. Children who are more controlled by their mother or perceive receiving less affection than their siblings are more likely to be anxious or depressed. These children also tend to be more difficult. Differential parental treatment alone may not produce the entirety of these reported outcomes (Feinberg et al., 2000). Rather, the **interactional perspective** suggests a bidirectional causality. For instance, a difficult child may lead parents to become more controlling or, yet, more permissive (Moilanen et al., 2009), especially when compared to his or her siblings (Lam et al., 2012a). Or such children may be treated more harshly (Richmond et al., 2005). It may also be that a more ambitious child attracts paternal attention and encouragement. That is, his or her ambitions create or *evoke* the favoured attention rather than vice versa. It is also possible that it is the perception and interpretation of differences rather than the actual differential treatment that cause the problems for the child who feels deprived.

In great part, except for gender roles, parents respond to their children according to their personalities and behaviours, as seen in the preceding chapter. Thus, Bank et al. (1996) found that parents behave differently with a boy who is aggressive and oppositional than with his easy-going sibling. In their experimental study, one group of families had both a difficult and an easy-going boy while the other set of families had two "easy" children. The researchers observed family interactions when the difficult son was present and then when he was absent. The two samples showed different parental treatment of their children when the difficult boy was included. But when only the parents and the easy-going child were considered together, there was no difference between the two samples of families in the way parents treated their children. This result illustrates the impact of a child on family dynamics and on the creation of differential parental treatment.

It would be important to study parents' differential treatment in the **context** of other variables, such as marital happiness, number and spacing of offspring, and marital status (Jenkins et al., 2005b). It is not known, for instance, if differential treatment has a more negative impact in a poor quality environment or in a more privileged environment, or in families that have children of only one sex or of both. Moreover, differential treatment may produce effects that vary according to parental personality, overall level of parenting involvement, and relative parental power within the family. For example, Lam et al. (2012a) have found that fathers may be more reactive to children's unique behaviours because fathers' role may be less engaged and voluntary and "therefore more conditioned by offspring's characteristics." As well illustrated by the following mature student, some children seem to perceive their mother's lower social prominence and "shrug off" her differential behaviours toward them, yet are affected when the father does not treat them equally, however small the slight might be:

> *"At home, I am in a rather unfortunate situation: Although I am always available to the children and am really their maid, when their father is around I am just as good as not there. They hang on to his every word and find him so interesting. He doesn't even have to ask them to do something, they just do it. One or the other children gets very upset if he doesn't talk to him or her or gives unequal treatment. They're like courtesans around a king. Me, what am I? Nothing! So if I yell at one, that one doesn't even notice it. If I give him a compliment, they shrug it off. It has more or less always been like that: My husband is quite the social butterfly, looks good, and is known to a lot of people. In contrast, I am the somewhat mousy wife about whom people wonder, 'Whatever did he find in her?'"*

ADULT AND STEPSIBLING RELATIONSHIPS

Personalities and lifestyles are fairly important in determining the quality of adult sibling bonds, particularly in view of the fact that these relationships are largely optional (Connidis, 2007, 2010). Furthermore, the literature on remarriage has been so focused on problems of adult and child adjustment that little attention has been devoted to the new relationships that are formed among children from the merging families. Not only is there little information on the relationship between stepsiblings, but there is equally little on that between halfsiblings (i.e., when new children are born in a remarriage).

Although there is some research on middle-aged and older siblings, there is still relatively little literature devoted to sibling relationships during the young adult years, after siblings have established their own families, especially during the years of childrearing. Neither is the role and influence of cousins studied, in part because researchers in western societies do not pay as much attention to the extended family system as perhaps they should.

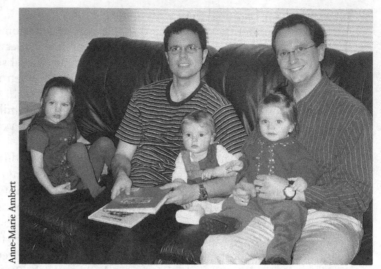

Anne-Marie Ambert

Among adults in North America, proximity increases contact among siblings and the potential for both conflict and closeness. When no other family member lives nearby, proximity also increases the exchange of help between siblings. Different lifestyles and resources can create barriers to closeness (Connidis, 2007). Cicirelli (1996) points out that older persons like to reminisce about the past. They can do so far better with like-minded siblings than with their adult children. Thus, siblings remain important confidants as well as sources of emotional support, especially after widowhood, but are less central in terms of companionship (Campbell et al., 1999; Connidis, 2010). One area of sibling relationships that requires far more research at all age levels pertains to the homosexuality of one sibling, as well as her or his living in a same-sex union (Connidis, 2003b).

We return here to the theme of **gender** in the sibling relationship. Overall, bonds are closer between sisters than between brothers, although there are many exceptions (Spitze and Trent, 2006; Weaver et al., 2004). Further, sisters provide more help to each other as well as to other family members than do brothers (White, 2001); this pattern is more obvious in some ethnic groups than others. For males, a good relationship with their sisters is also important for their morale: Elderly men who have more sisters feel happier and more secure (Cicirelli, 1989). This result probably stems from the greater familial cohesiveness that exists in families that have females and from the nurturing role to which women are socialized. Sisters provide moral support to their brothers and this contributes to the latter's sense of well-being. But sisters do not benefit equally from fraternal support, as brothers have not generally been socialized to be nurturing and supportive.

Siblings are more likely to be supportive of one another when parents are also supportive (Voorpostel and Blieszner, 2008). But, as seen above, differential parental treatment that was perceived to be unfair when the children were growing up often extends its negative consequences into adulthood and is reflected in the siblings' later relationships. In some cases, jealousy continues into old age, even though there never was any factual basis for it—it was simply a matter of perception, which one male student deplores:

"I have never been able to understand why my older brother and sisters are still so jealous of me. It's very painful to me at this age [about 23] because I have never done anything and neither have my parents to attract this attitude. I was sick more often as a child and my parents had to worry about me more. But the older ones had a lot more freedom and they got much more financially: They didn't have to pay for school as I am doing. At my age they all had cars and I don't. I should be the one who is jealous, really. It's just in their heads and it's upsetting because they certainly don't go out of their way to encourage my little nephews and nieces to accept me."

Stepsibling relationships have, on average, a greater potential for conflict (Jenkins et al., 2005b). However, remarriages are often brief and stepchildren do not always live in the same household, so that many of these relationships simply do not have the time or the opportunity to blossom. A nonresidential father's children may feel some degree of animosity toward his new wife's children who live with him. This animosity or jealousy can be provoked by the fact that many nonresident fathers see their own children rarely or do not support them unless forced to by the government:

"My feelings for my father . . . I can't say with 100% certainty that I love him because we have always been his invisible children. . . . I can't stand his wife's children after all those years because they have it all: My father has been very good to them and they've always been in the way, like we can't see him without these two being there and grabbing all the attention."

"So I have a stepsister who is two years older than I am. At first, we hated each other. . . . Now we are not close but we get along quite well now that we don't have to see each other often."

When the remarriage lasts, stepsiblings often become companionable and supportive, and maintain some level of connectedness into adulthood (Anderson, 1999).

"My two stepbrothers were then 2 and 4 years younger than me and they looked up to me so that I soon ended up playing big brother. For a 10-year-old who is rather upset at what has happened to his parents, that was a great thing. We got along famously well and have been a team to this day."

The stepsibling relationship is closer when there are no full siblings. Halfsiblings and stepsiblings may be better able to bond when the type of solidarity that generally exists between two full siblings, whether biological or adopted, is absent. Still, even among older cohorts, more conflict is reported between halfsiblings and stepsiblings than between full siblings, perhaps in part because they have at least one parent they do not share. Halfsiblings and stepsiblings also help one another less in old age than do full siblings. All in all, in adulthood, the longer stepsiblings have lived together as children, the closer the bond. Having lived with one's mother and stepfather also leads to more contact than having lived with one's father and a stepmother—again indicating the salience of relationships that are maintained by a mother: Halfsiblings who share a mother tend to be closer than those who share a father (Bernstein, 1997). This brief presentation highlights the necessity for research in these domains.

NATURE AND NURTURE

As anticipated through the autobiographical vignette at the beginning of the chapter, we now turn to investigate the role that genes and the environment play in human development. We return to the theory of behaviour genetics and, in so doing, we also look into the question of why siblings can be so different.

How Can Siblings Be So Different?

Many studies have documented how dissimilar siblings generally are on at least some important personality characteristics and related behaviours (for review, Horwitz and Neiderhiser, 2011). Everyday experience also presents the reader with many opportunities to observe such differences between two brothers or two sisters who are only one to three years apart. Yet, children in the same family are exposed to a **shared environment*** that includes family structure, family routines and events, values and teachings emphasized by parents, as well as the effects of parents' personalities on family functioning (Lemelin et al., 2007). The traditional socialization perspective predicts that this shared environment should make siblings quite similar in terms of personality characteristics, values, behaviours, and even adult lifestyles. Further-more, each child inherits 50 percent of his or her genetic makeup from the mother and the other 50 percent from the father. Thus, siblings inherit their genetic makeup from the combined gene pool of a same mother and father—hence, one more reason for them to be similar. Why are they not? There are three reasons.

First, siblings who are not identical twins are different because each inherits a different **combination** of their **parents' gene pool**. We should add that the more simi-lar the biological parents are to each other, the more likely it is that siblings will be similar because they may inherit two copies of many genes. (Think of hair colour here.) Second, siblings are different because of the **nonshared environment***, which essentially refers to environmental influences or experiences that differ for each child, including intra-uterine quality, birth accidents, birth order, peers, school experi-ences, and accidents and illnesses that affect one sibling but not the other—and the timing of birth in the family life course (East and Jacobson, 2000; Hareven, 2000). As we have seen, even their own relationship can constitute a nonshared experience: Siblings often treat one another differently.

A third reason why siblings are different is that many transform much of their shared or familial environment into a nonshared one. This occurs when siblings, while partaking together of their shared familial environment, such as parental teach-ings or even divorce, attach **different meanings** (symbolic interactionism) to it because of their individual personalities and what they have learned outside the family. For instance, Dunn and McGuire (1994) compared the impact on siblings of 256 events that had occurred in the families they had observed over a three-year period. These shared events affected the siblings differently in nearly 70 percent of the cases. Thus, only 30 percent of the events produced a common effect.

Let's take the fictive example of two fraternal twins. Although their parents treat them similarly, twin Bob perceives that he receives less love, whereas twin

Harry does not see any difference in the way they are treated. This perceptual gap is the result of twin Bob being more sensitive, anxious, and rebellious than Harry. This perceptual difference produces another consequence: Bob's sense of resentment and then distancing from parents. In effect, because of his reaction, Bob is creating for himself a family climate different from that of his twin. This divergent family climate will become part of their nonshared environment. In turn, this nonshared environment interacts with each twin's predispositions and will create different ways of behaving toward others, including their parents. For instance, Bob becomes even more rebellious and anxious as a result of the nonshared environment he has in great part created—although he has done so unconsciously. In turn, these disparate reactions not only strengthen their personality differences but also create a private environment—that is, one that they do not share with their siblings. This nonshared environment contributes to maintaining or even widening the differences between them.

Such examples fit very well within the perspectives of interactional theories. In summary, siblings are dissimilar to some extent in terms of personalities, appearance, and physical constitution because of a different combination of genes. (By the same token, however, they are more similar among themselves than to unrelated persons of the same age in their neighbourhood.) As well, psychological traits are influenced by several genes combined (polygene*), and the effect of genes can change over time. Second, siblings are also different because of the nonshared environment, such as different friends. And third, their different perceptions of and reactions to their shared environment reinforce their differences and create new ones.

Twins as Natural Experiments

We now expand this discussion to look at the combined factors that contribute to siblings' development. Molecular or biological genetics can occasionally pinpoint exactly which sets of genes are related to specific health conditions, abilities, and certain behaviours (e.g., Guo et al., 2008), as well as psychological vulnerability or susceptibility to negative environments (Brody et al., 2013; Wickrama and O'Neal, 2013). However, until this can be done for more behaviours and personality predispositions, geneticists have to rely on sophisticated statistical guesswork. The best natural experiment that life provides at this point resides in twin and adoption situations (D'Onofrio and Lahey, 2010; Horwitz and Neiderhiser, 2011; Leve et al., 2010b).

The rationale behind research with twins and adopted siblings is to take advantage of degrees of genetic relatedness (Leve et al., 2010a): *Identical twins share all of their genes; fraternal twins and other siblings share 50 percent. Halfsiblings as well as cousins who are the children of identical twins share 25 percent of their genes, while the children of fraternal twins share 12.5 percent.* For their part, stepsiblings and adopted children have no specific genetic background in common—except as human beings (Leve et al., 2010b). The more closely related two persons are genetically, the more likely they are to be similar (Reiss, 2003; see Family Research 11.2). Further, research designs comparing identical twins within a same family allow for the study of the separate and combined role played by genetics, the shared environment,

Potential Problems in Twin Studies

Many studies have, by now, compared pairs of adoptive siblings with pairs of biological siblings, including twins, on various characteristics and behaviours. For our purposes here, we are interested in the potential problems of twin studies. For instance, one can wonder whether it is valid to assume that twins' family environment is equivalent to that of siblings who are not twins. The equivalency assumption is a necessary one if the results of behaviour genetics studies are to be valid. Yet, one can easily see that parenting two or more same-age children (twins) may create a different familial climate, which would violate the assumption of an equivalent family environment.

Furthermore, identical twins may be more likely to copy each other's behaviour than fraternal twins or even just regular siblings. This situation could artificially increase the genetic influence. Twins, particularly when they are identical, are more likely to share a similar environment, which would again contribute to increasing their similarity (Iervolino et al., 2005). Thus, methodological problems may exist in the research on twins and may reduce researchers' ability to draw solid and generalizable conclusions about the role of genetics and environment in human development (Lam et al., 2012a). However, studies of twins reared separately in different families do not suffer from this possible methodological complication.

and the nonshared environment. An interesting extension of the twin experimental approach is well illustrated in a study on family conflict: This research included adult pairs of twins of the same sex, their spouses, and one adolescent child in each unit. This study established that close to 40 percent of family conflict is genetically related (Horwitz et al., 2010).

Thus, researchers "experiment" with degrees of genetic closeness and degrees of shared environments: Twins who have been adopted into separate families present an ideal experimental situation. This particular twin research design is illustrated in Table 11.1. This table is fictive in the sense that the numbers are invented for teaching purposes. However, the numbers presented follow the general line of reasoning of such studies. This table focuses on *personality characteristics* because they, along with cognitive abilities and certain conditions such as reading disability, autism, and schizophrenia, are more likely to be genetically influenced than are lifestyles and activities—and identical twins are very similar in the former respects (Miller, 2012). Other traits depend far more on the available environment, both shared and nonshared (Lemelin et al., 2007). As well, when individuals have extreme characteristics, whether pathologies or gifts, these traits tend to be more heavily influenced by genetics rather than environment (Viding et al., 2005), which does not mean that early intervention cannot help, for instance, in the case of psychopathology (Bezdjian et al., 2011).

Higher percentages in Table 11.1 mean that the twins are more similar. Thus, twins who would be totally similar in terms of personality characteristics would have a 100 percent similarity. As well, if genes were the main source of personality formation, the percentages for identical twins would be close to 100 percent to indicate

TABLE 11.1	**Fictive Percentages of Overall Personality Similarity among Identical and Fraternal Twins Who Were Raised Together or Separately***			
	Identical Twins Raised Together (Group 1)	Identical Twins Raised Separately (Group 2)	Fraternal Twins Raised Together (Group 3)	Fraternal Twins Raised Separately (Group 4)
	80%	60%	50%	30%

*The fictive subjects are four groups, each containing 100 pairs of same-sex twins aged 14.

near perfect similarity whether they were raised together or separately—because they share all their genes. But the highest figure in the table is 80 percent for identical twins raised together compared to 60 percent for those raised separately. This more or less means that around 60 percent of the identical twins' personalities is produced by their genes because, even though they are raised in different environments, they are still 60 percent similar. Or, looking at twins reared together (Groups 1 and 3), if genes played no role, identical and fraternal twins would be equally similar because, in each set, both share the same environment: But they are not.

So we also see, in Table 11.1, that the family environment plays a role. For instance, although identical twins are still very similar when they have been raised in different families—by 60 percent—at least 20 percent of personality traits come from the shared familial environment (difference between Groups 1 and 2). We also see that even fraternal twins are more similar, by 20 percent, when raised together (difference between Groups 3 and 4).

Interestingly, other studies show that identical adult twins who had been adopted separately and thus raised apart give many similar answers when they are asked to describe the homes in which they have been reared (Hur and Bouchard, 1995:339). Their **perceptions** are more similar than are those of fraternal twins also raised apart. In view of the fact that the homes were different, how can this be? This similarity of perceptions is the result of a combined genetic and environmental effect. To begin with, it is likely that these identical twins' different sets of adoptive parents were reacting fairly similarly to the twins' identical physical appearances and relatively similar personalities when they were growing up—this is called the "evocative effect" that influences parents (Barnes and Beaver, 2012:22). Although living in different homes, the identical twins may then have developed more similar relationships with their two sets of parents and thus naturally perceive these homes more similarly than do fraternal twins (Harlaar et al., 2008). The latter were less alike in terms of appearance and personalities, and consequently elicited **different reactions** from their two sets of adoptive parents (Horwitz and Neiderhiser, 2011).

As the reader can see, these processes are also easily understood through both symbolic interactionism and interactional theories: People create reactions from others that then become part of their environment, and this environment in turn helps create their personalities and perceptions. All in all, *these studies indicate that genes indirectly play a role in the creation of a person's environment:* Genes and environment, both shared and nonshared, act together. There are also indications that the familial or shared environment marks children more as they get older in some domains while, in others, genes become more important with age (Haworth et al., 2009).

What about the **nonshared** environment? In Table 11.1, none of the percentages that combine the effect of genes and shared family environment on personalities reaches 100 percent. For instance, we see in Group 1 that genes and family account for about 80 percent of identical twins' personalities. The remaining 20 percent indicates the effect of unique experiences the twins do not share—and this could start even in the uterus. Such unique experiences are likely to be more numerous for twins who are not identical. As well, one can see that siblings who are not twins will be far more affected by their nonshared environments because they have different age, birth order, classrooms, and peers (Lemelin et al., 2007). They were born at different stages of their families' and their parents' life course (Elder, 1998; Hareven, 2000).

Very recent research has also discovered yet another factor that contributes to making even identical twins different. This is called an epigenetic tag or switch. These tags or switches are "chemical mechanisms that can express (activate or suppress) genes to different degrees" (Miller, 2012). They do not change the DNA—and the twins still have the same genes—but may make a gene dormant in one twin or, yet, activate it in only one twin: Autism and schizophrenia in only one of the identical twins are good examples. What leads the switches to turn the genes on or off may be environmental influences or simply random mutations. Some scientists even suspect that some of these tags may be inherited. More progress is expected in this new field of epigenetics—which applies to all persons, not just twins.

THE CONTEXTS OF PARENTAL INFLUENCE

Socialization theories indicate that parents are extremely important in the formation of their children's personalities, behaviours, and well-being. Yet, most studies based on this premise find real but only moderate correlations between various child outcomes and parents' socialization practices—which does not mean that they do not count. *Socialization does count, but within its genetic and environmental contexts.* In essence, what in the past has been assumed to be strictly the result of parenting is now better understood as an interplay between parents' and children's genetic predispositions, parenting practices linked to reciprocal gene/environment effects, as well as between all these variables and the general environment in which families are located (Horwitz and Neiderhiser, 2011).

In other words, parents influence their offspring, both biological and adopted, both similar and different. But they do so within the *limits* set by their children's genetic predispositions, perceptions, and reactions (Reiss, 2003). Rutter (1997:393) correctly puts this into perspective when he points out that parents produce an effect but it is different for each child because each child is different from birth.

For example, twin Mia is impulsive, quick to react, and pays little attention to what is said. With the help of her mother, Mia learns to become less impulsive than she would be were she living in a family that provides little structure. In the latter family, she would become more impulsive. Her twin Alan is totally differ-ent: He is quiet, shy, and learns quickly. With their mother's help, he becomes more engaging socially, thus less shy. Because he is a quick learner, their mother can teach him many skills, so that Alan learns even better than he would in a family with a less invested mother.

Although both twins remain different, each improves under maternal influence, even though his or her basic personality remains. Parents can, in many circumstances, compensate for children's genetic vulnerabilities and enhance their gifts (Guo et al., 2008; Shanahan, M. J., et al., 2008). For instance, adopted children whose biological parents have shown pathology are much less likely to be similar to them when their adoptive family provides an environment that offsets these genetic risks (Reiss et al., 2009). As we soon see, some parents are more successful than others at influencing their children, in part because they have more personal resources and the social context they live in is more compatible with their values (Lamborn et al., 1996). *Disadvantaged and criminogenic environments often prevent children from benefiting from their genetic strengths and their parents' positive influence—and thus these children frequently do not fulfill their genetic potential* (Ambert, 1998; Beaver, 2011; Nielsen, 2006; Tucker-Drob and Harden, 2012). Further, children unconsciously (and later consciously) filter their parents' teachings through their own predispositions or personalities (Udry, 2003).

This said, *the fact remains that some families provide more shared socialization experiences for their children than do most other families.* To begin with, some fathers and mothers are quite similar to each other as a result of **assortative mating*** (Nisbett et al., 2012:137; Chapter 7). Such parents pass on more similar genes to their children; they are also likely to reinforce each other's teachings and provide a more uniform home climate that leaves less room for differentiation among siblings than when parents hold different views (Feinberg et al., 2005). Second, we can use Thornton and Lin's (1994) theory of **family integration** as an explanation. Parents who engage in many activities with their children, both at home or elsewhere, provide siblings with a more cohesive and integrative learning experience—and more social closure as proposed in Coleman's theory (1990a) following Bourdieu's (1977) own suggestions on cultural transmission. For instance, parents may take their children along on vacations and to libraries or museums, and they may engage in specific sports activities as a family group. All these activities combined contribute to family integration, which tightens up the children's shared environment. The shared activities also limit the time children spend in nonshared activities and in environments that could lead to different perceptions and learning experiences.

Third, this shared effect becomes even more powerful when parents and children together engage in activities *with other parents and their children as a group*; the entire family then experiences more shared elements. These activities can include religious worship, sports, communal picnics, and visits to other families' homes. The end result is that parents and offspring interact with others their age within the same context that, in turn, reinforces parental teachings—a matter of **collective socialization** (Coleman and Hoffer, 1987). Fourth, when parents are able to send their children to schools that replicate their own value system and lifestyle, siblings and parents have a more expanded, shared learning environment (Chapter 6). Then, school and the family essentially overlap in what the children learn, each agent of socialization reinforcing the other and, in rational theory terms, offering social closure against the rest of the world. Such a form of social capital may compensate for a child's negative genetic predispositions (Shanahan, M. J., et al., 2008). Or, else, it can reinforce negative predispositions when this capital is a deficit (deviant, for instance), as seen below.

Although each child in such families benefits from the common environment somewhat differently because of his or her personality, the fact remains that these siblings are surrounded by a "wrap-around" lifestyle that is shared by parents, relatives, friends, friends' parents, parents' friends, and even teachers. This shared environment becomes an **effective community** where everyone more or less pitches in and socializes its children similarly. *Collective socialization is a far more powerful agent of socialization than isolated parental efforts at home*, which can be diminished by different sets of values and behaviours as soon as children step outside. The shared environment becomes a more powerful source of influence on offspring. Siblings then become more similar with regard to lifestyle, education, values, beliefs, and occupational achievement. One sees such examples among communities of rural Amish and Mennonite families where children who remain home replicate their parents' particular rural and religious lifestyle. As well, collective socialization tends to be the norm rather than the exception in rural areas of economically developing countries (Hewlett and Lamb, 2005; Kitayama and Cohen, 2007). Not only are the villages and settlements smaller, but there are fewer consumerist challenges, and value consensus is higher—not to omit the fact that lifestyles are uniform from one family to the next.

At the negative level, such a powerful collective socialization also exists among traditional Mafia families that interact among themselves and where male children learn to engage in illegal activities. This expanded shared environment can also occur by default in geographically isolated pockets of rural poverty or in distant Aboriginal villages deprived of their traditional economies, where all the children fall under the same influences that mould their perceptions and narrow their life alternatives. They consequently grow up to replicate their parents' and their neighbours' poverty, despite having different personalities and innate abilities (Rowe et al., 1999). These abilities may not be allowed to flourish (Ambert, 1998).

Thus, parents hold *one* key to their child's development: Both genes and the non-shared environment (siblings, peers, media, teachers, illnesses, traumas) contribute the other keys. Finally, one has to recall that certain parental effects on children are derived from their own genes; thus *even the familial environment is partly genetic* (Kim-Cohen et al., 2004; Reiss et al., 2009). But, as we have seen when discussing parental influence in the previous chapter, external environmental forces counteracting parental influence are today far more powerful in child socialization than they were a century ago: The family then constituted a larger part of a child's environment. As well, the rest of the community tended to hold values that were generally compatible with those reflected in the family, thus providing a larger component of closure from other influences and a more powerful shared environment (Côté, 2000).

Similarly, one has to consider that, via families, various types of cultures will encourage the development of attitudes, skills, and values that are very different.

Thus, to give a hypothetical example, twins with similar genetic predispositions may develop even more differently when raised separately, one in Canada and one in an African village. This issue of cultural impact on personality formation is one that is not sufficiently recognized and remains the purview of cultural psychologists (Kagitcibasi, 2007; Kitayama and Cohen, 2007).

CONCLUSIONS: NATURE AND NURTURE

In western countries, sibling interactions are far more varied and optional than parent-child relationships because they are less scripted culturally. The sibling relationship reflects gender roles whereby females are already kin-keepers. This relationship is also affected by the familial context and later on by the peer network and other social groups. We have also seen that the influence of siblings on one another is underrated: It is quite possible that, at least for the younger child in a family, it is greater than parental influence in many domains of life.

The study of siblings, particularly twins and adopted children, has been directed toward better understanding the role that genes and the environment jointly play in human development. For sociologists, this new knowledge can be utilized to soften long-held views on the presumably all-powerful role that parents play in their child's socialization—and consequently to rectify the blame parents have received when a child turns out "wrong." The reality is that parents influence their children, but they do so within a specific context (their culture, social class, neighbourhood, peer group, media), and in conjunction with the genetic material or predispositions inherited by their children as well as their children's interpretations of reality. The latter are also influenced by genetic and environmental factors. Thus, there is a constant interplay between nature and nurture and the diversity of this interplay remains to be studied in societies that are still agrarian and non-western.

Summary

1. The determinants of sibling relationships are discussed. Older siblings are compared to younger ones in terms of their behaviours toward each other. It is possible that effects that have been attributed to parental practices are actually the result of the handling a child has received from siblings. Gender plays a very important role in sibling relations. Overall, siblings do not perceive their relationship similarly.

2. Siblings' influence on one another, particularly older ones toward younger ones, is discussed. The sharing of friends contributes to sibling similarity and influence. Supportive sibling relationships are studied.

3. Differential parental treatment of siblings is discussed as are its effects.

4. The various facets of adult sibling relationships in western societies are studied. Stepsibling relationships are presented.

5. The study of sibling differences returns us to the issues raised by behaviour genetics. Despite a shared home environment and genes inherited from the same parents, siblings are different because each inherits a particular combination of their parents' gene pool and has a different nonshared environment, including birth order as well as peer and school experiences. Further, because of their individual personalities, children perceive and

interpret their shared environment (such as parental teachings) differently. Families that provide a more powerful shared environment are described.

6. In order to study the joint effect of genes and environment on human development, twin and adoption studies are used because they present degrees of genetic closeness. Twins reared apart also present degrees of environmental closeness. The totality of the studies indicates that combined environmental forces are generally more important than biology. Yet, parents influence their offspring, both biological and adopted, but they can do so only within the limits set by the children's genetic predispositions, perception, and reactions.

7. Various themes are discussed within the context of parental influence, as is the relationship between nature and nurture.

Analytical Questions

1. Do you think there are advantages to large family size in terms of personality development? Would your answer differ for the 21st century compared to the 19th?

2. Families are becoming smaller (related to lower fertility). Analyze this development from a life course perspective.

3. Why are siblings different from one another? And are they more different from one another than they are from the other kids in the same neighbourhood?

4. What role do perceptions play in the distinction of what constitutes the shared versus the nonshared environment?

5. Do you agree or disagree with behaviour geneticists when some rule out parental influence (or the shared environment) as a key element in children's development? Justify your answer.

6. What role does collective socialization play in human development?

7. How do rational theories contribute to understanding human development?

CHAPTER 12

Divorce, Widowhood, and Remarriage

tigra62/Fotolia

OUTLINE

Divorce Rates and Trends
Age at Divorce and Duration of
Dissolved Marriages
Multiple (Serial) Divorces
Number of Children Involved
*Who Is Responsible for Children
after Divorce?*

Factors Contributing to Divorce
Sociocultural Factors
Demographic Factors
Reasons People Give for Divorcing

Adults' Life after Divorce
Changes in Ex-Spouses' Social Networks

**What Are the Effects of Divorce on
Children?**

**Theories Explaining How Divorce Affects
Children**
Economic Explanation
Disruption of Parenting
The Role of Parental Conflict
Preexisting Child Conditions
Genetic Influence

Widowhood and Bereavement
Consequences of a Parent's Death for
Children

Remarriage and Repartnering
Life after Remarriage and Repartnering
*The New Spouse and the Ex-Spouse
Adjustment to Remarriage and
Stepparenting*
What Are the Effects of Parental
Remarriage on Children?

**Grandparenting after Divorce and
Step-Grandparenting**

**Conclusions: The Familial and Social
Implications of Divorce**

Summary
Analytical Questions

"I really didn't see it coming [his marriage breaking up]. *I guess I was too busy."*

"Oh, I was so unhappy with him, you have no idea. He has no idea either." [The above man's ex-wife]

"My divorce was a pathetic waste, a waste of time and a psychological waste. We could have stayed together; instead we chose to subject each other to all manner of psychological warfare." [This man was happily remarried.]

"Am I better off now? I am not any happier. It's hard to raise children on your own when that wasn't in the planning. But at least I don't have to put up with his constant rejection and abuse."

"I used to think that a woman my age was too old for me. I dated much younger women, you know the stereotypical bachelor. I liked the ego boost these girls gave me. But when the party was over and time came to face life, I went for a woman my age . . . otherwise the life goals, long-term life goals, would have been too different."

"He shares in the upbringing of our children whereas I had to do it all in my previous marriage. He is thoughtful and we plan everything together. In my first marriage, it was all his life; his home was his castle. I was a fringe benefit."

"I love my stepchildren. Now I have a very large family and more grandchildren."

"I'd rather not have my stepsons. Mind you, I care for them and I am attached to them but I never set out to have children, and having someone else's children is a burden; I often resent it."

I have selected these quotes from the thousands available in the files of my longitudinal study on divorce to represent the various stages from divorcing, to repartnering or remaining single, and to stepparenting. These quotes illustrate how divorce is an experience that is both very individual and yet, as we soon see, carries similarities across cases: A first divorce is, at the very least, a marking event in a person's life. It represents a transition in an individual and a family life course. However, family development theories suggest that it rarely is an event that is timely in the life trajectory (Hareven, 2000:128).

In previous centuries, single-parent families were a common occurrence. For instance, in 1900, 25 percent of all children under the age of 15 had lost a parent (Nett, 1993). *Until the Second World War, the death of a spouse remained the leading cause of family disruption, at which point it was surpassed by divorce.* It is because of this historical shift that divorce, rather than widowhood, is the main focus of this chapter. Although divorce rates have not increased recently in Canada, the number of divorced persons is nevertheless increasing with population growth. In 2007, there were 972,183 divorced women and 712,531 divorced men in the population (Statistics Canada, 2007f). This gender difference stems from the fact that divorced men repartner more and sooner than women and also because women outlive men. The divorced account for 5.1 percent of the population versus 4.8 percent for the widowed. In 2007, of Canadians aged 50 to 65, one-quarter had experienced at least one divorce and 13.8 percent at least one cohabitational dissolution (Hébert and Uriarte-Landa, 2012).

The history of the legalization of divorce in Canada predates that of its colonial overseer, England, where it was only in 1857 that divorce was legislated, mainly on grounds of adultery. Nova Scotia, New Brunswick, and Prince Edward Island respectively enacted divorce laws in 1761, 1791, and 1837, generally on grounds of adultery (Wu and Schimmele, 2009). It was not until 1968 that Canada enacted its first unified federal *Divorce Act*, which was followed by the more liberal or "no fault" act of 1985. But the history of divorce is still unfolding as we now have to consider divorce among same-sex couples (Tyler, 2004).

DIVORCE RATES AND TRENDS

Statistics Canada has stopped tracking marriage and divorce rates because of budgetary constraints—a very shortsighted action on the part of the government. Therefore, some of the figures in this chapter could not be updated. However, the latest estimates for recently married couples put the risk of divorce at **40.7 percent** *by the 30th wedding anniversary* for the country as a whole—ranging from 25 percent in Newfoundland and Labrador to 47.4 percent in Quebec and 59.7 percent in the Yukon, as illustrated in Table 12.1 (Kelly, 2012). These estimates include persons who are divorcing for the first time as well as others who are divorcing for a second time or more. The probability of divorcing is lower for a *first marriage* and is higher for a remarriage (Bohnert, 2011). The low rates for the Maritimes may be the result of a higher level of social integration and a more effective community (Durkheim, 1897). Demographic variables such as an older population are also implicated. The higher rates for Quebec may stem from a combination of variables including widespread cohabitation before marriage, lower religiosity, and more liberal and individualistic attitudes.

Calculating divorce rates on the basis of couples who have been married for 30 years is the most accurate measure (Ambert, 2009). With this method, we see that persons who are about to marry have a much higher chance of staying together than of divorcing. However, this statistical method is a recent and sophisticated one that is not used everywhere. Therefore, in order to be able to compare divorce rates over

TABLE 12.1	Total Divorce Rates, per 100 Marriages, by the 30th Wedding Anniversary by Provinces and Territories				

	1998	2000	2002	2004	2008
Canada	**36.1**	37.7	37.6	37.9	40.7
Newfoundland and Labrador	23.2	22.9	21.8	21.6	25.0
Prince Edward Island	26.4	26.9	25.2	29.1	31.7
Nova Scotia	28.2	30.4	30.4	30.2	31.1
New Brunswick	26.9	31.9	27.2	26.9	29.7
Quebec	45.2	47.4	47.6	48.4	47.4
Ontario	33.0	34.6	34.9	35.5	42.1
Manitoba	30.1	34.6	30.3	30.6	31.5
Saskatchewan	31.5	31.4	28.7	27.6	30.3
Alberta	39.0	41.5	41.9	41.9	46.0
British Columbia	40.0	40.6	41.0	41.8	37.1
Yukon	55.2	33.6	43.4	34.5	59.7
Northwest Territories and Nunavut	37.5	40.7	31.2	35.5	33.1

Source: Statistics Canada, 2008f; Kelly, 2012. From Statistics Canada.

time and across cultures, a less sophisticated method is used: The *crude divorce rate* based on divorce per 1,000 population. Table 12.2 presents yearly trends per 1,000 population. We see that rates had already begun climbing before the Second World War, so that by the 1968 *Divorce Act*, divorce was more common, although still rare. Rates then increased spectacularly after the 1968 Act and peaked in 1987 at 3.6 divorces per 1,000 population—compared to 5.2 American divorces in 1981, which was the peak year in the U.S.

Thereafter, the rates declined to the point where, in the 2000s, they were equivalent to those of the late 1970s. Similar downward trends are evident in the U.S., although with rates always higher than in Canada. **Cross-culturally**, statistics from the United Nations (2008) and CDC (2012) indicate that Canadian crude rates (2.2) are comparable to those of Sweden (2.2) and are lower than British (2.8) and especially American ones (3.6). The American rates are the highest in the western world except for the Russian ones (4.5).

Before we examine other statistics about divorce, several points have to be emphasized to better understand **conjugal dissolution** (cohabitations and marriages that end). Cohabitation is now more common than marriage in Quebec as a first union and after divorce: Currently, 65 percent of Quebec couples are married versus 87 percent in the rest of Canada (Girard, 2008). In contrast to divorce, when a cohabiting union breaks up, the dissolution does not appear in official statistics. However, these rates of dissolution are very high, except for those cohabitations occurring later in life after a divorce (Bohnert, 2011). *But one can ask if the breakup of a cohabitation is equivalent to divorce.* This is important in order to measure the

| TABLE 12.2 | **Canadian Crude Divorce Rates per 1,000 Population since 1921** |

Years	Numbers	Rates per 1,000 population
1921	558	0.06
1941	2,462	0.21
1961	6,563	0.36
1968*	11,343	0.55
1970	26,093	1.23
1981	67,671	2.71
1985**	61,980	2.53
1986	78,304	2.99
1987*	**96,200**	**3.62**
1990	80,998	2.96
1995	77,636	2.62
1997	67,400	2.25
2000	71,144	2.31
2002	70,155	2.23
2005	71,269	2.20

Source: Adapted from Statistics Canada throughout the years; last one 2008f.

Divorce Act; **Reform of Divorce Laws; ***Peak Year

true extent of conjugal dissolution. The answer is not a simple one. Indeed, including all cohabitations as a form of marriage, for instance, may be misleading and so would be equating their breakup with divorce. In fact, as seen in earlier chapters, many cohabitations last a few months and merely constitute temporary or day-to-day arrangements lacking any long-term commitment as is explicit in marriage. Therefore, at which point should a cohabitation that breaks up be registered in statistics? After one year or two? And how to register these breakups?

Another factor to consider is that an unknown number of married couples separate but never divorce. This type of conjugal dissolution may be as consequential as a divorce, yet it does not appear in divorce statistics. It may also be increasing among those who separate and go on to cohabit fairly rapidly after their separation. So, when these two caveats are put together, *at least* one out of every two *unions* ends in dissolution—with lower rates in the Maritimes and Prairies and higher ones in Quebec. The dissolution percentage may continue to rise if younger cohorts continue to enter in greater numbers into cohabitation as a first union.

Statistics are not yet available for **same-sex divorce**. One question that will arise is the extent to which patterns and rates of divorce among gay and lesbian couples resemble those of heterosexual couples. Given that same-sex marriage has only recently become legal, a good proportion of these marriages involve couples who had been in long-term relationships. As such, one could reasonably predict that their divorce rate would be lower than that of married couples who are heterosexual. However, it should be noted that in Sweden and Norway, gay registered partnerships have higher divorce rates than heterosexual ones; in addition, lesbian partnerships have a 77 percent higher risk than gay ones. Andersson et al. (2006:96) explain this higher rate among homosexuals by the fact that they are less likely to have children than are heterosexual couples. Also, women's same-sex partnerships may be more at risk of divorce because of a "stronger sensitivity to the quality of relationships" by women than by men "regardless of sexual orientation."

Age at Divorce and Duration of Dissolved Marriages

Another recent trend in divorce rests on the fact that couples are now on average older at divorce than in the past: In 2005, the average **age at divorce** was 44 years for men and 41.4 for women. This age may rise again to reflect the fact that men and women now marry later. The average duration of marriages ending in divorce in 2005 was **14.5 years** or 1.7 years longer than a decade earlier (Statistics Canada, 2008f). In Ontario, it was 13.8 years versus 16.7 years in P.E.I. Lengthier marriages before divorce are also occurring in other western countries, such as the U.K. (In contrast, between 2001 and 2006, dissolved cohabitations that were reported in surveys had lasted 4.3 years—Beaupré and Cloutier, 2007.) As well, Statistics Canada indicates that the highest number of divorces occurs after the third anniversary—or 30 per 1,000 marriages (Kelly, 2012). After that, the rate decreases for each additional year married and, by the 40th anniversary, only 1.19 divorces occur per 1,000 marriages.

But we do have to be careful when we consider divorce statistics by duration because, among older persons, a divorce at age 60 or older may be a first one after a long marriage or a second or higher-order one. For instance, for men 65 to 87 who divorced in 1990–92, the average duration of their first marriage was 37.8 years, while subsequent divorces occurred after an average of 14 years of remarriage (Gentleman and Park, 1997). The more frequently people divorce and remarry, the shorter each subsequent remarriage (Ambert, 1989).

Multiple (Serial) Divorces

Sixteen percent of divorcing women and men in 2005 had been divorced at least once before (Statistics Canada, 2008f). These rates are lower in Newfoundland (because they have a much lower divorce rate) and Quebec (because the divorced tend to cohabit rather than remarry). The highest rates of serial divorces are in B.C., Alberta, and the Yukon. Therefore, *over 20 percent of all divorces in Canada are a repeat divorce for at least one of the spouses*. Both here and in the U.S., people who divorce many times seem to differ from the once-divorced on some personality dimensions (Disney et al., 2012). Some have more personal problems while others are less committed to marriage (Booth and Amato, 2001). For instance, Clark and Crompton (2006) have found that people who experience multiple divorces are much less likely to believe that marriage is important to them and to their happiness. They are not willing or ready to make adjustments or concessions that could lead to stability, as illustrated in the quotes below:

"Women expect too much out of marriage. I sure as hell can't live out their dreams." [Man in his fourth marriage]

"My wife says I have to work at our marriage. I don't agree with her. Marriage is supposed to be pleasant and if it isn't, well, it's not my problem." [Man in his third marriage]

In comparison, most respondents who had divorced only once expressed feelings of hurt, guilt, and even regret. While interviewing persons who had divorced several times within a short time span, I often had the impression that their marriages were part of the throw-away culture: If it's of no use, then get rid of it. However, the serially divorced did not all differ from those who had divorced only once: Some had simply had the misfortune of remarrying a "divorce-prone" spouse. Moreover, there are persons who make a mistake early on and divorce in their twenties, remarry, have children, and divorce again in their forties or fifties. There is no research comparing such persons who divorce a second time after years of stability with those, such as in my study, who had divorced two to four times within 15 years or less. One can reasonably assume that the former may be more stable and more responsible spouses and parents than the latter.

Number of Children Involved

The number of dependent children involved in a parental divorce was 36,252 in 1998—the total number of divorces had been 69,088. The *yearly* numbers are probably equivalent today. Strohschein et al. (2009) have estimated that about 20 percent of the 1984 birth cohort of Manitoba children had experienced their parents' divorce by age 18. For their part, Juby et al. (2005b) estimated that nearly 30 percent of Canadian children also born in 1984 had experienced the dissolution of their parents' *marriage or cohabitation* by age 15. The 2009 CAMH study obtained a self-report of about 24 percent of students in grades 7 to 12 who lived with a single parent or no parent (Paglia-Boak et al., 2010). Of Quebec children born in the late 1990s, 22 percent had experienced a parental conjugal dissolution by age 8 (Desrosiers et al., 2012).

Only about half of couples who divorce have children, due to the fact that a good proportion of divorces occur within the first few years of marriage. As well, only about a third of couples who dissolve a cohabitation have children (Beaupré and Cloutier, 2007). Further, the divorced who have children do not have as many, on average, as couples of their age who remain married. It is not clear whether this is because couples who have a stable marriage are more likely to add a second or third child to their family or if a larger number of children inhibits divorce, at least during the children's young years (Vanderschelden, 2006). But what we know is that the presence of children at home is related to a lower divorce rate (Clark and Crompton, 2006). Paradoxically, in remarriages, the presence of a woman's children from a previous union increases the risk of divorce (Teachman, 2008).

For Canada, there are no estimates of the number of children who experience multiple parental separations, including dissolved cohabitations. We know, however, that children who live in cohabitational families are more likely to experience a parental separation than children whose parents are married. Le Bourdais and her colleagues (2004) have found that Quebec and other Canadian children whose parents cohabit have, respectively, a threefold and a fivefold chance of going through a parental separation. Similar results have been found in the U.S. (Osborne et al., 2007).

Who Is Responsible for Children after Divorce?

In 1986, 15 percent of custody awards went to fathers exclusively but only 8.5 percent did in 2003 because by then 42 percent were **joint legal custody** (Statistics Canada, 2004j). But in most of these instances, *children still live with their mother*. Although joint legal custody may involve children living on alternate weeks or months with each parent, it generally simply involves equal rights of access and decision for both parents while the children remain with one parent. For their part, children prefer equal time with each parent as do young adults retrospectively (Fabricius, 2003). Mothers prefer sole custody, but are favourable to joint custody when they perceive their ex-husbands to be good parents and when the post-marital relationship is not conflictual (Wilcox et al., 1998). In this respect, in February 2005, the Ontario Court of Appeal ruled that joint custody should not be granted when parents cannot communicate effectively with each other about the care of their child(ren).

Custodial fathers compared to custodial mothers are more likely to be remarried or have another adult living with them (Goldscheider and Sassler, 2006). Overall, custodial fathers have fewer resident children, and fewer young ones, than custodial mothers (Beaupré et al., 2010; Rapoport and Le Bourdais, 2006): Fathers who have young children or many children tend not to seek their custody (Drapeau et al., 2000). Residence with their children tends to result in a better father-child relationship and contributes to fathers' mental health (Arendell, 1995). Resident fathers experience fewer feelings of lack of control over their paternal situation than nonresident fathers. But resident fathers are more likely to find their role constraining—they have less freedom and more demands placed on them. So far, it is difficult to conclude how living with a father compared to a mother relates to children's development. There are indications that heterosexual single fathers may be somewhat less hands-on, less supervisory, more permissive, and perhaps less warm than mothers. These hands-off styles, and comparative lack of family routines, often increase with the presence of a father's cohabitational partner (Bronte-Tinkew et al., 2010). As a result, these adolescents may have higher rates of delinquency (Biblarz and Stacey, 2010:16).

Both in terms of numbers and the social construction of motherhood, **noncustodial mothers** are non-normative (Walker and McGraw, 2000). Among them are mothers who relinquish custody because of financial hardship and a few who do so in order to have more freedom or to remarry someone who does not want children at home. In other cases, the father has won custody after a lengthy and often costly legal battle. Other mothers are involuntarily noncustodial as a result of ill health, mental problems, drug addiction, incarceration, child neglect, or because the child has been kidnapped by the father. In the U.S., nonresident mothers maintain more frequent telephone, letter, and extended visitation contacts with their children than nonresident fathers (Stewart, 1999b). But, overall, this is one instance when adolescents are closer to their fathers (King, 2007). However, both sets of nonresident parents tend to engage largely in leisure activities with their children (Stewart, 1999a). Further, neither mothers nor fathers pay all the child support they owe.

In the U.S., nearly 30 percent of fathers never visit their children (Amato et al., 2009) versus about 15 percent in Canada, while another 25 percent do so only irregularly (Marcil-Gratton, 1999). As well, parents in common-law unions that dissolve with children are far less likely to provide child support than formerly married ones (Child Support Team, 2000). Some researchers suggest that there is something in the structure of being a nonresident parent that inhibits active parenting as well as economic support for children outside of marriage (Gaudet and Devault, 2006; Manning et al., 2004). Other barriers to involvement include geographical distance and duration of separation (Manning and Smock, 2000). Low income is a key factor working against active parenting because it often places severe constraints on a father's time, resources, lodging, and availability (Sinkewicz and Garfinkel, 2009; Swiss and Le Bourdais, 2009). The presence of "new" children is another barrier (Smock and Greenland, 2010). Nonresident fathers whose ex-partner has a new child from a new union or they themselves have a new child are less likely to provide informal material and monetary support to their child from the previous union (Meyer and Cancian, 2012). This is particularly so when their child had been from a previous union that was non-marital—as discussed in Chapter 8 in terms of multi-partnered fertility. Overall, only a minority of nonresident fathers (whether divorced, separated, or single) display high levels of involvement (Carlson, 2006). This is especially evident among single fathers after their relationship with the mother ends and even more so after she repartners (Tach et al., 2010). (See also Family Research 12.1 below.)

As well, interactional theories suggest that children's characteristics play a role in these parent-child dynamics (Ambert, 2001). For instance, recent studies indicate that fathers are less likely to be closely involved with nonresident adolescents who have behavioural, mood, and academic problems (Hawkins et al., 2007). Such adolescents may discourage their fathers from getting involved, may be aversive, and may place obstacles to visiting with them. In turn, in a causality feedback perspective,

FAMILY RESEARCH 12.1

The Pitfalls of Measuring Father Involvement

Carlson (2006:150) hypothesizes that, when adolescents are interviewed about the level of their fathers' involvement in their lives, they may hold a different standard for fathers who live elsewhere compared with those who live at home. They may have higher standards for live-in fathers and describe as "close" their relationship with a nonresident father for less involvement on his part than do adolescents for their resident fathers. This is an important area for future research. Indeed, were it true that children's standards differ, then their answers might not be comparable in the two types of families.

this means that these same adolescents then have less support, which may compound their problems: Research is unanimous to the effect that children do far better cognitively and behaviourally when their father remains an active parent (Allard et al., 2005). Amato and Gilbreth (1999) suggest that children of divorce have better outcomes when nonresident fathers are more than "Sunday daddies" and participate more fully *as parents*—that is, when they provide emotional and practical support, make behavioural demands, place limits on what can be done, and administer consistent discipline.

FACTORS CONTRIBUTING TO DIVORCE

Multiple, interlocking factors have contributed to the rapid rise of divorce in Canada and other western countries in the second part of the 20th century. These same factors have contributed to the maintenance of relatively high rates of divorce into the 21st century as well as to increasing rates of cohabitation and cohabitational dissolution. Below, various cultural and demographic contributing factors are discussed, and then linked to the personal reasons people give for divorcing.

Sociocultural Factors

As seen in previous chapters, sociocultural factors are broad social and cultural variables that affect several aspects of people's lives and influence the ways in which families perceive and experience their relationships. Divorce rates were already inching upward in the early 20th century as a result of **secularization trends,** the **liberalization of norms** concerning individual choice, and **lower religiosity.** This is often referred to as the "desacralization of marriage." For many, marriage has become an individual choice rather than a covenant before God and this change has contributed to the acceptance of its temporal nature (Cherlin, 2004). These sociocultural trends later came to influence the passage of **more liberal divorce laws.** In turn, easier divorce laws, such as those promulgated in 1968 and 1985, are followed by an increase in divorce (see Table 12.2). Such laws signalled the normalization of divorce, which then lost its stigma and became more socially acceptable. These cultural and legal factors have made it easier for people to be less attached to marriage as an **institution*** and consequently to turn to divorce as a solution.

The trends toward **individualism** that began two centuries ago have resulted in an emphasis on rights rather than duties. When individualism is coupled with an ideology of gratification, particularly sexual and psychological, where people are encouraged to be "happy" and "fulfilled," it follows that spouses' mentality about their marriage is affected. Marriage is less likely to be seen as an institution centred on mutual responsibilities and is more likely to be based on the pursuit of happiness and companionship. More is demanded of marriage in terms of **personal gratification.** As Amato (2007) puts it, in individualistic marriages, spouses view the marriage as valuable as long as it meets their needs for self-actualization: "If the marital relationship no longer meets these needs, then spouses feel justified in jettisoning the relationship to seek out new partners who better meet these needs" (p. 309). Perhaps, as Durkheim (1897) might explain it, individualistic marriages and unions in general are less stable because they are more **anomic*** or normless, less bound by imperatives of social cohesion. Relatedly, a culture of narcissism may be another factor (Twenge and Campbell, 2010). As a consequence of these trends, Canadians and most Westerners have developed a **lower threshold of tolerance** when their marriage does not meet with their expectations for personal fulfillment. All things considered, *while more is expected of marriage, couples are also less tolerant about its challenges and less willing to shoulder the compromises it may require.*

Demographic Factors

Given the cultural variables facilitating divorce, we now look at *demographic factors through which vulnerability to divorce is expressed.* We have seen in Chapter 4 how poverty multiplies individual risks in general, reduces life opportunities, and increases stressors. All of these factors have a negative impact on the marital relationship. Thus, **low-income** couples are at a higher risk of divorcing (Amato and Previti, 2004; (Shaffer and James, 2013; 0 Strohschein, 2012). This risk is very present among couples on welfare (Frenette and Picot, 2003:15) and those who are unemployed (Bohnert, 2011). But we have also seen that divorce contributes to poverty. This means that divorce and poverty are two variables that reinforce each other in the causality chain. This said, higher-income women are more likely to leave an abusive marriage than are other women (Kraeger et al., 2013).

Youthful marriage or cohabitation also increases the risk of divorcing or breaking up (Desrosiers et al., 2012; NCHS, 2010; Provencher et al., 2006). Couples who marry during their teens and even early twenties generally have low incomes and **low educational** levels, which are contributing factors to divorce (Clark and Crompton, 2006) as are large educational differences (Schwartz, 2010b). Moreover, very young couples often marry for reasons that differ from those of couples who are more mature. They may also lack the maturity and experience to cope with the demands of a marital relationship. Their personalities have not yet stabilized so that their needs may change and upset the balance of their new marriage.

Another demographic factor related to divorce is **solo motherhood:** Mothers who have children without a partner are more likely to be young and poor and to cohabit serially before marrying—thus combining many risk factors for divorce when they later marry (Luong, 2008). **Remarriages** are a risk factor for divorce, in great part because of a higher propensity to have recourse to divorce, the complexities of reconstituted families, and, therefore, stressors unique to stepfamilies (Schramm and Adler-Baeder, 2012). In stepfamilies, relationships are more difficult to negotiate and negative family processes are exacerbated (Jenkins et al., 2005b). Further, families with a resident stepfather are less stable than families with a resident stepmother (Marcil-Gratton et al., 2003).

The **sex ratio*:** Men are more likely to divorce when there is a high proportion of unmarried women with them in the labour force and the same applies to women who work in domains with a male preponderance (South et al., 2001). These conditions raise married persons', especially men's, chances of sexual infidelity and of forming new relationships. Similarly, when there is a sex ratio imbalance favouring men in a particular ethnic group in a city, this group may also have higher rates of serial cohabitation and divorce (Harknett, 2008).

Parental divorce correlates with lower marital commitment among some children once adults and this is then reflected in higher divorce rates later (Li and Wu, 2008; Whitton et al., 2008). One study has even found that this occurs especially when the parental marriage had a low level of conflict—such parents may divorce simply because they are less committed to marriage as an institution and may transmit this value to their offspring (Amato and DeBoer, 2001).

Cohabitation prior to marriage has constituted until now a strong risk factor to a first divorce (Clark and Crompton, 2006; Marcil-Gratton et al., 2003) and for a remarriage (Xu et al., 2006). But there is recent evidence that cohabiting *with a future spouse* may *not* increase the risk of divorcing (Teachman, 2008). This is especially when cohabiting follows an engagement or official commitment (Jose et al., 2010; NCHS, 2010:13; Stanley et al., 2010). It may even be a stabilizing element in remarriages (Reinhold, 2010). But there is still not enough information on the most recent trends for current cohorts to draw solid conclusions (Hewitt and de Vaus, 2009). Nevertheless, the fact is that, as cohabitation increases in a population, it is less likely to be selective of divorce-prone persons (NCHS, 2010; Reinhold, 2010). For instance, in a study of 16 European countries, Liefbroer and Dourleijn (2006) found that, as a result of selection, cohabitation before marriage is related to a higher risk of divorce only in countries in which cohabitation is a small minority phenomenon, such as Spain and Italy, or when it is a majority phenomenon, such as Norway and Finland. Yet, in Quebec, children born to parents who have cohabited before their marriage are 3.96 times more likely to experience their parents' divorce (and 5.71 times in the rest of Canada) than children whose parents have not cohabited before marrying (Marcil-Gratton et al., 2003).

Other studies still show that some individuals select themselves into cohabitation because it requires, in their opinion, less sexual faithfulness than in marriage, or because cohabitation is viewed as an alternative to the lifelong commitment assumed by marriage. This situation occurs even in countries such as Sweden and Norway where cohabitation is widespread (Wiik et al., 2009). Cohabitation is easier to get into and easier to get out of than marriage. Therefore, there is less reason to "work" at maintaining a relationship that may never have been viewed as a lifelong commitment to begin with. Yet, many such less committed couples drift into marriage. As a result, they have a higher chance of divorcing.

Not only is there a selection process—although it is diminishing—but there is also evidence of a **causality effect**. That is, the experience of a less committed, and at times less faithful cohabitation, shapes subsequent marital behaviour (Dush et al., 2003). Such couples continue to live their marriage through the perspective of the low commitment, and even lack of fidelity, of their prior cohabitation. Others simply learn to accept the temporary nature of relationships (Smock and Gupta, 2002). The result is a marriage at risk. This is especially so when children were born during a prior cohabitation (Tach and Halpern-Meekin, 2009). Cohabitation may also reduce religiosity, an important factor of stability (Eggebeen and Dew, 2009).

Therefore, people select themselves into cohabitation, especially serial cohabitations, because of both personal and demographic characteristics. In turn, cohabitations that *lack commitment* shape subsequent marital behaviours in ways that may be detrimental to marital relationships. Hence, the increased divorce rates. However, as cohabitation is becoming more institutionalized*, both as a prelude to marriage and as a relationship in itself, its behavioural contents will evolve so that commitment, sexual fidelity, and feelings of security may be equivalent to those found in marriage. For instance, in Australia, where cohabitations are now of longer duration, this new development may be reducing the risk of divorce (Hewitt and de Vaus, 2009). However, even in Sweden and Norway, cohabitants with no intention of marrying their current partner report a far less committed relationship than those with marital intentions (Wiik et al., 2009). This is also what the most recent U.S. statistics indicate (NCHS, 2010).

For its part, **serial cohabitation** represents a particularly high risk for divorce (Lichter and Qian, 2008). More young people as well as more post-divorce adults engage in **serial** cohabitations than was the case in the past, at times accumulating many such relationships over the years (Sassler, 2010). Just as persons who divorce multiple times seem to differ on some key dimensions compared to the once-divorced, one should expect that future research will find similar results for serial cohabitants. In other words, the process of selection and of behavioural shaping will continue to characterize serial cohabitants.

Finally, one has yet to study the possible impact of serial **casual sexual relationships**, such as hook-ups and friends with benefits, and the "churning" in and out of relationships (Halpern-Meekin et al., 2013), on the stability of future serious relationships such as cohabitation and marriage. For the same reason that serial cohabitations may be more likely to be a risk factor to marital stability, so could prior serial casual relationships. Further, one could hypothesize, these relationships may constitute a risk for the children they may eventually have. Children suffer from their parents' multiple conjugal transitions as they are then less likely to have a home and parental environment that is child oriented (Cherlin, 2009).

Reasons People Give for Divorcing

It should be noted that, since divorce has become easier to obtain and is no longer stigmatized, a majority of conjugal dissolutions are from unions that are unsatisfactory rather than very conflictual or abusive (Desrosiers et al., 2012). Thus, when asked what led to their divorce, most people mention "irreconcilable differences," "didn't get along," "no longer loved each other," and fighting and quarrelling about money, children, and their relationship. In the U.S., Amato and Previti (2004) found that infidelity was the reason most often given while Allen and Atkins (2012) found that perhaps half of men and woman who have been unfaithful divorce. In the study I conducted, there were several cases in which a casual and unplanned extramarital affair, such as those occurring at out-of-town conventions, caused an enormous blow-up when the other spouse accidentally learned of it; separation was practically immediate. I refer to these as "**accidental**" or "**useless**" divorces (Ambert, 1989). These divorces may never have otherwise occurred because the relationships were sound and both ex-spouses reported a high level of marital happiness (see Family Research 12.2). Infidelities plant seeds of doubt and insecurity that are too difficult

FAMILY RESEARCH 12.2

Asking Both Ex-Spouses about Their Past Marital Happiness

You may recall reading in Chapter 9 that few studies examine the marital happiness of a *couple*. Generally, only one spouse is interviewed and then husbands and wives are compared as two separate groups. But these husbands and wives are not married to each other. Therefore, little can be said about the couple. The same problem occurs in studies of divorce. In order to compensate for this deficit, I have interviewed both ex-spouses and their new spouses (when my respondents had remarried) three times over a period of six years (Time 1, Time 2, and Time 3). This allowed me to derive a classification of ex-couples depending on both ex-spouses' reported level of marital happiness in their past marriage:

High happiness ex-marriages	13%
Mid-level happiness ex-marriages (mixture of near high and average)	52%
High unhappiness ex-marriages	35%

At the time, these results surprised me, but they have since been replicated in the U.S. and Canada. In other words, in only one-third of the cases did both ex-spouses recall having been very to fairly unhappy in their past marriage (Amato et al., 2007:245–6). Furthermore, at least one divorce in 10 occurred to couples in which both partners had been happy or very happy (Ambert, 1989). Analyses at the couple level could shed light on many issues that, until now, have been studied with only one or the other spouse as the basis.

to overcome for persons who may have fewer psychological resources or may have other alternatives.

Other reasons people give are physical abuse, mental cruelty, religious differences, and alcoholism. Drug addiction, gambling, mental illness, criminality, "he's never home," and child-related problems, such as the stress of caring for a child with a disability, are occasionally mentioned. Domestic violence as one of the reasons for divorce is less often mentioned than in the past in Canada and in other western countries (de Graaf and Kalmijn, 2006). This finding is consistent with studies showing a decline in conjugal violence between 1993 and 2004 (Laroche, 2007; Statistics Canada, 2006d).

In most cases of divorce, one spouse wants out far more than the other (Hopper, 2001). One spouse is happier with the relationship (Waite and Gallagher, 2000). Often it is husbands who are surprised when their marriage breaks down (Hetherington, 2003).Women generally find more problems with their marriage than husbands do and decide to divorce more often than men, even though they are the ones who carry the larger burden afterwards.

The personal reasons or explanations that people give for their divorce, as seen above, actually flow from the sociocultural and demographic factors discussed earlier. For instance, without an emphasis on individualism and gratification, people would not divorce as often because they "fell out of love." In countries where marriage is embedded within a context of family solidarity, these reasons would be considered frivolous. In a society where divorce is more difficult to obtain and less acceptable, or where marriage may represent the only legitimate means of forming and maintaining a family or obtaining economic security, only reasons such as abuse and abandonment are tolerated. *Therefore, before people decide to divorce on particular grounds, a social and cultural climate has to exist that offers a legitimate framework for their reasons.* It should also be added that many psychological characteristics such as difficult temperaments, higher distress, and inability to communicate, among others, are also related to less satisfying marriages (Lavner and Bradbury, 2010) and high divorce rates (Markman et al., 2010). But even these variables can increase divorce only within societies that facilitate divorce legally and culturally.

ADULTS' LIFE AFTER DIVORCE

Divorce reduces adults' economic situation: We have already seen that poverty increases the risk of divorce. In turn, divorce also increases the risk of poverty for a large proportion of women and their children and so does the dissolution of cohabitations (Avellar and Smock, 2005; Hay, 2009). Rotermann (2007a) found that, within two years after a separation/divorce, 43 percent of women had experienced a decrease in household income compared to 15 percent of men. In contrast, 29 percent of men and only 9 percent of women had experienced an increase. As well, men who divorce are more likely to exit welfare while women are more likely to go on welfare (Frenette and Picot, 2003). Even three years after divorce, women's household income remains below what it had been during marriage and far below their ex-husbands' current income. However, as more women are employed and earn better salaries, this income decline is less painful than before, though still evident—even in retirement, particularly among women from higher-income families (Statistics Canada, 2012e). As well, in a decade when most families have two breadwinners, men who divorce lose far more economically than in the past, especially those married to a high-earning wife. As child support payments become better enforced, economic factors may contribute in the long run to dissuade some men and women from ending their marriage.

Divorce drastically reduces many adults' mental and physical health, often over the life course (Hughes and Waite, 2009). Alcohol abuse increases among divorced men and mothers with young children. A large study found that the negative effect of divorce on psychological well-being especially affected parents of young children, particularly women. Parental strains, economic problems, and the stressors of having to maintain contact with the ex-spouse are explanatory factors (Williams and Dunne-Bryant, 2006). Depression as well as a general feeling of being less healthy often occur among divorced women (Wu and Hart, 2002). Rotermann (2007a) reports even more depression among men after divorce.

Many divorced persons admit that they are not any happier while others are even unhappier than during their marriage. In fact, Waite et al. (2002) have found that even unhappily married people were not necessarily happier five years after their divorce than those who had remained married. Another study found that persons in high-distress marriages were happier after divorce whereas those who had been in relatively comfortable marriages were unhappier (Amato and Hohmann-Marriott, 2007). Divorce generally involves a period of stress, instability, loneliness, hurt feelings, and often hostility. That period of transition is often related to health problems (Dupré and Meadows, 2007). Longer studies are needed to see whether these effects diminish over time. One also has to consider that some effects, both for adults and children, may not appear until later in life (Hughes and Waite, 2009). As well, recent research suggests that some of the negative effects of a divorce are still evident two generations later among grandchildren (Amato and Cheadle, 2005).

However, one should keep in mind that marital conflict is a significant risk for mental and physical problems so that remaining in a bad marriage can have an important negative impact on the immune system (D'Onofrio and Lahey, 2010). Thus, a stressful marriage produces noxious effects (Choi and Marks, 2008). Leaving such a marriage may increase well-being (Waite et al., 2009). However, Rotermann's (2007a) longitudinal study included bad marriages, and episodes of depression were still more prevalent after divorce. An interesting perspective is that adults' divorces negatively affect their own mothers, but not significantly their fathers (Kalmijn and de Graff, 2012)—in other words, divorce has an upward as well as downward negative effect on the generations of a family.

Often, as soon as separation or divorce occurs, a relationship that was rather placid becomes conflictual; it is during this period that women are at greater risk of being assaulted and even killed by their former partner (Fleury et al., 2000; GSS, 2000). This may be particularly so for cohabiting women who leave (Sev'er, 2002). Overall, *divorce is much more stressful and requires a great deal of adjustment*, at least for *one spouse*, when a couple has children who still live at home; a couple jointly owns a home and shares other assets; the marriage was long and many habits have to be changed; a couple is older, thus less flexible, and perhaps no longer employed; there is a loss of financial resources and economic status; a husband and wife share all their friends; one or both spouses is in ill health, an alcoholic, or a drug abuser. As well, when respective families take sides, each ex-spouse then loses half of her or his extended kin group. A loss of friends makes adjustment more difficult because social support deteriorates at a time of emotional need.

Changes in Ex-Spouses' Social Networks

Persons' social networks after divorce are rarely studied. In order to modestly remedy this lack of information, I am using qualitative data from my longitudinal study of divorce (Ambert, 1989; see Family Research 12.2). With divorce, many couples lose the in-law kin system, so that each ex-spouse now has a reduced kin network. More women than men reported losing friends after separation, particularly in long-term marriages during which friendships had been shared as a couple. Mutual friends remained with the ex-husband more often than with the ex-wife. Two women explained this situation thusly:

> *"His wife* [a friend's wife] *feels more secure with Paul I think than with me. As a single woman, I am a threat to her. . . . I just never realized that she'd be so jealous the minute her husband looked at me."*

> *"My ex-husband is more fun to be with because he has more money to do things and go out."*

However, very few women had lost those friends whom they had already had before their marriage or had maintained separately during the marriage. The workplace became an important source of moral support at that time. As pointed out in the next quote, in a couple-oriented society, social support is more readily extended to coupled individuals and, after divorce, to men, unless women have a strong, independent network of female friends. Married men seem less threatened by their divorced male friends than married women are by their divorced women friends. Men reported either little change or an increase in visiting, particularly being invited over for dinner and for outings when their children were with them. Custodial fathers definitely received more offers of help from friends and colleagues, and even from their children's teachers, than custodial mothers. They received far more sympathy than custodial mothers.

At Time 2, and particularly Time 3, of the follow-up, three and six years later respectively, a great proportion of respondents had remarried. These remarriages provided an excellent opportunity to see if changes in social networks had occurred. Remarried women had seen a substantial increase in their social activities involving new friends. The change had been practically instantaneous for many. One woman sarcastically put it this way:

> *"Remarriage puts a woman back where she belongs; she's no longer a threat to other women, no longer a temptation to their husbands. But I also think that socially a woman has value because of her married status; I could feel it. I mean, I felt so bitter about it when I was divorced, it was so obvious. From a couple's point of view a divorced woman is more than useless, and all adults are couples so that leaves you nowhere."* [Now?] *"I am part of a couple again."*

When adults remarry or repartner, they gain another set of in-laws; then, they often acquire each other's friends and this explains in part their increased social network and activities. Again, to paraphrase the last woman's quote, this increase is also in part explained by the fact that, for other couples, a couple is a safer and more valued unit for friendship than a divorced individual. The **status** of marriage or *of being part of a couple* certainly enhances a person's social acceptability.

WHAT ARE THE EFFECTS OF DIVORCE ON CHILDREN?

In a nutshell, although most children do not experience developmental problems, divorce is certainly a strong risk factor and a source of stressors. Divorce is, above all, an emotionally **difficult transition** and, as Kelly and Emery (2003) point out, it can "create lingering feelings of sadness, longing, worry, and regret that coexist with competent psychological and social functioning" (p. 359). Connidis (2003a) remarks that relationships are changed after divorce and have to be renegotiated many times over the years; the effects are felt across several living generations within a family.

Although average differences are not huge, children whose parents are divorced (and especially after they are remarried or repartnered) are *more likely* than children whose parents remain together to suffer from depression, anxiety, and other emotional disorders; exhibit behavioural problems including hyperactivity, aggressiveness, fighting, and hostility; become young offenders; do less well in school and do not remain in school as long; and experience more relationship problems and instability, in part due to their behavioural problems (Cavanagh et al., 2008; Desrosiers et al., 2012; Oldehinkel et al., 2008; Sun and Li, 2008). The negative consequences of divorce are particularly apparent within the context of poverty (Côté et al., 2003).

Adults whose parents divorced during their childhood and teen years, compared to adults from intact two-parent families, tend to have had a child out of wedlock more often, particularly during adolescence; achieve lower educational levels; be more often unemployed and do less well economically; have higher cohabitation rates; enter into a first union earlier; have more marital problems and divorce more; be more likely to have lost contact with their father and to report a less happy childhood (Amato, 2003; Hetherington, 2003; Martin et al., 2005; Provencher et al., 2006; Williams, 2001b). As well, a study by Boyd and Norris (1995) has found that children of divorced parents leave home earlier than others. They leave home in even greater numbers when their custodial parent remarries and more so when both parents remarry. (We have no information about cohabitation; however, the results are probably more salient—Brown, 2006; Fagan, 2013.) A consequence is that it becomes too expensive to continue their education past secondary school. This, in turn, leads to lower occupational skills and higher unemployment.

Divorce also increases negative interactions between siblings (Kim et al., 1999). In fact, a conflictual relationship between parents is more likely to lead to, or be accompanied by, greater sibling conflict (Poortman and Voorpostel, 2009). Conger and Conger (1996) find that "it is the actual disruption of marriage rather than the degree" of parental conflict in intact marriages "that most adversely affects relations between brothers and sisters" (p. 119). This effect of divorce on the sibling relationship is one that is infrequently mentioned in the more recent literature on the consequences of marital breakup.

As indicated in Table 12.3, when children who have experienced their parents' marital dissolution reach adulthood, their relationship with their parents is less likely to be warm. They are also less frequently in touch with their fathers when he has stepchildren (Noël-Miller, 2013) and when he has had more than two marital dissolutions (Ménard and Le Bourdais, 2012). Amato and Booth (1997) have found that adult children of divorce fare even less well in this respect than children whose parents remained in an unhappy marriage. Longitudinal studies following children up to age 33 indicate that, when emotional problems develop, the effect of parental divorce may last and can even intensify (Cherlin et al., 1998). Because these studies were longitudinal, the researchers were able to measure other family and child characteristics

TABLE 12.3 | **Recalled Childhood Quality for Men and Women Who Experienced Parental Structure Change versus Those Who Did Not***

	Men		Women	
	No change	Change	No change	Change
Very happy childhood	93%	74%	91%	71%
Very close emotionally to mother	92	83	87	76
Very close emotionally to father	73	53	75	49

Source: Statistics Canada; Williams, 2001c. From Statistics Canada.

* Includes all individuals who began life with two parents (biological or adoptive).

that could have influenced the development of emotional problems. Yet, even after they had considered these other influences, their results still showed that the divorce itself had increased the likelihood of emotional problems, including later on in adulthood. Divorce even contributes negative effects two generations down to grand-children (Amato and Cheadle, 2005). A new couple's risk of divorcing is even higher when their two sets of parents had divorced during their childhood or adolescence (Amato, 1996).

The research indicates that **multiple family transitions** correlate with declining well-being in children and an increase in behavioural problems (Amato and Sobolewski, 2001; Fomby and Cherlin, 2007). Some of the hardships caused to children stem mainly from their own parents' first divorce. Remarriages end more quickly than first marriages; thus, children may not have had sufficient time to bond with their temporary stepparent to suffer from this loss. However, repeated divorces affect adults, which in turn may affect their ability to parent adequately (Hetherington, 2003). Moreover, multiple divorces may constitute a **socialization experience** for children who see their parents divorce so rapidly and so often: They may fail to learn adequate conflict resolution techniques. Such children may learn to quarrel or to give up without resolving differences. They may also learn to think that marriage is a personal choice of a temporary nature.

In summary, most children survive their parents' divorce well developmentally, even though they may be worried, stressed, and unhappy. Pedro-Carroll (2001) points out that *one has to differentiate between distress and disorder*. Most children of divorce experience a certain level of distress, which often lasts for over a decade. For instance, they miss the other parent and, when little, they may feel that they are partly to blame for the divorce; some desperately try to get their parents together again; they are sad; some cry a lot while others lash out and develop temporary behavioural problems. But, despite their distress, most still function well, that is, do not experience "*disorders*" (Laumann-Billings and Emery, 2000). Indeed, whatever statistics one reads concerning the negative outcomes of children of divorce, they do *not* apply to *all* these children (Corak, 2001). Rather, what these statistics indicate is that children of divorced parents *in general* have a greater risk of developing problems or of not reaching their full potential than children whose parents remain together. One needs to add that a parental remarriage often contributes another set of stressors and risks, as we see later.

THEORIES EXPLAINING HOW DIVORCE AFFECTS CHILDREN

Several theories explaining the negative consequences of divorce for children receive support in the research. These explanations are complementary rather than mutually exclusive, because *each fits some children better than others.*

Economic Explanation

As documented in Chapter 4, a majority of children experience a reduction in their standard of living after divorce and many become poor. Poverty contributes to amplifying the negative effects of divorce on the mother-child family unit, on the father-child relationship, and on children's life chances. When all variables are considered, post-divorce poverty is at least as strong a source of lower cognitive ability and school achievement as is the divorce itself (Strohschein et al., 2009). In some European societies, particularly Norway and Sweden, the **social safety net** compensates greatly so that single-mother families have a (low) rate of poverty that is close to that of two-parent families. Thus, in countries with a more equitable income distribution, the negative consequences of divorce for children do not disappear but are less pronounced than they are in Canada, the U.S., and the U.K.

A 20 to 40 percent income loss for women and children after divorce leads to many **concurrent changes**. To begin with, a great proportion of Canadian women and their children move after separation, often to more crowded and dilapidated housing, where there is more noise and pollution. Children and their mothers may be less healthy as a result and more stressed (see Kohen et al., 2008). The neighbourhood may be less safe and have more children who are equally poor, do less well in school, and engage more in delinquency (Chapter 5). Having to adjust to a new and often more difficult peer group can create a great deal of problems—loneliness, bullying, school avoidance, and delinquency. All of these changes are a lot to ask of children, especially.

Disruption of Parenting

The economic theory is not in itself sufficient to explain divorce effects: Living in a breaking-up family still produces an independent negative effect of its own (Wu, 1996). Thus, a second theory that also receives a great deal of research support sees parenting behaviours as either a direct causative variable or as a mediator variable (Osborne and McLanahan, 2007). In a nutshell, this theory posits that parents who divorce or break up experience a great deal of stressors and have to adjust to a new lifestyle that gives them less social support as individuals and as parents. Moreover, the custodial mother may have to work long hours to make ends meet. When she returns home, she may be tired, preoccupied, and have less time to devote to her children. As a result, children of divorced mothers who are poor or near poor may receive less attention, guidance, supervision, encouragement, and affection than other children. Parenting skills and availability suffer. Many become less tolerant of misbehaviour and are more prone to have screaming fits, while others become depressed and withdraw from their children (Forgatch et al., 1996). Divorced parents tend to be preoccupied or busy, which means less time for children—less time for advice, for love, and for monitoring. Sons often become defiant, disobedient, disrespectful, and even abusive. Similarly, the situation where parenting changes when a father or mother experiences several relation transitions should be studied because children's outcomes often deteriorate under these circumstances; we also know that these parents may differ from others who experience only one divorce (Bronte-Tinkew et al., 2010; Disney et al., 2012; Sun and Li, 2011).

Amato and Gilbreth (1999) suggest that children of divorce have better outcomes when nonresident fathers provide emotional and instrumental support, make behavioural demands, place limits on what can be done, and administer consistent discipline. When nonresident fathers remain **active parents,** as opposed to "Sunday daddies" or their children's "pals," they complement and reinforce custodial mothers' socialization efforts. Children receive the same message of support and authority from both parents, an ideal situation rarely achieved. Basically, what counts in child outcomes is neither the custodial arrangement nor the frequency of visitation, but the **quality of parenting** and parents' psychological functioning (Wallerstein, 1998). However, we know that ex-husbands are more likely to remain involved if they feel supported by their ex-wives in their parenting role (Sobolewski and King, 2005).

The Role of Parental Conflict

The third theory overlaps with the second theory to some extent. It focuses on parental conflict both during marriage and after divorce. Conflict is so detrimental that children who remain in a conflict-ridden family have more negative outcomes than those whose parents divorce to eliminate the tension (Amato et al., 1995; Yu et al., 2010). Parental conflict is particularly painful when adolescents or children hear their parents fight about them: They feel caught in the middle. In at least one study looking at situations of high parental conflict, boys who were in regular contact with their nonresident parent tended to have more problems than boys for whom this contact was limited (Amato and Rezac, 1994). As expressed in the following male student quote, conflict is extremely painful for children of all ages, both while parents are married and after the divorce:

> *"When I was 11, my parents separated. This has been the most difficult period of my short life until now and it still hurts to this day. But when I was 11 it was worse because my life became so different. My sister seemed to cope better but I just couldn't stand the fighting. They'd fight over the phone about everything and when my father would pick us up for the weekend they'd go at it some more and I'd be shaken up for the entire weekend and it would start all over when he would drop us off and on top of it all, they used to talk against each other and say awful things about each other in front of me. To this day, my skin crawls when I know that they'll talk to each other which is rare now that we're older.*

My sister's wedding was a nightmare of tension and as far as I'm concerned I'll just elope one day because I just couldn't go through with it. I have been a nervous wreck since that time [age 11]."

In fact, Buchanan et al. (1996) have found that the *worst thing that can happen to a child is that his or her parents remain locked in conflict after divorce*. In such cases, divorce fulfills no positive function for the child; rather, it exacts a heavy price for which there is no compensation. In contrast, amicable coparenting after divorce may shield children from the stressors of divorce. Fewer marriages ending in divorce are highly conflictual than in the past (Kerr and Michalski, 2007). But, as we saw, low-conflict marriages that end in divorce appear to have a strong negative effect on children, whereas divorce for high-conflict couples may have a beneficial effect (Booth and Amato, 2001). But, in many cases, "intense anger and conflict is ignited by the separation itself and the impact of highly adversarial legal processes" (Hopper, 2001; Kelly and Emery, 2003:353). Overall, there is research consensus that pre- and post-divorce conflict is detrimental to children but that the divorce itself contributes an additional source of potential problems (Hanson, 1999). We also need research to differentiate the effect on children of parental conflict within marriage from that following separation: Parental conflict following separation/divorce may be an independent cause of some children's negative outcomes.

Although this concept is not new (Gardner, 1987), we are now hearing about an extreme problem that has recently been "discovered": **Parental alienation** occurs when one parent more or less brainwashes a child against the other parent and effectively prevents that parent from seeing the child and the child from loving that parent. The child may in fact come to reject the hapless parent (Gagné et al., 2005). The consequences for the child's future mental health can be dire.

Preexisting Child Conditions

A fourth explanation has evolved from longitudinal studies of children who were in intact families at the time of the first interview, or Time 1. Throughout the years, some of these children's parents divorced. This allowed the researchers at subsequent stages of the study to return to what they had observed at Time 1 and compare the behaviour and mental health of children whose parents stayed together to those of children whose parents eventually divorced (Desrosiers et al., 2012). Two of these studies found that, years before the divorce occurred, children of divorce already exhibited more problems than children whose parents stayed together (Block et al., 1988). This led these authors to warn that some of what is interpreted to be consequences of divorce may have actually existed before the divorce or may have been consequences of conflict within the marriage.

Subsequent studies, however, have established that the functioning of children and adolescents often changes negatively after their parents' separation, even when researchers control for the child's predivorce characteristics or difficulties (Aseltine, 1996; Morrison and Cherlin, 1995). In other words, the pre- and postdivorce differences "can be attributed to parental divorce and its accompanying disruption of family processes" (Forehand et al., 1997:157). This conclusion is reaffirmed by Cherlin and colleagues (1998) whose data indicate that predivorce characteristics cannot entirely explain children's problems after divorce. Nevertheless, it appears that, in many cases, children are already more difficult before the divorce, which makes sense, considering that their parents may have been fighting or were at the very least preoccupied (Strohschein, 2012). Exiting a dysfunctional* marriage may actually decrease children's antisocial behaviour (Strohschein, 2005). But, overall, anxiety and depression arise after separation but less so for those children whose familial functioning was very poor (Desrosiers et al., 2012).

Genetic Influence

A fifth theory relates to the genetic inheritance of problematic predispositions. A proportion of people who divorce or end a cohabitation do so because they are temperamental, conflictual, or impulsive individuals who pass on these predispositions to their children via genetic inheritance. These children are then both predisposed to being problematic and live in a home environment that is conflict-ridden, disorganized, and fosters their negative predispositions. When divorce happens in these situations, children's existing problems are exacerbated in a circular or feedback model of causality (Guo et al., 2008). In these cases, negative effects of divorce are caused both by the environment that divorce produces and genetic frailties passed on to the next generation (D'Onofrio et al., 2007).

Offspring of divorce "are more likely to have an interpersonal style marked by . . . problems with anger, jealousy, hurt feelings, communication, [and] infidelity" (Amato, 1996:638). These interpersonal behaviours may be both learned and genetically transmitted. Indeed, Hetherington (2003) found moderate correlations between parents' personality risks and offspring's personality risks. Genetic transmission would be particularly relevant to the offspring of parents whose divorce is caused by alcoholism, mental illness, and difficult personality characteristics (Rutter, 2002). When children are already genetically vulnerable, the environment created by the divorce exacerbates their vulnerabilities. They receive less attention, monitoring, and guidance, so that their genetic liabilities often find fertile ground upon which to grow (Horwitz et al., 2010). In contrast, children who have more positive predispositions and also have more stable parents are far less likely to develop problems after divorce—and their parents are also less likely to divorce to begin with.

WIDOWHOOD AND BEREAVEMENT

There were 1,261,100 widowed women but only 312,357 widowed men in Canada in 2006 (Statistics Canada, 2007f). At all age levels, women are more likely to be widowed than men and this difference widens with age. In fact, 45 percent of all women over the age of 65 are widows. Looked at differently, in 2001, 61 percent of senior men lived with a spouse or partner compared to only 35 percent of senior women (Statistics Canada, 2002b). As well, widowed men remarry or begin cohabiting far sooner than do widowed women, even within the younger age groups (Wu, 1995). Widowhood is therefore a **gendered stage** that affects women far more than men. Widowed women are also more likely than their male counterparts to become poor, especially elderly women who are living alone. However, they may have long-term friendships and are more likely than men to make new acquaintances (Martin-Matthews, 1991).

The death of a partner requires much readjustment in addition to the great emotional pain it brings. Age, health status, and level of independence may prolong or shorten bereavement. Adaptation to widowhood also depends on the income that is available, as a drop in income may add a tremendous burden to the afflicted person (Statistics Canada, 2004m). Among seniors, the loss of a spouse is often followed by some mental confusion, helplessness, depression, and general physical vulnerability, as well as a loss of interest in life. Health care costs generally rise following widowhood (Prigerson et al., 2000). The length of the grieving period depends on personal resources, the social support received, and how well prepared the bereaved spouse was for the death. With a long terminal illness, the spouse often begins mourning before death occurs. Thus, having been the caregiver for the deceased spouse also affects bereavement (Larkin, 2009). The loss of a spouse may bring feelings of relief and newly acquired freedom among older women (Hurd, 1999).

The quality of the relationship is also an important element in the grieving process, but may produce different results. Some may be relieved by the death of a partner who has made their lives miserable, while others may feel guilty. Spouses who took care of an ailing partner are often vulnerable (Schulz et al., 2008). When a good relationship existed, some spouses are inconsolable for a long period, yet others are thankful for the years they shared. Others are angry (Carr and Boerner, 2009). At least one longitudinal study has found that happy marriages are associated with more traumatic grief symptoms (Prigerson et al., 2000). Another study found that men and women who had been quite dependent on their spouse during marriage experienced a great deal of personal growth in widowhood (Carr, 2004).

Consequences of a Parent's Death for Children

Because widowhood occurs later in life than it did even 50 years ago, most young children are spared the loss of a parent by death. In Bibby's (2001) survey of adolescents, only 3 percent had a deceased parent while 25 percent had parents who were no longer living together. In terms of outcomes, in most western countries, children and adolescents of widowhood do as well as those in two-parent families or, at the very least, far better than children of divorced and single parents (Biblarz and Gottainer, 2000; Provencher et al., 2006; Steele et al., 2009). This is not to say that children do not grieve and miss their deceased parent. But they benefit from several social, familial, and personal advantages over children of divorce (Teachman, 2004). First, they are less likely to have been subjected to parental conflict before the death and are certainly not affected by it after. Second, the remaining parent is often left in a more favourable economic situation and may also be helped by life insurance benefits so that poverty occurs less frequently. This relative economic security also protects children from a host of accompanying stressors, such as having to move and change schools. Third, following death, there are social rites of bonding through which sympathy is bestowed upon children, which is quite a contrast to what happens to children in cases of parental divorce.

Fourth, the remaining parent's task of grieving, of caring for the children's own pain, and of behaving as a proper widow or widower delays his or her re-entry to the mating scene. Children are not faced with a parent who is suddenly unavailable because of the demands of his or her social life. There is no immediate competition for the parent's love. A fifth element protecting children of widowhood is that a good proportion of the deaths occur to couples who had a stable marriage. Thus, the individuals involved may not have included so many parents with difficult personalities as may be the case in situations of divorce (Simons et al., 1996). Consequently, the children themselves have greater chances of being stable individuals. They also tend to live with a very positive evaluation of the deceased parent (Krampe and Newton, 2012).

Children of widowhood may also adapt better to their parent's remarriage later because this loss makes them more receptive to acquiring a substitute parent. Bereaved children no longer have another parent, whether visiting or custodial, whose place seems to be usurped by a stepparent. No visitations are involved; there is only one home, one set of rules, and one family. With peers and teachers, a formerly widowed parent with children and a new spouse more easily pass for a "real" family.

REMARRIAGE AND REPARTNERING

Remarriage has become less common both because of the increasing tendency to cohabit after divorce, especially in Quebec (Beaupré, 2008), and to remain single later in life, again, particularly in Quebec (Charton and Lapierre-Adamcyc, 2010). Wu and Schimmele (2009) have estimated that 10 years after a divorce or breakup, only 52.5 percent of women and 70 percent of men are repartnered (also Shaffer and James, 2013). Interestingly enough, this pattern was already evident in the early 18th century in Quebec: Brun (2011) found that, while 41.6 percent of widowed women remarried, 68 percent of widowed men did. Currently, those separated from a cohabitation repartner more quickly, followed by the divorced, and then the widowed (Sweeney, 2010). Remarriage is more common among immigrants than Canadian-born citizens. As well, cohabitation rates after divorce are lower for women than men (Belleau, 2007:15). Rates of remarriage decline with age for both genders but more acutely so for women because men prefer younger women (England and McClintock, 2009; Sassler, 2010).

Life after Remarriage and Repartnering

Although heterosexual remarriages are as happy as first marriages, controlling for the number of years married, remarriages after a divorce have a higher rate of dissolution (Sweeney, 2010). However, this may not necessarily be the case among gay couples (van Eeden-Moorefield et al., 2012). Remarriages that are preceded by cohabitation are even less stable, although this finding is not unanimous (Teachman, 2008; Xu et al., 2006). Why are remarriages less stable? First, remarriages include persons who have already divorced, may be more accepting of divorce as a solution, and may be more ready to have recourse to it a second time. Second, spouses in remarriages may be less willing to compromise and may become disenchanted more rapidly. Third, there are fewer norms that guide these relationships, making it more difficult for the spouses to feel secure within their respective roles. Fourth, the structure itself of remarriage is a more complex one when children are brought in along with ex-spouses and ex-in-laws (Teachman, 2008). Indeed, remarriages without children from previous unions or only with children born to the union have a rate of divorce equivalent to that of first marriages.

A remarriage after divorce generally enhances the quality of adults' lives, emotionally, socially, and financially—the latter especially for women, but not as much as is the case for a first marriage (Sweeney, 2010). Many mother-headed families exit poverty through remarriage (Wilmoth and Koso, 2002). However, one should not ignore the fact that many divorced and widowed middle-aged and older women may prefer to remain single. These women's level of well-being should be quite high. When a remarriage or cohabitation endures, it may far outlast the first marriage. After years of remarriage or cohabitation, many spouses even forget that they have been married to someone else, particularly when there were no children from the first union. With time and more research, we will also develop a perspective regarding remarriage among same-sex couples.

The New Spouse and the Ex-Spouse

In 2002, 34 percent of all marriages included at least one spouse who had been previously married and nearly 46 percent of remarriages were remarriages for both spouses (Statistics Canada, 2006d). A remarried person whose spouse has children may need to relate to the children's other parent—the "ex"—particularly when there is shared custody as is the case in 47 percent of custody situations (Vézina, 2012). Relatively little research exists on this complex relationship, so I have borrowed from my fieldwork. It is obvious from the quotes that follow as well as from the entire research data that a husband's ex-wife or a wife's ex-husband is not overly popular among current wives and husbands or partners:

> *"We don't socialize. It's strictly business for the children's sake. I didn't marry my husband to acquire his ex-wife or her new husband, and my husband certainly does not want to be saddled with my ex-husband and his girlfriend. No. These relationships are nice on a TV screen but not in real life."*

The new husband or wife often resents the help the spouse has to give his or her ex, especially financial help. Noncustodial fathers frequently expressed serious concerns about their ex-wife's new partner who had become their children's live-in stepparent. They worried about the way the new stepfather treated the children, the example he provided, as well as the potential for sexual abuse:

> *"My ex-wife's husband is a burden to me in a way [he is an alcoholic]. I told my wife, my ex-wife, that she's got to be very careful never to let the girls alone with him. She was offended but she got the point. I just don't trust him."*

In some instances, the new wife and the ex-wife have to cooperate in order to raise the children and to arrange visitation schedules:

> *"We have a lot of planning to do to arrange her children's visits. . . . So we have a lot to talk about. But I think she must appreciate me because I don't have to have his children over as often as I do especially so since I have three of my own,*

Remarriages are as happy as first marriages; they are, however, more fragile and likely to end in another divorce. The structural complexity of remarriages—including the presence of children belonging to each partner—certainly contributes to their instability.

Rob Walls/Alamy

so actually I babysit for her. She doesn't [interfere], *not exactly, but what can you expect with so many children, it's a real interference even if they're quite good."*

Overall, the study unearthed a great deal of uneasiness about the possibility of having a close relationship with the ex, in part because of the threat of instability in the new union. For instance, a man's ex-spouse more easily accepts his new wife when the latter had not been involved with him in an adulterous relationship. Obviously, boundary maintenance is a key element in the success of remarriages.

Adjustment to Remarriage and Stepparenting

In Canada, the term "stepfamilies" includes both marital and cohabitational situations: In 2011, 48 percent of stepfamilies were common-law (Vézina, 2012). Thus, just over one-half of stepfamilies are remarriages. In Quebec, nearly 75 percent of all stepfamilies are common-law unions. In 2001 and 2011, 12 percent and 12.6 percent, respectively, of *families* composed of a couple with children were stepfamilies. Most are simple stepfamilies (children of only one of the spouses, generally the mother), while others are complex stepfamilies, that is, a mixture of children from both spouses and a "new" child of both parents. The proportion of parents in complex stepfamilies had increased by 2011, in part because a greater proportion have a new child than in the past (Vézina, 2012). (About 10 percent of Canadian *children* under the age of 15 are living in a stepfamily—Statistics Canada, 2012a.)

When neither spouse has children, adjustment to remarriage is no different than in a first marriage. It becomes more complex with stepchildren, and the complexity increases when there are both live-in and visiting stepchildren. In 2011, 32 percent of stepfamilies had children living at home part of the time only (Vézina, 2012). The period of readjustment takes several years before a stepfamily is stabilized. However, we have no research data concerning cohabitational stepfamilies compared to married ones.

Being a stepparent is not a role one expects to occupy and for which one is prepared, and it is not an **institutionalized** one (Cherlin, 1978). With stepchildren, the newlyweds have to adapt to two key roles simultaneously, parent and spouse, while these two roles are generally initiated separately in first unions. Stepparenthood is also a vilified role when one thinks of the "wicked stepmother" in fairy tales. The role is considered inferior to that of mothers. No norms or rules guide the behaviour of a "good" stepparent, as is the case for a good parent. Each stepparent more or less has to reinvent the role and the relationship, which can be both an advantage and a disadvantage. These remarks also apply to stepparenting in same-sex marriages (Nelson, 1996). Overall, the quality of parent-child relationships remains lower in stepfamilies over the years (Ward et al., 2009). In later life, having stepchildren is related to lower health outcomes and more caregiving problems (Pezzin et al., 2013; Sherman et al, 2013).

What Are the Effects of Parental Remarriage on Children?

This question is complicated by the fact that nearly as many divorced parents cohabit as marry (Vézina, 2012). As well, it is only recently that studies have focused on the fact that, when the parents repartner, *the child becomes a stepchild*. This familial restructuring requires a great deal of adjustment on the stepchild's part (Juby et al., 2005a). As well, in 43 percent of stepfamilies, a new child is born who is the couple's shared child (Vézina, 2012). Therefore, at some point after one of their parents' repartnering, *many stepchildren become halfsiblings* (Marcil-Gratton et al., 2003). When it is their father who has a new child, the older children who do not reside with him are likely to experience a decrease in paternal involvement (McGene and King, 2012) that follows into adulthood (Noël-Miller, 2013).

Stepchildren do not generally have better outcomes than those who remain with their divorced parent, except perhaps financially while they live at home (Brown, 2004; Tillman, 2008). Rather, they tend to have higher rates of problems, including delinquency (Savoie, 2007; Statistics Canada, 2007i; Zeman and Bressan, 2008). Hetherington (1988) found that the presence of a stepfather is often accompanied by fractious sibling interactions. Children, and especially boys, reaching adolescence disengage more from their siblings in remarried than in married families. However, parental cohabitation rather than remarriage seems to be associated with more child problems (Brown, 2006). This may stem from a lower stepfather investment in situations of cohabitation and the biological father's lesser involvement after the mother's repartnering (Guzzo, 2009b). One reason for the negative effects may be that stepchildren are likely to live in families that have or will have more conjugal unions than intact families, thus *more transitions* (Fagan, 2013): In 2011, 22 percent of parents in a stepfamily were in a *third union* compared to only 3 percent among parents in an intact family (Vézina, 2012). In contrast, there is a correlation between high stepfather involvement in remarriage and mothers' reports of fewer behavioural problems among children (Amato and Rivera, 1999).

When girls had a close relationship with their single mother, they are more likely to fare poorly in the remarriage. They miss the attention their mother lavished on them and may resent the intruder. For them, the remarriage constitutes a loss. As adults, estrangement from fathers also occurs more often among daughters than sons, and many daughters interpret this distancing to be the result of their father's remarriage (Ahrons and Tanner, 2003). In fact, 57 percent of young women and 30 percent of young men in remarried families leave home at a younger age than average (Beaupré et al., 2008). Aquilino (2005) has found that *remarried parents and stepparents are less inclined than other parents to feel that they have to support their children once they are older*. Moreover, stepdaughters are more at risk of being abused sexually by their stepfather or their mother's boyfriend than are daughters in intact families (Turner et al., 2007). This may stem from the fact that roles are more blurred than in biological families. Further, stepfathers have a low involvement in child care, which increases the risk for sexual abuse, even among fathers (in Giles-Sims, 1997). Stepfathers often become acquainted with the child only when she is older and can be perceived as an object of sexual attraction. It should be added, however, that *children in stepfamilies (and in single-parent families) have higher rates of several types of victimization* (see Chapter 13).

Boys adjust better than girls to being a stepchild, perhaps because they are at home less or because many benefit from the presence of a stepfather. Nevertheless, Pagani et al. (1997) have found that boys living with a recently remarried parent were the most hyperactive at school of all categories of boys aged 12 to 16. This latter result has also been revealed in the U.S. by Coughlin and Vuchinich (1996), who documented higher rates of early delinquency among boys who had lived in either a single-parent or stepparent family at age 10.

Overall, younger children usually adapt better, especially when they have always known the stepparent (Hofferth and Anderson, 2003). Many children and adolescents have a close relationship with their resident stepfather and this relates to better outcomes, especially when they also maintain a supportive relationship with their nonresident father (King, 2006). Many boys are advantaged by the addition of an authoritative (not to be confused with authoritarian) adult male role model in the family. Others, however, resent the intrusion of one more authority figures in their lives at a time when they may be seeking autonomy from their family (Hetherington and Kelly, 2002). Even small children benefit when a resident stepfather is involved with them (Bzostek, 2008). Yet, on many measures, young stepchildren still fare less well than other children (Kerr and Michalski, 2007).

There is evidence that a **parental cohabitation**, rather than remarriage, may be even less functional for stepchildren, especially when it takes place rapidly after parental separation (Fagan, 2013; Juby et al., 2007). Cohabitation may bring additional stressors to children's lives when it heightens a mother's or father's sense of insecurity and diminishes the quality of her or his parenting. Cohabiting stepparent families bring far more boundary ambiguity than married ones (Brown and Manning, 2009) and probably result in far less support from kin, at least at the outset—and this might be especially so with multiple prior cohabitations that each resulted in fertility (Bronte-Tinkew et al., 2009). Indeed, in general in Quebec and the rest of Canada, about 15 percent of second-born children become a halfsibling to an older child, that is, a child from another father (Duchesne, 2007). Overall, the research has consistently shown that children who live with their original *married* parents have fewer behavioural problems than other children, including children who live with their own cohabiting parents (Hofferth, 2006; Kerr and Michalski, 2007).

New children born to blended families may have more problems than children living with their still-married parents (Halpern-Meekin and Tach, 2008). "New" children born to a family reconstituted via cohabitation are over twice as likely as children born in an intact family to have their parents separate (Marcil-Gratton et al., 2003). Children in a remarriage, whether they are stepchildren or a new child born to the remarriage with stepchildren, have on average less positive outcomes than children whose parents have never divorced (Halpern-Meekin and Tach, 2008; Hofferth, 2006; Mac Con, 2006). These results are fairly consistent throughout the western world (Marks, 2006). At this point, no solid explanation exists because this research is very new.

Studies of young adults whose custodial parent's *remarriage has endured* have shown that these offspring were strongly attached to their family and benefited emotionally from it. It is thus possible that some of the positive effects of a parent's good and lasting remarriage do not appear until later in adulthood (see Sun and Li, 2008). Adult children remain more attached to stepparents they have lived with than to other stepparents, even after their parent divorced again (Schmeeckle et al., 2006).

GRANDPARENTING AFTER DIVORCE AND STEP-GRANDPARENTING

There are three separate situations in terms of grandparenting after divorce: Grandparenting after the divorce of an adult child; grandparenting after one has divorced at some earlier point, often long before the grandchildren arrive; and divorcing after one already is a grandparent. The available research pertains only to the first two situations, particularly the first one.

Maternal grandparents often help their divorcing children, especially daughters, both emotionally and instrumentally, particularly in terms of child care. But many other grandparents lose touch with grandchildren after a divorce because the custodial parent moves too far away or is not cooperative; others because their son, who is the visiting parent, more or less relinquishes his responsibilities. Such grandparents often experience a sharp decrease in well-being (Drew and Silverstein, 2007). This is yet another example of how adult children's marital or parental transitions create related transitions in the older generation: In the latter instance, grandparents lose their grandchildren.

Grandparents' visitation rights have been legalized in the Yukon and four provinces: Alberta, British Columbia, New Brunswick, and Quebec (Campbell and Carroll, 2007). In theory, in-laws, who are one's children's grandparents, should be a prime source of help. However, in my study, fewer than 20 percent of custodial parents actually talked to their former in-laws in a week's time, had visited them in a month's time, or had received some help from them (Ambert, 1989). Some 60 percent of respondents talked of former in-laws who were hostile toward them; 35 percent of the respondents felt that their former in-laws projected their negative attitude, either verbally or behaviourally, to their *grandchildren*. The most prominent difficulties were situations in which the ex-in-laws openly accused the custodial parent of having caused the failure of the marriage (48 percent). The second difficulty most frequently mentioned was ex-in-laws' comments concerning custodial parents' fitness as parents (46 percent). These accusations, gossip, and remarks ranged from stating that the parent was "unfit," was a "bad" mother or father, did not spend enough time with the children, left them alone too much, and was unfair or cruel to the father (or mother). These accusations were often extended to other areas of life, such as "poor money manager," "sexually loose," or "unable to hold down a job." Or grandparents would ask their grandchildren: *"Does she go out? Whom with?" "Is she home when you come home from school?" "Does she drink?"* One 14-year-old girl shouted at her mother, *"Grandma says you sleep with anyone so I don't see why you can tell me that I can't go out tonight!"*

Even when words were not spoken, grandparents' refusal to talk to or see the other parent was a behavioural indicator that did not go unnoticed by the children. It has been suggested that, where relevant, grandparents should visit their grandchildren at both their homes, and many do. Such visits contribute to legitimize the children's two-home nuclear family. Grandchildren would retain a psychologically intact family and would not feel torn between the two sides of their kinship group. It is regrettable that not enough research has been carried out on grandparenting after an adult child's divorce (Henderson and Moran, 2001), particularly on those who are helpful, even financially.

Another gap in the research exists in terms of grandparents who have themselves divorced. Divorced or remarried grandparents have a lower frequency of contact with their children (Uhlenberg and Hammill, 1998). Therefore, they, and especially grandfathers, are less involved with their grandchildren than nondivorced ones. But, in part, a good relationship between parents and grandparents compensates for the negative effect of divorce in the older generation (King, 2003a). In other words, these studies confirm the long-term consequences of divorce on family life later on and across generations (Connidis, 2003a).

For its part, step-grandparenting is a role that is even less culturally delineated than that of regular grandparenting, although at least 12 percent of Canadian families include a step-grandparent. A step-grandparent is created when an adult child remarries a person who has children. But a person may also marry a grandparent (who may be widowed or divorced) and thus becomes a step-grandparent to his or her grandchildren. Only the first situation has been studied, albeit very little.

In my research, stepmothers often went to see their own parents when their husband's children were visiting. In part, there was the desire to allow the stepchildren to receive as much attention as possible from their father without interference from the stepmother and her own children. In some cases, women knew that stepchildren and their mother resented them and they preferred to distance themselves from the situation. Thus, in many instances of nonresident fathers' remarriages, the stepmother and her kin effectively remain in the background. Her parents are step-grandparents in name only, and the termination of her marriage to him affects them very little as step-grandparents.

On the other hand, it may be easier for children and adolescents to accept a step-grandparent when they rebel against having a stepparent at home. This is a less threatening and far more benign relationship. When the remarried custodial parent visits with the new in-laws and brings the children along, the latter may indirectly acquire a sense of normalization of family relationships. Thus, step-grandparents may contribute to the integration of the reconstituted family and fulfill the same functions as actual grandparents (Attar-Schwartz et al., 2009; Connidis, 2010).

CONCLUSIONS: THE FAMILIAL AND SOCIAL IMPLICATIONS OF DIVORCE

According to Furstenberg and Cherlin (1991), divorce creates a **structural ambiguity** in that "the social and psychological tasks of divorce directly collide with the normal expectations of parenthood" (p. 28). Divorce represents a solution to conjugal unhappiness and misery. But *what is a solution for adults is not necessarily one for their children* (Beaujot, 2000). We also saw that the same can be said of remarriage and, especially, repartnering. Nevertheless, results on the effect of divorce on children have to be interpreted with caution. First, not all children are affected by their parents' divorce, whether positively or negatively. Some children had no problems before and acquire none after. Others had problems before and have the same or worse ones after. Yet others do better after the divorce of highly conflictual parents. Second, among children who are affected, the magnitude and duration of the effects differ greatly. There is also a great deal of difference in terms of the domains of life that are touched. For instance, some children are affected emotionally, others behaviourally, and still others in terms of school performance. The impact on the most affected touches on all these and other fronts. In many cases, the effects are lifelong. In general, it can be said that most marital status transitions are detrimental to children, if only temporarily—whether it is from marriage to single parenting, to divorce, to cohabitation, or to remarriage and another divorce (Fomby and Cherlin, 2007).

Contrary to expectations from various opposite corners of the ideological spectrum, "the increase in marital instability has not brought society to the brink of chaos, but neither has it led to a golden age of freedom and self-actualization" (Amato, 2000:1282). Apparently, neither has remarriage or repartnering after divorce become a cornucopia of blessings, especially for children.

Summary

1. The rates of divorce are discussed along with geographic region. Topics presented are the length of marriages before divorce, age at divorce, serial divorces, and the number of children implicated as well as the type of custody.

2. The sociocultural factors related to a high divorce rate are multiple and interlinked.

3. At the demographic level, the first four years of marriage are the most vulnerable to divorce. Besides poverty, there are several additional demographic risks to divorce. Selection and causality effects of cohabitation help explain its relationship to divorce. Reasons for divorcing vary.

4. The many factors associated with an easier adjustment to divorce among adults are described. Women who are younger and have remained employed are advantaged in the process of adjustment. After divorce, changes occur in ex-spouses' social networks.

5. At the individual level, children exhibit a wide range of effects of divorce, from being very negatively affected to benefiting from it. On average, however, children whose parents divorce experience higher rates of behavioural, emotional, and achievement problems, even into adulthood, than children raised by their two parents. The main theories explaining these negative consequences are presented.

6. Early widowhood is far less common than it was even in the 1920s. But widowhood is more common among women than men in middle age and after. It is a gendered stage. The stages and length of bereavement vary. In the long term, children of widowhood have outcomes similar to those whose parents remain together.

7. The rates of remarriage and repartnering are given. The structure of a remarriage is often more complex and related to higher divorce rates. The relationship between, say, a man's wife and ex-wife is described as are the effects of remarriage on children. Grandparenting after divorce and step-grandparenting are discussed.

8. Divorce and remarriage are adult institutions that often create a structural ambiguity that collides with the requisites of effective parenting. The factors associated with divorce and remarriage may evolve over time.

Analytical Questions

1. What relationships would you establish among the reasons people give for their own divorce and the sociocultural factors related to divorce?

2. How can young women organize their lives to prevent some of the negative consequences of divorce for themselves later on, if it ever occurs?

3. Of the theories meant to explain the negative effects of parental divorce on children, which would particularly apply to children whose parents have remarried and why?

4. Some politicians, especially south of the border, want to return to a time when divorce was difficult to obtain. What do you think the consequences would be? What, rather, should be done?

CHAPTER 13

Family Violence, Abuse, and Neglect

Artem Furman/Fotolia

OUTLINE

Dating and Courtship Violence

Verbal and Psychological Abuse of Partners

Spousal and Partner Physical Abuse
Factors Facilitating Spousal Abuse
The Effect of Spousal Violence on
Children

Child Abuse and Neglect by Parents
Child Abuse by Parents
*Consequences for Children of Abuse
by an Adult*
*Do Abused Children Become Abusive
Parents?*
Child Neglect by Parents

Child Sexual Abuse by Adults
Who and Where Are the Sexual Abusers?
Consequences of Sexual Abuse for the
Child: The Life Course Perspective

Sibling Violence
Sibling Physical Violence
Sibling Sexual Abuse

Peer Abuse
Peer Sexual Harassment and Abuse

Abuse of Parents by Children
Physical Abuse of Parents by Young
Children and Adolescents
Abuse of Elderly Parents by Adult
Children

Conclusions: The Larger Context of
Family Violence

Summary
Analytical Questions

A 16-year-old rapes his 15-year-old girlfriend in his car on the way back from the movies. He felt that they had been going out long enough and it was time "to go all the way." (Abstract from student autobiography)

A police officer brings a 14-year-old girl back home after finding her doing drugs with two older males at a strip mall. It's 3 a.m. She lives in an affluent suburban home. Her parents did not know that she was out. (Abstract from student autobiography)

A 10-year-old girl has been fondled, kissed in the genital area, and convinced to "touch" the genitals of her father's best friend. He is "part of the family," and often babysits the two children, a boy and a girl. One day, he forces the girl to practise oral sex on him when the boy, age 11, walks in. He later tells his parents who call the police. (Abstract from student autobiography)

A man stalks his wife after she leaves him for battery. Despite a restraining order preventing him from coming within 300 feet, he savagely stabs her as she returns home from work. She leaves two children. (Canadian newscast)

Social workers are called to a home where they find five children ranging in age from two to 10 in a filthy and barely furnished home. The children are hungry and cold, and the level of functioning of all but the oldest one indicates delay due to neglect. The two parents involved have been out on a crack-induced "trip" for three days. (American newscast)

A man is beaten up by his gay partner so severely that he requires emergency surgery. The battering has been going on for two years. (American newscast)

What these vignettes share in common is either violence or neglect. In order to form a more complete picture of abuse and neglect afflicting Canadian families, to these situations one can add sibling violence and peer abuse—which are the most common types of maltreatment—and the less well-known child-to-parent abuse (Duffy and Momirov, 2005). In this chapter, various forms of family violence and neglect are analyzed as reflections of cultural norms that foster such behaviours and of social inequalities that oppress some groups more than others (Marx, 1867). Indeed, not everyone in our society is equally vulnerable to being an abuser and/or a victim: Social inequalities by class, race/ethnicity, religion, marital status, and especially gender and age come to the fore. Females of all ages and all races are more likely to be abused (DeKeseredy and Dragiewicz, 2007; Sev'er, 2002). Hence, feminist theories are particularly relevant. A methodological note is necessary: A majority of cases of family, dating, and peer violence goes unreported. Second, reported cases can be difficult to interpret, even in official statistics, which often originate from several sources: police statistics and reports from victims and aggressors in population surveys.

DATING AND COURTSHIP VIOLENCE

While family violence and partner abuse have become more socially and politically visible, dating abuse is only beginning to emerge in the public consciousness. For a substantial segment of Canadian youths, dating and now hook-ups are a fertile ground upon which to continue their aggressive behaviours toward their peers. For others, particularly among males, it is an opportunity to discover a new arena in which to exercise **power**. Most incidents of courtship or dating violence are not reported to authorities or to parents, but estimates are that over 20 percent of women university students are assaulted in a broad sense. In 2010, the police reported about 54,100 victims of dating violence compared to 48,700 victims of spousal violence (Statistics Canada, 2012f). Overall, eight out of 10 victims are women. *Both men and women are more at risk of violence by dating partners than by spouses* (Statistics Canada 2013a). Younger men and women aged 15 to 24 are more likely to be victims of violent crime in general than other age groups (Statistics Canada, 2013d).

Many youths actually consider acts of violence a normal part of the "excitement" of the dating process:

> *"We both have strong personalities and don't let people walk all over us and that goes for each other. I don't mind punching him in the stomach or kicking his legs if he's too fresh and he does the same, except that he's bigger and it hurts more. My mother gets on my nerves about this because she says, 'If that's the way the both of you behave now think what it's going to be like in 5 years.'"*

Other women students are not so complacent:

> *"I'd rate myself as unhappy at this point because I have to decide if I'll stay with my boyfriend of three years. Once in a while he calls me names but recently he's grabbed me and shoved me in the car and once against the wall another time and I am afraid that I'll end up a battered wife."*

Indeed, dating violence predicts domestic abuse later on, whether it occurs in cohabitation or marriage. Perhaps the most surprising aspect of courtship violence, as is the case for spousal abuse, is that both men and women are involved in inflicting harm, often within a same couple, especially among younger partners (Renner and Whitney, 2010; Swinford et al., 2000). However, women sustain most of the injuries and much of the violence carried out by women is in self-defence or *reactive* (Warner, 2010). In contrast, men are more likely to use violence as an exercise of power or as an attempt to regain control (DeKeseredy and Dragiewicz, 2007). Unstable dating relationships (in and out) or "churning" are more related to abuse than are those that are stable or break up definitely (Halpern-Meekin et al., 2013).

Date rape is an issue that is also rarely reported. The situation of date and even acquaintance rape became more complex in the 1990s with the arrival of readily available chemicals that, when dropped in a woman's drink, secure her compliance. The woman cannot later recall much of what occurred. These situations happen on campuses as well as in bars and nightclubs where the purpose is to meet members of the opposite sex. They include gang rape, even in high schools and college campuses. Gang rape is the ultimate in terms of a "power trip" and **male dominance**. These instances well illustrate young males' readiness to circumvent decency and legality in order to secure their own sexual gratification and to be able to justify their acts.

The sources of dating violence are still debated. Most studies have turned to psychological and familial explanations while excluding social and cultural influences. This omission of factors at the sociocultural level distorts reality and prevents us from acquiring a full understanding of how particular behaviours emerge (Sev'er, 2002). For instance, in certain peer groups, including professional athletes who have been much in the news in recent years with respect to violence, the **social construction of masculinity** includes violent attitudes in general, and particularly toward females. It also involves a mentality of sexual entitlement (Hartwick et al., 2007). Thus, a feminist perspective indicates that, among heterosexual couples, the overall gender stratification provides an open-door policy for violence against women. This type of cultural climate is reflected in the media. As well, much pornographic material, to which many men and boys are exposed, contains graphically detailed violent sex. Similarly, as we soon see, children engage in a great deal of peer abuse that can easily be transposed into dating relationships. This construction of masculinity should also be related to the fact that too many males, particularly disadvantaged ones, as seen in Chapter 8, feel entitled to have babies they rarely support.

Studies on childhood exposure to interparental violence as the key factor in the origins of dating violence are inconclusive: Some find a relationship between the two but others do not (Foshee et al., 2005). The least that can be said is that exposure to parental violence during adolescence and young adulthood certainly constitutes a risk factor. So does prior abuse in childhood (Wekerle et al., 2009). On average, males who engage in dating violence were more aggressive as boys and more likely to have committed delinquent acts and used drugs than other males (Capaldi and Clark, 1998; Simons et al., 1998). Many exhibited behavioural problems as children and may still be out of control; the same pattern occurs among some abusive females. These results corroborate those of other researchers who report two categories of married abusers: those who limit their abuse to the home and those who are violent in other contexts as well (Delsol et al., 2003).

Although rape is herein discussed in the context of dating relationships, one should not forget that, across the world in countries where civil wars rage, whether Syria, Afghanistan, and especially in some countries of Africa, rape is and has always been "one of the spoils" of war (show of power and revenge). Reports from the *Toronto Star* (2011a) and *The Economist* (2011b) estimate that in the Congo thousands of females are being raped daily, ranging in age from 3 to 80: "At worst, rape is a tool of ethnic cleansing and genocide as in Bosnia, Darfur and Rwanda." Many of these women are then rejected by their family and community because they have ruined the family honour. As well, it is estimated that 80 percent of these rapes target girls under 18 and that, of these, 20 percent are under the age of 11 (Aubert and Holder, 2013).

VERBAL AND PSYCHOLOGICAL ABUSE OF PARTNERS

Verbal abuse consists of repeatedly addressing one's partner with epithets, foul language, berating and demeaning put-downs, threats, and criticisms, even in public (DeKeseredy, 2000). Its purpose is to dominate, to exercise power, and to show who is "the boss." It is also used to rationalize or excuse one's bad behaviour by demeaning the other. Verbal abuse marks the **erosion of civility** and sets a precedent upon which physical abuse can be added. Indeed, physical abuse is generally accompanied or preceded by verbal insults and attempts by one partner or both to intimidate or control the other. Males particularly tend to practise both types of abuse in severe cases of psychological and physical assaults (Hamby and Sugarman, 1999). The 2009 General Social Survey showed that 34 percent of Aboriginal women and 17 percent of non-Aboriginal women had suffered psychological, verbal, and financial abuse from their spouse (Brennan, 2011). Of all these psychologically abused women,

61 percent had suffered put-downs, name calling

60 percent had a partner who needed to know where she was at all times

56 percent had a partner who did not want her to talk to others

45 percent were forced to limit contact with her family/friends

30 percent had had damages or destruction of some of her possessions or property

15 percent were prevented from knowledge of and access to family income

Verbal abuse is quite salient in music videos favoured by youths, and it is nearly always directed against women because, *in a subtle way, culture defines women as legitimate targets of male violence.* The words "bitch" and "ho" are widespread in a growing segment of younger cohorts; they are often used as soon as a quarrel erupts. It is not unusual to hear young couples calling each other foul and demeaning names; such insults were rarely overheard just 20 years ago. These exchanges represent a dangerous escalation, a lack of civility, part of what Garbarino (1995) refers to as the "toxic" environment surrounding families raising children.

Psychological abuse is often reciprocal, underreported, and its effects on the parties are underestimated (Follingstad and Edmundson, 2010). When it is bilateral, both spouses often have high scores on dominance, jealousy, and psychological aggression (Kar and O'Leary, 2013). Renzetti (1997) has discovered among same-sex couples that this type of abuse is often tailored to fit a partner's vulnerabilities. Coercive control can occur without physical violence with damaging consequences (Anderson, 2008). During my study on divorce, ex-spouses, particularly ex-wives, frequently mentioned that such verbal violence had been a pattern in their past marriage:

> One woman who was obese was repeatedly called a "fat slob" and a "pile of lard" by her husband. He would tell her to "move your fat ass" or order her to "sit on your god-damn fat ass, I have something to tell you." At the dinner table, she had to eat like a bird lest he observed to the children, "There goes your mother, stuffing her fat face."

This tailoring of verbal abuse can focus on facial features, body shape, clumsiness, lack of mental agility, as well as unemployment and financial difficulties: One ex-wife had repeatedly taunted her unemployed husband in front of their children as *"good for nothing"* and *"you're no real man."* Verbal abuse can also take the form of threats and become a form of psychological blackmail:

> One divorced woman recalled that her ex-husband used to threaten to tell her children that she had given up her first-born for adoption—disregarding the fact that the infant had been his and he had not wanted him (this was before they married). . . . One ex-husband was threatened by his ex-wife of legal exposure if he did not "cough up" more monthly support; at some point in the past, he had defrauded his former employers in order to meet his wife's extravagant demands but had never been caught. Now that she was his ex-wife, she used his illegal past activities as leverage to get more money.

Psychological abuse can turn into physical abuse and even life-threatening situations (Renzetti, 1997). Emotionally abusive relationships often lead to physical violence (Frye and Karney, 2006). In 2004, the prevalence of physical violence was 34 percent for females and 26 percent for males in emotionally abusive relationships but 1 percent when there was no emotional abuse (Brzozowski and Brazeau, 2008).

Verbal and psychological abuse is an issue that is particularly important among adolescents who begin dating at an early age, as described in Chapter 7. Young girls are easy prey to being manipulated, ordered around, having their whereabouts controlled, and may even consider their boyfriends' possessiveness and extreme jealousy as proof of love—and, now, the ubiquitousness of texting and sexting expands the scope of this problem. Thus, the dating process may have negative effects on the personal development of some teenagers and on the dynamics of their intimate relationships later. There is little research on these aspects of dating and, also, of hook-ups.

SPOUSAL AND PARTNER PHYSICAL ABUSE

Spousal or partner physical abuse covers quite a range of acts, so that one has to exercise caution when interpreting statistics. The Conflict Tactics Scale (CTS) devised by Straus (1979) is commonly used and includes the following acts, in ascending order of severity:

> Threw something at spouse; pushed, grabbed, or shoved spouse; slapped spouse; kicked, bit, or hit spouse with fist; hit or tried to hit spouse with something; beat up spouse; choked spouse; threatened spouse with a knife or gun; used a knife or a gun on spouse.

However, this and similar scales have several drawbacks. For instance, it is not a valid instrument for determining whether an act is committed in self-defence or what its consequences are.

In the 2009 General Social Survey, 6.4 percent of Canadian women and 6 percent of men reported that they had experienced spousal abuse *in the past five years*, with a higher proportion for previous than current unions (Statistics Canada, 2011f): Indeed, spousal violence is four times more likely to have occurred between ex-partners than current partners in *the past five years*. In contrast, 21 percent of Aboriginal persons in Nunavut and the Northwest Territories reported spousal abuse (Paletta, 2008) as did

15 percent of Aboriginal women in the provinces (Perreault, 2011). As well, approximately 75 percent of spouses who report having been a victim of violence also admit to having been an offender (Laroche, 2007:72). In 2004, 44 percent of female victims reported having been **injured** compared to 19 percent of male victims; 14 and 11 percent of these injuries resulted in hospital services (Laroche, 2007:93). As well, 34 percent of females feared for their lives versus 10 percent of males (Brzozowski and Brazeau, 2008). Here, as well, these figures are twice as high among Aboriginals (Perreault, 2011). Overall, Aboriginal women in the provinces, and particularly in the territories, are about three times as likely to be victims of violence in general than are other Canadian women (Brennan, 2011). Yet, General Social Survey respondents overwhelmingly admit that they do not report incidents of spousal abuse (Brennan, 2011).

Data from the 1999 and 2004 General Social Surveys also show a decline in the overall rate of *self-reported* spousal victimization (Brzozowski and Brazeau, 2008). In these statistics, the word "spousal" includes a current as well as an ex-spouse, whether by marriage or cohabitation. These numbers are still extremely high in the Northwest Territories and Nunavut, followed by Saskatchewan (because of the elevated Aboriginal rates), and lowest in Ontario and the Maritimes. Although rare in Canada, nearly half of all family homicides are spousal. However, spousal homicides have declined since 1978 by more than half. Between 1998 and 2008, there were 753 such homicides: The victims were women in 80 percent of the cases. Common-law partners, both men and women, were more likely to be victims than married partners (Ogrodnik, 2009).

Often, once a wife becomes a target of abuse, she is at risk of becoming a repeat victim. In 2009, 50 percent of the Aboriginal victims of spousal violence reported being victimized more than three times in the past five years compared to 29 percent of other Canadians (Perreault, 2011). Women are even attacked during pregnancy, which, of course, does not show in the CTS (Sev'er, 2002). However, in 1999 in Canada, over 60 percent of violence was not repeated during *the following year* (Laroche, 2007:84). Therefore, it would be important to have longitudinal studies showing the evolution of the beginning, continuation, or cessation of incidents of violence within couples.

The fact that wives also commit acts of violence does not mean that they are more violent than or even as violent as husbands or dates. Women who are truly and forcefully violent and abuse their male partners are still the exception. Above all, women may fear painful retaliation if they hit their partners. They attack with far less force and energy than men. They are generally less muscular, tall, heavy, and strong; thus, the results of their aggressiveness are generally inconsequential physically and their partners may not even take these assaults seriously.

Rape is another aspect of spousal violence (Duffy, 2004). Men who are very violent toward their wives often combine physical battering with sexual assault. This is the ultimate way of establishing one's power over the other. Browne (1997) points out that women whose partners are sexually aggressive are also at a higher risk of suffering more severe physical aggression than women with male partners who are physically but not sexually violent.

Another example of the effect of abuse on women is the existence of **shelters** for abused women. On April 15, 2010, there were 593 such shelters in Canada with

4,645 resident women and 426 others who had been turned away that day. Nearly one-third of these women were repeat admissions. On average, each woman reported five reasons for seeking admission. The most common reasons were emotional abuse (66 percent) and physical abuse (53 percent); issues of lack of housing, mental health, and drug/alcohol dependency were also involved but in lower proportions (Statistics Canada, 2011g).

Many batterers are actually quite pathological: But *pathology is culturally influenced* or even created. In our society, as in many others, pathology can lead to interpersonal violence or abuse. As was the case for dating, both men and women who engage in spousal violence are more likely than nonviolent spouses to have been involved in delinquency and to have been considered troublemakers when adolescents (Giordano et al., 1999).

Johnson distinguished between two types of interpartner violence. The first is a matter of self-regulation and is situational or **reactive** (Johnson and Leone, 2005). The second pertains to **power and control**; it is what Johnson called "intimate terrorism." This type of violence, generally against women, is less frequent but predominates among victims who seek refuge in shelters (Laroche, 2007:170); it may be why some women are at risk of being battered when they try to separate or after they have separated from their boyfriend or husband (DeKeseredy, 2009). As a result, women often have to seek a restraining court order (Duffy, 2004). Despite this, some are killed. This is a reflection of a patriarchal ideology concerning intimate relations and abuse of women (DeKeseredy and Dragiewicz, 2007).

Men who lack the material and status ability "of expressing and maintaining power within their intimate relationships may engage in violence as a means of reestablishing their domestic position" (Anderson, 1997:668). The cultural framework allows them to have recourse to violence as an ego booster. Men in stressful occupations may compensate against their partners while others in physically violent occupations, such as the police and the military, may bring the controlling techniques into the home (Melzer, 2002).

Factors Facilitating Spousal Abuse

As we saw above, spousal abuse, as with dating abuse, is facilitated by our **culture of oppression and violence** as well as by ideologies of masculine dominance over women. Spousal abuse is in large part the result of a desire to control women, although women are not exempt from this motive (Migliaccio, 2002). Within this broad cultural context, other factors come into play. For instance, a proportion of dating and domestic violence is committed under the influence of **alcohol** or other substances (Brzozowski and Brazeau, 2008), including among elderly couples (Ma and Rietschlin, 2012). This is reported by one-half of Aboriginal victims of spousal violence compared to one-third in the rest of the victimized Canadian population (Statistics Canada, 2006e). Many batterers and even their victims construct alcohol as a socially acceptable excuse for violence. It is part of the **social construction of masculinity** (Peralta et al., 2010). Alcohol facilitates abuse because it de-inhibits control. When both the batterer and the victim have been drinking, they may not even notice the presence of their children. Alcohol and drugs are involved in a majority of the cases *when the police are called*, perhaps because women are more afraid of the violence and, if they have also been drinking, they may be less inhibited and less inclined to excuse their partner.

In North America, social inequalities pertaining not only to gender but also to income, wealth, status, and power constitute the main factors related to spousal abuse. For instance, very **low-income** couples and women with relatively little schooling are at an increased risk for partner violence (DeKeseredy, 2009) and are more likely to stay in a violent marriage (Kraeger et al., 2013). A lack of social control may in part explain the following (DeMaris et al., 2003): Poor couples who live in **disadvantaged neighbourhoods** are more at risk of spousal abuse (and, as seen later, child abuse) than similar couples who live in economically secure environments (Miles-Doan, 1998). This is also the case for spousal abuse among seniors, perhaps because of social isolation (Ma and Rietschlin, 2012). The presence of social problems in some neighbourhoods and lack of an effective community, as described in Chapter 5, are highly applicable to partner violence (Browning, 2002). In contrast, the absence of visible violence in relatively comfortable areas may act as a deterrent against domestic abuse. In fact, *poor neighbourhoods exhibit higher rates of violence of all sorts, and this includes spousal abuse*. Children in low-income households witness physical violence twice as often as others (Statistics Canada, 2003e). However, this should not be taken to mean that domestic abuse never occurs among the more affluent. It does.

Few studies focus on ethnicity. Yet, in the U.S., one study indicates substantial levels of cohabitant and spousal abuse among blacks (Uzzell and Peebles-Wilkins, 1989). Domestic violence among **oppressed minorities** may have sources compounding those among whites (Baskin, 2003). For instance, blacks are differentially located in society because of their devalued colour. Prejudice and discrimination may be internalized among a segment of black males, who then demean black women and express their general rage toward them rather than projecting it elsewhere (Crenshaw, 1994). One cannot overlook the fact that, in some countries with a more rigid patriarchal structure, women as a group are more likely to be abused—and this pattern is pursued once they settle in Canada (Papp, 2010; Sev'er, 2002). For instance, particularly among Muslims and Hindus, the prerogatives of patriarchy include violence against female kin—in order to keep them "in line" and to save the family's honour (Sev'er, 2002). This includes murder or honour killings (Sev'er and Yurdakul, 2001). This culturally-driven violence is frequently transplanted to Canada (Papp, 2010). In a study in Egypt, Yount and Li (2009) reported that half of the wives justified wife beating, especially rural women and dependent wives. Research by *The Globe and Mail* in Afghanistan shows widespread female abuse, 82 percent of which is committed by family members (Leeder, 2009). Thus, one would also need research on other minority groups, particularly immigrants who hail from countries where wife abuse is rampant, such as Pakistan and Afghanistan, as well as India where rape of women by strangers is a large problem (Dutta and Malhotra, 2013). Such women are particularly vulnerable as they are unlikely to be in a position to report their "problems" to the police, because they would then be socially ostracized by their group.

Aboriginal spousal violence deserves special mention. The consensus of the sparse research on this topic is that it is extremely high. However, as pointed out in the 2006 Department of Justice report, no one knows how high (Chartrand and

McKay, 2006): Estimates range from 25 percent of women and 13 percent of men (Patterson, 2003) to as high as 90 percent among women in other studies—versus 7 percent in Canada in general. Complicating the issue of gathering information is the fact that underreporting of violence in general is even more widespread among Aboriginals than among other Canadians because *more Aboriginals are victims of someone they know* (Statistics Canada, 2006e). Therefore, fear of reprisals and ostracism within the community is widespread as well as a lack of hope that anyone can do anything to prevent it (Lane et al., 2002; Stewart et al., 2001).

In turn, the high rates of Aboriginal spousal violence are related to widespread childhood and youth abuse, including sexual victimization (Hylton, 2002). Most of this violence occurs at the hand of other Aboriginals (Statistics Canada, 2006c). This has resulted in a "normalization" of domestic violence in some communities (Lane et al., 2002; Stewart et al., 2001). Thus, overall, females have extremely high rates of victimization (Levan, 2001) along with youth (ANAC, 2002). These forms of brutalization as well as high criminal rates are interrelated and result from past colonization of Aboriginals and their culture, as detailed in Chapter 2 (ANAC & RCMP, 2001; Chartrand and McKay, 2006). In turn, this violence becomes a form of internal colonization.

Two other factors that facilitate spousal violence are related to couple structure. For one, **same-sex-partner** violence is as much a matter of power and control as it is in heterosexual couple violence, except that gender or patriarchal ideologies are not an issue. The rate of violence among same-sex couples is higher than that among heterosexuals (Cameron, 2003). Indeed, gays, lesbians, and bisexuals suffer more from partner abuse than do heterosexuals (Balsam et al., 2005). In Canada, in 2004, 15 percent of gays and lesbians and 28 percent of bisexuals reported being victims of spousal abuse compared to 7 percent of heterosexuals (Beauchamp, 2008). More research is needed to explain this phenomenon but it is possible that social isolation, stigmatization, and a lack of an effective community in these respects are contributing factors.

For their part, **cohabiting couples** have the highest rate of partner violence and cohabiting women often suffer more severe abuse than married ones (Brown and Bulanda, 2008; Brownridge and Halli, 2001). Both in Quebec and the rest of Canada, even men have a much higher risk of being victimized in cohabitations than in marriages (Laroche, 2007:121; Statistics Canada, 2011f). These facts undermine the claim of those who portray marriage per se as a "licence to hit." We do not know what causes the link between abuse and cohabitation: Is the abuse taking place in short-term cohabitations with a lesser commitment? Or do some individuals with a tendency for aggressiveness channel themselves into these types of cohabitation?

The Effect of Spousal Violence on Children

Statistics Canada (2012f) reports that, in 2009, 52 percent of victims of spousal abuse who had children said that their children heard or witnessed at least one of these assaults in the previous five years. This was up from 43 percent in 2004. Further, children tended to witness the more severe spousal assaults, often with resulting injuries. Because the reports pertained to the past five years, a great proportion of what children witnessed occurred before their parents separated (Perreault, 2011). Many children thus watch or hear their father beat their mother or both parents throw projectiles at each other and engage in mutual slapping and punching, with much yelling and name calling. Some effects on children are immediate (Minze et al., 2010), others are delayed until certain life transitions occur, and many are long lasting (Sev'er, 2002). One immediate effect is fear, and an urge to run away or to help the victimized parent. Children may throw themselves between parents, and older sons may try to fend off a father. Many children are injured in the process. Other children call for neighbours' help or even the police. A few others take the abuser's side, as explained by an older woman student:

> *"Ever since I can recall, my father always beat up my mother and in those days (1960–70) women had to put up with it. I used to hide when it would start and then I would run to my mother and hug her and kiss her and cry with her. As a result, I have always been a sad child and to this day I tend to be anxious and easily pessimistic. But perhaps the saddest part is that my older brother never felt sorry for my mom. He used to tell her like my father did, 'That serves you right, next time do as he says.' My brother . . . grew up just like [my father] and he often beat me up too and a couple of times he slapped my mother. . . . [He] beat up his ex-wife and he's tried it on many women but he's such a hypocrite: At work he's a model citizen."*

Even if children do not witness partner abuse, the resulting familial atmosphere may be tense, difficult, and coparenting may be impossible. Resulting harsh parenting may become another risk factor for children (Graham et al., 2012).

On average, children of abused mothers have more behavioural and psychological problems and exhibit less interpersonal sensitivity (Moss, 2004). Other long-lasting effects include lower psychological well-being in adulthood, increased risk for depression, as well as poor parent-child relationships (Russell et al., 2010). These consequences may be exacerbated by the negative effect of battering on the mothers

Parental disagreements that are resolved amicably present a positive context for children to learn about peaceful conflict resolution. However, verbal abuse and destructive quarrels are not only traumatic for children but also constitute a negative learning context.

goodluz/Fotolia

themselves, including health issues (Sillito, 2012). Women who are repeatedly abused have high rates of sleep disorders, depression, illness, and even suicide attempts. These severe maternal symptoms are likely to disrupt mothers' ability to parent and, consequently, negatively affect at least some aspects of many children's personal development (Zerk et al., 2009). Partner violence may also lead to the neglect of small children via a mother's consequent reduced well-being and ability to provide care and nurturance (Nicklas and Mackenzie, 2013) as well as reduced ability to coparent (Kan et al., 2012).

The greatest negative impact of interparental violence occurs in those families where parents are the most violent toward each other *and* engage in the entire spectrum of abusive activities (McDonald et al., 2009). By the age of 18, offspring from these dysfunctional families have generally been exposed to *other* adversities, including poverty, divorce, parental alcoholism, and even criminality and childhood abuse. Once these contextual circumstances are controlled for, the direct negative effect of interparental violence is substantially reduced but does not disappear entirely (Fergusson and Horwood, 1998). The follow-ups from the Canadian National Longitudinal Survey of Children and Youth showed that children who had witnessed some physical violence (parents, siblings) at home were more aggressive at the time, especially boys, and that their chances of being aggressive and/or anxious were still higher two and four years later (Statistics Canada, 2003e).

The matter of the **intergenerational transmission of violence**—that is, from witnessing parental violence to committing dating and partner violence later on—is much discussed. Pertaining to Aboriginals, McGillivray and Comaskey (1999) pointed out that witnessing violent parental behaviour "begins the process of brutalization and violent coaching that may lead to a transgenerational cycle of intimate violence and to offending outside the family setting" (p. 72). But the evidence is not unanimous, and some researchers do not find more violence in the family background of spousal abusers than nonabusers (Delsol et al., 2003). In a sample of 340 men charged with assault of a female partner, a third had witnessed parental violence or been maltreated themselves. The authors concluded that perpetrators "with a family violence history more strongly endorse ideas that present women and feminine attributes in a negative light" (Lee et al., 2013:85). Others point out that "the most typical outcome for individuals exposed to violence in their families of origin is to be nonviolent in their adult families" (Heyman and Slep, 2002:860). Even researchers who support the cycle of violence theory recognize that "the mechanisms by which violence is transmitted appear to be complex and multidimensional" (O'Keefe, 1998:41). As well, certain children are more **resilient** than others because of an easier temperament and higher cognitive abilities (Martinez-Torteya et al., 2009).

O'Keefe distributed questionnaires to 1,012 high school students in the Los Angeles area. She asked them about parental violence, their own dating experience, their attitude toward dating violence, and the type and frequency of violence they witnessed in their community and at school. She then centred her research on the 232 students who reported a great deal of interparental violence in order to see what would characterize those who followed the parental example. She found that 49 percent had inflicted violence against a dating partner at least once. As well, 55 percent reported having been victimized at least once. Among males, those who had inflicted or been the victim of dating violence tended to be of lower socioeconomic status (SES) and reported more exposure to community and school violence. Among females, those who had followed the parental example or who had been victimized were characterized by exposure to community and school violence, poor school performance, and having been abused as a child.

Therefore, the exposure to a *high level* of parental violence places youths at a great risk of committing similar acts and/or being victimized themselves. But there are **other risk factors** at the social level that increase the likelihood of such occurrences in the students' own lives (Onyskiw and Hayduk, 2001). The variable of exposure to **community and school violence** is particularly significant because it appears as a risk factor for both genders. Conversely, the protective factors that intervene to prevent the transmission of violence across the two generations are higher SES and low community and school violence. Thus, O'Keefe's results on dating violence confirm those of studies finding *more spousal and child abuse in disadvantaged areas where other types of violence exist.* These results also help to understand the higher rates of abuse in Aboriginal communities. It should be noted that, so far, there is no research on the effect of spousal violence on children who live in same-sex-parent families.

CHILD ABUSE AND NEGLECT BY PARENTS

Physical violence and sexual abuse of children are generally investigated separately and are then partitioned between adult perpetrators versus peer and, only recently, sibling perpetrators. Unfortunately, this partitioning prevents a more comprehensive understanding of the role of maltreatment *in general* in a child's life course (Finkelhor et al., 2009). Indeed, children who are distressed by prior victimization often become at greater risk for re-victimization by yet other sources (Cuevas et al., 2010). In 1998, the incidence of cases of abuse and neglect *investigated* by welfare agencies was estimated to be 21.5 per 1,000 children—40 percent of which constituted neglect, particularly failure to supervise (Health Canada, 2001). The Ontario Health Supplement Study found that 31 percent of male and 21 percent of female respondents aged 15 and over reported some abuse that had occurred while they were growing up (MacMillan et al., 1997) and 31 percent of adolescents in Bibby's (2001) study reported that a close friend had been physically abused at home. In 2011, Statistics Canada found that 9.6 percent of women and 4.1 percent of men whose parents had had *no* alcohol or drug problems reported physical abuse at home. In contrast, 35 percent of women and 24 percent of men whose parents had had addiction problems reported abuse (Langlois and Garner, 2013).

It is customary in textbooks to begin discussions of child abuse with abuse by parents, even though, as they enter the school system, children are far more likely to be maltreated by their siblings and peers (right part of Figure 13.1). Only very small children are maltreated mainly by their parents or a caregiver (left part of Figure 13.1)—more by fathers than mothers for assaults, *and more by fathers in terms of neglect when they are absent. But the latter situation is never entered in the statistics.* AuCoin (2005) reports that, according to police data, children who are physically

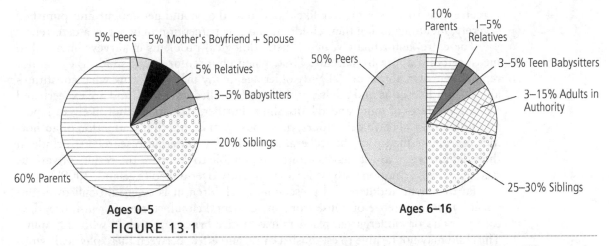

FIGURE 13.1

Estimates of the Main Sources of Child Maltreatment up to Age 16

assaulted within the family are so by a father in 44 percent of the cases, mothers 21 percent, and brothers 15 percent. Figure 13.1 presents a reasonable estimate of the overall sources of child abuse up to age 16 in terms of who tends to maltreat children the most frequently.

Child Abuse by Parents

In Canada, Children's Aid Societies were given the right to remove abused or neglected children from their homes for the first time in Ontario in 1893. Yet, child abuse in general was brought to the public's attention only in the 1960s by doctors who coined the concept of the *battered-child syndrome* (Kempe et al., 1962). It is therefore impossible to estimate how widespread it was before that date. In 2007, there were 41,000 reported cases of physical violence against children up to age 18, of which 9,000 were family related: 5,300 were caused by a parent, generally a father (Nemr, 2009). At the extreme of child abuse are child homicides by parents. Ogrodnik (2009) reports 336 cases of a child killed by a parent between 1998 and 2008, with an equal number of boys and girls. The perpetrator was a father in 65 percent of the cases. *(The term "father" includes stepfathers and live-in mothers' boyfriends.)* Infants are at a higher risk of fatal abuse from their mothers up to age four months, from their fathers between four to 10 months, and from their stepfathers or mothers' boyfriends from 10 to 25 months.

According to Finkelhor and Jones (2006), the period between 1998 and 2004 saw a decrease in the rate of child abuse even though all estimates are lower than reality. Demographic changes alone are consonant with the notion of a decrease: Families have fewer children and especially fewer unplanned children than in the past and parents are older at their first birth. Thus, being more mature helps them put their children's needs ahead of their own. Parents are more aware of some of the literature on child development, at least at the middle-class level, and may try to avoid any situation that could traumatize their children. Further, parents certainly perceive that there is a greater likelihood that they could get caught and punished severely, including losing their children, and this perception may act as a deterrent.

There are, unfortunately, many methodological problems in surveys intended to measure child abuse by parents. First, when children are very small, they cannot report their own abuse; at a slightly older age, many may not know what constitutes abuse. As adolescents and adults, problems of recollection set in, and are exacerbated by current states of mind and relationships. Further, parents are not likely to report all of their own abusive behaviours, thus abuse that comes to the attention of authorities represents the tip of the iceberg. As well, what different researchers include in their definitions of abuse makes it often impossible to compare the results of various studies. Finally, emotional abuse is too frequently overlooked (Egeland, 2009).

Further, with toddlers and preschool-age children, it is often difficult to distinguish a *first* occurrence of abuse from an accidental circumstance. For instance, daycare workers or kindergarten teachers may notice bruises or a child who is limping. The child may not be able to establish a cause and effect between these physical symptoms and the fact that he or she was punched or thrown against a piece of furniture the day before. Parents generally explain that the child fell into the bathtub, off the toilet seat, or down the staircase. These explanations are plausible because nearly all small children sooner or later have such accidents and some children are more accident prone than others, particularly when they are active as well as impulsive.

Once again, the economic structure of our society is at the forefront of this problem: Child abuse and neglect are more common in low-income families, especially in **neighbourhoods** with a high concentration of **poverty** and **violence**. Three decades ago, Garbarino and Sherman (1980) had already found that living in a high-risk neighbourhood correlated with child abuse, even after controlling for family characteristics (Turner et al., 2007). In these neighbourhoods, the lack of an effective community means that each set of parents, or each single parent, is more socially isolated, lacks support, and is deprived of elements of social control (Bogenschneider and Corbett, 2010:795). Were all these missing elements present, parents would be prevented from lashing out at their children as often and cruelly as some do. Further, children with disabilities are also more vulnerable (Owen, 2010:213).

Many studies link parents' daily stressors and psychological distress to distant, rejecting, and punitive parenting. Among single mothers, particularly, the adverse effects of poverty increase maternal depression and, in turn, punishment of adolescents (Turner et al., 2007). All in all, the daily stressors of poverty exacerbate difficult temperaments and may activate predispositions to violence, while simultaneously inhibiting controls against violence. In conditions of poverty, coping mechanisms are unduly taxed by daily irritants that cumulate to form an explosive situation. Depending on the temperament of the individuals affected and the characteristics of the child who is targeted, either explosive or apathetic behaviours may result (Elder et al., 1994). Poverty aside, a parental history of severe mental illness and especially antisocial behaviour may increase the risk of child abuse (Walsh et al., 2002).

Consequences for Children of Abuse by an Adult

The literature on child abuse unavoidably focuses on children's developmental outcomes rather than on their current suffering, struggles, and small victories—as researchers could not ethically study these children without intervening to help them. Hence, the everyday life of these children is not well documented. What is known is that, on average, children who have been or are abused do less well in school, are more frequently delinquent, have more peer-related problems, and are less reciprocal in their relations (Salzinger et al., 1993; Sternberg et al., 1993). Understandably, they become hyper-vigilant to danger and threat, and as a result tend to often attribute hostile intent to others and be more aggressive. They frequently experience conflict with authority figures (Stouthamer-Loeber et al., 2001). As adults, they are also likely to suffer from psychological problems and substance abuse (Herrenkohl et al., 2013; MacMillan et al., 2001), and many see interpersonal violence as normal (Valdez et al., 2013).

In other words, *these children share some of the outcomes mentioned earlier about children who witness interparental violence.* The two types of abuse are frequently related. For instance, fathers who abuse their wives physically are more likely to abuse their children (McDonald et al., 2009). In turn, abused mothers use harsh punishment more often than nonabused mothers. Women who have been abused as children have a higher chance of marrying an abusive husband. Together, these factors mean that child abuse often **coexists** or overlaps with spousal abuse and related difficulties (Moylan et al., 2010). As well, it can be said that witnessing parental violence is an indirect form of abuse (Finkelhor et al., 2009). This combination of factors may explain the similarity between the long-term effects of child abuse and those of interparental violence. It also makes it difficult to determine the effects specific to child abuse alone.

However, children who have been abused generally fare less well than those who witness interparental violence (see Margolin, 1998) and they are also at risk of being abusive later on in romantic relationships (Swinford et al., 2000). Miller et al. (2002) have found that harsh parenting is related to greater anxiety among young children of low SES than children of high SES. Thus, when children are small, *low SES makes them even more vulnerable to the consequences of ill treatment.* Children who have mental disabilities that are invisible, particularly those suffering from fetal alcohol spectrum disorders (FASD) are frequently victimized by their parents and all their kin (Chudley et al., 2005; Petersilia, 2001). This is particularly prevalent among Aboriginals who, later, often become offenders and inmates in the penal system (Fraser and McDonald, 2009).

Instead of becoming aggressive, adults who have been abused as children at times become depressed, withdrawn, and addicted to drugs. Others may become warm and particularly altruistic. Certain types of abuse and degrees of severity affect personal development, whereas other types of abuse affect subsequent parenting behaviours or interpersonal relations. Still other patterns of abuse are linked to antisocial behaviour or are causally linked to all such negative outcomes. However, the initial "causative" factor (the abuse) may be outweighed by personality resilience, happy circumstances in the person's life course, and a general lack of subsequent stressors. As well, various types of abuse may coexist: For instance, emotional abuse is not as often studied and in itself surely contributes negative effects (Wekerle et al., 2009).

Therefore, *the path between a variable believed to be causal and its resulting outcome depends on many other factors along the life course,* including SES (Zielinski, 2009). **Protective factors** must exist for severely abused children who turn out well, whereas risk factors must exist for children who are not abused but go on to become abusive as adults (Schultz et al., 2009). These protective and risk factors may be found at the individual level (the child's personality and genetic inheritance—Jaffee et al., 2005); at the family level (supportive siblings or one parent who is warm); or at the societal level (prosocial schools and neighbourhoods).

Do Abused Children Become Abusive Parents?

Just as is the case for interparental violence, one of the consequences of child abuse that is much studied and debated involves its reproduction in the next generation. As it turns out, abusive parents themselves, compared to nonabusive parents, have, on average, been more frequently abused or harshly treated as children (Pears and Capaldi, 2001). Abusive parents, especially those who are sexually exploitative, lack empathy for their child and entertain unrealistic expectations of what the child can do for them (Bert et al., 2009). Despite these parental drawbacks, *most abused children do not grow up to be abusive,* although severe and persistent child abuse probably always leaves long-term traces of psychological misery.

The **transmission rate** of family violence across generations has been estimated to be about 30 percent or less (Möhler et al., 2009). Abuse is not unavoidably transmitted because, as just mentioned, several factors enter into play in the chain of transmission (Berlin et al., 2011). This includes the meaning that people attach to having been abused: Some children who are beaten interpret this as justifiable punishment, yet, because it has hurt them, decide later on to utilize other forms of punishment with their own children. Attachment to a partner and children as well as the perceived disapproval of friends and relatives concerning family violence also prevent individuals who suffered or witnessed violence in their families from committing it themselves. In other instances, a spouse intervenes and resocializes the potential abuser into utilizing more appropriate punishment.

Although some violent parents are more at risk of transmitting this pattern than others, the mechanisms through which this occurs are still poorly understood. In this respect, Simons and colleagues proposed in 1995 that a **parent's antisocial orientation** may well be a mediating factor in the transmission of violence to the next generation. Thus, it is possible that abusive parents who have *other* antisocial characteristics are more likely to transmit various abusive and violent behaviours to their children than adults who, except for being abusive parents, are otherwise prosocial. Antisocial parents might abuse their spouse, pick fights with others, or engage in criminal activity, for instance. In other words, they provide a stronger negative socialization experience for their children. In a small core of families, it may also be that physical abuse as well as other antisocial activities are transmitted across generations by **genetic heredity**—that is, parents pass on to their children severe predispositions for aggressiveness or for other partly genetically influenced traits, such as low self-control or high impulsivity (see Jaffee et al., 2005; Jespersen et al., 2009). However, heredity does not mean unavoidability. *Most people born with a predisposition to aggressiveness are not condemned or forced to act it out. But they are more likely to act it out when their environment encourages violence.*

In a previous section, we have seen that exposure to community and school violence represents risk factors in the transmission of violence. We have also noted earlier that spousal and child abuse more frequently occur in poor neighbourhoods, along with many other forms of violence and antisocial behaviours. It is therefore quite likely that children who were abused *and* still live in a high-crime area will be more at risk of reproducing this pattern of violence in their own families than similar children who grow up in peaceful neighbourhoods where visible violence is practically nonexistent.

Child Neglect by Parents

Neglect involves not so much what parents do to their offspring but what they fail to do; it is a passive form of maltreatment. Straus and Kaufman-Kantor (2005) have defined it as "behavior by a caregiver that constitutes a failure to act in ways that are presumed by the culture of a society to be necessary to meet the developmental needs of a child and which are the responsibility of a caregiver to provide" (p. 20). Neglect includes failing to feed children, not clothing them adequately in cold weather, allowing toddlers to roam outside without supervision, failing to keep dangerous substances and firearms out of their reach, and not sending them to school. At the more psychological level, neglectful parents fail to give their children a chance at getting an education or neglect them emotionally by ignoring them most of the time and not interacting with them. Other parents fail to reprimand their children and their adolescents when they engage in antisocial or badly inappropriate behaviours.

Neglect of adolescents is a situation that is less easily detected and less reported than abuse. For instance, adolescents are neglected when they are given all the freedom they want to experiment with sex, alcohol, drugs, and even criminal activities. Not surprisingly, many of these youths do not define their parents as neglectful; they often see them as being "understanding" and "cool." Their parents may actually define themselves along the same lines. Adolescents are far more likely to complain about supervisory than permissive parents, even though the former are more invested parents. Although child neglect, particularly at the adolescent stage, is less discussed than child abuse, it is more common than child abuse (Health Canada, 2001). Neglect can have serious consequences: It can lead to peer abuse and excessively premature motherhood, for instance.

When parents are under stress or hold jobs that keep them away from home a great deal of the time, children go unsupervised. In other societies, such as Scandinavian countries, leaving children home alone has not been, until now, a problem. But this is often not the case here due to the potential risks involved and because professionals have become hyper-vigilant, thus frightening parents. Leaving children alone, then, becomes child neglect unless parents supervise their children's activities by phone, for instance, and set strict rules of safety and behaviours to be followed during their absence.

In the U.S., child neglect accounts for nearly half of child deaths related to maltreatment (McCurdy and Daro, 1994). Physical child neglect is often related to parents' drug addiction and mental illness (Marquis et al., 2008). Above all, it stems from **poverty** as well as the stressors and social isolation created by poverty (Wulczyn, 2009). When families are forced to remain in or move to a poor neighbourhood with social problems, children are immediately at risk of physical and psychological harm as well as bad examples. The dangers are so numerous that parents have to be extremely vigilant, which is not a normal state—for parents or for children (Garbarino et al., 1991). Therefore, it is easy for such parents to not be cautious enough, although they may be doing everything they can. Pelton (1991) points out that *poverty sets up a double standard of parenting* "in that we implicitly ask impoverished parents to be more diligent in their supervisory responsibility than middle-class parents, because greater protection is required to guard children from the dangerous conditions of poverty than from the relatively safer conditions of middle-class homes and neighbourhoods" (p. 3).

Children often suffer from abuse and neglect together or from physical and emotional neglect combined. This overlap makes it nearly impossible to attribute specific effects. The consequences of neglect range from insecurity to aggressiveness toward peers, behaviour problems, and lack of school readiness. In general, neglectful families function less adequately than other families. They often receive less social support from their immediate kin network, and mothers perceive their children to be more difficult (Harrington et al., 1998). Yet, in spite of all these and their own problems, children who are neglected do not necessarily perceive their family differently than other children. They may have no basis for comparison, particularly if other families around them are similar to theirs. In other instances, children do not wish to report neglect to social workers because they fear being placed out of their homes.

CHILD SEXUAL ABUSE BY ADULTS

Sexual abuse is the commission of a sex act without a person's consent or when a person is too young or immature to understand what is asked of or done to him or her. This broad definition involves inappropriate touching as well as penetration for the perpetrator's sexual gratification. Most of the sexual offences reported (81 percent) are of the less severe form (Brennan and Taylor-Butts, 2008). The incidence of child sexual abuse is even more complex to estimate than that of physical abuse because of the elements of victims' shame or ignorance, perpetrators' complete secrecy, and lack of visible physical cues. As well, new types of crimes have recently been added, more specifically, "luring a child via a computer," which is increasing.

As indicated below, of all cases of sexual assaults and other sex-related crimes reported to the police in Canada, a staggering 61 percent have youth younger than 18 as victims (AuCoin, 2005):

0–5 age group: 1,261 reported cases or 8 percent of all reported cases

6–10 age group: 2,251 reported cases or 15 percent of all reported cases

11–13 age group: 2,556 reported cases or 17 percent of all reported cases

14–17 age group: 3,284 reported cases or 21 percent of all reported cases

It is estimated that 90 percent of sexual offences are never reported to the police. However, it is not known whether adult victims underreport more or less than child/youth victims. Girls constitute 85 percent of reported occurrences and 13 is the peak age for girls (Statistics Canada, 2003c). It may be earlier for boys (Dorais, 2002). Adolescent girls who work have a high risk of being harassed sexually as have women

| TABLE 13.1 | **Perpetrators of Sexual Assaults and Offences against Children Reported to Police Services, by Age and Gender of Child, 2003** | | | | | | | |

Ages	0–5		6–10		11–13		14–17	
Sex of child	F	M	F	M	F	M	F	M
Perpetrators	%	%	%	%	%	%	%	%
A parent	26	17	15	11	11	10	10	9
A sibling	13	18	17	16	10	8	4	6
Other family	11	14	14	11	9	7	6	6
Friend, etc.	36	38	39	46	53	57	52	57
Stranger/unknown	13	12	17	17	18	18	28	23

Source: AuCoin, 2005. Adapted from Tables 1 and 3. Statistics Canada.

in their twenties and thirties (Fineran and Gruber, 2009). Overall, the consensus is that about one out of every four females is sexually abused before she reaches age 16. A late-1980s American national survey revealed that 27 percent of the women and 16 percent of the men interviewed reported having been sexually abused as children (Finkelhor et al., 1990). Although no question was asked about this topic, the female students' autobiographies revealed a range from 15 to 25 percent, depending on the year; rare instances surfaced among the less numerous male students. In the U.S., *substantiated* cases of child sexual abuse have declined by a third between 1992 and 1999 (Jones et al., 2001).

Who and Where Are the Sexual Abusers?

Turning to Table 13.1, we see that, for the youngest victims, the abusers are more likely to be a relative. As children age, they become prey to peers, casual acquaintances, and strangers (Statistics Canada, 2013a). The focus has often been on fathers as the sexual abusers—especially on TV talk shows. But we have to take four facts into consideration. First, where it says that a "parent" was the abuser, in 95 percent of the cases it was the "father." Second, however, the term "father" includes stepfathers, mothers' live-in boyfriends, as well as foster fathers. Third, these fathers together are involved in 9 to 26 percent of these sexual crimes whereas friends/acquaintances account for 36 to 57 percent. Fourth, it is possible that sexual abuse committed by fathers of very young children is underreported when it is not visible, even to mothers.

Other perpetrators within the family include older sisters' boyfriends, siblings, grandfathers, uncles, and cousins. Children are also sexually abused by fathers' friends; in foster care, daycare, and group care institutions; by babysitters, coaches, and clergymen; as well as by peers. A majority of the **perpetrators are males**, but victimization by a mother, a sister, or a female babysitter, as well as a stepmother, occasionally occurs. In the students' autobiographies, only four cases of father-daughter incest came to light in about 1,500 autobiographies. It is possible, however, that students did not want to discuss it because it was too painful and private—but I doubt this because a great deal of other very sensitive material was divulged. Rather, such cases probably occur more in school-age and clinical samples than in university student samples, because this is a type of abuse that carries the most serious consequences (see also Hyman, 2000). Three of the four reported cases had occurred in immigrant families in which many problems coexisted or who were from patriarchal societies (Duffy, 2004).

In a clinical intervention for 50 adolescent girls who had been sexually abused, the fathers had been the offenders in 16 percent of the cases, whereas stepfathers and mothers' boyfriends had been in 32 percent of the cases (Morrison and Clavenna-Valleroy, 1998). Over half of these girls' mothers also reported having been sexually abused as children, an extremely high rate that coincides with a high rate of these mothers' partners having abused their daughters. This **double female victimization** *across the generations* relates to other research findings showing that a proportion of women who are abused as girls marry partners who abuse them and may also abuse their daughters. The abuse carries from one generation to the next through the transmission of risk factors and victimization from mother to daughter. In fact, children who live with an abused mother are over 12 times more likely to be sexually abused (McCloskey et al., 1995).

Once again, children from **low-income** families are more likely to be victimized than others and often come from more troubled families (Dorais, 2002). As well, among Aboriginals, this is a form of victimization that is quite prevalent but about which no one speaks (Hylton, 2002). This brings us back to Chapter 6, where we saw that a proportion of girls who became mothers by age 15 had been coerced into sex, and most were poor. Further, males who have been sexually abused as boys are more likely to impregnate a teenager at some point in their lives (Rosenberg, 2001). In addition, Chapter 5 indicates that, in areas with a high level of poverty, children may be less well supervised and more at risk of victimization. The presence of transient males in a family combined with overcrowding can also contribute to explain this difference in child sexual abuse by social class.

It should be added that police-reported sexual assaults against youth under the age of 13 occur the most frequently *between 3 and 7 p.m. after school* and, we presume, before the return home of parents (AuCoin, 2005; Brennan and Taylor-Butts, 2008). In contrast, the 14 to 17 age group is victimized more frequently between 1 and 5 p.m. (related to truancy from school and homes that have no adult presence), as well as between 10 p.m. and 2 a.m. (AuCoin, 2005).

Consequences of Sexual Abuse for the Child: The Life Course Perspective

Within a life course sociological framework, *sexual abuse constitutes an inappropriate sexual socialization*. Sexual contact with an adult focuses the child on his or her own sexuality from a less than healthy perspective very early on in life. The abuse constitutes a precocious initiation into sexuality and powerlessness and brings a **premature foreclosure in identity**: The young child begins to define herself in terms of sexuality and perhaps material gains (Dorais, 2002). This may open the door to deviant opportunities and close the door to a normal life course. In turn, these "opportunities" may lead to early sexual relations with older peers and pregnancy (Roosa et al., 1997). *These children are often re-victimized* (Barnes et al., 2009). They have more sexual partners among older peers, and are at greater risk of contracting sexually transmitted infections and becoming homeless. The same path may lead to prostitution, both female and male (Kingsley and Mark, 2000). As adults, those who have been sexually abused when children have higher rates of serial partners, unwanted pregnancies, abortions, and STIs (Boden et al., 2009; van Roode et al., 2009). They are also more likely to become victims of intimate partners later on (Daigneault et al., 2009). In addition, incarcerated women are found to have had a high incidence of childhood sexual abuse (Johnson and Lynch, 2013).

As Browning and Laumann (1997) explain, adult sexual contact with a young girl "seems to provide access to sexuality without cultivating the emotional and cognitive skills to manage sexual experiences" (p. 557). The girls' (or boys') subsequent deviant behaviour often arises from the fact that their **self-perception** has been distorted as a result of the abuse. Some of these children may grow up believing that others have the right to their body or that early sexuality is normal. As we see in the case below, this is actually one of the discourses that child abusers hold with their victim. They explain that the act is "normal" or that the relationship is a "special" one in order to convince the child to be victimized and, later on, to justify the abuser's behaviour.

> *A student devoted many pages detailing the sexual abuse she began suffering at age six when her grandparents were babysitting her. Although her grandmother was nearby in the kitchen, the grandfather regularly coerced the child into performing oral sex in the family room because "it made him feel good and he used to tell me that I was his special girl." The poor little girl gagged and gagged and had to submit to further indecencies. "At the time I was convinced that I was special and he had me promise not to tell anyone so that I was essentially isolated and didn't know any better." As she grew up, she became more and more repulsed and begged her mother to find her another sitter. The abuse stopped when she was 10 years old. By early adolescence, she feared men, and by late adolescence, she had to seek therapy because sex disgusted her. She began suffering from depressive episodes. "I will never let any old man babysit my children."*

Browning and Laumann (1997) find that, when child abuse does not give rise to an early, risky sexual life, the victims are less likely to experience adverse outcomes later in life. The authors conclude that *the long-term effects of child sexual abuse are probably indirect through the negative life course that they often generate*; redirecting sexual trajectories at an early age might cancel most of the severe and long-term negative consequences of sexual abuse.

Most children who are sexually abused do not follow a deviant life course. Parental or peer support, personal strength, and appropriate therapy may be instrumental in resocializing children and helping them build their lives constructively. Still, many such children develop emotional and behavioural problems, both as children and later on as adults. As illustrated in the student vignette, depression is a common sequel that can appear as early as adolescence. Sexual abuse may trigger problems in a child who may not otherwise be at risk, or it may increase pre-existing problems, even later on in life. Studies show that adult sex offenders who abuse children have had particularly high rates of sexual abuse in their past (Jespersen et al., 2009).

Many children grow up to forget or repress the abuse. For instance, Williams and Banyard (1997) followed up men and women who, in the early 1970s, had been examined in a hospital emergency room for sexual abuse. After 17 years, 38 percent of the women and 55 percent of the men had no recollection of the abuse. Widom and Morris (1997) found similar numbers when they followed up court-substantiated instances of child sexual abuse that had taken place 20 years earlier. Perhaps children who grow up to forget have particular strengths. Perhaps the fact that the abuse has been forgotten means that, at the time, it had not been vested with tragic overtones by the child who may not even have realized what was happening to her or him. This would go counter to claims that any sexual gesture toward a child is traumatic. The actual fact is that we have no proof of the effect, if any, of certain types of sexual encounters with children—even though they are morally reprehensible. Above all, perhaps children who grow up to forget are more likely to have had a normal life course, as a result of early parental intervention (Browning and Laumann, 1997).

SIBLING VIOLENCE

In this section, sibling violence is divided into physical and sexual: Psychological abuse was covered to some extent in Chapter 12. But, in either case, these are neglected topics of research, both in terms of their incidence and consequences (AuCoin, 2005; Tucker et al., 2013). Negative consequences often ensue for the child who is victimized (Kiselica and Morrill-Richards, 2007). We also have to consider that the abusive child is allowed to grow into a role that may repeat itself later on in other aspects of life and against other victims such as dates and spouses or even children.

Sibling Physical Violence

Straus and colleagues (1980) sampled 1,224 pairs of siblings ranging in age from three to 17 years. Pushing and shoving were the most frequently mentioned acts of physical violence at the less serious end of the continuum. At the other extreme, 14 percent reported having beaten up their sibling and 5 percent reported using a gun, either to threaten or to hurt. This survey took place in 1975. The level of violence among children in general has since risen, and, because adult presence at home has diminished, these figures could be higher today. The result that sister pairs were the least aggressive of all sibling pairs is still true today (Tucker et al., 2013). But here as well, one can expect higher frequencies than in the 1970s because there has been an increase in violence perpetrated by girls. The main difference is that families are now smaller so that children have fewer siblings than in the 1970s. Yet, in 2010, 99,000 Canadians were victims of *reported* family violence: 11 percent was committed by siblings (Statistics Canada, 2012f).

The media, the public, professionals, and researchers have all paid a great deal of attention to child abuse by parents when, actually, sibling abuse is more common (Wallace, 1999). This selective inattention stems from widespread beliefs that it is simply part of growing up. It is considered normal. Siblings hurt one another so frequently that no one pays much attention to it. Parents are concerned, however, but many believe that they should not interfere in their children's lives and that "they have to learn on their own." This attitude is stronger toward male than female children as the former receive greater social support toward aggressiveness (Tucker et al., 2012). This type of reasoning leads to the conclusion that sibling violence is not "real" violence that one has to prevent, when, in reality, it is the most common form of intimate abuse (Button and Gealt, 2010). The parallel with hockey violence comes to mind. These parents' beliefs about nonintervention are reinforced by the lack of professional concern. Because of this widespread **adult tolerance**, children are far less likely to report sibling abuse to their parents or other authority figures than is the case for abuse by adults. The stronger of the two siblings is encouraged on this path because he or she benefits from advantages over the other and no one intervenes. As a result, later on, adults who are asked about victimization in their past often fail to equate sibling beatings with assault. Strangely, when perpetrators and victims of sibling aggression become adults, they are more accepting of this type of abuse (Hardy et al., 2010). Once more, this leads to the underrepresentation of sibling violence in official surveys. Further, it is only recently that a few studies have been able to look at the developmental conse-quences of everyday sibling abuse: It is related to behavioural problems, above and beyond genetic inheritance and parental treatment (Natsuaki et al., 2009).

However, not all families experience sibling abuse (excluding, here, the usual quarrels) or tolerate it. For instance, in a large sample of high-school students, Button and Gealt (2010) found, as have others, that sibling victimiza-tion occurs more in families where there are other forms of violence. Thus, there are high rates of **co-occurrence** of several types of abu-sive and problematic behaviours. This means that sibling violence is often part of a family's culture and perhaps genetic background. In turn, sibling violence is also related to increased odds of delinquency, aggression, and even substance abuse. Sibling violence does not occur randomly.

Courtesy of Pearson Education

While abuse by peers is finally receiving serious attention (the phenomenon of "bullying"), sibling violence and abuse still remain to be studied in-depth and recognized socially.

Sibling Sexual Abuse

The following student quote serves as an introduction to a topic that is equally overlooked or taboo: Sibling sexual abuse or sibling incest, which is probably more common than parent-child incest:

> *"The most painful time in my life was the period between the ages of 6 to 10: My brother was six years older than me and my parents counted on him to babysit me. . . . At first I did not understand what was happening to me, however difficult this is to explain with hindsight, but my brother got me into performing intimate acts for him and later on after a year of this his best friend used to come over and they would both share me. This is all I can write here because this is very painful. This went on for two years until I became strong enough to resist and threaten to tell my parents which of course I never did because I was too ashamed. At school I was ashamed too because I saw this boy. . . . Now I harbour intensely negative feelings about my brother who seems to have forgotten all about these years. . . . It would kill my parents if I told them. I went into therapy when I got to this university and have come to terms with the situation, which is not to say that I accept it but I can live with it and go on with my life."*

Sibling incest is a mainly brother-to-sister initiated or coerced phenomenon, but incest between siblings of the same sex also occurs. We are not talking here of "playing doctor," which many small children engage in out of curiosity and from which they have to be distracted and directed to other more prosocial activities. (These incidents can also be used by parents to explain what is inappropriate touching.) As is the case for all types of sexual abuse, sibling incest is found more in clinical than in survey populations. This would indicate that it results in serious psychological consequences for many abused brothers and sisters. As well, sibling sexual abuse may perhaps occur more among already vulnerable and malfunctioning families. Such families simply cannot supervise their children because of various burdens. It can also result from the way parental roles are carried out. Visible extramarital affairs and open sexuality between parents that children observe, for instance, are related to sibling incest: Children may copy what they see.

O'Brien (1991) compared adolescent sex offenders whose victims were siblings with other adolescent sex offenders whose victims were children outside the family. Adolescents who had sexually abused a sibling had done it more often and for a much longer period of time (one year) than adolescents who had abused a child outside the family, because of the availability of the little brother or sister at home (as illustrated in the student quote). As well, their sibling victim was much younger, between four and nine years of age, than the victims of the other abusers. This young age allowed for greater accessibility, because a small child can more easily be coerced than an older child. The frequency of the abuse resulted in nearly half of the sibling cases progressing to anal or vaginal penetration. This occurred rarely when the victim was not a sibling, for it is easier to progress to penetration within the context of long-term availability and within the privacy of the home.

In the families with sibling incest, O'Brien uncovered a phenomenon we have already encountered for child sexual abuse by a father or a stepfather, where both mother and daughter have been abused: Parents of incest perpetrators, particularly mothers, had been more often abused sexually as children than was the case among the parents of the other sex offenders; 42 percent of the incestuous offenders had been abused sexually, although generally outside the family. Thus, in these families, many parents had themselves been vulnerable during their childhood. Further, some of their sons had also been sexually abused, and of those many had gone on to abuse their siblings. The **transmission** from one generation to the next was one of **vulnerability** for sexual victimization in many of these families.

PEER ABUSE

As we have seen in Figure 13.1, older children are more likely to be abused by their peers than by anyone else. Examples of cruel, destructive, and even violent peer behaviours are mentioned in the newscasts on a weekly basis, are posted on YouTube or Facebook, and in some cases, result in murder or suicide (Hinduja and Patchin, 2010). When this abuse takes place on the Internet it has come to be referred to as **cyberbullying***. Peer abuse in general is a situation that severely depletes a child's social capital outside the home and often endangers the development of his or her human capital—especially now that it so often occurs on Facebook or in texting, from which the victims cannot escape, even in the privacy of their home (e.g., Christofides et al., 2012). Thus, it also affects family dynamics. In 2010 in Canada, there were at least three lawsuits by the parents of a traumatized child against schools for allegedly failing to protect their child against bullying (Hammer, 2010).

A conservative estimate might be that a minimum of 20 percent of children are *seriously* abused by peers during their young lives—and this does not refer to normal conflicts, disagreements, and teasing. Most adolescents are both victims and abusers, although not necessarily at the same time. Most children bully at one point but few do so persistently (Pepler et al., 2008). In Ontario, 29 percent of Grade 7 to 12 students reported being bullied *at school* during the current academic year, which was a decrease since 2003 (Paglia-Boak, 2010).

In the autobiographies, students recalled far more peer maltreatment that they described as having had detrimental and *lasting* consequences on their development than was the case for maltreatment by parents. That is, these peer experiences had affected them negatively for several years, often up to the present time (Ambert, 1994a). Further, such mentions increased as time went on. In the autobiographies as well as in magazines, one reads about students who had been happy and well adjusted, but quite rapidly began deteriorating psychologically, sometimes to the point of becoming physically ill and incompetent in school or even delinquent. For many, the impact of peer maltreatment leads to avoidance of school (Kochenderfer and Ladd, 1996). In other instances, it contributes to poor school performance (Hodges et al., 1997) as well as anxiety and depression or alcohol use (Peleg-Oren et al., 2012), and conduct problems (Loukas and Pasch, 2013). As one student recalls it (see also another similar case on p. 303), even school work can be disrupted, as young victims become too distraught and often too fearful to focus on anything else:

"The years between 12 and 16 were the worst in my life. I was surely the most unpopular boy at my school. There was a group of boys with some girls too who

used to pick on me and no one would have dared be nice to me after that. They'd steal my lunch, force me to hand over my pocket money, they'd laugh and snicker when I passed by. . . . It got to the point where I felt so terrorized that I couldn't even pay attention to what the teacher said in class and my marks suffered and of course my parents weren't too sympathetic because they hadn't a clue that this was going on until I got really sick with chronic stomach problems, but by then the years had gone by and my life had been ruined. I feel insecure to this day and always sit at the back to avoid being noticed."

Peer abuse is not merely a psychological situation created by a victim and an abuser because of two sets of personality characteristics. Rather, it is influenced by the **clique** structure of schools and by what children have learned elsewhere, including the media—whether television, video games, or the Internet—and siblings. For instance, Espelage and colleagues (1996) find that adolescent bullies watch more violent television, are more difficult at home, spend less time with adults, and have more exposure to gang activities than other children. Being a bully also negatively affects school performance (Ma et al., 2009) and may persist into young adulthood as does victimization (Pontzer, 2010). A third of bullies had a single parent and another third lived with a stepparent. Thus, it would seem that *serious bullies* escape adult influence and control, especially when it comes to social bullying (Brendgen et al., 2008:26). However, teachers' intervention in school can lower victimization rates and effects (Hektner and Swenson, 2012) as can bullying intervention programs among peers (Espelage et al., 2012). The **culture of violence** in the society at large is implicated along with reduced social control. This is well illustrated in the fact that bisexuals and homosexuals are more often abused by their peers when in school (Balsam et al., 2005). Peer abuse is a situation created by opportunity. It is, above all, a cultural phenomenon and a reflection of a lack of an effective community, including lack of school supervision (Wienke Totura et al., 2009). And it is now given additional outlets with cell phones, Facebook, and other new modes of communication as they become available each year.

Peer Sexual Harassment and Abuse

Sexual harassment, mainly by boys toward girls, is a particularly pernicious form of abuse that may begin early. It generally goes undetected, may even be approved of by boys' parents *("he's all boy")*, and some girls may be led by their peers into believing that it is flattering (*"he likes you, silly"*) or simply the normal price one has to pay for popularity. It is the forecaster of date and partner abuse. Many adolescents and even preadolescent girls are coerced into sexuality by male peers (Chapter 7). The degree of coercion ranges from outright rape to subtle pressure in a relationship where the girl is afraid to lose her date. Adolescents are particularly at risk when they score high on scales of conformity to peers (Small and Kerns, 1993): They become vulnerable because they need their peers' approval more than a less conforming adolescent does. Many girls who do not want sexual intercourse end up complying because of peer pressure (Laumann, 1996). Some of this pressure comes from female peers who may already be sexually active or pretend to be. This creates a **cultural climate** that is very potent; a teenager eager for peer acceptance will follow suit.

Victimization from severe forms of sexual abuse, rape, or coercion into unwanted sexuality is more likely to occur to adolescents who live in neighbourhoods that have a high rate of social problems and whose parents cannot supervise or protect them adequately. Girls from single-parent families, particularly when they are disadvantaged, as well as those who have parents who suffer from alcoholism, for instance, are at a higher risk of sexual victimization in general, including by peers (Moore et al., 1989). Peer sexual abuse, as is the case for peer abuse in general, is very much a **crime of opportunity**. It is done by and occurs to children and adolescents while they are unsupervised by adults, whether at school, at home, in an abandoned building, or in a car (AuCoin, 2005). Peer sexual abuse is the result of media influences and disengagement from adults, including teachers and parents—in other words, a generalized lack of an effective community.

ABUSE OF PARENTS BY CHILDREN

Two additional types of familial abuse exist: Ill treatment of parents by their young children and adolescents as well as the abuse of elder parents by their adult offspring. In 2010, of the 99,000 Canadians who were victims of *reported* family violence, 9 percent had been the victim of one of their children, generally an adult child (Statistics Canada, 2012f). The literature is thin concerning these topics, particularly that pertaining to young children as abusers. Why is this? Perhaps because we tend to socially construct children as victims (Gallagher, 2004a, b). Perhaps because we fail to understand that children are social actors and make choices (Ambert, 2001). Or perhaps we view parents as more powerful than they are and, at times, we stereotype them as the natural abusers of their children.

Physical Abuse of Parents by Young Children and Adolescents

Already in 1979, Harbin and Madden used the phrase, "battered parents." Yet, the topic has largely remained taboo both for families and mental health professionals. Estimates of children who have physically assaulted their parents range from 1 to 16 percent (Laurent and Derry, 1999). As well, the relative absence of research on this topic is perplexing in view of the fact that small children are generally more physically aggressive than older ones (Onyskiw and Hayduk, 2001). They spend more time with parents, especially **mothers**, thus giving them more opportunities for abuse. In fact, the few studies that exist are unanimous to the effect that mothers are the most common victims (Gallagaher, 2004a; Nock and Kazdin, 2002; Straus and Ulma, 2003).

Violent young offenders often target their own families. Those who aggress their parents are more likely to belong to gangs and associate with peers who own guns (Kennedy et al., 2010). Several teens in one of my studies repeatedly yelled at their mother that she was "stupid" and even a "bitch." (If the mothers were the ones doing the name-calling, *they would be censured*.) A few mothers were bearing bruises from the beatings received at the hand of a teenage son. The mothers were single and poor; one was in a wheelchair. The latter was also called a "scumbag" by her

16-year-old son. One can also witness severe physical assault of mothers by children as young as age three (Straus and Ulma, 2003). These observations are made in public areas—such as sidewalks, parks, and subway platforms—for everyone to see, a sign that children do not fear public condemnation in this respect: There is an *entitlement mentality* among some children and adolescents when it comes to mothers. This stems from our social construction of motherhood.

> I observed the following scene in a subway train. A well-dressed mother, age 25 to 30, walked in with an equally well-groomed little boy, age four or five. The little boy was screaming at his mother at the top of his lungs:
>
> B: *You hurt my feelings!*
>
> M: (bending down to soothe him) *I'm so sorry, honey, I apologize.*
>
> B: *I hate you, I hate you!* (He was red in the face with rage and was hitting his mother with his fists.)
>
> M: (softly) *Again, I'm sorry honey; it won't happen again.*
>
> B: *You're stupid.* (He kicked her with his booted foot.)

The mother had tears in her eyes. The boy was not in the least bit deterred by the staring disapproval from passengers as he continued punching and yelling. I doubt that anyone had ever told him that this was wrong. The cases observed in public involved higher-SES mothers with small children: The few studies on this topic point out that this is mainly an upper-middle-class phenomenon as well as a white one—at least, up to this point in time. It may be related to parenting permissiveness where proper boundaries of authority and right versus wrong are absent (Gallagher, 2004a; Laurent, 1997). Gelles (1997:112) points out that clinical observations of abusive adolescents reveal deficiencies in the authority structure of families whereby adolescents have been granted too much control and decision-making power (see Chapter 10). Studies also indicate that the young abusers tend to be more difficult oppositional children, who stress parents, and who are very demanding of them. Such children burden their familial environment and, as a result, their parents become less competent at setting limits (Nock and Kazdin, 2002).

In Massachusetts, between September 1992 and June 1993, nearly one-third of all restraining court orders issued were requested by parents against children, mainly by mothers against sons (reported in Gelles, 1997). In a 1996 British Crime Survey, one in 10 mothers reported having been assaulted by her children—some of these offspring were over age 18 (Mirrlees-Black et al., 1996).

Abuse of Elderly Parents by Adult Children

The construct of elder abuse and neglect is a fairly recent one arising from the particular socioeconomic context of the middle of the 20th century (Harbison et al., 2012). Basically, ageism was created with forced retirement of workers on the basis of chronological age as a result of the need to ensure productivity. Age and retirement then became constructed as decline and disengagement. Overall, neglect and abuse of seniors remain poorly understood by the public (Roger and Ursel, 2009; Walsh and Ma, 2012) and do not receive the support that child abuse does, for instance, even when it involves frail and ill elders (Harbison et al., 2012). Rates of elder abuse range from 2 to 10 percent depending on studies (Sev'er, 2009). In general, seniors have the lowest rate of victimization. When they are victims of crime, the perpetrator is usually someone they know, too often a family member, particularly grown children and then spouses (Brennan, 2013)—or, yet, a caretaker in a seniors' home (Phillips et al., 2013). Women outlive men, and one of the consistent findings on elder abuse within the family is that *most victims are women* (Biggs et al., 2009; Krienert et al., 2009). Abuse and neglect of elders takes many forms, including physical and sexual abuse, emotional abuse, neglect, financial exploitation, refusal of health services, as well as violation of rights (Harbinson et al., 2012). This heterogeneity contributes to its underreporting (Walsh and Ma, 2012). Until now, explanations for elder abuse within the family have emphasized the elderly person's caregivers: The line of reasoning is that the frustrated and burdened caregiver lashes out at the frail dependent parent. However, elderly parents are often abused by an adult child who lives with them because of that child's own dependency (Carp, 2000). In that case, the adult child depends on the parent financially or for shelter, because he or she is unemployed or is mentally delayed, physically challenged, emotionally disturbed, or addicted (Walsh and Ma, 2012). Indeed, after discharge from hospital care, 85 percent of unmarried adult children who are mentally ill move in with their elderly parents (Greenberg et al., 1993). The potential for abuse certainly exists.

Courtesy of Pearson Education

Elderly parents who are abused by their adult children rarely report the situation. They feel ashamed and may fear retaliation. They are often socially isolated and have no one in whom to confide.

Hence, researchers may have placed too much emphasis on the dependence of the elderly as a source of abuse even though it constitutes a serious risk factor (Walsh and Ma, 2012); the elderly who have a dependent and physically stronger spouse or child living with them should be considered at particular risk (Carp, 2000; Ma and Rietschlin, 2012). Other explanations propose that elder abuse is spousal abuse "grown old" or that it stems at least in part from prejudicial attitudes and beliefs toward the elderly (Harbison, 1999).

Police-reported data for the year 2007 showed that **men** are the most frequent perpetrators of violence against an older family member—80 percent of such cases. Older men were more frequently victimized by their adult children whereas older women were as likely to be abused by their spouse or adult children (Vaillancourt, 2009). As well, younger seniors were more frequently victimized by family members than those aged 85 to 98 who are probably more often victimized within institutions:

They are too isolated or in ill health to report it (Turcotte and Schellenberg, 2007). Indeed, a study in Michigan showed that, when elders moved into a nursing home, their risk tripled (Page et al., 2009). A more recent study in the same state obtained 24 percent of respondents who reported *at least one* incident of physical abuse by nursing staff (Schiamberg et al., 2012). In yet another study, the authors concluded: "The results show that elder mistreatment" in assisted living facilities "is seriously underidentified, even by state inspectors" (Phillips et al., 2013). In the 1999 Canadian General Social Survey, 7 percent of seniors reported emotional abuse, while 1 percent reported financial abuse, and another 1 percent physical or sexual violence (Dauvergne, 2003). In Ontario in 2010, the *Toronto Star* investigated 3,000 complaints, including severe physical abuse and neglect (McLean and Welsh, 2011). Medical abuse is at times perpetrated when the caregiving adult child does not seek assistance for a sick or suffering elderly parent—to safeguard the entirety of the inheritance or precipitate its occurrence. Material forms of abuse by adult children are motivated by greed, personal debts or addictions, or the financial demands of an adult child's spouse or children. Material abuse includes siphoning off parental revenues, walking out with parents' possessions, or controlling the parents' house (Biggs et al., 2009).

Elder abuse has very **low visibility**: In fact, parents may be less likely to report abuse than would a maltreated adolescent or even a child (Payne and Gainey, 2006). Actually, perhaps as few as 5 percent report it (Tatara, 1993). Elderly parents may be ashamed of their situation and may have no one else to turn to for help. An attempt to report the abuse might fail and result in dreaded retaliation. Moreover, while abused children grow up and may eventually denounce their parents, the elderly parent dies with the secret. Thus, abuse of elderly parents is a relatively easy act to commit and can have even less social visibility than abuse of school-age children. The elderly who are most at risk are often socially isolated: They are no longer connected to their social networks, such as church, work, or even friends. No one may notice the abuse, and physicians who see bruises may be told that the senior person fell, something that occurs quite often in old age. (The parallel with small children is obvious here.) It is not known if the model of the intergenerational transmission of violence is a valid explanatory framework for elder abuse. As well, this perspective does not address larger sociological issues of society's role in preventing the abuse of frail elders.

CONCLUSIONS: THE LARGER CONTEXT OF FAMILY VIOLENCE

Neglect and intimate violence are better explained within a framework that includes several theoretical perspectives jointly. To begin with, political economy theories point to violence as a result of social inequalities and resulting from poverty: Certain groups, such as devalued minorities and Aboriginals with a long history of oppression, are overrepresented in the statistics on intimate violence. Closely related is the focus of feminist approaches on females as the most frequent victims and on the social construction of male advantage, of masculinity, and the role of extreme patriarchy in some cultures (Papp, 2010). Violence within the family is a reflection of violence within society, including its "colonization by the media," as Habermas would put it (1987). The psychological aspects of violence generally used as explanatory frameworks are, in turn, largely dependent upon the political and cultural forces present in society and in the world at large. One can also note that abusive situations would not be so prevalent in a society where civility, altruism, and a sense of communal responsibility were the valued forms of interaction. Second, within such a civilized and less competitive-aggressive environment, even impulsive persons would learn to respect others rather than maltreat them.

Other larger sociocultural forces that are implicated in family violence include the fact that the family is the only institution that is single-handedly responsible for the well-being of its dependent members—whether children, the disabled, or the frail elderly. The family has too many responsibilities—particularly too many caregiving functions—while it receives too little social support from the very complex, expensive, and competitive society in which it is embedded. In other words, we have come full circle, and these remarks return us to the theoretical perspectives presented in Chapter 1 and to the discussion on the multiple roles that families are burdened with in Chapter 3.

Five salient themes emerge from this chapter. Females of all ages are the most frequent victims of all types of violence. Males are the most frequent offenders. Several types of violence often co-exist within one family (because of an amalgam of genetic predispositions within difficult environments, such as poverty). Both offender and victim roles are, in some families, transmitted intergenerationally. Finally, violence in one's environment, whether neighbourhood or school, is often a key factor in the transmission of violence to the next generation.

Summary

1. Courtship and dating violence are discussed, with respect to reported cases, both genders, and causes. Date rape is also discussed.

2. Verbal and psychological abuse of partners is not as easy to measure as physical abuse. It has also been less researched. It is quite salient in music videos favoured by adolescents. This form of abuse is often tailored to fit partners' vulnerabilities.

3. At the spousal level, along with cultural influences, physical violence by a partner is a situational matter as well as an issue of power. Cohabiting couples have the highest rate of partner violence. Poor couples, particularly those living in unsafe neighbourhoods, are more at risk of partner violence. Domestic violence among oppressed minorities may have causes that do not exist among whites. Same-sex-partner violence is discussed.

4. On average, children of abused mothers have more behavioural and psychological problems. However, the intergenerational transmission of violence depends on many variables, and only a minority of these children grow up to repeat the pattern in their own families.

5. Statistics are presented on child and adolescent abuse, as well as its consequences. Child abuse and neglect are more common in low-income families, especially in areas with a high concentration of poverty and violence. The intergenerational transmission of abuse is discussed.

6. Child neglect is more widespread and involves not so much what parents do to their offspring as what they fail to do. Physical neglect is particularly related to poverty and has many consequences.

7. There may have been a decrease in child abuse by parents in the last two decades of the 20th century. However, child neglect has probably increased.

8. Child sexual abuse tends to occur more within the family among girls and outside the family among boys. A proportion of women who are abused as girls marry partners who abuse them or their daughters. Again, children from low-income families are at a higher risk of sexual abuse. The consequences for the child depend on the nature of the abuse and who the perpetrator is. Sexual abuse of a child is analyzed as an inappropriate sexual socialization.

9. Sibling violence is discussed as well as sibling incest, which is predominantly a brother-to-sister situation.

10. Abuse of children by their peers is probably the most common form of abuse in society. It carries many negative consequences and can be explained by sociocultural factors.

11. A number of children and adolescents assault their parents, particularly their mothers, both verbally and physically, but this topic is not given much attention in research. Among the elderly who are abused by their adult children, most are mothers. The types as well as the contexts of elder abuse are discussed.

12. Violence within the family is a reflection of violence in the society at large and is exacerbated by social inequalities. It also results from the fact that the family is burdened with responsibilities for which it receives little societal support.

Analytical Questions

1. The intergenerational transmission of violence and abuse is a recurrent theme in this chapter. It is also much emphasized in the media. How are the contents of this chapter different from the media emphases? (The answer may not be in the text.)

2. What role does culture play in partner abuse?

3. Cohabiting couples have high rates of partner violence. Explain why this is so, using information from this chapter and perhaps Chapters 7 and 12.

4. Why can permissiveness be analyzed as a form of child or adolescent neglect?

5. What, for you, is the most salient result of this chapter? Justify your response.

6. Give three different topics for further research suggested in this chapter, which would increase our knowledge of the issues discussed.

7. How do many of the results in this chapter fit in feminist *and* political economy theories and which are these results?

CHAPTER 14

Family Futures and Social Policies

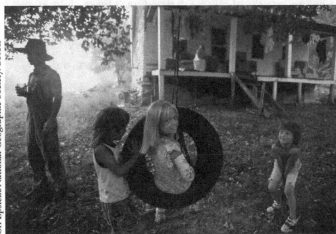

Lori Epstein/National Geographic Society/Corbis

OUTLINE

Salient Themes Revisited
Social Inequalities and Gender
Stratification
Diversity of Families
A Surfeit of Family Responsibilities
The Effective Community
The Cultural Context

What Does the Future Hold?
Fertility, Sex Ratio Imbalance, and Age
Distribution
A Crisis in Caring
Cohabitation, Marriage, and Divorce
Singlehood and Family Formation
by Singles
Immigration and Transnational Families
Families' Natural Environment
The Longer Time Frame

Social Policies Pertaining to Families
Focus of "Family Policies"

**Reducing Poverty and Economic
Inequality**
A Critique of Current Policies
Creating Green Jobs
Facilitating Adequate Housing
Expansion of Child Care Programs
After-School Care and Improved
Schooling
Consequences and Limitations
of Programs

Supporting the Parental Role

Facilitating the Care of Elders

Conclusions: The Family in Contexts
Inertia of Political Systems
Family Responsibilities and Their Contexts

Summary
Analytical Questions

"Where will I be at in ten years from now? I am on my way to becoming a politician but for this I first have to go to Law School and this is my next step. I have always wanted to be a politician since my uncle lost his job because his company brought in more automation. It has always seemed to me that politicians should be there to help the private sector help average citizens rather than those that are in power."

"In ten years from now I'd like to write that I will be married with three children but I know that I will not be able to afford the three children, perhaps two at most because I'll have to work along with my husband to make ends meet. But before that I want to travel and experiment with different types of jobs to see what I'd like best to do."

"My head spins when I think about 10 years from now because honestly I don't know where I will be at. For sure I will have to help my family financially because our parents have made a lot of sacrifices to allow us to live here and go to university. I'll be a nurse for sure but I can't even think beyond that. Married? Hopefully. Children? Hopefully. But the future seems so insecure."

"If you had asked this question to my older now 33 years old brother, he would have had no problem answering because the future 10 years ago was pretty obvious. But it's not so obvious to me right now. I want to become a criminologist, on the technological side of it but I don't know if I will get a job when I am finished school. Getting a job is not what it used to be. It seems that the requirements change all the time and the jobs come and go."

"In 10 years from now I will be taking care of my parents, both of them probably seeing how things already are at this state. I am the youngest of five and my parents are already in their 70s for my father and late 60s for my mother and they are in poor health with no savings because they gave everything to us. My father already has Alzheimer and we can't find a place that would help us just a bit, like putting him in respite care once in a while to give my mother and myself some breathing space and my mother has a heart problem."

This concluding chapter builds on the material presented in the entire book. As the students' quotes above illustrate, the future is less certain than it used to be. Some see that they will not be able to have the number of children they want while others are already facing taking care of parents because society is not helping. We begin with a return to the key themes that inform this text and that were initially outlined in the first chapter. Future trends in family life are then predicted on a modest scale. Family-related policies are discussed within the context of some of the main themes outlined, as well as some of the problems defined in previous chapters.

SALIENT THEMES REVISITED

The key sociodemographic variables of social class, gender, and race/ethnicity are part of the fabric of the various themes that recur throughout this text.

Social Inequalities and Gender Stratification

It is a key underlying theme that *families' major problems are largely, but not exclusively, created by economic, ethnic, and gender inequalities*. These pertain to issues of power and are examined within a combination of political economy and feminist theories. These structural challenges are evident as families struggle to survive economically, or to overcome racial discrimination, or to manage the difficulties of child socialization or even couple dynamics. Gender inequalities cut across ethnic and class divides. Therefore, gender stratification and roles were in evidence in most chapters. The text highlighted the extent to which females, at all age levels, are the nurturers and kin-keepers and how much more invested in various couple and family domains they generally are compared to males. Basic child socialization and care, as well as familial problems and interactions, affect mothers more than fathers, wives more than husbands, sisters more than brothers, and grandmothers more than grandfathers (e.g., Burton et al., 2006).

The gender "revolution," as England (2010) puts it, has stalled in many domains and kin-keeping is one of them. As a result, when social structures fail to meet the needs of fragile families, mothers can be blamed as a political expedient (Ambert, 2001; Robson, 2005). Indeed, in their parenting roles, **mothers** *are far more subject to moral policing than are fathers* (e.g., Knaak, 2005), particularly when they are single (Gazso, 2012). Further, social inequalities based on gender stratification mean that women are paid less than men for equivalent work (Beaujot, 2000). As well, women often channel themselves into part-time work and less well-paid jobs with no benefits because of the unequal division of household labour and lack of regulated child care. This double factor contributes to keeping a large proportion of mother-headed families at or under the poverty level. As well, the types of jobs and the structure of the jobs to which women have access reinforce inequality at home (England, 2010). In this and other respects, feminist political theories posit that production and social reproduction are subsidized by women as well as by the poor and the socially marginalized (Arat-Koç, 2011; Luxton, 2006a).

Diversity of Families

The theme of family diversity resides not only at the ethnic level but also at the cultural level, including religion, ideologies, and beliefs. As well, family diversity encompasses structure and modes of family formation: stepfamilies, single-mother-headed units, foster families, same-sex-parent families, and families created by adoption or with the help of reproductive technologies. *Because of current socioeconomic conditions*, certain types of family structures—namely, single parent and, to some extent, blended and cohabiting structures—are less well equipped than others to invest in children's well-being and future (Hofferth, 2006; Kerr and Michalski, 2007). At this point in time, research suggests that a child in a stable parental marriage is the context that is the most favourable to that child's development and adult well-being (Halpern-Meekin and Tach, 2008; Mac Con, 2006). Hence, extending the right to marriage to same-sex-parent families has been a step forward and in children's best interest. Overall, there is a great deal of *similarity* among diverse types of families because families, as defined in this text, are institutions centred on intergenerational filiation, reproduction, socialization, nurturance, caring, and the expression of emotions. *Whatever their structure, they are similar in the responsibilities they shoulder.*

A Surfeit of Family Responsibilities

This third theme arose from the recurring observation that the family has not lost its roles but, rather, has acquired new responsibilities—in great part because a lack of effective social policies is expanding the range of family care and duties (Beaujot, 2000, 2004). The new social structure based on an unbridled market economy, information technology, and government cutbacks to helpful policies has bestowed upon the family a new set of responsibilities. This multiplication of family functions was documented in many chapters, whether we discussed neighbourhood and school quality, peer and media influences, or the lack of adequate care provided by society to its children, frail seniors, and challenged or disabled adults. Accordingly, we have seen that families are **burdened** with responsibilities imposed by the deficits of the social structure and the poverty of the political culture. As a result, too great a proportion of families are ill equipped to shoulder the responsibilities of caring for their members, protecting them, and maintaining them within a normative life course. There are five major causes for this situation.

First, at the juncture of the personal and societal levels of analysis is the absence of an effective community surrounding families, as discussed below. A second cause, based on political economy theories, resides in the market structure of our societies, that is in the **lack of social and political support** that would provide more resources to parents, children, and other family members with special needs—a situation to which we soon return. A third cause, also systemic*, refers to those countless families that are forgotten by society and relegated to segregated enclaves in poor neighbourhoods. The fourth source of individual families' inability to fulfill their functions is related to the previous ones: Too many families are headed by parents, often young and single, who do not have the financial, educational, and maturity resources to raise children. Finally, at the personal level, and within the context of so many social inequalities, parents often become so burdened by their own dramas and the need to make a living for their fractured family that their children are not sufficiently supported, even if only for a brief but crucial period of time.

The Effective Community

We have seen in many chapters that more and more research points to the necessity of having parents supported by a community that cares for its children—all of its children, regardless of social class, race, religion, and parents' marital status and gender. There is convergence among researchers from several disciplines as to the necessity of collective forms of socialization (Frempong and Willms, 2002; Sampson, 1997). Such communities are even more necessary now that we face the dire consequences of economic uncertainties, as discussed in Chapter 4. As suggested by proponents of rational theories, an effective community links parents and teachers together and prevents them from being isolated and unaware of children's activities (Coleman, 1990a). In turn, within such a context, what children learn at home is reinforced at their friends' homes or in schools. Within the shelter of this effective community and informal social control, there are fewer opportunities for non-normative behaviours that would take adolescents off the path of prosocial development. This description of the effective community is one that fits reality less and less, particularly in cities and their new suburbs. Thus, the past decades have seen the **erosion of the community** as a result of urbanization, individualism, dependency on expert knowledge, interest groups, and the technological market economy (Etzioni, 1994). All of these forces have contributed to weaken the community that would be so needed in times of cultural changes, increased media exposure, as well as an insecure economy.

The Cultural Context

First, in view of the greater cultural diversity of new Canadian families, particularly in terms of countries of origin and religion, the importance of this cultural context is present in all chapters, although especially in Chapter 2. The traditional religions in Canada, since its rediscovery, have been Christianity and Judaism. Later on, in the 19th century and early in the 20th century, immigration from China brought Buddhist and Confucian influences, among others, and later Hindu, Sikh, and Muslim religions became more salient in the Canadian cultural landscape. The theme of cultural context was also reflected in the recourse to social constructionism as an explanatory framework. It is the sociocultural context that defines what is proper behaviour and what are masculine and feminine roles, for instance. Cultures evolve and construct and reconstruct people's perceptions of the roles of mothers, children, adolescents, and the elderly throughout the centuries. More recently, we have seen the concept of emerging adulthood as a new life stage in perspectives on adult development.

The cultural theme is particularly evident in Chapter 3, which focused on the cultural revolution constituted by the audiovisual **media** (television, videos, cell phones, the Internet). Concerns about the advisability of exposing children to contents including physical violence, sexist and homophobic abuse, foul language, exploitative sexuality, and low-quality programming have not been taken seriously by the industries in question (Garbarino, 1995). Parental roles have become far more difficult to fulfill within such a cultural climate—a conclusion that reinforces the previous theme of families' inability to fulfill their functions adequately and to raise their children according to their **values** and not those of a consumerist and competitive society (Côté and Allahar, 2006; Doherty, 2000). The media *structure* (visual, constant, rapid, individualized) and contents may result in what Habermas (1987) saw as the opposite of human emancipation. These may also contribute to creating an environment of anomie* and lowered social solidarity among future adults (Durkheim, 1893, 1897).

WHAT DOES THE FUTURE HOLD?

No responsible sociologist can peer into a crystal ball and predict the future of the family beyond the next five to ten years because rapid change, rather than stability, is the hallmark of our society. We live in a **technology-driven** rather than a socially or morally driven world. The pace of technology is rapidly distancing humanity's ability to control it, plan for it, and adjust to it. The family is immersed in a global economy buffeted by the winds of speculation, where profits are paramount, and where the less educated become a surplus population—a perfect model for political economy theories (Bartels, 2008; Marx, 1867; Stiglitz, 2012). Under such circumstances, there are not many rules; therefore, predictions of the distant future are impossible. A few demographic trends constitute sociology's only secure source of predictions for the next decade.

Fertility, Sex Ratio Imbalance, and Age Distribution

The Canadian fertility rate, currently standing at 1.66, was even lower, at 1.5, a decade ago and could dip again, especially if environmental pollutants and various lifestyle activities reduce men's fertility and women's ability to conceive and bring to term a viable fetus. Fertility rates depend particularly on the economic situation, stable unions, and on the age at first marriage (Beaujot and Kerr, 2004). Low fertility rates were already well in place two decades ago in technologically advanced Asian countries such as Japan, South Korea, China, and have even spread to Vietnam. Low rates are now evident on all continents and are particularly noticeable in countries such as in Iran, Lebanon, Tunisia, Turkey, as well as the United Arab Emirates and Singapore, because they are culturally unexpected in these societies (Kotkin, 2012).

Cross-culturally and from a feminist perspective, one should also be concerned about the added burden on many societies of the low numbers of female children that are born in China and India, as well as the fact that this situation may be spreading to other countries, including Vietnam and former Soviet republics—now the countries of Azerbaijan, Georgia, and Armenia, among others (Hvistendahl, 2011). This demographic phenomenon, 10 to 20 years from now, will be an added burden on societies that already have a very low fertility rate. Indeed, perhaps as many as an additional 20 percent of men will not be able to find a wife; trafficking of women already occurs; and violence generally increases historically when males predominate in terms of numbers in a population (Seccombe, 2013). **Female feticide*** a concept used by Indian demographers, represents another form of feminine subjugation. This is a very paradoxical form of subjugation in countries where girls and woman are becoming more equal and educated, yet they still contribute to getting rid of some of their potential daughters in order to have sons or a son (Aulakh, 2013; Ram, 2012).

As more seniors live longer and are in better health, they will constitute a larger proportion of the population because their growing numbers are not accompanied by similar numbers of births at the other end of the age structure, except, for the time being, in Sub-Saharan Africa. As is the case in many western countries with a low fertility rate, the Canadian population is aging, except for that of the Northwest Territories and Nunavut. For instance, in July 2012, the **median*** age in Canada had reached an all-time high of 40.0 years versus 25.4 years in 1966 (Statistics Canada, 2012g). The population is youngest in the Territories and the three prairie provinces and highest in the Maritimes (because of out migration for work). Persons aged 65 and over account for 14.4 percent of the population, and it is projected that this segment will reach 20 percent by 2026 (Turcotte and Schellenberg, 2007). Children outnumber seniors by nearly half a million compared to nearly 2.6 million in 1992 (Statistics Canada, 2012g). The group that is increasing the fastest is the 85-and-over age bracket. In addition, later age at marriage and its accompanying low fertility mean that the family takes the vertical or "bean-pole" form: In the future, children will have fewer uncles, aunts, and cousins. *The extended family network will be substantially reduced. Thus, a key source of familial support is decreasing throughout the world,* as is already evident in China and Japan.

What concerns people in terms of the **aging of the population** is the cost of dependency. However, most of the elderly live on their own and are in reasonably good health. This being said, however, policies will have to be devised so that the frail elderly are well taken care of and do not become the sole responsibility of families.

A Crisis in Caring

It flows from the above that a **crisis in caring** will soon be affecting most European countries as well as China, South Korea, and is already upon Japan, among many others—although not India to the same extent because of higher fertility (Ram, 2012). Indeed, one of the consequences of the aging of the population is the looming reduction of the available pool of potential workers. This means that, in a very near future, there may be full employment of the qualified with resulting greater power of the workforce. But, on the negative side of the equation, this also means that there may not be enough workers, volunteers, and loving adults to care for the frail elders and as well as persons of all ages who have disabilities (Luxton, 2006b; Mandell and Wilson, 2011). Further, studies show that caring for family members with disabilities results in a great deal of work-family conflict in terms of responsibilities and scheduling (Stewart, 2013). Currently, many societies in Europe and the Americas, as well as Japan, import immigrants from less advantaged countries to reduce shortages of nurses and other care-related professionals (Arat-Koç, 2011). But, as all societies may eventually develop lower fertility rates, at least temporarily, citizens of less affluent countries may find work at home and may no longer need or wish to emigrate. As well, there will no longer be enough adult children to provide this labour of love.

The crisis in caring, which is a result of the aging of the population, is exacerbated by social policies that do not provide sufficient human and technical resources to maintain persons in their home or, in the case of severely impaired children and adults with physical or mental disabilities, to shelter them in special institutions, at least for respite care. This looming crisis in caring is one of the reasons why Japanese entrepreneurs are developing "companion" pet robots and robots that can lift disabled persons and carry them. They are also seeking to develop more sophisticated robots that would provide a greater variety of "emotions" and help, particularly in terms of feeding, picking up objects, and entertaining the elderly.

One can also be concerned that the very disabled and the sick "old" elderly may be deprived of certain medical treatments (Boyle, 2011). This already occurs in a form of triage away from some forms of aggressive but life-saving treatments of the very elderly and frail (Grignon et al., 2012). Within a political theory analysis, one can see that a society's rationale would be to reduce the cost of these treatments and to put a term to lives that might be considered burdens (or a **"surplus" population**) on the labour force and on a society's economy where everything has a price—where everything and everyone is a commodity (Hochschild, 2012). The world will need more ethicists to prevent such occurrences as market economy imperatives and ideologies can twist human values.

Cohabitation, Marriage, and Divorce

Will cohabitation rates increase? Probably, at least in the short term, because the current trends in this direction have not yet peaked. At the same time, marriage rates will dip accordingly among young adults. But over the entire lifespan, a majority of people will continue to marry at least once, although at a later age and in smaller numbers. Factors that could soften this trend toward cohabitation are increased immigration from Muslim and Hindu countries—which could also increase marriage and decrease single parenthood (Biles and Ibrahim, 2005). Better economic opportunities for the relatively unskilled might also foster stable relationships rather than unstable cohabitation (NCHS, 2010). Indeed, because of poverty, marital commitment is often not an option for the less affluent segments of the population (Goldstein and Kenney, 2001). Research also suggests that more cohabitational relationships are becoming as committed and as stable as marriages, at least for a segment of the population. Were this trend to spread, couples' and children's well-being would be equally well served in both types of unions.

What about the divorce rate? Some factors herald lower rates in the future while others herald higher rates. In the balance, the next decade should not bring a marked decline or increase in divorce in Canada. For instance, delaying marriage may act as a preventive measure to those divorces that are related to youthful marriages. However, we have also seen that marriages that are preceded by *uncommitted* cohabitations are more likely to end in divorce. As well, one can be concerned about the rise of serial cohabitations and casual relationships such as hook-ups and friends with benefits. Such relationships may contribute to lowering commitment in *future* cohabitations and marriages. As well, where Internet dating and special apps lead to constant availability for partnering, one again can be concerned about commitment, which research indicates to be one of the key ingredients in successful and lasting relationships (Fincham et al., 2017a).

As women continue to make gains on the labour market, the financial losses of divorce for men may slowly increase over time as they will stand to lose more than previous cohorts of men whose wives depended nearly entirely on them (Fry and Cohn, 2010; McManus and DiPrete, 2001). Whether this trend will contribute to reducing divorce remains to be seen. Were men to behave more equitably at home, and were the cultural assumptions about men's and women's roles changed in society at large, women might be more rewarded by and more inclined to remain in their marriage.

Singlehood and Family Formation by Singles

The trends internationally, including in Eastern Asia, are for an increase in the proportion of adults who will be single all their lives, whether by choice or circumstances (Kotkin, 2012). As well, the number of cohabiting Canadians and Europeans is increasing and we know that these unions are not yet as stable as marriage—another factor that is contributing to a rise in the number of single persons (NCHS, 2010; Provencher et al., 2006). As we soon see in Table 14.1 (on page 421), unattached individuals have higher poverty rates. Thus, one can justifiably be concerned that poverty rates will increase among future seniors, especially among women who have been poor and single, or poor mothers, and/or poor immigrants. We can also be concerned that the Canada Pension Plan may no longer be able to compensate.

The rate of births to single women has remained stable and has even decreased recently, particularly among adolescents, both in Canada and the U.S. (McKay and Barrett, 2010). This decrease seems to be related to more widespread recourse to contraception and, in the U.S., to a higher level of abstinence. Let's recall here that, because of economic circumstances and lack of appropriate social policies, nonmarital motherhood is generally neither in the best interest of a mother or a child, particularly at a young age. On the other hand, nonmarital fatherhood is not immediately detrimental to individual men (Nock, 1998a). So long as this gender-role imbalance survives, women remain entirely responsible for the reduction of nonmarital fertility. This inequity makes it more complicated to alter the pattern because women's good intentions may be thwarted by men's desire for immediate gratification without consequent responsibilities. Factors that could reduce the rate of births to single women include higher educational attainment, and better job prospects in pockets of poverty for both men and women (Bingoly-Liworo, 2010). As well, a change in cultural values, more adequate utilization of contraception, and male cooperation are also necessary. *Fertility needs to be de-gendered in terms of responsibilities.*

Immigration and Transnational Families

It is difficult to predict what the Canadian government will decide in terms of immigration levels in the next decade or so. Much will depend on our economy as well as the economy and political situation of countries from which a great proportion of our immigrants originate. Currently, poverty, lack of employment opportunities, political instability, civil wars, terrorism, and undemocratic governments bloated with corruption are key reasons why people are pushed out and migrate. More and more, climate change (lack of water, droughts, heat, loss of territory) will become an additional push for migration, often from the same set of countries. On the other side of the ledger, the aging of the population is a reason why Canada and other countries need immigrants. Thus, immigration levels will vary depending on these variables.

So will the number of transnational families or, perhaps, their type. That is, these families may be separated in order to take advantage of options to further their opportunities or, simply, as is especially the case for women immigrants and temporary workers, to provide a basic living for their disadvantaged families back home. At least for the next decade, while the segment of our population that needs caring increases, we will see an increase of transnational families at the lower end of the economic scale: women who come to Canada to do caring work and leave their children behind—nannies, health care workers, home helpers or attendants in seniors' homes, and even maids—whether from the Philippines, Latin America, or Sri Lanka and the Caribbean (Arat-Koç, 2011). The families they leave behind, in turn, suffer from a crisis in caring (Parreñas, 2002). In many cases, our own crisis in caring boomerangs abroad.

Families' Natural Environment

Families depend on the environment for their health, water, food, space, and cultural contents. In turn, the environment depends on families for its survival even though various financial and business concerns often work against this interdependence. In terms of predictions for the near future, global warming is a looming problem (*The Economist*, 2012c). As our economy is polluting and depleting the environment of its non-renewable resources in order to meet a spiralling series of consumer "needs," counter-movements of minimalist living and environmental protection are emerging. These movements, along with the limitations of our planet, may eventually have to put the brakes on consumerism and change children's "needs" that are fuelled by advertising.

Schools are helping to socialize children in terms of issues such as waste, recycling, and composting. Children in turn bring these concerns home. Still, Canadians use far too much electricity and oil, create too much garbage, and use too much water per capita—in fact, we are at the top of the consumption ladder in the world. In addition, the sprawl of our suburbs eats up the best farmland, which is our local source of food (Josey, 2008). This could become particularly important if global warming continues and creates recurrent droughts in the south: At that point, Canadian resources of water and arable land could be dangerously stretched. Studies show that, as countries in Asia, for instance, become economically advantaged, people's diet changes toward more meat eating, thus requiring more land to produce food. As well, it is estimated that, both in rich and poor countries, a staggering 30 to 50 percent of all food produced either rots away uneaten or is thrown away (*The Economist*, 2011c).

The Longer Time Frame

The possible trends just presented pertain to a future that is nearly here. Surely within a longer time frame, perhaps 20 years, more momentous changes in family life may take place. Consider the domains of the division of labour at home (more egalitarian?); families' growing dependency on or rejection of technology (virtual sex? robotic nurses and companions? robotic pets?); increased or decreased unemployment; reproductive modes and technologies (in vitro wombs? cloning?). It is with some interest that I recently reread a passage from a 1973/1976 book where I predicted artificial wombs or *in vitro pregnancies* (Ambert, 1976:207). I went on to discuss the health advantages for women and fetuses—a situation that would help women whose health is fragile and would replace surrogate motherhood. I was ahead of the times. . . !

Most of the changes that will occur in families in general will be largely dictated by the combination of technological developments and an economy that has become based more on speculation and takeovers than on production and services that could create jobs (Stiglitz, 2012). It is also an economy that benefits only a very small class, which controls most of the means of production on a world-wide scale (Marx, 1867). However, a point may be reached whereby unbridled technology so saturates life and degrades its humaneness that other societal forces might reassert themselves, including social planning, humanitarian philosophies, religion, morality, and community rather than economic values. What one must not forget is that technology and the market economy are **ideologies.** Such ideologies could be rejected as determinants of people's lives and societies could more judiciously choose technologies that can enhance rather than ruin the environment and family life. This is a choice that humanity will have to make at some point if it is to remain humane.

SOCIAL POLICIES PERTAINING TO FAMILIES

The reader will note that this section is not entitled "Family Policies" because Canada (as well as the U.S. and Great Britain) really does not have a coherent and purposive set of family policies (Beaujot, 2000). In fact, there is no equivalent to a Ministry of the Family, except in Quebec, which is the province that is also the most advanced in this domain (Albanese, 2011). Rather, what we have in Canada are social policies that directly or indirectly affect families. Policies in general and family policies in particular are **social choices.** Such choices are heavily influenced by the economic ideologies and the values espoused by a political system at a given time (Béland, 2010; Langille, 2009; van Kersbergen and Manow, 2009). For instance, there are generally vast differences in the policies enacted by a Conservative- versus a Liberal-controlled Parliament (or a NDP one) both at the federal and the provincial levels. Thus, there are also differences among provinces (Meilleur and Lapierre-Adamcyk, 2006). There are also vast differences among various western countries because of their ideologies as well as their historical backgrounds (Aysan and Beaujot, 2009; Hay, 2009; Raphael, 2011).

Anne-Marie Ambert

Government budget cuts will more and more require that the entire care of frail seniors be subsidized by families, thus extending family responsibilities throughout the generations. Adult grandchildren become particularly helpful in this intergenerational chain and contribute to the senior generation's well-being and happiness.

Focus of "Family Policies"

Overall, social policies that can be termed "family policies" largely focus on five areas of family life. These policies generally originate from various ministries at the provincial or territorial level, except for a few domains such as First Nations issues that are more frequently dealt with at the federal level.

1. **Family creation or reproduction:** An example is the bonus for families that the Quebec government previously initiated at the birth of a child, with a larger amount for subsequent children in order to raise the fertility rate. The bonus was more recently replaced with a different system focusing more on pro-family than pro-natalism (Krull, 2007). For Canada as a whole, the Child Tax Benefit and various child care allowances and deductions are helpful to low-income and middle-class families. Other family policies include laws pertaining to adoption: for instance, open adoption records and immigration requirements for international adoptions. Regulations concerning surrogate motherhood, sperm banks, and other aspects of assisted reproduction technologies also fit in this category.

2. **Family reunification or reconstitution:** Examples are the emphasis in the *Immigration and Protection Act* of 2001 on reuniting immigrants with their immediate families (Cottrell and VanderPlaat, 2011; Dench, 2006). At the provincial

level, an example is the emphasis of children's aid societies on returning children who have been abused or severely neglected to their original families.

3. **Childrearing and care or social reproduction:** The legislation of parental leave falls in this category. Partly paid parental leave is a Canadian social policy that is very useful to parents before and after the birth of a child. It prevents poverty in some families. The *Unemployment Insurance Act* of 1940 (now the *Employment Insurance Act*) was amended in 1971 to allow mothers up to 15 weeks of maternal leave, with a proportion of their salaries paid. In December 2000, this was increased to 35 weeks for either parent (Marshall, 2006). Currently, mothers can take from six months to a year off. Amendments are being considered for self-employed mothers. However, mothers who work too few hours cannot receive these benefits. Mitchell (2003:16) also found that women with salaries below $20,000 tended to return to work more rapidly than others—probably because their leave benefits are too low to sustain their family. Quebec has been administering its own, and more generous, Parental Insurance Plan since 2006 (Beaujot and Wang, 2010).

   In the 2010–11 Survey of Young Canadians, 90 percent of mothers reported taking a maternity leave averaging 44 weeks (Findlay and Kohen, 2012). More fathers took a parenting leave in Quebec than in the remainder of Canada: 76 versus 26 percent. For very small children, subsidized parental leave may be a more appropriate social policy in large cities than subsidized child care centres (Maccoby and Lewis, 2003). Indeed, parents would like to spend more time with small children (Beaujot and Ravanera, 2009). Nevertheless, the creation of inexpensive and regulated care centres is especially important here. Quebec has its $7.00 a day system but the waiting list is very long. Ontario began, in September 2010, offering extended child care before and after kindergarten hours for five-year-olds. But, overall, as seen in Chapter 6, child care spaces are totally inadequate and subject to cuts when government deficits grow.

4. **Caregiving for the frail and elderly:** Governments in the recent past undertook steps toward strong contributions in this domain. However, budget cuts are resulting in increased reliance on family members (Chappell and Funk, 2011; Connidis, 2010; Mandell and Wilson, 2011). The provision of free time to attend to the care of the elderly and the sick, as well as the availability of services such as visiting homemakers, also fall in this category, as does the maintenance of subsidized seniors' homes. One area of care that needs far more attention in terms of policies is that pertaining to the growing number of autistic children who move into adolescence and adulthood. A proportion needs specialized care and constant supervision. Yet, institutions are not forthcoming while others are closing; some parents are forced to abandon these adolescent children to the state so that they can get care.

5. **Economic support:** This includes such initiatives as the Child Tax Benefit, the National Child Benefit Supplement, the Universal Child Care Benefit, and Old Age Security (with its components), as well as the Canada Pension Plan (Hay, 2009). For instance, for 67 percent of senior families, government transfers constitute their principal source of income (Williams, 2003). Without this income, a

high proportion of seniors, particularly single women, would be poor. However, as poor children age and move out of the nest, their disadvantaged parents, particularly single mothers, may become even poorer because of the loss of child-related benefits (Krull, 2007). As well, low-income youth would need subsidies to attend higher education: Increases in fees have gone beyond their grasp (Coelli, 2009). In Quebec, the system of support provides more money to families with one as opposed to two parents in order to compensate for the number of parents present (Krull, 2007). As well, as indicated in Table 14.1, better Employment Insurance provisions are needed for younger unattached individuals because this group has very high poverty rates (Statistics Canada, 2009j). In the following sections, we look at suggestions on how to eliminate poverty, support the parental role, and facilitate the care of our elders.

REDUCING POVERTY AND ECONOMIC INEQUALITY

We have seen throughout the text that social inequalities resulting in poverty are the root cause of a multiplicity of social problems, family misery, and individual deficits (Raphael, 2011; Vall and Thompson, 2012). Overall, *poverty makes couples and families vulnerable* (Conger et al., 2010) and affects seniors' health and degree of isolation (Gilmour, 2012). Mothers and their small children, as well as unattached persons (living alone), are particularly affected, as indicated in Table 14.1, which summarizes the 2007 poverty rates for various types of families and individuals (Statistics Canada, 2009i). But families scoring $100 above will not be considered poor, yet such families are in the same predicament as the "truly poor" ones. There are probably as many families near the poverty level as below it. Thus, "poverty" is more widespread than indicated in these statistics alone.

The gendered situation among single-parent families illustrated in Table 14.1 holds across all cultures. It has given rise to the concept of the **feminization of poverty**. Even in Sweden, poverty is transmitted from generation to generation, albeit to a lesser extent, when families have single mothers and/or criminal fathers (Stenberg, 2000). France also has a higher poverty rate among mother-headed families, despite more aggressive *prestations sociales* (Dell et al., 2003). The same can be observed in Quebec despite more progressive policies. In Quebec, the higher rates of cohabitation leave many women financially marginalized when their union breaks up (Meilleur and Lapierre-Adamcyk, 2006). As indicated in Table 14.1, some children are at much higher risk of poverty than others. Poverty rates are much higher in large cities, particularly those where disadvantaged groups are located. For instance, in 2006 for Winnipeg, 46 percent of Aboriginal households were poor and so were 26 percent of households with a child under six (CCPA, 2009).

A Critique of Current Policies

Within a context of political economic theories, policies to reduce economic *inequalities* would need to be much deeper and more revolutionary than what is discussed here, as the entire system of the market economy is implicated (Langille, 2009; Marx, 1867; Stiglitz, 2012). Hence our more modest focus is on eliminating poverty. This said,

TABLE 14.1 | **Poverty Rates after Income Tax Cut-Offs for Families and Persons in Canada, 2007**

Types of families and persons	%*
ADULTS	
Couples without children	4.7
Senior couples	0.9
Unattached women below 65 years	35.1
Unattached men below 65 years	29.7
Unattached senior women	14.3
Unattached senior men	13.9
CHILDREN**	
In two-parent families	6.5
In male single-parent families	9.2
In female single-parent families	26.6
Immigrant children	33.0
Aboriginal children not on reserves	28.0

Sources: Data from National Council of Welfare. 2009a, "Poverty trends by family type, 1976–2007," Ottawa, November and National Council of Welfare 2009b. A snapshot of children living in poverty. Ottawa, November.

* After income tax cut-offs. Poverty rates before income tax would be higher than shown here because low-income persons receive tax credits which help some rise above the poverty level.

** Below the age of 18.

policies aimed at truly preventing and reducing poverty rather than simply displacing it (to jails, for instance) or shifting it to private agencies and food banks, would benefit the entire society (Lindsey and Martin, 2003). How to reduce poverty? The overarching answer begins with increasing the income of the working poor, of those near the poverty line, and providing more adequate welfare payments to the unemployed.

Low wages create poverty, and some families living on such wages hold two or three jobs to make ends meet and still have recourse to food banks. There is a great deal of political and business-community resistance to raising minimum wages to acceptable levels because this would reduce corporations' profits and affect small employers (Coburn, 2010). This returns us to Chapter 4 where we saw that the ease with which companies relocate their plants and services abroad, where wages are very low, is probably one of the main factors that prevents provincial governments from raising wages more substantially than they do. Under these circumstances, raising the minimum wage might result in layoffs and simply displace poverty from country to country.

However, governments could make up the difference by topping low wages so that they reach a minimum that is sufficient—according to the cost of living in different areas—or a **guaranteed minimum income**. In other words, monthly wage supplements would allow families a release from working overtime or three jobs that prevent some couples from spending enough time together and others from having another child (Nyberg et al., 2010). Such a program has been shown to bring behavioural and school-related benefits to children (Bogenschneider and Corbett, 2010:792).

Families affected by unemployment should receive welfare payments until they are able to be self-sufficient (Gennetian and Morris, 2003). Currently, in order to qualify for welfare, people have to exhaust all their assets and earn practically nothing (Monsebraaten, 2010). Welfare payments should be socially reconstructed as a form of *salary* given to families that have been marginalized by the economy, discrimination, or even their own frailties. It is an investment in the nation's youth, education, and in future seniors. *Society would benefit, even economically, in the next generation.* Unfortunately, the next generation is not generally a priority among politicians.

Pong et al. (2003) have shown that the gap in academic achievement between children from one- and two-parent families narrowed in those countries that have policies aimed at equalizing economic resources between families (see, also, Brady and Burroway, 2012). Adequate welfare payments that raise families above the poverty level can prevent the transmission of poverty, rather than perpetuating it, by enhancing children's cognitive development, which later contributes to their economic success (Duncan and Brooks-Gunn, 1997). In turn, this situation could lower the rates of unmarried motherhood for, as we have seen, this is largely a poverty-related phenomenon. As well, adequate support may actually be correlated with lower homicide rates (DeFronzo, 1997). Such programs are preferable to investing in prisons, which are not a remedy.

Similarly, research suggests revamping the health care system and orienting it toward the prevention of disease and chronic conditions. Only about 20 percent of persons over the age of 45 report having received information that could prevent illness. Patients with chronic conditions account for two-thirds of all health spending—no matter their age. But, as people age, without preventive medicine, they acquire more chronic problems (Picard, 2011). Hence, current policies do not address these key issues, which risk bankrupting our health care system in the long term.

Creating Green Jobs

In Canada, even more than in many European countries, employment is the most important factor to avoiding poverty (Hay, 2009). Nearly seven out of 10 households with no employment are poor. With one wage earner, 21 percent are poor while only four percent are when two or more persons are gainfully employed. Our new economy, based on the service sector, information technology, and financial speculation no longer provides well paid **entry-level jobs** that young people can turn to and then be in a position to establish families they can support (Beaujot, 2006). Many social thinkers advance that our governments need to invest in new industries and technologies that are environmentally friendly (such as solar energy) and more democratic (Rifkin, 2011). Once energy concerns are addressed, other jobs can follow to create new materials that are environmentally neutral, which can go into more durable roads, residences, and cars, or even clothes and printing paper, as other instances.

At the same time, it is suggested that governments should enter into partnerships with the private sector to retain jobs here. *Each country should be able to provide work for its citizens, above and beyond the ideology of globalization.* This is important for Canada because it is a country that is too dependent on the consumerism of other nations, particularly the U.S., for its exports and too dependent on the depletion of its own natural resources (gas, oil, wood, and minerals), the extraction and processing of which pollute the environment. In this vein, helping farmers produce more but with better incomes would help provide many jobs for young people who do not have the ability, desire, or means to acquire higher education—hence the economic marginalization of too many (Côté and Allahar, 2006; National Council of Welfare, 2009). Some are much happier and productive doing manual work. Hence the rationale for creating a greater variety of jobs even if this means retaining, resuscitating, or repatriating certain industries, such as shoe or electronic manufacturing, that can provide basic labour.

Facilitating Adequate Housing

One component of poverty, and even of average income, is the lack of affordable housing, especially in expensive metropolitan areas such Toronto and Vancouver (CBoardC, 2010; CERA, 2013). We have seen in Chapter 5 that neighbourhoods that have high proportions of low-income families are related to more problematic family dynamics and child outcomes. For instance, Kohen et al. (2002a) have found that disadvantaged children benefit from living in a neighbourhood that has a greater proportion of economically secure residents. In contrast, social housing, as currently designed, tends to increase an area's already existing poverty.

Thus, one suggestion is that poor families receive **subsidies** that would allow them to find lodgings in a range of neighbourhoods. This could be accompanied by subsidies that would offer a proportion of stable low-income families the opportunity to buy a housing unit. Individual development accounts would assist families by providing them with monthly supplements to pay their mortgage and/or a down payment (Boyle, 2002). *Options for Homes*, for instance, uses innovative financing to make **home ownership** more affordable, even in high-rises (CBoardC, 2010). *Habitat for Humanity* is another helpful example. These policies would have the triple advantage of mixing social classes, empowering the poor via home ownership, and allowing them to move out of nefarious neighbourhoods. At the same time, governmental costs for building, managing, and maintaining public housing would decrease. Green and White (1997) suggest that home ownership itself forces people to acquire new management skills related to property maintenance, financial planning, and interpersonal functioning that, in turn, may be transferred to more successful parenting practices. Indeed, there are indications that parents who are homeowners become more hopeful and future oriented; their children benefit in terms of adaptive behaviours (Boyle, 2002).

However, it is difficult to know what the effect of such policies would be in terms of the neighbourhoods themselves. First, what would it do to areas that are currently devastated by poverty and even criminality? Would the truly disadvantaged families be left behind in the difficult areas creating ghettoes of even more acute deprivation (Fletcher, 2007)? There is also the possibility, based on an earlier study, that low-income youths moved to higher-income areas may feel excluded; they may react by becoming even more antisocial (Boyle et al., 2007). Or, yet, would policies that help disadvantaged families move out displace problems to areas that are stable, as may have happened in the U.S. (Rosin, 2008)? These possibilities might be the case if these families do not receive scaffolding support to equip them with coping mechanisms necessary to function in more stable neighbourhoods.

> *A small example of this possibility occurred in a condo located in a stable neighbourhood in Toronto when a family with two teenagers and one school-age child moved in as renters after having lived in a notorious area of town. The teenagers promptly used the stairwells to smoke, drink, and have sex and began intimidating other residents who tried to put a stop to these activities. Many other nonresident teens began visiting this apartment and then loitered in corridors harassing residents. The younger child began playing ball in the unit and the neighbours below developed headaches. Then adults were showing up as guests at all hours of the night. The police became frequent visitors. After a month of hearing complaints from residents and the terrorized janitorial as well as security staff, the president of the board of this condo discussed the issue with two owners of the same race as the new residents. The family was called in and it became very obvious that they were elated at having "escaped" from their "jungle" but had no idea as to how to behave according to the norms of their new area. The rules were explained to them: The teenagers were sneering (as they had always done when confronted with adult authority). After a while, they understood that, if they wanted to stay in this area, they had to change their behaviours. The two owners volunteered to mentor them. They also introduced the family to a new peer group and to adjacent sports and library facilities, among others. The situation improved drastically.*

Although the outcome was positive, it was so only because of extensive informal intervention. This example highlights the necessity of preventing cultural and social isolation and divisions created by poverty and class segregation from emerging.

Another problem related to housing pertains to the fact that Aboriginals who live on reserves do not own their homes, which is a disadvantage in a private property economy. A recent agreement between the Nisga'a band and British Columbia may have set a precedent. As well, a reserve near Vancouver has become a free township with property rights. Home ownership would allow for the accumulation of wealth and the transmission of this capital to the next generation as is the prerogative of other Canadians. It would also provide some capital for Aboriginals who move away from a reserve and settle in a city. As owners, inhabitants of reserves would have a stake in maintaining their properties so that the standards of housing that are now so low in many of these communities might rise. With this, other problems might be easier to solve, provided that a level of home ownership mentoring takes place.

Expansion of Child Care Programs

Universal and inexpensive child care would be particularly important in the prevention of poverty and as a remedy when it occurs (Kershaw et al., 2005). It would also lower the burdens of parenting in an economy that necessitates two salaries.

Furthermore, it is needed to redress the gender imbalance against women in the domain of child care and hence contribute to the reconciliation of work and family life (Thévenon, 2011). An inexpensive and quality child care system can also create jobs and promote the economy of an area (Albanese, 2006, 2011). It may encourage fertility where it is needed.

Yet, we have seen in Chapter 6 that only 20 percent of Canadian pre-schoolers have access to *regulated* child care (Beach et al., 2009). As a first step, child care should be available to all low-income families: Early poverty is the most detrimental for child, family, and society because it prevents the formation of skills needed in schools (Duncan et al., 1998; Sawhill et al., 2012). This step has already been widely suggested (Friendly et al., 2006; Pascal, 2009), and it consists of providing enriched care to all children aged one to five in poor and near-poor families, all day long (Rushowy, 2004).

Two immediate results would follow. First, we know from Chapter 6 that disadvantaged children in such programs develop more human resources, both behaviourally and cognitively, that prepare them for school (Pascal, 2009). Later on, they do better in terms of earnings and provide more revenues to society via taxes (Reynolds et al., 2011). Second, since child care constitutes mothers' main roadblock to self-sufficiency, this program would make it easier for mothers to find and retain jobs. For mothers on welfare, pursuing some postsecondary training would be an excellent investment, which current welfare policies do not necessarily encourage, but which extended child care programs could make feasible. However, one also has to be cautious in proclaiming institutional child care as the solution to all problems as so much of *its results depend on the quality of the educators, the peer group, and the families involved*. As well, as seen in Chapter 6, too many hours at child care centres may be difficult for small children in terms of adaptation to all the stimuli involved: There are indications that behavioural problems emerge (Belsky et al., 2007).

After-School Care and Improved Schooling

To extend the benefits of early childhood education, a second phase of the program would provide after-school care and tutoring through junior high school (Pascal, 2009). These have been shown to improve academic competence (Mahoney et al., 2005). This would, at the same time, provide children with much needed supervision and reduce opportunities for delinquency. Indeed, physical and sexual assaults against school-age children too frequently occur between 3 and 6 p.m.—that is, between the end of the school day and a parent's return home from work (AuCoin, 2005:68). Such programs could also reduce parenting stress (Barnett and Gareis, 2006). Extended after-school hours already exist in Quebec and have been implemented on an experimental scale in some areas in Ontario. One in particular is the Peel District School Board's Early Years Hubs and Readiness Centres, located in areas of need and which also involve parents (Grieve and Hogarth, 2009). The Pascal report in Ontario (2009) also suggests extended programs during the summer in areas where 15 or more families request it.

As well, the quality of schools should be improved in areas of poverty. This might begin in primary school, and when the "improved" cohort of children moves on, then the program would be extended throughout high school. Each high school at risk might include incentive programs, at least on a trial basis, as exist in some American states and in some cities in Canada. For instance, adolescents from low-income families could be given a "salary" to remain in school in good standing (no truancy, no disruptive conduct, and all homework done). As well, students who achieve an A or B+ could be guaranteed scholarships for higher education. Such incentives might have the unanticipated result of creating a school and peer culture that values rather than denigrates education. If this were to happen, material incentives would no longer be needed in the next cohort of children.

Consequences and Limitations of Programs

Each one of the preceding policies in isolation is insufficient to lift a sizable number of children out of poverty. It is the total configuration that counts (Vall and Thompson, 2012). The financial costs of such multipronged, proactive, preventive policies may appear high initially, but their **long-term results** would make them cost effective. To begin with, welfare outlays would rapidly diminish as better-educated parents are able to secure and maintain jobs. Health costs would certainly be reduced after a while, and so would costs stemming from child abuse and foster care (Pelton, 1997). Over $65,000 a year is needed to maintain a young person in a correctional institution. Thus, within a few years, the costs incurred for law enforcement and penal institutions would fall along with delinquency.

Further, an unintended consequence of enriched programs and school reform in disadvantaged areas might be a further reduction in the rate of family formation by young mothers. This could result from a greater interest of children in school

The effects of poverty on children differ, not only because of their familial and personal characteristics, but also depending on the era in which poverty occurs. This boy grew up in a rural area during the Great Depression and may even have been a **Home Child**.

Library of Congress Prints and Photographs Division [LC-USZ62-53754]

achievement and extracurricular activities generated by school quality and financial incentives toward postsecondary education. As children mature into adolescents who have been supported by appropriate structures since age one, their enhanced educational capital would lead to jobs. In turn, we already know that increased income constitutes an incentive to stable relationships before procreation and that two-parent families are less likely to become poor.

Not everyone can become economically independent. Some individuals are not sufficiently gifted by nature and need to be supported. They are not responsible for their deficits of human capital. Further, not all poverty can be eradicated. The ideology that has contributed to the initial creation of poverty would still survive. Indeed, poverty is created, as we have seen in Chapter 4, by social incqualitics stemming from global socioeconomic forces that now include "smart" technology requiring higher educational credentials. It is also created by corporations that are guided by an ever-increasing profit motive for their shareholders, largely disregarding human costs (Langille, 2009). Currently, repayment of government debts siphon off monies that could be used to help young families. The combined ideologies of racism and sexism also contribute to poverty, such as the poverty of minority women who cannot find employed males to help support their children. All women are disadvantaged on the labour market in terms of wages.

SUPPORTING THE PARENTAL ROLE

Even before we begin discussing supporting parents, we have first to discuss how the issue of low fertility rates could be addressed. As we have seen, the desired fertility level is over two children but the achieved one is 1.6 (Edmonston et al., 2010). This discrepancy between desired and achieved fertility means that there are policies that employers and governments could develop to facilitate family life and perhaps contribute to increasing fertility (Beaujot, 2004; Kotkin, 2012). Unless governments quickly adopt policies more favourable to youths, young families, and the reconciliation of work and family life, one can predict that young families will continue having few children and more couples will choose to remain childless (Thévenon, 2011). In other words, we need to reduce the costs of having children. Feminists have long alerted us about the devaluation of reproductive work in all societies (Daniels, 1987; DeVault, 1991; D. Smith, 1999). Now, many economists and demographers are recognizing this inequity (e.g., Romaniuk, 2010). Many are suggesting that, if we want men and women to have more than one child, women in particular will have to receive a salary from the state for their parenting work. Or, yet, both parents will have to receive a valued compensation for their care work. After all, parents are doing the reproductive work for society and the economy in terms of the future work force and tax contributors. In other words, *parents are subsidizing the economy and the ruling class.* Above all else, availability of low-cost and high-quality child care, including after school hours, is essential and has been related to fertility increases, albeit modest, in Norway and Quebec, for instance (Rindfuss et al., 2010). Adjustment in work hours and the entire production system may be key (Beaujot, 2006:124). Under such circumstances, *the interests of adults would compete less with those of children,* and parents, especially women, would find their situation more equitable than is currently the case. Overall, it is difficult to predict which amalgam of policies or cultural change could encourage higher fertility (McQuillan, 2006). But it would be unrealistic to expect any upward shift that might go beyond a rate of two children per woman. However, even such an increase would result in positive demographic consequences for several generations to come and would bring a slow and orderly population decline, which would be helpful to the environment.

Only 42 percent of Canadian parents of young children agree that "Canada values its young children" (Invest in Kids, 2002). Research suggests that parents should be respected and better supported by schools, professionals, welfare agencies, and law enforcement personnel (see also Adams et al., 2002). In other words, the parental role needs to be more adequately institutionalized and more positively **reconstructed socially**. Invest in Kids (2002) also found that parents were not confident in their role and often lacked knowledge, that many were distressed, and too many utilized ineffective parenting practices. Chao and Willms (2002) noted that only about a third of parents are authoritative. Perhaps parents should all receive official reinforcement and even training, no matter their social class.

But we also recall that interactional theories view children as coproducers in their development. Within this perspective, *it is suggested that professionals help youngsters cooperate in their upbringing rather than evade their responsibilities* (Brody et al., 2004). If children were encouraged from all quarters, including the media, to value their **parents' moral authority**, the family would become a more effective institution, whatever its structure and size (Doherty, 2000). Within such a context, children would more easily accept and internalize norms of behaviour and would be more inclined to cooperate in their upbringing (Ambert, 2001). As a result, parental investment and monitoring would be facilitated, and behavioural problems, drug and alcohol abuse, as well as delinquency would diminish substantially.

Within the framework of political economy perspectives, another parenting problem deserves a mention here: It is that parents have been forced to enter an era of competitive parenting due to the demands of the technological economy. Others call it hyper-parenting (Honoré, 2008), or intensive parenting, particularly mothering (Hays, 1996), or "concentrated cultivation" (Lareau, 2011). This is parenting guided by experts to "optimize" children's outcomes ("the best") in terms of skills, particularly academic skills (Bodovski and Farkas, 2008)—*children as products*. We have seen that, in English-speaking western countries, childrearing has become professionalized to promote children's acquisition of traits that are valued in our type of society (Alwin, 1986; Arnett, 2008). These traits include individualism, self-esteem, self-sufficiency, and independence (Harkness and Super, 2002). Yet, this "expertise" has resulted in children's lives becoming more structured in terms of extracurricular activities and less spontaneous—and, paradoxically, this promotes dependence on parents. Yet, what is needed is interdependence between the generations (Kitayama and Cohen, 2007; Tsai and Dzorgbo, 2012). This type of parenting is demanding, both of parents and of children. It induces insecurity among parents, a sense of never doing enough, and a fear that one's child will miss out on opportunities. Children become managed children as well as **products**. These norms are set by various experts who gain a great deal in the bargain. This is part of the culture of the type of economy we live in: competitive, acquisitive, and driven. Parents are encouraged to use an authoritative style by some but a permissive style by others. As a result, many parents, afraid of assuming their role, choose permissive or "wavering-negotiating" styles (Chapter 10). These trends are pronounced mainly at the middle-class and upper-class levels, which are the social strata that are the most successfully embedded in the economic system of production and consumerism. Working-class and disadvantaged parents, in general, hold different values of cooperation, obedience, and familism, as do many immigrants. They are also more group oriented and use childrearing practices that fit within the exigencies of their more constrained lifestyles. Sociologist Annette Lareau (2011) calls this the "accomplishment of natural growth" in contrast to the "process of concerted cultivation" enacted by middle-class parents.

Supporting the parental role will also involve providing more affordable and roomier housing than what developers are building in our cities—small condos. In other words, nations need to increase their supply of appropriate housing. Basically, we need to change our societies so that the economy is more favourable to parents and, in general, offer better working conditions with fewer hours of paid employment to reduce the time crunch. Finally, we should add that, by offering better alternatives to parents, a society will encourage others to become parents. While we cannot backtrack to earlier fertility rates—the world could not support this—very low rates are not sustainable over an extended time. Kotkin (2012) ends by saying, "In the coming decades, success will accrue to those cultures that preserve the families' places, not as the exclusive unit in society, but as the one truly indispensable for the ages" (p. 35).

Thus, failure to help parents and families may result in a further decrease in fertility and in a society where children are "rare" (Christiansen, 2013). One has to consider that a society with relatively few children may become even more individualistic culturally because fewer persons then have the opportunity to care and nurture young lives. Hence, very low fertility rates do endanger certain family responsibilities and, within a few generations, many families will cease to exist. From an environmental perspective (population pressure, pollution, and mismanagement of our natural resources), population decline is a positive aspect. The earth needs fewer persons. But from an economic perspective, negative population growth *after the large cohort of baby boomers* means a shortfall in the labour force: In the near future, jobs will not find workers. This is fine when it comes to producing goods because humanity produces too much materially. However, the problem that arises is that there are and will be too few persons of working age to care for the sick, the frail, the disabled, and the elderly.

FACILITATING THE CARE OF ELDERS

Persons aged 65 and older account for 13 percent of the Canadian population. Of these, only 7.4 percent are in residences for seniors or health care facilities, and this occurs generally during their oldest years (after age 85) or when they become very frail and dependent in the last year of life. In 2011, 31 percent of those 85 and older were in a collective dwelling (Statistics Canada, 2012h), but in many instances, the waiting lists are too long for nursing homes (Walkom, 2012). Gilmour (2012) also shows that 20 percent of seniors who are 75 and over do volunteer work in the community. Overall, 31 percent of all seniors engage in **volunteer work** (CIW, 2010). Thus, while nearly 30 percent of seniors received help for transportation and errands, another 19 percent provided this same help to someone else and over 10 percent did housework for someone else not living with them. As discussed in Chapter 10, the flow of help is bidirectional throughout families—as seniors also help the younger generations—and this help is largely based on altruistic and filiation motives (Beaujot, 2006; Rajulton and Ravanera, 2006b). Overall, most seniors are **independent,** live on their own, and are still active citizens—far from the social construct of a socially disengaged age category (Harbison et al., 2012).

Most seniors who receive assistance because of a long-term health problem, receive it in part or totally from informal sources such as relatives (Luxton, 2006b). As seniors age and their problems become more serious, they receive more assistance from formal sources, whether government, paid employees, or non-government organizations. In 2002, the GSS showed that seniors tended to receive more of their help from informal sources when they had many living children. After spouses, **daughters** provided more in terms of housework and personal care and shared with sons in terms of transportation, shopping, and the payment of bills. Personal care was more often carried out via organizations and paid employees.

The 2007 GSS completed this profile, focusing on **caregivers** 45 years and older and care recipients 65 years and older. Cranswick and Dosman (2008) report that women relatives are more often caregivers than men and do more of the tasks requiring *regular* assistance (such as meal preparation and medical-related care). This continues the cycle of social reproduction intergenerationally (Mandell and Wilson, 2011). These tasks compete with women's work schedule. Cranswick and Dosman also point out that wives' care of their elderly husbands is vastly underreported as it is simply seen as part of the household routine. In the same study, mature adult caregivers had been providing assistance for 5.4 years while older caregivers had been doing so for an average of 6.5 years. A British study has found that many caregivers had played this role at least twice before. Larkin (2009) used the term "serial carer." Finally, and perhaps surprisingly, they found that caregiving occurs more often when an older person enters a collective dwelling for seniors. This can in part be explained by the fact that institutions offer a limited range of free services and, in some cases, the caregiving is substandard and abusive (e.g., McLean and Welsh, 2011; Reid, 2008). An American study reported by Gallagher (2010) found that family members "actually provide higher-quality service than unrelated workers" (p. 272). In turn, the "clients" of these institutions feel more secure with the care provided by relatives.

There will soon be more middle-aged caregivers who belong to the **sandwich generation** as children are born later and stay home longer. As Duxbury et al. (2009) point out, just over one in 10 Canadians provide some form of help for an elderly person who lives nearby or in another location. This help tends to be given as a labour of love. In 2007, about 1.65 million Canadians aged 45 and over were providing assistance to a parent or a parent-in-law. About 22 percent of adult children were helping a parent who lived at least an hour away by car (Vézina and Turcotte, 2010). This situation required more financial outlays on the part of the adult children and 40 percent of them had to miss work compared to 28 percent of those living closer. Yet, employment tends to mitigate the stress of caregiving (Rubin and White-Means, 2009).

What all this information indicates is a *concern for future seniors* with no or few children—as is becoming more and more the norm (Légaré and Décarie, 2012). Thus, social inequalities among seniors will exist both in terms of physical assets and social capital (Keating and Dosman, 2009). As well, more seniors will need help from organizations. Informal caregivers, whether spouses, daughters, or daughters-in-law, will need more formal support to carry out their role. Beaujot (2004:22) suggests a world that is less centred on work and where family has priority, with work leaves for the caretaking of disabled or challenged children and adults as well as elderly relatives. But such a world also needs to be complemented with one in which consumer aspirations are reduced; however, trends are definitely going in the opposite direction currently. Our society, therefore, needs to develop more flexible workplaces so that children and relatives can assist their elderly parents more efficiently and with a lesser sense of stress. This is particularly necessary in view of the fact that not all adult children will be inclined to help their parents or feel the necessity to reciprocate for previous help they might have received (Ménard and Le Bourdais, 2012). As well, new government policies toward instituting a longer **"care leave"** for adults who need to take a more hands-on role in the help or care of a parent would be particularly helpful and timely. This would prevent financial difficulties for the caregivers and reduce the strain of doing two jobs at the same time: Although helping one's frail relatives, as is the case for child care, is an altruistic act, it is also an economic act and *benefits the entire society* (see Funk and Kobayashi, 2009).

CONCLUSIONS: THE FAMILY IN CONTEXTS

The family represents an experience lived by all people, making each individual an "expert" on the topic. But as we have seen, this personal expertise is insufficient, for family life has many faces, speaks many languages, harbours a multitude of cultures, and involves different cohorts and dynamics. It entails great happiness and cradles painful dramas. It appears so simple but in its totality it is so very complex because it depends on so many external contexts.

Inertia of Political Systems

On the whole, it is safe to advance that our political system makes it very difficult to adopt policies that would prevent social problems: Such policies require a great deal of planning, thus the political will to invest in the future (Béland, 2010). Also required is a certain level of consensus on what family policy means and what the goals are. Unfortunately, the future needs of families clash with the current political reality of getting votes and, now, of reducing deficits. For instance, the government has stopped excellent surveys by Statistics Canada that provide scientific information upon which policies can be based (Bednar and Stabile, 2012). Indeed, social policies pertaining to families should be the object of evaluation or research to ascertain the extent to which the explicit goals have been reached and to seek unintended (negative or positive) consequences (Bogenschneider and Corbett, 2010). But here as well, such necessities do not fit well with the short attention span of politicians. Further, our political systems, at all levels, are becoming more polarized, more divisive—perhaps following the example of the American electoral media wars or verbal sluggings between the left and the right. Polarization is certainly a poor basis for policy making in terms of investment in future generations. Overall, **political expediency** forces the adoption of stop-gap policies to solve a few problems that are identified by public opinion polls. But even remedial policies can take a very long time to produce a visible effect that can be assessed by research and appreciated by the public. In contrast, politicians need immediate or foreseeable results if their party is to remain in power. They also need results that will not offend the powerful groups that are often the same ones that subsidize political parties—in other words, legalized corruption. This returns us to political economy theories explaining how a powerful class controls not only modes of production but the political system that supports it (Bartels, 2008; Raphael, 2011).

Family Responsibilities and Their Contexts

The research summarized and evaluated in this book does not support the pessimistic view of a family decline. Rather, the research supports pessimism concerning *individual families' ability* to fulfill their *ever-increasing* responsibilities adequately, particularly that of the socialization of children and the care of frail elders. On the one hand, the family as an institution is highly valued, and exacting demands are placed on it in terms of its responsibilities in many domains. On the other hand, this same exacting socioeconomic context generally fails to provide individual families with equivalent moral support, resources, and practical help that could allow them to fulfill their responsibilities.

For instance, society is choosing to embrace market capitalism and information technology as a value and as a way of life (Côté and Allahar, 2006). Unavoidably, there are high costs to such a choice, and families bear a disproportionate burden in this respect, especially those that are marginalized by poverty and lack of access to the new types of jobs (Phillips and Phillips, 2000). As Blank (1997) phrases it, when a society "has chosen a market-oriented economy, it has a responsibility to those who cannot survive in the market on their own" (p. 198). This responsibility should not be displaced onto families. Unfortunately, this is exactly what continues to happen. Above all, in western societies, the family is a small and relatively isolated unit that is much affected by its various environments. In recent decades, this cultural and socioeconomic context has broadened considerably because of globalization and a more pervasive as well as intrusive technology. Empowering and assisting families, no matter their structure, is one of the key social challenges of the 21st century.

Summary

1. The three key sociodemographic variables of social class, gender, and race/ethnicity are part of the fabric of the various themes that have recurred throughout this text.

2. Trends in the very near future of family life are described.

3. Areas of family life addressed by policies are presented, and a critique of the political system is offered, including critiques of policies concerning poverty. Suggestions for the reduc-tion of poverty are provided. Other suggestions focus on better supporting the parental role and facilitating elder care.

4. The research presented in this book does not support the pessimistic view of the decline of the family, but does support pessimism concerning individual families' abilities to fulfill these ever-increasing responsibilities adequately.

Analytical Questions

1. Why are more and more families unable to meet their diverse responsibilities?

2. The concept of the effective community has been used repeatedly in this text. What could be done to put it into practice and what would be the consequences?

3. How does this chapter present a critique of our political system? How could this system be improved for the benefit of families and their members?

4. Relate the sections on the facilitation of elder care to their counterpart sections in Chapter 10—particularly the concepts of burden and care.

5. What are some key concerns that sociologists of the family should entertain regarding fertility?

Glossary

Anomie (anomic): Occurs when individuals are unable to follow the norms of their society. The word "normlessness" is often used instead of anomie. This is an important concept in Durkheim's theory (1897). It can also be used to refer to a situation whereby a society is in transition and norms are either lacking or not clear so that individuals are left in a state of anomie or normlessness.

Ascribed status: Synonymous with assigned status. For instance, a man who becomes a father is automatically ascribed this status. Children's social class is also ascribed in that they belong to their parents' class.

Assortative mating: Refers to selecting spouses or mates in a nonrandom fashion; marrying persons who have similar given characteristics. The characteristics may be physical appearance, IQ, values, one or several personality traits, or even social class. The opposite of assortative mating is random mating.

Authoritarian parenting: Refers to parental behaviours and attitudes that are predominantly controlling and punishing. At the extreme, they can be even harsh and rejecting. The authoritarian approach does not appeal to a child's sense of reasoning or morality. It is a "do-as-I-say-or-you'll-get-smacked" type of upbringing. Authoritarian parents may also be inconsistent: They may threaten to punish but do not follow through with the punishment.

Authoritative parenting: Combines both warmth and monitoring of children's activities and whereabouts. Authoritative parents make maturity demands on their children. They explain the reasons behind their demands or rules. Once they have explained the reasons and the consequences, they consistently follow through with enforcement of those rules.

Cohort: A group of people who were born around the same time and who therefore go through life experiencing similar sociohistorical conditions. For example, people born during the Great Depression form a cohort.

Commodify (to): Refers to the situation whereby private services, such as the care of family members, become services that can be bought and paid for.

Coparenting: This concept has so far been used to measure the extent to which parents support each other in their role or cooperate with each other psychologically and facilitate each other's role (e.g., Szabó et al., 2012).

Correlations: Correlations exist between two factors or variables, such as poverty and violence, when, as one increases or decreases, the other also changes. When both change in the same direction (e.g., both increase), this is a positive correlation. A negative correlation exists when one factor increases at the same time that the other decreases, as in the example of a decreasing number of cases of serious delinquency with an increasing level of socioeconomic status. Correlation is a statistical test, which is schematically illustrated in Figure 5.1 on page 127.

Critical mass: Refers to a proportion of well-functioning families that is necessary in a neighbourhood if that neighbourhood is to remain a good environment in which to raise children. The term can also refer to the proportion of children who are good students that is necessary in a classroom if learning is to take place. Researchers have not yet been able to determine what this exact proportion should be: 30 percent? 40 percent? 60 percent? (This term can also be used to refer to the negative as in "a critical mass of antisocial adolescents.")

Cyberbullying: "The use of electronic communications technology to threaten, harass, embarrass, or socially exclude others" (Mishna et al., cited in Scheelar, 2012).

Dilution of parental resources: This concept is used to explain the finding that children in large families do less well, on average, than those in smaller families. The rationale is that, in large families, parents have fewer resources to place at the disposal of each child: The resources are scattered over several children, or diluted.

Dysfunction: See *Function*. Dysfunctional behaviours are those that impair a person's functioning and success. They are maladaptive either for society, the family, the person concerned, or all of these. Persons or groups can be dysfunctional for their family or society, for instance.

Effective community: Refers to parents' links to other parents and to members of the community who maintain a prosocial set of values and are in contact with one another. The sharing of values, socialization goals, instrumental help, and collective supervision of children are characteristics of an effective community.

Endogamy: When people date, cohabit, or marry within their own social class, race, religion, or even language group.

Ethnic group: A group that is set apart from others because of its unique cultural patterns, history, language, as well as its sense of distinctiveness.

Ethnocentric: Refers to the judgments of social situations and people that individuals make based on their experiences within the culture of their own ethnic or cultural group. It can also be the assumption that one's own way of life is superior to that of other cultures or groups.

Exogamy: Marrying out of one's group; the opposite of *endogamy*. Interracial and interreligious marriages are examples of exogamy.

Failed states: States where the rule of law no longer exists and, generally, where there are civil wars, atrocities, and terrorism, as well as widespread poverty. There is relatively little in terms of political, legal, educational, and economic structures or institutions.

Female feticide: The killing of a female fetus, usually by abortion, after the sex of the fetus has been determined via ultrasound testing.

Friends with benefits: Involve "ongoing sexual activity occurring between partners who do not identify the relationship as romantic" (Weaver et al., 2011).

Function: What an institution or group does for society, for families, or for individuals.

Gender roles: Norms or rules that define how males and females should think and behave. Gender roles represent the social definition of what a society constructs as appropriately masculine or feminine in terms of behaviour.

Homogamy: See *Assortative mating*.

Hook-ups: Involve occasional sexual encounters.

Human capital: The entirety of abilities, skills, education, and positive human characteristics that a person possesses or has achieved. Synonymous with human assets.

Hypothesis: A testable proposition or sentence. For instance, "Wives who have been employed all their married lives adjust better to divorce than do homemakers or women who have been employed irregularly." Hypotheses are often designed to test theories.

Indicator: Indicators are used to measure variables, such as conjugal conflict. They are sentences, numbers, or observations that serve to illustrate a variable. Indicators are often coded (given a number) to derive statistics. Indicators of conjugal conflict can be the number of times spouses say they quarrel and how long their quarrels last.

Individuation: A psychological concept referring to the process by which children gain a sense of identity separately from their connection to their parents. This is a western concept related to individualism, which means the process of separating from the group.

Institution: A recognized area of social life that is organized along a system of norms (or rules) regulating behaviours that are widely accepted in a society. Examples of institutions are the family, schools, and the banking system. On a larger scale, institutions include the political, economic, and religious systems of a society as well as the military.

Institutionalized: Said of a situation or arrangement or activity that is widely accepted in a society and is organized around a set of norms defining the behaviours of the participants. A structural aspect of family life, such as marriage, is said to be institutionalized because it is governed by rules that are also widely accepted by society, or socially recognized. Such a structure is well scaffolded by society and its legal system.

Longitudinal studies: Consist of studying the same people over time. For instance, people may be interviewed at age 18 and studied again at ages 25 and 35. This research design contrasts with cross-sectional or one-time studies and surveys. Synonymous with panel study.

Macrosociology: The study of the family within its broader sociocultural context to see how global forces such as the class system, the economy, and religion shape family structure and dynamics. In other words, "large" sociology or the study of large-scale phenomena and developments in a society, and its social structure and organization.

Median: The middle number in a set of numbers that are arranged in order of magnitude.

Métissage: Refers to racial mixing. In Canada, this refers specifically to the mixing of white and Aboriginal partners, usually historically rather than currently—hence the origins of the Métis nation.

Microsociology: The study of interactions between individuals within specific and generally smaller contexts, such as the family or a group of friends. It is also the study of the internal dynamics of small groups, including the family.

Minority group: This generally refers to a group that is not as large as others. Or it can be a group that is given inferior status and less power in a society because of race, ethnicity, cultural practices, or religion. In Canada, this term generally refers to people other than white or Aboriginal.

Nonshared environment: Generally refers to experiences that differ for each sibling in a family. These can be different school, peer, and street experiences or environment. Within the home, the term refers to experiences that are specific to each child, such as differential parental treatment, the presence of the other siblings, or the chores given to a child because of his or her age or gender.

Polygenic: Refers to a trait, characteristic, or illness that can occur only when several specific genes are present.

Reference group: A group or category of persons whom people look up to, whose behaviour they imitate and emulate, and according to whose standards they evaluate themselves.

Shared environment: Generally refers to the home environment that siblings have in common or share. This could include parental behaviours, teachings, family routines and special occasions, and transitions, such as divorce or the death of a grandparent. It refers to the familial atmosphere. However, this shared environment is often perceived somewhat differently by each sibling, depending on his or her age, gender, and personality: The environment is shared but its impact differs.

Sex ratio: The proportion of males to females in a population. A ratio of one would mean that there is an equal number of males and females in a population or within an age group or in a year. A sex ratio over one, for instance 1.30, means that for each 100 females, there are 130 males or 30 more males than females. This is a very high sex ratio. A normal sex ratio at birth consists of 105 males per 100 females.

Social capital: A resource that resides in relationships, particularly family and community relations, that benefits child socialization. In Coleman's (1988) theory, social capital refers both to the positive interactions between a child's parents and between the child and his or her parents, as well as the relationships that parents maintain outside of the family that can benefit children or the entire family. Synonymous with social assets.

Social causation: Refers to theories that explain, for example, the high rates of well-being and economic success found among the married compared to the nonmarried, as a result of the benefits of marriage.

Social construct: A socially acceptable definition of a situation held by a group or a society. It is a cultural creation or invention. Social constructs concerning a phenomenon such as adolescence generally differ across history and across cultures.

Social reproduction: In this text, this concept, which is key to feminist theories, particularly political economy feminists, refers to activities and responsibilities surrounding the raising of children, including household maintenance, emotional work, as well as the care of the sick, disabled, and elderly family members. These activities sustain the future and current labour force and contribute to a society's economic productivity—as counted in the gross national product. This concept thus links productivity and reproduction work and closes the traditional analytical separation between work performed in the labour market and in homes. Motherhood is the key site of social reproduction. It should be noted that this concept has a somewhat different meaning in education theories where it largely refers to the transmission of a society's or a family's cultural capital as per Bourdieu's (1986) theory.

Socialization: Refers to the process whereby a child learns to think and behave according to the ways of the society and the group into which he or she is born.

Social mobility: The passage from one social stratum to another or from one social class to another. Downward mobility occurs when individuals fall below their parents' stratum (intergenerational mobility) or below the one they have themselves occupied earlier (intragenerational mobility). Upward mobility takes place when individuals achieve a higher socioeconomic status than that of their parents. In other words, they "move up" in the class system.

Socioeconomic status (SES): The ranking of people on a scale of prestige on the basis of occupation, income, and education. SES is often used as a synonym for social class.

Stratification: Refers to the ranking that people occupy in a system. Social stratification can be based on gender, race, or social class. For instance, families that belong to the higher social class have more resources, power, and prestige than others.

Systemic: Refers to a problem that is built into a system, an institution, or a society. Solutions to such problems often require a restructuring of the institution, a difficult enterprise at best.

Theory: A set of interrelated propositions that explain a particular phenomenon. A theory is a sophisticated explanation that can be tested against facts to see if it fits. A good theory should withstand the test of research.

Bibliography and Author Index*

*The boldfaced numbers are the pages on which these citations appear.

Abada, T., Hou, F., and Rani, B. 2009. Ethnic differences in educational attainment among the children of Canadian immigrants. *Canadian Journal of Sociology, 34*, 1–30. **110**

Ablow, J. C., et al. 2009. Linking marital conflict and children's adjustment: The role of young children's perceptions. *Journal of Family Psychology, 23*, 485–499. **277**

Abramson, I., et al. 2012. What helps couples rebuild their relationship after infidelity? *Journal of Family Issues, 33*, 1494–1519. **214**

Abu-Laban, S., and McDaniel, S. A. 2004. Aging, beauty, and status. In N. Mandell (Ed.), *Feminist issues: Race, class, and gender*, 4th Ed. (pp. 100–126). Toronto: Prentice Hall. **83, 189, 307, 308**

Acemoglu, D., and Robinson, J.A. 2012. *Why nations fail.* New York: Crown Business. **12, 41**

Adachi, P., and Willoughby, T. 2013. Do video games promote positive youth development? *Journal of Adolescent Research, 28*, 155–165. **87**

Adams, G. R., Côté, J., and Marshall, S. 2002. *Parent/Adolescent relationships and identity development.* Ottawa: Health Canada. **428**

Adler-Baeder, F., et al. 2005. *Marital transitions in military families: Their prevalence and their relevance for adaptation to the military.* U.S. Military Family Research Institute, Purdue University. **77, 78**

Adoption Council of Canada. 2003 and 2007. *Canadians adopt almost 20,000 children from abroad. U.S. Census asks about adopted children.* **246, 247**

Adoption Council of Canada. 2003. International adoptions steady: 1,891 in 2002. Ottawa. **242, 246, 247**

Ahearn, L. A. 2001. *Invitations to love: Literacy, love letters and social change in Nepal.* Ann Arbor, MI: The University of Michigan Press. **62**

Ahrons, C. R., and Tanner, J. L. 2003. Adult children and their fathers: Relationship changes 20 years after parental divorce. *Family Relations, 52*, 340–351. **369**

Aird, E. G. 2001. On rekindling a spirit of "home training": A mother's notes from the front. In S. A. Hofferth, N. Rankin, and C. West (Eds.), *Taking parenting public* (pp. 13–28). New York: Rowan & Littlefield. **15**

Albanese, P. 2006. Small town, big benefits: The ripple effect of $7/day child care. *The Canadian Review of Sociology and Anthropology, 43*, 125–141. **425**

Albanese, P. 2011. Addressing the interlocking complexity of paid work and care: Lessons from changing family policy in Quebec. In C. Krull and J. Sempruch (Eds.), *A life in balance? Reopening the family-work debate* (pp. 130–143). Vancouver: University of British Columbia Press. **417, 425**

Aldous, J. 1996. *Family careers: Rethinking the developmental perspective.* Thousand Oaks, CA: Sage. **23**

Aldous, J., and Ganey, R. F. 1999. Family life and the pursuit of happiness: The influence of gender and race. *Journal of Family Issues, 20*, 155–180. **174, 263**

Aliaga, D. E. 1994. Italian immigrants in Calgary: Dimensions of cultural identity. *Canadian Ethnic Studies, 26*, 141–148. **48**

Al-Krenawi, A., Graham, J. R., and Al-Krenawi, S. 2002. The psychological impact of polygamous marriages on Palestinian women. *Women & Health, 34*, 1–16. **10**

Al-Krenawi, A., Slonim-Nevo, V., and Graham, J. R. 2006. Polygyny and its impact on the psychosocial well-being of husbands. *Journal of Comparative Family Studies, 37*, 173–189. **8, 10**

Allard, F. L., et al. 2005. Maintien de l'engagement paternel après une rupture conjugale: Point de vue des pères vivant en contexte de pauvreté. *Enfances, familles, générations, 3*, 1–42. **350**

Allen, E. S., and Atkins, D. 2012. The association of divorce and extramarital sex in a representative U.S. sample. *Journal of Family Issues, 33*, 1477–1493. **353**

Allen, E. S., et al. 2005. Intrapersonal, interpersonal, and contextual factors in engaging in and responding to extramarital involvement. *Clinical Psychology: Science and Practice, 12*, 101–130. **214**

Allen, E. S., et al. 2010 Hitting home: Relationships between recent deployment, posttraumatic stress symptoms, and marital functioning for army couples. *Journal of Family Psychology, 24*, 280–288. **77**

Allen, R. E. S., and Wiles, J. L. 2013. How older people position their late-life childlessness: A qualitative study. *Journal of Marriage and Family, 75*, 206–220. **236**

Alwin, D. F. 1986. From obedience to autonomy: Changes in traits desired in children, 1924–1978. *Public Opinion Quarterly, 52*, 33–52. **428**

Alwin, D. F. 1990. Cohort replacement and changes in parental socialization values. *Journal of Marriage and Family, 52*, 347–360. **301**

Alwin, D. F. 2001. Parental values, beliefs, and behavior: A review and promulga for research into the new century. In S. L. Hofferth and T. J. Owens (Eds.), *Children at the millennium: Where have we come from, where are we going?* (pp. 97–139). Oxford, UK: Elsevier. **301**

American Academy of Pediatrics. 2011. Policy statement on "media use by children younger than 2 years." Council on Communications and Media. *Pediatrics, 128*, 1040–1045. **90**

Amato, P. R. 1996. Explaining the intergenerational transmission of divorce. *Journal of Marriage and Family, 58*, 628–640. **359, 363**

Amato, P. R. 2000. The consequences of divorce for adults and children. *Journal of Marriage and Family, 62*, 1269–1287. **372**

Amato, P. R. 2003. Reconciling divergent perspectives: Judith Wallerstein, quantitative family research, and children of divorce. *Family Relations, 52*, 332–339. **358**

Amato, P. R. 2007. Transformative processes in marriage: Some thoughts from a sociologist. *Journal of Marriage and Family, 69,* 305–309. **350**

Amato, P. R., and Booth, A. 1997. *A generation at risk: Growing up in an era of family upheaval.* Cambridge, MA: Harvard University Press. **358**

Amato, P. R., and Cheadle, J. 2005. The long reach of divorce: Divorce and child well-being across three generations. *Journal of Marriage and Family, 67,* 191–206. **356, 359**

Amato, P. R., and DeBoer, D. D. 2001. The transmission of marital instability across generations: Relationship skills or commitment to marriage? *Journal of Marriage and Family, 63,* 1038–1051. **352**

Amato, P. R., and Gilbreth, J. G. 1999. Nonresident fathers and children's well-being: A meta-analysis. *Journal of Marriage and Family, 61,* 557–573. **350, 361**

Amato, P. R., and Hohmann-Marriott, B. 2007. A comparison of high- and low-distress marriages that end in divorce. *Journal of Marriage and Family, 69,* 621–638. **356**

Amato, P. R., and Previti, D. 2004. People's reasons for divorcing: Gender, social class, the life course, and adjustment. *Journal of Family Issues, 24,* 602–606. **111, 351, 353**

Amato, P. R., and Rezac, S. J. 1994. Contact with nonresident parents, interparental conflict, and children's behavior. *Journal of Family Issues, 15,* 191–207. **361**

Amato, P. R., and Rivera, F. 1999. Paternal involvement and children's behavioral problems. *Journal of Marriage and Family, 61,* 375–384. **368**

Amato, P. R., and Rogers, S. J. 1997. A longitudinal study of marital problems and subsequent divorce. *Journal of Marriage and Family, 59,* 612–624. **177**

Amato, P. R., and Sobolewski, J. M. 2001. The effects of divorce and marital discord on adult children's psychological well-being. *American Sociological Review, 66,* 900–921. **359**

Amato, P. R., Meyers, C. E., and Emery, R. E. 2009. Changes in nonresident father-child contact from 1976 to 2002. *Family Relations, 58,* 41–53. **349**

Amato, P. R., Spencer-Loomis, L. S., and Booth, A. 1995. Parental divorce, marital conflict, and offspring well-being during early adulthood. *Social Forces, 73,* 895–915. **361**

Amato, P. R., et al. 2003. Continuity and change in marital quality between 1980 and 2000. *Journal of Marriage and Family, 65,* 1–22. **261, 266, 272**

Amato, P. R., et al. 2007. *Alone together. How marriage in America is changing.* Cambridge, MA: Harvard University Press. **256, 261, 354**

Ambert, A.-M. 1976. *Sex structure,* 2nd Ed. Toronto: Longman. **417**

Ambert, A.-M. 1989. *Ex-spouses and new spouses: A study of relationships.* Greenwich, CT: JAI Press. **346, 353, 354, 356, 370**

Ambert, A.-M. 1994a. A qualitative study of peer abuse and its effects: Theoretical and empirical implications. *Journal of Marriage and Family, 56,* 119–130. **399**

Ambert, A.-M. 1994b. An international perspective on parenting: Social change and social constructs. *Journal of Marriage and Family, 56,* 529–543. **17, 287**

Ambert, A.-M. 1998. *The web of poverty: Psychosocial perspectives.* New York: Haworth. **108, 118, 337, 338**

Ambert, A.-M. 2001. *The effect of children on parents,* 2nd Ed. New York: Haworth. **19, 26, 277, 286, 303, 349, 401, 409, 428**

Ambert, A.-M. 2006. *One-parent families: Characteristics, causes, consequences, and issues.* Ottawa: Vanier Institute of the Family. **226**

Ambert, A.-M. 2007. *The rise in the number of children and adolescents who exhibit problematic behaviours.* Ottawa: Vanier Institute of the Family. **14**

Ambert, A.-M. 2009. *Divorce: Facts, causes, and consequences.* Ottawa: Vanier Institute of the Family. **343**

Ambert, A.-M., et al. 1995. Understanding and evaluating qualitative research. *Journal of Marriage and Family, 57,* 879–893. **31**

ANAC (Aboriginal Nurses Association of Canada) and the RCMP (Royal Canadian Mounted Police). 2001. *Family violence in Aboriginal communities: A review.* Ottawa: Aboriginal Nurses Association of Canada. **53, 383**

ANAC (Aboriginal Nurses Association of Canada). 2002. Exposure to violence in the home: Effects on Aboriginal children. *Conference Proceeding Report.* Ottawa: Aboriginal Nurses Association of Canada. **383**

Anderson, C. A., Gentile, D. A., and Buckley, K. E. 2007. *Violent video game effects on children and adolescents: Theory, research, and public policy.* New York: Oxford University Press. **86**

Anderson, C. A., et al. 2004. Violent video games: Specific effects of violent content on aggressive thoughts and behavior. *Advances in Experimental Social Psychology, 36,* 199–249. **86**

Anderson, E. R. 1999. Sibling, half sibling, and stepsibling relationships in remarried families. In E. M. Hetherington, S. H. Henderson, and D. Reiss (Eds.), *Adolescent siblings in stepfamilies: Family functioning and adolescent adjustment* (pp. 101–126). *Monographs of the Society for Research in Child Development, 259,* 64, no. 4. **331**

Anderson, K. L. 1997. Gender, status, and domestic violence: An integration of feminist and family violence approaches. *Journal of Marriage and Family, 59,* 655–669. **381**

Anderson, K. L. 2008. Is partner violence worse in the context of control? *Journal of Marriage and Family, 70,* 1157–1168. **20, 378**

Anderssen, E. 2011. The perils of praise. *Globe and Mail,* September 9, L3. **287**

Anderssen, E., and McIlroy, A. 2004. Starting from ten: Part 5. *Globe and Mail.* April 10, A1, A7. **55**

Andersson, G., et al. 2006. The demographics of same-sex marriages in Norway and Sweden. *Demography, 43,* 79–98. **210, 223, 346**

Andreasen, M. S. 1994. Patterns of family life and television consumption from 1945 to the 1990s. In D. Zillman, J. Bryant, and A. C. Huston (Eds.), *Media, children, and the family* (pp. 19–36). Hillsdale, NJ: Erlbaum. **82**

Aneshensel, C. S., et al. 2011. The urban neighborhood and cognitive functioning in late middle age. *Journal of Health and Social Behavior, 52,* 163–179. **123**

Anisef, P., and Kilbride, K. M. 2003. Overview and implications of the research. In P. Anisef and K. M. Kilbride (Eds.), *Managing two worlds: The experiences & concerns of immigrant youth in Ontario* (pp. 235–272). Toronto: Canadian Scholars' Press. **157, 166**

Anisef, P., et al. 2000. *Opportunity and uncertainty.* Toronto: University of Toronto Press. **161**

Ansen, J. 2000. Nationalism and fertility in francophone Montreal: The majority as minority. *Canadian Studies in Population, 27,* 377–400. **55**

Aquilino, W. S. 2005. Impact of family structure on parental attitudes toward the economic support of adult children over the transition to adulthood. *Journal of Family Issues, 26,* 143–167. **369**

Arat-Koç, S. 2011. Whose social reproduction? Transnational motherhood and challenges to feminist political economy. In M. Gleason et al. (Eds.), *Rethinking Canada: The promise of women's history,* 6th Ed. (pp. 414–425). Toronto: Oxford University Press. **12, 13, 22, 72, 73, 76, 409, 413, 416**

Arendell, T. 1995. *Fathers and divorce.* Newbury Park, CA: Sage. **348**

Arendell, T. 2000. Conceiving and investigating motherhood: The decade's scholarship. *Journal of Marriage and Family, 62,* 1192–1207. **17**

Ariès, P. 1962. *Centuries of childhood: A social history of family life.* New York: Knopf and Random House. **16**

Arnett, J. J. 2001. *Adolescence and emerging adulthood: A cultural approach.* Upper Saddle River, NJ: Prentice Hall. **296**

Arnett, J. J. 2008. The neglected 95%: Why American psychology needs to become less American. *American Psychologist, 63,* 602–614. **10, 242, 287, 292, 297, 301, 428**

Arnold, M. S. 1995. Exploding the myths: African-American families at promise. In B. B. Swadener and S. Lubeck (Eds.), *Children and families "at promise"* (pp. 143–162). Albany: State University of New York Press. **115**

Aseltine, R. H., Jr. 1996. Pathways linking parental divorce with adolescent depression. *Journal of Health and Social Behavior, 37,* 113–148. **362**

Atkin, C. 1978. Observation of parent-child interaction in supermarket decision making. *Journal of Marketing, 42,* 41–45. **88**

Atkins, D. C., and Kessel, D. E. 2008. Religiousness and infidelity: Attendance, but not faith and prayer, predict marital fidelity. *Journal of Marriage and Family, 70,* 407–418. **172**

Attané, I. 2006. The demographic impact of a female deficit in China, 2000–2050. *Population and Development Review, 32,* 755–770. **8**

Attar-Schwartz, S., et al. 2009. Grandparenting and adolescent adjustment in two-parent biological, lone-parent, and step-families. *Journal of Family Psychology, 23,* 67–75. **371**

AuCoin, K. 2005. *Children and youth as victims of violent crime.* Ottawa: Statistics Canada. Catalogue no. 85-002-XIE, vol. 25, no. 1. **386, 392, 393, 394, 397, 401, 425**

Aubert, V., and Holder, A. 2013. *Unspeakable crimes against children: Sexual violence in conflict.* London: Save the Children. **205, 377**

Audas, R., and McDonald, T. 2004. Rural-urban migration in the 1990s. *Canadian Social Trends, 73,* 17–24. **144, 145**

Aulakh, R. 2009. Birth ratio in the GTA favours sons. *Toronto Star,* October 3, A1, A23. **238**

Aulakh, R. 2009. Forced marriage. *Toronto Star.* November 14, A1, A18. **62**

Aulakh, R. 2013. India doctors choosing sons over daughters. *Toronto Star,* February 16, A20. **238, 413**

Avellar, S., and Smock, P. J. 2005. The economic consequences of the dissolution of cohabiting unions. *Journal of Marriage and Family, 67,* 315–327. **355**

Averett, P., Nalavany, B., and Ryan, S. 2009. An evaluation of gay/lesbian and heterosexual adoption. *Adoption Quarterly, 12,* 129–151. **224**

Aysan, M. F., and Beaujot, R. 2009. Welfare regimes for aging populations: No single path for reform. *Population and Development Review, 35,* 701–720. **417**

Baber, K. M. 2010. Reconceptualizing gender: A review essay. *Journal of Family Theory & Review, 2,* 88–94. **22**

Baca Zinn, M. 2007. Feminist rethinking from racial-ethnic families. In S. J. Ferguson (Ed.), *Shifting the centre: Understanding contemporary families* (pp. 18–27). New York: McGraw-Hill. **22**

Bachman, H. J., and Chase-Lansdale, P. L. 2005. Custodial grandmothers' physical, mental, and economic well-being: Comparisons of primary caregivers from low-income neighborhorhoods. *Family Relations, 54,* 475–487. **312**

Bachman, H. J., et al. 2012. Low-income mothers' patterns of partnership instability and adolescents' socioemotional well-being. *Journal of Family Psychology, 26,* 263–273. **221**

Bachman, J. G., et al. 1997. *Smoking, drinking, and drug use in young adulthood.* Mahwah, NJ: Erlbaum. **199**

Badinter, E. 2010. *Le conflit: La femme et la mère.* Paris: Flammarion. **16, 17, 18, 287**

Bahr, H. M., and Bahr, K. S. 2001. Families and self-sacrifice: Alternative models and meanings for family theory. *Social Forces, 79,* 1231–1258. **10, 14, 242**

Bailey, J. A., et al. 2009. Parenting practices and problem behavior across three generations: Monitoring, harsh discipline, and drug use in the intergenerational transmission of externalizing behavior. *Developmental Psychology, 45,* 1214–1226. **294**

Baillargeon, R., Tremblay, R., and Willms, J. D. 2002. Physical aggression among toddlers: Does it run in families? In J. D. Willms (Ed.), *Vulnerable children* (pp. 71–103). Edmonton: University of Alberta Press. **322**

Bakan, A. B., and Stasiulis, D. (Eds.). 1997. *Not one of the family: Foreign and domestic workers in Canada.* Toronto: University of Toronto Press. **22**

Bakan, J. 2011. *Childhood under siege.* London, U.K.: Allen Lane. **82, 287**

Baker, D. 2010. Korean religiosity in comparative perspective. In L. DeVries et al. (Eds.), *Asian religions in British Columbia* (pp. 164–183). Vancouver: University of British Columbia Press. **173**

Baker, M. 2001. *Families, labour and love.* Vancouver: University of British Columbia Press. **160**

Bala, N., et al. 2005. *Polygamy in Canada: Legal and social implications for women and children—An international review of polygamy.* Ottawa: Status of Women Canada. **10**

Balakrishnan, T. R., Maxim, P., and Jurdi, R. 2005. Social class versus cultural identity as factos in the residential segregation of ethnic groups in Toronto, Montreal and Vancouver for 2001. *Canadian Studies in Population, 32,* 203–227. **132**

Balsam, K. F., Rothblum, E. D., and Beauchaine, T. P. 2005. Victimization over the life span: A comparison of lesbian, gay, bisexual, and heterosexual siblings. *Journal of Consulting and Clinical Psychology, 73,* 474–487. **211, 383, 400**

Baluja, T. 2011. The steep social costs of vertical living. *The Globe and Mail,* November 5, M7. **142**

Banerjee, S., and Coward, H. 2005. Hindus in Canada: Negotiating identity in a "different" homeland. In P. Bramadat and D. Siljak (Eds.), *Religion and ethnicity in Canada,* (pp. 30–51). Toronto: Pearson. **172**

Bank, L., Patterson, G. R., and Reid, J. B. 1996. Negative sibling interaction patterns as predictors of later adjustment problems in adolescent and young adult males. In G. H. Brody (Ed.), *Sibling relationships: Their causes and consequences* (pp. 197–230). Norwood, NJ: Ablex. 328

Bankston, C. L., III, and Caldas, S. J. 1998. Family structure, schoolmates, and racial inequalities in school achievement. *Journal of Marriage and Family, 60,* 715–724. 158

Barber, J. G., and Delfabbro, P. H. 2009. The profile and progress of neglected and abused children in long-term foster care. *Child Abuse & Neglect, 33,* 421–428. 251

Barber, J. S., and East, P. L. 2009. Home and parenting resources available to siblings depending on their birth intention status. *Child Development, 80,* 921–934. 238

Barbieri, C., Mahoney, E., and Butler, L. 2008. Understanding the nature and extent of farm and ranch diversification in North America. *Rural Sociology, 73,* 205–230. 138

Bar-Haim, Y., et al. 2007. Threat-related attentional bias in anxious and nonanxious individuals: A meta-analytic study. *Psychological Bulletin, 113,* 1–24. 280

Baril, R., Lefebvre, T., and Merrigan, P. 2000. Quebec family policy: Impact and options. *Choices: Family Policy, 6,* 4–52: IRPP. 55

Barkan, S. E. 2006. Religiosity and premarital sex in adulthood. *Journal for the Scientific Study of Religion, 45,* 407–417. 208

Barman, J. 2003. Schooled for inequality: The education of British Columbia Aboriginal children. In N. Janovicek and J. Parr (Eds.), *Histories of Canadian children and youth* (pp. 212–235). Toronto: Oxford University Press. 44

Barnes, G., et al. 2006. Effects of parental monitoring and peer deviance on substance use and delinquency. *Journal of Marriage and Family, 68,* 1084–1104. 289

Barnes, J. C., and Beaver, K. M. 2012. Marriage and desistance from crime: A consideration of gene-environment correlation. *Journal of Marriage and Family, 74,* 19–33. 27, 335

Barnes, J. E., et al. 2009. Sexual and physical revictimization among victims of severe childhood sexual abuse. *Child Abuse & Neglect, 33,* 412–420. 27, 395

Barnett, O. W., et al. 2005. *Family violence across the lifespan: An introduction,* 2nd Ed. Thousand Oaks, CA: Sage. 293

Barnett, R. C., and Gareis, K. C. 2006. Parental after-school stress and psychological well-being. *Journal of Marriage and Family, 68,* 101–108. 425

Barrow, C. 1996. *Family in the Caribbean: Themes and perspectives.* Kingston, Jamaica: Ian Randle Publishers. 7, 18, 57, 79

Bartels, L. M. 2008. *Unequal democracy. The political economy of the new gilded age.* New York: Russell Sage. 12, 13, 95, 412, 432

Bartholet, E. 1993. *Family bonds: Adoption and the politics of parenting.* Boston: Houghton Mifflin. 243

Bartholet, E. 2010. International adoption: The human rights issues. In M. B. Goodwin (Ed.), *Baby markets* (pp. 94–117). New York: Cambridge University Press. 247

Bartowski, J. P., Xu, X., and Levin, M. L. 2008. Religion and child development: Evidence from the Early Childhood Longitudinal Study. *Social Science Research, 37,* 18–36. 174

Baskin, C. 2003. From victims to leaders: Activism against violence towards women. In K. Anderson and B. Lawrence (Eds.), *Strong stories:*

Native vision and community survival (pp. 213–287). Vancouver: Sumach Press. 382

Batson, C. D., Quian, Z., and Lichter, D. 2006. Interracial and intraracial patterns of mate selection among America's diverse Black populations. *Journal of Marriage and Family, 68,* 658–672. 186

Baumer, E. P., and South, S. J. 2001. Community effects on youth sexual activity. *Journal of Marriage and Family, 63,* 540–554. 130

Baumrind, D. 1967. Child care practices anteceding three patterns of preschool behavior. *Genetic Psychology Monographs, 75,* 43–88. 288

Baumrind, D. 1990. Parenting styles and adolescent development. In R. M. Lerner, J. Brooks-Gunn, and A. C. Petersen (Eds.), *The Encyclopedia of adolescence* (pp. 746–758). New York: Garland Press. 288

Baumrind, D. 1991. Effective parenting during the early adolescent transition. In P. A. Cowan and M. E. Hetherington (Eds.), *Family transitions* (pp. 111–163). Hillsdale, NJ: Erlbaum. 290

Baute, N. 2010. Late-blooming lesbians find different kind of partnership. *Toronto Star,* September 2. 185, 210

Bawin-Legrow, B., and Gauthier, A. 2001. Regulation of intimacy and love semantics in couples living apart together. *International Review of Sociology, 11,* 39–46. 79

Beach, J., et al. 2009. *Early childhood education and care in Canada 2008.* 8th Ed. Toronto: Childcare Resource and Research Unit. 152, 425

Beauchamp, D. L. 2008. *Victimization amongst gays, lesbians and bisexuals.* Ottawa: Statistics Canada, Canadian Centre for Justice Statistics. 383

Beaujot, R. 2000. *Earning & caring in Canadian families.* Peterborough: Broadview Press. 29, 269, 372, 409, 410, 417

Beaujot, R. 2004. *Delayed life transitions: Trends and implications.* Ottawa: Vanier Institute of the Family. 25, 233, 304, 410, 427, 431

Beaujot, R. 2006. Delayed life transitions: Trends and implications. In K. McQuillan and Z. R. Ravanera (Eds.), *Canada's changing families. Implications for individuals and society* (pp. 105–132). Toronto: University of Toronto Press. 303, 305, 422, 427, 430

Beaujot, R., and Bélanger, A. 2001. *Perspective on below replacement fertility in Canada: Trends, desires, accommodations.* Paper presented at the International Union for the Scientific Study of Population, Tokyo, March 2001. 202

Beaujot, R., and Kerr, D. 2004. *Population change in Canada,* 2nd Ed. Toronto: Oxford University Press. 51, 54, 75, 233, 412

Beaujot, R., and McQuillan, K. 1982. *Growth and dualism: The demographic development of Canadian society.* Toronto: Gage Publishing. 40

Beaujot, R., and Muhammad, A. 2006. Transformed families and the basis for childbearing. In K. McQuillan and Z. R. Ravanera (Eds.), *Canada's changing families. Implications for individuals and society* (pp. 15–48). Toronto: University of Toronto Press. 233

Beaujot, R., and Ravanera, Z. 2009. Family models for earning and caring: Implications for childcare and for family policy. *Canadian Studies in Population, 36,* 145–166. 419

Beaujot, R. and Wang, J. 2010. Low fertility in Canada: The Nordic model in Quebec and the U.S. model in Alberta. *Canadian Studies in Population, 37,* 441–443. 419

Beaupré, P. 2008. I do. Take two? Changes in intentions to remarry among divorced Canadians during the past 20 years. *Matter of Fact,* Ottawa: Statistics Canada, July 19. 365

Beaupré, P., and Cloutier, E. 2007. Navigating family transitions: Evidence from the General Social Survey. *Canadian Social Trends,* June 13. 234, 346, 347

Beaupré, P., Dryburgh, H., and Wendt, M. 2010. Making fathers "count." *Canadian Social Trends, 90,* June 8. 348

Beaupré, P., et al. 2008. *When is junior moving out? Transitions from the parental home to independence.* Ottawa: Statistics Canada. 136, 176, 369

Beaupré, P., Turcotte, P., and Milan, A. 2006. When is junior moving out? *Canadian Social Trends,* August. 303, 304, 319

Beaute, N. 2009. Adoptees can find mom, but not dad. *Toronto Star,* December 10, A1, A16. 242, 249

Beaver, K. 2011. Environmental moderators of genetic influences on adolescent delinquent involvement and victimization. *Journal of Adolescent Research, 26,* 84–114. 337

Beaver, K. M., et al. 2009. Gene-environment interplay and delinquent involvement. *Journal of Adolescent Research, 24,* 147–168. 303

Beavon, D., and Cooke, M. 2003. An application of the UN Human Development Index and registered Indians in Canada, 1996. In J. White et al. (Eds.), *Aboriginal conditions: Research as a foundation for public policy.* Vancouver, BC: University of British Columbia Press. 110

Beck, A. N., et al. 2010. Partnership transitions and maternal parenting. *Journal of Marriage and Family, 72,* 219–233. 222

Becker, G. S. 1974. A theory of social interactions. *Journal of Political Economy, 82,* 1063–1093. 14

Beckett, C., et al. 2006. Do the effects of early severe deprivation persist into early adolescence? Findings from the English and Romanian adoptees study. *Child Development, 77,* 696–711. 247

Bednar, V., and Stabile, M. 2012. Good policy needs good data. *Toronto Star,* July 11. 31, 432

Béland, D. 2010. *What is social policy? Understanding the Welfare State.* Cambridge: Polity Press. 417, 431

Bélanger, A., and Oikawa, C. 1999. Who has a third child? *Canadian Social Trends, 53,* 23–26. 233

Bélanger, A., Morency, J. D., and Spielauer, M. 2010. A microsimulation model to study the interaction between fertility and union formation and dissolution: An application to Canada and Quebec. *Canadian Studies in Population, 37,* 339–373. 221, 233, 236

Belanger, Y. D. 2008. *Gambling with the future: The evolution of Aboriginal gambling in Canada.* Saskatoon: Punch Publishing. 54

Belle, M., and McQuillan, K. 1994. Births outside marriage: A growing alternative. *Canadian Social Trends, 33,* 14–17. 225–226

Belleau, H. 2007. *L'union de fait et le mariage au Québec: analyse des différences et similitudes.* Québec: Institut national de la recherche scientifique. Urbanisation, Culture et Société. 190, 191, 193, 365

Belot, M., and Francesconi, M. 2013. Dating preferences and meeting opportunities in mate choice decisions. *Journal of Human Resources, 48,* 474–508. 188

Belsky, J., Conger, R., and Capaldi, D. M. 2009. The intergenerational transmission of parenting: Introduction to the Special Edition. *Developmental Psychology, 45,* 1201–1204. 294

Belsky, J., and Pluess, M. 2009. Beyond diathesis stress: Differential susceptibility to environmental influences. *Psychological Bulletin, 135,* 885–908. 28

Belsky, J., et al. 2007. Are there long-terms effects of early child care? *Child Development, 78,* 681–701. 153, 154, 425

Beltran, A. 2001. [A review of several books on] Empowering grandparents raising children: A training manual for group leaders/

Grandparents raising grandchildren: Theoretical, empirical, and clinical perspectives. *The Gerontologist, 41,* 559–563. 312

Bengtson, V. L. 2001. Beyond the nuclear family: The increasing importance of multigenerational bonds. *Journal of Marriage and Family, 63,* 1–16. 310

Bennett, J. W., and Seena, B. K. 1995. *Settling the Canadian-American west, 1890–1915: Pioneer adaptation and community building. An anthropological history.* Lincoln, NE: University of Nebraska Press. 48

Berardo, F. M. 1998. Family privacy: Issues and concepts. *Journal of Family Issues, 19,* 4–19. 143

Berger, L., et al. 2009. Estimating the "impact" of out-of-home placement on child well-being: Approaching the problem of selection bias. *Child Development, 80,* 1856–1876. 250

Berger, P. L., and Luckmann, T. 1966. *The social construction of reality: A treatise in the sociology of knowledge.* New York: Doubleday. 16

Berlin, L. J., et al. 2009. Correlates and consequences of spanking and verbal punishment for low-income White, African American, and Mexican American toddlers. *Child Development, 80,* 1403–1420. 230, 293, 294

Berlin, L. J., et al. 2011. Intergenerational continuity in child maltreatment: Mediating mechanisms and implications for prevention. *Child Development, 82,* 162–176. 390

Bernard, A. 2013. Unemployment dynamics among Canada's youth. Ottawa: Statistics Canada, *The Daily,* June 11. 96, 98

Bernstein, A. C. 1997. Stepfamilies from siblings' perspectives. *Marriage and Family Review, 26,* 153–176. 331

Berry, M., et al. 1998. The role of open adoption in the adjustment of adopted children and their families. *Children and Youth Services Review, 20,* 151–171. 248

Bert, S. C., et al. 2009. The influence of maternal history of abuse on parenting knowledge and behavior. *Family Relations, 58,* 176–187. 390

Berthet, T. 1992. *Seigneurs et colons de Nouvelle France: l'émergence d'une société distincte au XVIIIème siècle.* Cachan, Éditions de l'E.N.S. 42

Bertotti, A. M. 2013. Gendered divisions of fertility work: Socioeconomic predictors of female versus male sterilization. *Journal of Marriage and Family, 75,* 13–25. 236

Bessant, K. C. 2006. A farm household conception of pluriactivity in Canadian agriculture: Motivation, diversification and livelihood. *Canadian Review of Sociology and Anthropology, 43,* 51–73. 138

Bezanson, K., and Luxton, M. (Eds.). 2006. *Social reproduction: Feminist political economy challenges neo-liberalism.* Montreal: McGill-Queen's University Press. 20, 70, 91, 100

Bezdjian, S., et al. 2011. The genetic and environmental covariation among psychopathic personality traits, and reactive and proactive aggression in childhood. *Child Development, 82,* 1267–1281. 334

Bharadwaj, P., and Lakdawala, L. K. 2013. Discrimination begins in the womb: Evidence of self-selective prenatal investments. *Journal of Human Resources, 48,* 71–113. 63

Bianchi, S. M., Robinson, J. P., and Milkie, M. A. 2006. *Demographic rhythms in American family life.* New York: Russell Sage Foundation. 269, 276

Bibby, R. W. 2001. *Canadian teens: Today, yesterday, and tomorrow.* Toronto: Stoddart. 203, 364, 386

Bibby, R. W. 2002. *Restless gods: The Renaissance of religion in Canada*. Toronto: Stoddart. 170, 184

Bibby, R. W. 2004. *The future families project*. Ottawa: Vanier Institute of the Family. 193, 293

Bibby, R. W. 2009. *The emerging millennials: How Canada's newest generation is responding to change and choice*. Lethbridge, Alberta: Project Canada Books. 168

Bibby, R. W., and Posterski, D. C. 2000. *Teen trends: A nation in motion*. Toronto: Stoddart. 203, 298, 305

Biblarz, T. J., and Gottainer, G. 2000. Family structure and children's success: A comparison of widowed and divorced single-mother families. *Journal of Marriage and Family, 62*, 533–548. 364

Biblarz, T. J., and Savci, E. 2010. Lesbian, gay, bisexual, and transgender families. *Journal of Marriage and Family, 72*, 480–497. 211, 224

Biblarz, T. J., and Stacey, J. 2010. How does the gender of parents matter. *Journal of Marriage and Family, 72*, 3–22. 348

Bierman, A., Fazio, E. M., and Milkie, M. A. 2006. A multifaceted approach to the mental health advantage of the married. *Journal of Family Issues, 27*, 554–582. 198

BIFHSGO (British Isles Family History Society of Greater Ottawa). n.d. *Origins of the Home Children sent to Canada*. Accessed online March 18, 2010. 46, 47

Biggs, S., et al. 2009. Mistreatment of older people in the United Kingdom: Findings from the First National Prevalence Study. *Journal of Elder Abuse & Neglect, 21*, 1–14. 403, 404

Biles, J., and Ibrahim, H. 2005. Religion and public policy: Immigration, citizenship, and multiculturalism—Guess who's coming to dinner? In P. Bramadat and D. Seljak (Eds.), *Religion and ethnicity in Canada* (pp. 154–177). Toronto: Pearson. 28, 171, 414

Billette, J.- M., Le Bourdais, C., and Laplante, B. 2011. An assessment of heterogeneity in first home-returning trends of young Canadians. *Canadian Studies in Population, 38*, 19–41. 305

Binda, K. P. 2001. Native diaspora and urban education: Intractable problems. In S. K. Binda and S. Calliou (Eds.), *Aboriginal education in Canada* (pp. 179–194). Mississauga: Canadian Educators' Press. 132, 167

Bingoly-Liworo, G. 2010. The influence of characteristics of men's job on the timing of the first birth in Canada. *Canadian Studies in Population, 37*, 77–105. 415

Binnema, T. 1996. Old swan, big man, and the Siksika bands, 1794–1815. *Canadian Historical Review, 77*, 1–32. 37

Binnema, T. 2001. Migrant from every direction: communities of the Northwestern Plains to 1750. In T. Binnema (Ed.), *Common and contested ground: A human and environmental history of the Northwestern Plains*. Norman, OK: University of Oklahoma Press. 37

Binstock, G., and Thornton, A. 2003. Separations, reconciliations, and living apart in cohabiting and marital unions. *Journal of Marriage and Family, 65*, 432–443. 79, 193

Birditt, K. S., Fingerman, K. L., and Zarit, S. H. 2010. Adult children's problems and successes: Implications for intergenerational ambivalence. *Journal of Gerontology: Series B, 65B*, 145–153. 306

Birditt, K. S., et al. 2010. Marital conflict behaviors and implications for divorce over 16 years. *Journal of Marriage and Family, 72*, 1188–1204. 264

Black, D. A., et al. 2000. Demographics of the gay and lesbian population in the United States: Evidence from available systematic data sources. *Demography, 37*, 139–154. 210

Blair, C., et al. 2011. Salivary cortisol mediates effects of poverty and parenting on executive functions in early childhood. *Child Development, 82*, 1970–1984. 117

Blake, J., Richardson, B., and Bhattacharya, J. 1991. Number of siblings and sociability. *Journal of Marriage and Family, 53*, 271–284. 319

Blank, R. M. 1997. *It takes a nation: A new agenda for fighting poverty*. New York: Russell Sage. 91, 432

Blau, P. 1964. *Exchange and power in social life*. New York: Wiley. 13

Bledsoe, C. H., and Souv, P. 2011. Back to Africa: Second chances for the children of West African immigrants. *Journal of Marriage and Family, 73*, 747–762. 288, 289, 293

Block, J. H., Block, J., and Gjerde, P. F. 1988. Parental functioning and the home environment of families of divorce: Prospective and current analyses. *Journal of the American Academy of Child and Adolescent Psychiatry, 27*, 207–213. 362

Blood, R. O., and Wolfe, D. M. 1960. *Husbands and wives. Dynamics of married living*. New York: The Free Press. 13

Blumer, H. 1969. *Symbolic interactionism: Perspective and method*. Englewood Cliffs, NJ: Prentice Hall. 25

Blumstein, P., and Schwartz, P. 1990. Intimate relationships and the creation of sexuality. In D. McWhirter, S. Sanders, and J. Reinisch (Eds.), *Homosexuality/heterosexuality: Concepts of sexual orientation* (pp. 96–109). New York: Oxford University Press. 213–214

Boden, J. M., Fergusson, D. M., and Horwood, L. J. 2009. Experience of sexual abuse in childhood and abortion in adolescence and early adulthood. *Childhood Abuse & Neglect, 33*, 870–876. 395

Bodovski, K., and Farkas, G. 2008. "Concerted cultivation" and unequal achievement in elementary school. *Social Science Research, 37*, 903–919. 428

Boekhoven, B. 2009. *"Caution! Kids at play?" Unstructured time use among children and adolescents*. Ottawa: The Vanier Institute of the Family. 150

Bogenschneider, K., and Corbett, T. J. 2010. Family policy: Becoming a field of inquiry and subfield of social policy. *Journal of Marriage and the Family, 72*, 783–803. 15, 70, 73, 113, 119, 156, 388, 422, 432

Bogle, K. 2008. *Hooking up: Sex, dating, and relationships on campus*. New York: New York University Press. 183

Bohnert, N. 2011. Examining the determinants of union dissolution among married and common-law unions in Canada. *Canadian Studies in Population, 38*, 75–92. 343, 344

Bolick, K. 2011. All the single ladies. *The Atlantic*, November. 202

Bonds, D. D., and Gondoli, D. M. 2007. Examining the process by which marital adjustment affects maternal warmth: The role of coparenting support as a mediator. *Journal of Family Psychology, 21*, 288–296. 279

Bonduelle., M., et al. 2005. A multi-centre cohort study of the physical health of 5-year-old children conceived after intracytoplasmic sperm injection, *in vitro*, fertilization and natural conception, *Human Reproduction, 20*, 413–419. 240

Bonell, C. 2004. Why is teenage pregnancy conceptualized as a social problem? A review of quantitative research from the USA and UK. *Culture, Health & Sexuality, 6*, 255–272. 227

Bonnycastle, C., and Prentice, S. 2011. Childcare and caregiving: Overlooked barriers for northern post-secondary women learners. *The Canadian Journal of Native Studies, 31*, 1–16. 156

Booth, A., and Amato, P. R. 2001. Parental predivorce relations and offspring postdivorce well-being. *Journal of Marriage and Family, 63*, 197–212. **346, 362**

Booth, A., and Edwards, J. M. 1992. Starting over: Why remarriages are unstable. *Journal of Family Issues, 13*, 179–194. **266**

Booth, A., Carver, K., and Granger, D. A. 2000. Biosocial perspectives on the family. *Journal of Marriage and the Family, 62*, 1018–1034. **27**

Booth, B., et al. 2007. *What we know about army families: 2007 update.* U.S. Army, MWR. **77, 78**

Bopp, M., Bopp, J., and Lane, P., Jr. 2003. *Aboriginal domestic violence in Canada.* The Aboriginal Healing Foundation. **54**

Borders, L. D., Penny, J. M., and Portnoy, F. 2000. Adult adoptees and their friends: Current functioning and psychosocial well-being. *Family Relations, 49*, 407–418. **244**

Bornstein, M. H., and Putnick, D. L. 2012. Cognitive and socioemotional caregiving in developing countries. *Child Development, 83*, 46–61. **17, 287**

Borrell, K., and Karlsson, S. G. 2002. *Reconceptualizing intimacy and ageing: Living apart together.* Paper presented at the International Symposium on Reconceptualising Gender and Ageing, University of Surrey: Centre for Research on Ageing and Gender, June. **79**

Bos, H. M. W., et al. 2007. Child adjustment and parenting in planned lesbian-parent families. *American Journal of Orthopsychiatry, 77*, 38–48. **224**

Bos, H. M. W., et al. 2008. Children in planned lesbian families: A cross-cultural comparison between the United States and the Netherlands. *American Journal of Orthopsychiatry, 78*, 211–219. **224**

Bould, S. 2004. Caring neighborhoods: Bringing up the kids together. *Journal of Family Issues, 24*, 427–447. **130**

Bourdieu, P. 1977. *Reproduction in education, society, culture.* (Translated). Thousand Oaks, CA: Sage. **14, 15, 116, 160, 167, 337**

Bourdieu, P. 1984. *Distinction: A social critique of the judgment of taste.* (Translated by R. Nice). London: Routledge and Kegan Paul. **15, 157**

Bourdieu, P. 1986. The forms of capital. In J. G. Richardson (Ed.), *Handbook for theory and research for the sociology of education* (pp. 241–258). Westport, CT: Greenwood. **437**

Boyce, W. F., Gallupe, O., and Fergus, S. 2008. Characteristics of Canadian youth reporting a very early age at first sexual intercourse. *The Canadian Journal of Human Sexuality, 17*, 97–109. **209**

Boyce, W., et al. 2006. Sexual health of Canadian youth: Findings from the Canadian Youth, Sexual Health and HIV/AIDS Study. *The Canadian Journal of Human Sexuality, 15*, 59–68. **204, 206, 206, 207, 209, 211**

Boyd, M., and Cao, X. 2009. Immigrant language proficiency, earnings, and language policies. *Canadian Studies in Population, 36*, 63–86. **109**

Boyd, M., and Li, A. 2003. May–December: Canadians in age-discrepant relationships. *Canadian Social Trends, 70*, 29–33. **189**

Boyd, M., and Norris, D. 1995. Leaving the nest? The impact of family structure. *Canadian Social Trends, 38*, 14–19. **358**

Boyle, M. H. 2002. Home ownership and the emotional and behavioral problems of children and youth. *Child Development, 73*, 883–892. **423**

Boyle, M. H. and Lipman, E. L. 2002. Do places matter? Socioeconomic disadvantage and behavioral problems of children in Canada. *Journal of Counseling and Clinical Psychology, 70*, 378–389. **118**

Boyle, M. H., et al. 2007. Neighborhood and family influences on educational attainment: Results from the Ontario Child Health Study Follow-Up 2001. *Child Development, 78*, 168–189. **128, 424**

Boyle, T. 2011. Seniors, women may lose out on trauma centre treatment. *Toronto Star*, August 2, A2. **414**

Boylestein, C., and Hayes, J. 2012. Reconstructing marital closeness while caring for a spouse with Alzheimer's. *Journal of Family Issues, 33*, 584–612. **268**

Brabant, C., Bourdon, S., and Jutras, F. 2004. L'école à la maison au Québec: l'expression d'un choix familial marginal. *Enfances: Familles, Générations*, Fall. **169**

Bradbury, B. 1996. *Working families: Age, gender, and daily survival in industrializing Montreal.* Toronto: Oxford University Press. **21, 100**

Bradbury, B. 2000. Gender at work at home: Family decisions, the labour market, and girls' contribution to the family economy. In B. Bradbury (Ed.), *Canadian family history* (pp. 177–198). Toronto: Irwin Publishing. **100**

Brady, D., and Burroway, R. 2012. Targeting, universalism, and single-mother poverty: A multilevel analysis across 18 affluent democracies. *Demography, 49*, 719–746. **111, 422**

Brady, D., and Kall, D. 2008. Nearly universal, but somewhat distinct: The femininization of poverty in affluent Western democracies, 1969–2000. *Social Sciences Research, 37*, 976–1007. **226**

Braithwaite, S. R., Selby, E. A., and Fincham, F. D. 2011. Forgiveness and relationship satisfaction: Mediating mechanisms. *Journal of Family Psychology, 25*, 551–559. **265**

Bramadat, P., and Seljak, D. (Eds.). 2005. *Religion and ethnicity in Canada.* Toronto: Pearson. **174, 175**

Bramlett, M. D., Radel L. F., and Blumberg, S. J. 2007. The health and well-being of adopted children. *Pediatrics, 119S*, S54–60. **244**

Brandáo, J. A. 2003. *Nation Iroquoise: A seventeenth-century ethnography of the Iroquois.* Lincoln, NE: University of Nebraska Press. **37**

Brauner-Otto, S. R., and Axinn, W. G. 2010. Parental family experiences, the timing of first sex, and contraception. *Social Science Research, 39*, 875–893. **208**

Brendgen, M., et al. 2002. Same-sex peer relations and romantic relationship during early adolescence: Interactive links to emotional, behavioral, and academic adjustment. *Merril-Palmer Quarterly, 48*, 77–103. **184**

Brendgen, M., et al. 2008. Linkages between children's and their friends' social and physical aggression: Evidence for a gene-environment interaction? *Child Development, 79*, 13–29. **400**

Brendgen, M., et al. 2011. Gene-environment processes linking aggression, peer victimization, and the teacher-child relationship. *Child Development, 82*, 2021–2036. **157**

Brenna, J. 2012. *A shrinking universe: How concentrated corporate power is shaping income inequalities in Canada.* Ottawa: Canadian Centre of Policy alternatives. **12, 95, 96, 107, 119**

Brennan, S. 2013. Family violence against seniors. Ottawa: Statistics Canada: *Juristat*, June. **403**

Brennan, S. 2011. Violent victimization of aboriginal women in the Canadian provinces, 2009. Statistics Canada: *Juristat*, May. **52, 378, 380**

Brennan, S., and Taylor-Butts, A. 2008. *Sexual assault in Canada, 2004–2007.* Canadian Centre for Justice Statistics Profile Series, Catalogue no. 85F0033M, no. 19. **392, 394**

Brewaeys, A., et al. 2005. Anonymous or identity-registered sperm donors? A study of Dutch recipients' choices. *Human Reproduction, 20,* 820–824. **239**

Brewer, D. J., Eide, E. R., and Ehrenberg, R. G. 1999. Does it pay to attend an elite private college? Cross-cohort evidence of the effects of college type on earnings. *Journal of Human Resources, 34,* 104–123. **168**

Briggs, A., and Lee, C. R. 2012. *Poverty costs: An economic case for a preventive poverty reduction in Alberta.* Calgary: Vibrant Communities Calgary and Action to End Poverty in Alberta. **113**

Brody, G. H., and Flor, D. L. 1998. Maternal resources, parenting practices, and child competence in rural, single-parent African American families. *Child Development, 69,* 803–816. **290**

Brody, G. H., and Murry, V. M. 2001. Sibling socialization of competence in rural, single-parent African-American families. *Journal of Marriage and Family, 63,* 996–1008. **290, 322**

Brody, G. H., et al. 2004. The strong African American families program: Translating research into prevention programming. *Child Development, 75,* 900–917. **428**

Brody, G. H., et al. 2013. Supportive family environments, genes that confer sensitivity, and allostic load among rural African American emerging adults : A prospective analysis. *Journal of Family Psychology, 27,* 22–29. **333**

Brodzinski, D. M., and Brodzinski, A. B. 1992. The impact of family structure on the adjustment of adopted children. *Child Welfare, 71,* 69–76. **244**

Broman, C. L. 2005. Marital quality in Black and White marriages. *Journal of Family Issues, 26,* 431–441. **263**

Bronfenbrenner, U. 1979. *The ecology of human development.* Cambridge, MA: Harvard University Press. **286**

Bronfenbrenner, U. 1985. Freedom and discipline across the decades. In G. Becker, H. Becker, and L. Huber (Eds.), *Ordnung und unordnung (Order and disorder)* (pp. 326 339). Berlin: Beltz. **290**

Bronfenbrenner, U. 1989. Ecologial systems theory. In R. Vasta (Ed.), *Six theories of child development* (pp. 185–246). Greenwich, CT: JAI Press. **26**

Bronte-Tinkew, J., et al. 2009. Fathering with multiple partners: Links to children's well-being in early childhood. *Journal of Marriage and Family, 71,* 608–631. **19, 229, 369**

Bronte-Tinkew, J., et al. 2010. Single custodial fathers involvement and parenting: Implications for outcomes in emerging adulthood. *Journal of Marriage and Family, 72,* 1107–1127. **348, 361**

Brooks, D. 2001. The organization kid. *The Atlantic Monthly,* April, 40–54. **287**

Brooks-Gunn, J. 2003. Do you believe in magic?: What we can expect from early childhood intervention programs. *Social Policy Report* (Society for Research in Child Development), *17,* 3–13. **155**

Brown, D. T., et al. 2012. The role of parental personality traits in differential parenting. *Journal of Family Psychology, 26,* 542-553. **326**

Brown, J. D, et al. 2006. Sexy media matters: Exposure to sexual content in music, movies, television, and magazines predicts black and white adolescents' sexual behavior. *Pediatrics, 117,* 1018–1027. **89**

Brown, L. 2012. Summer makes poor children poorer readers. *Toronto Star,* July 25, A1, A8. **163**

Brown, S. L. 2002. Child well-being in cohabiting families. In A. Booth and A. C. Crouter (Eds.), *Just living together* (pp. 173–187). Mahwah, NJ: Erlbaum. **196, 221, 222**

Brown, S. L. 2004. Family structure and child well-being: The significance of parental cohabitation. *Journal of Marriage and Family, 66,* 351–367. **221, 368**

Brown, S. L. 2006. Family structure transitions and adolescent well-being. *Demography, 43,* 447–461. **358, 368**

Brown, S. L., and Bulanda, J. R. 2008. Relationship violence in young adulthood: A comparison of daters, cohabitors, and marrieds. *Social Sciences Research, 37,* 73–87. **383**

Brown, S. L., and Kawamura, S. 2010. Relationship quality among cohabitors and marrieds in older adulthood. *Social Science Research, 39,* 777–786. **197**

Brown, S. L., and Manning, M. D. 2009. Family boundary ambiguity and the measurement of family structure: The significance of cohabitation. *Demography, 46,* 85–102. **369**

Brown, S. L., et al. 2012. Transitions into and out of cohabitation in later life. *Journal of Marriage and Family, 74,* 774–793. **197**

Browne, A. 1997. Violence in marriage: Until death do us part? In A. P. Cardarelli (Ed.), *Violence between intimate partners* (pp. 48–69). Boston: Allyn & Bacon. **380**

Browning, C. R. 2002. The span of collective efficacy: Extending social disorganization theory to partner violence. *Journal of Marriage and Family, 64,* 833–850. **382**

Browning, C. R., and Laumann, E. O. 1997. Sexual contact between children and adults: A life course perspective. *American Sociological Review, 62,* 540–560. **395, 396**

Brownridge, D., and Halli, S. S. 2001. *Explaining violence against women in Canada.* Lanham, NJ: Lexington Books. **383**

Brun, J. 2011. Gender, family, and mutual assistance in New France: Widows, widowers, and orphans in eighteenth-century Quebec. In M. Gleason et al. (Eds.), *Rethinking Canada: The promise of women's history,* 6th Ed. (pp. 40–56). Toronto: Oxford University Press. **365**

Brunk, M. A., and Henggeler, S. W. 1984. Child influences on adult controls: An experimental investigation. *Developmental Psychology, 20,* 1074–1081. **296**

Bryant, T. 2009. Housing and health: More than bricks and mortar. In D. Raphael (Ed.), *Social determinants of health: Canadian perspectives* 2nd Ed. (pp. 235–249). Toronto: Canadian Scholars' Press. **140**

Bryant, C. M., et al. 2008. Marital satisfaction among African Americans and Black Caribbeans: Findings from the National Survey of American Life, *Family Relations, 57,* 239–253. **57, 263**

Bryceson, D., and Vuorela, U. 2002. Transnational families in the twenty-first century. In D. Bryceson and U. Vuorela (Eds.), *The transnational family* (pp. 3–30). New York: Oxford University Press. **75**

Brzozowski, J.-A., and Brazeau, R. 2008. *What are the trends in self-reported spousal violence in Canada?* Statistics Canada, November. **195, 379, 380, 381**

Buchanan, C. M., Maccoby, E. E., and Dornbusch, S. M. 1996. *Adolescents after divorce.* Cambridge, MA: Harvard University Press. **362**

Buchignani, N., and Armstrong, C. E. 1999. Informal care and older Native Canadians. *Ageing and Society, 19,* 3–32. **52-53**

Buckles, K. S., and Munnich, E. L. 2012. Birth spacing and sibling outcomes. *Journal of Human Resources, 47,* 613–642. **319**

Buckley, K. E., and Anderson, C. A. 2006. *A theoretical model of the effects and consequences of playing video games.* In P. Vorderer and J. Bryant (Eds.), *Playing video games: Motives, responses, and consequences* (pp. 363–378). Mahwah, NJ: Earlbaum. **87**

Buehler, C., Lange, G. M., and Franck, K. L. 2007. Adolescents' cognitive and emotional responses to marital hostility. *Child Development, 78,* 775–789. **278, 280**

Bumpass, L. 2001. The changing contexts of parenting in the United States. In J. C. Westman (Ed.), *Parenthood in America: Undervalued, underpaid, under siege* (pp. 211–219). Madison, WI: The University of Wisconsin Press. **72**

Bumpass, L. L., and Lu, H.-H. 2000. Increased cohabitation changing children's family settings. *Research on Today's Issues,* NICHD, *13,* September. **193, 221**

Bumsted, J. M. 2010. *The peoples of Canada: A pre-Confederation history.* 3rd Ed. Toronto: Oxford University Press. **38, 40, 43**

Bundy-Fazioli, K., et al. 2009. Placement outcomes for children removed for neglect. *Child Welfare, 88,* 85–103. **251**

Burgess, E. W., Locke, H. J., and Thomes, M. M. 1963. *The family: From traditional to companionship.* New York: American Book. **261**

Burke, R., and Weir, T. 1976. Relationship of wives' employment status to husband, wife and pair satisfaction and performance. *Journal of Marriage and Family, 38,* 279–287. **272**

Burnette, D. 1999. Social relationships of Latino grandparent caregivers: A role theory perspective. *The Gerontologist, 39,* 49–58. **312**

Burney, S. 1995. *Coming to Gum San: The story of Chinese Canadians.* Toronto: Health Canada (for the Multicultural History Society of Ontario). **60**

Burstyn, V. 1999. *The rites of men: Manhood, politics, and the culture of sport.* Toronto: University of Toronto Press **87.**

Burt, S. A., et al. 2005. How are parent-child conflict and childhood externalizing symptoms related over time? Results from a genetically informative cross-lagged study. *Development and Psychopathology, 17,* 145–165. **294**

Burt, S. A., McGue, M., and Iacono, W. G. 2009. Nonshared environmental mediation of the association between deviant peer affiliation and adolescent externalizing behaviors over time: Results from a cross-lagged monozygotic twin differences design. *Developmental Psychology, 45,* 1751–1760. **303**

Burton, L. M., and Jarrett, R. L. 2000. In the mix, yet on the margins: The place of families in urban neighborhoods and child development research. *Journal of Marriage and Family, 62,* 1114–1135. **131**

Burton, P., Lethbridge, L., and Phipps, S. 2006. Children with disabilities and chronic conditions and longer-term parental health. Statistics Canada, *The Daily,* November 22. **409**

Bushman, B. J. and Anderson, C. A. 2001. Media violence and the American public: Scientific facts versus media misinformation. *American Psychologist, 56,* 477–489. **83**

Bushman, B., J., and Huesmann, L. R. 2001. Effects of televised violence on aggression. In D. G. Singer and J. L. Singer (Eds.), *Handbook of children and the media* (pp. 223–254). Thousand Oaks, CA: Sage. **85**

Bushman, B. J., and Huesmann, L. R. 2006. Short-term and long-term effects of violent media on aggression in children and adults. *Archives of Pediatrics and Adolescent Medicine, 160,* 348–352. **85**

Bushnik, T., et al. 2012a. Estimating the prevalence of infertility in Canada. *Human Reproduction, 27,* 738–746. **235**

Bushnik, T., et al. 2012b. Seeking medical help to conceive. Statistics Canada, *Health Reports, 23, December.* **231**

Buss, D. M., et al. 2001. A half century of mate preferences: The cultural evolution of values. *Journal of Marriage and Family, 63,* 491–503. **189**

Butala, S. 2005. *Lilac moon.* New York: HarperCollins. **48, 49**

Butler, A. 2005. Gender differences in the prevalence of same-sex sexual partnering: 1988–2002. *Social Forces, 84,* 421–448. **210**

Butler-Sweet, C. 2011. "A healthy Black identify": transracial adoption, middle-class families, and racial socialization. *Journal of Comparative Family Studies, 42,* 193–213. **246**

Button, D. M., and Gealt, R. 2010. High risk behaviors among victims of sibling violence. *Journal of Family Violence, 25,* 131–140. **397**

Buxton, B. 2004. *Damaged angels.* Toronto: Alfred A. Knopf. **244**

Bzostek, S. 2008. Social fathers and child well-being. *Journal of Marriage and Family, 70,* 950–961. **369**

CACUSS (Canadian Association of College and University Student Services). 2013. *Data on health behaviours of Canadian post-secondary students.* Copyrighted by the American College Health Association. June. **90, 183, 205, 210**

CAIS (Canadian Association of Independent Schools). 2009. *Statistics summary 1998–2009/2010.* **168**

CCPA (Canadian Centre for Policy Alternatives). 2009. *State of the inner city, 2009.* Manitoba, December 9. **110, 132, 420**

CDC (Center for Disease Control and Prevention). 2012. *National marriage and divorce rate trends.* Atlanta, GA: CDC. **197, 344**

Calasanti, T. M. 2004. Feminist gerontology and old men. *Journals of Gerontology, 59B,* S305–314. **268**

Calgary Homeless Foundation. 2012. *The State of homelessness in Calgary in 2012.* April. **132**

Calixte, S. J., Johnson, J. L., and Motapanyane, J. M. 2010. Liberal, socialist, and radical feminism: An introduction to three theories about women's oppression and social change. In N. Mandell (Ed.), *Feminist issues: Race, class, and gender,* 5th Ed. (pp. 1–39). Toronto: Prentice Hall. **16, 20**

Call, V., Sprecher, S., and Schwartz, P. 1995. The incidence and frequency of marital sex in a national sample. *Journal of Marriage and Family, 57,* 639–652. **211, 212**

Callahan, K. L., et al. 2011. Neighborhood disadvantage as a moderator of the association between harsh parenting and toddler-aged children's internalizing and externalizing problems. *Journal of Family Psychology, 25,* 68–76. **126, 129**

Callaway, E. 2012. Fathers bequeath more mutations as they age. *Nature News, August 22,* 439, 488. **231**

Calliste, A. 2003. Black families in Canada: Exploring the interconnections of race, class, and gender. In M. Lynn (Ed.), *Voices: Essays on Canadian families,* 2nd Ed. (pp. 199–220). Scarborough, ON: Thomson Nelson. **45, 56, 57**

Cameron, P. 2003. Domestic violence among homosexual partners. *Psychological Reports, 93,* 410–416. **383**

Campaign 2000. *2010 Report card on child and family poverty in Canada: 1989–2010.* www.campaign2000.ca. **105, 106, 106, 108, 114, 151**

Campbell, A. 2005. *Polygamy in Canada. How have policy approaches to polygamy responded to women's experiences and rights? An international comparative analysis.* Status of Women Canada. **9**

Campbell, L. D., and Carroll, M. 2007. Aging in Canadian families today. In D. Cheal (Ed.), *Canadian families today* (pp. 117–133). Toronto: Oxford University Press. **370**

Campbell, L. D., Connidis, I. A., and Davies, L. 1999. Sibling ties in later life: A social network analysis. *Journal of Family Issues, 20,* 114–148. **330**

Campbell, S. B., and Renshaw, K. D. 2012. Distress in spouses of Vietnam veterans: Association with communication about deployment experiences. *Journal of Family Psychology, 26*, 18–25. **79**

Campos, B., et al. 2009. Opportunity for interaction? A naturalistic observation study of dual-earner families after work and school. *Journal of Family Psychology, 23*, 798–807. **276**

Canada Year Book, 2011. Ottawa: Statistics Canada. **140, 235**

Canada Year Book, 2012. Ottawa: Statistics Canada. **98, 151, 247**

Canadian Council on Social Development. 2006. *Families: A Canadian profile.* **309**

Canadian Forces. 2008. *Annual Report 2007–2008, for the year ending 31 March.* **77**

Cancian, M., et al. 2011. The evolution of family complexity from the perspective of nonmarital children. *Demography, 48*, 957–982. **229**

Cantor, J., and Nathanson, A. I. 2001. The media and parents: Protecting children from harm. In J. C. Westman (Ed.), *Parenthood in America: Undervalued, underpaid, and under siege* (pp. 232–241). Madison, WI: The University of Wisconsin Press. **86**

Capaldi, D. M., and Clark, S. 1998. Prospective family predictors of aggression toward female partners for at-risk young men. *Developmental Psychology, 34*, 1175–1188. **377**

Card, N. A., et al. 2011. A meta-analytic review of internalizing, externalizing, and academic adjustment among children of deployed military service members. *Journal of Family Psychology, 25*, 508–520. **77**

Carey, E. 2001. Kids' special needs often unmet: Study. *Toronto Star.* November 21. **119**

Carey, E. 2004. Homeless women "crisis." *Toronto Star.* April 13, A1, A4. **134**

Carlson, M. J. 2006. Family structure, father involvement, and adolescent behavioral outcomes. *Journal of Marriage and Family, 68*, 137–154. **349**

Carlson, M. J., and Furstenberg, F. F., Jr. 2006. The prevalence and correlates of multipartnered fertility among U.S. parents. *Journal of Marriage and Family, 68*, 718–732. **229**

Carlson, M. J., et al. 2011. Couples as partners and parents over children's early years. *Journal of Marriage and Family, 73*, 317–334. **278**

Carmalt, J. H., et al. 2008. Body weight and matching with a physically attractive romantic partner. *Journal of Marriage and Family, 70*, 1287–1296. **189**

Carothers, S. S., et al. 2005. Religiosity and the socioemotional adjustment of adolescent mothers and their children. *Journal of Family Psychology, 19*, 263–275. **175**

Carp, E. W. 2008. Does opening adoption records have an adverse social impact? Some lessons from the U.S., Great Britian, and Australia, 1953–2007. *Adoption Quarterly, 10*, 29–52. **247**

Carp, F. M. 2000. *Elder abuse in the family.* New York: Springer. **403**

Carr, D. 2004. Gender, preloss marital dependence, and older adults' adjustment to widowhood. *Journal of Marriage and Family, 66*, 220–235. **364**

Carr, D., and Boerner, K. 2009. Do spousal discrepancies in marital quality assessments affect psychological adjustment to widowhood? *Journal of Marriage and Family, 71*, 495–509. **364**

Carroll, J. A., et al. 2005. Theorizing about marriage. In V. L. Bengtson et al. *Sourcebook of family theory & research* (pp. 263–266). Thousand Oaks, CA: Sage. **14, 262**

Carroll, J. S., Badger, S., and Yang, C. 2006. The ability to negotiate or the ability to love? *Journal of Family Issues, 27*, 1001–1032. **264**

Carter, S. 2008. *The importance of being monogamous: Marriage and nation building in Western Canada to 1915.* Edmonton: The University of Alberta Press. **44, 48, 52**

Cartier, G. 2008. City of Quebec 1608–2008: 400 years of censuses. *Canadian Social Trends,* June 3. **39, 40**

Casad, B. J., et al. 2012. Younger age at first childbirth predicts mothers' lower economic and psychological well-being later in life. *Journal of Family and Economic Issues, 33*, 421–435. **232**

Casey, P., et al. 2013. Families created by donor insemination: Father-child relationship at age 7. *Journal of Marriage and Family, 75*, 858–870. **241**

Castaneda, C. 2002. *Figurations: Child bodies worlds.* Durham, NC: Duke University Press. **74**

Castellano, M. 2002. *Aboriginal family trends: Extended families, nuclear families, families of the heart.* Ottawa: Vanier Institute of the Family. **52**

Castells, 2010. 2nd Ed. *The rise of the network society.* Chichester, U.K.: Wiley-Blackwell. **80**

Cavanagh, S. E. 2011. Early pubertal timing and the union formation behaviours of young women. *Social Forces, 89*, 1217–1238. **208**

Cavanagh, S. E., Crissey, S. R., and Raley, R. K. 2008. Family structure history and adolescent romance. *Journal of Marriage and Family, 70*, 698–714. **358**

CBoardC (Conference Board of Canada). 2010. *Building from the ground up: Enhancing affordable housing in Canada.* Ottawa, March. **423**

CCPA (Canadian Centre for Policy Alternatives). 2009. *State of the inner city, 2009.* Manitoba, December 9. **421**

CDC (Center for Disease Control and Prevention). 2012. *National marriage and divorce rate trends.* Atlanta, GA: CDC. **344**

Cebello, R., et al. 2004. Gaining a child: Comparing the experiences of biological parents, adoptive parents, and stepparents. *Family Relations, 53*, 38–48. **232, 246**

Celdran, M., et al. 2012. When grandparents have dementia: Effects on their grandchildren's family relationships. *Journal of Family Issues, 33*, 1218–1239. **308**

CERA (Centre for Equality of Rights in Accommodation). 2013. Accessed online June, 2013. **423**

Chabot, J. M., and Ames, B. D. 2004. "It wasn't 'let's get pregnant and go do it'": Decision making in lesbian couples planning motherhood via donor insemination. *Family Relations, 53*, 348–356. **239**

Chan, R. W., Raboy, R. C., and Patterson, C. J. 1998. Psychosocial adjustment among children conceived via donor insemination by lesbian and heterosexual mothers. *Child Development, 69*, 443–457. **224**

Chandra, A, et al. 2008. Does watching sex on television predict teen pregnancy? *Pediatrics, 122*, 1047–1054. **89**

Chao, R. K., and Willms, J. D. 2002. The effects of parenting practices on children's outcomes. In *Vulnerable children* (pp. 149–166). Edmonton: University of Alberta Press. **291, 428**

Chappell, N. L., and Dujela, C. 2008. Caregiving: Predicting at-risk status. *Canadian Journal on Aging, 27*, 169–179. **308**

Chappell, N. L., and Funk, L. M. 2011. Social support, caregiving, and aging. *Canadian Journal on Aging, 30*, 355–370. **307, 419**

Chappell, N. L., and Penning, M. J. 2001. Sociology of aging in Canada: Issues for the millennium. *Canadian Journal on Aging, 20,* 82–110. **21**

Chappell, N., McDonald, L., and Stones, M. 2010. *Aging in contemporary Canada.* 2nd ed. Toronto: Prentice-Hall. **310**

Charles, G., Stainton, T., and Marshall, S. 2012. Young careers in Canada: The hidden costs and benefits of young caregiving. Ottawa: The Vanier Institute of the Family. **299, 300**

Charron, M. 2009. Neighbourhood characteristics and distribution of police-reported crime in Toronto. *Crime and Justice Research Paper Series.* Statistics Canada Research Catalogue 85-561-M2009018. Ottawa. **126**

Charton, L., and Lapierre-Adamcyk, E. 2010. Low fertility and contraceptive sterilization. The Canadian case. Canadian Studies in Population, 37, 373–410. **235, 365**

Chartrand, L. N., and McKay, C. 2006. *A review of research on criminal victimization and First Nations, Métis, and Inuit Peoples 1990 to 2001.* Ottawa: Department of Justice, Research and Statistics Division, Policy Centre for Victim Issues. **44, 52, 53, 382–383**

Chartrand, L. N., Logan, T. E., and Daniels, J. D. 2006. *Métis history and experience in residential schools in Canada.* The Aboriginal Healing Foundation. **43, 44, 54**

Cheadle, J. E., Amato, P. R., and King, V. 2010. Patterns of non-resident father contact. *Demography, 47,* 205–225.

Cheah, C. S., et al. 2009. Authoritative parenting among immigrant Chinese mothers of preschoolers. *Journal of Family Psychology, 23,* 311–320. **61**

Chen, F., and Liu, G. 2012. The health implications of grandparents caring for grandchildren in China. *The Journals of Gerontology, 67,* 99–113. **312**

Chen, W. H., Myles, J., and Picot, G. 2011. *Why have poorer neighbourhoods stagnated economically while the richer have flourished?* Edmonton, AB: Edmonton Social Planning Council and Canadian Labour Market and Skills Research Network. **96, 123**

Chen, Y., and Li, H. 2013. Prenatal sex selection and missing girls in China: Evidence from the diffusion of diagnostic ultrasound. *Journal of Human Resources, 48,* 36–70. **59**

Cherlin, A. J. 1978. Remarriage as an incomplete institution. *American Journal of Sociology, 84,* 634–651. **368**

Cherlin, A. J. 2004. The deinstitutionalization of American marriage. *Journal of Marriage and Family, 66,* 848–861. **350**

Cherlin, A. J. 2009. *The marriage-go-around.* New York: Alfred A. Knopf. **353**

Cherlin, A. J., Chase-Lansdale, P., and McRae, C. 1998. Effects of parental divorce on mental health throughout the life course. *American Sociological Review, 63,* 239–249. **358, 362**

Chesler, P. 1989. *The sacred bond: The legacy of Baby M.* New York: Vintage. **242**

Chetty, R., et al. 2011. How does your kindergarten classroom affect your earnings? Evidence from Project STAR. *The Quarterly Journal of Economics, 126,* 1593–1660. **157**

Child Support Team. 2000. *Selected statistics on Canadian families and family law: Second edition.* Ottawa: Department of Justice. **349**

Chiu, S., et al. 2009. The health of homeless immigrants. *Journal of Epidemiology and Community Health, 63,* 943–948. **132, 133**

Choi, H., and Marks, N. F. 2008. Marital conflict, depressive symptoms, and functional impairment. *Journal of Marriage and Family, 70,* 377–390. **356**

Christakis, D. A. 2009. The effects of infant media usage: What do we know and what should we learn? *Acta Paediatrica, 98,* 8–16. **81, 90**

Christensen, A., et al. 2006. Cross-cultural consistency on the demand/withdraw interaction pattern in couples. *Journal of Marriage and Family, 68,* 1029–1044. **264, 265**

Christensen, D. 2000. *Ahtahkakoop: The epic account of a Plains Cree head chief, his people, and their struggle for survival, 1816–1896.* Shell Lake, SK: Ahtahkakoop. **37**

Christiansen, S. 2013. A nation without children: A discussion of fertility decline in Japan. *Family Focus, 58,* Spring, F18–F20. **236, 286, 429**

Christofides, E., et al. 2012. Risky disclosures on Facebook: The effect of having a bad experience on online behavior. *Journal of Adolescent Research, 27,* 714–731. **399**

Chudley, A. E., et al. 2005. Fetal Alcohol Spectrum Disorder: Canadian guidelines for diagnosis. *Canadian Medical Association Journal, 12,* Supplement 5, S1–S21. **389**

Chui, T. 2011. Immigrant women. In V. Ferrao and C. Williams (Eds.): Women in Canada, 6th Ed. Statistics Canada: *The Daily,* July 26. **109**

Chung, A. 2010. Wounded warriors. *Toronto Star,* November 10, A6. **77**

Chung, H. L., and Steinberg, L. 2006. Relations between neighborhood factors, parenting behaviors, peer deviance, and delinquency among serious juvenile offenders. *Developmental Psychology, 42,* 319–331. **129**

Chun, J. J., and Cheong, A. 2011. *Immigrants and low-paid work: Persistent problems, enduring consequences.* British Columbia: Metropolis British Columbia. **109**

Chunn, D. E. 2000. "Politicizing the personal": Feminism, law, and public policy. In N. Mandell and A. Duffy (Eds.), *Canadian families: Diversity, conflict, and change,* 2nd Ed. (pp. 225–259). Toronto: Harcourt Brace. **20**

CIBC (Canadian Imperial Bank of Commerce). 2013. *CIBC poll: Parents delaying retirement, taking on debts to help kids pay for education.* August 22. **97**

Ciccarelli, J. C., and Beckman, L. J. 2005. Navigating rough waters: An overview of psychological aspects of surrogacy. *Journal of Social Issues, 61,* 21–43. **241**

Ciccarelli, J. K., and Ciccarelli, J. C. 2005. The legal aspects of parental rights in Assisted Reproductive Technology. *Journal of Social Issues, 61,* 127–137. **240, 241**

Cicirelli, V. G. 1989. Feelings of attachment to siblings and well-being in later life. *Psychology and Aging, 4,* 211–216. **330**

Cicirelli, V. G. 1996. Sibling relationships in middle and old age. In G. H. Brody (Ed.), *Sibling relationships: Their causes and consequences* (pp. 47–74). Norwood, NJ: Ablex. **330**

CIW (Canadian Index of Wellbeing). 2010. *Caught in the time crunch: Time use, leisure and culture in Canada.* **90, 102, 103, 298, 430**

Clairmont, D. H. J., and Magill, D. 1999. *Africville: The life and death of a Canadian black community,* 3rd Ed. Toronto: Canadian Scholars' Press. **46**

Clampet-Lundquist, S., et al. 2011. Moving teenagers out of high-risk neighborhoods: How girls fare better than boys. *American Journal of Sociology, 116,* 1154–1189. **130**

Clark, D. J. 2001. *Surfing for seniors: Report of the National Council on Family Relations.* March, F18, F20. 84

Clark, J., et al. 2006. The role of low expectations in health and education investment and hazardous consumption. *Canadian Journal of Economics, 39,* 1151–1172. 112

Clark, L. A., Kochanska, G., and Ready, R. 2000. Mothers' personality and its interaction with child temperament as predictors of parenting behavior. *Journal of Personality and Social Psychology, 79,* 274–285. 285

Clark, S. 1999. What do we know about unmarried mothers? In J. Wong and D. Checkland (Eds.), *Teen pregnancy and parenting* (pp. 10–24). Toronto: University of Toronto Press. 230

Clark, W. 1998. Religious observance, marriage and family. *Canadian Social Trends, 50,* 2–7. 172

Clark, W. 2002. Time alone. *Canadian Social Trends, 66,* 2–6. 141

Clark, W., and Crompton, S. 2006. Till death do us part? The risk of first and second marrage dissolution. *Canadian Social Trends, 11,* Summer. 102, 346, 347, 351, 352

Clark, W., and Schellenberg, G. 2006. Who's religion? *Canadian Social Trends, 11,* May. Ottawa: Statistics Canada. 171

Clarke, A. Y. 2011. *The inequalities of love: College-educated black women and the barriers to romance and fertility.* Durham, NC: Duke University Press. 57, 186

Clarke, L. 2003. Hijab according to the Hadith: Text and interpretation. In S. S. Alvi, H. Hoodfar, and S. McDonaugh (Eds.), *The Muslim veil in North America* (pp. 214–286). Toronto: Women's Press. 178

Cleveland, H. H., and Wiebe, R. P. 2003. The moderation of adolescent-to-peer similarity in tobacco and alcohol use by school levels of substance use. *Child Development, 74,* 279–291. 158

Clio Collective 1987. *Quebec women: A history.* Toronto: Women's Press. 40

Coakley, J., and Donnelly, P. 2004. *Sports in society: Issues and controversies.* Toronto: McGraw-Hill Ryerson. 87, 150

Coburn, D. 2010. Health and health care: A political economy perspective. In T. Bryant, D. Raphael, and M. Rioux (Eds.), *Staying alive: Critical perspectives on health, illness, and health care.* 2nd Ed. (pp. 239–263). Toronto: Canadian Scholars' Press. 11, 95, 119, 421

Coelli, M. B. 2009. Tuition fees and equality of university enrolment. *Canadian Journal of Economics, 42,* 1072–1099. 420

Cohen, P. N., and Petrescu-Prahova, M. 2006. Gendered living arrangements among children with disabilities. *Journal of Marriage and Family, 68,* 630–638. 19

Cohen, S., et al. 2012. Eye of the beholder: The individual and dyadic contributors of empathic accuracy and perceived empathic effort to relationship satisfaction. *Journal of Family Psychology, 26,* 236–245. 265

Coleman, J. S. 1988. Social capital in the creation of human capital. *American Journal of Sociology, 94,* S95–S120. 14, 159, 161

Coleman, J. S. 1990a. *Foundations of social theory.* Cambridge, MA: Harvard University Press. 14, 116, 337, 411

Coleman, J. S. 1990b. *Equality and achievement in education.* Boulder, CO: Westview Press. 14

Coleman, J. S., and Hoffer, T. 1987. *Public and private schools: The impact of communities.* New York: Basic Books. 15, 167, 337

Coley, R. L. 2001. (In)visible men: Emerging research on low-income, unmarried, and minority fathers. *American Psychologist, 56,* 743–753. 19

Coley, R. L., et al. 2011. Do children's behavior problems limit poor women's labor market success? *Journal of Marriage and Family, 73,* 33–45. 298

Collins, M. E., Paris, R., and Ward, R. L. 2008. The permanence of family ties: Implications for youth transitioning from foster care. *American Journal of Orthopsychiatry, 78,* 54–62. 251

Collins, P. H. 1990. *Black feminist thought: Knowledge, consciousness, and the politics of empowerment.* Boston: Unwin Hyman. 298

Collins, P. H. 1992. Black women and motherhood. In B. Thorne and M. Yalom (Eds.), *Rethinking the family,* rev. Ed., (pp. 215–245). Boston: Northeastern University Press. 18

Collins, S. B. 2010. *Sofas, shelters and strangers: A report on youth homelessness in Niagara.* Niagara Region Community Services, May 13. 133

Coloma, R. S., et al. (Eds.) 2012. *Filipinos in Canada: Disturbing invisibility.* Toronto: Toronto University Press. 64

Coltrane, S. 2000. Research on household labor: Modeling and measuring the social embeddedness of routine family work. *Journal of Marriage and Family, 62,* 1208–1233. 272

Conger, R. D., and Conger, K. J. 1996. Sibling relationships. In R. Simons and Associates (Eds.), *Understanding differences between divorced and intact families* (pp. 104–121). Thousand Oaks, CA: Sage. 325, 358

Conger, R. D., Conger, K. J., and Martin, M.J. 2010. Socioeconomic status, family processes, and individual development. *Journal of Marriage and the Family, 72,* 685–704. 26, 116, 420

Connell, C. M., et al. 2009. Maltreatment following reunification: Predictors of subsequent Child Protective Services contact after children return home. *Child Abuse & Neglect, 33,* 218–228. 250

Connidis, I. A. 2003a. Divorce and union dissolution: Reverberations over three generations. *Canadian Journal on Aging, 22,* 353–368. 358, 371

Connidis, I. A. 2003b. Bringing outsiders in: Gay and lesbian family ties over the life course. In S. Arber, K. Davidson, and J. Ginn (Eds.), *Gender and ageing: Changing roles and relationships* (pp. 79–94). Maidenhead, UK: Open University Press. 310, 330

Connidis, I. A. 2007. Negotiating inequality among adult siblings: Two case studies. *Journal of Marriage and Family, 69,* 482–499. 329, 330

Connidis, I. A. 2010. *Family ties & aging,* 2nd Ed. Thousand Oaks, CA: Sage. 306, 307, 309, 312, 317, 329, 330, 371, 419

Connidis, I. A., and McMullin, J. A. 2002a. Sociological ambivalence and family ties: A critical perspective. *Journal of Marriage and Family, 64,* 558–567. 306

Connidis, I. A., and McMullin, J. A. 2002b. Ambivalence, family ties, and doing sociology. *Journal of Marriage and Family, 64,* 594–601. 306

Contenta, S., and Monsebraaten, L. 2009. Canada "guest workers." *Toronto Star,* November 1, A1, A6–A7. 75

Cook, C., and Willms, J. D. 2002. Balancing work and family life. In J. D. Willms (Ed.), *Vulnerable children* (pp. 183–198). Edmonton: University of Alberta Press. 160

Cook, D. 2004. *The commodification of childhood: The children's clothing industry and the rise of the child consumer.* Durham, NC: Duke University Press. 104

Cook, D. A., and Fine, M. 1995. "Motherwit": Childrearing lessons from African-American mothers of low income. In B. B. Swadener and S. Lubeck (Eds.), *Children and families "at promise"* (pp. 118–142). Albany: State University of New York Press. 114

Cooke, M. 2009. A welfare trap? The duration and dynamics of social assistance use among lone mothers in Canada. *The Canadian Review of Sociology, 46*, 179–206. 112

Cooksey, E. C., and Craig, P. H. 1998. Parenting from a distance: The effects of paternal characteristics on contact between nonresidential fathers and their children. *Demography, 35*, 187–200. 251

Cooley, C. H. 1902. *Human nature and the social order.* New York: Scribner. 25

Coombs, R. H. 1991. Marital status and personal well-being: A literature review. *Family Relations, 40*, 97–102. 198

Cooney, T. M., and Dunne, K. 2001. Intimate relationships in later life. *Journal of Family Issues, 22*, 838–858. 197

Coontz, S. 1992. *The way we never were: American families and the nostalgia trap.* New York: Basic Books. 81

Coontz, S. 2000. Historical perspectives on family studies. *Journal of Marriage and Family, 62*, 283–297. 71, 143, 151, 251

Coontz, S. 2006. *Fact sheet on polygamy.* US: Council on Contemporary Families. 8

Cooper, A. 2011. Acts of resistance: Black men and women engage slavery in Upper Canada, 1793–1803. In M. Gleason et al. (Eds.), *Rethinking Canada: The promise of women is history*, 6th Ed. (pp. 71–79). Toronto: Oxford University Press. 45

Corak, M. 1998. Getting ahead in life: Does your parents' income count? *Canadian Social Trends, 49*, 6–10. 71

Corak, M. 2001. Death and divorce: The long-term consequences of parental loss on adolescents. *Journal of Labor Economics, 19*, 682–716. 359

Corbin, J., and Strauss, A. 2008. *Basics of qualitative research: Techniques and procedures for developing grounded theory.* Thousand Oaks, CA: Sage. 31

Corliss, H. L., et al. 2009. Age of minority sexual orientation development and risk of childhood maltreatment and suicide attempts in women. *American Journal of Orthopsychiatry, 79*, 511–521. 211

Cornish, M. 2012. *A living wage as a human right.* Ottawa. Canadian Centre for Policy Alternatives, October 5. 105

Corsaro, W. A. 1997. *The sociology of childhood.* Thousand Oaks, CA: Pine Forge Press. 26

Côté, J. E. 2000. *Arrested adulthood: The changing nature of maturity and identity.* New York: New York University Press. 104, 303, 338

Côté, J., and Allahar, A. L. 1994. *Generation on hold: Coming of age in the late twentieth century.* Toronto: Stoddart. 297

Côté, J., and Allahar, A. L. 2006. *Critical youth studies. A Canadian focus.* Toronto: Pearson. 150, 303, 305, 412, 423, 432

Côté, S., Tremblay, R. E., and Vitaro, F. 2003. Le devéloppement de l'agression physique au cours de l'enfance: Différences entre les sexes et facteurs de risque familaux. *Sociologie et Sociétés, 35*, 203–219. 358

Cottrell, B., and VanderPlaat, M. 2011. My kids want to eat pork: Parent-teen conflicts in immigrant families. In E. Tastsoglou and P. S. Jaya (Eds.), *Immigrant women in Atlantic Canada* (pp. 267–296). Toronto: Canadian Scholars' Press. 72, 292, 298, 301, 418

Coughlin, C., and Vuchinich, S. 1996. Family experience in preadolescence and the development of male delinquency. *Journal of Marriage and Family, 58*, 491–501. 369

Coyne, A. 2011. The $25,000 cow. *Maclean's Magazine,* August 22, 16–18. 137

Cranswick, K. 1997. Canada's caregivers. *Canadian Social Trends, 47*, 2–6. 308

Cranswick, K., and Dosman, D. 2008. Eldercare: What we know today. *Canadian Social Trends,* October, 47–57. 430

Crenshaw, K. W. 1994. Mapping the margins: Intersectionality, identity politics, and violence against women of color. In M. A. Fineman and R. Mykitiuk (Eds.), *The public nature of private violence.* New York: Routledge. 382

Criss, M. M., and Shaw, D. S. 2005. Sibling relationships as contexts for delinquency training in low-income families. *Journal of Family Psychology, 19*, 592–600. 323

Cristi, M. 2012. Durkheim on moral individualism, social justice, and rights: A gendered construction of rights. Canadian Journal of Sociology, 37, 409–438. 11

Critchley, K. A., et al. 2007. Building healthy Mik'mac communities in Prince Edward Island. *The Canadian Journal of Native Studies, 27*, 1–17. 38

Crockenberg, S., and Leerkes, E. 2003. Infant negative emotionality, caregiving, and family relationships. In A. C. Crouter and A. Booth (Eds.), *Children's influence on family dynamics* (pp. 57–78). Mahwah, NJ: Erlbaum. 286

Crosnoe, R. 2004. Social capital and the interplay of families and schools. *Journal of Marriage and Family, 66*, 267–280. 161

Crosnoe, R., and Elder, G. H., Jr. 2002. Adolescent twins and emotional distress: The interrelated influence of nonshared environment and social structure. *Child Development, 73*, 1761–1774. 174, 326

Crotty, M. 1998. *The foundations of social research.* London: Sage. 16

Crouter, A. C., et al. 1999. Conditions underlying parents' knowledge about children's daily lives in middle childhood: Between and within-family comparisons. *Child Development, 70*, 246–259. 326

Crowder, K. D., and Tolnay, S. E. 2000. A new marriage squeeze for Black women: The role of racial intermarriage by Black men. *Journal of Marriage and Family, 62*, 792–807. 186

Cuber, J., and Harroff, P. B. 1965. *The significant American.* New York: Hawthorn. 257, 258, 259

Cuevas, C. A., et al. 2010. Psychological distress as a risk factor for re-victimization in children. *Child Abuse & Neglect, 34*, 235–243. 386

Cui, M., and Donnellan, M. B. 2009. Trajectories of conflict over raising adolescent children and marital satisfaction. *Journal of Marriage and Family, 71*, 478–494. 277

Cui, M., Conger, R. D., and Lorenz, F. O. 2005. Predicting change in adolescent adjustment from change in marital problems. *Developmental Psychology, 41*, 812–823. 278

Cummings, E. M., and Davies, P. T. 2010. Marital conflict and children: An emotional security perspective. New York: Guilford Press. 278

Curry-Stevens, A. 2009. When economic growth doesn't trickle down: The wage dimensions of income polarization. In D. Raphael (Ed.) *Social determinants of health: Canadian perspectives,* 2nd Ed. (pp. 41–60). Toronto: Canadian Scholars' Press. 108

Curtis, L. J., et al. 2004. Child well-being and neighbourhood quality: Evidence from the Canadian Longitudinal Survey of Children and Youth. *Social Science and Medicine, 58*, 1917–1927. 128

Daddis, C. 2011. Desire for increased autonomy and adolescents' perception of peer autonomy: "Everyone else can; Why can't I?" *Child Development, 82*, 1310–1326. **302**

Dahrendorf, R. 1959. *Class and class conflict in industrial society.* Stanford, CA: Stanford University Press. **11**

Daigneault, I., Hébert, M., and McDuff, P. 2009. Men's and women's childhood sexual abuse and victimization in adult partner relationships: A study of risk factors. *Child Abuse & Neglect, 33*, 638–647. **395**

Daly, K. 2003. Family theory versus the theories families live by. *Journal of Marriage and Family, 65*, 771–784. **25, 104-105**

Daly, K. 2004. *The changing culture of parenting.*Ottawa: The Vanier Institute of the Family. **301**

Damaske, S. 2011. *For the family? How class and gender shape women's work.* New York: Oxford University Press. **99, 100**

Daneshpour, M. 2013. A mini-narrative about my praxis as a Muslim feminist. *Family Focus*, Winter, F2–3. **22, 174**

Daniels, A. K. 1987. Invisible work. *Social Problems, 34*, 403–415. **328, 427**

Daniels, D. 1987. Differential experiences of children in the same family as predictors of adolescent sibling personality differences. *Journal of Personality and Social Psychology, 51*, 339–346. **328**

Danvers, G. D. 2001. Gendered encounters: Warriors, women and William Johnson. *Journal of American Studies, 35*, 187–202. **37**

Das Gupta, M., Chung, W., and Shuzhuo, L. 2009. Evidence for the incipient decline in numbers of missing girls in China and India. *Population and Developmental Review, 35*, 401–416. **8, 59, 63**

Das Gupta, T. 2000. Families of Native people, immigrants, and people of colour. In N. Mandell and A. Duffy (Eds.), *Canadian families: Diversity, conflict, and change*, 2nd Ed. (pp. 146–187). Toronto: Harcourt Brace. **22, 44, 49, 52**

Daubs, K. 2009. Tasty idea to keep kids off the streets. *Toronto Star*. November 21, GT8. **156**

Dauvergne, M. 2003. Family violence against seniors. *Canadian Social Trends, 68*, 10–14. **404**

Dauvergne, M. 2012. Adult correctional statistics in Canada, 2010–2011. Statistics Canada: *Juristat*, October 11. **113**

Davidson, P. 2012. University is still the surest path to prosperity. *Globe and Mail*, September 12. **97**

Davis, K. D., et al. 2008. Nonstandard work schedules, perceived family well-being, and daily stressors. *Journal of Marriage and Family, 70*, 991–1003. **99**

Davis, S. N., et al. 2007. Effects of union type on division of household labor. Do cohabiting men really perform more housework? *Journal of Family Issues, 28*, 1246–1272. **195**

DeAngelis, T. 2002. A new generation of issues for LGBT clients. *Monitor on Psychology, 33*, February. **190, 225**

Dearing, E., McCartney, K., and Taylor, B. A. 2009. Does higher quality early child care promote low-income children's math and reading achievement in middle childhood? *Child Development, 80*, 1329–1349. **154**

DeFina, R., and Hannon, L. 2010. For incapacitation, there is no time like the present: The lagged effects of prisoner reentry on property and violent crime rates. *Social Science Research, 39*, 1004–1014. **130**

DeFronzo, J. 1997. Welfare and homicide. *Journal of Research in Crime and Delinquency, 34*, 395–406. **422**

DeGarmo, D. S. 2010. Coercive and prosocial fathering, antisocial personality, and growth in children's postdivorce noncompliance. *Child Development, 81*, 503–516. **295**

de Graaf, P. M., and Kalmijn, M. 2006. Divorce motives in a period of rising divorce. *Journal of Family Issues, 27*, 483–505. **354**

Dei, G. J. 1993. Narrative discourses of Black/African-Canadian parents and the Canadian public school system. *Canadian Ethnic Studies, 25*, 45–54. **56**

Dej, E. 2011. What once was sick is now bad: The shift from victim to deviant identity for those diagnosed with fetal alcohol spectrum disorder. *Canadian Journal of Sociology, 36*, 137–160. **16, 250**

Dekel, R., and Goldblatt, H. 2008. Is there intergenerational transmission of trauma? The case of combat veterans' children. *American Journal of Orthopsychiatry, 78*, 281–289. **77**

DeKeseredy, W. S. 2000. Current controversies on defining nonlethal violence against women in intimate heterosexual relationships: Empirical implications. *Violence Against Women, 6*, 728–746. **378**

DeKeseredy, W. S. 2009. Patterns of violence in the family. In M. Baker (Ed.), *Families: Changing trends in Canada,*6th Ed. (pp. 179–205). Toronto: McGraw Hill Ryerson. **381, 382**

DeKeseredy, W. S., and Dragiewicz, M. 2007. Understanding the complexities of feminist perspectives on woman abuse: A commentary on Donald G. Dulton's Rethinking Domestic Violence. *Violence Against Women 13*, 874–884. **376, 381**

Dell, F., Legendre, N., and Ponthieux, S. 2003. *La pauvreté chez les enfants.* Paris: INSEE. **420**

Delsol, C., Margolin, G., and John, R. S. 2003. A typology of maritally violent men and correlates of violence in a community sample. *Journal of Marriage and Family, 65*, 635–651. **377, 385**

DeMaris, A., et al. 2003. Distal and proximal factors in domestic violence: A test of an integrated model. *Journal of Marriage and Family, 65*, 652–667. **382**

DeMino, K. A., Appleby, G., and Fisk, D. 2007. Lesbian mothers with planned families: A comparative study of internalized homophobia and social support. *American Journal of Orthopsychiatry, 77*, 165–173. **224**

Demos, J. 1971. Developmental perspectives on the history of childhood. *The Journal of Interdisciplinary History, 2*, 315–327. **297**

den Boggende, B. 1997. Alone in the province: The Cobourg ladies' seminary of Burlington Ladies' Academy 1842–1851. *Ontario History, 89*, 53–74. **42**

Dench, J. 2006. Ending the nightmare: Speeding up refugee family reunification. *Canadian Issues*, Spring, 53–56. **418**

Denissen, J. J. A., van Aken, M. A. G., and Dubas, J. S. 2009. It takes two to tango: How parents' and adolescents' personalities link to the quality of their mutual relationship. *Developmental Psychopathology, 45*, 928–941. **295, 298**

Derne, S. 2008. *Globalization on the ground: Media and the transformation of culture, class, and gender in India.* London: Sage. **62, 261**

Desrosiers, H., Cardin, J.-F., and Belleau, L. 2012. *L'impact de la séparation des parents sur la santé mentale des jeunes enfants.* Fascicule, 3. Québec: Institut de la statistique du Québec, Novembre. **347, 351, 353, 358, 362, 363**

DeVault, M. L., 1991. *Feeding the family: The social organization of caring and gendered work.* Chicago: University of Chicago Press. **427**

DeVries, L., Baker, D., and Overmyer, D. (Eds.) 2010. *Asian religions in British Columbia*. Vancouver: University of British Columbia Press. **61, 172**

Dew, J. 2008. Debt change and marital satisfaction change in recently married couples. *Family Relations, 57,** 60–71. **265**

Dew, J., and Wilcox, W. B. 2011. If momma ain't happy: Explaining declines in marital satisfaction among new mothers. *Journal of Marriage and Family, 73,* 1–12. **273, 276, 277**

de Wolff, A. 2006. Bargaining for collective responsibility for social reproduction. In K. Bezanson and M. Luxton (Eds.), *Social reproduction: Feminist political economy challenges neo-liberalism* (pp. 93–116). Montreal: McGill-Queen's University Press. **13**

Dickason, O. 2002. *Canada's First Nations: A history of founding peoples from the earliest times.* 3rd Ed. Don Mills, ON: Oxford University Press. **39**

Diener, E., and Biswas-Diener, R. 2002. Will money increase subjective well-being? *Social Indicators Research, 57,* 119–169. **125**

Dion, K. K., and Dion, K. L. 2001. Gender and cultural adaptation in immigrant families. *Journal of Social Issues, 57,* 511–521. **22**

Disney, K. L., et al. 2012. Personality disorder symptoms are differentially related to divorce frequency. *Journal of Family Psychology, 26,* 959–965. **346, 361**

Dittman, M. 2002. *Running on Ritalin.* New York: Bantam Books. **88**

DND (2012). CF Human Resources Management System. Ottawa: DND/Department of National Defence. **77**

Doherty, J., Norton, E., and Veney, J. 2001. China's one-child policy: The economic choices and consequences faced by pregnant women. *Social Science and Medicine, 52,* 745–761. **59**

Doherty, W. J. 2000. Family science and family citizenship: Toward a model of community partnership with families. *Family Relations, 49,* 319–325. **412, 428**

Doherty, W. J., Kouneski, E. F., and Erickson, M. F. 1998. Responsible fathering: An overview and conceptual framework. *Journal of Marriage and Family, 60,* 277–292. **20**

Doherty, W. J., Kouneski, E. F., and Erickson, M. F. 2000. We are all responsible for responsible fathering: A response to Walher and McGraw. *Journal of Marriage and Family, 62,* 570–574. **20**

Dolbin-MacNab, M. L., and Keiley, M. K. 2009. Navigating interdependence: How adolescents raised solely by grandparents experience their family relationships. *Family Relations, 58,*162–175. **311**

Domina, T. 2005. Levelling the home advantage: Assessing the effectiveness of parental involvement in elementary school. Sociology of Education, 78, 233–249. **158**

Dondorp, W. J., De Wert, G. M., and Janssens, P. M. W. 2010. Shared lesbian motherhood: A challenge of established concepts and frameworks. *Human Reproduction, 25,* 812–814. **223**

Donnerstein, E., and Linz, D. 1995. The media. In J. Q. Wilson and J. Petersilia (Eds.), *Crime* (pp. 257–266). San Francisco, CA: Institute for Contemporary Studies. **85**

D'Onofrio, B. M., and Lahey, B. B. 2010. Biosocial influences on the family: A decade review. *Journal of Marriage and Family, 72,* 762–782. **28, 333, 356**

D'Onofrio, B. M., et al. 2007. A genetically informed study of the intergenerational transmission of marital instability. *Journal of Marriage and Family, 69,* 793–809. **363**

Doolittle, R. 2009. Mayhem's ground zero. *Toronto Star.* September 1, A1. **127**

Dorais, M. 2002. *Don't tell: The sexual abuse of boys.* Translated by I. D. Meyer. Montreal: McGill-Queen's University Press. **32, 392, 394, 395**

Dorow, S. K. 2006. *Transnational adoption.* New York: New York University Press. **247**

Doucet, A. 2006. *Do men mother? Fathering, care, and domestic responsibility.* Toronto: University of Toronto Press. **16, 19, 20**

Doucet, A. 2009. Gender equality and gender differences: Parenting, habits, and embodiment (The 2008 Porter Lecture). *The Canadian Review of Sociology, 46,* 103–113. **269**

Douthat, R, 2008. Is pornography adultery? *The Atlantic,*October, 81–85. **215**

Downey, D. B. 2001. Number of siblings and intellectual development: The resource dilution explanation. *American Psychologist, 56,* 497–504. **319**

Downey, D. B., and Condron, D. J. 2004. Playing well with others in kindergarten: The benefit of siblings at home. *Journal of Marriage and Family, 66,* 333–350. **319**

Drapeau, S., et al. 2000. Siblings in family transitions. *Family Relations, 49,* 77–85. **348**

Dreby, J. 2010. *Divided by borders: Mexican migrants and their children.* Berkeley: University of California Press. **19, 76**

Drefahl, S. 2012. Do the married really live longer? The role of cohabitation and socioeconomic status. *Journal of Marriage and the Family, 74,* 462–475. **199**

Drew, L. M., and Silverstein, M. 2007. Grandparents' psychological well-being after loss of contact with their grandchildren. *Journal of Family Psychology, 21,* 372–379. **370**

Drew, L. M., Berg, C., and Wiebe, D. J. 2010. The mediating role of extreme peer orientation in the relationships between adolescent-parent relationship and diabetes management. *Journal of Family Psychology, 24,* 299–306. **302**

Dribe, M., and Stanfors, M. 2009. Does parenthood strengthen a traditional household division of labor? Evidence from Sweden. *Journal of Marriage and Family, 71,* 33–45. **269**

Drolet, M. 2003. Motherhood and paycheques. *Canadian Social Trends, 68,* 19–21. **99**

Drolet, M. 2010. Why has the gender wage gap narrowed? Ottawa: Statistics Canada, *Perspectives on Labour and Income,* December. **98, 99**

Druckerman, P. 2012. *Bringing up bébé.* New York: Penguin Press. **16, 17**

Dua, E. 1999. Beyond diversity: Explaining the ways in which the discourse of race has shaped the institution of the nuclear family. In E. Dua (Ed.), *Scratching the surface: Canadian anti-racist feminist thought* (pp. 237–260). Toronto: Women's Press. **22**

Dua, E. 2011. Exclusion through inclusion: Female Asian migration in the making of Canada as a white settler nation. In M. Gleason et al. (Eds.), *Rethinking Canada: The promise of women's history,* 6th Ed. (pp. 176–193). Toronto: Oxford University Press. **49**

Dubeau, D. 2002. *Portraits of fathers.* Ottawa: The Vanier Institute of the Family. **19**

Duchesne, L. 2007. *Un nouvel enfant d'un autre père.* Québec: Institut de la statistique du Québec. **369**

Duffy, A. 2004. Violence against women. In N. Mandell (Ed.), *Feminist issues: Race, class, and gender*, 4th Ed. (pp. 127–159). Toronto: Prentice Hall. 380, 381, 394

Duffy, A., and Momirov, J. 2005. Family violence: A twenty-first century issue. In N. Mandell and A. Duffy (Eds.), *Canadian families*. Toronto: Thomson Nelson. 375

Duffy, A., and Pupo, N. 2011. Employment in the new economy and the impact on Canadian families. In C. Krull and J. Sempruch (Eds.), *A life in balance? Reopening the family-work debate* (pp. 98–114). Vancouver: University of British Columbia. 96, 98

Dufur, M. J., et al. 2008. Capital and context: Using social capital at home and at school to predict child social adjustment. *Journal of Health and Social Behavior, 49,* 146–161. 157

Dumont, M. 1995. Women of Quebec and the contemporary constitutional issue. In F. P. Gingras (Ed.), *Gender politics in contemporary Canada* (pp. 153–175). Toronto: Oxford University Press. 54

Dunaway, W. A. 2003. *The African-American family in slavery and emancipation*. Cambridge, New York: Maison des sciences de l'homme/Cambridge University Press. 45

Duncan, B. 2013. Economic incentives and foster child adoption. *Demography, 50,* 933–954. 250

Duncan, G. J. 2010. Early-childhood poverty and adult attainment, behavior, and health. *Child Development, 81,* 306–325. 117

Duncan, G. J., and Brooks-Gunn, J. 1997. Income effects across the life span: Integration and interpretation. In G. J. Duncan and J. Brooks-Gunn (Eds.), *Consequences of growing up poor* (pp. 596–610). New York: Russell Sage. 422

Duncan, G. J., et al. 1998. How much does childhood poverty affect the life chances of children? *American Sociological Review, 63,* 406–423. 425

Duncan, L. 2010. Money and membership: Effects of neighbourhood poverty, income inequality and individual income on voluntary association membership in Canada. *Canadian Journal of Sociology, 35,* 573 593. 125

Dunifon, R., and Kowaleski-Jones, L. 2002. Who's in the house? Race differences in cohabitation, single parenthood, and child development. *Child Development, 73,* 1249–1264. 225

Dunn, J. 1994. Temperament, siblings, and the development of relationships. In W. B. Carey and S. C. McDevitt (Eds.), *Prevention and early intervention* (pp. 50–58). New York: Bruner/Mazel. 318, 321, 322

Dunn, J. 1996. Brothers and sisters in middle childhood and early adolescence: Continuity and change in individual differences. In G. H. Brody (Ed.), *Sibling relationships: Their causes and consequences* (pp. 31–46). Norwood, NJ: Ablex. 322

Dunn, J., and McGuire, S. 1994. Young children's nonshared experiences: A summary of studies in Cambridge and Colorado. In E. M. Hetherington, D. Reiss, and R. Plomin (Eds.), *Separate social worlds of siblings* (pp. 111–128). Hillsdale, NJ: Erlbaum. 322, 332

Dunn, J., Plomin, R., and Daniels, D. 1986. Consistency and change in mothers' behavior to two-year-old siblings. *Child Development, 57,* 348–356. 326

Dunn, J., et al. 1994. Adjustment in middle childhood and early adolescence: Links with earlier and contemporary sibling relationships. *Journal of Child Psychology and Psychiatry, 35,* 491–504. 321

Dupéré, V., et al. 2008. Neighborhood poverty and early transition to sexual activity in young adolescents: A developmental ecological approach. *Child Development, 79,* 1463–1476. 131

Dupéré, V., et al. 2012. Neighborhood processes, self-efficacy, and adolescent mental health. *Journal of Health and Social Behavior, 53,* 183–198. 130

Dupré, M. E., and Meadows, S. O. 2007. Disaggregating the effects of marital trajectories on health. *Journal of Family Issues, 27,* 623–652. 356

Dupuis, S. L., and Norris, J. E. 2001. The roles of adult daughters in long-term care facilities: Alternative role manifestations. *Journal of Aging Studies, 15,* 27–54. 308

Durkheim, E. 1895. Revue critique: L'origine du mariage dans l'espèce humaine, d'après Westermarck. *Revue philosophique XL,* 606–623. 3, 4

Durkheim, E. 1897 (1951). *Suicide*. New York: Free Press. 10, 14, 170, 174, 343, 351, 412, 434

Durkheim, E. 1893 (1964). *The division of labor in society*. New York: Free Press. 10, 125, 412

Durkheim, E. 1912 (1965). *The elementary forms of religious life*. New York: Free Press. 170

Du Rocher Schudlich, T. D., Papp, L. M., and Cummings, E. M. 2004. Relations in husbands' and wives' dysphoria to marital conflict resolution strategies. *Journal of Family Psychology, 18,* 171–183. 274

Durrat, J. E., Rose-Krasnor, L., and Broberg, A. G. 2003. Physical punishment and maternal beliefs in Sweden and Canada. *Journal of Comparative Family Studies, 34,* 585–604. 293

Dursun, S., and Sudom, K. 2009. *Impacts of military life on families: Results from the Perstempo survey of Canadian Forces spouses*. Ottawa: Director General Military Personnel Research & Analysis, National Defence, DGMPRA TR 2009-001, November. 78

Dush, C. K., and Taylor, M. 2012. Trajectory of marital conflict across the life course: Predictors and interactions with marital happiness trajectories. *Journal of Family Issues, 33,* 341–368. 257, 268

Dush, C. M. K., Cohan, C. L., and Amato, P. R. 2003. The relationship between cohabitation and marital quality and stability: Change across cohorts? *Journal of Marriage and Family, 65,* 539–549. 352

Dush, C. M. K., Taylor, M. G., and Kroeger, R. A. 2008. Marital happiness and psychological well-being across the life course. *Family Relations, 57,* 211–226. 263, 273

Dutta, S., and Malhotra, A. 2013. A rape map of India. Derived from Indian Crime Statistics. *India Real Time,* January 9. 382

Duvall, E. M. 1957. *Family development*. Philadelphia: Lippincott. 22

Duxbury, L., and Higgins, C. 2012. *Revisiting work-life issues in Canada: The 2012 National Study of balancing work and caregiving in Canada*. Ottawa: Carleton University. 103

Duxbury, L., Higgins, C., and Schroeder, B. 2009. *Balancing paid work and caregiving responsibilities: A closer look at family caregivers in Canada*. Ottawa: Canadian Policy Research Networks. 307, 430

Dzara, K. 2010. Assessing the effect of marital sexuality on marital disruption. *Social Science Research, 39,* 715–724. 213

Eamon, M. K. 2002. Effects of poverty on mathematics and reading achievement of young adolescents. *Journal of Early Adolescence, 22,* 49–74. 117

East, P. L. 1999. The first teenage pregnancy in the family: Does it affect mothers' parenting attitudes, or mother-adolescent communication? *Journal of Marriage and Family, 61,* 306–319. 323

East, P. L., and Jacobson, L. J. 2000. Adolescent childbearing, poverty, and siblings: Taking new directions from the literature. *Family Relations, 49,* 287–292. 25, 227, 332

East, P. L., Felice, M. E., and Morgan, M. C. 1993. Sisters' and girlfriends' sexual and childbearing behavior: Effects on early adolescent girls' sexual outcomes. *Journal of Marriage and the Family, 55,* 953–963. **323**

East, P. L., Reyes, B. T., and Horn, E. J. 2007. Association between adolescent pregnancy and a family history of teenage births. *Perspectives on Sexual and Reproductive Health, 39,* 108–115. **228**

East, P. L., et al. 2012. Adolescents' pregnancy intentions, wantedness, and regret: Cross-lagged relations with mental health and harsh parenting. *Journal of Marriage and Family, 74,* 167–185. **230**

Easterbrook, G. 2003. *The progress paradox: How life gets better while people feel worse.* New York: Random House. **104**

Edin, K., and Kefalas, M. 2005. *Promises I can keep.* Berkeley, CA: University of California Press. **198**

Edin, K., Nelson, T., and Reed, J. M. 2011. Daddy, baby, momma maybe: Low-income urban fathers and the "package deal" of family life. In M. J. Carlson and P. England (Eds.), *Families in an unequal society* (pp. 85–107). Palo Alto, CA: Stanford University Press. **116**

Edmonston, B., Lee, S. M., and Wu, Z. 2010. Fertility intentions in Canada: Change or no change? *Canadian Studies in Population, 37,* 297–337. **232, 233, 427**

Edwards, M. E., et al. 2009. Paradoxes of providing rural social services: The case of homeless youth. *Rural Sociology, 74,* 330–356. **136**

Egeland, B. 2009. Taking stock: Childhood emotional maltreatment and developmental psychopathology. *Child Abuse & Neglect, 33,* 22–26. **388**

Egeland, G., et al. 2010. Food insecurity among Inuit preschoolers: Nunavut Inuit Child Health Survey, 2007–2008. *Canadian Medical Association Journal, 182,* 243–248. **110, 114**

Eggebeen, D. J, and Dew, J. 2009. The role of religion in adolescence for family formation in young adulthood. *Journal of Marriage and Family, 71,* 108–121. **352**

Eggebeen, D. J., and Knoester, C. 2001. Does fatherhood matter for men? *Journal of Marriage and Family, 63,* 381–393. **19**

Eggertsen, L. 2008. Primary factors related to multiple placements for children in out-of-home care. *Child Welfare, 87,* 71–91. **251**

Ehrenreich, B., and Hochschild, A. R. 2002. (Eds.). *Global women* (Introduction, pp. 1–13). New York: John Holt and Company. **102**

Eichler, M. 1997. *Family shifts: Families, policies, and gender equality.* Toronto: Oxford University Press. **22**

Elder, G. H., Jr. 1995. The life course paradigm and social change: Historical and developmental perspectives. In P. Moen, G. H. Elder, Jr., and K. Lüscher (Eds.), *Perspectives on the ecology of human development* (pp. 101–140). Washington, DC: American Psychological Association. **145, 231**

Elder, G. H., Jr. 1998. The life course as developmental theory. *Child Development, 69,* 1–12. **23, 336**

Elder, G. H., Jr., Caspi, A., and Nguyen, T. V. 1994. Resourceful and vulnerable children: Family influences in stressful times. In R. K. Silbereisen and K. Eyferth (Eds.), *Development in context: Integrative perspectives on youth development.* New York: Springer-Verlag. **388**

Elgar, F. J., et al. 2003. Antecedent-consequence conditions in maternal mood and child adjustment problems: A four-year cross-lagged study. *Journal of Clinical Child and Adolescent Psychology, 32,* 362–374. **286**

Elliott, D. S., et al. 2006. *Good kids from bad neighborhoods.* New York: Cambridge University Press. **128**

Elliott, W., Jung, H., and Friedline, T. 2010. Math achievement and children's savings: Implications for child development accounts. *Journal of Family and Economic Issues, 31,* 171–185. **104**

Ellison, C. G., Burdette, A. M., and Hill, T. D. 2009. Blessed assurance: Religion, anxiety, and tranquility among US adults. *Social Science Research, 38,* 656–667. **174**

Ellison, C., Burdette, A. M., and Wilcox, W. B. 2010. The couple that prays together: Race and ethnicity, religion, and relationship quality among working-age adults. *Journal of Marriage and Family, 72,* 963–975. **177**

Emberley, J. V. 2001. The bourgeois family, Aboriginal women, and colonial governance in Canada: A study in feminist historical and cultural materialism. *Signs, 27,* 59–85. **43**

Engeland, J., Lewis, R., and Schellenberg, G. 2005. Evolving housing conditions in metropolitan areas, 1991 to 2001. Statistics Canada, *The Daily,* January 5. **143, 144**

Engelbrecht, W. 2003. *Iroquoia: The development of a Native world.* Syracuse, NY: Syracuse University Press. **37**

Engelhart, K. 2013. True loves. *Maclean's Magazine,* February 4, 46–50. **187**

Engels, F. 1884 (1972). *The origins of the family, private property and the state.* New York: International Publishers. **11, 20, 58**

Engels, J. W. 1995. Marriage in the People's Republic of China: Analysis of a new law. In M. Rank and E. Kain (Eds.), *Diversity and change in families: Patterns, prospects and policies* (pp. 57–67). Englewood Cliffs, NJ: Prentice Hall. **58**

England, P. 2000. Marriage, the costs of children and gender inequality. In L. J. Waite et al. (Eds.), *The ties that bind: Perspectives on marriage and cohabitation* (pp. 320–342). New York: Aldine de Gruyter. **199**

England, P. 2010. The gender revolution. *Gender & Society, 24,* 149–166. **99, 409**

England, P., and McClintock, E. A. 2009. The gendered double standard of aging in US marriage markets. *Population and Developmental Review, 35,* 797–816. **189, 365**

England, P., et al. 2011. Birth control use and early, unintended births: Evidence for a class gradient. In M. J. Carlson and P. England (Eds.), *Social class and changing families in an unequal America* (pp. 21–49). Stanford, CA: Stanford University Press. **112, 225**

Engler, K., et al. 2005. An exploration of sexual behaviour and self-definition in a cohort of men who have sex with men. *Canadian Journal of Human Sexuality, 14,* 87–105. **211**

Entwisle, D. R., Alexander, K. L., and Olson, L. S. 1997. *Children, schools, and inequality.* Boulder, CO: Westview Press. **155, 162, 164**

Erdwins, C. J., et al. 2001. The relationship of women's role strain to social support, role satisfaction, and self-efficacy. *Family Relations, 50,* 230–238. **156**

Erickson, B. H. 1996. Culture, class and connections. *American Journal of Sociology, 102,* 217–251. **15**

Erickson, R. J. 2005. Why emotion work matters: Sex, gender, and the division of household labor. *Journal of Marriage and Family, 67,* 337–351. **274**

Errington, E. J. 1995. *Wives and mothers, schoolmistresses and scullery maids: Working women in Upper Canada, 1790–1840.* Montreal: McGill-Queen's University Press. **42**

Ertl, H. 2000. Parental involvement and children's academic achievement in the National Longitudinal Survey of Children and Youth, 1994–1996. *Education Quarterly Review, 6,* 35–50. **160**

Espelage, D., et al. 1996. Paper presented at the annual meeting of the American Psychological Association, reported in the APA *Monitor,* 41. **400**

Espelage, D., et al. 2012. Willingness to intervene in bullying episodes among middle school students: Individual and peer-group influences. *The Journal of Early Adolescence, 32,* 776–801. **400**

Esteve, A., et al. 2012. The Latin American cohabitation boom. *Population and Development Review, 38,* 55–81. **191**

Etzioni, A. 1994. *The spirit of community: Rights, responsibilities, and the new communitarian agenda.* New York: Crown. **411**

Evans, C., Jordan, A., and Horner, J. 2011. Only two hours? A qualitative study of the challenges parents perceive in restricting child television time. *Journal of Family Issues, 32,* 1223–1244. **72, 88**

Evans, G. W. 2004. The environment of childhood poverty. *American Psychologist, 59,* 77–92. **117**

Evans, P. M. 1996. Single mothers and Ontario's welfare policy: Restructuring the debate. In J. Brodie (Ed.), *Women and public policy.* Toronto: Harcourt Brace. **21**

Evenhouse, E., and Reilly, S. 2012. Multiple-father families and welfare. *Journal of Family Issues, 33,* 966–995. **229**

Eyer, D. E. 1992. *Mother-infant bonding.* New Haven, CT: Yale University Press. **17**

Fabricius, W. V. 2003. Listening to children of divorce: New findings that diverge from Wallerstein, Lewis, and Blakeslee. *Family Relations, 52,* 385–396. **348**

Fagan, J. 2013. Effects of divorce and cohabitation dissolution on preschoolers' literacy. *Journal of Family Issues, 34,* 460–483. **358, 368, 369**

Farnam, K. 1998. The westlings: Swedish pioneers. *Alberta History, 46,* 10–14. **48**

Faulkner, M., and Madden, E. E. 2012. Open adoption and postadoption birth family contact: A comparison of non-relative foster and private adoptions. *Adoption Quarterly, 15,* 35–56. **248**

Feigelman, W. 1997. Adopted adults: Comparisons with persons raised in conventional families. *Marriage and Family Review, 25,* 199–223. **244**

Feinberg, M. E., et al. 2000. Sibling comparison of differential parental treatment in adolescence: Gender, self-esteem, and emotionality as mediators of the parenting adjustment association. *Child Development, 71,* 1611–1628. **328**

Feinberg, M. E., et al. 2005. Differential association of family subsystem negativity on siblings' maladjustment: Using behavior genetic methods to test process theory. *Journal of Family Psychology, 19,* 601–610. **337**

Fenton, W. N. 1998. *The great law and the longhouse: A political history of the Iroquois confederacy.* Norman, OK: University of Oklahoma Press. **37**

Fergusson, D. M., and Horwood, L. J. 1998. Exposure to interparental violence in childhood and psychosocial adjustment in young adulthood. *Child Abuse & Neglect, 22,* 339–357. **385**

Fergusson, D. M., Boden, J. M., and Horwood, L. J. 2007. Abortion among young women and subsequent life outcomes. *Perspectives on Sexual and Reproductive Health, 39,* 6–12. **238**

Ferree, M. M. 2010. Filling the glass: Gender perspectives on families. *Journal of Marriage and Family, 72,* 420–439. **21, 22**

Ferree, M. M., Lorber, J., and Hess., B. B. (Eds.). 1999. *Revisioning gender.* Thousand Oaks, CA: Sage. **16**

Ferrer, A., and Riddell, W. C. 2008. Education, credentials, and immigrant earnings. *Canadian Journal of Economics, 41,* 186–216. **109**

Fincham, F. D. 1998. Child development and marital relations. *Child Development, 69,* 543–574. **278**

Fincham, F. D., and Beach, S. R. H. 2010. Marriage in the new millennium: A decade in review. *Journal of Marriage and Family, 72,* 630–649. **177, 214, 215**

Fincham, F. D., Beach, S. R. H., and Davila, J. 2007a. Longitudinal relations between forgiveness and conflict resolution in marriage. *Journal of Family Psychology, 21,* 542–545. **261, 265, 415**

Fincham, F. D., Stanley, S. M., and Beach, S. R. H. 2007b. Transformative processes in marriage: An analysis of emerging trends. *Journal of Marriage and Family, 69,* 275–292. **256**

Findlay, L. C., and Kohen, D. E. 2011. *Child care for First Nations children living off reserve, Métis children, and Inuit children.* Ottawa: Statistics Canada, Pub. No. 11-008-X. **151**

Findlay, L. C., and Kohen, D. E. 2012. Leave practices of parents after the birth or adoption of young children. *Canadian Social Trends,* Winter, 94. Ottawa: Statistics Canada. **99, 419**

Fineran, S., and Gruber, J. E. 2009. Youth at work: Adolescent employment and sexual harassment. *Child Abuse & Neglect, 33,* 550–559. **393**

Fingard, J. 1992. Race and respectability in Victorian Halifax. *Journal of Imperial and Commonwealth History, 20,* 169–195. **46**

Fingerhut, A. W., and Maisel, N. C. 2010. Relationship formalization and individual and relationship well-being among same-sex couples. *Journal of Social and Personal Relationships, 27,* 956–969. **201**

Fingerman, K., et al. 2009. Giving to the good and the needy: Parental support of grown children. *Journal of Marriage and Family, 71,* 1220–1233. **306, 319**

Fingerman, K. L., et al. 2012a. Helicopter parents and landing pad kids: Intense parental support of grown children. *Journal of Marriage and Family, 74,* 880–896. **304**

Fingerman, K. L., et al. 2012b. Only as happy as the least happy child: Multiple grown children's problems and successes and middle-aged parents' well-being. *The Journals of Gerontology, 67,* 184–194. **306**

Finkelhor, D., and Jones, L. 2006. Why have child maltreatment and child victimization declined? *Journal of Social Issues, 62,* 685–716. **387**

Finkelhor, D., Ormrod, R. K., and Turner, H. A. 2009. Lifetime assessment of poly-victimization in a national sample of children and youth. *Child Abuse & Neglect, 33,* 403–411. **386, 389**

Finkelhor, D., et al. 1990. Sexual abuse in a national survey of adult men and women: Prevalence, characteristics, and risk factors. *Child Abuse & Neglect, 14,* 19–28. **393**

Fischer, D. G. 1993. Parental supervision and delinquency. *Perceptual and Motor Skills, 56,* 635–640. **130**

Fisher, W. A., et al. 2005. Characteristics of women undergoing repeat induced abortion. *Canadian Medical Association Journal, 172,* 637–641. **237**

Fiske, J., and Johnny, R. 2003. The Lake Babini First Nation family: Yesterday and today. In M. Lynn (Ed.), *Voices: Essays on Canadian families,* 2nd Ed. (pp. 181–198). Scarborough, ON: Thomson Nelson. 43, 44, 52

Fisman, R., et al. 2006. Gender differences in mate selection: Evidence from a speed dating experiment. *The Quarterly Journal of Economics, 121,* 673–697. 190

Fitzgerald, R. 2009. *Self-reported violent delinquency and the influence of school, neighbourhood and student characteristics.* Statistics Canada. Publication 85-561-M. no. 17. September 15. 165, 288, 302

Fitzgerald, R. 2010. *Parenting, school contexts and violent delinquency.* Ottawa, Statistics Canada, Canadian Centre for Justice Statistics, Catalogue no. 85-561-M, no. 19, January. 288

Fitzgerald, R., Wisener, M., and Savoie, J. 2004. Neighbourhood characteristics and the distribution of crime in Winnipeg. *Crime and Justice Research Paper Series.* Statistics Canada Catalogue no. 85-561-MIE. no. 4. Ottawa. 126

Fletcher, A. C., Steinberg, L., and Williams-Wheeler, M. 2004. Parental influence on adolescent problem behavior: Revisiting Stattin and Kerr. *Child Development, 75,* 781–796. 289

Fletcher, J. M. 2007. Social multipliers in sexual initiation decisions among U.S. high school students. *Demography, 44,* 373–388. 423

Fleury, E., and Fernet, M. 2012. An exploratory study of gang-affiliated young men's perceptions and experiences of sexuality and gender relations. *The Canadian Journal of Human Sexuality, 21,* 1–15. 127, 209

Fleury, R. E., Sullivan, C. M., and Bybee, D. I. 2000. When ending the relationship does not end the violence. *Violence Against Women, 6,* 1363–1383. 356

Fluke, J. D., et al. 2010. Placement decisions and disparities among aboriginal groups: An application of the decision making ecology through multi-level analysis. *Child Abuse & Neglect, 34,* 57–69. 250

Folbre, N. 1994. *Who pays for the kids?* New York: Routledge. 252

Foley, K. 2012. Can neighbourhoods change the decisions of youth on the margins of university participation? *Canadian Journal of Economics, 45,* 167–188. 116

Follingstad, D. R., and Edmundson, M. 2010. Is psychological abuse reciprocal in intimate relationships? Data from a national sample of American adults. *Journal of Family Violence, 25,* 495–508. 378

Fomby, P., and Cherlin, A. J. 2007. Family instability and child well-being. *American Sociological Review, 72,* 181–204. 359, 372

Fong, E., and Cao, X. 2009. Effects of foreign education on immigrant earnings. *Canadian Studies in Population, 36,* 87–110. 109

Fong, V. A. 2002. China's one-child policy and the empowerment of urban daughters. *American Anthropologist, 104,* 1098–1109. 59

Food Banks Canada. 2009. *Hunger Count 2009.* 105, 110, 113, 141

Forbes, S. 2003. "Why have just one?" An evaluation of the anti-polygamy laws under the establishment clause. *Houston Law Review, 39,* 1517–1547. 9

Forehand, R., Armistead, L., and David, C. 1997. Is adolescent adjustment following parental divorce a function of predivorce adjustment? *Journal of Abnormal Child Psychology, 25,* 157–164. 362

Forehand, R., et al. 2002. African American childrens's adjustment: The roles of maternal and teacher depressive symptoms. *Journal of Marriage and Family, 64,* 1012–1023. 157

Forgatch, M. S., Patterson, G. R., and Roy, J. A. 1996. Stress, parenting, and adolescent psychopathology in nondivorced and stepfamilies: A within-family perspective. In E. M. Hetherington and

E. A. Blachman (Eds.), *Stress, coping, and resilience in children and families* (pp. 39–66). Mahwah, NJ: Erlbaum. 361

Fombe, P., and Cherlin, A. J. 2007. Family instability and child well-being. *American Sociological Review, 72,* 181–204. 359

Fortin, P., Godbout, L., and St-Cerny, S. 2011. *Economic consequences of Quebec's educational childcare policy.* Toronto: Early Years Economic Forum, June 22. 156

Fosco, G. M., and Grych, J. H. 2010. Adolescent triangulation into parental conflicts: Longitudinal implications for appraisals and adolescent-parent relations. *Journal of Marriage and Family, 72,* 254–266. 277

Foshee, V. A., et al. 2005. The association between family violence and adolescent dating violence onset. *Journal of Early Adolescence, 25,* 317–344. 293, 377

Fournier, S., and Crey, E. 1997. *Stolen from our embrace: The abduction of First Nations children and the restoration of Aboriginal communities.* Vancouver/Toronto: Douglas and McIntyre. 52

Fouts, H. N., Hewlett, B. S., and Lamb, M. E. 2005. Parent-offspring weaning conflicts among the Bofi farmers and foragers of Central Africa. *Current Anthropology, 46,* 29–50. 17, 18, 294

Fox, B. J. 2001. Reproducing difference: Changes in the lives of partners becoming parents. In B. J. Fox (Ed.), *Family patterns, gender relations,* 2nd Ed. (pp. 287–302). Toronto: Oxford University Press. 16

Fox, B. 2006. Motherhood as a class act: The many ways in which 'intensive mothering' is entangled with social class. In K. Bezanson and M. Luxton (Eds.), *Social reproduction: Feminist political economy challenges neo-liberalism* (pp. 231–262). Montreal: McGill-Queen's University Press. 287

Fram, M., et al. 2012. Early care and prekindergarten care as influences on school readiness. *Journal of Family Issues, 33,* 478–505. 153

Frasch, K. M., Brooks, D., and Barth, R. P. 2000. Openness and contact in foster care adoptions: An eight-year follow-up. *Family Relations, 49,* 435–446. 248

Fraser, C., and McDonald, S. 2009. *Identifying the issues: Victim services' experiences working with victims of Fetal Alcohol Spectrum Disorder.* Ottawa: Departement of Justice, October 10. 389

Freeman, T., et al. 2009. Gamete donation: Parents' experiences of searching for their child's donor siblings and donor. *Human Reproduction, 24,* 505–516. 240

Frempong, G., and Willms, J. D. 2002. Can school quality compensate for socioeconomic disadvantage? In J. D. Willms (Ed.), *Vulnerable children* (pp. 277–304). Edmonton: University of Alberta Press. 161, 411

Frenette, M., and Picot, G. 2003. *Life after welfare: The economic wellbeing of welfare leavers in Canada during the 1990s.* Statistics Canada, Catalogue no. 11F0019, no. 192. 111, 351, 355

Frenette, M., Green, D. A., and Milligan, K. 2007. The tale of tails: Canadian income inequality in the 1980s and 1990s. *Canadian Journal of Economics, 40,* 734–764. 96

Frenette, M., Picot, G., and Sceviour, R. 2004. *How long do people live in low-income neighbourhoods? Evidence for Toronto, Montreal and Vancouver.* Statistics Canada, Catalogue no. 11F001MIE, no. 216. 125

Frideres, J. S. 2000. Revelation and revolution: Fault lines in Aboriginal-White relations. In M. A. Kalbach and W. E. Kalbach (Eds.), *Perspectives on Ethnicity in Canada* (pp. 207–237). Toronto: Harcourt Brace. 51

Frideres, J. S. 2011. First Nations in the twenty-first century. Toronto: Oxford University Press. **44, 51, 52, 110, 113**

Friendly, M. 2000. Child care as a social policy issue. In L. Prochner and N. Howe (Eds.), *Early childhood education and care in Canada* (pp. 252–272). Vancouver: University of British Columbia Press. **152**

Friendly, M., Doherty, G., and Beach, J. 2006. *Quality by design: What do we know about quality in early learning and childcare, and what do we think? A literature review.* University of Toronto: Childcare Resource and Research Unit. **425**

Friendly, M., Halfon, S., Beach, J. & Forer, B. (2013). Early childhood education and care in Canada 2013. Toronto, ON: Childcare Resource and Research Unit. Retrieved from "http://childcarecanada.org/publications/ecec-canada/13/08/early-childhood-education-and-care-canada-2012". 151

Friesen, J. 2011. A quiet rise to the top of immigration rolls. *The Globe and Mail*, March 19, A12. **64**

Friesen, J. W. 1999. *First Nations of the Plains: Creative, adaptable, enduring.* Calgary, AB: Detselig Enterprises. **37**

Frisco, M. L., and Williams, K. 2004. Perceived housework equity, marital happiness, and divorce in dual-earner households. *Journal of Family Issues, 24,* 51–73. **272**

Froese, E. 2012. When dad is also the boss: Challenges in farm family business continuity. Ottawa: Vanier Institute of the Family, *Transition,* Spring. **137**

Fry, R., and Cohn, D. 2010. *Women, men and the new economics of marriage.* Pew Research Center, January 10. **415**

Frye, N. E., and Karney, B. R. 2006. The context of aggressive behavior in marriage: A longitudinal study of newlyweds. *Journal of Family Psychology, 20,* 12–20. **379**

FSAT (Family Service Association of Toronto and Community Social Planning Council of Toronto). 2004. *Falling fortunes: A report on the status of young families in Toronto.* Toronto. **71, 96, 106**

Fuchs, V. R. 1990. Are Americans underinvesting in children? In D. Blankenhorn et al. (Eds.), *Rebuilding the nest: A new commitment to the American family* (pp. 53–72). Milwaukee, WI: Family Service America. **103**

Fulkerson, J. A., et al. 2010. Longitudinal associations between family dinner and adolescent perceptions of parent-child communication among racially diverse urban youth. *Journal of Family Psychology, 24,* 261–270. **298**

Fuller, C. J., and Narasimhan, H. 2008. Companionate marriage in India: The changing marriage system in a middle-class Brahman subcaste. *Journal of the Royal Anthropological Institute, 14,* 736–754. **61, 261**

Funk, J. B., Buchman, D. B., and Germann, J. N. 2000. Preference for violent electronic games, self-concept, and gender differences in young children. *American Journal of Orthopsychiatry, 70,* 233–241. **87**

Funk, L. M., and Kobayashi, K. M. 2009. "Choice" in filial care work: Moving beyond a dichotomy. *The Canadian Review of Sociology, 46,* 235–252. **431**

Furman, W., and Lanthier, R. P. 1996. Personality and sibling relationships. In G. H. Brody (Ed.), *Sibling relationships: Their causes and consequences* (pp. 127–172). Norwood, NJ: Ablex. **321**

Furstenberg, F. F., Jr., and Cherlin, A. J. 1991. *Divided families: What happens to children when parents part?* Cambridge, MA: Harvard University Press. **372**

Furstenberg, F. F., Jr., et al. 1994. How families manage risk and opportunity in dangerous neighborhoods. In W. J. Wilson (Ed.), *Sociology and the public agenda* (pp. 231–258). Newbury Park, CA: Sage. **131**

Gagné, M.-A., Drapeau, S., and Hénault, R. 2005. L'aliénation parentale: Un bilan des connaissances et des controverses, *Canadian Psychology, 46,* 73–87. **362**

Gagnon, A. 1994. Our parents did not raise us to be independent: The work and schooling of young Franco-Albertan women, 1890–1940. *Prairie Forum, 19,* 169–188. **48**

Galabuzi, G.-E. 2006. *Canada's economic apartheid.* Toronto: Canadian Scholars' Press. **11, 12, 109**

Galabuzi, G.-E. 2009. Social exclusion. In D. Raphael (Ed.), *Social determinants of health: Canadian perspectives,* 2nd Ed. (pp. 252–268). Toronto: Canadian Scholars' Press. **108**

Gallagher, E. 2004a. Parents victimised by their children. *Australian & New Zealand Journal of Family Therapy, 25,* 1–12. **401, 402**

Gallagher, E. 2004b. Youth who victimize their parents. *Australia & New Zealand Journal of Family Therapy, 25,* 94–105. **401**

Gallagher, M. 2010. *Why do parents have rights? The problem of kinship in liberal thought.* In M. B. Goodwin (Ed.), Baby markets (pp. 164–176). New York: Cambridge University Press. **251, 430**

Galloway, G. 2004. Black population growth dramatic, report shows. *Globe and Mail.* March 10, A11. **56, 57**

Games, A. 1999. *Migration and the origins of the English Atlantic world.* Cambridge, MA: Harvard University Press. **41**

Ganiban, J. M., et al. 2009. Understanding the role of personality in explaining associations between marital quality and parenting. *Journal of Family Psychology, 23,* 646–660. **280, 295**

Ganong, L., and Coleman, M. 1994. *Remarried family relationships.* Newbury Park, CA: Sage. **266**

Gans, D., Silverstein, M., and Loweinstein, A. 2009. Do religious children care more and provide more care for older parents? A study of filial norms and behaviors across five nations. *Journal of Comparative Family Studies, 40,* 187–205. **175**

Garbarino, J. 1995. *Raising children in a socially toxic environment.* San Francisco: Jossey-Bass. **378, 411**

Garbarino, J. 1999. *Lost boys: Why our sons turn violent and how we can save them.* New York: Free Press. **22, 86**

Garbarino, J. 2006. *See Jane hit.* New York: Penguin Press. **82, 87, 90**

Garbarino, J., and Sherman, D. 1980. High-risk neighborhoods and high-risk families: The human ecology of child maltreatment. *Child Development, 51,* 188–198. **388**

Garbarino, J., Kostelny, K., and Dubrow, N. 1991. *No place to be a child: Growing up in a war zone.* Lexington, MA: Lexington Books. **392**

Garcia, L. T. 2006. Perceptions of sexual experience and preferences for dating and marriage. *The Canadian Journal of Human Sexuality, 15,* 85–95. **207**

Gardner, R. A. 1987. *The parental alienation syndrome and the difference between false and genuine child sex abuse.* Cresskill, NJ: Creative Therapeutics. **362**

Garriguet, D. 2005. Early sexual intercourse. Statistics Canada, *Health Reports, 16,* May. **208**

Gartrell, N., et al. 2005. The National Lesbian Family Study. 4 Interviews with the 10-year-old children. *American Journal of Orthopsychiatry, 75,* 518–524. **224, 225, 244**

Gaspar, D. R., and Hine, D. C. (Eds.). 1999. *More than chattel: Black women and slavery in the Americas.* Bloomington: Indiana University Press. **45**

Gates, G. J. 2011. Family formation and raising children among same-sex couples. *Family Focus, Winter*, F2–F4. **223**

Gaudet, J., and Devault, A. 2006. Quelles sont les conditions associées à une bonne adaptation au rôle paternal post-rupture?: Parcours paternels et points de vues des pères. *Revue Canadienne de Santé Mentale, 25*, 17–32. **349**

Gaudin, S. 2011. Son preference in Indian families: Absolute versus relative wealth effects. *Demography, 48*, 343–370. **238**

Gauthier, A. H., Smeeding, T. M., and Furstenberg, F. F., Jr. 2004. Are parents investing less time in children? Trends in selected industrialized countries. *Population and Development Review, 30*, 647–672. **103**

Gazso, A. 2010. Mothers' maintenance of families through market and family care relations. In N. Mandell (Ed.), *Feminist Issues*, 5th Ed. (pp. 219–246). Toronto: Pearson Canada. **19, 70**

Gazso, A. 2012. Moral codes of mothering and the introduction of welfare-to-work in Ontario. *Canadian Review of Sociology, 49*, 26–49. **19, 225, 226, 409**

Ge, X., et al. 2008. Bridging the divide: Openness in adoption of postadoption psychosocial adjustment among birth and adoptive parents. *Journal of Family Psychology, 22*, 529–540. **248**

Gee, E. M. 2000. Voodoo demography, population aging, and social policy. In E. M. Gee and G. M. Gutman (Eds.), *The overselling of population aging* (pp. 1–25). Toronto: Oxford University Press. **306**

Gee, E. M., Mitchell, B. A., and Wister, A. V. 2003. Home leaving trajectories in Canada: Exploring cultural and gendered dimensions. *Canadian Studies in Population, 30*, 245–270. **304**

Gelles, R. J. 1997. *Intimate violence in families*, 3rd Ed. Thousand Oaks, CA: Sage. **402**

Gennetian, L. A., and Morris, P. A. 2003. The effects of time limits and make-work-pay strategies on the well-being of children: Experimental evidence from two welfare reform programs. *Children and Youth Services Review, 25*, 7–54. **422**

Gennetian, L. A., Lopoo, L. M., and London, A. S. 2008. Maternal work hours and adolescents' school outcomes among low-income families in four urban countries. *Demography, 45*, 31–53. **118**

Gentile, D. A., et al. 2009. The effects of prosocial video games on prosocial behaviors: International evidence from correlational, longitudinal, and experimental studies. *Personality and Social Psychology Bulletin, 35*, 752–763. **87**

Gentleman, J. F., and Park, E. 1997. Divorce in the 1990s. Statistics Canada, *Health Reports, 9*, 53–58. **346**

Gergen, K. J., et al. 1996. Psychological science in cultural context. *American Psychologist, 51*, 496–503. **16**

Gershoff, E. T., et al. 2012. Longitudinal links between spanking and children's externalyzing behaviors in a national sample of white, black, Hispanic, and Asian American families. *Child Development, 83*, 838–843. **293**

Gewirtz, A. H., et al. 2009. Parenting, parental mental health, and child functioning in families residing in supportive housing. *American Journal of Orthopsychiatry, 79*, 336–347. **134**

Ghandour, B., and Perry-Jenkins, M. 2008. Differences between European and Lebanese Americans' values about marriage. *Journal of Human Subjectivity, 6*, 49–76. **276**

Giles, W., and Hyndman, J. (Eds.) 2004. *Sites of violence: Gender and conflict zones*. Berkeley, CA: University of California Press. **22**

Giles-Sims, J. 1997. Current knowledge about child abuse in stepfamilies. *Marriage and Family Review, 26*, 215–230. **369**

Gilgun, J. F. 2013. Qualitative family research: Enduring themes and contemporary variation. In G. W. Peterson and K. R. Bush (Eds.), *Handbook of marriage and the family* (pp. 91–119). Thousand Oaks, CA: Sage. **31**

Gillis, J. 1996. *A world of their own making: Myth, ritual and the quest for family values*. New York: Basic Books. **25**

Gionet, L. 2009. *First Nations people: Selected findings of the 2006 Census*. Ottawa: Statistics Canada, July 27. **144, 219, 311**

Gilmour, H. 2012. Social participation and the health and well-being of Canadian seniors. Ottawa: Statistics Canada, Health Reports, 23, December. **113, 420, 430**

Giordano, P. C., et al. 1999. Delinquency, indentity, and women's involvement in relationship violence. *Criminology, 37*, 17–37. **381**

Girard, C. 2008. *Le bilan démographique du Québec, 2008*. Québec: Institut de la statistique du Québec. **55, 190, 197, 219, 344**

Glantz, M. J., et al. 2009. Gender disparity in the rate of partner abandonment in patients with serious medical illness. *Cancer, 115*, 5237–5242. **256**

Gleason, M., Myers, T., and Perry, A. 2011. *Rethinking Canada: The promise of women's history*, 6th Ed. Toronto: Oxford University Press. **45**

Glenn, N. D., 1991. The recent trends in marital success in the United States. *Journal of Marriage and Family, 5*, 261–270. **266**

Glick, P. C. 1947. The family cycle. *American Sociological Review, 12*, 164–174. **22**

Goffman, E. 1959. *The presentation of self in everyday life*. New York: Doubleday. **25**

Goldberg, A. F. 2007. (How) Does it make a difference? Perspectives of adults with lesbian, gay, and bisexual parents. *American Journal of Orthopsychiatry, 77*, 550–562. **225**

Goldberg, A. E., et al. 2008. Perceptions of children's parental preferences in lesbian two-mother households. *Journal of Marriage and Family, 70*, 419–434. **224**

Goldberg, A. E. 2010. *Lesbian and gay parents and their children*. Washington, D.C.: American Psychological Association. **185, 201, 224, 225, 239, 275, 276**

Goldberg, A. E., et al. 2011. Lesbian, gay and heterosexual couples in open adoption arrangements: A qualitative study. *Journal of Marriage and Family, 2011*, 502–518. **248**

Goldberg, A. E., et al. 2012. The division of labor in lesbian, gay, and heterosexual new adoptive parents. *Journal of Marriage and Family, 74*, 812–828. **270**

Goldberg, A. E., Smith, J. Z., and Kashy, D. A. 2010. Preadoptive factors predicting lesbian, gay, and heterosexual couples' relationship quality across the transition to adoptive parenthood. *Journal of Family Psychology, 24*, 221–232. **185**

Goldscheider, F., and Sassler, S. 2006. Creating stepfamilies: Integrating children into the study of union formation. *Journal of Marriage and Family, 68*, 275–291. **348**

Goldstein, A. L., et al. 2011. *Youth on the street and youth involved with child welfare*. University of Toronto. **132, 133**

Goldstein, J. R., and Kenney, C. T. 2001. Marriage delayed or marriage forgone? New cohort forecasts of first marriage for U.S. women. *American Sociological Review, 66*, 506–519. **414**

Golombok, S., and Badger, S. 2010. Children raised in mother-headed families from infancy: A follow-up of children of lesbian and single heterosexual mothers, at early adulthood. *Human Reproduction, 25,* 150–157. **224, 226**

Golombok, S., et al. 2002. Families with children conceived by donor insemination: A follow-up at age twelve. *Child Development, 73,* 952–968. **239, 240**

Golombok, S., et al. 2006. Non-genetic and non-gestational parenthood: Consequences for parent-child relationship and the psychological well-being of mothers, fathers, and children at age 3. *Human Reproduction, 21,* 1918–1924. **241**

Golombok, S., et al. 2007. Parenting and the psychological development of a representative sample of triplets conceived by assisted reproduction. *Human Reproduction, 25,* 150–157. **241, 320**

Gorder, C. 1996. *Home schools: An alternative.* Mesa, AZ: Blue Bird. **170**

Gordon, J., et al. 2012. Balancing caregiving and work: Role conflict and role strain dynamics. *Journal of Family Issues, 33,* 662–689. **307**

Gore, A. 2006. *An inconvenient truth.* New York: Rodale Books. **74**

Gorman, T. 1997. Canadian television in transition. *Canadian Social Trends, 44,* 19–23. **80**

Gosa, T. L., and Alexander, K. L. 2007. Family (dis)advantage and the educational prospects of better off African American youth: How race still matters. *Teachers College Record, 109,* 285–321. **57**

Gottfredson, G. D., et al. 2005. School climate predictors of school disorder: Results from a national study of delinquency prevention in schools. *Journal of Research in Crime and Delinquency, 42,* 412–444. **165**

Goulet, L., Dressyman-Lavallee, M., and McCleod, Y. 2001. Early childhood education for Aboriginal children: Opening petals. In K. P. Binda and S. Calliou (Eds.), *Aboriginal education in Canada* (pp. 137–153). Mississsauga: Canadian Educators' Press. **154, 158**

Graham, A. M., Kim, H. K., and Fisher, P. A. 2012. Partner aggression in high-risk families from birth to age 3 years: Associations with harsh parenting and child maladjustment. *Journal of Family Psychology, 26,* 105–114. **294, 384**

Grant, A. 2004. *Finding my talk: How fourteen Native women reclaimed their lives after residential school.* Calgary: Fifth House Ltd. **51**

Gray, M. R., and Steinberg, L. 1999. Unpacking authoritative parenting: Reassessing a multidimensional construct. *Journal of Marriage and Family, 61,* 574–587. **288**

Green, A. I. 2010 Queer unions: Same-sex spouses marrying tradition and innovation. *Canadian Journal of Sociology, 35,* 399–436. **201, 270**

Green, K., et al. 2012. Marriage trajectories and health risk behaviors throughout adulthood among urban African Americans. *Journal of Family Issues, 33,* 1598–1618. **198**

Green, R. K., and White, M. J. 1997. Measuring the benefits of homeowning: Effects on children. *Journal of Urban Economics, 41,* 441–461. **423**

Greenberg, B. S., and Busselle, R. W. 1996. Soap operas and sexual activity: A decade later. *Journal of Communication, 46,* 153–160. **88**

Greenberg, J. S., Seltzer, M. M., and Greenlay, J. R. 1993. Aging parents of adults with disabilities: The gratifications and frustrations of later-life caregiving. *The Gerontologist, 33,* 542–549. **403**

Greenberg, L., and Normandiu, C. 2011. Disparities in life expectancy at birth. Ottawa: Statistics Canada, *The Daily,* April 24. **123**

Greitemeyer, T. 2009. Effects of songs with prosocial lyrics on prosocial thoughts, affect, and behavior. *Journal of Experimental Social Psychology, 45,* 186–190. **87**

Greitemeyer, T., and Osswald, S. 2010. Effects of prosocial video games on prosocial behaviour. *Journal of Personality and Social Psychology, 98,* 211–221. **87**

Grieve, J., and Hogarth, B. 2009. Opportunity to transform early learning in Ontario. *Toronto Star.* June 16, A19. **425**

Grignon, M. et al. 2012. *L'âge du patient influence-t-il le choix du traitement d'un infarctus du myocarde aigu?* In S. Rheault and J. Poirier (Eds.), Le vieillissement démographique (pp. 207–224). Québec: Institut de la statistique du Québec. **414**

Grona, M. 2009. Canada Survey of Giving, Volunteering and Participating. Statistics Canada, *The Daily,* June 8. **173**

Grotevant, H. D., et al. 2008. Many faces of openness in adoption: Perspectives of adopted adolescents and their parents. *Adoption Quarterly, 10,* 79–101. **248**

GSS (General Social Survey). 2000. Family violence. Statistics Canada, *The Daily.* **356**

Guèvremont, A., and Kohen, D. 2013. The physical and mental health of Inuit children of teenage mothers. Ottawa: Statistics Canada, *Health Reports,* November, 23. **230**

Guilmoto, C. Z. 2009. The sex ratio transition in Asia. *Population and Development Review, 35,* 519–549. **8, 59, 63**

Guo, G., Roettger, M. E., and Cai, T. 2008. The integration of genetic propensities into social-control models of delinquency and violence among male youths. *American Sociological Review, 73,* 543–568. **333, 337, 363**

Gusarova, I., Fraser, V., and Alderson, K. 2012. A quantitative study of "friends with benefits" relationships. *The Canadian Journal of Human Sexuality, 21,* 41–59. **183**

Guzzo, K. B. 2009a. Marital intentions and the stability of first cohabitations. *Journal of Family Issues, 30,* 179–205. **193**

Guzzo, K. B. 2009b. Maternal relationships and nonresidential father visitation of children born outside of marriage. *Journal of Marriage and Family, 71,* 632–649. **368**

Guzzo, K. B., and Furstenberg, F. F., Jr. 2007a. Multipartnered fertility among American men. *Demography, 44,* 583–601. **111, 112, 228, 229**

Guzzo, K. B., and Furstenberg, F. F., Jr. 2007b. Multipartnered fertility among young women with a nonmarital first birth: Prevalence and risk factors. *Perspectives on Sexual and Reproductive Health, 39,* 29–38. **227**

Habermas, J. 1987. *The theory of communicative action: Lifeworld and system: A critique of functionalist reason* (vol. 2, translated by T. McCarthy). Boston: Beacon Press. **89, 404-405, 412**

Hall, A. 2007. Organic farming, gender, and the labor process. *Rural Sociology, 72,* 289–317. **138**

Halpern-Meekin, S., and Tach, L. 2008. Heterogeneity in two-parent families and adolescent well-being. *Journal of Marriage and Family, 70,* 435–451. **370, 410**

Halpern-Meekin, S., et al. 2013. Relationship churning, physical violence, and verbal abuse in young adult relationships. *Journal of Marriage and Family, 75,* 2–12. **183, 353, 376**

Hamby, S. L., and Sugarman, D. B. 1999. Acts of psychological aggression against a partner and their relations to physical assault and gender. *Journal of Marriage and Family, 61,* 959–970. **378**

Hamill, S. 2012. Caring for grandparents with Alzheimer's disease: Help from the "forgotten" generation. *Journal of Family Issues, 33,* 1195–1217. **308**

Hamilton, B. E., et al. 2012. Births: Preliminary data for 2011. *National Vital Statistics Reports,* October 3. U.S. Department of Health and Human Services. **226, 234**

Hamilton, L., and Armstrong, E. A. 2009. Gendered sexuality in young adulthood. *Gender & Society, 23,* 589–616. **183**

Hamilton, L., Cheng, S., and Powell, S. 2007. Adoptive parents, adaptive parents: Evaluating the importance of biological ties for parental involvement. *American Sociological Review, 72,* 95–116. **246**

Hamilton, R. 1988. *Feudal society and colonization: The historiography of New France.* Gananoque, ON: Langdale Press. **39**

Hamilton, R. 2005. *Gendering the vertical mosaic: Feminist perspectives on Canadian society,* 2nd Ed. Toronto: Pearson Prentice Hall. **20**

Hamilton Spectator. 2011. Mothers too soon. November 19. **111**

Hammer, K. 2010. Lawsuits question schools' responses to bullying. *The Globe and Mail.* February 17, A7. **111, 227, 399**

Hamplova, D., and Le Bourdais, C. 2008. Educational homogamy of married and unmarried couples in English and French Canada. *Canadian Journal of Sociology, 33,* 845–872. **189**

Hampton, M. R., McWatters, R., and Jeffery, B. 2005. Influence of teens' perceptions of parental disapproval and peer behaviour on their initiation of sexual intercourse. *The Canadian Journal of Human Sexuality, 14,* 105–122. **209**

Hansen, K. V. 2005. *Not-so-nuclear families: Class, gender, and networks of care.* New Brunswick, NJ: Rutgers University Press. **14**

Hansen, M., et al. 2005. Assisted reproductive technologies and the risk of birth defects—a systematic review. *Human Reproduction, 20,* 328–338. **240**

Hansen, T., Mourn, T., and Shapiro, T. 2007. Relational and individual well-being among cohabitors and married individuals in midlife. *Journal of Family Issues, 28,* 910–933. **197**

Hanson, T. L. 1999. Does parental conflict explain why divorce is negatively associated with child welfare? *Social Forces, 77,* 1283–1315. **362**

Harbin, H., and Maddin, D. 1979. Battered parents: A new syndrome. *American Journal of Psychiatry, 136,* 1288–1291. **401**

Harbison, J. 1999. Models of intervention for elder abuse and neglect: A Canadian perspective on ageism, participation, and empowerment. *Journal of Elder Abuse & Neglect, 10,* 1–17. **403**

Harbison, J., et al. 2012. Understanding 'elder abuse and neglect': A critique of assumptions underpinning responses to the mistreatment and neglect of older people. *Journal of Elder Abuse & Neglect, 24,* 88–103. **16, 402, 403, 430**

Harden, B. J. 2004. Safety and stability for foster children: A developmental perspective. *The Future of children, 14,* 31–47. **250**

Harden, K. P., et al. 2007. Marital conflict and conduct problems in children of twins. *Child Development, 78,* 1–18. **265, 281**

Hardie, J. H., and Lucas, A. 2010. Economic factors and relationship quality among young couples: Comparing cohabitation and marriage. *Journal of Marriage and Family, 72,* 1141–1154. **265**

Harding, D. J. 2009. Violence, older peers, and the socialization of adolescent boys in disadvantaged neighborhoods. *American Sociological Review, 74,* 445–464. **130**

Harding, D. J. 2010. Collateral consequences of violence in disadvantaged neighborhoods. *Social Forces, 88,* 757–785. **128**

Hardy, M., et al. 2010. Personal experience and perceived acceptability of sibling aggression. *Journal of Family Violence, 25,* 65–71. **397**

Hareven, T. K. 1994a. Continuity and change in American family life. In A. S. Skolnick and J. H. Skolnick (Eds.), *Family in transition,* 8th Ed. (pp. 40–46). New York: HarperCollins. **69, 300**

Hareven, T. K. 1994b. Aging and generational relations: A historical and life course perspective. *Annual Review of Sociology, 20,* 437–461. **300, 305**

Hareven, T. K. 2000. *Families, history, and social change: Life-course and cross-cultural perspectives.* Boulder, CO: Westview Press. **16, 23, 43, 75, 98, 150, 231, 285, 303, 305, 313, 332, 336, 342**

Harkness, S., and Super, C. M. 2002. Culture and parenting. In M. H. Bornstein (Ed.), *Handbook of parenting,* 2nd Ed, (pp. 253–280). Mahwah, NJ: Erlbaum. **18, 428**

Harknett, K. 2008. Mate availability and unmarried parent relationships. *Demography, 45,* 555–571. **57, 352**

Harknett, K., and Knab, J. 2007. More kin, less support: Multipartnered fertility and perceived support among mothers. *Journal of Marriage and Family, 69,* 237–253. **229**

Harlaar, N., et al. 2008. Retrospective reports of parental physical affection and parenting style: A study of Finnish twins. *Journal of Family Psychology, 22,* 605–613. **335**

Harper, S., and Martin, A. 2013. Transnational migratory labor and Filipino fathers: How families are affected when men work abroad. *Journal of Family Issues, 34,* 270–290. **281, 295**

Harrington, D., et al. 1998. Child neglect: Relation to child temperament and family context. *American Journal of Orthopsychiatry, 68,* 108–116. **392**

Harrison, D. 2006. The role of military culture in military organizations responses to woman abuse in military families. *The Sociological Review, 54,* 546–574. **78**

Harrison, D., and Laliberté, L. 1994. *No life like it: Military wives in Canada.* Toronto: James Lorimer. **78**

Harrison, T. W., and Friesen, J. W. 2004. *Canadian society in the twenty-first century: A historical sociological approach.* Toronto: Pearson-Prentice Hall. **43, 51, 54, 110**

Hartley, S. L., et al. 2012. Marital satisfaction and life circumstances of grown children with autism across 7 years. *Journal of Family Psychology, 26,* 688–697. **277**

Hartwick, C., Desmarais, S., and Hennig, K. 2007. Characteristics of male and female victims of sexual coercion. *The Canadian Journal of Human Sexuality, 16,* 31–45. **377**

Hassouneh-Phillips, D. 2001. Polygamy and wife abuse: A qualitative study of Muslim women in America. *Health Care for Women International, 22,* 735–748. **10**

Hatch, L. R., and Bulcroft, K. 2004. Does long-term marriage bring less frequent disagreements? Five explanatory frameworks. *Journal of Family Issues, 25,* 465–495. **265**

Hawkins, D. N., Amato, P. R., and King, V. 2007. Nonresident father involvement and adolescent well-being: Father effects or child effects? *American Sociological Review, 72,* 990–1010. **349**

Hawkins, D. N., and Booth, A. 2005. Unhappily ever after: Effects of long-term, low-quality marriages on well-being. *Social Forces, 84,* 451–470. **263**

Haworth, C. M. A., Dale, P. S., and Plomin, R. 2009. The etiology of science performance decreasing heritability and increasing importance of the shared environment from 9 to 12 years of age. *Child Development, 80,* 662–673. **336**

Hay, D. I. 2009. *Poverty reduction policies and programs.* Ottawa: Canadian Council on Social Development. **355, 417, 419, 422**

Hayes, C. 2012. *Twilight of the elites: America after meritocracy.* New York: Crown Publishers. **95, 97**

Haynie, D. L., and South, S. J. 2005. Residential mobility and adolescent violence. *Social Forces, 84,* 370–373. **145**

Hays, S. 1996. *The cultural contradictions of motherhood.* New Haven, CT: Yale University Press. **17, 18, 19, 72, 100, 163, 286, 428**

Hays, S. 1998. The fallacious assumptions and unrealistic prescriptions of attachment theory: A comment on "Parents' socioemotional investment in children." *Journal of Marriage and Family, 60,* 782–795. **18**

Health Canada. 2000. *1998/1999 Canadian sexually transmitted disease (STD) surveillance report.* **207–208**

Health Canada. 2001. *The Canadian incidence study of reported child abuse and neglect.* **386, 391**

Heath, D. T. 1995. The impact of delayed fatherhood on the father-child relationship. *Journal of Genetic Psychology, 155,* 511–530. **232**

Hébert, B.-P., and Uriarte-Landa, J. 2012. Influence des antécédents familiaux et professionnels sur l'âge de la retraite. In S. Rhéault and J. Poirier, *Le vieillissement démographique: de nombreux enjeux à déchiffrer* (pp. 31–43). Québec: Institut de la statistique du Québec. **268, 343**

Heflin, C. M., and Pattillo, M. 2006. Poverty in the family: Race, siblings, and socioeconomic heterogeneity. *Social Science Research, 35,* 804–822. **57**

Heimdal, K. R., and Houseknecht, S. K. 2003. Cohabiting and married couples' income organization: Approaches in Sweden and the United States. *Journal of Marriage and Family, 65,* 525–538. **194**

Hektner, J., and Swenson, C. 2012. Links from teacher beliefs to peer victimization and bystander intervention: Tests of mediating process. *The Journal of Early Adolescence, 32,* 516–536. **400**

Helliwell, J. F., and Barrington-Leigh, C. P. 2010. Viewpoint: Measuring and understanding subjective well-being. *Canadian Journal of Economics, 43,* 729–753. **124**

Henderson, T. L., and Moran, P. B. 2001. Grandparent visitation rights: Testing the parameters of parental rights. *Journal of Family Issues, 22,* 619–638. **371**

Henry, R. G., Miller, R. B., and Giarrusso, R. 2005. Difficulties, disagreements, and disappointments in late-life marriages. *International Journal on Aging and Human Development, 61,* 243–264. **268**

Herrenkohl, T., I., et al. 2013. Developmental impacts of child abuse and neglect related to adult mental health, substance abuse, and physical health. *Journal of Family Violence, 28,* 191–199. **389**

HERI (Higher Education Research Institute). 2003. *College freshmen spend less time studying and more time surfing the net, UCLA survey reveals.* Los Angeles, CA: UCLA Graduate School of Education and Information Studies. **90**

Herrington, D. L. 2009. *Prevention of spousal abuse in the Canadian Forces.* Canadian Forces. **78**

Hetherington, E. M. 1988. Parents, children, and siblings: Six years after divorce. In R. A. Hinde and J. Stevenson-Hinde (Eds.), *Relationships within families: Mutual influences* (pp. 311–331). Oxford: Oxford University Press. **368**

Hetherington, E. M. 2003. Intimate pathways: Changing patterns in close personal relationships across time. *Family Relations, 52,* 318–331. **266, 278, 354, 358, 359, 363**

Hetherington, E. M., and Kelly, J. 2002. *For better or for worse: Divorce reconsidered.* New York: Norton. **369**

Hewitt, B., and de Vaus, D. 2009. Change in the association between premarital cohabitation and separation, Australia 1945–2000. *Journal of Marriage and Family, 71,* 353–361. **352, 353**

Hewlett, B. S., and Lamb, M. E., (Eds.). 2005. *Hunter-gatherer childhoods.* New Brunswick, CT: Aldine Transaction. **16, 17, 151, 338**

Hewlett, S. A., and West, C. 1998. *The war against parents.* Boston: Houghton Mifflin. **91**

Heyman, R. E., and Slep, A. M. S. 2002. Do child abuse and interparental violence lead to adulthood family violence? *Journal of Marriage and Family, 64,* 864–870. **385**

Heyman, R. E., et al. 2009. Desired change in couples: Gender differences and effects on communication. *Journal of Family Psychology, 23,* 474–484. **264**

Hill, E. J., Hawkins, A. J., Ferris, M., and Weitzman, M. 2001. Finding an extra day a week: The positive influence of perceived job flexibility on work and family life balance. *Family Relations, 50,* 49–58. **102**

Hill, T. D, Ross, C. E., and Angel, R. J. 2005. Neighborhood disorder, psychophysiological distress, and health. *Journal of Health and Social Behavior, 46,* 170–186. **128**

Hillier, L., and Harrison, L. 2007. Building realities less limited than their own: Young people practicing same-sex attraction on the Internet. *Sexualities, 10,* 82–100. **185**

Hinduja, S., and Patchin, J. W. 2010. Bullying, cyberbullying and suicide. *Archives of Suicide Research, 14,* 206–221. **399**

Hirji, A. 2012. Islam's role in family (and life) education. *Family Focus,* Summer, F11-12. **174**

Hochschild, A. R. 1983. *The managed heart.* Berkeley: University of California Press. **274**

Hochschild, A. R. 1997. *The time bind.* New York: Metropolitan Books. **100**

Hochschild, A. R. 2012. *The outsourced self.* New York: Metropolitan Books. **13, 16, 414**

Hochschild, A. R., with Machung, A. 1989. *The second shift.* New York: Avon. **46, 100**

Hodges, E. V. E., Malone, M. J., and Perry, D. G. 1997. Individual risk and social risk as interacting determinants of victimization in the peer group. *Developmental Psychology, 33,* 1032–1039. **399**

Hoekstra, C., et al. 2008. Dizygotic twinning. *Human Reproduction Update, 14,* 37–47. **320**

Hofferth, S., and Anderson, K. G. 2003. Are all dads equal? Biology versus marriage as a basis for paternal investment. *Journal of Marriage and Family, 65,* 213–232. **369**

Hofferth, S. L. 2006. Residential father family type and child well-being: Investment versus selection. *Demography, 43,* 53–77. **369, 370, 410**

Hofferth, S. L. 2010. Home media and children's achievement and behavior. *Child Development, 81,* 1598–1619. **86**

Hofferth, S. L., and Goldscheider, F. 2010. Family structure and the transition to early parenthood. *Demography, 47,* 415–437. **230**

Hofferth, S. L., and Sandberg, J. F. 2001. Changes in American children's time, 1981–1997. In S. L. Hofferth and T. J. Owens (Eds.), *Children at the millennium: Where have we come from, where are we going?* (pp. 193–229). Oxford, UK: Elsevier. **102, 270**

Hoffman, F., and Taylor, R. 1996. *Much to be done: Private life in Ontario from Victorian diaries.* Toronto: Natural Heritage/Natural History Inc. **41, 42, 46**

Hoffman, R., and Robinson, A. 2010. Nisga'a self-government: A new journey has begun. *The Canadian Journal of Native Studies, 30,* 387–405. **54**

Hohmann-Marriott, B. E. 2006. Shared beliefs and the union stability of married and cohabiting couples. *Journal of Marriage and Family, 68,* 1015–1028. **193**

Homans, G. C. 1961. *Social behavior: Its elementary forms.* New York: Harcourt, Brace, and World. **13**

Home Children, 1869–1930. Accessed online December 18, 2009. **46**

Homma, Y., et al. 2012. A profile of high school students in rural Canada who exchange sex for substances. *The Canadian Journal of Human Sexuality, 21,* 29–40. **205**

Honoré, C. 2008. *Under pressure: How the epidemic of hyper-parenting is endangering childhood.* Toronto: Alfred A. Knopf Canada. **428**

Hopper, J. 2001. The symbolic origins of conflict in divorce. *Journal of Marriage and Family, 63,* 430–435. **354, 362**

Horn, E. E., et al. 2012. Accounting for the physical and mental health benefits of entry into marriage: A genetically informed study of selection and causation. *Journal of Family Psychology, 26,* October, special issue. **198**

Horwitz, A. V. 1993. Adult siblings as sources of social support for the seriously mentally ill: A test of the serial model. *Journal of Marriage and Family, 55,* 623–632. **325**

Horwitz, A. V., and Raskin White, H. 1998. The relationship of cohabitation and mental health: A study of a young adult cohort. *Journal of Marriage and Family, 60,* 505–514. **199**

Horwitz, B. N., and Neiderhiser, J. M. 2011. Gene-environment interplay, family relationships, and child adjustment. *Journal of Marriage and Family, 73,* 804–816. **286, 294, 332, 333, 335, 336**

Horwitz, B. N., et al. 2010. Genetic and environmental influences on global family conflict. *Journal of Family Psychology, 24,* 217–220. **334, 363**

Hostetler, J. A. 1993. *Amish society,* 4th Ed. Baltimore: Johns Hopkins University Press. **73**

Hou, F. 2010. Homeownership over the life course of Canadians: Evidence from Canadian Census of population. Statistics Canada, *The Daily,* June 6. **141**

Hou, F., and Milan, A. 2003. Neighbourhood ethnic transition and its socio-economic connections. *Canadian Journal of Sociology, 28,* 387–410. **132**

Hou, F., and Myles, J. 2004. Neighbourhood inequality and self-perceived health status. Statistics Canada, *The Daily,* September 27. **128**

Hou, F., and Myles, J. 2007. Study: Changing role of education in the marriage market in Canada and the United States. Statistics Canada, *The Daily,* May 18. **188**

Hou, F., and Myles, J. 2008. The changing role of education in the marriage market: assortative marriage in Canada and the United States since the 1970s. *Canadian Journal of Sociology, 33,* 337–366. **188**

Hou, F., and Picot, G. 2004. Visible minority neighbourhoods in Toronto, Montreal, and Vancouver. *Canadian Social Trends, 72,* 8–13. **132**

Hou, F., and Wu, Z. 2009. Racial diversity, minority concentration, and trust in Canadian urban neighborhoods. *Social Science Research, 38,* 693–716. **132**

Houseknecht, S. K., and Macke, A. 1981. Combining marriage and career: The marital adjustment of professional women. *Journal of Marriage and the Family, 43,* 651–661. **272**

Housseaux, F. 2003. *La famille, pilier des identités.* Paris: INSEE. **71**

HRSD (Human Resources and Skills Development). 2009. *Low-income in Canada: 2000–2007, Using the Market Basket Measure.* Gatineau, Que: HRSD Canada, August. Catalogue no. SP-909-07-09E. **105**

Huebner, A. J., and Mancini, J. A. 2005. *Adjustments among adolescents in military families when a parent is deployed.* U.S. Military Family Research Institute, Purdue University. **77**

Huebner, A. J., et al. 2009. Shadowed by war: Building community capacity to support military families. *Family Relations, 58,* 216–228. **78**

Huesmann, L. R., et al. 2003. Longitudinal relations between children's exposure to TV violence and their aggressive and violent behavior in young adulthood: 1977–1992. *Developmental Psychology, 39,* 201–221. **86**

Huey, L. 2012. *Invisible victims: Homelessness and the growing security gap.* Toronto: University of Toronto Press. **133**

Hughes, M. E., and Waite, L. J. 2009. Marital biography and health in mid-life. *Journal of Health and Social Behavior, 50,* 344–358. **355, 356**

Hughes, M. E., et al. 2007. All in the family: The impact of caring for grandchildren on grandparents' health. *The Journals of Gerontology: Series B, 62B,* S108–120. **311**

Huh, D., et al. 2006. Does problem behavior elicit poor parenting? A prospective study of adolescent girls. *Journal of Adolescent Research, 21,* 185–204. **286, 289, 295, 296**

Huijts, T., and Kraaykamp, G. 2011. Religious involvement, religious context, and self-assessed health in Europe. *Journal of Health and Social Behavior, 52,* 91–106. **174**

Hulchanski, J. D. 2011. The vanishing middle. *Toronto Star,* October 26, A23. **123**

Humble, A. M. 2003. "*Doing weddings*": Couples' gender strategies in wedding preparation. Oregon State University: Doctoral dissertation. **185, 274**

Hummer, R. A., Hack, K. A., and Raley, R. K. 2004. Retrospective reports of pregnancy wantedness and child well-being in the United States. *Journal of Family Issues, 25,* 404–428. **238**

Hummer, R. A., et al. 1999. Religious involvement and U.S. adult mortality. *Demography, 36,* 273–285. **174**

Hunter, J. 2011. B. C. Native school overcomes long odds. *The Globe and Mail,* April 13, A3. **167**

Hur, Y.-M., and Bouchard, T. J., Jr. 1995. Genetic influences on perceptions of childhood family environment: A reared apart twin study. *Child Development, 66,* 330–345. **335**

Hurd, L. C. 1999. "We're not old!": Older women's negotiation of aging and oldness. *Journal of Aging Studies, 13,* 419–439. **364**

Hurd, N. M., et al. 2012. Natural mentors, racial identity, and educational attainment among African American adolescents: Exploring pathways to success. *Child Development, 83,* 1196–1212. **166**

Hurst, M. 2011. Debt and family type in Canada. Ottawa: Statistics Canada, *Canadian Social Trends, 91,* April. **111**

Hussain, A., and Scott, J. S. 2012. Moslims. In J. S. Scott (Ed.), *The religions of Canadians* (pp. 167–218). Toronto: University of Toronto Press. 50, 172

Hvistendahl, M. 2011. *Unnatural selection*. New York: Public Affairs. 59, 237, 412

Hylton, J. 2002. *Aboriginal sex offending in Canada*. Ottawa: Aboriginal Healing Foundation. 383, 394

Hyman, B. 2000. The economic consequences of child sexual abuse for adult lesbian women. *Journal of Marriage and Family, 62,* 199–211. 394

Iannaccone, L. R. 1990. Religious practice: A human capital approach. *Journal for the Scientific Study of Religion, 29,* 297–314. 174

Iervolino, A., et al. 2005. Genetic and environmental influences on sex-typed behavior during the preschool years. *Child Development, 76,* 826–840. 334

Illick, J. E. 2002. *American childhoods*. Philadelphia: University of Pennsylvania Press. 18

Ingersoll-Dayton, B., Neal, M. B., and Hammer, L. B. 2001. Aging parents helping adult children: The experience of the sandwich generation. *Family Relations, 50,* 262–271. 309

Ivanova, I. 2011. *The cost of poverty in B.C.* Vancouver: Canadian Centre for Policy Alternatives. 117

Invest in Kids. 2002. *A national survey of parents of young children*: Invest in Kids Foundation. June. 103, 294, 428

Jackson, E., and Whittington, L. 2012. You're safer than you think. *Toronto Star,* July 25. 128

Jadva, V., et al. 2009a. "Mom by choice, single by life's circumstances ..." Findings from a large scale survey of the experiences of single mothers by choice. *Human Fertility, 12,* 175–184. 226

Jadva, V., et al. 2009b. The experiences of adolescents and adults conceived by sperm donation: Comparisons by age of disclosure and family type. *Human Reproduction Advance, 1,* 1–11. 241

Jadva, V., et al. 2012. Surrogacy families 10 years on: Relationship with the surrogate, decisions over disclosure and children's understanding of their surrogacy origins. *Human Reproduction, 27,* 3008–3014. 241

Jaeger, M. M. 2009. Equal access but unequal outcomes: Cultural capital and educational choice in a meritocratic society. *Social Forces, 87,* 1943–1972. 160

Jaffee, S. R., et al. 2005. Nature x nurture: Genetic vulnerabilities interact with physical maltreatment to promote conduct problems. *Developmental Psychopathology, 17,* 67–84. 390

Jamieson, K. 1986. Sex discrimination and the Indian Act. In J. R. Ponting (Ed.), *Arduous journey: Canadian Indians and decolonization*. Toronto: McClelland & Stewart. 39

Jamil, V., and Rousseau, C. 2012. Subject positioning, fear, and insecurity in South Asian Muslim communities in the war on terror context. *Canadian Review of Sociology, 49,* 370–388. 64

Janosz, M., et al. 2013. *Elementary school students at risk of dropping out of high school: Characteristics at 12 years of age and predictors at 7 years of age.* Québec: Institut de la Statistique, 7, 2, February. 164

Janssens, P. M. W. 2006. A new Dutch law regulating provision of identifying information of doners to offspring: background, content and impact. *Human Reproduction, 21,* 852–856. 239

Javed, N. 2008. GTA's secret world of polygamy. *Toronto Star.* May 24, A10, ID1. 7

Javed, N. 2013. Is pornography changing how teens view sex? *Toronto Star,* April 20, IN1, IN6. 215

Jaya, P., and Porter, M. 2011. Asking for apples from a lower tree: Experiences of immigrant women in Newfoundland and Labrador. In E. Tastsoglou and P. S. Jaya (Eds.), *Immigrant women in Atlantic Canada* (pp. 111–141). Toronto: Canadian Scholars' Press. 298

Jayakody, R., and Phuong, P. 2013. Social change and fathering: Change or continuity in Vietnam? *Journal of Family Issues, 34,* 228–249. 295

Jendrek, M. P. 1993. Grandparents who parent their grandchildren: Effects on lifestyle. *Journal of Marriage and Family, 55,* 609–621. 312

Jenkins, J. M., et al. 2005a. Change in maternal perception of sibling negativity: Within- and between-family influences. *Journal of Family Psychology, 19,* 533–541. 286, 328

Jenkins, J., et al. 2005b. Mutual influence of marital conflict and children's behavior problems: Shared and nonshared family risks. *Child Development, 76,* 24–39. 276, 277, 329, 331, 351

Jenkins-Tucker, C., McHale, S. M., and Crouter, A. C. 2001. Conditions of sibling support in adolescence. *Journal of Family Psychology, 15,* 254–271. 323, 324

Jensen, A.-M. 1995. Gender gaps in relationships with children: Closing or widening? In K. O. Mason and A.-M. Jensen (Eds.), *Gender or family change in industrialized countries* (pp. 223–242). Oxford: Clarendon. 21

Jeong, J., and Bélanger, D. 2012. *Kirogi* families as virtual "families": Perspectives and experiences of *Kirogi* mothers. In S. Noh, A. H. Kim, and M. S. Noh (Eds.), *Korean immigrants in Canada* (pp. 259–284). Toronto: University of Toronto Press. 75

Jepsen, L. K., and Jepsen, C. A. 2002. An empirical analysis of the matching patterns of same-sex and opposite-sex couples. *Demography, 39,* 435–453. 189

Jespersen, A. F., Lalumière, M. L., and Seto, M. C. 2009. Sexual abuse history among adult sex offenders and non-sex offenders: A meta-analysis. *Child Abuse & Neglect, 33,* 179–192. 390, 396

Joël, J. 2012. 'Nagging wife' revisited: Women and the fur trade in New France. In M. Gleason et al. (Eds.), *Rethinking Canada: The promise of women's history,* 6th Ed. (pp. 28–37). Toronto: Oxford University Press. 40, 42

John Howard Society of Toronto. 2010. *Homeless and jailed: Jailed and homeless.* August. 133

Johnson, B. R., et al. 2001. Does adolescent religious commitment matter? A reexamination of the effects of religiosity on delinquency. *Journal of Research in Crime and Delinquency, 38,* 22–44. 174

Johnson, E. I., and Easterling, B. 2012. Understanding unique effects of parental incarceration on children: Challenges, progress, and recommendations. *Journal of Marriage and Family, 74,* 342–356. 58, 126

Johnson, J. G., et al. 2002. Television viewing and aggressive behavior during adolescence and adulthood. *Science, 295,* 2468–2471. 85

Johnson, J. K. 1994. Friends in high places: Getting divorced in Upper Canada. *Ontario History, 86,* 201–218. 42

Johnson, K. A., and Lynch, S. M. 2013. Predictors of maladaptive coping of incarcerated women who are survivors of childhood sexual abuse. *Journal of Family Violence, 28,* 43–52. 395

Johnson, M. P., and Leone, J. M. 2005. The differential effects of intimate terrorism and situational couple violence. *Journal of Family Issues, 26,* 322–349. 381

Johnston, P. 1983. *Native children and the child welfare system.* Toronto: Canadian Council on Social Development, in association with James Lorimer and Company. **52**

Jones, F. 2000. Community involvement: The influence of early experience. *Canadian Social Trends, 57,* 15–19. **124, 175**

Jones, G. W. 2007. Delayed marriage and very low fertility in Pacific Asia. *Population and Development Review, 33,* 453–478. **79, 232, 235, 304**

Jones, G. W., and Gubhaju, B. 2009. Factors influencing changes in mean age at first marriage and proportion never marrying in the low fertility countries of East and Southeast Asia. *Asian Population Studies, 3,* 237–268. **202**

Jones, L. M., Finkelhor, D., and Kopiec, K. 2001. Why is sexual abuse declining? A survey of state child protection administrators. *Child Abuse & Neglect, 25,* 1139–1158. **393**

Jose, A., O'Leary, D., and Moyer, A. 2010. Does premarital cohabitation predict subsequent marital stability and marital quality? A meta-analysis. *Journal of Marriage and Family, 72,* 105–116. **352**

Josey, S. 2008. Farmland in GTA is diminishing. *Toronto Star.* September 8. **136, 416**

Joussemet, M., et al. 2008. Controlling parenting and physical aggression during elementary school. *Child Development, 79,* 411–425. **289**

Joy, L. A., Kimball, M. M., and Zabrack, M. L. 1986. Television and children's aggressive behavior. In T. M. Williams (Ed.), *The impact of television: A natural experiment in three communities* (pp. 303–360). Orlando, FL: Academic Press. **86**

Joyner, K., and Udry, J. R. 2000. You don't bring me anything but down: Adolescent romance and depression. *Journal of Health and Social Behavior, 41,* 369–391. **184**

Juby, H., Marcil-Gratton, N., and Le Bourdais, C. 2005a. *Moving on: The expansion of the family network after parents separate.* Ottawa: Department of Justice, Catalogue no. 2004-FCY-9E. **221, 368**

Juby, H., Marcil-Gratton, N., and Le Bourdais, C. 2005b. *When parents separate: Further findings from the National Longitudinal Survey of Children and Youth.* Ottawa: Department of Justice. **347**

Juby, H., et al. 2007. Nonresident fathers and children: Parents' new unions and frequency of contact. *Journal of Family Issues, 28,* 1220–1245. **369**

Judge, S. 2003. Determinants of parental stress in families adopting children from Eastern Europe. *Family Relations, 52,* 241–248. **247**

Juffer, J., and van Izjendoorm, M. H. 2005. Behavior problems and mental health referrals of international adoptees. *Journal of the American Medical Association, 293,* 2501–2515. **247**

Justice, L. M., et al. 2011. Peer effects in preschool classrooms: Is children's language growth associated with their classmates' skills? *Child Development, 82,* 1768–1777. **156**

Kaczynski, K. J., et al. 2006. Marital conflict, maternal and paternal parenting, and child adjustment: A test for mediation and moderation. *Journal of Family Psychology, 20,* 199–208. **278**

Kaestle, C. E., Morisky, D. E., and Wiley, D. J. 2002. Sexual intercourse and the age difference between adolescent females and their romantic partners. *Perspectives on Sexual and Reproductive Health, 34,* 304–309. **209**

Kağıtçıbasi, C. 2007. *Family, self, and human development across cultures.* Mahwah, NJ: Erlbaum. **29, 74, 290, 339**

Kaiser Family Foundation. 2003. *Sex on TV3.* Menlo Park, CA: H. J. Kaiser Family Foundation. **88**

Kalbach, M. A. 2000. Ethnicity and the altar. In M. A. Kalbach and W. E. Kalbach (Eds.), *Perspectives on ethnicity in Canada: A reader* (pp. 111–121). Toronto: McClelland & Stewart. **186**

Kale, R. 2012. Pregnant women face intense pressure. *Toronto Star,* April 25, A17. **238**

Kalmijn, M., de Graaf, P. M., and Janssen, J. P. G. 2005. Intermarriage and the risk of divorce in the Netherlands: The effects of differences in religion and in nationality, 1974–94. *Population Studies, 59,* 71–85. **188**

Kalmijn, M., and de Graaf, P. M. 2012. Life course changes of children and well-being of parents. *Journal of Marriage and Family, 74,* 269–280. **356**

Kan, M., Feinberg, M., and Solmeyer, A. 2012. Intimate partner violence and coparenting across the transition to parenthood. *Journal of Family Issues, 33,* 115–135. **385**

Kapinus, C. A., and Pellerin, L. A. 2008. The influence of parents' religious practices on young adults' divorce attitudes. *Social Science Research, 37,* 801–814. **177**

Kaplan, S. J., Skolnik, L., and Turnbull, A. 2009. Enhancing the empowerment of youth in foster care: supportive services. *Child Welfare, 88,* 133–162. **251**

Kar, H. L., and O'Leary, K. D. 2013. Patterns of psychological aggression, dominance, and jealousy within marriage. *Journal of Family Violence, 28,* 109–119. **378**

Karazin, C. D., and Littlejohn, J. R. 2012. *Swirling: How to date, mate, and relate mixing race, culture and creed.* New York: Atria. **186**

Karney, B., et al. 2012. Comparing marital status and divorce status in civilian and military populations. *Journal of Family Issues, 33,* 1572–1594. **78**

Karney, B. R., and Bradbury, T. N. 2005. Contextual influences on marriage: Implications for policy and intervention. *Current Directions in Psychological Science, 14,* 171–174. **256**

Karraker, A., and DeLamater, J. 2013. Last-year sexual inactivity among older married persons and their partners. *Journal of Marriage and Family, 75,* 142–163. **211, 212**

Kasper, J. D., et al. 2008. Effects of poverty and family stress over three decades on the functional status of older African American women. *The Journals of Gerontology: Series B, 63B,* S201–211. **228**

Kasser, T. 2002. *The high price of materialism.* Cambridge, MA: MIT Press. **125**

Katz, L. F., Kling, J. R., and Liebman, J. B. 2001. Moving to opportunity in Boston: Early results of a randomized mobility experiment. *Quarterly Journal of Economics, 116,* 655–680. **130**

Keating, N., and Dosman, D. 2009. Social capital and the care networks of frail seniors. *The Canadian Review of Sociology, 46,* 301–318. **431**

Keating, N., et al. 2003. Understanding the caring capacity and informal networks of frail seniors. *Ageing and Society, 23,* 115–127. **21**

Keijsers, L., et al. 2009. Developmental links of adolescent disclosure, parental solicitation, and control with delinquency: Moderation by parental support. *Developmental Psychology, 45,* 1314–1327. **292, 295, 298**

Keizer, R., and Schenk, N. 2012. Becoming a parent and relationship satisfaction: A longitudinal dyadic perspective. *Journal of Marriage and Family, 74,* 759–773. **277**

Kelly, J. B., and Emery, R. E. 2003. Children's adjustment following divorce: Risk and resilience perspectives. *Family Relations, 52,* 352–362. **357, 362**

Kelly, M. B. 2012. Divorce cases in civil court, 2010/2011. *Juristat,* Ottawa: Statistics Canada, Cat. No. 85-002-X. **343, 344, 346**

Kemp, C. 2004. Grand expectations: The experience of grandparents and adult grandchildren. *Canadian Journal of Sociology, 29,* 499–526. **310**

Kemp. C. 2012. Married couples in assisted living: Adult children's experiences providing support. *Journal of Family Issues, 33,* 639–661. **308**

Kempe, C., et al. 1962. The battered child syndrome. *Journal of the American Medical Association, 181,* 17–24. **387**

Kennedy, T., et al. 2010. The clinical and adaptive features of young offenders with histories of child-parent violence. *Journal of Family Violence, 25,* 509–520. **401**

Kenney, C. T., and McLanahan, S. S. 2006. Why are cohabiting relationships more violent than marriages? *Demography, 43,* 127–140. **195**

Keown, L.-A. 2009. *2008 General Social Survey report. Social networks help Canadians deal with change.* Statistics Canada, Publication no. 11-008-X. **84**

Kern, L. 2010. *Sex and the revitalized city: Gender, condominium development, and urban citizenship.* Vancouver: University of British Columbia Press. **13, 141, 142**

Kerr, D. C. R., et al. 2009. A prospective three generational study of fathers' constructive parenting: Influences from family of origin, adolescent adjustment, and offspring temperament. *Developmental Psychology, 45,* 1257–1275. **295**

Kerr, D., and Michalski, J. H. 2007. Family structure and children's hyperactivity problems: A longitudinal analysis. *Canadian Journal of Sociology, 32,* 85–106. **362, 369, 410**

Kerr, D., Moyser, M., and Beaujot, R. 2006. Marriage and cohabitation: Demographic and socioeconomic differences in Quebec and Canada. *Canadian Studies in Population, 33,* 83–117. **190**

Kerr, M., and Stattin, H. 2003. Parenting of adolescents: Action or reaction? In A. C. Crouter and A. Booth (Eds.), *Children's influence on family dynamics* (pp. 121–152). Mahwah, NJ: Erlbaum. **289, 296**

Kershaw, P., and Anderson, R. 2011. *Raising a family is harder but retiring is easier for Canadians today than in the '70s.* Vancouver: University of British Columbia: Human Early Learning Parnership. **96, 97**

Kershaw, P., Irwin, L., and Hertzman, T. K. 2005. *The BC Atlas of Child Development.* Human Early Learning Partnership, Western Geographical Press. **52, 424**

Kessen, W. 1979. The American child and other cultural inventions. *American Psychologist, 34,* 815–820. **16**

Kett, J. F. 1977. *Rites of passage: Adolescence in America 1790 to present.* New York: Basic Books. **297**

Khan, S. R. 2010. The making of an adolescent elite at St. Paul's School. Princeton: Princeton University Press. **168**

Kharas, H., and Rogerson, A. 2012. *Horizon 2025.* New York: The Brookings Institution and London U.K.: Overseas Development Institute. **107**

Khasawneh, O. M., and Hijazi, A. H. Y. 2011. Polygamy and its impact on the upbringing of children: A Jordanian perspective. *Journal of Comparative Family Studies, 42,* 563–578. **9**

Kiecolt, K. J. 2003. Satisfaction with work and family life: No evidence of a cultural reversal. *Journal of Marriage and Family, 65,* 23–35. **102**

Kiecolt-Glaser, J. K., and Newton, T. L. 2001. Marriage and health: His and hers. *Psychological Bulletin, 127,* 472–503. **102, 274**

Kiepal, L., Carrington, P. J., and Dawson, M. 2012. Missing persons and social exclusion. *Canadian Journal of Sociology, 37,* 137–168. **52, 134**

Kilmer, R. P., et al. 2008. Siblings of children with severe emotional disturbances: Risks, resources, and adaptation. *American Journal of Orthopsychiatry, 78,* 1–10. **325**

Kim, A. H. 2009. *The social context of residential integration: Ethnic groups in the United States and Canada.* El Paso, TX: LFB Scholarly Publishing. **132**

Kim, J. 2010. Neighborhood disadvantage and mental health: The role of neighborhood disorder and social relationships. *Social Science Research, 39,* 260–271. **128**

Kim, J. E., Hetherington, E. M., and Reiss, D. 1999. Associations among family relationships, antisocial peers, and adolescents' externalizing behaviors: Gender and family type differences. *Child Development, 70,* 1209–1230. **358**

Kim, J.-Y., et al. 2006. Longitudinal course and family correlates of sibling relationships from childhood through adolescence. *Child Development, 77,* 1746–1761. **322**

Kim, P. G. 2010. *Preserving ethnicity through religion in America: Korean Protestants and Indian Hindus across generations.* New York: New York University Press. **172**

Kimball, M. M. 1986. Television and sex-role attitudes. In T. M. Williams (Ed.), *The impact of television* (pp. 265–301). New York: Academic Press. **86**

Kim-Cohen, J., et al. 2004. Genetic and environmental processes in young children's resilience and vulnerability to socioeconomic deprivation. *Child Development, 75,* 651–668. **118, 338**

Kim-Spoon, J., et al. 2012. Adolescents who are less religious than their parents are at risk for externalizing and internalizing symptoms: The mediating role of parent-adolescent relationship quality. *Journal of Family Psychology, 26,* 636–641. **175**

Kimmel, M. S. 2000. *The gendered society.* New York: Oxford University Press. **327**

King, V. 2003a. The legacy of a grandparent's divorce: Consequences for ties between grandparents and grandchildren. *Journal of Marriage and Family, 65,* 170–183. **371**

King, V. 2003b. The influence of religion on fathers' relationships with their children. *Journal of Marriage and Family, 65,* 382–395. **175**

King, V. 2006. The antecedents and consequences of adolescents' relationships with stepfathers and nonresident fathers. *Journal of Marriage and Family, 68,* 910–928. **369**

King, V. 2007. When children have two mothers: Relationships with non-resident mothers, stepmothers, and fathers. *Journal of Marriage and Family, 69,* 1178–1193. **349**

King, V., and Elder, G. H., Jr. 1995. American children view their grandparents: Linked lives across three rural generations. *Journal of Marriage and Family, 57,* 165–178. **310**

King, V., and Scott, M. E. 2005. A comparison of cohabiting relationships among older and younger adults. *Journal of Marriage and Family, 67,* 271–285. **197**

King, V., et al. 2004. Relations with grandparents: Rural Midwest versus urban Southern California. *Journal of Family Issues, 24,* 1044–1069. **137**

Kingsley, C., and Mark, M. 2000. *Sacred lives: Canadian Aboriginal children & youth speak out about sexual exploitation: Save the Children Canada.* National Aboriginal Project. Retrieved online January 21, 2010. **395**

Kingston, A. 2013. The dangers of older dads. *Maclean's Magazine,* March 4, 58–61. **231, 235**

Kirk, D. S., and Papachristos, A. V. 2011. Cultural mechanisms and the persistence of neighborhood violence. *American Journal of Sociology, 116,* 1190–1233. **128**

Kirkorian, H., et al. 2009. The impact of background television on parent-child interaction. *Child Development, 80,* 1350–1359. **82**

Kirmayer, L. J., et al. 2007. *Suicide among Aboriginal People in Canada.*The Aboriginal Healing Foundation. **51**

Kiselica, M. S., and Morrill-Richards, M. 2007. Sibling maltreatment: The forgotten abuse. *Journal of Counseling and Development, 85,* 148–160. **396**

Kitayama, S., and Cohen, D. 2007. *Handbook of cultural psychology.* New York: Guilford Press. **29, 338, 339, 428**

Klebanov, P. K., et al. 1998. The contribution of neighborhood and family income to developmental test scores over the first three years of life. *Child Development, 69,* 1420–1436. **130**

Klinenberg, E. 2012. *Going solo.* New York: Penguin. **201**

Kluwer, E. S. 2010. From partnership to parenthood: A review of marital change across the transition to parenthood. *Journal of Family Theory & Review, 2,* 105–125. **201, 277**

Knaak, S. 2005. Breast-feeding, bottle-feeding and Dr. Spock: The shifting context of choice. *Canadian Review of Sociology and Anthropology, 42,* 197–216. **18, 409**

Knighton, T., and Mirza, S. 2002. Postsecondary participation: The effects of parents' education and household income. *Education Quarterly Review, 8,* 25–32. **160, 161**

Knoester, C., Haynie, D. L., and Stephens, C. M. 2006. Parenting practices and adolescents' friendship networks. *Journal of Marriage and Family, 68,* 1247–1260. **302**

Kochenderfer, B. J., and Ladd, G. W. 1996. Peer victimization: Cause or consequence of school maladjustment? *Child Development, 67,* 1305–1317. **399**

Koenig, H. G., McCullough, M. E., and Larson, D. B. 2001. *Handbook of religion and health.* New York: Oxford University Press. **171**

Kohen, D. E., et al. 2002a. Neighborhood income and physical and social disorder in Canada: Associations with young children's competencies. *Child Development, 73,* 1844–1860. **123, 129, 423**

Kohen, D., Hertzman, C., and Willms, J. D. 2002b. The importance of quality child care. In J. D. Willms (Ed.), *Vulnerable children* (pp. 261–276). Edmonton: University of Alberta Press. **153**

Kohen, D. E., et al. 2008. Neighborhood disadvantage: Pathways of effects for young children. *Child Development, 79,*156–169. **131, 360**

Kohler Riessman, C. 2000. Stigma and every day resistance practices: Childless women in South India. *Gender and Society, 14,* 111–135. **63**

Kohler, H. P., Behrman, J. R., and Skytthe, A. 2005. Partner + children = happiness? The effects of partnerships and fertility on well-being. *Population and Development Review, 31,*407–443. **309**

Kohler, J. K., Grotevant, H. D., and McRoy, R. G. 2002. Adopted adolescents' preoccupation with adoption: The impact on adoptive family relationships. *Family Relations, 64,* 93–104. **248**

Kollmeyer, C., and Pichler, F. 2013. Is deindustrialization causing high unemployment in affluent countries? Evidence from 16 OECD countries, 1970–2003. *Social Forces, 91,* 785–812. **96**

Kotkin, J. 2012. *The rise of post-familism: Humanity's future?* Singapore: Civil Service College. **21, 96, 202, 234, 235, 412, 415, 427, 429**

Kovan, N. M., Chung, A. L., and Sroufe, L. A. 2009. The intergenerational continuity of observed early parenting: A prospective, longitudinal study. *Developmental Psychology, 45,*1205–1213. **296**

Kraeger, D. A., et al. 2013. Women's education, marital violence, and divorce: A social exchange perspective. *Journal of Marriage and Family, 75,* 565–581. **351, 382**

Krakauer, I.D., and Rose, S. M. 2002. The impact of group membership on lesbians' physical appearance. *Journal of Lesbian Studies, 6,* 31–43. **190**

Kramer, L., and Ramsburg, D. 2002. Advice given to parents on welcoming a second child: A critical review. *Family Relations, 51,* 2–14. **317**

Krampe, E., and Newton, R. 2012. Reflecting on the father: Childhood family structure and women's paternal relationships. *Journal of Family Issues, 33,* 773–800. **365**

Kremarik, F. 2000a. The other side of the fence. *Canadian Social Trends, 57,* 20–24. **124**

Kremarik, F. 2000b. A family affair: Children's participation in sports. *Canadian Social Trends, 58,* 20–24. **87**

Kremarik, F. 2002. A little place in the country: A profile of Canadians who own vacation property. *Canadian Social Trends, 65,* 12–14. **139**

Kremarik, F., and Williams, C. 2001. Mobile homes in Canada. *Canadian Social Trends, 62,* 14–17. **142**

Krienert, J. L, Walsh, J. A., Walsh, J. A., and Turner, M. 2009. Elderly in America: A descriptive study of elder abuse examining National Incident-Based Reporting System (NIBRS) data, 2000–2005. *Journal of Elder Abuse & Neglect, 21,* 325–345. **403**

Krull, C. 2003. Pronatalism, feminism and family policy in Quebec. In M. Lynn (Ed.), *Voices: Essays on Canadian families,* 2nd Ed. (pp. 245–265). Scarborough, ON: Thomson Nelson. **40, 55**

Krull, C. 2007. Families and the State: Family Policy in Canada. In D. Cheal (Ed.), *Canadian families today* (pp. 254–272). Toronto: Oxford University Press. **418, 420**

Krull, C., and Sempruch, J. (Eds.). 2011. *A life in balance? Reopening the family-work debate.* Vancouver: University of British Columbia Press. **21**

Krull, C., and Trovato, F. 2003a. Collapse of the cradle: A comprehensive framework of fertility decline in Quebec: 1941–1991. *Canadian Studies in Population: Special Issue in Honor of Anatole Romaniuc, 40,* 193–220. **40, 235**

Krull, C., and Trovato, F. 2003b. Where have all the children gone? Quebec's fertility decline: 1941–1991. *Canadian Studies in Population, 30,* 193–220. **42**

Kühhirt, M., and Ludwig, V. 2012. Domestic work and the wage penalty for motherhood in West Germany. *Journal of Marriage and Family, 74,* 186–200. **99**

Kumar, M. B., and Janz, T. 2010. An exploration of cultural activities of Métis in Canada. *Canadian Social Trends, 89.* **54**

Kuperberg, A. 2012. Reassessing differences in work and income in cohabitation and marriage. *Journal of Marriage and Family, 74,* 688–707. **195**

Kupersmidt, J. B., et al. 1995. Childhood aggression and peer relations in the context of family and neighborhood factors. *Child Development, 66,* 360–375. **130**

Kurdek, L. A. 1990. Divorce history and self-reported psychological distress in husbands and wives. *Journal of Marriage and Family, 52,* 701–708. **266**

Kurdek, L. A. 1994. Areas of conflict for gay, lesbian, and heterosexual couples: What couples argue about influences relationship satisfaction. *Journal of Marriage and Family, 56,* 923–934. **264, 275**

Kurdek, L. A. 2008. Change in relationship quality for partners from lesbian, gay male, and heterosexual couples. *Journal of Family Psychology, 22,* 701–711. **275, 277**

Lachance-Grzela, M., and Bouchard, G. 2009. La cohabitation et le marriage, deux mondes à part? Un examen des caractéristiques démographiques, individuelles et relationnelles. *Canadian Journal of Behavioural Science, 41,* 37–44. **195**

Ladurantaye, S. 2010. Trailer park cash. *The Globe and Mail,* September 8, 1, B6. **142, 143**

Lai, D. C., Paper, J., and Paper, L. C. 2005. The Chinese in Canada: Their unrecognized religion. In P. Bramadat and D. Seljah (Eds.), *Religion and ethnicity in Canada* (pp. 89–110). Toronto: Pearson. **172**

Laird, R. D., et al. 2003. Parents' monitoring-relevant knowledge and adolescents' delinquent behavior: Evidence of correlated developmental changes and reciprocal influences. *Child Development, 74,* 752–768. **289**

Lam, C. B., et al. 2012a. Sibling differences in parent-child conflict and risky behavior: A three-wave longitudinal study. *Journal of Family Psychology, 26,* 523–531. **286, 295, 326, 327, 328, 329, 334**

Lam, C. B., et al. 2012b. The division of household labor: Longitudinal changes and within-couple variation. *Journal of Marriage and Family, 74,* 944–952. **273**

Lam, V. 2011. *Tommy Douglas.* Toronto: Penguin. **170**

Lamb, K. A., Lee, G. R., and DeMaris, A. 2003. Union formation and depression: Selection and relationship effects. *Journal of Marriage and Family, 65,* 953–962. **195**

Lamborn, S. D., Dornbusch, S. M., and Steinberg, L. 1996. Ethnicity and community context as moderators of the relations between family decision making and adolescent readjustment. *Child Development, 67,* 283–301. **337**

Lane, P., et al. 2002. *Mapping the healing journey: The final report of a First Nation research project on healing in Canadian Aboriginal communities.* Ottawa: Solicitor General of Canada, Aboriginal Corrections Policy Unit. **54, 383**

Laner, M. R., and Ventrone, N. A. 1998. Egalitarian daters/traditionalist dates. *Journal of Family Issues, 19,* 468–477. **184-185**

Langille, D. 2009. Follow the money: How business and politics shape our health. In D. Raphael (Ed.), *Social determinants of health: Canadian perspectives,* 2nd Ed. (pp. 305–317). Toronto: Canadian Scholars' Press. **13, 95, 417, 420, 427**

Langille, D. B., et al. 2003. Association of socio-economic factors with health risk behaviours among high school students in rural Nova Scotia. *Canadian Journal of Public Health, 94,* 442–448. **220**

Langlois, K. A., and Garner, R. 2013. Trajectories of psychological distress among Canadian adults who experienced parental addiction in childhood. Statistics Canada: *Health Reports, 24,* March 20. **386**

Lansford, J. E., et al. 2001. Does family structure matter? A comparison of adoptive, two-parent biological, single-mother, stepfather, and stepmother households. *Journal of Marriage and Family, 63,* 840–851. **244**

Lansford, J. E., et al. 2009. Trajectories of physical discipline: Early childhood antecedents and developmental outcomes. *Child Development, 80,* 1385–1402. **287, 293, 294, 296**

Lansford, J. E. et al. 2012. Forms of spanking and children's externalyzing behaviors. *Family Relations, 61,* 224–236. **293**

Laplante, B. 2006. The rise of cohabitation in Quebec: Power of religion and power over religion. *Canadian Journal of Sociology, 31,* 1–24. **190**

Laplante, B., Miller, C., and Malherbe, P. 2006. The evolution of beliefs and opinions on matters related to marriage and sexual behaviour among French-speaking Catholic Quebecers and English-speaking Protestant Ontarians. *Canadian Studies in Population, 33,* 209–239. **54**

Lareau, A. 2011. *Unequal childhoods: Class, race, and family life,* 2nd Ed. Berkeley: University of California Press. **17, 18, 159, 160, 292, 428, 429**

Larkin, M. 2009. Life after caring: The post-caring experiences of former carers. *British Journal of Social Work, 39,* 1026–1042. **364, 430**

Laroche, D. 2007. *La violence conjugale envers les hommes et les femmes, au Québec et au Canada, 1999.* Québec: Gouvernement du Québec, Institut de la Statistique. **354, 380, 381, 383**

LaRossa, R. 2005. Grounded theory methods and qualitative family research. *Journal of Marriage and Family, 67,* 837–857. **31**

Larson, R. W., and Richards, M. H. 1994. *Divergent realities: The emotional lives of mothers, fathers, and adolescents.* New York: Basic Books. **102, 270, 274, 298, 299**

Larzelere, R. E., et al. 1998. Punishment enhances reasoning's effectiveness as a disciplinary response to toddlers. *Journal of Marriage and Family, 60,* 388–403. **288, 293**

Laszloffy, T. A. 2002. Rethinking family development theory: Teaching with the systemic family development (SFD) model. *Family Relations, 51,* 206–214. **23**

Lau, C. Q. 2012. The stability of same-sex cohabitation, different-sex cohabitation, and marriage. *Journal of Marriage and Family, 74,* 973–988. **201**

Laumann, E. O. 1996. Early sexual experiences: How voluntary? How violent? In M. D. Smith et al. (Eds.), *Sexuality and American social policy.* Menlo Park, CA: Henry J. Kaiser Family Foundation. **400**

Laumann, E. O., et al. 1994. *The social organization of sexuality: Sexual practices in the United States.* Chicago: University of Chicago Press. **210, 212, 214**

Laumann-Billings, L., and Emery, R. E. 2000. Distress among young adults from divorced families. *Journal of Family Psychology, 14,* 671–687. **359**

Laurent, A. 1997. À propos des familles ou les parents sont battus par leur enfant. *Archives de Pédiatrie, 4,* 468–472. **402**

Laurent, A., and Derry, A. 1999. Violence of French adolescents towards their parents: Characteristics and contexts. *Journal of Adolescent Health, 25,* 21–26. **401**

Lavee, Y., and Katz, R. 2002. Division of labor, perceived fairness, and marital quality: The effect of gender ideology. *Journal of Marriage and Family, 64,* 27–39. **29**

Lavner, J. A., and Bradbury, T. N. 2010. Patterns of change in marital satisfaction over the newlywed years. *Journal of Marriage and Family, 72,* 1171–1187. **263, 355**

Lavoie, Y. 1981. *L'émigration des Québécois aux États-Unis de 1830 à 1940.* Québec: Conseil de la langue française, direction des études et recherches. **43, 144**

Lawrence, B. 2004. *"Real" Indians and others: Mixed-blood urban Native Peoples and Indigenous nationhood.* Vancouver: University of British Columbia Press. **51**

Lawrence, C. R., Carlson, E. A., and Egeland, B. 2006. The impact of foster care on development. *Development and Psychopathology, 18,* 57–76. **250, 251**

Lawrence, E., et al. 2008. Marital satisfaction across the transition to parenthood. *Journal of Family Psychology, 22,* 41–50. **276**

Lawrence, R. 2007. *School Crime and Juvenile Justice,* 2nd Ed. New York: Oxford University Press. **165**

Le Bourdais, C., Lapierre-Adamcyk, E., and Pacaut, P. 2004. Changes in conjugal life in Canada: Is cohabitation progressively replacing marriage? *Journal of Marriage and Family, 66,* 929–942. **348**

Le Bourdais, C., et al. 2000. The changing face of conjugal relationship. *Canadian Social Trends, 56,* 14–17. **190**

LeClere, F. B., and Kowalewski, B. M. 1994. Disability in the family: The effects on children's well-being. *Journal of Marriage and Family, 56,* 457–468. **325**

Leathers, S. J. 2003. Parental visiting, conflicting allegiances, and emotional and behavioral problems among foster children. *Family Relations, 52,* 53–63. **248, 250**

Lebner, A. 2000. Genetic "mysteries" and international adoption: The cultural impact of biomedical technologies on the adoptive family experience. *Family Relations, 49,* 371–377. **242**

Lee, C. T., et al. 2011. The impact of marital discord of parents on Taiwanese adolescents' academic achievement: The mediating and moderating effect of maternal parenting practice. *Journal of Comparative Family Studies, 42,* 827–850. **278**

Lee, K. S. 2012. Marriage, cohabitation, and happiness: A cross-national analysis of 27 countries. *Journal of Marriage and Family, 74,* 953–972. **199**

Lee, R. D., et al. 2013. Behavioral and attitudinal factors differentiating male intimate partner violence perpetrators with and without a history of childhood family violence. *Journal of Family Violence, 28,* 85–94. **385**

Lee, S. M., and Boyd, M. 2008. Marrying out: Comparing the marital and social integration of Asians in the US and Canada. *Social Science Research, 37,* 311–329. **186**

Lee, Y. 2009. Early motherhood and harsh parenting: The role of human, social, and cultural capital. *Child Abuse & Neglect, 33,* 625–637. **230**

Leeder, J. 2009. "The husband can abuse you, he can do anything." *The Globe and Mail,* September 24, A14. **382**

Lefebvre, S. 2003. Housing: An income issue. *Canadian Social Trends, 68,* 15–18. **140**

Légaré, J., and Décarie, Y. 2012. Les mutations démographiques de la famille et leurs répercussions sur l'entourage des personnes âgées au Canada. In S. Rheault and J. Poirier (Eds.), *Le vieillissement démographique* (pp. 147–153). Québec: Institut de la statistique du Québec. **431**

Lemelin, J.-P., et al. 2007. The genetic-environmental etiology of cognitive school readiness and later academic achievement in early childhood. *Child Development, 78,* 1855–1869. **28, 332, 334, 336**

Lenton, R. L. 1990. Techniques of child discipline and abuse by parents. *Canadian Review of Sociology and Anthropology, 27,* 157–185. **294**

Leon, I. G. 2002. Adoption losses: Naturally occurring or socially constructed? *Child Development, 73,* 652–663. **244, 245**

Leon, K. 2003. Risk and protective factors in young children's adjustment to parental divorce: A review of the research. *Family Relations, 52,* 258–270. **157**

Leopold, T. 2012. The legacy of leaving home: Long-term effects of coresidence on parent-child relationships. *Journal of Marriage and Family, 74,* 399–412. **305**

Letourneau, N., et al. 2007. Longitudinal study of social-environmental predictors of behavior: Children of adolescent and older mothers compared. *Canadian Studies in Population, 34,* 1–27. **230**

Levan, M. B. 2001. *Creating a framework for the wisdom of the community: Victim services in Nunavut: Needs and recommendations.* Ottawa: Departement of Justice, Research and Statistics Division, Policy Centre for Victim Issues., RR03vic-3. **383**

Leve, L. D., et al. 2010a. Infant pathways to externalizing behavior: Evidence of genotype x environment interaction. *Child Development, 81,* 340–356. **286, 333**

Leve, L. D., et al. 2010b. The Early Growth and Development Study: Using the prospective adoption design to examine genotype-environment interplay, *Behaviour Genetics, 40,* 306–314. **291, 333**

Levey, G. 2009. Lament for the iGeneration. *Toronto Life,* October, 33–38. **90**

Levin, I., and Trost, J. 1999. Living apart together. *Community, Work, and Family, 2,* 279–294. **79**

LeVine, R. A. 1990. Infant environments in psychoanalysis: A cross-cultural view. In J. W. Stigler, R. A. Shweder, and G. Herd (Eds.), *Cultural psychology: Essays on comparative human development* (pp. 454–476). New York: Cambridge University Press. **17, 120, 288, 290, 292**

Lewis, M. 1997. *Altering fate:Why the past does not predict the future.* New York: Guilford Press. **286**

Li, J.-C. A., and Wu, L. L. 2008. No trend in the intergenerational transmission of divorce. *Demography, 45,* 875–883. **352**

Li, P. S. 2008. The role of foreign credentials and ethnic ties in immigrants' economic performances. *Canadian Journal of Sociology, 33,* 291–310. **109**

Lichter, D. T., and Carmalt, J. H. 2009. Religion and marital quality among low-income couples. *Social Science Research, 38,* 168–187. **177**

Lichter, D. T., and Qian, Z. 2008. Serial cohabitation and the marital life course. *Journal of Marriage and Family, 70,* 861–878. **196, 353**

Lichter, D. T., et al. 2010. National estimates of the rise in serial cohabitation. *Social Science Research, 39,* 754–765. **192, 195**

Liefbroer, A. C., and Dourleijn, E. 2006. Unmarried cohabitation and union stability: Testing the role of diffusion using data from 16 European countries. *Demography, 43,* 203–221. **352**

Lin, I.-F. 2008. Consequences of parental divorce for adult children's support of their frail parents. *Journal of Marriage and Family, 70*, 113–128. 306

Lin, K.-H., and Tomaskovic-Devey, D. 2013. Financialization and U.S. income inequality, 1970–2008. *American Journal of Sociology, 118*, 1284–1329. 95

Lindsay, C. 2006. Women in Canada. Statistics Canada, *The Daily*, March 7. 99

Lindsay, C. 2008. Canadians attend weekly religious services less than 20 years ago. Ottawa: Statistics Canada, *The Daily*, June 26. 173

Lindsey, D., and Martin, S. K. 2003. Deepening child poverty: The not so good news about welfare reform. *Children and Youth Services Review, 25*, 165–173. 421

Lipps, G., and Frank, J. 1997. The social context of school for young children. *Canadian Social Trends, 47*, 22–26. 161

Little, M. H. 2011. The invisibility of mothering. In C. Krull and J. Sempruch (Eds.), *A life in balance? Reopening the family-work debate.* (pp. 194–205). Vancouver: University of British Columbia Press. 21, 112, 226

Liu, H., and Reczek, C. 2012. Cohabitation and U.S. adult mortality: An examination by gender and race. *Journal of Marriage and Family, 74*, 794–811. 203

Liu, H., and Umberson, D. J. 2008. The times they are 'a-changin': Marital status and health differentials from 1972 to 2003. *Journal of Health and Social Behavior, 49*, 239–253. 199

Liu, M., et al. 2005. Autonomy- vs. connectedness-oriented parenting behaviours in Chinese and Canadian mothers. *International Journal of Behavioral Development, 29*, 489–495. 61

Livesey, B. 2012. *Thieves of Bay Street*. Toronto: Random House. 12, 95, 97, 124

Livingston, G., and Cohn, D'. V. 2012. *U.S. birth rate falls to a record low; decline is greatest among immigrant women*. Pew Research Center. 234

Lockhead, C. 2000. The trend toward delayed first childbirth: Health and social implications. *ISUMA: Canadian Journal of Policy Research*, Autumn, 41–44. 232

Lodge, A. C., and Umberson, D. 2012. All shook up: Sexuality of mid-to later life married couples. *Journal of Marriage and Family, 74*, 428–443. 212

Logan, J. R., Alba, R., and Zhang, W. 2002. Immigrant enclaves and ethnic communities in New York and Los Angeles. *American Sociological Review, 67*, 299–322. 132

Logan, J., and Smith, C. 2005. Face-to-face contact post adoption: Views from the triangles. *British Journal of Social Work, 35*, 3–35. 248

Longmore, M. A., Manning, W. D., and Giordano, P. G. 2001. Preadolescent parenting strategies and teens' dating and sexual initiation: A longitudinal analysis. *Journal of Marriage and Family, 63*, 322–335. 183

Longmore, M. A., et al. 2009. Parenting and adolescents' sexual initiation. *Journal of Marriage and Family, 71*, 969–982. 208

Loukas, A., and Pasch, K. 2013. Does school connectedness buffer the impact of peer victimization on early adolescents' subsequent adjustment problems? *The Journal of Early Adolescence, 33*, 245–266. 399

Love, J., et al. 2005. The effectiveness of early Head Start for 3 year-old children and their parents: Lessons for policy and programs. *Developmental Psychology, 41*, 885–901. 155

Low, S. 2012. The role of economic strain on adolescent delinquency: A microsocial process model. *Journal of Family Psychology, 26*, 576–584. 118

Lowe Vandell, P., et al. 2010. Do effects of early child care extend to age 15 years? Results from the NICHD study of early child care and youth development. *Child Development, 81*, 737–756. **153, 155**

Lowenstein, A., Katz, R., and Gur-Yaish, N. 2007. Reciprocity in parent-child exchange and life satisfaction among the elderly: A cross-national perspective. *Journal of Social Issues, 63*, 865–883. 309

Lowry, D. T., and Towles, D. W. 1989. Soap opera portrayals of sex, contraception, and sexually transmitted diseases. *Journal of Communication, 39*, 76–83. 88

Ludwig, J., Duncan, G., and Hirshfeld, P. 2001. Urban poverty and juvenile crime: Evidence from a randomized housing mobility experiment. *Quarterly Journal of Economics, 116*, 655–680. 130

Lukasiewicz, K. 2002. Ethnicity, politics and religion: Polish societies in Edmonton in the inter-war years. *Alberta History, 50*, 2–12. 48

Lundquist, J. H., and Smith, H. L. 2005. Family formation among women in the U.S. military: Evidence from the NLSY. *Journal of Marriage and Family, 67*, 1–13. 78

Luneau, K. 2013. Don't just sit there. *Maclean's*, January 14, 54–56. 83

Luo, Y., et al. 2012. Grandparents providing care to grandchildren: A population-based study of continuity and change. *Journal of Family Issues, 33*, 1143–1167. 310

Luong, M. 2008. Study: Life after teenage motherhood. Statistics Canada, *The Daily*, May 23. **228, 351**

Luong, M. 2010. Study: The financial impact of student loans. Statistics Canada, *Perspectives on Labour and Income 11*, January. **97, 304**

Luong, M. 2011. The wealth and finances of employed low-income families. *Perspectives on Labour and Income, 23*, July. Ottawa: Statistics Canada. 105

Luster, T., and Oh, S. M. 2001. Correlates of male adolescents carrying handguns among their peers. *Journal of Marriage and Family, 63*, 714–726. 127

Luthar, S. S. 2003. The culture of affluence: Psychological costs of material wealth. *Child Development, 74*, 1581–1593. 125

Luthar, S. S., and Becker, B. E. 2002. Privileged but pressured: A study of affluent youth. *Child Development, 73*, 1593–1610. **124, 125**

Luxton, M. 1997. Feminism and families: The challenge of neo-conservatism. In M. Luxton (Ed.), *Feminism and families* (pp. 10–26). Halifax: Fernwood. **22, 70**

Luxton, M. 2006a. Feminist political economy in Canada and the politics of social reproduction. In K. Bezanson and M. Luxton (Eds.), *Social reproduction: Feminist political economy challenges neo-liberalism* (pp. 11–44). Montreal: McGill-Queen's University Press. **12, 13, 20, 70, 108, 124, 226, 233, 308, 409**

Luxton, M. 2006b. Friends, neighbours, and community: A case study of the role of informal caregivers in social reproduction. In K. Bezanson and M. Luxton (Eds.), *Social reproduction: Feminist political economy challenges neo-liberalism* (pp. 263–292). Montreal: McGill-Queen's University Press. **74, 413, 430**

Luxton, M. 2009. Conceptualizing families: Theoretical frameworks. In M. Baker (Ed.), *Families: Changing trends in Canada*, 6th Ed. (pp. 26–48). Toronto: McGraw-Hill Ryerson. **11, 20**

Luxton, M., and Corman, J. 2001. *Getting by in hard times: Gendered labour at home and on the job*. Toronto: University of Toronto Press. 18

Lynch, S. K., et al. 2006. A genetically informed study of the association between harsh punishment and offspring behavioral problems. *Journal of Family Psychology, 20,* 190–198. **293, 294**

Ma, C. P., and Rietschlin, J. 2012. Intimate partner victimization among adults aged 60 and older: An analysis of the 1999 and 2004 General Social Survey. *Journal of Elder Abuse & Neglect, 24,* 120–137. **381, 382, 403**

Ma, L., Lerner, J., and Lerner, R. M. 2009. Academic competence for adolescents who bully and who are bullied. *Journal of Early Adolescence, 29,* 862–897. **400**

Ma, X., and Zhang, Y. 2002. *A national assessment of effects of school experiences on health outcomes and behaviours of children.* Technical Report. Ottawa: Health Canada. **157, 158, 159**

Mac Con, K. 2006. The impact of family context on adolescent emotional health during the transition to high school. In K. McQuillan and Z. R. Ravanera (Eds), *Canada changing families. Implications for individuals and society* (pp. 160–178). Toronto: University of Toronto Press. **370, 410**

Maccoby, E. E., and Jacklin, C. N. 1983. The "person" characteristics of children and the family as environment. In D. D. Magnusson and V. L. Allen (Eds.), *Human development: An interactional perspective* (pp. 75–92). New York: Academic Press. **26**

Maccoby, E. E., and Lewis, C. C. 2003. Less day care or different daycare? *Child Development, 74,* 1069–1075. **153, 419**

Maccoby, E. E., and Martin, J. 1983. Socialization in the context of the family: Parent-child interaction. In E. M. Hetherington (Ed.), *Handbook of child psychology: vol. 4. Socialization, personality, and social development* (pp. 1–101). New York: Wiley. **291**

MacDermid, S. M., et al. 2004. *Child care use and satisfaction among military families with preschool children.* U.S. Military Family Research Institute, Purdue University. **78**

Macdonald, C. L. 2010. *Shadow mothers.* Berkeley, CA: University of California Press. **13, 18, 102, 270**

MacDonald, M. A. 1990. *Rebels and royalists: The lives and material culture of New Brunswick's early English-speaking settlers, 1758–1783.* Fredericton, NB: New Ireland Press. **41**

MacDougall, K., et al. 2013. Age shock: Misperceptions of the impact of age on fertility before and after IVF in women who conceive after age 40. *Human Reproduction, 28,* 350–356. **231**

MacIntosh, H., and Andruff, H. 2010. Same-sex marriage in Canada: The impact of legal marriage on the first cohort of gay and lesbian Canadians to wed. *The Canadian Journal of Human Sexuality, 19,* 79–90. **201**

Mackenzie, C. S., et al. 2009. Associations between psychological distress, learning, and memory in spouse caregivers of older adults. *The Journals of Gerontology: Series B, 64B,* 742–750. **268**

Mackenzie, H. 2012a. *Canada's CEO elite 100: The 0.01%.* Canadian Centre for Policy Alternatives. **12, 96**

Mackenzie, H. 2012b. Inequality frays the ties that bind. *Toronto Star,* December 31. **97**

MacKinnon, C. 2005. *Women's lives, men's laws.* Cambridge, MA: Harvard University Press. **21**

MacKinnon, C. 2006. *Are women human? And other international dialogues.* Cambridge, MA: Harvard University Press. **22**

MacMillan, H. L., et al. 1997. Prevalence of child physical and sexual abuse in the community: Results from the Ontario Health Supplement. *Journal of the American Medical Association Abstracts, 9,* July 9. **386**

MacMillan, H. L., et al. 2001. Childhood abuse and lifetime psychopathology in a community sample. *American Journal of Psychiatry, 158,* 1878–1883. **389**

Macmillan, R., and Copher, R. 2005. Families in the life course: Interdependency or roles, role configurations, and pathways. *Journal of Marriage and Family, 67,* 858–879. **23**

MacQueen, K. 2009. What Canadians really believe. *Maclean's,* November 30, 46–50. **7, 214**

MacQueen, K. 2011. Success, one student at a time. *Maclean's,* November 7, 72–78. **167**

MacQueen, K. 2012. The value of giving in the Valley. *Maclean's,* January 9, 18. **173**

MacTavish, K. 2007. The wrong side of the tracks: Social inequality and mobile home park residence. *Community Development, 38,* 74–91. **142**

Madden-Derdich, D. A., and Leonard, S. A. 2000. Parental role identity and fathers' involvement in coparental interaction after divorce: Fathers' perspectives. *Family Relations, 49,* 311–318. **20**

Madhavan, S. 2002. Best of friends and worst of enemies: Competition and collaboration in polygamy. *Ethnology, 41,* 69–84. **10**

Magee, K. 2008. "They are the life of the nation": Women and war in traditional Nadouek society. *The Canadian Journal of Native Studies, 28,* 185–199. **37**

Magee, K. 2011. 'They are the life of the nation': Women and war in traditional Nadoueh society. In M. Gleeson et al. (Eds.), *Rethinking Canada: The promise of women's history* (pp. 13–22). Toronto: Oxford University Press. **37**

Mahmood, S. 2005. *The politics of piety.* Princeton: Princeton University Press. **22**

Mahoney, J. L., Lord, H., and Carryl, E. 2005. An ecological analysis of after-school program participation and the development of academic performance and motivational attributes for disadvantaged children. *Child Development, 76,* 811–825. **425**

Maisel, N. C., and Karney, B. R. 2012. Socioeconomic status moderates associations among stressful events, mental health, and relationship satisfaction. *Journal of Family Psychology, 26,* 654–600. **118**

Maldonado-Carrēno, C., and Votruba-Drzal, E. 2011. Teacher-child relationships and the development of academic and behavioral skills during elementary school: A within-and between-child analysis. *Child Development, 82,* 601–616. **157**

Mallett, S., Rosenthal, D., and Keys, D. 2005. Young people, drug use, and family conflict: Pathways into homelessness. *Journal of Adolescence, 28,* 185–199. **133**

Mallon, G. P. 2005. *Gay men choosing parenthood.* New York: Columbia University Press. **251**

Malszecki, G., and Cavar, T. 2004. Men, masculinities, war & sport. In N. Mandell (Ed.), *Feminist issues: Race, class, and gender,* 4th Ed. (pp. 160–187). Toronto: Prentice Hall. **83, 87**

Man, G. 2001. From Hong Kong to Canada: Immigration and the changing family lives of middle-class women from Hong Kong. In B. Fox (Ed.), *Family patterns, gender relations,* 2nd Ed. (pp. 420–438). Toronto: Oxford University Press. **60**

Mandelbaum, D. J. 1979. *The Plains Cree: An ethnographical, historical and comparative study.* Regina: Canadian Plains Research Centre. **36**

Mandell, N., and Sweet, R. 2004. Homework as home work: Mothers' unpaid educational labour. *Atlantis, 28.2,* 7–18. **71, 158**

Mandell, N., and Wilson, S. 2011. Intergenerational carework: Mothering, grandmothering, and eldercare. In C. Krull and J. Sempruch (Eds)., *A life in balance? Reopening the family-work debate.* (pp. 30–46). Vancouver: University of British Columbia Press. **73, 74, 108, 236, 308, 310, 413, 419, 430**

Manganello, J. A., and Taylor, C. A. 2009. Television exposure as a risk factor for aggressive behavior among 3-year-old children. *Archives of Pediatrics & Adolescent Medicine, 11,* 1037–1045. **86**

Manlove, J., et al. 2002. *Preventing teenage pregnancy, childbearing, and sexually transmitted diseases: What the research shows.* Washington, DC: Child Trends Research Brief. May. **158, 208**

Manlove, J., et al. 2008a. Factors associated with multiple-partner fertility among fathers. *Journal of Marriage and Family, 70,* 536–548. **111, 229**

Manlove, J., et al. 2008b. Pathways from family religiosity to adolescent sexual activity and contraceptive use. *Perspectives on Reproductive Health, 40,* 105–117.

Mann, C. C. 2011. *1493.* New York: Alfred A. Knopf. **175**

Mannheim, K. 1936. *Ideology and Utopia.* London: Routledge & Kegan Paul. **16**

Manning, W. D. 2002. The implications of cohabitation for children's well-being. In A. Booth and A. C. Crouter (Eds.), *Just living together* (pp. 121–152). Mahwah, NJ: Erlbaum. **221**

Manning, W. C., and Cohen, J. A. 2012. Premarital cohabitation and marital dissolution: An examination of recent marriage. *Journal of Marriage and Family, 74,* 377–387. **196**

Manning, W. D., and Lamb, K. A. 2003. Adolescent well-being in cohabiting, married, and single-parent families. *Journal of Marriage and Family, 65,* 876–893. **221, 222**

Manning, W. D., and Smock, P. J. 2000. "Swapping" families: Serial parenting and economic support for children. *Journal of Marriage and Family, 62,* 111–122. **349**

Manning, W. D., Stewart, S. D., and Smock, P. J. 2004. The complexity of father's parenting responsibilities and involvement with non-residential children. *Journal of Family Issues, 24,* 645–667. **349**

March, K. 1995a. Perception of adoption as social stigma: Motivation for search and reunion. *Journal of Marriage and Family, 57,* 653–660. **244, 249**

March, K. 1995b. *The stranger who bore me.* Toronto: University of Toronto Press. **249**

Marcil-Gratton, N. 1998. *Growing up with mom and dad? The intricate life course of Canadian children.* Ottawa: Statistics Canada, Catalogue no. 89–566. **221**

Marcil-Gratton, N. 1999. Growing up with mom and dad? Canadian children experience shifting family structures. *Transition, 29,* September, 4–7. **349**

Marcil-Gratton, N., et al. 2003. Du passé conjugal des parents au devenir familial des enfants: Un example de la nécessité d'une approche longitudinale. *Sociologie et sociétés, 35,* 143–164. **351, 352, 368, 370**

Marcussen, K. 2005. Explaining difference in mental health between married and cohabiting individuals. *Social Psychological Quarterly, 68,* 239–257. **193**

Margolin, G. 1998. Effects of domestic violence on children. In P. K. Trickett and C. J. Schellenback (Eds.), *Violence against children in*

the family and the community (pp. 57–101). Washington, DC: American Psychological Association. **389**

Marin, B. V. O., et al. 2006. Boyfriends, girlfriends and teenagers' risk of sexual involvement. *Perspectives on Sexual and Reproductive Health, 38,* 76–83. **209**

Markman, H. J., et al. 2010. The premarital communication roots of marital distress and divorce: The first five years of marriage. *Journal of Family Psychology, 24,* 289–298. **355**

Marks, G. N. 2006. Family size, family type and student achievement: Cross-national differences and the role of socioeconomic and school factors. *Journal of Comparative Family Studies, 37,* 18–24. **154, 319, 370**

Marks, L. 2004. Feminism and stay-at-home motherhood: Some critical reflections and implications for mothers on social assistance. *Atlantis, 28.2,* 73–83. **21, 100**

Marks, S. R. 2000. Teasing out the lessons of the 1960s: Family diversity and family privilege. *Journal of Marriage and Family, 62,* 609–622. **124**

Marquis, R. A., et al. 2008. The relationship of child neglect and physical maltreatment to placement outcomes and behavioral adjustment in children in foster care: A Canadian perspective. *Child Welfare, 87,* 5–26. **251, 391**

Marshall, A. R. 2011. *The way of the bachelor: Early Chinese settlement in Manitoba.* Vancouver: University of British Columbia Press. **7, 49, 172**

Marshall, B. L. 2011. The greying of "sexual health": A critical research agenda. *Canadian Review of Sociology, 48,* 390–413. **203, 212**

Marshall, K. 2006. General Social Survey: Paid and unpaid work. Statistics Canada, *Perspectives on Labour and Income, 7,* July. **101, 102, 419**

Marsiglio, W. 2004. When stepfathers claim stepchildren: A conceptual analysis. *Journal of Marriage and Family, 66,* 22–39. **246**

Marsiglio, W., and Roy, K. 2012. *Nurturing dads: Social initiatives for contemporary fatherhood.* New York: Russell Sage. **20, 251**

Martel, L., and Bélanger, A. 2000. Dependence-free life expectancy in Canada. *Canadian Social Trends, 58,* 26–29. **312**

Martikainen, P., et al. 2005. Differences in mortality by marital status in Finland from 1976 to 2000. *Population Studies, 59,* 99–115. **198**

Martin, A., Brooks-Gunn, J., and Ryan, R. M. 2010. When fathers' supportiveness matters most: Maternal and paternal parenting and children's school readiness. *Journal of Family Psychology, 24,* 145–155. **158**

Martin, G. 1974. British officials and their attitudes to the Negro community in Canada, 1833–1861. *Ontario History, 66,* 79–88. **45**

Martin, L., and Hou, F. 2010. Sharing lives: Women, marital trends and education. Statistics Canada. Ottawa: *The Daily,* September 9. **189, 191**

Martin, R. L. 2011. *Fixing the game.* Boston: Harvard Business Review Press. **95**

Martin, V., Mills, M., and Le Bourdais, C. 2005. The consequences of parental divorce on the life course outcomes of Canadian children. *Canadian Studies in Population, 32,* 29–51. **358**

Martinez-Torteya, C., et al. 2009. Resilience among children exposed to domestic violence: The role of risk and protective factors. *Child Development, 80,* 562–577. **385**

Martin-Matthews, A. 1991. *Widowhood in later life*. Toronto: Butterworths/Harcourt. **364**

Martin-Matthews, A. 2000. Change and diversity in aging families and intergenerational relations. In N. Mandell and A. Duffy (Eds.), *Canadian families: Diversity, conflict, and change* (pp. 323–360). Toronto: Harcourt Canada. **24, 305**

Martin-Matthews, A. 2001. *The ties that bind aging families*. Ottawa: The Vanier Institute of the Family. **308**

Martin-Matthews, A. 2007. Situating "home" at the nexus of the public and private spheres. *Current Sociology, 55*, 229–249. **21**

Marx, K. 1867 (1967). *Capital: A critique of political economy*. New York: International Publishers. **11, 95, 107, 108, 119, 157, 287, 288, 375, 412, 417, 420**

Mashburn, A. J., et al. 2008. Measures of classroom quality in pre-kindergarten and children's development of academic, language, and social skills. *Child Development, 79*, 732–749. **152**

Masten, C. L., Juvonen, J., and Spatzier, A. 2009. Relative importance of peers. Differences in academic and social behaviors at three grade levels spanning late childhood and early adolescence. *Journal of Early Adolescence, 29*, 773–799. **301**

Mata, F. 2011. *Lone-parent status among ethnic groups in Canada: Prevalence, composition and generational persistence*. Vancouver: Metropolis British Columbia. **220**

Mather, M., and Rivers, K. L. 2006. *The concentration of negative child outcomes in low-income U.S. neighbourhoods*. Population Reference Bureau. **130**

Maxim, P. S., White, J. P., and Gyimah, S. O. 2003. Earnings implications of person years lost life expectancy among Canada's Aboriginal peoples. *Canadian Studies in Population, 30*, 271–295. **128**

Mayberry, M., et al. 1995. *Home-schooling: Parents as educators*. Thousand Oaks, CA: Corwin. **169**

Mayer, L. 2008. Aboriginal women and education: Overcoming a legacy of abuse. *The Canadian Journal of Native Studies, 27*, 35–48. **35**

Mayfield, M. 2001. *Early childhood education and care in Canada*. Toronto: Prentice Hall. **154**

McCabe, K. M., et al. 2005. The relation between violence exposure and conduct problems among adolescents: A prospective study. *American Journal of Orthopsychiatry, 75*, 575–584. **128**

McCann, L. 1999. Seasons of labor: Family work and land in a nineteenth century Nova Scotia shipping community. *History of the Family, 4*, 485–527. **138**

McCarthy, E. D. 1996. *Knowledge as culture: The new sociology of knowledge*. London: Routledge. **16**

McCartney, K., et al. 1997. Social development in the context of typical center-based child care. *Merrill-Palmer Quarterly, 43*, 426–450. **153**

McCartney, K., et al. 2010. Testing a series of causal propositions relating time in child care to children's externalizing behavior. *Developmental Psychology, 46*, 1–17. **153, 154**

McClare, D. (Ed.) 1997. *The 1815 diary of a Nova Scotia farm girl, Louisa Collins of Colin Grove, Dartmouth*. Dartmouth, NS: Brook House Press. **42**

McClintock, E. A. 2010. When does race matter? Race, sex, and dating at an elite university. *Journal of Marriage and Family, 72*, 45–72. **185, 186**

McCloskey, L. A., Figueredo, A. J., and Koss, M. P. 1995. The effects of systemic family violence on children's mental health. *Child Development, 66*, 1239–1261. **394**

McCurdy, K., and Daro, D. 1994. Child maltreatment: A national survey of reports and fatalities. *Journal of Interpersonal Violence, 9*, 75–94. **391**

McDaniel, B. T., and Teti, D. M. 2012. Coparenting quality during the first three months after birth: The role of infant sleep quality. *Journal of Family Psychology, 26*, 886–895. **286**

McDaniel, S. A. 2002. Women's changing relations to the state and citizenship: Caring and intergenerational relations in globalizing Western democracies. *Canadian Review of Sociology and Anthropology, 39*, 1–26. **23**

McDaniel, S. A. 2003. Family/work challenges among mid-life and older Canadians. In M. Lynn (Ed.), *Voices: Essays on Canadian families*, 2nd. Ed. (pp. 152–176). Toronto: Thomson Nelson. **24, 307**

McDaniel, S. A. 2009. The family lives of the middle-aged and elderly in Canada. In M. Baker (Ed.), *Families: Changing trends in Canada*, 6th Ed. (pp. 225–242). Toronto: McGraw-Hill Ryerson. **21, 268, 274, 308, 317**

McDonald, K. B., and Armstrong, E. M. 2001. De-romanticizing Black intergenerational support: The questionable expectations of welfare reform. *Journal of Marriage and Family, 63*, 213–223. **130**

McDonald, R., et al. 2009. Children's adjustment problems in families characterized by men's severe violence toward women: Does other family violence matter? *Child Abuse & Neglect, 33*, 94–101. **385, 389**

McDonough, S., and Hoodfar, H. 2005. Muslims in Canada: From ethnic groups to religious community. In P. Bramadat and D. Seljak (Eds.), *Religion and ethnicity in Canada* (pp. 133–153). Toronto: Pearson. **173**

McGene, J., and King, V. 2012. Implications of new marriages and children for coparenting in nonresident father families. *Journal of Family Issues, 33*, 1619–1641. **19, 368**

McGillivray, A., and Comaskey, B. 1999. *Black eyes all the time: Intimate violence, aboriginal women, and the justice system*. Toronto: University of Toronto Press. **385**

McHale, S. M., and Crouter, A. C. 1996. The family contexts of children's sibling relationships. In G. H. Brody (Ed.), *Sibling relationships: Their causes and consequences* (pp. 173–196). Norwood, NJ: Ablex. **322**

McHale, S. et al. 2012. Sibling relationships and influences in childhood and adolescence. *Journal of Marriage and Family, 74*, 913–930. **317, 322**

McIlvane, J. M., Ajrouch, K. J., and Antonucci, T. C. 2007. Generational structure and social resources in mid-life: Influences on health and well-being. *Journal of Social Issues, 63*, 759–773. **306**

McIntosh, C. N., et al. 2009. Income disparities in health-adjusted life expectancy for Canadian adults, 1991 to 2001. Statistics Canada, *Health Reports, 20*, November. **114**

McIntosh, R. 2003. The boys in Nova Scotian coal mines: 1873–1923. In N. Janovicek and J. Parr (Eds.), *Histories of Canadian children and youth* (pp. 77–87). Toronto: Oxford University Press. **46**

McIntyre, L., et al. 2002. Food insecurity of low-income lone mothers and their children in Atlantic Canada. *Canadian Journal of Public Health, 93*, 411–416. **117**

McKay, A. 2005. Sexuality and substance use: The impact of tobacco, alcohol, and selected recreational drugs on sexual function. *The Canadian Journal of Human Sexuality, 14,* 47–57. **208**

McKay, A., and Barrett, M. 2010. Trends in teen pregnancy rates from 1996–2006: A comparison of Canada, Sweden, U. S. A., and England/Wales. *The Canadian Journal of Human Sexuality, 19,* 43–52. **226, 237, 415**

McLean, J., and Welsh, M. 2011. Nursing home neglect flourishes in secret. *Toronto Star,* November 18, A6. **404, 430**

McLeod, N. 2000. Plains Cree identity: Borderlands, ambiguous genealogies and narrative irony. *Canadian Journal of Native Studies, 20,* 437–454. **37**

McLoyd, V. C. 1998. Socioeconomic disadvantage and child development. *American Psychologist, 53,* 185–204. **118**

McLoyd, V. C., and Smith, J. 2002. Physical discipline and behavior problems in African American, European American, and Hispanic children: Emotional support as a moderator. *Journal of Marriage and Family, 64,* 40–53. **293**

McManus, P. A., and DiPrete, T. A. 2001. Losers and winners: The financial consequences of separation and divorce for men. *American Sociological Review, 66,* 246–268. **415**

McNeil, J. 1975. Feminism, femininity and the television shows: A content analysis. *Journal of Broadcasting, 19,* 259–269. **81**

McNulty, J. K. 2008. Forgiveness and marriage: Putting the benefits into context. *Journal of Family Psychology, 22,* 171–175. **265**

McNulty, J. K., Neff, L. A., and Karney, B. R. 2008. Beyond initial attraction: Physical attractiveness in newlywed marriage. *Journal of Family Psychology, 22,* 135–143. **190**

McPherson, B. D. 1998. *Aging as a social process,* 3rd Ed. Toronto: Harcourt Brace. **53, 310**

McPherson, C. J., Wilson, K. G., and Murray, M. A. 2007. Feeling like a burden: Exploring the perspectives of patients at the end of life. *Social Science and Medicine, 64,* 417–427. **309**

McQuillan, K. 2006. Conclusion: Family change and the challenge for social policy. In K. McQuillan and Z. R. Ravanera (Eds.), *Canada's changing families. Implications for individuals and society* (pp. 293–306). Toronto: University of Toronto Press. **428**

McWey, L. M., and Mullis, A. K. 2004. Improving the lives of children in foster care: The impact of supervised visitation. *Family Relations, 53,* 293–300. **250**

McWhinnie, A. 2001. Should offspring from donated gametes continue to be denied knowledge of their origins and antecedents? *Human Reproduction, 16,* 807–817. **239**

Mead, G. H. 1934. *Mind, self and society.* Chicago: University of Chicago Press. **25**

Mead, M. 1928. *Coming of age in Samoa.* New York: William Morrow. **297**

Meaney, M. J. 2010. Epigenetics and the biological definition of gene x environment interactions. *Child Development, 81,* 41–79. **28**

Meier, A. M. 2007. Adolescent first sex and subsequent mental health. *American Journal of Sociology, 112,* 1811–1847. **207**

Meier, A., Hull, K. E., and Ortyl, T. A. 2009. Young adult relationship values and the intersection of gender and sexuality. *Journal of Marriage and Family, 71,* 510–525. **210**

Meijer, A. M., and van den Wittenboer, G. L. H. 2007. Contribution of infants' sleep and crying to marital relationship of first-time parent couples in the 1st year after childbirth. *Journal of Family Psychology, 21,* 49–57. **276**

Meilleur, N., and Lapierre-Adamcyk, E. 2006. Single parenthood and labour force participation: The effect of social policies. In K. McQuillan and Z. R. Ravanera (Eds.), *Canada's changing families. Implications for individuals and society* (pp. 210–236). Toronto: University of Toronto Press. **417, 420**

Mejer, L., and Robert-Bobée, I. 2003. *Mortalité des femmes et environnement familial.* Paris: INSEE, April. **140**

Melzer, S. A. 2002. Gender, work, and intimate violence: Men's occupational violence spillover and compensatory violence. *Journal of Marriage and Family, 64,* 820–832. **381**

Menaghan, E. G., and Parcel, T. L. 1995. Social sources of change in children's home environments: The effects of parental occupational experiences and family conditions. *Journal of Marriage and Family, 57,* 69–84. **113**

Ménard, F.-P., and Le Bourdais, C. 2012. Impact de la diversification des trajectoires familiales sur les échanges intergénérationnels. In S. Rhéault and J. Poirier, (Eds.), *Le vieillissement démographique: de nombreux enjeux à déchiffrer* (pp. 131–146). Québec: Institut de la statistique du Québec. **305, 306, 358, 431**

Mendle, J., et al. 2009. Associations between father absence and age of first sexual intercourse. *Child Development, 80,* 1463–1480. **208, 231**

Mendleson, R. 2013. Peel faces big-city woes. *Toronto Star,* Section GT, April 6. **123**

Menon, M., et al. 2007. The developmental costs of high self-esteem for antisocial children. *Child Development, 78,* 1627–1639. **17**

Merton, R. K. 1968. *Social theory and social structure.* New York: Free Press. **10**

Messner, M. 1997. *The politics of masculinity: Men in movements.* Thousand Oaks, CA: Sage. **22**

Metz, M. E., Rosser, B. R. S., and Strapko, N. 1994. Differences in conflict-resolution styles among heterosexual, gay, and lesbian couples. *Journal of Sex Research, 31,* 293–308. **264**

Metzger, J. 2008. Resiliency in children and youth in kinship care and family foster care. *Child Welfare, 87,* 115–121. **251**

Meyer, D. R., and Cancian, M. 2012. "I'm not supporting his kids": Nonresident fathers' contributions given mothers' new fertility. *Journal of Marriage and Family, 74,* 132–151. **349**

Miall, C. E., and March, K. 2005. Open adoption as a family form: Community assessment and social support. *Journal of Family Issues, 26,* 380–410. **242**

Michelson, W., and Tepperman, L. 2003. Focus on home: What time-use data can tell you about caregiving to adults. *Journal of Social Issues, 59,* 591–610. **308**

Middelburg, M. J., et al. 2008. Neuromotor, cognitive, language, and behavioural outcome in children born following IVF or ICSI—a systematic review. *Human Reproduction Update, 14,* 219–231. **240**

Migliaccio, T. A. 2002. Abused husbands: A narrative analysis. *Journal of Family Issues, 23,* 26–52. **381**

Milan, A. 2000. One hundred years of families. *Canadian Social Trends, 56,* 2–12. **193, 212, 234**

Milan, A. 2003. Would you live common-law? *Canadian Social Trends, 70,* 2–6. **191, 192**

Milan, A., and Hamm, B. 2003. Across the generations: Grandparents and grandchildren. *Canadian Social Trends, 71,* 2–7. **24, 311**

Milan, A., and Hamm, B. 2004. Mixed unions. *Canadian Social Trends, 73,* 2–6. **132**

Milan, A., and Peters, A. 2003. Couples living apart. *Canadian Social Trends, 69,* 2–6. **79, 193**

Milan, A., Maheux, H., and Chui, T. 2010. A portrait of couples in mixed unions. *Canadian Social Trends, 80,* April 20. **185, 186, 189**

Milan, A., Vézina, M., and Wells, C. 2009. *2006 Census: Family portrait: Continuity and change in Canadian families and households in 2006.* Statistics Canada, Demography Division, November 30. **311**

Milardo, R. 2009. *The forgotten kin: Aunts and uncles.* New York: Cambridge University Press. **6**

Milburn, N. G., et al. 2005. Predictors of close family relationships over one year among homeless young people. *Journal of Adolescence, 28,* 263–275. **134**

Miles-Doan, R. 1998. Violence between spouses and intimates: Does neighborhood context matter? *Social Forces, 77,* 623–645. **382**

Miller, A. B. K. 2012. Leaving home: an example of the disappearance of childhood and its end as a predictable set of uniform experiences. In N. Lauster and G. Allan (Eds.), *The end of children?* (pp. 105–120), Vancouver: University of British Columbia Press. **304**

Miller, B. C., et al. 2000. Comparisons of adopted and nonadopted adolescents in a large nationally representative sample. *Child Development, 71,* 1458–1473. **243, 244, 245**

Miller, B. D. 2005. *Cultural anthropology,* 3rd Ed. Boston: Pearson. **7, 17, 242, 243**

Miller, F., Jenkins, J., and Keating, D. 2002. Parenting and children's behaviour problems. In J. D. Willms (Ed.), *Vulnerable children* (pp. 167–182). Edmonton: University of Alberta Press. **389**

Miller, K. S., Forehand, R., and Kotchick, B. A. 1999. Adolescent sexual behavior in two ethnic minority samples: The role of family variables. *Journal of Marriage and Family, 61,* 85–98. **205**

Miller, L. C. 2005. International adoption, behavior, and mental health. *Journal of the American Medical Association, 293,* 2533–2536. **243**

Miller, P. 2012. A thing or two about twins. *National Geographic,* January, 46–65. **334, 336**

Miller, P. J. E., Caughlin, J. P., and Huston, T. L. 2003. Trait expressiveness and marital satisfaction: The role idealization processes. *Journal of Marriage and Family, 65,* 978–995. **263**

Miller, T. 2011. *Making sense of fatherhood: Gender, caring and work.* New York: Cambridge University Press. **19**

Minze, L. C., et al. 2010. Making sense of family conflict: Intimate partner violence and preschoolers' externalizing problems. *Journal of Family Psychology, 24,* 5–11. **384**

Mirrlees-Black, C., Mayhew, P., and Percy, A. 1996. *The 1996 British Crime Survey: England and Wales.* London: Home Office Statistical Bulletin, no. 19–96. **402**

Mitchell, B. A. 2000. The refilled "nest": Debunking the myth of families in crisis. In E. M. Gee and G. M. Guttman (Eds.), *The overselling of population aging* (pp. 80–99). Toronto: Oxford University Press. **303**

Mitchell, B. A. 2003. Would I share a home with an elderly parent? Exploring ethnocultural diversity and intergenerational support relations during young adulthood. *Canadian Journal on Aging, 22,* 69–82. **6, 419**

Mitchell, B. A. 2004. Home, but not alone: Socio-cultural and economic aspects of Canadian young adults sharing parental households. *Atlantis, 28,* 2, 115–125. **73, 305**

Mitchell, B. A. 2010. Midlife marital happiness and ethnic culture: A life course perspective. *Journal of Comparative Family Studies, 41,* 167–192. **263**

Mitchell, B. A., and Gee, E. M. 1996. Young adults returning home. Implications for social policy. In B. Galaway and J. Hudson (Eds.), *Youth in transition: Perspectives on research and policy* (pp. 61–71). Toronto: Thompson. **305**

Mitchell, K. J., Finkelhor, D., and Wolak, J. 2001. Risk factors for and impact of online sexual solicitation on youth. *Journal of the American Medical Association, 285,* June 20, 3011–3014. **88**

Mitnick, D. M., Heyman, R. E., and Smith Slep, A. M. 2009. Changes in relationship satisfaction across the transition to parenthood: A meta-analysis. *Journal of Family Psychology, 23,* 848–852. **263, 277**

Modell, J., and Goodman, M. 1990. Historical perspectives. In S. S. Feldman and G. R. Elliott (Eds.), *At the threshold: The developing adolescent* (pp. 93–122). Cambridge, MA: Harvard University Press. **297**

Mody, P. 2002. Love and the law: Love-marriage in Delhi. *Modern Asian Studies, 36,* 223–256. **62**

Moen, P., and Roehling, P. 2005. *The career mystique.* New York: Rowman & Littlefield. **95, 101**

Moffitt, T. E., et al. 2002. Males on the life-course-persistent and adolescence-limited antisocial pathways: Follow-up at age 26. *Development and Psychopathology, 14,* 179–206. **229**

Moghissi, H., Rahnema, S., and Goodman, M. J. 2009. *Diaspora by design.* Toronto: University of Toronto Press. **61, 64, 177, 264, 298**

Mohammed, P. 2002. (Ed.). *Gendered realities. Essays in Caribbean feminist thought.* Barbados: University of the West Indies Press. **22**

Möhler, E., et al. 2009. Mothers with a history of abuse tend to show more impulsiveness. *Child Abuse & Neglect, 33,* 123–126. **390**

Moilanen, K. L., et al. 2009. Growth and predictors of parental knowledge of youth behavior during early adolescence. *Journal of Early Adolescence, 29,* 800–825. **296, 302, 328**

Mollborn, S., and Morningstar, E. 2009. Investigating the relationship between teenage childbearing and psychological distress using longitudinal evidence. *Journal of Health and Social Behavior, 50,* 310–326. **228**

Monna, B., and Gauthier, A. H. 2008. A review of the literature on the social and economic determinants of parental time. *Journal of Family and Economic Issues, 29,* 634–653. **116**

Monsebraaten, L. 2009. Native children flooding into aid societies. *Toronto Star.* November 22, A1, A14. **52**

Mousebraaten, L. 2010. Welfare vise quashes hope of recovery, report finds. *Toronto Star,* December 14, A1, A19. **422**

Monsebraaten, L. 2011. Working for peanuts, going unpaid. *Toronto Star,* May 12. **109**

Monsebraaten, L. 2012. More help urged for Crown wards. *Toronto Star,* March 1, A8. **250**

Monserud, M. A. 2008. Intergenerational relationships and affectual solidarity between grandparents and young adults. *Journal of Marriage and Family, 70,* 182–195. **310**

Moore, K. A., Nord, C. W., and Peterson, J. L. 1989. Nonvoluntary sexual activity among adolescents. *Family Planning Perspectives, 21,* 110–114. **401**

Moore, M. R., and Chase-Lansdale, P. L. 2001. Sexual intercourse and pregnancy among African American girls in high-poverty neighborhoods: The role of family and perceived community environment. *Journal of Marriage and Family, 63*, 1146–1157. **131**

Moreno, M. A., et al. 2009. Display of health risk behaviors on MySpace by adolescents. *Archives of Pediatrics & Adolescent Medicine, 163*, 27–34. **90**

Morgan, L. H. 1877 (1963). *Ancient society.* New York: World Publishing Co. **12**

Morgan, S. P., Zhigand, G., and Hayford, S. R. 2009. China's below-replacement fertility: Recent trends and future prospects. *Population and Development Review, 35*, 605–629. **59, 235**

Morris, J. F., Balsam, K. F., and Rothblum, E. D. 2001. Lesbian and bisexual mothers and nonmothers: Demographics and the coming-out process. *Journal of Family Psychology, 16*, 144–156. **210, 225**

Morris, M. 2004. What research reveals about gender, home care, and caregiving: Overview and the case for gender analysis. In K. R. Grant et al. (Eds.), *Caring for/caring about* (pp. 91–114). Aurora, On: Garamond Press. **136**

Morissette, R. 2002. On the edge: Financially vulnerable families. *Canadian Social Trends, 67*, 13–17. **106, 113**

Morissette, R., and Hou, F. 2008. Does the labour supply of wives respond to husbands' wages? Canadian evidence from micro data and grouped data. *Canadian Journal of Economics, 41*, 1185–1210. **100**

Morissette, R., and Zhang, X. 2001. Experiencing low income for several years. *Perspectives on Labour and Income, 2*, March, 5–15. **112**

Morissey, T. W. 2009. Multiple child-care arrangements and young children's behavioral outcomes. *Child Development, 80*, 59–76. **151**

Morrison, D. R., and Cherlin, A. J. 1995. The divorce process and young children's well-being: A prospective analysis. *Journal of Marriage and Family, 57*, 800–812. **362**

Morrison, N. C., and Clavenna-Valleroy, J. 1998. Perceptions of maternal support as related to self-concept and self-report of depression in sexually abused female adolescents. *Journal of Child Sexual Abuse, 7*, 23–40. **394**

Moscovitch, A. 2007. *Good servant, bad master? Electronic media and the family.* Ottawa: The Vanier Institute of the Family. **72, 82, 87**

Moss, K. 2004. Kids witnessing family violence. *Canadian Social Trends, 73*, 12–16. **119, 384**

Moss, M. H. 1998. *Manliness and militarism: Educating young men for war in the province of Ontario.* Ed. D. dissertation, University of Toronto. **46**

Moyers, S., Farmer, E., and Lipscombe, J. 2006. Contact with family members and its impact on adolescents and their foster placements. *British Journal of Social Work, 36*, 541–559. **250**

Moylan, C. A., et al. 2010. The effect of child abuse and exposure to domestic violence on adolescent internalizing and externalizing behavior problems. *Journal of Family Violence, 25*, 53–63. **389**

Mueller, M. M., and Elder, G. H., Jr. 2003. Family contingencies across the generations: Grandparent-grandchild relationships in holistic perspective. *Journal of Marriage and Family, 65*, 404–417. **310**

Mulvaney, M. K., and Mebert, C. J. 2007. Parental corporal punishment predicts problems in early childhood. *Journal of Family Psychology, 21*, 389–397. **293**

Murdie, R. A., and Teixeira, C. 2003. Towards a comfortable neighbourhood and appropriate housing: Immigrant experiences in Toronto. In P. Anisef and M. Lanphier (Eds.), *The world in a city* (pp. 132–191). Toronto: University of Toronto Press. **131**

Murphy, J. 2012. *Home schooling in America.* Thousand Oaks, CA: Corwin. **169**

Murphy, R., et al. 2011. Son preference in rural China: Patrilineal families and socioeconomic change. *Population and Development Review, 37*, 665–690. **59**

Myers, D. G. 2000. *The American paradox: Spiritual hunger in an age of plenty.* New Haven, CT: Yale University Press. **124**

Myers, S. M. 2006. Religious homogamy and marital quality: Historical and generational patterns, 1980–1997. *Journal of Marriage and Family, 68*, 292–304. **189**

Myles, J., and Hou, F. 2004. Changing colours: Spatial assimilation and new racial minority immigrants. *Canadian Journal of Sociology, 29*, 29–55. **132**

Myles, J., and Picot, G. 2006. Employment and earnings among lone mothers. Statistics Canada, *The Daily*, June 7. **113**

Nadesan, M. H. 2002. Engineering the entrepreneurial infant: Brain science, infant development toys, and governmentality. *Cultural Studies, 16*(3), 401–432. **287**

Nathers, M., and Rivers, K. L. 2006. *The concentration of negative child outcomes in low-income U.S. neighborhoods.* Population Reference Bureau. **128**

National Council of Welfare. 2009. *Poverty trends by family type, 1976–2007.* Ottawa, November. **421, 423**

National Television Violence Study. 1998. *National televised violence study,* vol. 3. Santa Barbara: University of California, Center for Communication and Social Policy. **85**

Natsuaki, M. N., et al. 2009. Aggressive behavior between siblings and the development of externalizing problems: Evidence from a genetically-sensitive study. *Developmental Psychopathology, 45*, 1009–1018. **286, 397**

Naumann, D. 2008. Aboriginal women in Canada: On the choice to renounce or reclaim Aboriginal identity. *The Canadian Journal of Native Studies, 28*, 343–362. **51**

Nayar, K. E. 2004. *The Sikh Diaspora in Vancouver: Three generations amid tradition, modernity, and multiculturalism.* Toronto: University of Toronto Press. **63**

Nayar, K. E. 2010. The making of Sikh space: The role of the gurdwara. In L. DeVries et al. (Eds.), *Asian religions in British Columbia* (pp. 43–63). Vancouver: University of British Columbia Press. **61, 173**

NCHS (National Center for Health Statistics). 2010. *Marriage and cohabitation in the United States: A statistical portrait based on Cycle 6 (2002) of the National Survey of Family Growth.* Washington, DC: U.S. Department of Health and Human Services. **351, 352, 353, 414, 415**

Neff, C. 1996. Pauper apprenticeship in early nineteenth century Ontario. *Journal of Family History, 21*, 144–171. **47**

Neil, E. 2009. Post-adoption contact and openness in adoptive parents' minds: Consequences for child development. *British Journal of Social Work, 39*, 5–23. **248**

Nelson, A., and Robinson, B. W. 2002. *Gender in Canada,* 2nd Ed. Toronto: Pearson. **188**

Nelson, F. 1996. *Lesbian motherhood.* Toronto: University of Toronto Press. **368**

Nelson, H. L. 1997. Introduction. In H. L. Nelson (Ed.), *Feminism and families* (pp. 1–9). New York: Routledge. 21

Nelson, L. J., et al. 2007. "If you want me to treat you like an adult, start acting like one!" Comparing the criteria that emerging adults and their parents have for adulthood. *Journal of Family Psychology, 21,* 665–674. 303

Nelson, M. K. 2005. *The social economy of single motherhood: Raising children in rural America.* New York: Routledge. 14

Nelson, M. K. 2010. *Parenting out of control.* New York: New York University Press. 290, 292

Nemr, R. 2009. *Family violence in Canada. Section 3. Fact sheet—police-reported family violence against children and youth.* Statistics Canada. Publication no. 85-224-X. 387

Nesteruk, O. 2013. Intergenerational relationships in transnational Eastern European families. *Family Focus, 58,* 1, Spring, F20–F22. **75, 76**

Nett, E. M. 1981. Canadian families in social-historical perspective. *Canadian Journal of Sociology, 6,* 239–260. 68

Nett, E. M. 1993. *Canadian families: Past and present,* 2nd Ed. Toronto: Butterworths. **41, 68, 225, 343**

Netting, N. 2006. Two lives, one partner: Indo-Canadian youth between love and arranged marriages. *Journal of Comparative Family Studies, 37,* 129–146. 64

NICHD (National Institute of Child Health and Human Development). Early Child Care Research Network. 2004. Are child developmental outcomes related to before- and after-school care arrangements? Results from the NICHD Study of Early Child Care. *Child Development, 75,* 280–285. 153

NICHD (National Institute of Child Health and Human Development). Early Child Care Research Network. 2005. Duration and development timing of poverty and children's cognitive and social development from birth through third grade. *Child Development, 76,* 795–810. 117

NICHD (National Institute of Child Health and Human Development). Early Child Care Research Network. 2006. Child-care effect sizes for the NICHD study of early child care and youth development. *American Psychologist, 61,* 99–116. 153

Nicholas, A. B. 2001. Canada's colonial mission: The great white bird. In K. P. Binda and S. Calliou (Eds.), *Aboriginal education in Canada* (pp. 933–947). Mississauga: Canadian Educators' Press. 166

Nicholson, B. J. 1994. Legal borrowing and the origins of slave law in the British colonies. *American Journal of Legal History, 38,* 38–54. 45

Nicklas, E., and Mackenzie, M. J. 2013. Intimate partner violence and risk for child neglect during early childhood in a community sample of fragile families. *Journal of Family Violence, 28,* 17–29. 385

Nielsen, F. 2004. The ecological-evolutionary typology of human societies and the evolution of social inequality. *Sociological Theory, 22,* 292–314. 10

Nielsen, F. 2006. Achievement and ascription in educational attainment: Genetic and environmental influences on adolescent schooling. *Social Forces, 85,* 193–216. 337

Niranjan, S., Nair, S., and Roy, T. K. 2005. A socio-demographic analysis of the size and structure of the family in India. *Journal of Comparative Family Studies, 36,* 623–650. 61

Nisbett, R. E., et al. 2012. Intelligence: New findings and theoretical developments. *American Psychologist, 67,* 130–159. **155, 157, 160, 244, 246, 337**

Nock, M. K., and Kazdin, A. E. 2002. Parent-directed physical aggression by clinic-referred youths. *Journal of Clinical Child & Adolescent Psychology, 31,* 193–205. **401, 402**

Nock, S. L. 1998a. *Marriage in men's lives.* New York: Oxford University Press. 415

Nock, S. L. 1998b. *Marriage in men's lives.* New York: Oxford University Press. 176

Noël-Miller, C. M. 2011. Partner caregiving in older cohabiting couples. *Journals of Gerontology: Series B: Psychological Sciences and Social Sciences, 66,* 341–353. 197

Noël-Miller, C. M. 2013. Repartnering following divorce: Implications for older fathers' relations with their adult children. *Journal of Marriage and Family, 75,* 697–712. **358, 368**

Noh, S., Kim, A. H., and Noh, M. S. (Eds.). 2012. *Korean immigrants in Canada.* Toronto: University of Toronto Press. 79

Nokali, N. E. E., et al. 2010. Parent involvement and children's academic and social development in elementary school. *Child Development, 81,* 988–1005. 158

Nolen, S. 2011. The missing girls of India. *The Globe and Mail,* May 24, A12. 63

Nomaguchi, K. M. 2008. Gender, family structure, and adolescents' primary confidants. *Journal of Marriage and Family, 70,* 1213–1227. **298**

Nomaguchi, K. M., and DeMaris, A. 2013. Nonmaternal care's association with mother's parenting sensitivity: A case of self-selection bias? *Journal of Marriage and Family, 75,* 760–777. **155**

Nooner, K. B., et al. 2010. Youth self-report of physical and sexual abuse: A latent class analysis. *Child Abuse & Neglect, 34,* 146–154. 31

Northcott, H. C., and Wilson, D. M. 2008. *Dying and death in Canada.* Peterborough, ON: Broadview Press. **38, 308**

Notter, M. L., MacTavish, K. A., and Shamah, D. 2008. Pathways toward resilience among women in rural trailer parks. *Family Relations, 57,* 613–624. **142, 143**

Nyberg, G., et al. 2010. *Report of the Ontario Social Assistance Review Advisory Council.* Toronto: Ontario Ministry of Community and Social Services. 422

O'Brien, C.-A., and Goldberg, A. 2000. Lesbians and gay men inside and outside families. In N. Mandell and A. Duffy (Eds.), *Canadian families: Diversity, conflict, and change,* 2nd Ed. (pp. 115–145). Toronto: Harcourt Brace. 4

O'Brien, M. J. 1991. Taking sibling incest seriously. In M. Q. Patton (Ed.), *Family sexual abuse* (pp. 75–92). Newbury Park, CA: Sage. 398

Ocobock, A. 2013. The power and limits of marriage: Married gay men's family relationships. *Journal of Marriage and Family, 75,* 191–205. 201

Odgers, C. L., et al. 2009. The protective effects of neighborhood collective efficacy on British children growing up in deprivation: A developmental analysis. *Developmental Psychopathology, 45,* 942–957. 129-130

Offer, S. 2013. Family time activities and adolescents' emotional well-being. *Journal of Marriage and Family,75,* 26–41. 298

Ogbomo, O. 1997. *When men and women mattered: A history of gender relations among the Owan of Nigeria.* Rochester, NY: University of Rochester Press. 317

Ogilvie, M. 2010. Homeless and pregnant. *Toronto Star*. March 13, I1, 4–5. **132**

Ogilvie, M., and Aulakh, R. 2012. Population stats feed controversy over "feticide." *Toronto Star*, January 2, A1, A6. **238**

Ogrodnik, L. 2009. *Family violence in Canada*. Section 5: Fact sheet—family homicides. Statistics Canada, Catalogue no. 85-224-X. **195, 380, 387**

O'Keefe, G. S., and Clarke-Pearson, K. 2011. The impact of the social media on children, adolescents, and families. *Pediatrics, 127,* 800–804. **87, 89**

O'Keefe, M. 1998. Factors mediating the link between witnessing interparental violence and dating violence. *Journal of Family Violence, 13, 39–57.* **385**

Oldehinkel, A. J., et al. 2008. Parental divorce and offspring depressive symptoms: Dutch developmental trends during early adolescence. *Journal of Marriage and Family, 70,* 284–293. **358**

Oliver, L. N., and Kohen, D. E. 2012. Unintentional injury hospitalizations among children and youth in areas with a high percentage of aboriginal identity residents: 2001/2002 to 2005/2006. Ottawa: Statistics Canada, *Health Reports 2012, 23.* **119**

Oliver, L. N., Peters, P. A., and Kohen, D. E. 2012. Mortality rates among children and teenagers living in Inuit Nunangat, 1994 to 2008. Ottawa: Statistics Canada, *Health Reports,* Cat. No. 82-003-X. **125**

Ombelet, W., et al. 2006. Perinatal outcome of 12,021 singleton and 3,108 twin births after non-IVF-assisted reproduction: A cohort study. *Human Reproduction, 21,* 1025–1032. **240**

Ontario Heritage Foundation. 1997. *Home Children.* Accessed online January 12, 2010. **46**

Onysklw, J. E., and Hayduk, L. A. 2001. Processes underlying children's adjustment in families characterized by physical aggression. *Family Relations, 50,* 376–385. **184, 319, 386, 401**

Ornstein, M., and Stalker, G. 2013. Canadian families' strategies for employment and care for preschool children. *Journal of Family Issues, 34,* 53–84. **101**

Orpana, H. M., Lemyre, L., and Gravel, R. 2009. Income and psychological distress: The role of the social environment. Statistics Canada, *The Daily,* January 21. **18, 114**

Orsini, F. 2007. *Love in South Asia: A cultural history.* New Delhi: Cambridge University Press. **259, 261**

Orthner, D. K., and Rose, R. 2009. Work separation demands and spouse psychological well-being. *Family Relations, 58,* 392–403. **77**

Osborne, C., and McLanahan, S. 2007. Partnership instability and child well-being. *Journal of Marriage and Family, 69,* 1065–1083. **360**

Osborne, C., Manning, W. D., and Smock, P. J. 2007. Married and cohabiting parents' relationship stability: A focus on race and ethnicity. *Journal of Marriage and Family, 69,* 1345–1366. **221, 348**

Oster, E. 2009. Proximate sources of population sex imbalance in India. *Demography, 46,* 325–339. **63, 328**

Oswald, R. F., et al. 2008. Structural and moral commitment among same-sex couples: Relationship duration, religiosity, and parental status. *Journal of Family Psychology, 22,* 411–419. **177**

Ouellette, F.-R., and Belleau, H. 2001. *Family and social integration of children adopted internationally: A review of the literature.* Montréal: Institut national de la recherche scientifique. Université du Québec. **247**

Owasu, T. 1999. Residential patterns and housing choices of Ghanaian immigrants in Toronto, Canada. *Housing Studies, 14,* 77–97. **132**

Owen, M. 2010. Lack of support: Canadian families and disabilities. In D. Cheal (Ed.) 2nd Ed. *Canadian families today: New perspectives* (pp.200–237). Toronto: Oxford University Press. **101, 388**

Oxford, M. L., et al. 2005. Life course heterogeneity in the transition from adolescence to adulthood among adolescent mothers. *Journal of Research on Adolescence, 15,* 479–504. **228**

Oyen, N., et al. 1997. Combined effects of sleeping position and prenatal risk factors in Sudden Infant Death Syndrome: The Nordic Epidemiological SIDS study. *Pediatrics, 100,* 613–620. **220**

Ozawa, M. N., and Lee, Y. 2006. The net worth of female-headed households: A comparison to other types of households. *Family Relations, 55,* 132–145. **97**

Ozer, E. J. 2005. The impact of violence on urban adolescents: Longitudinal effects of perceived school connection and family support. *Journal of Adolescent Research, 20,* 167–192. **131**

Pagani, L., Boulerice, B., and Tremblay, R. E. 1997. The influence of poverty on children's classroom placement and behavior problems. In G. J. Duncan and J. Brooks-Gunn (Eds.), *Consequences of growing up poor* (pp. 311–339). New York: Russell Sage. **369**

Page, C., et al. 2009. The effect of care setting on elder abuse: Results from a Michigan survey. *Journal of Elder Abuse & Neglect, 21,* 239–252. **404**

Paglia-Boak, A., et al. 2010. *The mental health and well-being of Ontario students 1991-2009.* Toronto: CAMH (Centre for Addiction and Mental Health). **90, 164, 347, 399**

Palameta, B. 2003. Who pays for domestic help? *Perspectives on Labour and Income, 4,* August, 2–15. **101**

Paletta, A. 2008. *Understanding family violence and sexual assault in the Territories, First Nations, Inuit and Métis Peoples.* Ottawa: Department of Justice. **379**

Pallas, A. M. 2002. Educational participation across the life course: Do the rich get richer? *Advances in Life Course Research, 7,* 327–354. **161**

Paper, J. 2012. Aboriginals. In J. S. Scott (Ed.), *The religions of Canadians* (pp. 1–31). Toronto: University of Toronto Press. **36**

Papp, A. 2010. Culturally driven violence against women: A growing problem in Canada's immigrant communities. Winnipeg, MA: Frontier Centre for Public Policy, *Policy Series, 92,* July. **328, 382, 404**

Papp, L. M., Cummings, E. M., and Goeke-Morey, M. C. 2009. For richer, for poorer: Money as a topic of marital conflict in the home. *Family Relations, 58,* 91–103. **265**

Papp, L. M., Cummings, E. M., and Schermerhorn, A. C. 2004. Pathways among marital distress, parental symptomatology, and child adjustment. *Journal of Marriage and Family, 66,* 368–384. **280**

Pappano, L. 2001. *The connection gap—Why Americans feel so alone.* New Brunswick, NJ: Rutgers University Press. **141**

Parcel, T. L., Dufur, M. J., and Zito, R. C. 2010. Capital at home and at school: A review and synthesis. *Journal of Marriage and Family, 72,* 828–846. **157**

Park, R. E., and Burgess, E. W. 1925. *The city.* Chicago: University of Chicago Press. **123**

Parr, J. 1980. *Labouring children.* London: Croom Helm. **100**

Parr, J. 1994. *Labouring children: British immigrant apprentices to Canada 1869-1924.* Toronto: University of Toronto Press. **47**

Parr, J. 2000. Rethinking work and kinship in a Canadian hosiery town, 1910–1950. In B. Bradbury (Ed.), *Canadian family history* (pp. 220–240). Toronto: Irwin Publishing. **100**

Parr, J. 2003. Introduction. In N. Janovicek and J. Parr (Eds.), *Histories of Canadian children and youth* (pp. 1–7). Toronto: Oxford University Press. **16, 46**

Parreñas, R. S. 2002. The care crisis in the Philippines: Children and transnational families in the new global economy. In B. Ehrenreich and A. R. Hochschild (Eds.), *Global women* (pp. 39–54). New York: Henry Holt and Company. **102, 416**

Parsons, J. T., et al. 2012. Non-monogamy and sexual relationship quality among same-sex male couples. *Journal of Family Psychology, 26, 669–677*. **201**

Parsons, S. 2005. *Rational choice and politics*. London: Continuum. **14**

Parsons, T. 1951. *The social system*. New York: Free Press. **11**

Parsons, T., and Bales R. F. 1955. *Family, socialization and interaction process*. Glencoe, IL: Free Press. **11**

Pascal, C. E. 2009. *With our best future in mind. Implementing early learning in Ontario*. Toronto: Report to the Premier by the Special Advisor on Early Learning. **425**

Pasley, K., Futris, T. G., and Skinner, M. L. 2002. Effects of commitment and psychological centrality on fathering. *Journal of Marriage and Family, 64, 130–138*. **20**

Passmore, N. C., and Chipuer, H. M. 2009. Female adoptees' perceptions of contact with their birth fathers: Satisfactions and dissatisfactions with the process. *American Journal of Orthopsychiatry, 79, 93–102*. **249**

Passmore, N. C., and Feeney, J. A. 2009. Reunions of adoptees who have met both birth parents: Post-reunion relationships and factors that facilitate and hinder the reunion process. *Adoption Quarterly, 12, 100–119*. **249**

Patterson, C. J. 2000. Family relationships of lesbians and gay men. *Journal of Marriage and Family, 62, 1052–1069*. **203, 213, 225**

Patterson, J. 2003. Spousal violence. In H. Johnson and K. Au Coin (Eds.) *Family violence in Canada: A statistical profile 2003* (pp. 4–20). Ottawa: Ministry of Industry. **383**

Paul, P. 2004. The porn factor. *Time*, February 9, 75–76. **89**

Pauli-Pott, V., and Beckman, D. 2007. On the association of interparental conflict with developing behavioral inhibition and behavior problems in early childhood. *Journal of Family Psychology, 21, 529–532*. **280**

Paupanekis, K., and Westfall, D. 2001. Teaching Native language programs: Survival strategies. In K. P. Binda and S. Calliou (Eds.), *Aboriginal education in Canada* (pp. 89–104). Mississauga, ON: Canadian Educators' Press. **166**

Payne, B. K., and Gainey, R. R. 2006. *Family violence and criminal justice: A life-course approach*, 2nd Ed. Cincinnati: Anderson. **404**

Pearce, L. D., and Axinn, W. G. 1998. The impact of family religious life on the quality of mother-child relations. *American Sociological Review, 63, 810–828*. **175**

Pearce, L. D., and Thornton, A. 2007. Religious identity and family ideologies in the transition to adulthood. *Journal of Marriage and Family, 69, 1227–1243*. **174**

Pearce, M. J., et al. 2003. The protective effects of religiousness and parent involvement on the development of conduct problems among youth exposed to violence. *Child Development, 74, 1682–1696*. **175**

Pearce, T. 2012. What is TV teaching your child about bullying? *The Globe and Mail*, October 16, L2. **84**

Pears, K. C., and Capaldi, D. M. 2001. Intergenerational transmission of abuse: A two-generational prospective study of an at-risk sample. *Child Abuse & Neglect, 25, 1439–1461*. **390**

Pedro-Carroll, J. 2001. The promotion of wellness in children and families: Challenges and opportunities. *American Psychologist, 56, 993–1004*. **359**

Peleg-Oren, N., et al. 2012. An association between bullying behaviors and alcohol use among middle school students. *The Journal of Early Adolescence, 32, 761–775*. **399**

Pelkonen, S., et al. 2010. Perinatal outcome of children born after frozen and fresh embryo transfer: The Finnish cohort study 1995–2006. *Human Reproduction, 25, 914–923*. **240**

Pelton, L. 1991. Poverty and child protection. *Protecting Children, 7, 3–5*. **392**

Pelton, L. H. 1997. Child welfare policy and practice: The myth of family preservation. *American Journal of Orthopsychiatry, 67, 545–553*. **426**

Pena, D. 2000. Parent involvement: Influencing factors and implication. *Journal of Educational Research, 12, 68–89*. **158**

Pepler, D., et al. 2008. Developmental trajectories of bullying and associated factors. *Child Development, 79, 325–338*. **399**

Peralta, R. L., Tuttle, L. A., and Steele, J. L. 2010. At the intersection of interpersonal violence, masculinity, and alcohol use: The experiences of heterosexual male perpetrators of intimate partner violence. *Violence Against Women, 16, 387–409*. **381**

Peritz, I. 2010. Abortion. *The Globe and Mail*, June 19, A1, A15. **237**

Perreault, S. 2011. Violent victimization of Aboriginal people in the Canadian provinces, 2009. Ottawa: Statistics Canada. *Juristat, 85-002-X*, March. **380, 384**

Perry, Y. V., and Doherty, W. J. 2005. Viewing time through the eyes of overscheduled children and their underconnected families. In V. L. Bengtson et al., (Eds.), *Sourcebook of family theory & research* (pp. 255–258). Thousand Oaks, CA: Sage. **150**

Perry-Jenkins, M., and Crouter, A. 1990. Men's provider role attitudes: Implications for household work and marital satisfaction. *Journal of Family Issues, 11, 136–156*. **272**

Perry-Jenkins, M., and Claxton, A. 2011. The transition to parenthood and the reasons "mamma ain't happy." *Journal of Marriage and Family, 73, 23–28*. **277**

Peters, A. 2002. Is your community child-friendly? *Canadian Social Trends, 67, 2–5*. **128**

Petersilia, J. R. 2001. Crime victims with developmental disabilities: A review essay. *Criminal Justice and Behavior, 28, 655–694*. **389**

Petta, G. A., and Steed, L. G. 2005. The experience of adoptive parents in adoption reunion relationships: A qualitative study. *American Journal of Orthopsychiatry, 75, 230–241*. **249**

Pettit, G. S., et al. 1999. The impact of after-school peer contact on early adolescent externalizing problems is moderated by parental monitoring, perceived neighborhood safety, and prior adjustment. *Child Development, 70, 768–778*. **131**

Pettit, G. S., et al. 2007. Predicting the developmental course of mother-reported monitoring across childhood and adolescence from early proactive parenting, child temperament, and parents' worries. *Journal of Family Psychology, 21, 206–217*. **295**

Petts, R. J. 2012. Single mothers' religious participation and early childhood behavior. *Journal of Marriage and Family, 74,* 251–268. **174, 175**

PewIALP (Pew Internet & American Life Project). 2012. The best (and worst) of mobile connectivity. November 30, http://pewinternet.org/Reports/2012/ **85**

Pew Research Center. 2013. *The global divide on homosexuality.* June 4. **185**

Pezzin, L. E., et al. 2013. Complex families and late-life outcomes among elderly persons: Disability, institutionalization, and longevity. *Journal of Marriage and Family, 75,* 1084–1097. **368**

Phillips, L. R., et al. 2013. Elder mistreatment in U.S. residential care facilities: The scope of the problem. *Journal of Elder Abuse & Neglect, 25,* 19 39. **403, 404**

Phillips, P., and Phillips, E. 2000. *Women & work.* Toronto: James Lorimer. **432**

Picard, A. 2011. Being old doesn't have to mean being sick. *Globe and Mail,* January 28, L6. **422**

Pilkauskas, N. V. 2012. Three-generation family households: Differences by family structure at birth. *Journal of Marriage and Family, 74,* 931–943. **306**

Pitt, K. 2002. Being a new capitalist mother. *Discourse & Society, 13,* 251–267. **150, 160**

Ploeg, J., et al. 2003. Helping to build and rebuild secure lives and futures: Financial transfers from parents to adult children and grandchildren. *Canadian Journal on Aging, 23S,* S113–125. **306**

Plomin, R., et al. 2008. *Behavior genetics.* New York: Worth. **27**

Plotnick, R. D. 2009. Childlessness and the economic well-being of older Americans. *The Journals of Gerontology: Series B, 64B,* 767–773. **309**

Pole, J. D., and Flicker, S. 2010. Sexual behaviour profile of a diverse group of urban youth: An analysis of the Toronto Teen Survey. *The Canadian Journal of Human Sexuality, 19,* 145–156. **205, 208, 211**

Pogarsky, G., Thornberry, T. P., and Lizotte, A. J. 2006. Developmental outcomes for children of young mothers. *Journal of Marriage and Family, 68,* 332–344. **230**

Polgar, M. F., and North, C. S. 2009. Parenting adults who become homeless: Variations in stress and social support. *American Journal of Orthopsychiatry, 79,* 357–365. **134**

Pong, S. I. 1998. The school compositional effect of single parenthood on 10th-grade achievement. *Sociology of Education, 71,* 24–43. **158, 161**

Pong, S.-L., et al. 2003. Family policies and children's school achievement in single- versus two-parent families. *Journal of Marriage and Family, 65,* 681–699. **422**

Pontzer, D. 2010. A theoretical test of bullying behaviour: Parenting, personality, and the bully/victim relationship. *Journal of Family Violence, 25,* 259–273. **400**

Poonwassie, D. H. 2001. Parental involvement as adult education: A microstrategy for change. In K. P. Binda and S. Calliou (Eds.), *Aboriginal education in Canada* (pp. 155–165). Mississauga, ON: Canadian Educators' Press. **162, 167**

Poortman, A.-R., and Mills, M. 2012. Investments in marriage and cohabitation: The role of legal and interpersonal commitment. *Journal of Marriage and Family, 74,* 357–376. **193**

Poortman, A.-R., and Voorpostel, M. 2009. Parental divorce and sibling relationships. *Journal of Family Issues, 30,* 74–91. **358**

Popplewell, B. 2010. Broken people, broken policy. *Toronto Star,* October 31, A1, A8–A9. **110, 125**

Porter, C. 2003. A wedding story. *Toronto Star* (a series of articles ending September 14, A1 and A8, following a Canadian-Pakistani male through the steps leading to his arranged marriage in Pakistan). **63**

Portes, A. 1998. Social capital: Its origins and applications in modern sociology. *Annual Review of Sociology, 24,* 1–24. **15**

Potter, D. 2012. Same-sex parent families and children's academic achievement. *Journal of Marriage and Family, 74,* 556–571. **225**

Potter, J. 1996. *Representing reality: Discourse, rhetoric, and social construction.* London: Sage. **16**

Potter-MacKinnon, J. 1993. *While the women only wept: Loyalist refugee women.* Montreal, Kingston: McGill-Queen's University Press. **41**

Pougnet, E., et al. 2012. The intergenerational continuity of fathers' absence in a socioeconomically disadvantaged sample. *Journal of Marriage and Family, 74,* 540–555. **126, 228**

Powell, B. and Rankin, J. 2012. The ghosts of Galloway. *Toronto Star,* September 22, A1, A23. **127**

Powell, B., et al. 2006. Advancing age, advantaged youth: Parental age and the transmission of resources to children. *Social Forces, 84,* 1359–1390. **232**

Power, A. 2007. *City survivors: Bringing up children in disadvantaged neighbourhoods.* Bristol: The Policy Press. **128**

Preibisch, K. 2012. Migrant farm workers: Linking Canadian and international families. *Transition,* Spring, Ottawa: The Vanier Institute of the Family. **138**

Prentice, A., et al. 1988. *Canadian women: A history.* Toronto: Harcourt Brace. **46**

Presser, H. 1995. Are the interests of women inherently at odds with the interests of children and the family? A viewpoint. In K. Mason and A.-M. Jensen (Ed.), *Gender and family change in industrialized countries* (pp. 297–319). Oxford: Clarendon. **21**

Presser, S., and Stinson, L. 1998. Data collection mode and social desirability bias in self-reported religious attendance. *American Sociological Review, 63,* 137–145. **174**

Prigerson, H. G., Maciejewski, P. K., and Rosenbeck, R. A. 2000. Preliminary explorations of the harmful interactive effects of widowhood and marital harmony on health, health service use, and health care costs. *The Gerontologist, 40,* 349–357. **364**

Prioux, F. 2012. (*No title given.*) France: Institut national démographique. **190**

Prochner, L. 2000. A history of early education and child care in Canada, 1820–1966. In L. Prochner and N. Howe (Eds.), *Early childhood care and education in Canada* (pp. 252–272). Vancouver: University of British Columbia Press. **150**

Provencher, C., Le Bourdais, C., and Marcil-Gratton, N. 2006. Intergenerational transfer: The impact of parental separation on young adults' conjugal behaviour. In K. McQuillan and Z. R. Ravanera (Eds.), *Canada's changing families. Implications for individuals and society* (pp. 179–209). Toronto: University of Toronto Press. **177, 193, 351, 358, 364, 415**

Pruchno, R., Patrick, J. H., and Burant, C. J. 1997. African American and White mothers of adults with chronic disabilities: Caregiving burden and satisfaction. *Family Relations, 46,* 335–346. **308**

Pyke, K. 2000. "The normal American family" as an interpretive structure of family life among grown children of Korean and Vietnamese immigrants. *Journal of Marriage and Family, 62,* 240–255. **287**

Pyper, W. 2002. Falling behind. *Perspectives on Labour and Income,* 3, July, 17–23. **226**

Quane, J. M., and Rankin, B. H. 1998. Neighborhood poverty, family characteristics, and commitment to mainstream goals: The case of African American adolescents in the inner city. *Journal of Family Issues, 19,* 769–794. **130**

Quart, A. 2003. *Branded: The buying and selling of teenagers.* New York: Perseus. **88**

Raikes, H., et al. 2006. Mother-child book reading in low-income families: Correlates and outcomes during the first three years of life. *Child Development, 77,* 924–953. **155**

Rajkhowa, M., Mcconnell, A., and Thomas, G. E. 2006. Reasons for discontinuation of IVF treatment: A questionnaire study. *Human Reproduction, 21,* 358–363. **240**

Rajulton, F., and Ravanera, Z. R. 2006a. Social status polarization in the timing and trajectories to motherhood. *Canadian Studies in Population, 33,* 179–207. **14, 232**

Rajulton, F., and Ravanera, Z. R. 2006b. Family solidarity in Canada: An exploration with the General Social Survey on Family and Community Support. In K. McQuillan and Z. R. Ravanera (Eds.), *Canada's changing families. Implications for individuals in society* (pp. 239–263). Toronto: University of Toronto Press. **306, 430**

Raley, R. K., Crissey, S., and Muller, C. 2007. Of sex and romance: Late adolescent relationships and young adult union formation. *Journal of Marriage and Family, 69,* 1210–1226. **208**

Raley, S., Bianchi, S. M., and Wang, W. 2012. When do fathers care? Mothers' economic contribution and fathers' involvement in child care. *American Journal of Sociology, 117,* 1422–1459. **101**

Ram, B. 2010. Introduction to the special issue "Low Fertility in Comparative Perspectives." *Canadian Studies in Population, 37,* 3–4, 15–24. **231, 235**

Ram, B. 2012. Fertility decline and family change in India: A demographic perspective. *Journal of Comparative Family Studies, 43,* 11–39. **233, 238, 413**

Raneri, L. G., and Wiemann, C. M. 2007. Social ecological predictors of repeat adolescent pregnancy. *Perspectives on Sexual Reproductive Health, 39,* 39–47. **228**

Rankin, J., and Winsa, P. 2013. Sucked into the criminal justice system. *Toronto Star,* March 02, IN1, 4. **58**

Ranson, G. 2010. *Against the grain: Couples, gender, and the reframing of parenting.* Toronto: University of Toronto Press. **287**

Raphael, D. 2011. *Poverty in Canada,* 2nd Ed. Toronto: Canadian Scholars' Press. **105, 113, 417, 420, 432**

Rapoport, B., and Le Bourdais, C. 2006. Parental time, work schedules, and changing gender roles. In K. McQuillan and Z. R. Ravanera (Eds.), *Canada's changing families. Implications for individuals and society* (pp. 76–104). Toronto: University of Toronto Press. **348**

Raschick, M., and Ingersoll-Dayton, B. 2004. The costs and rewards of caregiving among aging spouses and adult children. *Family Relations, 53,* 317–325. **308**

Ratcliffe, C., and Vinopal, K. 2009. *Are families prepared for financial emergencies?* U.S. The Urban Institute. **106**

Ravanera, Z. R., and McQuillan, K. 2006. Introduction. In K. M. McQuillan and Z. R. Ravanera (Eds.), *Canada's changing families. Implications for individuals and society.* (pp. 3–11). Toronto: University of Toronto Press. **74**

Ravanera, Z., Beaujot, R., and Liu, J. 2009. Models of earning and caring: Determinants of the division of work. *Canadian Review of Sociology, 46,* 319–337. **269, 272**

Ravanera, Z. R., Rajulton, F., and Burch, T. K. 2003. Early life transitions of Canadian youth: Effects of family transformation and community characteristics. *Canadian Studies in Population, 30,* 327–353. **304**

Ravanera, Z. R., Rajulton, F., and Burch, T. K. 2004. Patterns of age variability in life course transitions. *Canadian Journal of Sociology, 29,* 527–542. **23**

Raver, C. C., et al. 2011. CSRP's impact on low-income preschoolers' preacademic skills: Self-regulation as a mediating mechanism. *Child Development, 82,* 362–378. **155**

Ray, B. D. 2001. Homeschooling in Canada. *Education Canada, 41,* 28–31. **169**

Ray, S. L., and Forchuk, C. 2011. *The experience of homelessness among Canadian Forces and Allied Forces veterans.* Ottawa: Human Resources and Skills Development Canada. Homeless Partnering Secretariat. **79**

Raymo, J. M. 2003. Premarital living arrangements and the transition to first marriage in Japan. *Journal of Marriage and Family, 65,* 302–315. **202**

Rayside, D., and Wilcox, C. 2011. (Eds.) *Faith, politics, and sexual diversity in Canada and the United States.* Vancouver: University of British Columbia Press. **178**

Rawlins, J. M. 2002. Middle-aged and older women in Jamaica. In P. Mohammed (Ed.), *Gendered realities: Essays in Caribbean feminist thought* (pp. 27–290). Barbados: University of the West Indies Press. **242**

RCAP (Report of the Royal Commission on Aboriginal Peoples). 1996. *Gathering Strength,* vol. 3. Ottawa: Canada Communication Group. **155**

Reardon, S. F., and Bischoff, K. 2011. Income inequality and income segregation. *American Journal of Sociology, 116,* 1092–1153. **123**

Reboucas, L. 2002. Brazil confronts adolescent sexual health issues. *Population Reference Bureau.* **89**

Recht, M. 1997. The role of fishing in the Iroquois economy, 1600–1792. *New York History, 78,* 429–454. **37**

Regnerus, M., and Uecker, J. 2011. *Premarital sex in America: How young Americans meet, mate, and think about marriage.* New York: Oxford University Press. **183**

Rehman, U. S., and Holtzworth-Munroe, A. 2007. A cross-cultural examination of the relation of marital communication behaviour to marital satisfaction. *Journal of Family Psychology, 21,* 758–763. **264**

Reichman, N. E., Corman, H., and Noonan, K. 2004. Effects of child health on parents' relationship status. *Demography, 41,* 569–584. **276**

Reid, C. R. 2008. Quality of care and mortality among long-term care residents with dementia. *Canadian Studies in Population, 35,* 1–3. **430**

Reinhold, S. 2010. Reassessing the link between premarital cohabitation and marital instability. *Demography, 47,* 719–733. **352**

Reiss, D. 2003. Child effects on family systems: Behavioral genetic strategies. In A. C. Crouter and A. Booth (Eds.), *Children's influence on family dynamics* (pp. 3–25). Mahwah, NJ: Erlbaum. **333, 336**

Reiss, D., et al. 2009. Understanding links between birth parents and the child they have placed for adoption: Clues for assisting families and for reducing genetic risk? In G. M. Wrobel and E. Neils (Eds.), *International advances in adoption research for practice* (pp. 199–243). Chichester, UK: John Wiley & Sons. **228, 244, 246, 294, 295, 337, 338**

Renner, L. M, and Whitney, S. D. 2010. Examining symmetry and intimate partner violence among young adults using socio-demographic characteristics. *Journal of Family Violence, 25*, 91–106. **376**

Renshaw, K. D., et al. 2011. Distress in spouses of service members with symptoms of combat-related PTSD: Secondary traumatic stress or general psychological distress? *Journal of Family Psychology, 25*, 461–469. **77**

Renzetti, C. M. 1997. Violence and abuse among same-sex couples. In A. P. Cardarelli (Ed.), *Violence between intimate partners* (pp. 70–89). Boston: Allyn & Bacon. **378, 379**

Reynolds, A. J., and Robertson, D. L. 2003. School-based early intervention and later child maltreatment in the Chicago Longitudinal Study. *Child Development, 74*, 3–26. **155**

Reynolds, A. J., and Temple, J. A. 1998. Extended early childhood intervention and school achievement: Age thirteen findings from the Chicago Longitudinal Study. *Child Development, 69*, 231–246. **155**

Reynolds, A. J., et al. 2011. Age 26 cost-benefit analysis of the Child-Parent Center early education program. *Child Development, 82*, 379–404. **156, 425**

Reynolds, C. 2004. The educational system. In N. Mandell (Ed.), *Feminist issues: Race, class, and gender*, 4th Ed. (pp. 247–265). Toronto: Prentice Hall. **150**

Rezai-Rashti, G. 2004. Unessential women: A discussion of race, class, and gender and their implications in education. In N. Mandell (Ed.), *Feminist issues: Race, class, and gender*, 4th Ed. (pp. 83–99). Toronto: Prentice Hall. **22**

Rhoades, G., et al. 2012. A longitudinal investigation of commitment dynamics in cohabiting relationships. *Journal of Family Issues, 33*, 363–390. **196**

Richmond, M. K., Stocker, C. M., and Rienks, S. L. 2005. Longitudinal associations between sibling relationship quality, parental differential treatment, and children's adjustment. *Journal of Family Psychology, 19*, 550–559. **321, 322, 328**

Rideout, V. J., Foehr, U. G., and Roberts, D. F. 2010. *Generation M2. Media in the lives of 8- to 18-year-olds.* The Kaiser Family Foundation. **82, 83**

Rifkin, J. 2011. *The third industrial revolution.* London, UK: Palgrave Macmillan. **12, 422**

Riina, E. M., and McHale, S. M., 2012. The trajectory of coparenting satisfaction in African American families: The impact of sociocultural stressors and supports. *Journal of Family Psychology, 26*, 896–905. **287**

Riley, D., and Steinberg, J. 2004. Four popular stereotypes about children in self-care: Implications for family life educators. *Family Relations, 53*, 95–101. **103**

Rindfuss, R. R., et al. 2010. Child-care availability and fertility in Norway. *Population and Development Review, 36*, 725–748. **427**

Ringstad, R. 2009. CPS: Client violence and client victims. *Child Welfare, 88*, 127–147. **251**

Rizk, C. 2003. *Le cadre des ménages les plus pauvres.* Paris: INSEE. **143**

Robinson, I. 2012. Jews. In J. S. Scott (Ed.), *The religions of Canada* (pp. 131–165). Toronto: University Toronto Press. **48**

Robison, J., et al. 2009. A broader view of family caregiving: Effects of caregiving and caregiver conditions on depressive symptoms, health, work, and social isolation. *The Journals of Gerontology: Series B, 64B*, 788–798. **308**

Robitaille, N., Guimond, E., and Boucher, A. 2010. Intergenerational ethnic mobility among Canadian Aboriginal populations in 2001. *Canadian Studies in Population, 37*, 151–174. **51**

Robson, K. 2005. Canada's most notorious bad mothers: The newspaper coverage of the Jordan Heikamp inquest. *Canadian Review of Sociology and Anthropology, 42*, 217–232. **19, 409**

Roche, K., and Ghazarian, S. 2012. The value of family routines for the academic success of vulnerable adolescents. *Journal of Family Issues, 33*, 874–897. **163**

Roger, K. S., and Ursel, J. 2009. Public opinion on mandatory reporting of abuse and/or neglect of older adults in Manitoba, Canada. *Journal of Elder Abuse & Neglect, 21*, 115–140. **402**

Rogers, S. J., and White, L. K. 1998. Satisfaction with parenting: The role of marital happiness, family structure, and parents' gender. *Journal of Marriage and Family, 60*, 293–308. **276**

Rolland, M., et al. 2013. Decline in semen concentration and morphology in a sample of 26,609 men close to general population between 1989 and 2005 in France. *Human Reproduction, 28*, 462–470. **236**

Rollings-Magnusson, S. 2008. Flax seed, goose grease, and gun powder: Medical practices by women homesteaders in Saskatchewan (1882–1914). *Journal of Family History, 33*, 388–410. **138**

Romaniuk, A. 2010. Fertility in an age of demographic maturity: An essay. *Canadian Studies in Population, 37*, 283–295. **427**

Ronson, A., Milhausen, R., and Wood, J. 2012. Reasons for having sex among lesbian women. *The Canadian Journal of Human Sexuality, 21*, 17–27. **185**

Roosa, M. W., et al. 1997. The relationship of childhood sexual abuse to teenage pregnancy. *Journal of Marriage and Family, 59*, 119–130. **395**

Roper, S. O., and Yorgason, J. B. 2009. Older adults with diabetes and osteoarthritis and their spouses: Effects of activity limitations, marital happiness, and social contacts on partner's daily mood. *Family Relations, 58*, 460–474. **268**

Rosenberg, J. 2001. Boyhood abuse increases men's risk of involvement in a teenager's pregnancy. *Family Planning Perspectives, 33*, 184–185. **394**

Rosenthal, C. J. 2000. Aging families: Have current changes been "oversold"? In E. M. Gee and G. M. Gutman (Eds.), *The overselling of population aging* (pp. 45–63). Toronto: Oxford University Press. **305, 307**

Rosenthal, C. J., and Gladstone, J. 2000. *Grandparenthood in Canada.* Ottawa: The Vanier Institute of the Family. **310**

Rosin, H. 2008. American murder mystery. *The Atlantic*, July/August, 40–54. **424**

Ross, C. E., and Mirowsky, J. 1999. Disorder and decay: The concept and measurement of perceived neighborhood disorder. *Urban Affairs Review, 34*, 412–432. **126**

Ross, C. E., and Mirowsky, J. 2009. Neighborhood disorder, subjective alienation, and distress. *Journal of Health and Social Behavior, 50,* 49–64. **129**

Ross, C. J. 2006. Foster children awaiting adoption under the *Adoption and Safe Families Act of 1997. Adoption Quarterly, 9,* 121–131. **250**

Rossi, A. S., and Rossi, P. H. 1990. *Of human bonding: Parent-child relations across the life course.* New York: Aldine de Gruyter. **301, 306, 312**

Rotermann, M. 2005. Sex, condoms and STDs among young people. Statistics Canada, *Health Reports, 16,* May. **207**

Rotermann, M. 2007a. Marital breakdown and subsequent depression. Statistics Canada, *Health Reports, 18,* 33–44. **111, 355, 356**

Rotermann, M. 2007b. Second or subsequent births to teenagers. Statistics Canada, *Health Reports, 18,* February. **227**

Rotermann, M. 2008. Trends in teen sexual behaviour and condom use. *Canadian Social Trends,* August 20. **204**

Rotermann, M. 2012. Sexual behaviour and condom use of 15- to 24-year-olds in 2003 and 2009/2010. Statistics Canada. Health Reports. 23 March. **204, 206n, 208**

Rothblum, E. D. 2002. "Boston marriage" among lesbians. In M. Yalom and L. L. Carstensen (Eds.), *Inside the American couple* (pp. 74–86). Berkeley, CA: University of California Press. **203, 210**

Rothermel, P. 2000. The third way in education: Thinking the unthinkable. *Education, 28,* 3–13. **170**

Rothman, B. K. 1989. *Recreating motherhood: Ideology and technology in a patriarchal society.* New York: W. W. Norton. **243**

Rowe, D. C., Jacobson, K. C., and Van den Oord, E. J. C. G. 1999. Genetic and environmental influences on vocabulary IQ: Parental education level as moderator. *Child Development, 70,* 1151–1162. **338**

Roxburgh, S. 2012. Parental time pressure and depression among married dual-earner parents. *Journal of Family Issues, 33,* 1027–1053. **103**

Roy, P. E. 2007. *The triumph of citizenship: The Japanese and Chinese in Canada, 1941–67.* Vancouver: University of British Columbia Press. **49**

Rubin, R. M., and White-Means, S. I. 2009. Informal caregiving: Dilemmas of sandwhiched caregivers. *Journal of Family and Economic Issues, 30,* 252–267. **431**

Rueter, M. A., et al. 2009. Family interactions in adoptive compared to nonadoptive families. *Journal of Family Psychology, 23,* 58–66. **243**

Ruggles, S. 2009. Reconsidering the Northwest European family system: Living arrangements of the aged in comparative historical perspective. *Population and Development Review, 35,* 249–273. **38**

Ruggles, S. 2010. Stem families and joint families in comparative perspective. *Population and Development Review, 36,* 563–577. **38**

Ruggles, S., and Heggeness, M. 2008. International coresidence in developing countries. *Population and Development Review, 34,* 253–281. **38, 304**

Rushowy, K. 2004. Pre-school crucial time. *Toronto Star.* March 27, pp. A1, A4. **156, 425**

Rushowy, K. 2011. Gay insults so common in schools, students feel unsafe, poll finds. *Toronto Star,* May 12. **185**

Ruspini, E. 2000. Lone mothers' poverty in Europe: The cases of Belgium, Germany, Great Britain, Italy, and Sweden. In A. Pfenning and

T. Bahle (Eds.), *Families and family policies in Europe* (pp. 221–244). Frankfurt am Main: Peter Lang. **252**

Russell, D., Springer, K. W., and Greenfield, E. A. 2010. Witnessing domestic abuse in childhood as an independent risk factor for depressive symptoms in young adulthood. *Child Abuse & Neglect, 34,* 448–453. **384**

Rutter, M. 2002. Nature, nurture, and development: From Evangelism through science toward policy and practice. *Child Development, 73,* 1–21. **27, 281, 286, 363**

Rutter, M. L. 1997. Nature-nurture integration: The example of antisocial behavior. *American Psychologist, 52,* 390–398. **336**

Ryan, S., et al. 2008. Older sexual partners during adolescence: Links to reproductive health outcomes in young adulthood. *Perspectives on Sexual and Reproductive Health, 40,* 17–26. **209**

Ryan, S., et al. 2009. Family structure history: Links to relationship formation behaviors in young adulthood. *Journal of Marriage and Family, 71,* 935–953. **222**

Sabatelli, R. M., and Bartle-Haring, S. 2003. Family-of-origin experiences and adjustment in married couples. *Journal of Marriage and Family, 65,* 159–169. **266**

Sabatelli, R. M., and Shehan, C. L. 1993. Exchange and resources theories. In P. G. Boss et al. (Eds.), *Sourcebook of family theories and methods: A contextual approach* (pp. 385–417). New York: Plenum Press. **13**

Sacher, J. A., and Fine, M. A. 1996. Predicting relationship status and satisfaction after six months among dating couples. *Journal of Marriage and Family, 58,* 21–32. **184**

Saewyc, E., et al. 2008a. Trends in sexual health and risk behaviours among adolescent students in British Columbia. *The Canadian Journal of Human Sexuality, 17,* 1–13. **211**

Saewyc, E., et al. 2008b. Stigma management? The links between enacted stigma and teen pregnancy trends among gay, lesbian, and bisexual students in British Columbia. *The Canadian Journal of Human Sexuality, 17,* 123–140. **211**

Salvation Army. 2011. *"Canada speaks": Exposing myths about the 150,000 Canadians living on the streets.* May 2011. **132, 133**

Salzinger, S., et al. 1993. The effects of physical abuse on children's social relationships. *Child Development, 64,* 169–187. **389**

Sameroff, A. 2010. A unified theory of development: A dialectic integration of nature and nurture. *Child Development, 81,* 6–22. **26**

Sampson, R. J. 1997. Collective regulation of adolescent misbehavior: Validation results from eighty Chicago neighborhoods. *Journal of Adolescent Research, 12,* 227–244. **130, 411**

Sampson, R. J., Morenoff, J. D., and Earls, F. 1999. Beyond social capital: Spatial dynamics of collective efficacy for children. *American Sociological Review, 64,* 633–660. **15, 130**

Sampson, R. J., Morenoff, J. D., and Gannon-Rowley, T. 2002. Assessing "neighbourhood effects": Social processes and new direction in research. *Annual Review of Sociology, 28,* 443–478. **126**

Sands, R. G., and Goldberg-Glen, R. S. 2000. Factors associated with stress among grandparents raising their grandchildren. *Family Relations, 49,* 97–105. **312**

Sanford, K. 2010. Assessing conflict communication in couples: Comparing the validity of self-report, partner-report, and observer ratings. *Journal of Family Psychology, 24,* 165–174. **257**

Sassler, S. 2004. The process of entering into cohabiting unions. *Journal of Marriage and Family, 66,* 491–505. **194**

Sassler, S. 2010. Partnering across the life course: Sex, relationships, and mate selection. *Journal of Marriage and Family, 72, 557–575.* **14, 188, 196, 353, 365**

Sassler, S., et al. 2012. The tempo of sexual activity and later relationship quality. *Journal of Marriage and Family, 74, 708–725.* **184**

Sastry, N., and Pebley, A. R. 2010. Family and neighborhood sources of socioeconomic inequality in children's achievement. *Demography, 47, 777–800.* **130**

Saunders, K. L. 2011. The hunt for justice: Métis harvesting rights and the pursuit of self-government. *The Canadian Journal of Native Studies, 31, 161–185.* **54**

Sauvé, R. 2008. *The current state of Canadian family finances—2007 Report.* Ottawa: The Vanier Institute of the Family. **107**

Sauvé, R. 2009a. *The current state of Canadian family finances—2008 Report.* Ottawa: The Vanier Institute of the Family. **111**

Sauvé, R. 2009b. The all-Canadian wealth test. *Canadian Business Online,* October 15. www.canadianbusiness.com **97**

Sauvé, R. 2012. *The current state of Canadian family finances, 2011–2012 Report.* Ottawa: Vanier Institute of the Family, March. **97**

Savoie, J. 2007. Youth self-reported delinquency, Toronto, 2006. *Juristat, 27, 6,* Statistics Canada Catalogue no. 85-002-XIE. Ottawa. **368**

Savoie, J. 2008. Neighbourhood characteristics and the distribution of crime: Edmonton, Halifax, and Thunder Bay. *Crime and Justice Research Paper Series.* Statistics Canada, Catalogue no. 85-561-M1E no. 10. Ottawa. **126**

Savoie, J., Bédard, F., and Colins, K. 2006. Neighbourhood characteristics and the distribution of crime on the Island of Montreal. *Crime and Justice Research Paper Series.* Statistics Canada Catalogue no. 85-561-MIE. no. 7. Ottawa. **126, 164**

Sawhill, I., et al. 2012. *Pathways to the middleclass.* The Social Genome Project. New York: Brookings Institution, September 20. **117, 425**

Saxbe, D. E., Repetti, R. L., and Graesch, A. P. 2011. Time spent in housework and leisure: Links with parents' physiological recovery from work. *Journal of Family Psychology, 25, 271–281.* **101**

Sayer, L. 2005. Trends in women's and men's paid work, unpaid work, and free time. *Social Forces, 84, 285–303.* **270**

Scaramella, L. V., et al. 2002. Evaluation of a social contextual model of delinquency: A cross-study replication. *Child Development, 73, 175–195.* **296**

Scaramella, L. V., et al. 2008. Consequences of socioeconomic disadvantage across three generations: Parenting behavior and child externalizing problems. *Journal of Family Psychology, 22, 725–733.* **114, 119**

Scarr, S. 1998. American child care today. *American Psychologist, 53, 95–108.* **18**

Scheelar, C. 2012. *Cyberbullying of young adults in Canada.* Edmonton Social Planning Council. June 19. **87, 435**

Schermerhorn, A. C., et al. 2007. Children's influence in the marital relationship. *Journal of Family Psychology, 21, 259–269.* **276**

Schiamberg, L. B., et al. 2012. Physical abuse of older adults in nursing homes: A random sample survey of adults with an elderly family member in a nursing home. *Journal of Elder Abuse & Neglect, 24, 65–83.* **404**

Schimmele, C. M., and Wu, Z. 2011. Cohabitation and social engagement. *Canadian Studies in Population, 38, 23–36.* **195**

Schindler, H. S. 2010. The importance of parenting and financial contributions in promoting fathers' psychological health. *Journal of Marriage and Family, 72, 318–332.* **116**

Schipper, E. J., de, et al. 2006. Effects of child-caregiver ratio on the interactions between caregivers and children in child-care centers: An experimental study. *Child Development, 77, 861–874.* **152**

Schlegel, A. 2003. Modernisation and changes in adolescent social life. In T. S. Saraswathi (Ed.), *Cross-cultural perspectives in human development* (pp. 236–257). New Delhi, India: Sage. **150, 301**

Schlegel, A., and Barry, H., III. 1991. *Adolescence: An anthropological inquiry.* New York: Free Press. **297**

Schmeeckle, M., et al. 2006. What makes someone family? Adult children's perceptions of current and former stepparents. *Journal of Marriage and Family, 68, 595–610.* **370**

Schmeer, K. K. 2011. The child health disadvantage of parental cohabitation. *Journal of Marriage and Family, 73, 181–193.* **220**

Schneewind, K. A., and Gerhard, A.-K. 2002. Relationship personality, conflict resolution, and marital satisfaction in the first 5 years of marriage. *Family Relations, 51, 63–71.* **265**

Schneider, B., Waite, L., and Dempsey, N. P. 2000. Teenagers in dual-career families. *Family Focus,* December, F11, F13. **103**

Schneider, D. 2011. Wealth and the marital divide. *American Journal of Sociology, 117, 627–667.* **112**

Schnittker, J. 2008. Happiness and success: Genes, families, and the psychological effects of socioeconomic position and social support. *American Journal of Sociology, 114,* S233–259. **27, 116**

Schober, P. S. 2012. Paternal child care and relationship quality: A longitudinal analysis of reciprocal associations. *Journal of Marriage and Family, 74, 281–296.* **272**

Schoen, R., and Cheng, Y.-H. A. 2006. Partner choice and the differential retreat from marriage. *Journal of Marriage and Family, 68, 1–10.* **198**

Schoppe-Sullivan, S. J., et al. 2007. Marital conflict and children's adjustment: Evaluation of the parenting process model. *Journal of Marriage and Family, 69,* 1118–1134. **279**

Schor, J. B. 2001. Time crunch among American parents. In S. A. Hewlett, N. Rankin, and C. West (Eds.), *Taking parenting public* (pp. 83–102). New York: Rowan & Littlefield. **103**

Schramm, D., and Adler-Baeder, F. 2012. Marital quality for men and women in stepfamilies: Examing the role of economic pressure, common stressors, and stepfamily-specific stressors. *Journal of Family Issues, 33, 1373–1397.* **351**

Schramm, D., et al. 2012. Religiosity, homogamy, and marital adjustment: An examination of newlyweds in first marriages and remarriages. *Journal of Family Issues, 33, 246–268.* **177, 178, 189**

Schteingart, J. S., et al. 1995. Homelessness and child functioning in the context of risks and protective factors moderating child outcomes. *Journal of Clinical Child Development, 24, 320–331.* **135**

Schudlich, T. D. D. R., et al. 2011. Observed infant reactions during live interparental conflict. *Journal of Marriage and Family, 73, 221–235.* **278**

Schultz, D., et al. 2009. The relationship between protective factors and outcomes for children investigated for maltreatment. *Child Abuse & Neglect, 33, 684–698.* **390**

Schulz, R., Boerner, K., and Hebert, R. S. 2008. Caregiving and bereavement. In M. S. Stroebe et al. (Eds), *Handbook of bereavement research and practice: Advances in theory and intervention* (pp. 265–285). Washington, DC: American Psychological Association. 364

Schwartz, C. R. 2010a. Earnings inequality and the changing association between spouses' earnings. *American Journal of Sociology, 115,* 1524–1557. 97

Schwartz, C. R. 2010b. Pathways to educational homogamy in marital and cohabiting unions. *Demography, 47,* 735–753. 189, 351

Schwartz, C. R., and Mare, R. D. 2012. The proximate determinants of educational homogamy: The effects of first marriage, marital dissolution, remarriage, and educational upgrading. *Demography, 49,* 629–650. 189

Schwartz, S. J., and Finley, G. E. 2006. Father involvement, nurturant fathering, and young adult psychosocial functioning. *Journal of Family Issues, 27,* 712–731. 246

Schwarz, B. et al. 2012. Does the importance of parent and peer relationships for adolescents' life satisfaction vary across cultures? *The Journal of Early Adolescence, 32,* 55–80. 301

SCIO (State Council Information Office of the People's Republic of China). 2000. *White paper—Fifty years of progress in China's human rights.* 58

Scott, J. S. 2012. Religions and the making of Canada. In J. S. Scott (Ed.), *The religions of Canadians* (pp.xi–xxvii). Toronto: University of Toronto Press. 48

Seabrook, J. A., and Avison, W. R. 2012. Socioeconomic status and cumulative disadvantage processes across the life course implications for health outcomes. *Canadian Review of Sociology, 49,* 50–68. 23, 27

Seccombe, K. 2013. China's one-child policy: Impressions of a Fullbrighter. *Family Focus,* Spring, 15–17. 412

Sedgh, G., et al. 2007. Legal abortion worldwide: Incidence and recent trends. *Perspectives on Sexual and Reproductive Health, 39,* 216–225. 237

Segrin, C., et al. 2012. The association between overparenting, parent-child communication, and entitlement and adaptive traits in adult children. *Family Relations, 61,* 237–252. 304

Seiter, E. 1993. *Sold separately: Children and parents in consumer culture.* New Brunswick, NJ: Rutgers University Press. 88

Seljak, D. 2005. Education, multiculturalism, and religion. In P. Bramadat and D. Seljak (Eds.), *Religion and ethnicity in Canada* (pp. 178–200). Toronto: Pearson. 167

Seltzer, J. A. 1998. Fathers by law: Effects of joint legal custody on nonresident fathers' involvement with children. *Demography, 35,* 135–146. 19

Seltzer, J. A. 2000. Families formed outside of marriage. *Journal of Marriage and Family, 62,* 1247–1268. 221

Seltzer, M. M., et al. 1997. Siblings of adults with mental retardation or mental illness: Effects on lifestyle and psychological well-being. *Family Relations, 46,* 395–405. 325

Selwyn, J., Frazer, L., and Quinton, D. 2006. Paved with good intentions: The pathway to adoption and the costs of delay. *British Journal of Social Work, 36,* 561–576. 244

Serbin, L. A., et al. 1998. Intergenerational transmission of psychosocial risk in women with childhood histories of aggression, withdrawal, or aggression and withdrawal. *Developmental Psychology, 34,* 1246–1262. 228, 230

Serbin, L. A., Peters, P. L., and Schwartzman, A. E. 1996. Longitudinal study of early childhood injuries and acute illness in the offspring of adolescent mothers who were aggressive, withdrawn, or aggressive-withdrawn in childhood. *Journal of Abnormal Psychology, 105,* 500–507. 230

Sercombe, H. 2009. The gift and the trap: Working the "teen brain" into our concept of youth. *Journal of Adolescent Research, 25,* 31–47. 28, 297

Sered, S. S. 1999. "Woman" as symbol and women as agents: Gendered religious discourses. In M. M. Ferree, J. Lorber, and B. B. Hess (Eds.), *Revisioning gender* (pp. 193–221). Thousand Oaks, CA: Sage. 178

Sev'er, A. 2002. *Fleeing the house of horrors: Women who have left abusive partners.*Toronto: University of Toronto Press. 195, 356, 376, 377, 380, 382, 384, 403

Sev'er, A. 2009. More than wife abuse that has gone old: A conceptual model for violence against the aged in Canada and the US. *Journal of Comparative Family Studies, 40,* 279–296. 403

Sev'er, A., and Yurdakul, G. 2001. Culture of honor, culture of change: A feminist analysis of honor killings in rural Turkey. *Violence Against Women, 7,* 964–998. 382

Shaffer, K., and James, S. L. 2013. Gender and socioeconomic status differences in first and second marriage formation. *Journal of Marriage and Family, 75,* 544–564. 351, 365

Shanahan, L., et al. 2008. Linkages between parents' differential treatment, youth depressive symptoms, and sibling relationships. *Journal of Marriage and Family, 70,* 480–494. 28, 328

Shanahan, M. J., et al. 2008. Environmental contingencies and genetic propensities: Social capital, educational continuation, and dopamine receptor gene DRD2. *American Journal of Sociology, 114,* S260–286. 337, 338

Shane, P. G. 1996. *What about America's homeless children?* Thousand Oaks, CA: Sage. 133

Sharma, A. R., McGue, M. K., and Benson, P. L. 1998. The psychological adjustment of United States adopted adolescents and their nonadopted siblings. *Child Development, 69,* 791–802. 243

Shauman, K. A. 2010. Gender asymmetry in family migration: Occupational inequality or interspousal comparative advantage? *Journal of Marriage and Family, 72,* 375–392. 146

Shephard, R. B. 1997. *Deemed unsuitable: Blacks from Oklahoma move to the Canadian Prairies in search of equality in the early twentieth century only to find racism in their new home.* Toronto: Umbrella Press. 45

Sherman, C. W., et al. 2013. Dementia caregiving in the context of late-life remarriage: Support networks, relationship quality, and well-being. *Journal of Marriage and Family, 75,* 1149–1163. 368

Shields, M. 2003. The health of Canada's shift workers. *Canadian Social Trends, 69,* 21–25. 99

Shields, M., and Tremblay, S. 2005. Community belonging and self-perceived health. Statistics Canada, *The Daily,* December 21. 124

Shippee, T. P., et al. 2012. Accumulated financial strain and women's health over three decades. *The Journals of Gerontology, 67,* 585–595. 113

Shirpak, K. R., Maticka-Tyndale E., and Chinichian, M. 2011. Post migration changes in Iranian immigrants' couple relationships in Canada. *Journal of Compartive Family Studies, 42,* 751–770. 261

Shook, S. E., et al. 2010. The mother-coparent relationship and youth adjustment: A study of African Amercian single-mother families. *Journal of Family Psychology, 24,* 243–251. 230

Shuey, K., and Hardy, M. A. 2003. Assistance to aging parents and parents-in-law: Does lineage affect family allocation decisions? *Journal of Marriage and Family, 65*, 418–431. 308

Shulman, J., et al. 2012. Will marriage matter? Effects of marriage anticipated by same-sex couples. *Journal of Family Issues, 33*, 158–181. 201

Shweder, R. A., et al. 2006. The cultural psychology of development: One mind, many mentalities. In W. A. Damon (Ed.), *Handbook of child development*, 5th Ed, vol. 1 (pp. 716–792). Chicago: University of Chicago Press. 74

Siennick, S. E. 2013. Still the favorite? Parents' differential treatment of siblings entering young adulthood. *Journal of Marriage and Family, 75*, 981–994. 328

Sieving, R. E., et al. 2006. Friends' influence on adolescents' first sexual intercourse. *Perspectives on Sexual and Reproductive Health, 38*, 13–19. 209

Sillito, C. 2012. Physical health effects of intimate partner abuse. *Journal of Family Issues, 33*, 1520–1539. 385

Silver, C. 2001. From sun-up to sundown: Work patterns of farming couples. *Canadian Social Trends, 61*, 12–15. 138

Silverstein, M., and Long, J. D. 1998. Trajectories of grandparents' perceived solidarity with adult grandchildren: A growth curve analysis over 23 years. *Journal of Marriage and Family, 60*, 912–923. 313

Silverstein, M., et al. 2010. Older parent-child relationships in six developed nations: Comparisons at the intersection of affection and conflict. *Journal of Marriage and Family, 72*, 1006–1021. 309

Simons, L. G., Simons, R. L., and Conger, R. D. 2004. Identifying the mechanisms whereby family religiosity influences the probability of adolescent antisocial behavior. *Journal of Comparative Family Studies, 35*, 547–563. 175, 296

Simons, R. L., et al. (Eds.). 1996. *Understanding differences between divorced and intact families*. Thousand Oaks, CA: Sage. 365

Simons, R. L., et al. 1994. The impact of mothers' parenting, involvement by nonresidential fathers, and parental conflict on the adjustment of adolescent children. *Journal of Marriage and Family, 56*, 356–374. 296

Simons, R. L., et al. 1995. A test of various perspectives on the intergenerational transmission of domestic violence. *Criminology, 33*, 141–172. 390

Simons, R. L., et al. 1998. A test of latent trait versus life-course perspectives on the stability of adolescent antisocial behavior. *Criminology, 36*, 217–244. 377

Simons, R. L., et al. 2002. Community differences in the association between parenting practices and child conduct problems. *Journal of Marriage and Family, 64*, 331–345. 129, 296

Singh, S., Darroch, J. E., and Frost, J. J. 2001. Socioeconomic disadvantage and adolescent women's sexual and reproductive behavior: The case of five developed countries. *Family Planning Perspectives, 33*, 258–268. 111

Sinkewicz, M., and Garfinkel, I. 2009. Unwed fathers' ability to pay child support: New estimates accounting for multipartner fertility. *Demography, 46*, 247–263. 229, 349

Skolnick, A. 1998. Solomon's children: The new biologism, psychological parenthood, attachment theory, and the best interests standard. In M. A. Mason, A. Skolnick, and S. D. Sugarman (Eds.), *All our families: New policies for a new century*. New York: Oxford University Press. 243

Slomkowski, C., et al. 2001. Sisters, brothers, and delinquency: Evaluating social influence during early and middle adolescence. *Child Development, 72*, 271–283. 323

Small, S. A., and Kerns, D. 1993. Unwanted sexual activity among peers during early and middle adolescence: Incidence and risk factors. *Journal of Marriage and Family, 55*, 941–952. 400

Smith, D. 1999. From women's standpoint to a sociology for people. In J. Abu-Lughod (Ed.), *Sociology for the twenty-first century* (pp. 65–82). Chicago: University of Chicago Press. 21, 427

Smith, D. E. 1993. The Standard North American family: SNAF as an ideological code. *Journal of Family Issues, 14*, 50–65. 16, 169

Smith, G. C., and Hancock, R. 2010. Custodial grandmother-grandfather dyads: Pathways among marital distress, grandparent dysphoria, parenting practice, and grandchild adjustment. *Family Relations, 59*, 45–49. 312

Smith, H. E. H., and Sullivan, L. M. 1995. Now that I know how to manage: Work and identity in the journals of Anne Langton. *Ontario History, 87*, 253–269. 41-42

Smith, S. L., et al. 2006. A post-ASFA examination of adoption disruption. *Adoption Quarterly, 9*, 19–44. 244

Smith, T. W. 1998. A review of church attendance measures. *American Sociological Review, 63*, 131–136. 172

Smits, A., van Gaalen, R. I., and Mulder, C. H. 2010. Parent-child coresidence: Who moves in with whom and for whose needs? *Journal of Marriage and Family, 72*, 1022–1033. 306

Smock, P. J., and Gupta, S. 2002. Cohabitation in contemporary North America. In A. Booth and A. C. Crouter (Eds.), *Just living together* (pp. 53–84). Mahwah, NJ: Erlbaum. 352

Smock, P. J., and Greenland, F. R. 2010. Diversity in pathways to parenthood: Patterns, implications, and emerging research directions. *Journal of Marriage and Family, 72*, 576–593. 221, 236, 349

Smock, P. J., and Manning, W. D. 1997. Cohabiting partners' economic circumstances and marriage. *Demography, 34*, 331–341. 191

Smyer, M. A., et al. 1998. Childhood adoption: Long-term effects in adulthood. *Psychiatry: Interpersonal and Biological Processes, 61*, 191–205. 244

Smylie, L., Medaglia, S., and Maticka-Tyndale, E. 2006. The effect of social capital and sociodemographics on adolescent risk and sexual health behaviours. *The Canadian Journal of Human Sexuality, 15*, 95–113. 209

Snyder, J., et al. 2008. Peer deviancy training and peer coercion: Dual processes associated with early-onset conduct problems. *Child Development, 79*, 252–268. 164

Sobolewski, J. M., and King, V. 2005. The importance of the coparental relationship for non-resident fathers' ties to children. *Journal of Marriage and Family, 67*, 1196–1212. 361

Soffen, L. n.d. The women of the United Arab Emirates. www.mtholyoke.edu/~skalmutt/uae/marriage.html. Accessed February 8, 2013. 202

South, S. J., and Haynie, D. L. 2004. Friendship networks of mobile adolescents. *Social Forces, 83*, 315–350. 145

South, S. J., Haynie, D. L., and Bose, S. 2005. Residential mobility and the onset of adolescent sexual activity. *Journal of Marriage and Family, 67*, 499–514. 144

South, S. J., Trent, K., and Shen, Y. 2001. Changing partners: Toward a macrostructural-opportunity theory of marital dissolution. *Journal of Marriage and Family, 63*, 743–754. 351

Spanier, G. B. 1976. Measuring dyadic adjustment: New scales for assessing the quality of marriage and similar dyads. *Journal of Marriage and Family, 42*, 15–27. **262**

Spar, D. L. 2010. Free markets, free choice? A market approach to reproductive rights. In M. B. Goodwin (Ed.), *Baby markets* (pp. 177–190). New York: Cambridge University Press. **238**

Spencer, M. B., et al. 1996. Parental monitoring and adolescents' sense of responsibility for their own learning: An examination of sex differences. *Journal of Negro Education, 65*, 30–43. **290**

Spitze, G., and Trent, K. 2006. Gender differences in adult sibling relations in two-child families. *Journal of Marriage and Family, 68*, 977–992. **330**

Sprechner, S. 2001. Equity and social exchange in dating couples: Associations with satisfaction, commitment, and stability. *Journal of Marriage and Family, 63*, 599–613. **14**

Sprey, J. 2009. Institutionalization of the family and marriage: Questioning their cognitive and relational realities. *Journal of Family Theory & Review, 1*, 4–19. **4**

Srinivasan, S., and Bedi, A. S. 2013. Census 2011 and child sex ratios in Tamil Nadu: A comment. *Journal of Human Development and Capabilities, 14*, 441–451. **238**

Sriram, R., and Sandhu, G. 2013. Fathering to ensure child's success: What urban Indian fathers do? *Journal of Family Issues, 34*, 159–181. **287**

St-Amour, 2012a. *Les écarts de fécondité selon la situation conjugale au Québec.* Québec: Institut de la statistique du Québec, 17, 2. **191, 233**

St-Amour, 2012b. *Mariages, nuptialité et situation conjugale.* Québec: Institut de la statistique du Québec. **191**

Stacey, J. 2011. *Unhitched.* New York: New York University Press. **8, 220, 221, 224, 248, 251**

Stacey, J., and Biblarz, T. J. 2001. (How) does the sexual orientation of parents matter? *American Sociological Review, 66*, 159–183. **225**

Stack, S., and Eshleman, J. R. 1998. Marital status and happiness: A 17-nation study. *Journal of Marriage and Family, 60*, 527–536. **198**

Staff, J., and Mortimer, J. T. 2012. Explaining the motherhood wage penalty during the early occupational career. *Demography, 49*, 1–21. **99**

Staley, R. 2011. When boys would rather not be boys. *Maclean's,* August 22, 45–50. **211**

Stambrook, F., and Hryniuk, S. 2000. Who were they really? Reflections on East European immigrants to Manitoba before 1914. *Prairie Forum, 25*, 215–232. **48**

Stanley, S. M., and Rhoades, G. 2009. "Sliding vs. deciding": Understanding a mystery. *Family Focus,* National Council on Family Relations, Summer. **194**

Stanley, S. M., Whitton, S. W., and Markman, H. J. 2004. Maybe I do: Interpersonal commitment and premarital or nonmarital cohabitation. *Journal of Family Issues, 25*, 496–519. **177, 195**

Stanley, S. M., et al. 2010. The timing of cohabitation and engagement : Impact on first and second marriages. *Journal of Marriage and Family, 72*, 906–918. **352**

Stanley, T. J. 2003. White supremacy, Chinese schooling, and school segregation in Victoria: The case of the Chinese students' strike, 1922–1923. In N. Janovicek and J. Parr (Eds.), *Histories of Canadian children and youth* (pp. 126–143). Toronto: Oxford University Press. **49**

Starrels, M. A., et al. 1997. The stress of caring for a parent: Effects of the elder's impairment on an employed adult child. *Journal of Marriage and Family, 59*, 860–872. **307, 308**

Statistics Canada. 2002a. *2001 Census of Canada: Profile of Canadian families and households: Diversification continues.* **3**

Statistics Canada. 2002b. 2001 Census: Marital status, common-law status, families, dwellings and households. Ottawa: *The Daily,* October 22. **141, 363,**

Statistics Canada. 2003c. Sexual offences. Ottawa: *The Daily,* July 25. **392**

Statistics Canada. 2003d. Household spending on domestic help. Ottawa: *The Daily,* August 26. **101**

Statistics Canada. 2003e. Witnessing violence: Aggression and anxiety in young children. Ottawa: *The Daily,* December 1. **382, 384**

Statistics Canada. 2003f. Grandparents and grandchildren. Ottawa: *The Daily,* December 9. **310**

Statistics Canada. 2004a. Study: How long do people live in low income neighbourhoods? Ottawa: *The Daily,* January 21. **125**

Statistics Canada. 2004e. Study: Student reading performance in minority-language schools. Ottawa: *The Daily,* March 22. **165**

Statistics Canada. 2004f. Induced abortions. Ottawa: *The Daily,* March 31. **237**

Statistics Canada. 2004h. Low income in census metropolitan areas. Ottawa: *The Daily,* April 7. **57**

Statistics Canada. 2004i. Births. Ottawa: *The Daily,* April 19. **234**

Statistics Canada. 2004j. Divorces. Ottawa: *The Daily,* May 4. **231, 348**

Statistics Canada. 2004k. Aboriginal Peoples Survey: Children who live in non-reserve areas. Ottawa: *The Daily,* July 9. **155, 160**

Statistics Canada. 2004l. General Social Survey: Social engagement. Ottawa: *The Daily,* July 6. **15, 113, 172**

Statistics Canada. 2004m. Study: Economic consequences of widowhood. Ottawa: *The Daily,* June 22. **364**

Statistics Canada. 2004n. Canadian community health survey. Ottawa: *The Daily,* June 15. **210**

Statistics Canada. 2005a. National Longitudinal Survey of Children and Youth: Home environment, income and child behaviour. Ottawa: *The Daily,* February 21. **112, 294**

Statistics Canada. 2005b. Adult correctional services. Ottawa: *The Daily,* December 16. **110**

Statistics Canada. 2005c. Social relationships in rural and urban Canada. Ottawa: *The Daily,* June 21. **135**

Statistics Canada. 2005d. Migration. Ottawa: *The Daily,* September 28. **144**

Statistics Canada. 2006a. Relationship between reading literacy and education outcomes. Ottawa: *The Daily,* June 7. **155**

Statistics Canada. 2006b. Readiness to learn at school among five-year-old children. Ottawa: *The Daily,* November 27. **155**

Statistics Canada. 2006c. Interreligious unions. Ottawa: *The Daily,* October 3. **189**

Statistics Canada. 2006d. *Report on the demographic situation in Canada: 2003 and 2004.* Catalogue no. 91-209-XIE. **354, 366**

Statistics Canada. 2006e. Aboriginal people as victims and offenders. Ottawa: *The Daily,* June 6. **381, 383**

Statistics Canada. 2007a. Study: Canada's immigrant labour market. Ottawa: *The Daily,* September 10. 109

Statistics Canada. 2007b. Study: Why are youth from lower-income families less likely to attend university? Ottawa: *The Daily,* February 8. 119

Statistics Canada. 2007c. Study: Time with the family. Ottawa: *The Daily,* February 13. 103

Statistics Canada. 2007d. *Mobility status 5 years ago, 2006 Census.* 144, 145

Statistics Canada. 2007e. Marriages. Ottawa: *The Daily,* January 17. 198

Statistics Canada. 2007f. *Population by marital status and sex.* Table 051–0010. 343, 363

Statistics Canada. 2007h. 2006 Census: Families, marital status, households and dwelling characteristics. Ottawa: *The Daily,* September 12. 200, 210

Statistics Canada. 2007i. Study: Self-reported delinquency among young people in Toronto. Ottawa: *The Daily,* September 25. 288, 368

Statistics Canada. 2008c. *Farm operators by highest level of educational attainment, by sex and primary occupation, by province, 2001 and 2006.* 136

Statistics Canada. 2008d. *Farm population and total population by rural and urban population, by province, 2001 and 2006.* 135

Statistics Canada. 2008e. Agriculture-population linkage data for the 2006 Census. Ottawa: *The Daily,* December 2. 136

Statistics Canada. 2008f. Divorces in Canada, 2005. Ottawa: *The Daily,* November 18. 344, 345, 346

Statistics Canada. 2008g. Children and youth. Ottawa: *The Daily,* October 18. 101

Statistics Canada. 2008h. Study: Health and development of children of older first-time mothers. Ottawa: *The Daily,* September 24. 219, 231

Statistics Canada. 2009a. Aboriginal peoples survey: School experiences of First Nations children aged 6 to 14 living off reserve. Ottawa: *The Daily,* January 16. 167

Statistics Canada. 2009c. *Canada's ethnocultural mosaic, 2006 Census: National Picture.* Ottawa: Statistics Canada, September 03. 56

Statistics Canada. 2009e. *Ethnic origin, single and multiple ethnic origin responses and sex for the population of Canada, 2006 Census.* Ottawa: Statistics Canada. July 26. 53

Statistics Canada. 2009f. Study: Hours and earnings of dual-earner couples. Ottawa: *The Daily,* April 24. 98

Statistics Canada. 2009g. Study: Earnings of women with and without children. Ottawa: *The Daily,* March 24. 99

Statistics Canada. 2009h. *Average earning by sex and work pattern.* Table 2002–0102. 99

Statistics Canada. 2009i. *Average total income by economic family types (2003–2007).* Table 202–0403. 420

Statistics Canada. 2009j. *Persons in low income before tax, by prevalence in percent (2003 to 2007).* Table 202–0802. 106, 113, 420

Statistics Canada. 2009k. Study: Immigrants' use of non-official languages in the workplace. Ottawa: *The Daily,* January 20. 109

Statistics Canada. 2009m. Off-farm work by farmers. Ottawa: *The Daily,* March 9. 138

Statistics Canada. 2009n. Canadian nine-year-olds at school, 2006–2007. Ottawa: *The Daily,* September 25. 155

Statistics Canada. 2009p. *Canada's ethnocultural mosaic, 2006 Census: National picture. Mixed unions.* September 3. 186

Statistics Canada. 2009r. *Therapeutic Abortion Survey.* Table 106–9005, October 16. 237

Statistics Canada. 2009s. *Crude birth rate, females 15 to 19 years, provinces and territories, for 2007.* Tables 102–4505. 226

Statistics Canada. 2010a. Chart 1. Religious attendance rates by sex, 1985 to 2008. *Canadian Social Trends,* Social Fact Sheet, 89, March 8. 173

Statistics Canada. 2010c. Study: The health of First Nations living off-reserve, Inuit and Métis adults. Ottawa: *The Daily,* June 23. 53

Statistics Canada. 2010d. Knowledge of Aboriginal languages among young First Nations children living off reserve. Ottawa: *The Daily,* September 9. 54

Statistics Canada. 2010e. Women in Canada: Paid Work. Ottawa: *The Daily,* December 9. 98

Statistics Canada. 2011a. Population projection by Aboriginal identity in Canada. Ottawa: *The Daily,* December 7. 51, 311

Statistics Canada. 2011b. General Social Survey: Time use. Ottawa: *The Daily,* July 12. 84

Statistics Canada. 2011c. Study: Commuting to work. Ottawa: *The Daily,* August 24. 135

Statistics Canada. 2011d. Births. Ottawa: *The Daily,* April 27. 51, 233, 234

Statistics Canada. 2011e. Study: Life-path outcomes associated with reading ability. Ottawa: *The Daily,* June 27. 155

Statistics Canada. 2011f. Family violence in Canada: A statistical profile. Ottawa: *The Daily,* January 27. 379, 383

Statistics Canada. 2011g. Shelters for abused women. Ottawa: *The Daily,* June 27. 381

Statistics Canada. 2012a. *Portraits of families and living arrangements in Canada.* Ottawa: online September 19, 2012. Cat. No. 98-312-X-2011001. Census Canada. 191, 200, 219, 220, 222, 249, 367

Statistics Canada. 2012b. Living arrangements of young adults aged 20 to 29. Ottawa: online September 19, 2012. Cat. No. 98-312-X-2011003. Census Canada. 6, 201, 303

Statistics Canada. 2012c. *Canada Year Book.* Ottawa: Minister of Industry.

Statistics Canada. 2012d. Study: Canada's immigrant labour market, 2008–2011. Ottawa: *The Daily,* December 14. 109, 138

Statistics Canada. 2012e. The impact of widowhood and divorce on income replacement among seniors, 1983 to 2007. Ottawa: *The Daily,* June 20. 355

Statistics Canada. 2012f. Family violence in Canada: A statistical profile, 2010. Ottawa: *The Daily,* January 22. 376, 383, 396, 401

Statistics Canada. 2012g. Canada's population estimates: Age and sex, July 1, 2012. Ottawa: *The Daily,* September 27. 413

Statistics Canada. 2012h. Living arrangements of seniors. Ottawa: *The Daily,* September 18. 430

Statistics Canada. 2012i. University tuition fees, 2012/2013. Ottawa: *The Daily,* September 12. 97

Statistics Canada. 2013a. 2011 National Household Survey: Immigration, place of birth, citizenship, ethnic origin, visible minorities, language and religion. Ottawa: *The Daily,* May 8. 50, 56-57, 59, 61, 96, 123, 171, 376, 393

Statistics Canada. 2013b. 2011 National Household Survey: Aboriginal peoples in Canada: First Nations people, Métis and Inuit. Ottawa: *The Daily,* May 8. 51, 250

Statistics Canada. 2013c. Study: Living apart together. Ottawa: *The Daily,* March 5. 79

Statistics Canada. 2013d. Violence against women, 2011. Ottawa: *The Daily,* January 25. 376

Statistics Canada. 2013e. High-income trends among Canadian tax filers, 1982 to 2010. Ottawa: *The Daily,* January 28. 96

Statistics Canada. 2013f. National Household Survey: Portrait of Canada's labour force. Ottawa: *The Daily,* June 26. 103

Steele, F., et al. 2009. Consequences of family disruption on children's educational outcomes in Norway. *Demography, 46,* 553–574. 364

Steinberg, L., Dornbusch, S., and Brown, B. 1992. Ethnic differences in adolescent achievement in ecological perspective. *American Psychologist, 47,* 723–729. 290, 292

Steinberg, L., et al. 1995. Authoritative parenting and adolescent adjustment: An ecological journey. In P. Moen, G. H. Elder, Jr., and K. Lüscher (Eds.), *Examining lives in context* (pp. 423–466). Washington, DC: American Psychological Association. 302

Steinberg, L., et al. 2006. Patterns of competence and adjustment among adolescents from authoritative, authoritarian, indulgent, and neglectful homes: A replication in a sample of serious juvenile offenders. *Journal of Research on Adolescence, 16,* 47–58. 291

Stenberg, S.-A. 2000. Inheritance of welfare recipiency: An intergenerational study of social assistance recipiency in postwar Sweden. *Journal of Marriage and Family, 62,* 228–239. 420

Sternberg, K. J., et al. 1993. Effects of domestic violence on children's behavior problems and depression. *Developmental Psychology, 29,* 44–52. 389

Steven, R. H., et al. 2012. Genetic moderation of contextual effects on negative arousal and parenting in African-American parents. *Journal of Family Psychology, 26,* 46–55. 28

Stevenson, K. 1999. Family characteristics of problem kids. *Canadian Social Trends, 55,* 2–6. 289

Stevens-Simon, C., Nelligan, D., and Kelly, L. 2001. Adolescents at risk of mistreating their children: Part 1: Prenatal identification. *Child Abuse & Neglect, 6,* 737–751. 230

Stewart, L. 2013. Family care responsibilities and employment: Exploring the impact of type of family care on work-family and family-work conflict. *Journal of Family Studies, 34,* 113–138. 413

Stewart, S. D. 1999a. Disneyland dads, Disneyland moms? How nonresident parents spend time with their absent children. *Journal of Family Issues, 20,* 539–556. 349

Stewart, S. D. 1999b. Nonresident mothers' and fathers' social contact with children. *Journal of Marriage and Family, 61,* 894–907. 349

Stewart, W., Huntly, A., and Blaney, F. 2001. *The implications of restorative justice for Aboriginal women and children survivors of violence: A comparison overview of five communities in British Columbia.* Vancouver, BC: Aboriginal Women's Action Network. 383

Stiglitz, J. E. 2012. *The price of inequality: How today's divided society endangers our future.* New York: W. W. Norton & Company. 12, 91, 95, 108, 412, 417, 420

Stimpson, J. P., Peek, M. K., and Markides, K. S. 2006. Depression and mental health among older Mexican American spouses. *Aging and Mental Health, 10,* 386–393. 274

Stobert, S., and Kemeny, A. 2003. Childfree by choice. *Canadian Social Trends, 69,* 7–10. 233

Stolzenberg, R. M., Blair-Loy, M., and Waite, L. J. 1995. Religious participation in early adulthood: Age and family life cycle effects on church membership. *American Sociological Review, 60,* 84–103. 176

Story, L. B., and Repetti, R. 2006. Daily occupational stressors and marital behavior. *Journal of Family Psychology, 20,* 690–700. 275

Stott, G. 2006. The persistence of family: A study of a nineteenth-century Canadian family and their correspondence. *Journal of Family History, 31,* 190–207. 4, 144

Stouffer, A. P. 1992. *The light of nature and the law of God: Anti-slavery in Ontario, 1833–1877.* Baton Rouge, LA: Louisiana State University Press. 45

Stouthamer-Loeber, M., et al. 2001. Maltreatment of boys and the development of disruptive and delinquent behavior. *Development and Psychopathology, 13,* 941–955. 389

Straus, M. A. 1979. Measuring intrafamily conflict and violence: The Conflict Tactics (CT) Scales. *Journal of Marriage and Family, 41,* 75–88. 379

Straus, M. A. 2008. Ending spanking can make a major contribution to preventing physical abuse. *Family Focus.* National Council on Family Relations. December. 293

Straus, M. A., and Kaufman-Kantor, G. 2005. Definition and measurement of neglectful behavior: Some principles and guidelines. *Child Abuse & Neglect, 29,* 19–29. 391

Straus, M. A., and Ulma, A. 2003. Violence of children against mothers in relation to violence between parents and corporal punishment by parents. *Journal of Comparative Family Studies, 34,* 41–60. 401, 402

Straus, M. A., Gelles, R. J., and Steinmetz, S. K. 1980. *Behind closed doors: Violence in the American family.* Garden City, NY: Anchor. 396

Strawbridge, W. J., et al. 1997. New burdens or more of the same? Comparing grandparents, spouse, and adult-child caregivers. *The Gerontologist, 37,* 505–510. 311

Strazdins, L., et al. 2006. Unsociable work? Nonstandard work schedules, family relationships, and children's well-being. *Journal of Marriage and Family, 68,* 394–410. 100

Strohschein, L. 2005. Parental divorce and child mental health trajectories. *Journal of Marriage and Family, 67,* 191–206. 117, 363

Strohschein, L. 2010. Generating heat or light? The challenge of social variables. *Journal of Marriage and Family, 72,* 23–28. 224, 251

Strohschein, L. 2012. Parental divorce and child mental health: Accounting for predisruption differences. *Journal of Divorce & Remarriage, 53,* 489–509. 351, 362

Strohschein, L., Noralou, R., and Bronwell, M. 2009. Family structure histories and high school completion: Evidence from a population-based registry. *Canadian Journal of Sociology, 34,* 83–104. 347, 360

Stromberg, B., et al. 2002. Neurological sequelae in children born after in-vitro fertilization: A population-based study. *Lancet, 359,* 461–465. 240

Strong-Boag, V. 2006. *Finding families, finding ourselves.* Toronto: Oxford University Press. 46, 47, 242, 247

Sturge-Apple, M., Davies, P. T., and Cummings, E. M. 2006. Hostility and withdrawal in marital conflict: Effects on parental emotional unavailability and inconsistent discipline. *Journal of Family Psychology, 20,* 227–238. **279**

Su, T. F., and Costigan, C. L. 2009. The development of children's ethnic identity in immigrant Chinese families in Canada. *Journal of Early Adolescence, 29,* 638–663. **61**

Sudom, K. 2010. *Quality of life among military families: Results from the 2008-2009 survey of Canadian Forces spouses.* Ottawa: Director General Military Personnel Research & Analysis, National Defence, DGMPRA TR 2010-017, August. **77**

Suitor, J. J., and Pillemer, K. 2000. Did mom really love you best? Exploring the role of within-family differences on parental favoritism. *Motivation and Emotion, 24,* 104–119. **325, 327**

Suitor, J. J., and Pillemer, K. 2007. Mothers' favoritism in later life: The role of children's birth order. *Research on Aging, 29,* 32–55. **325**

Suitor, J. J., Pillemer, K., and Sechrist, J. 2006. Within-family differences in mothers' support to adult children. *Journals of Gerontology, 61B,* S10–17. **306**

Suitor, J. J., et al. 2009. The role of perceived maternal favoritism in sibling relations in midlife. *Journal of Marriage and Family, 71,* 1026–1038. **328**

Sullivan, A. 1995. *Virtually normal: An argument about homosexuality.* New York: Alfred A. Knopf. **200**

Sullivan, E. A., et al. 2012. Single embryo transfer reduces the risk of perinatal mortality, a population study. *Human Reproduction, 27,* 3609–3615. **240**

Sum, A., et al. 2011. No country for young men: Deteriorating labor market prospects for low-skilled men in the United States. *The Annals of the American Academy of Political and Social Sciences, 635,* 24–55. **96**

Summer, A. 2012. *Where do the world's poor live? A new update.* London, U.K.: Institute of Development Studies. **106**

Sun, K. 2012. Fashioning the reciprocal norms of elder care: A case of immigrants in the United States and their parents in Taiwan. *Journal of Family Issues, 33,* 1240–1271. **76, 307, 308, 309**

Sun, Y., and Li, Y. 2008. Stable postdivorce family structures during late adolescence and socioeconomic consequences in adulthood. *Journal of Marriage and Family, 70,* 129–143. **358, 370**

Sun, Y., and Li, Y. 2011. Effects of family structure type and stability on children's academic performance trajectories. *Journal of Marriage and Family, 73,* 541–556. **361**

Suzuki, D., and Taylor, R. D. 2009. *The big picture: Reflections on science, humanity, and a quickly changing planet.* Vancouver: Greystone. **74**

Sweeney, M. M. 2010. Remarriage and stepfamilies: Strategic sites for family scholarship in the 21st century. *Journal of Marriage and Family, 72,* 667–684. **365, 366**

Sweet, R., and Anisef, P. (Eds.). 2005. *Preparing for post-secondary education: New roles for governments and families.* Montreal: McGill-Queen's University Press. **151**

Swinford, S. P., et al. 2000. Harsh physical discipline in childhood and violence in later romantic involvements: The mediating role of problem behaviors. *Journal of Marriage and Family, 62,* 508–519. **376, 389**

Swisher, R. R., et al. 1998. The long arm of the farm: How an occupation structures exposure and vulnerability to stressors across role domains. *Journal of Health and Social Behavior, 39,* 72–89. **137**

Swiss, L., and Le Bourdais, C. 2009. Father-child contact after separation: The influence of living arrangements. *Journal of Family Issues, 30,* 623–652. **349**

Szabó, N., et al. 2012. And baby makes four: The stability of coparenting and the effects of child temperament after the arrival of a second child. *Journal of Family Psychology, 26,* 554–564. **287, 434**

Szinovacz, M. E., and Davey, A. 2005. Retirement and marital decision-making: Effects on retirement satisfaction. *Journal of Marriage and Family, 67,* 387–398. **268**

Tach, L., and Halpern-Meekin, S. 2009. How does premarital cohabitation affect trajectories of marital quality? *Journal of Marriage and Family, 71,* 298–317. **352**

Tach, L., Mincy, R., and Edin, K. 2010. Parenting as a "package deal": Relationships, fertility, and nonresident father involvement among unmarried parents. *Demography, 47,* 181–204. **349**

Talbani, A., and Hasanali, P. 2000. Adolescent females between tradition and modernity: Gender role socialization in south Asian immigrant culture. *Journal of Adolescence, 23*(5), 615–627. **64**

Tamborini, C. R., et al. 2012. Women's earnings before and after marital dissolution: Evidence from longitudinal earnings records matched to survey data. *Journal of Family and Economic Issues, 31,* 69–82. **111**

Tan, T. X. 2009. School-age adopted Chinese girls' behavioral adjustment, academic performance, and social skills: Longitudinal results. *American Journal of Orthopsychiatry, 79,* 244–251. **247**

Tang, P. N., and Dion, K. 1999. Gender and acculturation in relation to traditionalism: Perceptions of self and parents among Chinese students. *Sex Roles, 41,* 17–29. **60**

Tanimura, M., et al. 2007. Television viewing, reduced parental utterance, and delayed speech development in infants and young children. *Archives of Pediatrics & Adolescent Medicine, 161,* 618–619. **90**

Tarver-Behring, S., and Barkley, R. A. 1985. The mother-child interactions of hyperactive boys and their normal siblings. *American Journal of Orthopsychiatry, 55,* 202–209. **295**

Tasker, F., and Golombok, S. 1995. Adults raised as children in lesbian families. American Journal of Orthopsychiatry, 65, 203–215. **224, 225**

Tasker, F. L., and Golombok, S. 1997. *Growing up in a lesbian family: Effects on child development.* New York: Guilford Press. **224**

Tastsoglou, E. 2011. Women, gender, and immigration: Focusing on Atlantic Canada. In E. Tastsoglou and P. S. Jaya (Eds.), *Immigrant women in Atlantic Canada* (pp.1–51). Toronto: Canadian Scholars' Press. **109**

Tatara, T. 1993. Understanding the nature and scope of domestic elder abuse with the use of state aggregate data: Summaries of the key findings of a national survey of state APS and aging agencies. *Journal of Elder Abuse and Neglect, 5,* 35–57. **404**

Tatum, B. D. 1999. *"Why are all the Black kids sitting together in the cafeteria?"* New York: Basic Books. **246**

Taylor, A. 2002. Keeping up with the kids in a wired world. *Transition,* Autumn, 3–6. **82, 84, 89, 90**

Taylor, C., and Peter, T. 2011. *Every class in every school.* Toronto: Egale Canada Human Rights Trust. **211**

Taylor, C., et al. 2011. *Every class in every school: The first national climate survey of homophobia, biphobia, and transphobia in Canadian schools. Final report.* Toronto: Egale Canada Human Rights Trust. **185, 224, 244**

Taylor, D. M., et al. 2004. "Street kids": Towards an understanding of their motivational context. *Canadian Journal of Behavioural Science, 36,* 1–16. **56, 133, 171, 172**

Taylor, J. E., and Norris, J. A. 2000. Sibling relationships, fairness, and conflict over transfer of the farm. *Family Relations, 49,* 277–283. **137**

Taylor, Z. E., et al. 2012. Familism, interparental conflict and parenting in Mexican-origin families: A cultural-contextual framework. *Journal of Marriage and Family, 74,* 312–327. **20, 279**

TDSB (Toronto District School Board). 2013. *The people for education.* Toronto, May. **161, 165**

Teachman, J. 2003. Childhood living arrangements and the formation of coresidential unions. *Journal of Marriage and Family, 65,* 507–524. **222**

Teachman, J. D. 2004. The childhood living arrangements of children and the characteristics of their marriages. *Journal of Family Issues, 25,* 86–111. **364**

Teachman, J. D. 2008. Complex life course patterns and the risk of divorce in second marriages. *Journal of Marriage and Family, 70,* 294–305. **347, 352, 365, 366**

Teachman, J. D., and Tedrow, L. 2008. Divorce, race, and military service: More than equal pay and equal opportunity. *Journal of Marriage and Family, 70,* 1030–1044. **78**

Thät, K., and Mills, M. 2012. Nonstandard work schedules, couple desynchronization, and parent-child interaction. A mixed-method analysis. *Journal of Family Issues, 33,* 1054–1087. **101**

The Economist. 2011a. Unmarried black women. October 15, 40. **186**

The Economist. 2011b. War's overlooked victims. January 15, 63–65. **377**

The Economist. 2011c. The 9 billion-people question: A special report on feeding the world. February 26. **416**

The Economist. 2012a. Measuring diversity: The London effect. December 15, 57–58. **186**

The Economist. 2012b. Islam and homosexuality. February 4, 63–64. **178**

The Economist. 2012c. The melting north. June 16. **416**

The Economist. 2013. Some are more equal than others. June 1, 47–48. **75, 106**

Theurer, K., and Wister, A. 2010. Altruistic behaviour and social capital as predictors of well-being among older Canadians. *Ageing and Society, 30,* 157–181. **15**

Thévenon, O. 2011. Family policies in OECD countries: A comparative analysis. *Population and Development Review, 37,* 57–87. **425, 427**

Thibaut, J. W., and Kelly, H. H. 1959. *The social psychology of groups.* New York: Wiley. **13**

Thomas, A., and Sawhill, I. 2005. For love and money? The impact of family structure on family income. *Future of Children, 15,* 57–74. **111**

Thomas, D. 2010. Foreign nationals working temporarily in Canada. *Canadian Social Trends, 90,* June 8. **109**

Thomas, D. E., et al. 2011. The influence of classroom aggression and classroom climate on aggressive-disruptive behavior. *Child Development, 82,* 751–757. **158**

Thompson, J., et al. 2011. *Survey on transition to civilian life: Report on Regular Force veterans.* Research Directorate, Veterans Affairs Canada, Charlottetown, and Director General Military Personnel and Analysis, Department of National Defence, Ottawa. January 4. **78**

Thompson, L. 2010. *Are you the descendant of a Home Child?* Ontario Historical Society, April 2010 Bulletin. **47**

Thorne, B. 1992. Feminism and the family: Two decades of thought. In B. Thorne and M. Yalom (Eds.), *Rethinking the family: Some feminist questions* (rev. Ed., pp. 3–30). Boston: Northeastern University Press. **20**

Thornton, A. 2005. *Reading history sideways.* Chicago: The University of Chicago Press. **6, 38, 69**

Thornton, A., and Lin, H.-S. 1994. *Social change and the family in Taiwan.* Chicago: University of Chicago Press. **337**

Thornton, A., and Young-DeMarco, L. 2001. Four decades of trends in attitudes toward family issues in the United States: The 1960s through the 1990s. *Journal of Marriage and Family, 63,* 1009–1037. **214**

Tieman, W., et al. 2008. Young adult international adoptees' search for birth parents. *Journal of Family Psychology, 22,* 678–687. **249**

Tillman, K. H. 2008. "Non-traditional" siblings and the academic outcomes of adolescents. *Social Science Research, 37,* 88–108. **368**

Tilly, L. A., and Scott, J. W. 2001. The family economy in modern England and France. In B. J. Fox (Ed.), *Family patterns, gender relations,* 2nd Ed. (pp. 78–107). Toronto: Oxford University Press. **41**

Tirone, S., and Sweatman, M. 2011. You suddenly have a different life: Leisure, gender, and the experience of immigrants living in Halifax, Nova Scotia. In E. Tastsoglou and P. S. Jaya (Eds.), *Immigrant women in Atlantic Canada* (pp. 325–353). Toronto: Canadian Scholars' Press. **64**

Tjepkema, M., and Wilkins, R. 2011. Remaining life expectancy at age 25 and probability of survival to age 75, by socio-economic status and Aboriginal ancestry. October. Ottawa: Statistics Canada, *Health Reports, 22.* **110, 114**

Tjepkema, M., et al. 2011a. Potential years of life lost at ages 25 to 74 among Status Indians, 1991 to 2001. Ottawa: Statistics Canada, *Health Reports, 22,* March. **53, 140, 144**

Tjepkema, M., et al. 2011b. Potential years of life lost ages 25 to 74 among Métis and non-status Indians, 1991 to 2001. Ottawa: Statistics Canada, *Health Reports, 22,* March. **53**

Topen, A. 2011. Selective welcome: Labour market experiences of immigrant women from Sub-Saharan Africa. In E. Tastsoglou and P. S. Jaya (Eds.), *Immigrant women in Atlantic Canada* (pp.143–173). Toronto: Canadian Scholars' Press. **109**

Tornello, S. L., et al. 2011. Predictors of parenting stress among gay adoptive fathers in the United States. *Journal of Family Psychology, 25,* 591–600. **244**

Toronto Star. 2011a. Sexual violence in Congo reaches astounding level. May 12. **377**

Toronto Star. 2011b. The high life. November 27. **142**

Torres, J. 2009. *Children & cities: Planning to grow together.* Ottawa: The Vanier Institute of the Family. **123**

Tough, P. 2012. *How children succeed: Grit, curiosity, and the hidden power of character.* Boston: Houghton Mifflin Harcourt. **117, 124, 125, 157, 287**

Trail, T. E., and Karney, B. R. 2012. What's (not) wrong with low-income marriages. *Journal of Marriage and Family, 74,* 413–427. **197**

Treas, J., and Giesen, D. 2000. Sexual infidelity among married and cohabiting Americans. *Journal of Marriage and the Family, 62,* 48–60. **177, 195, 214**

Treas, J., and Gubernskaya, Z. 2012. Farewell to moms? Maternal contact for seven countries in 1986 and 2001. *Journal of Marriage and Family, 74,* 297–311. **305**

Tremblay, J., et al. 2002. Valeur prévisionnelle de la différenciation de soi et des stratégies religieuses d'adaptation dans l'étude de la satisfaction conjugale. *Revue Canadienne des Sciences du Comportement, 34,* 19–27. **177**

Trentacosta, C. J., and Shaw, D. C. 2008. Maternal predictors of rejecting parenting and early adolescent antisocial behavior. *Journal of Abnormal Child Psychology, 36,* 247–259. **280**

Trudel, M. 1973. *The beginnings of New France 1524–1663.* Toronto: McClelland and Stewart. **38, 44**

Trussell, D., and Shaw, S. 2007. "Daddy's gone and he'll be back in October.": Farm women's experience of family leisure. *Journal of Leisure Research, 39,* 366–387. **48, 138**

Tsai, M.-C., and Dzorgbo, D.-B. S. 2012. Familial reciprocity and subjective well-being in Ghana. *Journal of Marriage and Family, 74,* 215–228. **8, 428**

Tu, W., et al. 2009. Time from first intercourse to first sexually transmitted infection diagnosis among adolescent women. *Archives of Pediatrics & Adolescent Medicine, 163,* 1106–1111. **208**

Tucker, C. J., Marx, J., and Long, L. 1998. "Moving on": Residential mobility and children's school lives. *Sociology of Education, 71,* 111–129. **145**

Tucker, C. J., McHale, S. M., and Crouter, A. C. 2003. Dimensions of mothers' and fathers' differential treatment of siblings: Links with adolescents' sex-typed personal quality. *Family Relations, 52,* 241–248. **326**

Tucker, C. J., et al. 2013. Sibling proactive and reactive aggression in adolescence. *Journal of Family Violence, 28,* 299–310. **396, 397**

Tucker-Drob, E. M., and Harden, K. P. 2012. Intellectual interest mediates gene x socioeconomic status interation on adolescent academic achievement. *Child Development, 83,* 743–757. **116, 337**

Turcotte, M., and Schellenberg, G. 2007. *A portrait of seniors in Canada.* Ottawa: Statistics Canada, Publication no 89-519-XWE, February 27. **307, 404, 413**

Turcotte, M., and Vézina, M. 2010. Migration from central to surrounding municipalities in Toronto, Montréal and Vancouver. *Canadian Social Trends, 90,* June 8. **144**

Turcotte, M. 2012. Charitable giving by Canadians. Ottawa. Statistics Canada: *Canadian Social Trends, 93,* Summer. **173**

Turcotte, P. 2002. Changing conjugal life in Canada. *The Daily,* July 11. **193**

Turner, H. A., Finkelhor, D., and Ormrod, R. 2007. Family structure variations in patterns and predictors of child victimization. *American Journal of Orthopsychiatry, 77,* 289–295. **369, 388**

Turney, K., and Carlson, M. J. 2011. Multipartnered fertility and depression among fragile families. *Journal of Marriage and Family, 73,* 570–587. **229**

Twenge, J. M., and Campbell, W. K. 2010. *The narcissism epidemic.* New York: Free Press. **17, 83, 86, 351**

Twenge, J. M., Campbell, W. K., and Foster, C. A. 2003. Parenthood and marital satisfaction: A meta-analytic review. *Journal of Marriage and Family, 65,* 574–583. **236**

Twum-Danso Imoh, A. 2012. From central to marginal? Changing perceptions of kinship fosterage in Ghana. *Journal of Family History, 37,* 351–363. **7, 9, 18, 242**

Tyler, K. A., and Bersani, B. E. 2008. A longitudinal study of early adolescent precursors to running away. *Journal of Early Adolescence, 28,* 230–251. **133**

Tyler, T. 2004. Ottawa backs gay divorce. *Toronto Star.* July 22, A1, A19. **343**

Tyyskä, V. 2001. *Long and winding road: Adolescence and youth in Canada today.* Toronto: Canadian Scholars' Press. **297**

Tyyskä, V. 2003. Solidarity and conflict: Teen-parent relationships in Iranian immigrant families in Toronto. In. M. J. Lynn (Ed.), *Voices: Essays on Canadian families,* 2nd Ed. (pp. 312–331). Toronto: Thomson Nelson. **289, 294**

UAPS (Urban Aboriginal Peoples Study). 2010. (Led by M. Adams.) Environics, April. **52**

Udry, J. R. 2003. How to string straw into gold. In A. C. Crouter and A. Booth (Eds.), *Children's influence on family dynamics* (pp. 49–54). Mahwah, NJ: Erlbaum. **337**

Uecker, J. E. 2008. Religion, pledging, and the premarital sexual behavior of married young adults. *Journal of Marriage and Family, 70,* 728–744. **208**

Uecker, J. E., and Stokes, C. E. 2008. Early marriage in the United States. *Journal of Marriage and Family, 70,* 835–846. **78**

Uhlenberg, P. 2009. Children in an aging society. *The Journals of Gerontology: Series B, 64B,* 489–497. **150**

Uhlenberg, P., and Hammill, B. G. 1998. Frequency of grandparent contact with grandchild sets: Six factors that make a difference. *The Gerontologist, 38,* 276–285. **371**

Umberson, D. 2003. *Death of a parent: Transition to a new adult identity.* Cambridge, UK: Cambridge University Press. **313**

Umberson, D., et al. 2005. As good as it gets? A life course perspective on marital quality. *Social Forces, 84,* 493–512. **260, 277**

Umberson, D., et al. 2006. You make me sick: Marital quality and health over the life course. *Journal of Health and Social Behavior, 47,* 1–16. **266**

United Nations. 2008. *Demographic yearbook.* New York: United Nations. **344**

United Way of Toronto. 2001. *A decade of decline: Poverty and income inequality in the City of Toronto in the 1990s.* **106**

U.S. Commission on Civil Rights. 1977. *Window dressing on the set: Women and minorities in television.* Washington, DC: A report of the U.S. Commission on Civil Rights. **81**

U.S. Department of Health and Human Services. 2002. *Trends in sexual risk behaviors among high school students—United States, 1991–2001.* Center for Chronic Disease, September 27. **89**

U.S. Department of Health and Human Services. 2010. *Marriage and cohabitation in the United States.* National Centre for Health Statistics. **193**

Uzzell, O., and Peebles-Wilkins, W. 1989. Black spouse abuse: A focus on relational factors and intervention strategies. *Western Journal of Black Studies, 13,* 10–16. **382**

Vaaler, M. L., Ellison, C. G., and Powers, D. A. 2009. Religious influences on the risk of marital dissolution. *Journal of Marriage and Family, 71,* 917–934. **177**

Vaillancourt, R. 2009. *Family violence in Canada. Section 4: Police-reported family violence against older adults.* Ottawa: Statistics Canada,Catalogue no. 85-224-X. **403**

Valdez, C. E., et al. 2013. "It's going to make the whole tower crooked": Victimization trajectories in IPV. *Journal of Family Violence, 28,* 131–140. **389**

Vall, C., and Thompson, A. 2012. *From getting by to getting ahead: Six levers for building the wellbeing of families with lower incomes.* Calgary: The United Way of Calgary and Area. **420, 426**

van den Akker, O. 2007. Psychosocial aspects of surrogate motherhood. *Human Reproduction Update, 31,* 53–62. **241**

Vanderschelden, M. 2006. *Les ruptures d'unions: plus fréquentes, mais pas plus précoces.* Paris: INSEE, 1107, Novembre. **347**

Van Die, M. 2005. *Religion, family, and community in Victorian Canada.* Montreal: McGill-Queen's University Press. **46, 144**

van Eeden-Moorefield, B., et al. 2012. Explaining couple cohesion in different types of gay families. *Journal of Family Issues, 33,* 182–201. **365**

Vanfraussen, K., et al. 2003. Family functioning of lesbian families created by donor insemination. *American Journal of Orthopsychiatry, 73,* 78–90. **224**

van Ijzendoorn, M. H., et al. 2005. Adoption and cognitive development: A meta-analytic comparison of adopted and non-adopted children's IQ and school performance. *Psychological Bulletin, 131,* 301–316. **244, 250**

Van Kersbergen, K., and Manow, P. (Eds.), 2009. *Religion, class coalitions, and welfare states.* New York: Cambridge University Press. **170, 417**

Van Kirk, S. 1992. The custom of the country: An examination of fur trade marriage practices. In B. Bradbury (Ed.), *Canadian family history.* Toronto: Copp Clark Pitman. **43**

van Roode, T., et al. 2009. Child sexual abuse and persistence of risky sexual behaviors and negative social outcomes over adulthood: Findings from a birth cohort. *Child Abuse & Neglect, 33,* 161–172. **395**

Vaughan, E., et al. 2013. Relationships between child emotional and behavioral symptoms and caregiving strain and parenting stress. *Journal of Family Issues, 34,* 534–554. **307**

Veblen, T. 1899. *The theory of the leisure class.* New York: Modern Library. **104**

Veldorale-Brogan, A., and Cooley, M. 2011. Child outcomes for children with LGBT parents. *Family Focus, Winter,* F15–16. **223, 225**

Vespa, J. 2012. Union formation in later life: Economic determinants of cohabitation and remarriage among older adults. *Demography, 49,* 1103–1125. **196**

Vetter, D. M., and Blimkie, M. 2011. Learning to teach in culturally responsive and respectful ways: The first steps in creating a First Nation, Métis and Inuit education infusion in a mainstream teacher education program. *The Canadian Journal of Native Studies, 31,* 173–185, 187, 189. **166**

Vézina, M. 2011. Quality of personal networks: Does living alone make a difference? *Canadian Social Trends,* Winter, 92. **203**

Vézina, M. 2012. *Being a parent in a stepfamily: A profile.* Ottawa: Statistics Canada, October. **198, 366, 367, 368**

Vézina, M., and Turcotte, M. 2009. *Forty-year-old mothers of pre-school children: A profile.* Ottawa, Statistics Canada. **231, 232**

Vézina, M., and Turcotte, M. 2010. Caring for a parent who lives far away: The consequences. Statistics Canada, *The Daily,* January 26. **431**

Viding, E., et al. 2005. Evidence for substantial genetic risk for psychopathy in 7-year-olds. *Journal of Child Psychology and Psychiatry, 46,* 592–597. **334**

VIF (Vanier Institute of the Family). 2002. *Sources of diversity: geography, ethnicity, gender, kinship ties and technology.* Ottawa: Vanier Institute of the Family. Accessed December 8. **242**

VIF (Vanier Institute of the Family). 2012a. *Trying to conceive: Infertility in Canada.* Ottawa, March 28. **235**

VIF (Vanier Institute of the Family). 2012b. *Teen pregnancy: Supporting young parents.* Ottawa. **226**

VIF (Vanier Institute of the Family). 2012c. *Families and technology.* Ottawa, September 20. **84**

Viner, R. M., and Tayler, B. 2005. Adult health and social outcomes of children who have been in public care: Population-based study. *Pediatrics, 115,* 894–899. **250**

Voisey, P. 1987. *Vulcan: The making of a Prairie community.* Toronto: University of Toronto Press. **48**

Volling, B. L. 1997. The family correlates of maternal and paternal perceptions of differential treatment in early childhood. *Family Relations, 46,* 227–236. **328**

Voorpostel, M., and Blieszner, R. 2008. Intergenerational solidarity and support between adult siblings. *Journal of Marriage and Family, 70,* 157–167. **330**

Vosko, L. F. 2002. Mandatory "marriage" or obligatory waged work. In S. Bashevkin (Ed.), *Women's work is never done* (pp. 165–199). New York: Routledge. **111, 252**

Votruba-Drzal, E., Coley, R. L., and Chase-Lansdale, P. L. 2004. Child care and low income children's development: Direct and moderated effects. *Child Development, 75,* 296–312. **153**

Votruba-Drzal, E., et al. 2010. Child care and the development of behavior problems among economically disadvantaged children in middle childhood. *Child Development, 81,* 1460–1474. **153**

Vroegh, K. S. 1997. Transracial adoptees: Developmental status after 17 years. *American Journal of Orthopsychiatry, 67,* 568–575. **246, 247**

Wagmiller, R. L., Jr., et al. 2006. The dynamics of economic disadvantage and children's life chances. *American Sociological Review, 71,* 847–866. **117**

Waite, L. J., and Gallagher, M. 2000. *The case for marriage.* Cambridge, MA: Harvard University Press. **354**

Waite, L. J., et al. 2002. *Does divorce make people happy?* Institute for American Values. **356**

Waite, L. J., Luo, Y., and Levin, A. C. 2009. Marital happiness and marital stability: Consequences for psychological well-being. *Social Science Research, 3,* 201–212. **356**

Walby, S. 1997. *Gender transformation.* London: Routledge. **252**

Walker, A. J., and McGraw, L. A. 2000. Who is responsible for responsible fathering? *Journal of Marriage and Family, 62,* 563–569. **348**

Walker, J. 1976. *The Black Loyalists: The search for a promised land in Nova Scotia and Sierra Leone, 1783–1807.* London: Longman. **45**

Walker, J. M. 1980. *A history of Blacks in Canada*. Ottawa: Minister of State for Multiculturalism and Supply and Services Canada. 44

Walkom, T. 2012. Nursing home flaws exposed. *Toronto Star*, December 15, A8. 430

Wall, C. S., and Madak, P. R. 1991. Indian students' academic self-concept and their perceptions of teacher and parent aspirations for them in a band-controlled school and a provincial school. *Canadian Journal of Native Education, 18*, 43–51. 166

Wall, G. 2001. Moral construction of motherhood in breastfeeding discourse. *Gender and Society, 15*, 592–610. 18

Wall, G. 2004. Is your child's brain potential maximized?: Mothering in an age of new brain research. *Atlantis, 28. 2*, 41–50. 17, 74, 160, 163, 287

Wall, G. 2009. Childhood and child-rearing. In M. Baker (Ed.), *Families: changing trends in Canada*, 6th Ed. (pp. 68–90). Toronto: McGraw-Hill Ryerson. 286

Wallace, H. 1999. *Family violence: Legal, medical, and social perspectives*, 2nd Ed. Boston: Allyn & Bacon. 397

Wallace, K. 2012. Newfoundland hockey officials force parents to take anger course. *Toronto Star*, September 19. 87

Wallace, M., Wisener, M., and Collins, K. 2006. *Neighbourhood characteristics and the distribution of crime in Regina. Crime and Justice Research Paper Series*. Ottawa, Statistics Canada Catalogue no. 85-561-MIE. no. 8. 126

Wallerstein, J. S. 1998. Children of divorce: A society in search of policy. In M. A. Mason, A. Skolnick, and S. D. Sugarman (Eds.), *All our families: New policies for a new century* (pp. 66–94). New York: Oxford University Press. 361

Walsh, C., MacMillan, H., and Jamieson, E. 2002. The relationship between parental psychiatric disorder and child physical and sexual abuse: Findings from the Ontario health supplement. *Child Abuse & Neglect, 26*, 11–22. 388

Walsh, C. A., and Ma, Y. 2012. Developing an empirical profile for elder abuse research in Canada. *Journal of Elder Abuse & Neglect, 24*, 104–119. 402, 403

Wang, Y., and Marcotte, D. E. 2007. Golden years? The labor market effects of caring for grandchildren. *Journal of Marriage and Family, 69*, 1283–1296. 312

Ward, C. 1998. Community resources and school performance: The Northern Cheyenne case. *Sociological Inquiry, 68*, 83–113. 166

Ward, O. 2010. Polygamy's reality often grim for wives. *Toronto Star*, November 28, A15. 8, 9

Ward, R. A., Spitze, G., and Deane, G. 2009. The more the merrier? Multiple parent-adult child relations. *Journal of Marriage and Family, 71*, 161–173. 368

Warman, C. 2007. Ethnic enclaves and immigrant earnings growth. *Canadian Journal of Economics, 40*, 401–422. 109

Warner, T. D. 2010. Violent acts and injurious consequences: An examination of competing hypotheses about intimate partner violence using agency-based data. *Journal of Family Violence, 25*, 183–193. 376

Wartella, E., Caplowitz, A. G., and Lee, J. H. 2004. From Baby Einstein to Leapfrog, from Doom to the Sims, from instant messaging to Internet chat rooms: Public interest in the role of interactive media in children's lives. *Social Policy Report, 18*, 3–19. 87

Watamura, S. E., et al. 2003. Morning-to-afternoon increases in cortisol concentrations for infants and toddlers at child care: Age differences and behavioral correlates. *Child Development, 74*, 1006–1020. 154

Watamura, S. E., et al. 2011. Double jeopardy: Poorer social-emotional outcomes for children in the NICHO SECCYD experiencing home and child-care environments that confer risk. *Child Development, 82*, 48–65. 153

Waters, J. L. 2002. Flexible families? Astronaut households and the experiences of mothers in Vancouver, British Columbia. *Social & Cultural Geography, 3*, 117–134. 75, 76

Weaver, A. D., et al. 2011. Experiences and perceptions of young adults in friends with benefits relationships: A qualitiative study. *The Canadian Journal of Human Sexuality, 20*, 41–53. 183, 435

Weaver, S. E., Coleman, M., and Ganong, L. H. 2004. The sibling relationship in young adulthood: Sibling functions and relationship perceptions as influenced by sibling pair composition. *Journal of Family Issues, 24*, 245–263. 330

Weber, M. P. 1905 (1958). *The Protestant ethic and the spirit of capitalism*. New York: Charles Scribner's Sons. 41, 170

Wegar, K. 1997. *Adoption, identity, and kinship: The debate over sealed birth records*. New Haven, CT: Yale University Press. 243

Wekerle, C., et al. 2009. The contribution of childhood emotional abuse to teen dating violence among child protective services-involved youth. *Child Abuse & Neglect, 33*, 45–58. 377, 389

Welsh, J. A., and Viana, A. G. 2012. Developmental outcomes of internationally adopted children. *Adoption Quarterly, 15*, 241–264. 247

Welsh, M. 2006. "The game." *Toronto Star*. April 29, A1, A26–27. 127

Wen, M., and Lin, D. 2012. Child development in rural China: Children left behind by their migrant parents and children of nonimmigrant families. *Child Development, 83*, 120–136. 75

Wentzel, K. R. 2002. Are effective teachers like good parents? Teaching styles and student adjustment in early adolescence. *Child Development, 73*, 287–301. 157

Westhead, R., and Aulakh, R. 2009. Lost brides. *Toronto Star*. Nov. 15. A1, A6. 63

Westoff, C. F., and Frejka, T. 2007. Religiousness and fertility among European Muslims. *Population and Development Review, 33*, 785–809. 171

Westoff, C. F., and Koffman, D. A. 2011. The association of television and radio with reproductive behavior. *Population and Development Review, 37*, 749–759. 89

Whalen, C. K., Henker, B., and Dotemoto, S. 1980. Methylphenidate and hyperactivity: Effects on teacher behavior. *Science, 208*, 1280–1282. 296

Whisman, M. A., and Snyder, D. K. 2007. Sexual infidelity in a national survey of American women: Differences in prevalence and correlates as a function of method of assessment. *Journal of Family Psychology, 21*, 147–154. 31

Whisman, M. A., Gordon, K. C., and Chatav, Y. 2007. Predicting sexual infidelity in a population-based sample of married individuals. *Journal of Family Psychology, 21*, 320–324. 214

White, D., and Mill, D. 2000. The child care provider. In L. Prochner and N. Howe (Eds.), *Early childhood education and care in Canada* (pp. 236–251). Vancouver: University of British Columbia Press. 152

White, J. M. 1999. Work-family stage and satisfaction with work-family balance. *Journal of Comparative Family Studies, 30,* 163–175. 272

White, J. M. 2005. *Advancing family theories.*Thousand Oaks, CA: Sage. 10, 15

White, J. M., and Klein, D. M. 2002. *Family theories,* 2nd Ed. Thousand Oaks, CA: Sage. 4, 13, 22, 25

White, L. 2001. Sibling relations over the life course: A panel analysis. *Journal of Marriage and Family, 63,* 555–568. 330

White, R. M. B., and Roosa, M. W. 2012. Neighborhood contexts, and Mexican American young adolescents' internalizing symptoms. *Journal of Marriage and Family, 74,* 152–166. 127

Whiteman, S. D., and Christiansen, A. 2008. Processes of sibling influence in adolescence: Individual and family correlates. *Family Relations, 57,* 24–34. 322

Whiteman, S. D., McHale, S. M., and Crouter, A. C. 2003. What parents learn from experience: The first child as a first draft? *Journal of Marriage and Family, 65,* 608–621. 326

Whiteman, S. D., McHale, S. M., and Crouter, A. C. 2007. Longitudinal changes in marital relationships: The role of offspring's pubertal development. *Journal of Marriage and Family, 69,* 1005–1020. 277

Whiting, B. B., and Edwards, C. P. 1988. *Children of different worlds.* Cambridge, MA: Harvard University Press. 17

Whiting, J. B., and Lee, R. E. 2003. Voices from the system: A qualitative study of foster children's stories. *Family Relations, 52,* 288–295. 250

Whitton, S. W., et al. 2008. Effects of parental divorce on marital commitment and confidence. *Journal of Family Psychology, 22,* 789–793. 352

Wickrama, K. A. S., and Bryant, C. M. 2003. Community context of social resources and adolescent mental health. *Journal of Marriage and Family, 65,* 850–866. 129

Wickrama, K. A. S., and O'Neal, C. W. 2013. Family of origin, rare/ethnicity, and socioeconomic attainment: Genotype and intraindividual processes. *Journal of Marriage and Family, 75,* 75–90. 27, 28, 116, 296, 333

Widmer, E. D. 1997. Influence of older siblings on initiation of sexual intercourse. *Journal of Marriage and Family, 59,* 928–938. 323

Widmer, E. D., Treas, J., and Newcomb, R. 1998. Attitudes toward nonmarital sex in 24 countries. *Journal of Sex Research, 35,* 349–358. 214

Widom, C. S., and Morris, S. 1997. Accuracy of adult recollections of childhood victimization: Part 2: Childhood sexual abuse. *Psychological Assessment, 9,* 34–36. 396

Wienke Totura, C. M., et al. 2009. Bullying and victimization among boys and girls in middle school. *Journal of Early Adolescence, 29,* 571–609. 400

Wiik, K. A., et al. 2009. A study of commitment and relationship quality in Sweden and Norway. *Journal of Marriage and Family, 71,* 465–477. 352, 353

Wiik, K. A., et al. 2012. Relationship quality in marital and cohabiting unions across Europe. *Journal of Marriage and Family, 74,* 389–398. 191, 193, 196

Wilcox, K. L., Wolchik, S. A., and Braver, S. L. 1998. Predictors of maternal preference for joint or sole legal custody. *Family Relations, 47,* 93–101. 348

Wilcox, W. B. 2002. Religion, convention, and parental involvement. *Journal of Marriage and Family, 64,* 780–792. 176

Wilcox, W. B., and Nock, S. L. 2006. What's love got to do with it? Equality, equity, commitment and women's marital quality. *Social Forces, 84,* 1321–1346. 256, 263, 273

Wiley, A. R., Warren, H. B., and Montanelli, D. S. 2002. Shelter in a time of storm: Parenting in poor rural African American communities. *Family Relations, 51,* 265–273. 175

Wilkie, J. R., Ferree, M. M., and Ratcliff, K. S. 1998. Gender and fairness: Marital satisfaction in two-earner couples. *Journal of Marriage and Family, 60,* 577–594. 270, 272

Wilkins, R., Bertholet, J.-M., and Ng, E. 2002. *Trends in mortality by neighbourhood income in urban Canada from 1971 to 1996.* Supplement for Health Reports, vol. 13, Catalogue no. 82–003. 128

Williams, A. L., and Merten, M. J. 2011. Family: Internet and social media technology in the family context. *Family and Consumer Sciences, 40,* 150–170. 84, 85

Williams, C. 2001a. Connected to the internet, still connected to life? *Canadian Social Trends, 63,* 13–15. 84

Williams, C. 2001b. Family disruptions and childhood happiness. *Canadian Social Trends, 62,* 2–5. 358, 359

Williams, C. 2002. Time or money? How high and low income Canadians spend their time. *Canadian Social Trends, 65,* 7–11. 103, 104

Williams, C. 2003. Finances in the golden years. *Perspectives on Labour and Income, 4,* November, 5–13. 419

Williams, C. 2008. Work-life balance of shift workers. *Perspectives on Labour and Income, 9.* 99

Williams, K., and Dunne-Bryant, A. 2006. Divorce and adult psychological well-being: Clarifying the role of gender and child age. *Journal of Marriage and Family, 68,* 1178–1196. 355

Williams, L. M., and Banyard, V. L. 1997. Gender and recall of child sexual abuse: A prospective study. In J. D. Read and D. S. Lindsay (Eds.), *Recollections of trauma: Scientific evidence and clinical perspective* (pp. 371–377). New York: Plenum Press. 396

Williams, S. T., Conger, K. J., and Blozis, S. A. 2007. The development of interpersonal aggression during adolescence: The importance of parents, siblings, and family economics. *Child Development, 78,* 1526–1542. 322

Williamson, H. C., et al. 2012. Communication behavior and relationship satisfaction among American and Chinese newlywed couples. *Journal of Family Psychology, 26,* 308–315. 261

Willms, J. D. 2002a. A study of vulnerable children. In J. D. Willms (Ed.), *Vulnerable children* (pp. 3–22). Edmonton: University of Alberta Press. 31

Willms, J. D. 2002b. Socioeconomic gradients for childhood vulnerability. In J. D. Willms (Ed.), *Vulnerable children* (pp. 71–103). Edmonton: University of Alberta Press. 31, 118, 161, 230

Willoughby, B., and Carroll, J. 2012. Correlates of attitudes toward cohabitation: Looking at the associations with demographics, relational attitudes, and dating behavior. *Journal of Family Issues, 33,* 1450–1476. 186, 194, 196

Wills, J. B., and Risman, B. J. 2006. The visibility of feminist thought in family studies. *Journal of Marriage and Family, 68,* 690–700. 20

Wilmoth, J., and Koso, G. 2002. Does marital history matter? Marital status and wealth outcomes among preretirement adults. *Journal of Marriage and Family, 64,* 254–268. 366

Wilson, A. E., Shuey, K. M., and Elder, G. H., Jr. 2003. Ambivalence in the relationship of adult children to aging parents and in-laws. *Journal of Marriage and Family, 65*, 1055–1072. **309**

Wilson, S. 2009. Partnering, cohabitation, and marriage. In M. Baker (Ed.), *Families: changing trends in Canada*, 6th Ed. (pp. 68–90). Toronto: McGraw-Hill Ryerson. **187**

Wilson, W. J. 1987. *The truly disadvantaged.* Chicago: University of Chicago Press. **112**

Wilson, W. J. 1996. *When work disappears: The world of the new urban poor.* New York: Knopf. **129**

WIN-Gallup International. 2013. *Global index of religiosity and atheism-2012.* Gallup International. http://wingia.com. **171**

Winks, R. W. 2000. *The Blacks in Canada: A history*, 2nd Ed. Montreal, Kingston: McGill-Queen's University Press. **45**

Winland, D., Gaetz, S., and Patton, T. 2011. *Family matters: Homeless youth and Eva's initiative's "Family Reconnect" Program.* Ottawa: Canadian Homeless Research Network Press. **133**

Wolak, J., et al. 2008. Online "predators" and their victims: Myths, realities, and implications for prevention and treatment. *American Psychologist, 63*, 111–128. **89**

Wolf, J. B. 2010. *Is breast best? Taking on the breast feeding experts and the new high stakes of motherhood.* New York: New York University Press. **18**

Wolff, E. N. 2001. The economic status of parents in postwar America. In S. A. Hewlett, N. Rankin, and C. West (Eds.), *Taking parenting public* (pp. 59–82). New York: Rowan & Littlefield. **103**

Wolkowicz, H. 2011. Transgendered: Struggling with jobs, inequality. *Toronto Star*, May 28, B1, B8. **211**

Woodward, L. J., Fergusson, D. M., and Horwood, L. J. 2006. Gender differences in the transition to early parenthood. *Development and Psychopathology, 18*, 275–294. **229**

Woodward, L., Fergusson, D. M., and Horwood, L. J. 2001. Risk factors and life processes associated with teenage pregnancy: Results of a prospective study from birth to 20 years. *Journal of Marriage and Family, 63*, 1170–1184. **228**

World Bank. 2012. *World development report 2012: Gender equality and development.* Washington: The World Bank. **98, 99**

Wright, C., et al. 2011. SketchUp™: A technology tool to facilitate intergenerational relationships for children with autism spectrum disorders (ASD). *Family and Consumer Sciences Research Journal, 40*, 135–149. **85**

Wu, Z., and Hart, R. 2002. The effects of marital and nonmarital union transition on health. *Journal of Marriage and Family, 64*, 420–432. **355**

Wu, L. L. 1996. Effects of family instability, income, and income instability on the risk of a premarital birth. *American Sociological Review, 61*, 386–406. **360**

Wu, Z. 1995. Remarriage after widowhood: A marital history study of older Canadians. *Canadian Journal on Aging, 14*, 719–736. **363**

Wu, Z. 2000. *Cohabitation: An alternative form of family living.* Toronto: Oxford University Press. **193, 197**

Wu, Z., and MacNeill, L. 2002. Education, work, and childbearing after age 30. *Journal of Comparative Family Studies, 33*, 191–213. **236**

Wu, Z., and Schimmele, C. M. 2003. Childhood family experience and completed fertility. *Canadian Studies in Population, 30*, 221–240. **225**

Wu, Z., and Schimmele, C. M. 2009. Divorce and repartnering. In M. Baker (Ed.), *Families: Changing trends in Canada*, 6th Ed., (pp. 154–178). Toronto: McGraw-Hill Ryerson. **343, 365**

Wu, Z., et al. 2000. Age-heterogamy and Canadian unions. *Social Biology, 47*, 277–293. **189**

Wu, Z., et al. 2004. "In sickness and in health": Does cohabitation count? *Journal of Family Issues, 24*, 811–838. **195**

Wulczyn, F. 2004. Family reunification. *The Future of Children, 14*, Winter, 95–113. **250**

Wulczyn, F. 2009. Epidemiological perspectives on maltreatment prevention. *The Future of Children, 19*, 39–65. **391**

Xinran. 2010. *Message from an unknown Chinese mother.* Transl. by N. Harmann. London: Chatto & Windus. **59, 247**

Xu, L., Gauthier, A. H., and Strohschein, L. 2009. Why are some children left out? Factors barring Canadian children from participating in extracurricular activities. *Canadian Studies in Population, 36*, 325–345. **125**

Xu, Q., and Yeung, W.-J. 2013. Hoping for a Phoenix: Shanghai fathers and their daughters. *Journal of Family Issues, 34*, 182–207. **287**

Xu, X., Hudspeth, C. D., and Bartkowski, J. P. 2006. The role of cohabitation in remarriage. *Journal of Marriage and Family, 68*, 261–274. **352, 365**

Yabiku, S. T., and Gager, C. T. 2009. Sexual frequency and the stability of marital and cohabiting unions. *Journal of Marriage and Family, 71*, 983–1000. **194, 212, 213**

Yalnizyan, A. 2010. *The rise of Canada's richest 1%.* Canadian Centre for Policy Alternatives. **12, 97**

Yaman, A., et al. 2010. Parenting and toddler aggression in second-generation immigrant families: The moderating role of child temperament. *Journal of Family Psychology, 24*, 208–211. **286**

Yanca, C., and Low, B. S. 2003. Female allies and female power: A cross-cultural analysis. *Evolution and Human Behavior, 25*, 9–23. **9**

Yancey, G. 2002. Who interracially dates?: An examination of the characteristics of those who have interacially dated. *Journal of Comparative Family Studies, 33*, 179–190. **187**

Yasuda, T., et al. 2011. Intergenerational coresidence in China, Japan, South Korea and Taiwan: Comparative analyses based on the East Asian Social Survey 2006 (1). *Journal of Comparative Family Studies, 42*, 703–722. **60**

Yax-Fraser, M. J. 2011. Mothering across cultures: Immigrant women's experiences in Halifax. In E. Tastsoglou and P. S. Jaya (Eds.), *Migrant women in Atlantic Canada* (pp. 297–323). Toronto: Canadian's Scholars' Press. **7, 19, 64, 72, 166, 293**

Ybarra, M. L., et al. 2009. Associations between blocking, monitoring, and filtering software on home computer and youth-reported unwanted exposure to sexual material online. *Child Abuse & Neglect, 33*, 857–869. **72**

Yee, S. 1994. Gender ideology and Black women as community-builders in Ontario, 1850–70. *Canadian Historical Review, 75*, 53–73. **46**

York, G. 2012. Developing world sees rise in unsafe abortions. *The Globe and Mail*, January 19, A16. **237**

Young, V. H. 1974. A Black American socialization pattern. *American Ethnologist, 1*, 415–431. **290**

Yount, K. M., and Li, L. 2009. Women's "justification" of domestic violence in Egypt. *Journal of Marriage and Family, 71,* 1125–1140. **382**

Yu, T., et al. 2010. The interactive effects of marital conflict and divorce on parents—Adult children's relationships. *Journal of Marriage and Family, 72,* 282–292. **278, 361**

Yucel, D., and Gassanov, M. A. 2010. Exploring actor and partner correlates of sexual satisfaction among married couples. *Social Science Research, 39,* 725–738. **215**

Zaidi, A. U., and Shuraydi, M. 2002. Perceptions of arranged marriages by young Pakistani Muslim women living in a Western society. *Journal of Comparative Family Studies, 33,* 495–514. **63, 206**

Zajonc, R. B. 2001. The family dynamics of intellectual development. *American Psychologist, 56,* 490–496. **317**

Zajonc, R. B., and Mullally, P. R. 1997. Birth order: Reconciling conflicting effects. *American Psychologist, 52,* 685–690. **319**

Zeman, K., and Bressan, A. 2008. *Factors associated with youth delinquency and victimization in Toronto, 2006.* Ottawa: Statistics Canada. **230, 368**

Zerk, D. M., Mertin, P. G., and Proeve, M. 2009. Domestic violence and maternal reports of young children's functioning. *Journal of Family Violence, 24,* 423–432. **385**

Zhao, Z., and Guo, Z. 2010. China's below replacement fertility: A further exploration. *Canadian Studies in Population, 37,* 525–562. **58-59, 235, 242**

Zhu, W. X., Lu, L., and Hesketh, T. 2009. China's excess males, sex selective abortion and one child policy: Analysis of data from 2005 national intercensus survey. *British Medical Journal, 338,* 1211–1217. **59**

Zielinski, D. S. 2009. Child maltreatment and adult socioeconomic well-being. *Child Abuse & Neglect, 33,* 666–678. **389**

Zimmerman, J. 2003. *Made from scratch: Reclaiming the pleasures of the American hearth.* New York: Free Press. **102**

Zine, J. 2008. *Canadian Islamic schools.* Toronto: University of Toronto Press. **22, 50, 158, 167, 171, 183, 206**

Zlotnick, C. 2009. What research tells us about the intersecting streams of homelessness and foster care. *American Journal of Orthopsychiatry, 79,* 319–325. **250**

Zuckerman, M. 2005. *Psychobiology and personality,* 2nd Ed. Cambridge, UK: Cambridge University Press. **280**

Zysk, K. G. 2002. *Conjugal love in India.* Boston: Brill. **259**

Subject Index

A

Abilities, skills, 15, 17, 117, 123, 129, 333, 334
Aboriginal families, 6, 52, 59, 242, 247, 418
  abuse, 44, 53
  alcohol, 43, 44, 110, 125
  band, 36, 37, 51, 52, 110
  childrearing, 51, 385
  children, 44, 46, 51, 247, 250, 311, 383, 385
  demographic profile, 36, 38, 51, 110
  discrimination, 48, 49, 125, 167
  education (schools), 43, 110, 151, 154–155, 158, 160, 162, 166
  elders, 53, 158
  family violence, 52, 53, 379–380, 381, 382–383, 404
  fertility, 51, 233
  First Nations families, 8, 219, 233, 247
  foster care, 52, 247
  Head Start, 151, 154–155
  health/health care, 38, 53, 110, 125
  history, 36–39, 43–46, 50–54, 64, 110, 167
  housing, 110, 144
  Indian Acts, 44, 51, 52
  inter-ethnic unions, 39, 43, 48, 49
  Inuit, 7, 14, 51, 73, 114, 219, 230
  kin orientation, 36, 44, 52–53, 166
  languages, 36, 43, 54, 156
  location, 47, 49, 51, 420
  Métis families, 38, 39, 43, 47, 49, 51, 53, 219, 233
  mortality, 110
  neighbourhoods, 119, 132,167, 238, 386, 420
  parenting, 18, 52, 166–167
  physical violence against, 52, 380, 381–383, 394
  poverty, 52, 63, 110, 113, 125, 219, 420
  reservation system, 44, 49, 51, 110,113, 125, 424
  residential school system, 43–44, 49–52, 54
  slavery, 43, 44
  women, 37, 39, 48, 52, 156
Abortion, 114, 218, 226, 236–238, 290
  of female fetuses, 59, 63, 233, 237, 238

Abuse, 111, 143, 222, 381 (see also Rape; Sexual abuse of children; Violence)
  of children, 111, 208, 222, 230, 250, 251, 383, 391–401, 419
  of children by parents, 230, 250, 251, 386–388
  of children by peers, 170, 377, 386
  of children by siblings, 386, 396–399
  dating/partner, 10, 111, 195, 260, 378–379, 381
  elder, 53, 307
  of parents by children, 292, 401–404
  psychological, 378–379
Achievement, 17, 104, 169 (see also School achievement)
Adolescence (ts), 83, 103, 237, 391, 419 (see also Child/Children; Childhood)
  as caregivers, 299–300, 324
  development, 222, 293
  difficult, 130, 230, 277, 288, 293, 302, 349, 387
  homeless, 133–134
  lengthened, 72, 183
  parenting, 227–229
  peers, 70, 130, 302
  pregnancy, 158, 192, 227
  relationship with parents, 51, 295–300, 301–303, 324, 388
  social construction, 27, 292, 293, 296–297, 303
Adolescent fathers, 112, 128, 228–229 (see also Adolescent mothers)
Adolescent mothers, 111, 112, 115, 175, 226–230, 311 (see also Single-mother families)
  Children of, 112, 227, 230 (see also Outcomes)
  children's fathers, 112, 128, 224
  mothers' own mothers, 175, 227–229
Adolescent sexuality, 89, 112, 175, 204–210, 211, 243, 324, 400–401
  control, 203–204, 207–209
  gender differences, 204–205, 207, 400–401
  peer effect on, 205, 208–210, 400–401
Adoption, 52, 202, 242–249, 333, 335, 337, 418
  adopted adults, 37, 43–44, 249, 335
  adopted children, 47, 243–246, 334, 337

  adoptive parents, 242, 244, 245, 246, 248, 335
  birth parents, 248, 337
  international/transracial, 246–247
  older children, 244, 247
  open, 247–248
  peer effects, 244–246
  reunions with birth parents, 243, 248–249
  siblings of, 244, 248
  social construction, 15, 29, 242–243, 245–246
Adult children,
  abuse of elderly parents, 53, 307
  death of parents, 312–313
  help from parents, 60, 303–305, 306, 307, 309, 395
  help to parents, 60, 305, 307–309, 408, 413, 430
  living at home (see Coresidence)
  problems, 306, 325
  relationship with parents, 305–309
  young adults, 176, 303–305
Adulthood, 303–309, 411
  emerging, 208, 303–304, 411
Adultery (see Sex/Sexuality)
Advertising, 13, 81, 83, 87–88, 90, 104, 416
Affluent (rich), 94, 95, 97, 103, 108, 116, 123, 128, 140, 159–161, 292, 402
Afghanistan, 3, 8, 61, 77, 107, 235, 264, 298, 377, 382
Africa, 7, 8, 9, 17, 18, 44, 50, 56, 98, 106, 107, 151, 171, 185, 202, 205, 220, 235, 242, 247, 260, 288, 294, 297, 320, 339, 377, 382, 412, 413
African-Canadians, 109 (see also Black families)
Age, 16, 137, 176, 184, 189, 201, 204, 208, 211–213, 298, 309–310, 316, 375, 402, 413
  at first birth, 78, 231, 233, 240, 387
  at marriage, 8, 55, 183, 212, 413
  older/elderly, 16, 53, 196–197, 413
  segregation by, 29, 150, 301
Aged parents, 71, 143, 402–404 (see also Adult children; Crisis in Caring; Elder care; Parent-child relations),

Aggressiveness, 85–87, 130, 153, 157, 228, 280, 293, 294, 319, 321, 323, 325, 376, 377, 383

Aging, 189, 211–213, 274

Aging of the population, 51, 137, 197, 220, 413–414, 416, 422

Agriculture, 12, 17, 39, 40, 48, 235, 288

Alberta, 45, 49, 113, 114, 144, 152, 161, 191, 197, 206, 219, 227, 303, 344, 370

Alcohol(ism), 43, 79, 125, 174, 199, 205, 208, 244, 250, 299, 311, 323, 355, 381

Altruism, altruistic, 14, 177, 242, 256, 261, 262, 288, 405, 430, 431

American (*see* United States)

Amish, 73, 137, 338

Anomie, 351, 412, 434

Antisocial, 130, 164–165, 228–229, 363, 390

Arab countries, 73, 75, 219

Armenia, 237, 412

Arranged marriages, 9, 58 (*see also* Forced Marriages)

Asia, Asians, 6, 7, 8, 9, 50, 62, 64, 79, 99, 109, 132, 149, 151, 186, 202, 234, 252, 260, 261, 287, 297, 320, 412, 416

Assets, 25, 41, 60, 96, 97, 124, 304, 305, 431

At risk (*see* Risk factors)

Attachment, 17, 224, 286, 290, 390

Attractiveness, 185, 190, 212

Australia, 97, 309, 353

Authority, 25, 220, 292, 300, 302, 389, 402

Autobiography (students'), 2, 30, 32, 57, 149, 184, 255, 298, 316, 399

Azerbaijan, 237, 412

B

Babies' fathers (*see* Adolescent mothers)

Behaviour genetics theories, 2, 26–28, 119, 231, 285, 320, 332–336 (*see also* Genes and environment; Genetic influence)

Behaviour problems, 130, 158, 198, 222, 230, 231, 247, 276, 277–278, 286, 288, 293, 296, 358, 384, 425, 428
  causes, 114, 117, 118, 129, 130, 151, 162, 165, 245
  consequences, 293, 295, 298

Bereavement, 363–365

Biology, biological, 239–241 (*see also* Behaviour genetics; Genetic influence)

Birth, 24–25, 111–113, 225–226, 240, 276, 285, 320–321
  rates, 51, 55, 233–235, 310, 413 (*see also* Fertility)

Birth control, 236, 237 (*see also* Family planning)

Birth parents, 243, 248, 249

Bisexual, 210–211 (*see also* Sex/Sexuality)

Black families, 18, 44–45, 48, 56–58, 81, 110, 223, 263, 290, 310, 382
  child outcomes, 57, 58, 160, 166, 246, 247, 290
  discrimination, 45, 57, 58, 382
  family structure, 44, 45, 46, 56, 57, 219
  fathers, 45, 58
  history, 44–46
  interracial unions, 57, 132, 186
  kin, 45, 57
  low-income, 57, 83, 132, 160
  origins, 56, 132
  neighbourhoods, 46, 57, 58, 132, 227
  religiosity, 56, 174, 175
  women, 46, 57, 186

Boundaries (family), 248, 367, 369

Boyfriends, 182, 184, 206, 207, 209, 222

Boys, 22, 42, 369, 392, 400–401

Brains, 90, 297

Brazil, 171, 235

Breadwinner, 96, 116, 259

British Columbia, 7, 36, 49, 52, 54, 97, 113, 137, 152, 170, 172–173, 191, 200, 206, 219, 226, 227, 231, 233, 304, 344, 370, 424

British (*see* Great Britain)

Brothers, 323, 324, 325, 327, 330, 331, 398, 409

Buddhists, 171, 172, 411

Bullying, 84, 87, 130, 164, 170, 303, 399–401 (*see also* Cyberbullying)

Burden, 116, 307, 308, 405, 414

C

Calgary, 105, 124, 304

California, 170, 223

Capital, 14, 132, 146, 174, 274, 304, 427
  cultural, 14, 116, 123, 157, 174, 252
  human, 14–15, 99, 116, 167, 220, 252, 399, 427, 435
  social, 14, 28, 113, 116, 123, 146, 157, 161, 165, 174, 176, 209, 220, 232, 252, 319, 324, 338, 399, 431, 436

Capitalism/capitalist(s), 10, 11, 12, 21, 41, 158, 160, 287, 288, 292, 432 (*see also* Market economy)

Caregiver (for adults), 299–300, 308, 368, 405, 430–431

Care, caring, 13, 72, 130, 252, 324, 410, 429 (*see also* Emotional work; Social Reproduction)
  crisis in caring, 72, 307, 410, 413–414, 416

Caregivers for elderly, 42, 197, 307–309, 413–414 (*see also* Elder care),
  spouse, 268, 307, 308

Caribbean communities, 18, 50, 56, 57, 58, 73, 76, 138, 153, 220, 242, 263, 290, 416

Casual sex, 183, 186, 208, 215, 353, 376, 414, 435

Catholic(s), 29, 40, 41, 42, 48, 49, 52, 54, 167, 171, 173, 189, 206, 215

Cellphones, 72, 73, 82, 84–85, 123, 165, 256, 266, 301, 305

CEOs, 95, 96

Child/children, 17–18, 101, 122, 151, 318, 360–363 (*see also* Adult children; Child development; Outcomes)
  activities, 102, 103, 123
  affluent parents, 97, 124–125, 150
  characteristics, 27, 116, 220, 285, 286, 349
  as caretakers, 17, 18, 51
  coproducers of their development, 26, 90, 286, 296, 428
  costs of, 235, 309, 427–429
  difficult, 130, 164–165, 296, 328–329 (*see also* Behaviour problems)
  effect on, 90, 277–281, 383–386 (*see also* Outcomes)
  effect on parents, 16, 17, 68, 265, 276–277, 285, 295, 296, 301, 353, 401–404
  first born, 276, 285, 317, 318
  investment in, 154, 220 (*see also* Parents)
  low-income, 82, 222
  needs, 17, 222, 239, 242, 243, 294, 305, 387, 410, 416
  neglect of, 143, 250, 251, 375
  older, 17, 18, 51, 76
  parental marital status, 219–220, 222, 229, 231
  preference for male, 233, 276, 327–329 (*see also* Female feticide)
  protection, 130, 131
  rights, 239, 293
  role, 51, 123, 151
  second-born, 317–319
  social actor, 26, 90
  violence against, 383, 386–388, 392–393, 396–401
  work, 42, 46, 47, 48, 101, 103, 138–139, 151, 235

Child abuse (*see* Abuse; Sexual abuse)

Child care, 17, 18, 60, 74, 78, 151, 267, 269–273, 409 (*see also* Division of household labour; Parenting)
  inadequate, 102, 151

Child care centres, 55, 70, 112, 150–156, 409, 419, 424–425
  effect on children, 153–156
  effect on parents, 156–157

Child custody (*see* Divorce)

Child development, 24, 26, 82, 90, 102, 116, 158, 224–225, 278–279, 323, 410 (*see also* Outcomes [child])
  intellectual/school, 117, 150, 153

Child economic support, 112, 116 (*see also* Fathers)

Childhood, 16, 17, 321

Childless, childlessness, 176, 218, 235–236, 286, 309

Childrearing practices, 16, 45, 57, 277, 287–288 (*see also* Parents/parenting; Outcomes; Socialization of children; Supervision of children)
China, Chinese, 7, 12, 58, 59, 64, 75, 96, 106, 150, 171, 186, 242, 247, 261, 411, 412, 413
  family size, 58–59, 235, 286
  filial piety, 60, 307–308, 309
  preference for male children, 58, 59, 233, 238, 247
Chinese-Canadian families, 35, 47, 48–50, 53, 59–61, 132, 172, 219, 290
Christian, 171, 172, 174, 276, 411
Church, 39, 191
Cities (*see* Urban)
Civility, 378, 405
Class (*see* Social class)
Cognitive impairment, 268, 307
Cohabitation, 79, 111, 116, 186, 189, 190–197, 199, 200, 208, 233, 257, 351, 353, 365
  breakup/dissolution, 193, 196, 197, 221, 233, 344–345, 348, 350, 356, 420
  and children, 221–222, 348, 349, 368, 370, 410
  and commitment, 183, 193, 194, 196, 197, 252, 345, 352–353, 414
  and divorce, 194, 196, 343, 345, 368–369
  and marriage, 193, 194, 196, 197, 212, 352, 365, 414
  long-term, 195, 197, 213
  rates, 190–191, 350, 415
  relationship, 116, 194–196, 197
  serial, 192, 193, 196, 221, 222, 225, 228, 351, 352–353, 414
  sex in, 194, 212–213
  stability/instability, 193, 221, 414, 415
  violence in, 195, 356, 383
Cohort, 99, 191, 200, 267–268, 286, 305, 310, 331, 414, 429, 434
Collective delusion, 209–210
Collective socialization, 15, 129, 130, 165, 167, 337, 338, 411, 431
Colombia, 50, 205
Commitment, 187, 198, 207, 214, 215, 220, 256, 277, 414
Commodifying, 13, 239, 414, 434
Common-law (*see* Cohabitation)
Communal life, 37, 44, 45
Communication, 73, 84–85, 263–264, 265
Communist, 12, 158
Community, 45, 56, 69, 73, 113, 122, 123, 124, 135, 142, 171, 175, 176, 252, 308, 319, 390–391, 411, 417 (*see also* Effective community)
Companionship, 255, 259, 262
Competitive, 84, 124, 160, 168, 301, 405, 428, 429
Computers, 68, 73, 85

Concentration, 94, 96, 97
Condos, 76, 109, 139, 141–142, 424, 429
Conflict, 11, 57, 86, 116, 144, 280, 296, 297, 298, 331, 334 (*see also* Divorce; Marital conflict; Parent-child relations; Outcomes; Same-Sex Marriage)
  conjugal/interpartner, 62, 116, 193
Confucianism, 58, 295, 411
Conjugal, 118, 255 (*see also* Conflict; Marital relationship)
  dissolution, 344–345
Consumerism/consumers/consumption, 13, 18, 41, 70, 72, 74, 83, 87–88, 100, 104–105, 151, 288, 292, 305, 338, 416, 429, 431
Context, 10, 31, 287, 292, 295, 300, 336, 339, 404–405, 431 (*see also* Culture; Sociocultural context; Socioeconomic context)
Contraception, 58, 227, 415 (*see also* Family Planning)
Control, 12, 196, 248, 289, 290, 294, 381, 383
Cooperation, 17, 81, 84, 87, 101, 153, 278, 288, 296, 319, 428, 429
Coparenting, 19–20, 45, 220, 229, 286, 287, 362, 384, 385, 434
Coping mechanisms, 77, 134, 424
Coresidence (with parents), 6, 202, 303–305, 306, 311, 403
Correctional system (*see* Incarceration)
Correlations, 31, 127, 209, 278–279, 434
Cottages, 139–140
Couples, 5–6, 97, 143, 184, 201, 214, 256, 257, 265, 282
  becoming parents, 276–277
  formation, 96, 184–201, 202
  interaction, relationships, 85, 183–184
  interracial, 185–186
Cousins, 330, 333, 413,
Courtship, 23, 187 (*see also* Dating; Partner selection)
Criminality, 85, 91, 113, 117, 125, 126, 128, 131, 140, 156, 164, 230, 338, 385, 391, 401, 420
Critical mass, 130, 179, 434
Crisis in caring, 72, 307, 410, 413–414, 419
Cross-cultural perspective/differences, 16, 151, 190, 202, 203, 261, 264, 276, 281, 282, 290, 292, 297, 301, 320, 338–339, 344, 412
Cuba, 73, 144
Culture(al), 26, 27, 29, 56, 57, 61, 69, 178, 184, 205, 206, 210, 215, 219, 252, 256, 260, 287, 288, 289, 290, 294, 297, 307, 313, 375, 381, 382, 400, 405, 411, 415, 416, 432

Custodial parents (*see* Fathers; Mothers; Parents/parental/parenting)
Cyberbullying, 84, 87, 165, 399, 435

D

Dating, 168, 183–185, 194, 258, 259, 376–377, 385–386 (*see also* Hook-Ups; Rape; Violence)
  early, 183, 209, 379
  gender roles, 184, 274
  inter-ethnic, 57, 186
  Internet, 185, 187, 414
Daughters, 42, 71, 249, 299–300, 307, 308, 327, 430
Day care (*see* Child care centres)
Death, 53, 63, 312–313, 343
Debt, 97, 105, 265, 304, 404
Delinquent/delinquency, 110, 115, 127–128, 130, 136, 164, 230, 293, 296, 302, 323, 358, 360, 369, 381
  prevention of, 156, 174, 288, 425, 426, 428
Depression, 103, 125, 174, 195, 229, 244, 286, 293, 306, 319, 328, 355, 356, 384–385, 388
Development (*see* Child development; Family development; Outcomes)
Developmental perspectives, 22–25
Disabilities, 29, 52, 53, 70, 72, 74, 133, 268, 410, 413, 429
  children with, 19, 243, 277, 307, 320, 324, 325, 388, 403, 414, 419
  parents with, 101, 299–300, 307, 308
  siblings with, 101, 299
Discrimination, 45, 48, 49, 245, 382, 409
Diversity, 35, 47–50, 136, 146, 207, 256, 288 (*see also* Family/Families)
Division of household labour and child care, 14, 16, 18–19, 21, 29, 60, 100–102, 138, 139, 163, 195, 236, 255, 265, 269–275, 276, 298, 409, 417
  equity/ inequity, 14, 21, 202, 269, 409
Divorce, 6, 14, 42, 48, 78, 255, 258, 260
  and age, 23, 212, 346
  causes of, 57, 111, 350–355
  child custody/support, 19, 116, 223, 246, 348–350
  children (number of), 317, 347
  conflict (before and after), 220, 353, 361–362
  correlates of, 177, 183, 263, 343
  effect on adults, 100, 199, 351, 355–357, 370
  effect on children, 133, 145, 220, 350, 352, 353, 357–363, 372
  first vs others, 343, 346–347
  gender differences, 346, 354, 355–357
  life after, 355–357, 358–360
  "new" children, 19
  and parenting, 19, 348–350
  and poverty, 111, 351, 355

Divorce (*continued*)
rates, 57, 183, 275, 343–346, 350, 414 (*see also* Conjugal Dissolution)
reasons given, 212, 353–355
same-sex, 224, 345–356
Domestic division of labour (*see* Division of household labour)
Domestic violence (*see* Abuse; Violence)
Domestic workers, 19, 22, 41, 42, 45, 49, 57, 58, 72, 73, 76, 101–102, 271, 416
Donor fertilization/insemination, 223, 224, 239–240
Drugs, 79, 115, 119, 125, 133, 134, 136, 164, 174, 199, 208, 228, 288, 290–291, 298, 311, 348, 375, 391, 428
Dysfunction/dysfunctional, 385, 435

E

Early childhood education (*see* Child Care Centres)
Eastern Europe (countries), 48, 73, 76, 237, 247, 412
Economic context/system, 2, 8, 10, 27, 28, 37, 74, 201–202, 234, 263, 294, 301, 303, 313, 415–416
Economics, economy, 11, 13, 19, 21, 54, 69, 94–119, 122, 156, 167, 179, 226, 257, 287, 360, 411, 414, 427, 429, 431 (*see also* Political Economy Theories; Poverty; Social Inequalities)
control over, 11–13, 95, 96, 108, 119, 417, 432
corporations, 83, 95, 119, 287, 421, 427
development, 46, 48, 416
globalization of, 94, 95, 150, 412
effects on families, 16, 17, 94, 95, 111, 119, 150, 252, 303, 409, 428–429
finances, 95, 265, 416
labour, 95, 414, 427
paper (speculative), 95, 412, 417
service sector, 73, 93, 95, 99, 304
Edmonton, 48, 123, 132, 304
Education(al), 3, 13, 54, 71, 112, 150–151, 172, 186, 188, 230–231, 287, 301, 426 (*see also* School[s]/Schooling)
higher, 90, 97, 109, 155, 160, 167, 169, 191, 193, 223, 228, 304, 427
the more educated, 95, 96, 97, 198
Effective community, 15, 29, 44, 130, 146, 157, 161, 165, 167, 177, 209, 288, 302, 324, 337–338, 343, 382, 388, 400, 401, 410, 411, 435
Effects on children (*see* Outcomes [child])
Elder care, 42, 53, 63, 72, 74, 136, 137, 403–404, 418, 419, 429–431 (*see also* Caregivers; Crisis in Caring)
neglect, 143, 307, 402–404
Elderly (in general), 84, 196–197, 235, 236, 267–268, 402, 413, 429, 431, 432 (*see also* Aged parents; Women)
Emerging adulthood, 208, 303–304, 411

Emotional problems, 133, 134, 198, 238, 247, 250, 311, 325, 336, 348, 358–359, 391 (*see also* Health)
Emotional work, 264, 274–275
Employment, 57, 95, 117, 301, 307, 413, 422 (*see also* Jobs; Work)
feminine, 69, 98–100, 156, 235, 255, 269 (*see also* Women and work)
maternal, 18–19, 98–100, 169, 298
Endogamy, 188, 189, 435
Environment (familial) (*see* Contexts)
extrafamilial, 26, 27, 71, 72, 86, 122, 280–281, 286, 313, 333, 334, 335, 336, 337, 338
natural, 36, 74, 136, 153, 236, 412, 416, 422, 429
nonshared, 332, 333, 336, 338, 436
shared, 27, 332, 336, 337, 338, 436
Epigenetic tag, 336
Ethnic/ethnicity, 26, 28, 35, 46, 53, 75, 113, 172, 185–186, 215, 310, 352, 382, 409, 435 (*see also* Intermarriage; Race)
diversity, 47–50, 81
Ethnocentric perspective, 183, 261, 435
Europe(an), 8, 12, 39, 97, 115, 126, 160, 171, 174, 175, 187, 199, 200, 234, 252, 294, 301, 305, 352, 413, 422
Exchange theories (*see* Rational theories)
Exclusion (*see* Social exclusion)
Ex-in-laws, 267, 366, 370–371
Exogamy, 185, 435
Experts, 16, 18, 88, 287, 292, 297, 301, 302, 325, 397, 411, 428 (*see also* Professionals)
Ex-spouses, 267, 273, 342, 354, 355, 356–357, 361, 366–367
Extended family, 5–7, 36, 44, 52, 60, 73, 141, 166, 251, 319, 330, 413
Extrafamilial environment (*see* Environment)
Extramarital affairs (*see* Sex/Sexuality)

F

Facebook, 80, 83, 84, 90, 165, 256, 399
Failed states, 107, 435
Family/families, 68–69, 70, 72, 131, 317, 319, 410, 417–420, 432 (*see also* Parents)
activities, 82, 332
affluent, 124–125, 152
binuclear, 4, 6
burdens, 68, 134, 149, 405, 410, 424, 432
change, 3, 317, 429
characteristics, 117, 130, 153, 157
cohabiting, 219, 221–222
definition, 3–4, 70
diversity, 3, 28, 47–50, 64, 124, 136, 137, 409–410, 431
dynamics, 68, 82, 197, 317, 324, 399, 431

empowering, 92, 428–429, 432
extended, 5–7, 36, 44, 52, 60, 73, 141, 166, 251, 319, 330, 413
formation, 70, 218, 220–249, 250–252, 256, 409, 418
foster, 7, 9, 52, 74, 133, 249–251, 311
future of, 3, 411–418, 431–432
honour, 183, 260 (*see also* Honour killings)
instability/stability, 220, 221–222
institution, 3–4, 64, 70, 74, 428, 432
interaction, 81, 82, 84, 85
integration, 337–338
investment in, 29, 119, 420–429
low-income, 78, 125–131, 150, 388, 394 (see also Poverty)
military, 73, 76–79 ,
nuclear, 4–6, 38, 41
processes, 197, 252
relevance, 69–75
responsibilities, 3, 11, 29, 64, 69, 70–75, 88, 91, 131, 151, 179, 405, 410, 412, 418, 429–431, 432
size, 40, 42, 55, 154, 286, 319–321
structure, 10, 38, 44, 55, 68, 69, 75, 97, 197, 218, 244, 252, 310, 368, 409–410, 413
time, 13, 80
transitions, 208, 225, 228, 305
two-earners, 96, 98–100, 266
two-parent, 113, 218, 221
unit of production, 70, 235
welfare agency, 72, 305, 413, 414, 430–431
Family development, 22–25, 176, 231, 309, 317–319, 342
Family planning, 232–236, 238, 252, 255
Farm families, farms, 70, 122, 135–139, 416, 423
FAS/FASD (fetal alcohol syndrome), 244, 250
Fathers/fatherhood, 11, 19, 100, 116, 222, 251, 255, 326, 348, 393–394, 415, 420 (*see also* Adolescent Fathers)
absence, 19, 111–113, 115–116, 126, 218, 299, 300, 311, 386
divorced, 116, 331, 358
investment in children, 16, 19–20, 101, 163, 232, 251, 287, 316, 349
multi-partnered fertility, 19, 128, 222, 228–229, 377
nonresidential, 331, 348–350, 361, 368
nurturing, 81, 232, 328
social construction of, 19–20, 116, 287
time with children, 101, 229, 316
transnational, 75–76, 316
versus mothers, 16, 19, 272, 278, 279, 298, 306, 327
Female feticide, 8, 59, 233, 237, 238, 412, 435
Females (*see* Gender roles; Girls; Women)

Feminism (feminist analysis, theories), 2, 11, 16, 20–22, 54, 55, 70, 100, 221, 242–243, 252, 272, 376, 377, 404, 409, 412, 427
Feminist political economic theories, 12, 13, 22, 241, 308, 409
Feminization, 21, 226
Fertility, 40, 51, 59, 68, 69, 96, 156, 221, 233–235, 415, 425, 427–428
    consequences for society, 218, 236, 252
    decline, 218, 220, 231, 413
    delayed, 96, 99, 233, 252
    desired vs achieved, 218, 233, 408, 427
    early, 128, 226, 233
    low rates, 218, 252, 286, 317, 413, 429
    multi-partnered, 19, 128, 222, 228–229, 377
    treatment for, 239–240, 320–321
Fetal alcohol syndrome (see FAS)
Filial piety, 60, 307, 308, 309
Filipinos, 12, 49, 50, 64, 73, 76, 108, 173, 186, 215, 219, 295, 416
Finland, 91, 115, 352
First Nations families (see Aboriginal families)
Food/food banks, 110, 113–114, 416, 421
Forced marriages, 62, 207, 260 (see also Arranged marriages)
Foster care/families, 7, 9, 52, 74, 133, 249–251, 311
France/French families/language, 9, 16, 18, 39, 40, 49, 64, 107, 140, 157, 160, 165, 171, 190, 191, 197, 200, 240, 420
Friendship, 15, 84, 145, 203, 299, 356
Friends with-benefits, 183, 215, 353, 414, 435
Functionalism (see Structural functionalism)
Functions/functional, 10–11, 16, 69–71, 172, 197, 252, 291, 302, 362, 369, 435 (see also Responsibilities)
Fur trade, 39–40, 41

G
Gangs of youths, 58, 110, 125, 127, 128, 131, 209, 401
Gap between rich and poor, 12, 91, 96, 107, 108, 119
Gay (see Homosexual; Same-sex couples; Same-sex families; Same-sex parenting)
Gender differences, 11, 22, 75, 174, 183–185, 191, 199, 201, 204–205, 207, 226, 249, 256, 264, 266, 273, 306, 330, 363, 365, 386–389, 392, 400–401, 409 (see also Daughters; Division of labour; Gender roles; Social Reproduction)
Gender division of labour, 99, 101, 102 (see also Division of household labour)
Gender ratio (see Sex ratio imbalance)
Gender relations, 9, 14, 21, 97

Gender roles, 11, 12, 16, 20, 22, 37, 46, 62, 64, 114, 137–139, 150, 195, 236, 269, 275, 298, 328, 330, 409, 411, 415, 435
Gender-role socialization, 22, 274, 327
Gender inequalities/stratification, 11, 16, 21, 22, 28, 52, 6, 178, 252, 308, 376, 377, 409, 420, 425
Generations, 4–7, 63, 119, 309, 310, 311, 312, 313, 356, 358, 418, 428, 429, 430, 432
    age condensed/gapped, 24–25, 232
    sandwich, 307, 430–431
Genes and environment, 27–28, 116, 225, 228, 231, 242, 280–281, 291, 296, 316, 335, 336–339, 363, 405
    sibling differences/similarities, 28, 332–336
Genetic influence, 71, 175, 265, 294, 295, 322, 332, 333, 336, 363, 390, 397 (see also Behaviour genetics theories)
    evocative effect, 328, 335
Genetic potential, 116, 146, 337
Germany, 48, 64, 99, 140, 160, 234
Girlfriends, 206, 207, 209
Girls, 35, 42, 369, 377, 392, 400–401 (see also Daughters)
Globalization, 74, 75, 92, 94, 95, 97, 150, 179, 412, 423, 432
Global level, 11, 16, 416
Government, 72, 77, 415, 417, 419, 421–423, 427
Grandchildren, 306, 308, 310, 311–312, 356, 359, 395, 418
Grandmothers, 15, 24, 58, 228, 241, 309, 310, 323
Grandparenting/grandparents, 24–25, 137, 304, 309–312, 371
    after divorce, 370–371
    raising grandchildren, 58, 76, 251, 311–312, 323
Gratification, 104, 256, 350, 355, 377, 415
Great Britain, 9, 12, 39, 41, 46, 47, 48, 50, 62, 186, 201, 239, 241, 246, 344, 402, 417, 430
Greece, 150, 234
Guest workers, 75, 109, 137, 138

H
Haiti, 56, 220, 247
Half-siblings, 229, 240, 329, 331, 333, 368, 369
Halifax, 41, 45, 105, 124, 304
Happiness, 198, 199, 203, 255, 309, 356, 418 (see also Marital happiness)
Health, 72–73, 83, 99, 105, 113, 117, 122, 125, 128, 135, 140, 157, 174, 198, 199, 203, 242, 256, 263, 266, 276, 307, 309, 310, 312, 320, 355, 416, 417
    care, 72–73, 74, 108, 111, 119, 136, 244, 403, 414, 422, 426
    mental, 77, 118, 119, 198, 355

Heredity (see Gene and environment; Genetic influence)
Hindus, 61, 62, 64, 150, 171, 172, 173, 189, 200, 215, 276, 382, 411, 414
Hispanics, 83, 174, 223
Historical periods/contexts, 11, 23, 36–64, 231, 237, 262, 281, 287, 300–304, 338, 343, 411
History/trends, 8, 16, 56, 59, 79, 100, 107, 150, 202, 218, 225, 233–234, 297
Holland, 48, 107, 153, 200
Home Children, 46–47, 48, 426
Home ownership, 132, 139, 140, 423
Homelessness, 132–135, 136, 395 (see also Shelters)
Homogamy/heterogamy, 188, 189, 435
Homosexual(ity), 178, 182, 185, 189, 190, 210–211, 214, 223, 224, 275–276, 307, 310, 330 (see also Lesbian; Same-sex couples; Same-sex marriage; Same-sex-parent families)
Hong Kong, 59, 75, 144, 235
Honour killing, 178, 207, 382
Hook-ups, 183, 186, 215, 353, 376, 414, 435
Households, 4, 6, 9, 38, 41, 45, 48, 60, 69, 125, 201, 311
Housework, 41, 45, 46, 48, 60, 99, 102, 195, 305, 306 (see also Division of household labour)
Housing conditions, 94, 96, 122, 126, 140–141, 423–424
    mobile homes, 142–143
    size of houses, 104, 140, 141, 429
Housing developments, 128, 129, 133, 423
Hunger, 110, 114 (see also Food banks)
Hypothesis, 29, 31, 199, 353, 435

I
Ideologies, 11, 13, 18, 28, 102, 146, 153, 160, 168, 200, 243, 297, 372, 381, 409, 414, 417, 423, 427
Immigrant families, 6, 9, 22, 58, 64, 72, 73, 80, 96, 109, 131–132, 144, 157, 166, 207, 215, 287, 298–299, 301, 304, 411, 413, 414, 415–416, 418 (see also Transnational families)
    adaptation of, 80, 109, 142, 261, 263, 287
    generations of, 35, 64, 108, 109, 174
    history, 41, 43, 48–50, 64
    marriages, 58, 257, 261, 263
    parents, 72, 166, 289, 292–293, 301
    poverty, 108–109, 114
    women, 9, 19, 109, 207, 382
Incarceration, 58, 113, 119, 126, 130, 133, 229, 250, 348, 395, 421, 426
Independence, 287, 292, 294, 301, 306, 428
India/Indo-Canadian families, 8, 12, 49–50, 59, 61–64, 106, 219, 233, 238
Indicators, 10, 171, 172, 174, 263, 435

Individualism/Individualistic, 10, 18, 38, 72, 74, 84, 91, 143, 160, 168, 194, 235, 256, 262, 287, 288, 292, 301, 319, 343, 350, 351, 355, 411, 428, 429
Individuation, 143, 177, 327, 435
Industrialization, 39, 41, 43, 46–50, 64, 94, 215
Industries, 43, 96, 108, 215, 411, 422, 423
Inequalities/inequities, 184, 186 (see also Division of household labour; Social inequalities)
Infertility, 207, 231, 235–236
Information technology (see Technological context; see also Media)
In-laws, 308, 309, 357
Institution, institutionalized, 2–4, 7, 8, 21, 32, 33, 64, 69, 73, 74, 78, 91, 149, 150, 151, 170, 183, 193, 200, 220, 221, 256, 287, 293, 368, 405, 410, 428, 432, 435–436
Intellectual/IQ, 15, 17, 116, 118, 130, 150, 153, 155, 160, 287
Interaction(s), Interactional-transactional perspective, 2, 26, 27, 29, 84–85, 102, 124, 277, 285–286, 287, 288, 296, 306, 328, 335, 349, 428
Intergenerational, 3–4, 15, 23, 32, 70, 76, 150, 236, 262, 306, 307, 309, 310, 410, 428 (see also Parent-child relations)
  transmission, 3, 140, 230, 231, 295, 337–338, 359, 385–386, 390–391, 394, 399, 404, 405, 420
Intermarriage, 57, 132, 246
Internalization, 175, 286, 287, 288, 428
Internet, 72, 75, 80, 82–83, 84, 89–90, 123, 185, 187, 287, 301, 305, 392, 400, 414
Inuit, 7, 14, 51, 73, 114, 219, 230 (see also Aboriginal families)
Interviews, 2, 30
In vitro fertilization, 239–241
Iran, Iran-Canadian families, 61, 142, 261, 264, 298, 412
Irish, 46, 48, 140
Islamic, 158 (see also Muslims)
Italy, Italian-Canadian families, 48, 132, 197, 234, 252

J

Jamaica, Jamaican-Canadian families, 56, 115, 220
Japan, Japanese-Canadian families, 49–50, 79, 150, 185, 198, 202, 219, 235, 252, 286, 308, 412, 413
Jewish, 48, 50, 132, 167, 174, 189, 206, 411
Jobs, 99, 408, 417, 427, 429
  creation of, 95, 108, 154, 415, 422–423
  loss of, 95, 96, 108
  low-paid, 96, 111, 304, 409
  part-time, 96, 99, 105, 304, 409
  rural, 136–139

well-paying, 96, 422
  with benefits, 95–96, 422
Jordan, 9, 205

K

Kin-keeping, 274, 310, 322, 409, 430
Kin/Kinship, 6, 7, 52–53, 137–139, 156, 157, 166, 228, 259, 260, 279, 300, 317, 319, 356, 392
Kingston, 41, 304
Knowledge, 15, 16, 220, 302
Koran (see Qur'an)
Korea, Korean-Canadian families, 50, 59, 75, 142, 219, 235, 261, 412, 413

L

Labour, 12, 41, 42, 46, 107, 108, 146, 150, 297
Language, 43, 52, 54, 56, 80, 90, 109, 129, 153, 155, 156, 166
Latin American, 7, 39, 50, 89, 171, 186, 191, 223, 235, 320, 416
LAT (living alone together), 5, 79
Leave of absence, 99, 269, 419, 431
Leisure, 101, 188, 236, 265, 266, 268, 277, 287, 325, 337, 349
Lesbian, 182, 189, 190, 203, 210–211, 214, 244, 264, 275–276, 307, 310 (see also Homosexuality; Same-sex couples; Same-sex families; Same-sex parenting)
Life course, 23, 117, 118, 161, 192, 210, 226, 236, 281, 293, 294, 303, 311, 312, 313, 316, 326, 328, 332, 336, 342, 386, 389, 410
Life course theories, 22–25, 27, 119, 145, 293, 305, 306, 394–396
Life expectancy, 69, 72, 110, 114, 128, 313
Lifespan, 26, 414
Longitudinal, 18, 23, 83, 85–86, 118, 153, 183, 200, 209, 213, 224, 246, 263, 268, 293, 355, 358, 362, 380, 436
Longevity, 72, 114, 198, 309, 310
Love, 62, 71, 175, 198, 205, 207, 228, 244, 245, 255, 258, 263, 264, 274, 281–282, 353, 430
Low-income families, 123, 125, 141, 142, 154–156, 162–165, 192, 308, 349, 382, 389, 419–420, 425, 429 (see also Poverty)

M

Macrosociology, 22, 23, 32–33, 436
Male bias/dominance, 16, 21, 70, 178, 184, 203, 255, 377, 404
Male vs female sphere, 11, 12, 274
Males (young), 127, 251
Manitoba, 43, 49, 51, 52, 113, 135, 152, 191, 197, 219, 227, 249, 344, 347
Manufacturing, 96, 98, 304
Marital conflict, 137, 220, 256, 259, 260, 264–265, 266, 273, 275, 279, 285 (see also Divorce)

Marital happiness/satisfaction, 29, 62, 184, 215, 236, 256, 261–263, 266, 267, 272, 276–277, 353–354
  and children, 220, 266, 267
Marital problems, 220, 230, 266, 294, 358
Marital relationship, 220, 232, 255–256, 261, 267–268, 277–279, 353
Marital status, 97, 306, 357, 375 (see also Single-parent families)
Maritime provinces, 36, 38, 41, 42, 45, 46, 124, 140, 299, 343, 345, 413
Market economy, 11–13, 14, 16, 18, 20, 27, 72, 74, 76, 91, 95, 158, 179, 288, 410, 411, 414, 417, 420, 432
Marriage, marital, 42, 186, 197–201, 266, 267–268, 346, 347, 350–351
  age at, 8
  arranged, 9, 38, 58, 259, 260
  benefits for children, 197, 220–221, 251, 410
  benefits for men, 197, 199, 200, 256
  benefits for society, 220–221, 262
  benefits for women, 197, 199, 200
  commitment, 177, 200, 215, 256, 261, 263, 264, 267, 346, 414
  communication, 261, 262, 355
  conflict, 111, 177, 220, 276, 277–279, 352, 353, 356, 362
  delayed, 183, 232, 414
  expectations of, 255–256, 258, 265, 266
  forced, 62, 207, 260
  formation, 112, 191
  Inequities in, 21, 199
  infidelities, 112, 191, 213–215, 353
  institution, 21, 220, 256, 262, 263, 350
  negative effects on children, 277, 278, 359, 363
  power, 13, 275–276
  quality, 177–178, 189, 255, 260, 266, 272–273, 274, 279–280, 363
  rates, 190, 197, 198, 219
  same-sex, 177, 200–201, 257
  sexuality in, 211–213, 250, 282
  stability, 177–178, 183, 193, 198, 201, 232, 255, 256, 350–353, 365
  types, 256–261
  value of, 196, 198, 215, 350, 357
Marxism, marxist, 11, 12
Masculinity, 46, 83, 87, 377, 381, 404
Maternal employment, 11, 18–19, 100
Materialistic, 75, 88, 104, 124–125, 288
Mate selection (see Partner selection)
Matrilineality, 12, 36, 37
Media, 13, 29, 68, 72, 79–91, 183, 214, 287, 300, 301, 411, 412 (see also Facebook; Internet; Television; Video games; Cellphones)
  influence, 70, 90, 203, 282, 338, 401, 404, 432
Men, 42, 96, 100, 137, 403, 404, 414 (see also Gender differences; Fathers)
Mennonites, 137, 167, 338
Mental illness (see Emotional problems)

Methods (research)/methodology, 25, 29–32, 244, 262, 376, 388
Métis, 38, 39 (*see also* Aboriginal families)
Métissage, 38, 43, 47, 53, 436
Mexico, Mexican, 7, 39, 50, 76, 138
Microsociology, 22, 23, 28, 32–33, 269, 436
Middle class, 12, 17, 18, 46, 97, 111, 114, 123, 128, 150, 160, 163, 260, 286, 292, 297, 429
Middle Eastern immigrants, 50, 62, 109, 150, 185, 260
Migration, 43, 75, 136, 309 (*see also* Immigrant families)
Military, 3, 39, 47, 50, 381
Military families, 73, 76–79
Minority(ies), 11, 46, 117–132, 292, 382, 404, 436
    racialized, 11, 114, 117
Mobile homes, 142–143
Money, 57, 94, 95, 116, 233, 265, 353
Monitoring (*see* Supervision of children)
Monogamy, monogamous, 5, 48, 201
Montreal, 39, 43, 46, 50, 105, 123, 124, 125, 126, 132, 144, 150, 173, 210, 228, 304
Morality, moral, 14, 48, 168, 169, 226, 238, 287, 290, 301, 412, 417
Mormons, 7, 8, 48, 167
Mortality, 174, 203, 220
Mother(s), 18, 71, 73, 169, 222, 287, 305, 419 (*see also* Adolescent mothers; Parents; Single-mother families; Women)
    abused, 294, 402
    blame of, 19, 409
    custodial/noncustodial, 348–349, 355
    education, 226, 229, 230, 232
    employment, 98–100
    lesbian, 223–225
    in poverty, 57, 113, 114–115, 298
    pressure on, 21, 46, 100, 101, 102
    relations with children, 19, 294, 298, 317, 326–327 (*see also* Parent-child relations)
    single, 19, 57, 100, 113
    social construction of, 16–19, 287
    surrogate, 224, 241–242, 417, 418
    transnational, 22, 75–76
    versus fathers, 20, 100–101, 114, 145, 331, 348–349, 401–402, 409
Motherhood, 17–20, 21, 46, 227, 287
Moving (*see* Residential mobility)
Multigenerational, 6, 60, 61
Multipartner fertility, 19, 128, 222, 228–229, 377
Muslims, 50, 56, 62, 63, 64, 150, 167, 168, 171, 172, 177, 178, 185, 189, 200, 206, 208, 215, 261, 276, 298, 382, 411, 414

N

Narcissism, 17, 53, 86, 288, 351
Natives (*see* Aboriginal families)

Natural environment, 36, 74, 136, 153, 236, 412, 416, 422, 429
Nature and nurture, 27–28, 313, 339 (*see also* Genes and environment)
Needs, 17, 83, 88, 165, 203, 256, 416
Neglect (*see* Aged parents; Child/children)
Neighbourhoods, 94, 122–132, 165
    affluent, 123, 124–125, 130, 288
    effects, 125–131, 133, 155, 281
    ethnic composition, 109, 131–132
    low-income, 58, 95, 113, 114, 117, 123, 125–131, 132, 146, 155, 227, 410, 423, 425–426
    perceptions of, 126, 128
    segregation by income, 123, 410
    with social problems, 58, 115, 117, 126–128, 131, 132, 382, 385–386, 388, 390–391, 401, 405, 424
Neighbours, 15, 124, 127
Networks, 4, 60, 174, 175, 202, 203, 356–357, 404
New Brunswick, 45, 113, 151, 191, 219, 227, 304, 343, 344, 370
New Zealand, 97, 160, 229
New children (*see* Half-siblings)
Newfoundland/Labrador, 7, 14, 38, 39, 41, 42, 73, 87, 114, 135, 137, 144, 151, 191, 219, 227, 343, 344, 346
Nonshared environment, 332, 333, 336, 338, 436
Norms, 15, 78, 129, 286, 302, 368
North America, 150, 160, 193, 222, 238, 242, 287–288, 292, 293, 301, 308, 382
Northwest Territories, 152, 191, 219, 227, 237, 249, 344, 413
Norway, Norwegians, 48, 91, 191, 200, 210, 221, 223, 346, 352, 353, 427
Nova Scotia, 38, 138, 152, 169, 191, 219, 227, 343, 344
Nunavut, 110, 114, 152, 191, 219, 226, 227, 233, 237, 249, 413

O

Old age (*see* Age; Elder)
Offshoring, 12, 95, 108, 421
Ontario, 10, 41, 45, 46, 49, 51, 113, 128, 137, 142, 144, 150, 152, 164, 167, 169, 173, 191, 197, 200, 219, 226, 227, 231, 242, 303, 304, 344, 346, 386, 387, 404, 425
Opportunities, 12–13, 28, 48, 57, 71, 95, 110, 112, 122, 125, 130, 149, 414, 416, 428
Ottawa, 48, 124, 128, 304
Outcomes (child), 9, 26, 83, 116, 146, 153–156, 157, 199, 243–246, 250, 301, 328–329 (*see also* Divorce; Peers; Poverty; Risk factors)
    of child abuse, 389–391, 394–401
    of difficult neighbourhoods, 114–115, 128, 130
    of parental conflict, 278–279, 280–281

of parental violence, 383–386 (*see also* Violence)
of parenting practices, 100, 114, 287, 288–292, 302
and parents' marital status, 197, 224–225, 228, 229–231, 350, 357–363
of poverty, 116–117, 229, 358
of sexual victimization, 392–396, 398 (*see also* Sexual abuse)
of siblings, 321–325, 396–398
Overcrowding, 135, 143

P

Pakistan, Pakistani-Canadians, 50, 61, 64, 171, 219, 235, 261, 264, 298
Parents/parental/parenting/parenthood, 6, 14, 227–229, 232, 295, 390, 423, 428–429 (*see also* Adolescence; Childrearing; Fathers; Mothers; Parent-Child Relations; Siblings; Same-sex parent families)
    abuse of, 401–404
    adaptation to children, 286, 317, 326
    affluent, 97, 116
    alienation, 362
    authoritarian, 61, 289, 434
    authoritative, 61, 279, 288, 292, 295, 302, 324, 350, 428, 429, 434
    authority, 228, 294, 301, 428
    blaming of, 176, 303, 339
    burdens, 68, 134, 149, 424
    conflict with each other, 116, 232, 277, 325, 361–362
    context, 287, 290, 292–293, 294–295, 327
    control, 183, 301, 328
    coparenting, 19–20, 45, 220, 229, 286, 287, 362, 384, 385, 434
    coresidence with, 6, 202, 303–305, 306, 311, 403
    death of, 312–313, 364–365
    delayed parenthood, 231–233
    determinants of, 294–296
    differential, 325–329
    disruption, 294, 360–361, 369, 410
    effects on, 149, 156–157, 301, 334
    effects on marriage, 267–268, 277
    elderly, 76, 141, 175, 305, 306–309, 402–404 (*see also* Aged parents; Elderly)
    empowerment, 129, 159, 176
    expectations for their children, 61, 119, 155, 158, 162
    genes, 27, 287 (*see also* Behaviour genetics; Genes and environment)
    influence of, 300–301, 336–339
    intensive, concerted, 18, 72, 100, 160, 286, 428
    investment, 160–161, 220, 396, 408
    involvement, 146, 157–164, 169, 287, 349
    middle-class, 17, 116, 160

Parents/parental/parenting (*continued*)
military, 76–78
monitoring by, 114, 131, 288, 326
neglect by, 391–392, 419
networks of, 129, 130, 288, 302, 337
no-nonsense, 289–290, 292, 295
permissive, 205, 290–291, 391, 429
personalities, 27, 294, 295–296, 326, 336
poor parenting, 114, 328, 361
proper parenting, 287, 292–294, 295
rejecting, 230, 291, 293, 294, 295, 296
relationship, 277–279, 295
role, 15, 26, 70, 176, 232, 300, 307, 339, 361, 411, 427–429
shared parenting, 9, 18, 37, 224
social isolation, 301–302 (*see also* Social isolation)
supervision, 61, 82, 83, 88, 114, 208, 286, 296, 391 (*see also* Supervision of children)
support for, 15, 153, 175–176, 408, 427–429
time, 71, 100–104, 116, 317
two, 220, 251, 420
values, 71, 301
wavering-negotiating, 291–292, 429
Parental resources, 156, 306 (*see also* Resources)
Parent-child relations, 26, 63, 84, 175, 293, 309, 312, 313, 328 (*see also* Adolescents; Adult children)
adolescents, 14, 205, 243, 295–300, 301, 303, 401–402
adult children, 149, 278, 303, 305–309, 310, 358, 402, 404 (*see also* Adult children)
conflict, 88, 243, 245, 293, 302
determinants of, 285, 301–302, 336
parental help, 60, 303–305, 306, 307, 309, 395
peer effects on, 301–303
young adults, 303–305
Parental leave, 99, 269, 419, 431
Partner selection, 62, 185–186, 188–190, 202, 337
Paternal (*see* Fathers)
Patriarchy (al), 20, 22, 36, 41, 60, 257, 259, 260, 275, 276, 279, 294, 381, 382, 404
Patrilineality, 12, 36, 137
Pay inequity, 98, 99, 108, 409
Pedophiles, 89, 393–396
Peers/peer group, 29, 60, 84, 85, 112, 130, 153, 155, 157–158, 174, 332, 395, 424, 425
abuse by, 303, 399–401
anti-social, 117, 135, 145
bullying, 225, 302, 399–401
choice of, 145, 174, 296
culture, 88, 151, 168, 301, 400, 426
effects of, 119, 126, 149, 154, 157–158, 298, 301, 323, 338
influence of, 70, 128, 169, 228, 292

peers' parents, 301–302
peers and parents, 301–302
pressure, 104, 400
Pension plans, 95, 96
Perceptions, 126, 127, 209, 257, 262, 293, 328, 332–333, 335, 336, 337, 395, 411
Personality, 27–28, 71, 118, 200, 265, 281, 288, 295–296, 298, 306, 313, 318, 321, 323, 328, 332, 333, 334, 335, 336, 351, 365, 390 (*see also* Predispositions; Temperament)
Philippines (*see* Filipinos)
Physical appearance, 189, 190
Police, 3, 302, 381, 382, 392, 394
Policies (*see* Social policies)
Political context, systems, 3, 13, 21, 70, 74, 95, 106–107, 173, 178, 251, 313, 405, 409, 410, 417, 422, 431–432 (*see also* Social policies)
Political corruption, 99, 416, 432
Political economy theories, 2, 11–13, 17, 20, 22, 23, 28, 74, 83, 91, 95, 119, 122, 146, 158, 226, 231, 287, 404, 409, 410, 412, 414, 420, 428, 432
Polygamy, 7–10, 49, 216
Polygenic, 333, 436
Pornography, 20, 89, 215, 377
Poverty, 11, 12, 42, 46, 47, 57, 91, 94, 98, 105–120, 142, 220, 337, 360
child, 116–119, 223, 229, 358, 420, 421, 422
consequences for adults, 113, 229, 350, 351, 414
consequences for children, 111, 112, 113, 116–119, 128, 163–165, 229, 250, 392
consequences for parents, 114–116, 250, 281, 312, 326, 392
costs to society, 113, 114, 119–120, 229, 250, 415, 421, 422, 426–427
early child poverty, 112, 113, 116–119, 420, 425
elderly women, 113, 415, 421
feminization of, 226, 251, 420
immigrant, 106, 108–109, 114, 421
intergenerational, 119, 222, 229, 230, 231, 312, 420
near poor, 74, 420, 421
one vs two parents, 106, 421
political choice, 107–110, 417, 422
poor countries, 106–107, 205, 247, 415
prevention/reduction, 156–157, 420–427 (*see also* Social policies)
single-mother families, 99, 106, 110, 111–113, 227, 409, 420
sources of, 74, 106–113
violence, 119, 385, 388, 404
working poor, 105, 106, 111, 421
Power, 9, 11, 13, 14, 16, 22, 40, 52, 60, 63, 107, 119, 128, 129, 199, 275, 321, 376–377, 380, 383, 408, 409, 413, 432

Prairies, 36, 49, 135, 140, 345
Predispositions, 128, 231, 244, 294, 324, 333, 336, 338
Pregnancy, 89, 130, 318, 380
Prince Edward Island, 105, 152, 173, 219, 227, 343, 344, 346
Prisons (*see* Incarceration)
Privacy, 143–144
Private property, 12, 54
Product, 18, 88, 428
Production, productivity, 12, 20, 41, 70, 99, 199, 233, 402, 409, 417, 429
Professionals (*see* Experts)
Profit motive, 74, 95, 412, 427
Propinquity, proximity, 188, 330
Prosocial, 15, 87, 88, 157, 174, 324, 411
Prostitution, 205, 395, 412
Protestants, 41, 48, 52, 174, 189
Psychology/ists, 13, 16, 30 (*see also* Experts)
Psychiatrists (*see* Experts)
Public and private spheres, 21, 91
Punishment, 288–289, 293–294

Q

Qualitative research, 30–31, 257
Quebec City, 39, 128
Quebec families, 41, 42, 54, 55, 97, 99, 124, 137, 169, 173, 197, 219, 226, 227, 237, 365
child care, 55, 151–152, 153, 156, 419, 425, 427
cohabitation, 55, 189, 190, 192, 195, 200, 221, 248, 367, 369, 370, 420
divorce, 54, 55, 222, 343, 344, 347
history, 6, 38–41, 54–55, 81, 150
family policies, 55, 240, 417, 418–420, 427
Qur'an, 8, 178

R

Race(ism), racial, 12, 21, 22, 28, 57, 89, 108, 114, 158, 173, 185–186, 202, 223, 375, 427
Rape, 87, 375, 377, 380, 400
Rational theories, 14–15, 25, 28, 29, 146, 157, 220, 274, 337, 338, 411
Reciprocity, 7, 14, 60, 76, 309, 325
Reconstituted families, 351 (*see also* Remarriage; Stepparent families)
Reference group, 25, 336
Regina, 105, 126, 128, 132, 304
Relationships, 80, 158, 184, 187, 328, 350 (*see also* Conflict; Marital relationships; Parent-child relations; Sibling relationships)
Relative deprivation, 104, 215
Relatives (*see* In-laws; Kinship)
Religion, 22, 28, 41, 42, 149–150, 167, 170, 171, 178, 179, 189, 215, 287, 301, 375, 409, 417
diversity, 47–50, 172, 207

Religiosity, 56, 149, 169, 171–178, 208
and family life, 174–176
and marital happiness, 172, 177, 276
and marital stability, 172, 177, 343, 350
Remarriage/repartnering, 69, 111,
177–178, 189, 212, 221–222,
266–267, 273, 365–370, 372
effects on children, 222, 246, 358, 359,
368–370
duration, 331, 346, 359
new children, 349, 368, 370
new spouse, 366–368
stability, 222, 267, 343, 347, 351, 365,
367, 370
Reproduction, 6, 12, 58, 70, 128, 236,
238–241, 257, 410, 417, 418, 427
Reproductive technologies, 238–240, 417
Research, researchers, 20, 29–32, 83, 183,
206, 256, 411, 428
critique of, 2, 21, 56, 200, 215, 223,
225, 238, 249, 256, 257, 262, 275,
287, 293, 296, 330, 334, 388
suggestions for, 79, 83, 84, 86–87, 88,
104–105, 116, 125, 139–140, 141,
142, 154, 170, 172, 174, 185, 187,
195, 199–200, 213, 246, 256, 279,
286, 292, 295, 306, 308, 310, 321,
322, 324, 329–330, 331, 345, 347,
353, 355, 362, 367, 379, 380, 432
Residential mobility, 144–146, 360
Resilience, 77, 114, 116, 118, 120, 129,
143, 157, 308, 323, 385
Resources, 11, 13, 14, 28, 41, 57, 113,
159–160, 246, 251, 294, 307, 317,
319, 337, 410–425, 432
dilution of, 131, 319, 320, 435
redistribution of, 91, 107, 108, 360
social, 15, 73, 113, 175, 199, 307, 410
Responsibilities (family), 3, 11, 19, 21, 56,
70–75, 150, 227, 297, 317, 415
Retirement, 97, 268, 355, 402
Rich (*see* Affluent)
Rights, 42, 91, 105, 227, 350, 403
Risk factors, 111, 116, 118, 128–131 (*see
also* Outcomes)
Robots, 414, 417
Role, 3, 11, 20, 23, 25–26, 40, 42, 48, 54,
63, 74, 151, 193, 268, 277, 300, 310,
368, 369, 411 (*see also* Gender roles)
models, 25, 286, 300, 319, 323
Rules, 82, 287, 288, 290
Ruling class (*see* Upper class)
Rural areas/families, 8, 59, 75, 135–140
Russia, 12, 96, 142, 144, 185, 191, 234, 344

S

Saint John, 105, 304
Salaries (*see* Wages)
Same-sex couples, 178, 189, 201, 214, 251,
264, 275–276, 282, 330, 366, 378
(*see also* Same-sex marriage;
Same-sex parenting)
dating, 184–185

Same-sex marriage, 200–201, 282, 368,
410
and children, 201, 223–225
Same-sex-parent families, 69, 201, 221,
222–225, 276
Samples (research), 31, 206, 329
Sandwich generation, 307, 430–431 (*see
also* Aged parents)
Saskatchewan, 49, 51, 113, 138, 152, 169,
191, 197, 219, 227, 233, 303, 344
Saskatoon, 128, 132, 304
School(s)/schooling, 131, 144, 151,
157–170, 209, 245, 297, 298, 300,
416, 425–426 (*see also* Education)
achievement, 90, 117, 118, 145, 155,
158, 205, 208, 288, 301, 316, 318,
399, 400, 422
and children, 54, 128, 149, 154, 162,
281
antisocial behaviours at, 164–165, 228,
399
before and after school care, 156, 425
completion, 144, 358
disengagement from, 135, 149
drop out, 118, 127, 131, 167, 358
extra-curricular activities, 149, 157,
167, 170
families and, 70, 157–164, 337
home schooling, 73, 168–170
parents and, 130, 131, 149, 155,
157–164, 179, 337
and poor children, 122, 129, 135,
425–426
preparation for, 81, 117, 154–155, 425
private, 167–168, 206
quality of, 117, 128, 179, 425–426
religious, 129, 172, 173, 206
violence, 385–386, 390–391, 400, 405
Secular humanism, 170, 173
Segregation, 74, 91, 117, 123, 132, 410
of children, 150, 151
gender, 178, 259, 260
Self-control, regulation, 112, 117, 289
Self-definition, 83, 184, 208, 224, 395
Self-esteem, 17, 18, 112, 116, 232, 244,
263, 293, 301, 428
Seniors (*see* Adult children; Elder)
Seniors` Homes, 308, 312, 403–404, 408,
430
Service sector, 73, 93, 95, 99, 304
SES (*see* Social class and Socioeconomic
status)
Sex/sexuality, 88–89, 182, 183, 184, 202,
203–215, 298, 299, 417 (*see also*
Adolescent sexuality)
attitudes, 127, 203
and aging, 211–213
casual (*see* Casual sex)
cohabitational, 194, 212–213
early, 112, 128, 174, 205, 207,
208–209, 290, 323, 395
exploitative, 72, 89, 127, 209, 215, 395
fidelity/infidelities, 193, 203, 213–215

gender differences, 203, 207, 213–214
high-risk, 89, 395
identities, 185, 210–211
intercourse, 88, 203, 204, 205, 206,
211–213, 323
marital, 211–215, 255, 282
multiple partners, 88, 183, 204–205,
395
nonmarital, 202, 203
oral, 204–205, 206
pressure, 182, 207, 208
recreational, 183, 205
STIs, 88, 205, 207, 208, 395
unprotected, 112, 205, 207, 208
Sex ratio, 8, 57, 59, 63, 186, 238, 247,
351–352, 412, 436
Sexting, 89, 379
Sexual abuse (of children), 222, 369,
392, 393–396, 398–399, 400–401,
425
Shanghai, 59, 235
Shared environment, 27, 332, 336, 337,
338, 436
Shelters, 132, 134–135, 380, 381 (*see also*
Homelessness)
Siblings, 28, 57, 299, 316, 336 (*see also*
Sibling relationships)
abuse by, 386, 396–399
adult, 329–331
birth order, 326–327, 332, 336
care of and by, 103, 200, 324–325
differences/similarities, 28, 316, 332,
336
effect of, 118, 321–322, 323, 339
first born, 317, 318
gender, 322, 325, 327–328, 330
influence, 322–324
older, 316, 319, 321
parents' treatment of, 318, 319, 320,
321, 325–329
relationships with parents, 317, 318
second born, 317–319
spacing, 317, 318, 319, 324
younger, 300, 316, 319, 322
Sibling relationships, 317, 321, 324, 328,
332, 339, 396–399
closeness, 317, 322, 330
conflict, 358, 368
determinants, 317, 318, 321, 322
helpful, 318–330
perceptions, 321, 322
and peers, 323–324
Sikhs, 61, 62, 64, 150, 167, 168, 171, 172,
189, 215, 276, 411
Singapore, 60, 235, 286
Single fathers, 111, 173 (*see also* Fathers/
fatherhood; Single-parent families)
Single-mother families, 130, 158, 223, 226,
251–252, 351 (*see also* Adolescent
mothers; Fathers)
births to, 70, 226, 415
child outcomes, 2, 18, 229–231, 415
(*see also* Outcomes)

Single-mother families (*continued*)
  mothers' boyfriends, 111, 222, 230 (*see also* Boyfriends)
  poverty, 110, 222, 226, 355, 409, 415, 422 (*see also* Poverty)
Singlehood/singles, 55, 192, 201–203, 304, 307, 415, 420, 421
Single-parent families, 69, 97, 126, 225–226, 251–252, 343, 410, 415, 420 (*see also* Single-mother families)
  children, 145, 218, 220 (*see also* Outcomes)
Sisters, 322, 327, 330, 331, 398, 409
Skype, 73, 84
Slavery, 12, 18, 43, 44–45, 47
Social assistance (*see* Welfare)
Social capital (*see* Capital)
Social change, 92, 313 (*see also* Sociocultural context)
Social class, 12, 47, 75, 76, 157, 158, 159–164, 202, 208, 223, 241, 271, 287, 306, 309, 319, 376, 409, 423 (*see also* Socioeconomic status; Social inequalities)
  reproduction of class system, 71, 157
Social conformity, 228, 229, 230, 301
Social closure, 15, 167, 337, 338
Social construction(ism), 2, 16–20, 22, 29, 286, 411
Social constructs, 16–20, 29, 46, 80, 116, 182, 203, 212, 227, 242–243, 245–246, 262, 282, 286, 287, 303, 307, 377, 381, 402, 404, 422, 428, 430, 436
  adolescence, 277, 292–293, 296–297, 303
  childhood, 16, 17, 46–47, 163, 287, 294
  motherhood, 21, 46, 227, 287, 348
  parenthood, 16–20, 286, 292, 401
Social control, 72, 126, 127, 145, 174, 177, 199, 220, 302, 382, 388, 411
Social exchange theories, 13–14, 29, 185, 196, 197
Social exclusion, 48, 49, 52, 74, 84, 91, 108, 110, 113, 125, 150, 229, 422
Social inequalities/inequities, 10, 11, 12, 21, 25, 28, 57, 91, 96, 97, 107, 123, 128, 141, 150, 158, 239, 247, 296, 308, 375, 382, 404, 409, 420–427, 431 (*see also* Economy; Gap between rich and poor; Gender stratification),
Social integration, 150, 168
Social isolation, 134, 301, 302, 382, 403–404, 424
Social media (*see* Media)
Social mobility, 71, 94, 97, 109, 168, 437
Social networks (*see* Networks)
Social policies, 4, 22, 30, 33, 131, 170, 312, 417–422, 432
  critique of, 19, 29, 31, 52, 70, 74, 97, 111, 115, 119, 235, 305, 307, 410, 414, 415, 420–422, 432
  incentives, 40, 55, 110, 423, 426, 427

and political systems, 49, 410, 417–420, 431–432 (*see also* Political context)
and poverty/social inequalities, 231, 420–427
  suggested, 157, 413, 422–427, 430–431
Social reproduction, 13, 20, 70, 91, 100, 108, 221, 233, 236, 252, 308, 310, 409, 430, 437
Social resources (*see* Resources)
Social safety net, 70, 107, 134, 360
Social stratification, 16, 22, 41, 48, 60, 71, 78, 168, 269
Social structure, 3, 21, 410
Social support, 60, 91, 92, 142, 174, 175, 176, 177, 214, 229, 241, 251, 300, 356, 388, 405, 410, 413, 432
Socialization, 3, 11, 15, 16, 17, 26, 27, 70, 71, 72, 88, 115, 129–130, 160, 167, 174, 175, 176, 183, 215, 251, 278, 287–296, 301, 302, 322–323, 327, 332, 336–337, 339, 359, 394, 409, 410, 432, 437 (*see also* Childrearing practices; Collective socialization)
Society(ies), 107, 129, 220–221, 223, 306
Sociocultural context/climate, 91, 92, 236, 256, 268, 286, 300, 313, 350–351, 354–355, 377, 411
Socioeconomic context, 16, 23, 79, 92, 98, 229, 251, 286, 287, 300, 402, 410, 432
Socioeconomic status (SES), 23, 28, 116, 129, 158, 168, 188, 244, 437 (*see also* Social class)
Sociology/sociologists/sociological, 13, 16, 26, 28, 104, 122, 149, 238, 256, 287, 412
Son preference, 55, 59, 233, 247, 276, 327–328, 412–413
South Africa, 8, 241
South America (*see* Latin America)
South Korea, Korean-Canadian families (*see* Korea)
Spain, 140, 234, 308, 352
Spousal relationship (*see* Marital relationship)
Status (ascribed and achieved), 9, 19, 52, 63, 71, 104, 112, 434
Stepchildren, 267, 273, 276, 331, 342, 347, 358, 366–368
Stepfamilies, 223, 351, 367–368
Stepparents/stepparenting, 69, 221, 273, 367–368
Stepparent families, 198, 222, 246, 306, 367–368
St. John's, 105, 304
Stratification, 11, 437 (*see also* Gender stratification; Social stratification)
Stress/stressors, 70, 90, 99, 102, 137, 156, 232, 247, 251, 274–275, 294, 307, 351, 355, 360, 388, 425
  and poverty, 113, 116, 222, 294, 326, 388

Structural functionalism, 10–11
Students (higher education), 208, 209–210, 394 (*see also* Debt; Education)
Suburbs, 60, 123, 125, 132, 135, 416
Suicide, 63, 125, 399
Supervision of children/adolescents, 74, 425
  by parents, 84, 127, 130, 205, 288, 324, 394
  collective, 129, 130, 324
Surplus, 12, 20
Surplus population, 412, 414
Surrogate motherhood, 224, 241–242, 417, 418
Surveys, 18, 30, 31, 118, 126, 171, 256, 266, 298, 388, 432
Sweden, 48, 91, 153, 191, 197, 200, 210, 214, 221, 223, 226, 240, 344, 346, 353, 420
Symbolic interactionism, 25–26, 27, 28, 83, 332, 335
Syrian refugees, 205, 377
Systemic/systems, 11, 301–302, 317, 410, 437

T

Taiwan, 59, 60, 75, 76, 142, 308, 309
Taxpayers/taxation system, 70, 91, 107, 156, 162, 425, 427
Teachers, 149, 155, 157, 159, 165, 166, 168, 296, 297, 338, 357, 400
Technological context/technology, 23, 69, 74, 91, 92, 94–95, 97, 102, 143, 160, 179, 287, 300, 410, 412, 417, 427, 432
Television, 68, 72, 79, 80–82, 85–86, 90, 104, 214, 287, 393, 400
Temperament, 118, 265, 280, 285, 293, 355 (*see also* Personality; Predispositions)
Theory(ies), 2, 10–28, 29, 31, 360–363, 404, 437
Therapists (*see* Experts)
Time/time pressure, 84, 100, 102, 104, 150, 152, 255
  family, 80, 82, 102–104, 298
  spent with the children, 100–101, 103–104, 116, 319, 419
Timing, 23, 182, 226, 323
Toronto, 7, 41, 46, 59, 63, 76, 105, 106, 123, 124, 125, 126, 128, 132, 142, 144, 150, 156, 161, 164, 172, 173, 210, 232, 238, 299, 304, 305
Traditional, 69, 70, 195, 199, 236
Transactional (*see* Interactional/ transactional perspectives)
Transitions (family/life), 23, 144, 146, 224, 225, 277, 286, 300, 304, 313, 342, 357, 359, 361, 368
  to parenthood, 224, 236, 312
Transnational families, 13, 22, 58, 73, 74–76, 295, 308, 309, 416 (*see also* Immigrant families)
Trends (*see* History)

Turkey, 50, 412
Twins, 28, 240, 320–321, 326, 333–336, 337

U

U-curve phenomenon, 267–268
Unattached individuals (*see* Singlehood)
Unemployment, 12, 91, 96, 105, 108–109, 110, 119, 127, 156, 211, 230, 358, 408, 417, 422
United Kingdom (*see* Great Britain)
United States/Americans, 8, 9, 18, 41, 43, 45, 78, 80–81, 87, 90, 95, 123, 125, 126, 153, 154, 169, 173, 183, 197, 201, 205, 210, 214, 226, 229, 237, 241, 246, 247, 272, 326, 344, 353, 391, 402, 415, 417, 432
Upper classes, 12, 42, 57, 95, 168, 183, 427, 429, 432
Urban/urbanisation, 41, 46, 48, 72, 74, 123, 202, 227, 235, 301, 305, 411

V

Values, 7, 10, 11, 15, 54, 60, 61, 69, 70, 71, 73, 81, 91, 124, 146, 149, 168, 177, 178, 184, 187, 206, 209, 215, 236, 252, 263, 287, 288, 294, 295, 300, 306, 307, 332, 337, 338, 414, 417, 432
Vancouver, 59, 76, 105, 123, 124, 125, 132, 142, 144, 173, 210, 232, 304, 305, 424
Variables (in research), 29, 126, 128, 153, 158, 167, 263, 350, 389
Victim(ization), 58, 127, 134, 157, 170, 294, 369, 380, 383, 394–396, 397, 403, 405 (*see also* Sexual abuse; Violence)
Video games/videos, 68, 82, 86–87, 123, 378, 400
Vietnam, 12, 73, 235, 247, 295, 412

Violence, 20, 78, 87, 119, 127–128, 288, 294, 377, 404–405, 412 (*see also* Abuse; Rape; Sexual abuse; Victimization)
  against children, 383, 386–388, 392–401
  against women, 356, 375, 376–377, 381, 382–383, 412
  among Aboriginal families, 379–380, 381
  conjugal/partner, 78, 111, 134, 237, 354, 375, 379–383
  culture of, 205, 378, 381, 400
  dating, 376–377
  domestic, 9, 133, 195, 294
  effects on children, 127, 128, 383–386, 388–392
  homicide (domestic), 195, 375, 380, 381, 387
  injuries, 68, 376, 380, 401, 404
  in media, 72, 83, 85–87, 90
  in neighbourhood, 126–128, 382
  peer, 68, 164–165
  same-sex, 375, 383
  sexual, 211, 375
  sibling, 396–399
Volunteer work, 15, 173, 413, 430
Vulnerabilities, 130, 184, 211, 280, 323, 333, 337, 351, 363, 375, 389, 399, 420

W

Wages, 12, 18, 96, 100, 251 (*see also* Jobs)
  low, 105, 152, 421, 427
  minimum, 105, 108, 420
War, 22, 37, 77, 234, 377, 415
Wealth, 107, 112, 140, 424 (*see also* Assets)
Wedding, 63, 185, 274
Welfare system, 47, 132, 226, 422
  inadequacies of, 91, 114, 305
  on welfare, 111, 112, 351

Well-being, 125, 174–175, 198, 199, 200, 414
  adult, 15, 156, 172, 220, 263, 323, 330, 355, 356, 418
  child, 220, 222, 287, 336, 410, 414
Western societies, 10, 17, 29, 69, 91, 107, 111, 150, 183, 190, 193, 198, 199, 203, 257, 262, 276, 287, 288, 292, 297, 301, 317, 320, 330, 339, 351
Western values/perspectives, 16, 203, 220, 261, 287, 292, 428
Widowhood/widowed, 42, 197, 309, 363–364
Wife battery (*see* Abuse; Violence)
Winnipeg, 48, 105, 123, 128, 132, 167, 304, 420
Women, 17–19, 40, 48, 54, 73, 100, 101, 109, 132–135, 178, 202, 305, 307, 377, 405, 414, 427 (*see also* Gender differences; Mothers)
  primary earners, 98, 355
  relative to men, 8, 12, 19, 37, 96, 101, 111, 184, 264, 266, 274, 403–404
  work, 19, 37, 48, 69, 78, 98–100, 137–139, 156, 255, 274–275, 416, 430
Women's Movement (*see* Feminism)
Work, 12, 70, 74, 99, 150, 151, 160, 268, 269, 300, 409, 425, 427, 431
Workers, 95, 96, 137, 413–414, 416
Working-class parents, 42, 46, 160
Work overload, 99, 100

Y

Young offenders (*see* Delinquency)
YouTube, 90, 399
Youth, 96, 98, 126, 127, 151, 176, 351, 420 (*see also* Adolescence)
Yukon, 152, 191, 219, 249, 344, 370